AN ENVIRONMENTAL LAW ANTHOLOGY

ANDERSON'S

Law School Publications

ADMINISTRATIVE LAW ANTHOLOGY
by Thomas O. Sargentich

ADMINISTRATIVE LAW: CASES AND MATERIALS
by Daniel J. Gifford

AN ADMIRALTY LAW ANTHOLOGY
by Robert M. Jarvis

ANALYTIC JURISPRUDENCE ANTHOLOGY
by Anthony D'Amato

AN ANTITRUST ANTHOLOGY
by Andrew I. Gavil

APPELLATE ADVOCACY: PRINCIPLES AND PRACTICE (Second Edition)
Cases and Materials
by Ursula Bentele and Eve Cary

A CAPITAL PUNISHMENT ANTHOLOGY (and Electronic Caselaw Appendix)
by Victor L. Streib

CASES AND PROBLEMS IN CRIMINAL LAW (Third Edition)
by Myron Moskovitz

THE CITATION WORKBOOK
by Maria L. Ciampi, Rivka Widerman, and Vicki Lutz

CIVIL PROCEDURE: CASES, MATERIALS, AND QUESTIONS
by Richard D. Freer and Wendy C. Perdue

COMMERCIAL TRANSACTIONS: PROBLEMS AND MATERIALS
Vol. 1: Secured Transactions Under the UCC
Vol. 2: Sales Under the UCC and the CISG
Vol. 3: Negotiable Instruments Under the UCC and the CIBN
by Louis F. Del Duca, Egon Guttman, and Alphonse M. Squillante

COMMUNICATIONS LAW: MEDIA, ENTERTAINMENT, AND REGULATION
by Donald E. Lively, Allen S. Hammond, Blake D. Morant, and Russell L. Weaver

A CONSTITUTIONAL LAW ANTHOLOGY
by Michael J. Glennon

CONSTITUTIONAL LAW: CASES, HISTORY, AND DIALOGUES
by Donald E. Lively, Phoebe A. Haddon, Dorothy E. Roberts, and Russell L. Weaver

THE CONSTITUTIONAL LAW OF THE EUROPEAN UNION
by James D. Dinnage and John F. Murphy

CONSTITUTIONAL TORTS
by Sheldon H. Nahmod, Michael L. Wells, and Thomas A. Eaton

CONTRACTS
Contemporary Cases, Comments, and Problems
by Michael L. Closen, Richard M. Perlmutter, and Jeffrey D. Wittenberg

A CONTRACTS ANTHOLOGY (Second Edition)
by Peter Linzer

CORPORATE AND WHITE COLLAR CRIME: AN ANTHOLOGY
by Leonard Orland

A CRIMINAL LAW ANTHOLOGY
by Arnold H. Loewy

CRIMINAL LAW: CASES AND MATERIALS
by Arnold H. Loewy

A CRIMINAL PROCEDURE ANTHOLOGY
by Silas J. Wasserstrom and Christie L. Snyder

Continued

THE LAW OF MODERN PAYMENT SYSTEMS AND NOTES
by Fred H. Miller and Alvin C. Harrell

LAWYERS AND FUNDAMENTAL MORAL RESPONSIBILITY
by Daniel R. Coquillette

MICROECONOMIC PREDICATES TO LAW AND ECONOMICS
by Mark Seidenfeld

PATIENTS, PSYCHIATRISTS AND LAWYERS
Law and the Mental Health System
by Raymond L. Spring, Roy B. Lacoursiere, M.D., and Glen Weissenberger

PROBLEMS AND SIMULATIONS IN EVIDENCE (Second Edition)
by Thomas F. Guernsey

A PRODUCTS LIABILITY ANTHOLOGY
by Anita Bernstein

PROFESSIONAL RESPONSIBILITY ANTHOLOGY
by Thomas B. Metzloff

A PROPERTY ANTHOLOGY
by Richard H. Chused

THE REGULATION OF BANKING
Cases and Materials on Depository Institutions and Their Regulators
by Michael P. Malloy

A SECTION 1983 CIVIL RIGHTS ANTHOLOGY
by Sheldon H. Nahmod

SPORTS LAW: CASES AND MATERIALS (Second Edition)
by Raymond L. Yasser, James R. McCurdy, and C. Peter Goplerud

A TORTS ANTHOLOGY
by Lawrence C. Levine, Julie A. Davies, and Edward J. Kionka

TRIAL PRACTICE
by Lawrence A. Dubin and Thomas F. Guernsey

TRIAL PRACTICE AND CASE FILES
by Edward R. Stein and Lawrence A. Dubin

TRIAL PRACTICE AND CASE FILES with *Video* Presentation
by Edward R. Stein and Lawrence A. Dubin

FORTHCOMING PUBLICATIONS

ALTERNATIVE DISPUTE RESOLUTON: STRATEGIES FOR LAW AND BUSINESS
by E. Wendy Trachte-Huber and Stephen K. Huber

BASIC ACCOUNTING PRINCIPLES FOR LAWYERS:
With Present Value and Expected Value
by C. Steven Bradford and Gary A. Ames

CONSTITUTIONAL CONFLICTS
by Derrick A. Bell, Jr.

EUROPEAN COMMUNITY LAW ANTHOLOGY
by Anthony D'Amato and Karen V. Kole

INTERNATIONAL HUMAN RIGHTS: LAW POLICY, AND PROCESS (Second Edition)
by Frank C. Newman and David Weissbrodt

PRINCIPLES OF EVIDENCE (Third Edition)
Irving Younger, Michael Goldsmith, and David A. Sonenshein

UNINCORPORATED BUSINESS ENTITIES
Larry E. Ribstein

An Environmental Law Anthology

Edited With Comments

By

Robert L. Fischman
Associate Professor
Indiana University School of Law—Bloomington

Maxine I. Lipeles
Professor
Washington University
School of Engineering & Applied Science

Mark S. Squillace
Winston S. Howard Professor
University of Wyoming College of Law

Anderson Publishing Co.
Cincinnati, Ohio

AN ENVIRONMENTAL LAW ANTHOLOGY

© 1996 by Anderson Publishing Co.

2035 Reading Road / Cincinnati, Ohio 45202
800-582-7295 / e-mail at andpubco@aol.com / Fax 513-562-8110

ISBN: 0-87084-009-6

Table of Contents

Preface

This environmental law anthology surveys the rich body of scholarship and commentary generated by pollution and natural resources management issues. Although environmental law can accurately be described as a collection of medium- or resource-based statutes, it is not best understood that way. Instead, this anthology is organized along the central and recurring themes that cut across many statutory, regulatory, and judicial debates. In selecting and discussing the material in the anthology, we have focused on the ideas that weave together the fragmented authorities in environmental law. We have avoided discussion of narrower operational aspects of specific laws and programs, which are covered adequately in more traditional environmental law texts.

This anthology is designed for a number of uses. It can provide supplemental reading for a traditional environmental law class using an existing casebook. By introducing students to the scholarly literature at an early point in their exploration of environmental law, teachers will impart a more coherent framework for understanding the issues involved in cases and statutes. The material and discussion notes in this anthology will also address the common student complaint that environmental law is a much drier subject than the issues would otherwise lead one to anticipate. This book presents the debates that cut to the heart of the compelling issues of environmental law. This anthology can also be the basis for an advanced seminar. Students who have had some exposure to environmental law can use these readings to examine critically what they have studied. Each chapter provides ready platforms for research topics that explore specific issues through the conceptual perspective of the chapter. Another pedagogic use of this anthology is to introduce non-law students to the core questions of environmental policy without having to wade through technical legal material. Students with backgrounds in environmental studies, the natural sciences, engineering, political science, economics, philosophy, policy analysis, and public health will all find some common ground in the excerpts and notes. Finally, this anthology should be a useful entree to scholars and professionals who may be unfamiliar with environmental law but seek to survey the field. People with existing skills in statutory interpretation and litigation will find these materials essential to understanding where a particular program fits into the larger scheme of environmental law.

In compiling, editing, and annotating this collection, we have tried to retain as much of the original text of the excerpts as space will allow in order to give readers a strong flavor of the style and substance of the scholarly discourse. We indicate material we have edited out of excerpts with three asterisks. Normal elipses indicate quoted material that an original author deleted. This anthology differs from most of the collections in the Anderson series in its extensive use of notes. Because this anthology is designed as a teaching tool, we have included notes that probe many related issues raised by the excerpts. Also, notes provide descriptions of and citations to other commentary that readers may want to pursue in researching particular topics in more detail. Finally, the notes seek to orient the excerpts in the context of the intellectual history of environmental law. Notes alert the reader to, for instance, whether an excerpt is representative of a particular school of thought, seminal in the field, or a minority position.

Chapter One explores the ethical dimensions of environmental law. It reviews historical and contemporary human attitudes towards nature, and considers how these attitudes have helped to shape environmental law. It also addresses problems of distributional justice—*i.e.* sharing environmental burdens across racial, economic, and intergenerational categories.

Chapter Two examines the role that governmental entities play in creating environmental law. It reviews the strengths and weaknesses of the Congress, the courts, and the Environmental Protection Agency as vehicles for advancing environmental goals. The chapter is concerned not just with the characteristics of these legal institutions but also with their dynamic interrelationships.

Chapter Three describes the economic approaches to and critiques of environmental law. Environmental law has become the subject of intense scrutiny by economists primarily concerned with achieving efficiency. The chapter discusses the important influence that economic thinking has had in creating marketing tools for implementing environmental law. It also presents criticisms of economic approaches based on their ethical underpinnings as well as their presumptions about the actual operation of environmental law.

Chapter Four discusses the vast literature that views the environment from a property law perspective. From this perspective, environmental problems are often seen as arising from shared ownership of air, water, and (sometimes) land. After discussing the characteristics of both private and common property that present problems, the chapter examines several remedies, including dividing common resources into privately owned property and limiting private uses through trust concepts. The chapter concludes with a discussion of the importance to environmental law of the Fifth Amendment's protection of private property.

Chapter Five examines the concept of risk. The chapter considers whether risk reduction is an appropriate guiding principle of environmental law. It also analyzes specific proposals for coordinating risk management across agencies and across different activities that pose hazards.

Chapter Six discusses the burgeoning area of international environmental law. Increasingly, environmental problems are not contained within national boundaries.

The instruments that have been drafted to govern these trans-boundary problems raise a number of issues discussed in the chapter.

Over the years we have been working on this book, a number of people have earned our profound gratitude for their assistance. In Bloomington, student research assistants Peter Dykstra, Christian Freitag, David Pantos, and Laurel Siegel, and secretaries Lisa McLean, Mary Jo Draglojovic, and Jennifer Underwood deserve great thanks. Kirk Emerson, a doctoral student at Indiana University, contributed immeasurably to the depth of the property chapter through her careful reading and wide-ranging intellect. In Laramie, we extend thanks to student research assistants Jim Schmehl and Dean Jessup, and secretary Julie Jenkins. In St. Louis, research assistants Michael Ford and Jodi Hirschfield, and support staff Elaine Halley and Donna Williams provided immeasurable assistance. In addition, special thanks go to William Darby, Vice Dean of the Washington University School of Engineering & Applied Science and Chair of the Department of Engineering & Policy, for his encouragement and multifaceted support. This project was also supported by generous grants from the Indiana School of Law—Bloomington, the George W. Hopper Research Fund at the University of Wyoming, and the Rocky Mountain Mineral Law Foundation.

A number of reviewers contributed enormously to the breadth of the notes in this anthology. Many thanks to Alison Del Rossi, Susanna Goodin, Paul Locke, Ed Sherline, Jeff Stake, and Susan Williams, who generously shared their expertise in reviewing chapters.

Finally, we would like to thank Sean Caldwell and Dee Dunn at Anderson Publishing for their patient efforts in nurturing this book.

Robert Fischman, Bloomington, Indiana   April, 1996
Maxine Lipeles, St. Louis, Missouri
Mark Squillace, Laramie, Wyoming

One
Ethical Dimensions

Our legal standards derive, in some sense at least, from our ethical values. Thus a careful study of environmental ethics should help to reveal the roots of environmental law. In the first essay of this chapter, Lynn White, a medieval historian, traces the history of our "ecological crisis" to early Western civilizations and Christian ethics. For White, the only way out of the crisis is to reassess and ultimately change traditional Christian values—a view that created quite a stir when first articulated in 1967. Although White's focus is on Western values and thus offers a somewhat limited perspective, his essay serves to underscore the profound influence of religious values on environmental ethics.

In his classic essay, *The Land Ethic,* Aldo Leopold offers a holistic alternative to the prevailing anthropocentric ethic of Western cultures. Leopold contends that the appropriateness of human actions can be gauged by asking whether they tend to preserve and protect the biotic community. Christopher Stone's question—whether trees should have standing to sue—offers a vehicle for establishing a legal doctrine which finds its roots in the ethical regimes endorsed by White and Leopold. Two essays then examine the issue of intergenerational equity—whether present generations of humans have a responsibility to future generations yet unborn, and if so, what that responsibility entails. The final article concerns environmental justice—a burgeoning legal issue with important ethical implications. Richard Lazarus offers a comprehensive look at the problems that arise when particular groups—primarily minority and lower income communities—bear a disproportionate share of the burden of environmental degradation.

There is a growing consensus that our planet faces some serious ecological problems. How have we reached this point, and what if anything can be done to redress these problems? Lynn White, Jr. offers the following explanation of the "roots" of these problems in an essay written more than a quarter of a century ago.

THE HISTORICAL ROOTS OF OUR ECOLOGIC CRISIS
Lynn White, Jr.
155 Science 1203 (1967)*

* * *

All forms of life modify their contexts. The most spectacular and benign instance is doubtless the coral polyp. By serving its own ends, it has created a vast undersea world favorable to thousands of other kinds of animals and plants. Ever since man became a numerous species he has affected his environment notably. The hypothesis that his fire-drive method of hunting created the world's great grasslands and helped to exterminate the monster mammals of the Pleistocene from much of the globe is plausible, if not proved. For 6 millennia at least, the banks of the lower Nile have been a human artifact rather than the swampy African jungle which nature, apart from man, would have made it. The Aswan Dam, flooding 5000 square miles, is only the latest stage in a long process. In many regions terracing or irrigation, overgrazing, the cutting of forests by Romans to build ships to fight Carthaginians or by Crusaders to solve the logistics problems of their expeditions, have profoundly changed some ecologies.

* * *

The history of ecologic change is still so rudimentary that we know little about what really happened, or what the results were. The extinction of the European aurochs as late as 1627 would seem to have been a simple case of overenthusiastic hunting. On more intricate matters it often is impossible to find solid information. For a thousand years or more the Frisians and Hollanders have been pushing back the North Sea, and the process is culminating in our own time in the reclamation of the Zuider Zee. What, if any, species of animals, birds, fish, shore life, or plants have died out in the process? In their epic combat with Neptune, have the Netherlanders overlooked ecological values in such a way that the quality of human life in the Netherlands has suffered? I cannot discover that the questions have ever been asked, much less answered.

People, then, have often been a dynamic element in their own environment, but in the present state of historical scholarship we usually do not know exactly when, where, or with what effects man induced changes came. As we enter the last third of the 20th century, however, concern for the problem of ecologic backlash is mounting feverishly. Natural science, conceived as the effort to understand the nature of things, had flourished in several eras and among several peoples. Similarly there had been an age-old accumulation of technological skills, sometimes growing rapidly, sometimes slowly. But it was not until about four generations ago that Western Europe and North America arranged a marriage between science and technology, a union of the theoretical and the empirical approaches to our natural environment. The emergence in widespread practice of the Baconian creed that scientific knowledge means technological power over nature can scarcely be dated before about 1850, save in the chemical industries, where it is anticipated

* Reprinted with permission from 155 Science 1203. Copyright 1967, American Association for the Advancement of Science.

in the 18th century. Its acceptance as a normal pattern of action may mark the greatest event in human history since the invention of agriculture, and perhaps in nonhuman terrestrial history as well.

Almost at once the new situation forced the crystallization of the novel concept of ecology; indeed, the word *ecology* first appeared in the English language in 1873. Today, less than a century later, the impact of our race upon the environment has so increased in force that it has changed in essence. When the first cannons were fired, in the early 14th century, they affected ecology by sending workers scrambling to the forests and mountains for more potash, sulfur, iron ore, and charcoal, with some resulting erosion and deforestation. Hydrogen bombs are of a different order: a war fought with them might alter the genetics of all life on this planet. By 1285 London had a smog problem arising from the burning of soft coal, but our present combustion of fossil fuels threatens to change the chemistry of the globe's atmosphere as a whole, with consequences which we are only beginning to guess. With the population explosion, the carcinoma of planless urbanism, the now geological deposits of sewage and garbage, surely no creature other than man has ever managed to foul its nest in such short order.

There are many calls to action, but specific proposals, worthy as individual items, seem too partial, palliative, negative: ban the bomb, tear down the billboards, give the Hindus contraceptives and tell them to eat their sacred cows. The simplest solution to any suspect change is, of course, to stop it, or, better yet, to revert to a romanticized past: make those ugly gasoline stations look like Anne Hathaway's cottage or (in the Far West) like ghost-town saloons. The "wilderness area" mentality invariably advocates deep-freezing an ecology, whether San Gimignano or the High Sierra, as it was before the first Kleenex was dropped. But neither atavism nor prettification will cope with the ecologic crisis of our time.

What shall we do? No one yet knows. Unless we think about fundamentals, our specific measures may produce new backlashes more serious than those they are designed to remedy.

As a beginning we should try to clarify our thinking by looking, in some historical depth, at the presuppositions that underlie modern technology and science. Science was traditionally aristocratic, speculative, intellectual in intent; technology was lower-class, empirical, action-oriented. The quite sudden fusion of these two, towards the middle of the 19th century, is surely related to the slightly prior and contemporary democratic revolutions which, by reducing social barriers, tended to assert a functional unity of brain and hand. Our ecologic crisis is the product of an emerging, entirely novel, democratic culture. The issue is whether a democratized world can survive its own implications. Presumably we cannot, unless we rethink our axioms.

THE WESTERN TRADITIONS OF TECHNOLOGY AND SCIENCE

One thing is so certain that is seems stupid to verbalize it: both modern technology and modern science are distinctively Occidental. Our technology has absorbed elements from all over the world, notably from China; yet everywhere today, whether in Japan or in Nigeria, successful technology is Western. Our science is the heir to all the sciences of the past, especially perhaps to the work of the great Islamic scientists of the Middle Ages, who so often outdid the ancient Greeks in skill and perspicacity: al-Razi in medicine, for example; or ibn-al-Haytham in optics; or Omar Khayyam in mathematics. Indeed, not a few works of such geniuses seem to have vanished in the original Arabic and to survive only in medieval Latin translations that helped to lay the foundations for later Western developments. Today, around the globe, all significant science is Western in style and method, whatever the pigmentation of language of the scientists.

A second pair of facts is less well recognized because they result from quite recent historical scholarship. The leadership of the West, both in technology and in science, is far older than the so-called Scientific Revolution of the 17th century or the so-called Industrial Revolution of the 18th century. These terms are in fact outmoded and obscure the true nature of what they try to describe—significant stages in two long and separate developments. By A.D. 1000 at the latest—and perhaps, feebly, as much as 200 years earlier—the West began to apply water power to industrial processes other than milling grain. This was followed in the late 12th century by the harnessing of wind power. From simple beginnings, but with remarkable consistency of style, the West rapidly expanded its skills in the development of power machinery, labor-saving devices, and automation. Those who doubt should contemplate that most monumental achievement in the history of automation: the weight-driven mechanical clock, which appeared in two forms in the early 14th century. Not in craftsmanship but in basic technological capacity, the Latin West of the later Middle Ages far outstripped its elaborate, sophisticated, and aesthetically magnificent sister cultures, Byzantium and Islam. In 1444 a great Greek ecclesiastic, Bessarion, who had gone to Italy, wrote a letter to a prince in Greece. He is amazed by the superiority of Western ships, arms, textiles, glass. But above all he is astonished by the spectacle of waterwheels sawing timbers and pumping the bellows of the blast furnaces. Clearly, he had seen nothing of the sort in the Near East.

By the end of the 15th century the technological superiority of Europe was such that its small, mutually hostile nations could spill out over all the rest of the world, conquering, looting, and colonizing.* * *

Since both our technological and our scientific movements got their start, acquired their character, and achieved world dominance in the Middle Ages, it would seem that we cannot understand their nature or their present impact upon ecology without examining fundamental medieval assumptions and developments.

MEDIEVAL VIEW OF MAN AND NATURE

Until recently, agriculture has been the chief occupation even in "advanced" societies; hence, any change in methods of tillage has much importance. Early plows, drawn by two oxen, did not normally turn the sod but merely scratched it. Thus, cross-plowing was needed and fields tended to be squarish. In the fairly light soils and semiarid climates of the Near East and Mediterranean, this worked well. But such a plow was inappropriate to the wet climate and often sticky soils of northern Europe. By the latter part of the 7th century after Christ, however, following obscure beginnings, certain northern peasants were using an entirely new kind of plow, equipped with a vertical knife to cut the line of the furrow, a horizontal share to slice under the sod, and a moldboard to turn it over. The friction of this plow with the soil was so great that it nominally required not two but eight oxen. It attacked the land with such violence that crossplowing was not needed, and fields tended to be shaped in long strips.

In the days of the scratch-plow, fields were distributed generally in units capable of supporting a single family. Subsistence farming was the presupposition. But no peasant owned eight oxen: to use the new and more efficient plow, peasants pooled their oxen to form large plow-teams, originally receiving (it would appear) plowed strips in proportion to their contribution. Thus, distribution of land was based no longer on the needs of a family but, rather, on the capacity of a power machine to till the earth. Man's relation to the soil was profoundly changed. Formerly man had been part of nature; now he was the exploiter of nature. Nowhere else in the would did farmers develop any analogous agricultural implement. Is it coincidence that modern technology, with its ruthlessness toward nature, has so largely been produced by descendants of these peasants of northern Europe?

* * *

These novelties seem to be in harmony with larger intellectual patterns. What people do about their ecology depends on what they think about themselves in relation to things around them. Human ecology is deeply conditioned by beliefs about our nature and destiny—that is, by religion. To Western eyes this is very evident in, say, India or Ceylon. It is equally true of ourselves and of our medieval ancestors.

The victory of Christianity over paganism was the greatest psychic revolution in the history of our culture. It has become fashionable today to say that, for better or worse, we live in "the post-Christian age." Certainly the forms of our thinking and language have largely ceased to be Christian, but to my eye the substance often remains amazingly akin to that of the past. Our daily habits of action, for example, are dominated by an implicit faith in perpetual progress which was unknown either to Greco-Roman antiquity or to the Orient. It is rooted in, and is indefensible apart from, Judeo-Christian teleology. The fact that Communists share it merely helps to show what can be demonstrated on many other grounds: that Marxism, like Islam, is a Judeo-Christian heresy. We continue today to live, as we have lived for about 1700 years, very largely in a context of Christian axioms.

What did Christianity tell people about their relations with the environment?

While many of the world's mythologies provide stories of creation, Greco-Roman mythology was singularly incoherent in this respect. Like Aristotle, the intellectuals of the ancient West denied that the visible world had had a beginning. Indeed, the idea of a beginning was impossible in the framework of their cyclical notion of time. In sharp contrast, Christianity inherited from Judaism not only a concept of time as nonrepetitive and linear but also a striking story of creation. By gradual stages a loving and all-powerful God had created light and darkness, the heavenly bodies, the earth and all its plants, animals, birds, and fishes. Finally, God had created Adam and, as an afterthought, Eve to keep man from being lonely. Man named all the animals, thus establishing his dominance over them. God planned all of this explicitly for man's benefit and rule: no item in the physical creation had any purpose save to serve man's purposes. And, although man's body is made of clay, he is not simply part of nature: he is made in God's image.

Especially in its Western form, Christianity is the most anthropocentric religion the world has seen. As early as the 2nd century both Tertullian and St. Irenaeus of Lyons were insisting that when God shaped Adam he was foreshadowing the image of the incarnate Christ, the Second Adam. Man shares, in great measure, God's transcendence of nature. Christianity, in absolute contrast to ancient paganism and Asia's religions (except, perhaps, Zoroastrianism), not only established a dualism of man and nature but also insisted that it is God's will that man exploit nature for his proper ends.

At the level of the common people this worked out in an interesting way. In Antiquity every tree, every spring, every stream, every hill had its own *genius loci*, its guardian spirit. These spirits were accessible to men, but were very unlike men; centaurs, fauns, and mermaids show their ambivalence. Before one cut a tree, mined a mountain, or dammed a brook, it was important to placate the spirit in charge of that particular situation, and to keep it placated. By destroying pagan animism, Christianity made it possible to exploit nature in a mood of indifference to the feelings of natural objects.

* * *

When one speaks in such sweeping terms, a note of caution is in order. Christianity is a complex faith, and its consequences differ in differing contexts. What I have said may well apply to the medieval West, where in fact technology made spectacular advances. But the Greek East, a highly civilized realm of equal Christian devotion, seems to have produced no marked technological innovation after the late 7th century, when Greek fire was invented. The key to the contrast may perhaps be found in a difference in the tonality of piety and thought which students of comparative theology find between the Greek and the Latin Churches. The Greeks believed that sin was intellectual blindness, and that salvation was found in illumination, orthodoxy—that is, clear thinking. The Latins, on the other hand, felt that sin was moral evil, and that salvation was to be found in right conduct. Eastern theology has been intellectualist. Western theology has been voluntarist. The Greek saint contemplates; the Western saint acts. The implications of Christianity for the conquest of nature would emerge more easily in the Western atmosphere.

The Christian dogma of creation, which is found in the first clause of all the Creeds, has another meaning for our comprehension of today's ecologic crisis. By revelation, God had given man the Bible, the Book of Scripture. But since God had made nature, nature also must reveal the divine mentality. The religious study of nature for the better understanding of God was known as natural theology. In the early Church, and always in the Greek East, nature was conceived primarily as a symbolic system through which God speaks to men: the ant is a sermon to sluggards; rising flames are the symbol of the soul's aspiration. This view of nature was essentially artistic rather than scientific. While Byzantium preserved and copied great numbers of ancient Greek scientific texts, science as we conceive it could scarcely flourish in such an ambience.

However, in the Latin West by the early 13th century natural theology was following a very different bent. It was ceasing to be the decoding of the physical symbols of God's communication with man and was becoming the effort to understand God's mind by discovering how his creation operates. The rainbow was no longer simply a symbol of hope first sent to Noah after the Deluge: Robert Grosseteste, Friar Roger Bacon, and Theodoric of Freiberg produced startlingly sophisticated work on the optics of the rainbow, but they did it as a venture in religious understanding. From the 13th century onward, up to and including Leibnitz and Newton, every major scientist, in effect, explained his motivations in religious terms. Indeed, if Galileo had not been so expert an amateur theologian he would have got into far less trouble: the professionals resented his intrusion.

And Newton seems to have regarded himself more as a theologian than as a scientist. It was not until the late 18th century that the hypothesis of God became unnecessary to many scientists.

* * *

AN ALTERNATIVE CHRISTIAN VIEW

We would seem to be headed toward conclusions unpalatable to many Christians. Since both *science* and *technology* are blessed words in our contemporary vocabulary, some may be happy at the notions, first, that, viewed historically, modern science is an extrapolation of natural theology and, second, that modern technology is at least partly to be explained as an Occidental, voluntarist realization of the Christian dogma of man's transcendence of, and rightful mastery over, nature. But, as we now recognize, somewhat over a century ago science and technology—hitherto quite separate activities—joined to give mankind powers which, to judge by many of the ecologic effects, are out of control. If so, Christianity bears a huge burden of guilt.

I personally doubt that disastrous ecologic backlash can be avoided simply by applying to our problems more science and more technology. Our science and technology have grown out of Christian attitudes toward man's relation to nature which are almost universally held not only by Christians and neo-Christians but also by those who fondly regard themselves as post-Christians. Despite Copernicus, all the cosmos rotates around our little globe. Despite Darwin, we are *not*, in our hearts, part of the natural process. We are superior to nature, contemptuous of it, willing to use it for our slightest whim. The newly elected Governor of California, like myself a churchman but less troubled than I, spoke for the Christian tradition when he said (as is alleged), "when you've seen one redwood tree, you've seen them all." To a Christian a tree can be no more than a physical fact. The whole concept of the sacred grove is alien to Christianity and to the ethos of the West. For nearly 2 millennia Christian missionaries have been chopping down sacred groves, which are idolatrous because they assume spirit in nature.

What we do about ecology depends on our ideas of the man-nature relationship. More science and more technology are not going to get us out of the present ecologic crisis until we find a new religion, or rethink our old one. The beatniks, who are the basic revolutionaries of our time, show a sound instinct in their affinity for Zen Buddhism, which conceives of the man-nature relationship as very nearly the mirror image of the Christian view. Zen, however, is as deeply conditioned by Asian history as Christianity is by the experience of the West, and I am dubious of its viability among us.

Possibly we should ponder the greatest radical in Christian history since Christ: St. Francis of Assisi. The prime miracle of St. Francis is the fact that he did not end at the stake, as many of his left-wing followers did. He was so clearly heretical that a General of the Franciscan Order, St. Bonaventure, a great and perceptive Christian, tried to suppress the early accounts of Franciscanism. The key to an understanding of Francis is his belief in the virtue of humility—not merely for the individual but for man as a species. Francis tried to depose man from his monarchy over creation and set up a democracy of all God's creatures. With him the ant is no longer simply a homily for the lazy, flames a sign of the thrust of the soul toward union with God; now they are Brother Ant and Sister Fire, praising the Creator in their own ways as Brother Man does in his.

Later commentators have said that Francis preached to the birds as a rebuke to men who would not listen. The records do not read so: he urged the little birds to praise God, and in spiritual ecstasy they flapped their wings and chirped rejoicing. Legends of saints, especially the Irish saints, had long told of their dealings with animals but always, I believe, to show their human dominance over creatures. With Francis it is different. The land around Gubbio in the Apennines was being ravaged by a fierce wolf. St. Francis, says the legend, talked to the wolf and persuaded him of the error of his ways. The wolf repented, died in the odor of sanctity, and was buried in consecrated ground.

* * *

I am not suggesting that many contemporary Americans who are concerned about our ecologic crisis will be either able or willing to counsel with wolves or exhort birds. However, the present increasing disruption of the global environment is the product of a dynamic technology and science which were originating in the Western medieval world against which St. Francis was rebelling in so original a way. Their growth cannot be understood historically apart from distinctive attitudes toward nature which are deeply grounded in Christian dogma. The fact that most people do not think of these attitudes as Christian is irrelevant. No new set of basic values has been accepted in our society to displace those of Christianity. Hence we shall continue to have a worsening ecologic crisis until we reject the Christian axiom that nature has no reason for existence save to serve man.

The greatest spiritual revolutionary in Western history, St. Francis, proposed what he thought was an alternative Christian view of nature and man's relation to it: he tried to substitute the idea of the equality of all creatures, including man, for the idea of man's limitless rule of creation. He failed. Both our present science and our present technology are so tinctured with orthodox Christian arrogance toward nature that no solution for our ecologic crisis can be expected from them alone. Since the roots of our trouble are so largely religious, the remedy must also be essentially religious, whether we call it that or not. We must rethink and refeel our nature and destiny. * * *

NOTES

1. White argues that "we shall continue to have a worsening ecologic crisis until we reject the Christian axiom that nature has no reason for existence save to serve man." White's criticism of the Christian tradition is most compelling when considered in the context of the classical Christian view that the human species should have dominion over all other creatures. This view is perhaps best illustrated by the familiar passage from the *Book of Genesis* where humans are admonished to "be fruitful and multiply, and fill the earth and subdue it, and have dominion over the fish of the sea and over the birds of the air and over every living thing." GENESIS, 1:28.

2. In *A Theology of the Earth,* Rene Dubos takes issue with White's thesis that the roots of our ecological crisis can be traced to the Judeo-Christian culture—

Despite my immense admiration for Lynn White's scholarship, I find it difficult to believe that the Judeo-Christian tradition has been as influential as he thinks in bringing about the desecration of the earth. One does not need to know much history to realize that the ancient Chinese, Greek and Muslim civilizations contributed their share to deforestation, to erosion, and to the destruction of nature in many other ways.

Rene Dubos, *A Theology of the Earth, reprinted in* WESTERN MAN AND ENVIRONMENTAL ETHICS 43 (Ian Barbour ed. 1973); *see also,* J. BAIRD CALLICOTT, IN DEFENSE OF THE LAND ETHIC 137-139 (1989). White responded to his critics by acknowledging that not all ecological damage is * * * rooted in religious attitudes. But, if anything, his message became more strident. He questioned, for example, whether a "prudential ethic" which would promote the protection of biotic systems because their demise might adversely affect the human species "can rightly be called an ethic." Lynn White, Jr., *Continuing the Conversation, reprinted in* WESTERN MAN AND ENVIRONMENTAL ETHICS 63 (Ian Barbour ed. 1973).

Christopher Stone takes the middle ground between Dubos and White:

[E]ven if it is extreme to blame Judeo-Christianity for the condition of our environment, it is not unlikely that it has made cultures which embrace it less sensitive than they would otherwise be to the dark side of what they are doing.

CHRISTOPHER D. STONE, THE GNAT IS OLDER THAN MAN 240 (1993). Why did such cultures become less sensitive? Arnold Joseph Toynbee explains it this way:

In popular pre-Christian Greek religion, divinity was inherent in all natural phenomena * * * . Divinity was present in springs and rivers and the sea; in trees * * * ; in mountains; in earthquakes and lightning and thunder. The godhead was diffuse * * *.

It was plural, not singular; a pantheon, not a unique almighty super-human person. When the Greco-Roman world was converted to christianity, the divinity was drained out of nature and was concentrated in one unique transcendent God.

Arnold Joseph Toynbee, *The Religious Background of the Environmental Crisis*, 3 INT'L J. ENVTL. STUD. 143 (1972).

3. Some who accept the view that the human species has rights superior to those of all other creatures, have nonetheless found a basis for eschewing the traditional view which suggests that nature exists only to serve the human species. For example, George Perkins Marsh, a 19th century conservationist from Vermont, has argued that Christianity imposes on humans a stewardship responsibility toward nature. "Man has too long forgotten," Marsh wrote, "that the earth was given to him for usufruct alone, not for consumption, still less for profligate waste." GEORGE PERKINS MARSH, MAN AND NATURE; OR, PHYSICAL GEOGRAPHY MODIFIED AS HUMAN ACTION 35 (1869). Lynn White, however, remained skeptical that stewardship alone could solve our ecological problems: "Mankind cannot be trusted to be trustee for the rest of nature. When we must decide whether to benefit lilies or sparrows or ourselves, we will recall that while our heavenly father is mindful of both lilies and sparrows, he cares even more deeply for us; so, in obedience to the divine preference, we opt for us." Lynn White, *The Future of Compassion,* 30 ECUMENICAL REV. 106, 107 (1978).

4. The stewardship ethic promoted by Marsh is the guiding principle of the Public Trust Doctrine, which is described at length in Chapter Four, Part C, *infra.* It has also won a number of modern adherents, including Rene Dubos and John Passmore. Dubos developed his ideas in a string of popular books, including especially WOOING THE EARTH (1980) and the Pulitzer Prize-winning SO HUMAN AN ANIMAL (1968). Dubos, who coined the term "think globally, act locally," was a medical scientist who believed that environmental problems would be solved only by adopting "a new social ethic—almost a new religion. Whatever form this religion takes, it will have to be based on harmony with nature as well as man, instead of the drive for mastery." SO HUMAN AN ANIMAL, *supra* at 7. Dubos then quotes passages from Genesis which support an alternative view of the human relationship with nature from that described by White. Dubos' alternative view analogizes nature to a garden and instructs humans to tend it. "This means * * * that [the earth] has been entrusted to our care. Technological societies thus far have exploited the earth; we must reverse this trend and learn to take care of it with love." *Id.*

John Passmore, an Australian philosopher, developed a similar theme of stewardship in MAN'S RESPONSIBILITY FOR NATURE (1974). Passmore rejects the notion of ecology "as being in essence mystical, as anti-scientific, or as entailing 'a philosophy of wholeness'". *Id.* at 174. On the contrary, Passmore argues that ecology is science, "that it *dispels* mysteries" and "that Western science is still fecund, still capable of contributing to the solution of problems which beset human beings, even when they are problems of the scientist's own making." *Id.* at 176-77 (emphasis in original). White, obviously, disagrees with this view. How does the Franciscan view of equality of all creatures, including humans, differ from the stewardship approach? How might this difference influence the objectives of environmental law?

5. While acknowledging that ecology is essentially science, Arne Naess, who coined the phrase "deep ecology", has argued that public policy must look beyond the science of ecology.

> The essence of deep ecology is to ask deeper questions. The adjective "deep" stresses that we ask why and how where others do not. For example, ecology as a science does not ask what kind of society would be best for maintaining a particular ecosystem—that is a question for value theory, for politics, for ethics * * * . What we need toady is a tremendous expansion of ecological thinking in what I call ecosophy. *Sophy* comes from the Greek term *sophis,* "wisdom," which relates to ethics, norms, rules and practice. Ecosophy, or deep ecology, then, involves a shift from science to wisdom.

BILL DEVALL & GEORGE SESSIONS, DEEP ECOLOGY 74 (1985) (quoting from an interview with Arne Naess). In their book, Devall and Sessions describe eight "basic principles" of the Deep Ecology movement, including among them—"(1) The well being and flourishing of human and non-human Life on Earth have value in themselves * * *. (3) Humans have no right to reduce this richness and diversity [of life] except to satisfy *vital* needs. (4) The flourishing of human life is compatible with a substantial decrease of the human population. The flourishing of non-human life requires such a decrease." *Id.* at 70 (emphasis in original). Arne Naess expanded on these principles in an interview with Devall and Sessions: "For deep ecology, there is a core democracy in the biosphere * * * . In deep ecology, we have the goal not only of stabilizing human population but also of reducing it to a sustainable minimum without revolution or dictatorship. I should think we must have no more than 100 million people if we are to have the variety of cultures we had one hundred years ago." *Id.* at 75-76. Is deep ecology the inevitable result of following Lynn White's ethical prescription? How might it differ? Is deep ecology compatible with capitalism?

6. Eco-feminism is a movement which seeks to bridge environmental ethics and feminism. Its essential characteristic is the belief that "there are important connections—historical, experimental, symbolic, theoretical—between the domination of women and the domination of nature." Karen J. Warren, *The Power and Promise of Ecological Feminism*, 12 ENVTL. ETHICS 125, 126 (1990). Eco-feminism shares with the deep ecology movement an "anti-hierarchical" approach toward nature. Ynestra King, *The Ecology of Feminism and the Feminism of Ecology*, 1 J. SOC. ECOLOGY 16, 17 (1983). But some supporters of eco-feminism have argued that deep ecology is flawed because of its failure to recognize "the intimate relationship between the domination of women and the domination of nature and the mutuality reinforcing nature of the two." Jim Cheney, *Eco-Feminism and Deep Ecology*, 9 ENVTL. ETHICS 115, 118 (1987); Ariel Kay Salleh, *Deeper Than Deep Ecology: The Eco-Feminist Connection*, 6 ENVTL. ETHICS 339 (1984).

Another difference between eco-feminism and deep ecology is that the eco-feminists stress nurturing and healing while deep ecologists focus more on a wild and natural world largely undisturbed by human intervention. "From the eco-feminist perspective it makes no sense to speak of caring for nonhuman beings apart from our capacity to care for each other." Michael Zimmerman, *Deep Ecology and Ecofeminism: An Emerging Debate, in* REWEAVING THE WORLD: THE EMERGENCE OF ECOFEMINISM 138, 152 (Irene Diamond & Gloria Orenstein eds., 1990). Starhawk argues that, although environmentalism should be concerned with wilderness preservation, the primary focus of deep ecologists, it must concern itself also with feeding the hungry and sheltering the homeless. According to Starhawk, a truly integrated environmental perspective links caring about these social issues to environmental concerns. Starhawk, *Power, Authority, and Mystery: Ecofeminism and Earth-based Spirituality, reprinted in* REWEAVING THE WORLD: THE EMERGENCE OF ECOFEMINISM 73, 82 (Irene Diamond & Gloria Orenstein eds., 1990).

7. The social ecology movement has much in common with eco-feminism. Both view "ecological destruction as related to social problems of control and dominance." JOSEPH R. DES JARDENS, ENVIRONMENTAL ETHICS 239 (1993). They differ primarily in that social ecology tends to look more broadly to various forms of social domination such as racism, sexism and capitalism to explain human domination of nature. Eco-feminism, by contrast, focuses more specifically on the oppression of women to explain human domination of nature. *Id.* at 240-41. The principal proponent of social ecology is Murray Bookchin. *See* MURRAY BOOKCHIN, THE PHILOSOPHY OF SOCIAL ECOLOGY (1990); MURRAY BOOKCHIN, THE ECOLOGY OF FREEDOM (1982).

8. Roderick Nash argues that the human species is continually expanding its recognition of persons or objects with rights. Initially, the human species recognized ethical obligations only towards family members; later these obligations were extended toward tribes or groups of families. Today, most societies recognize ethical obligations toward all members of the human species regardless of gender, race, or nationality. As deep ecology and similar movements suggest, much political discussion and debate is now ongoing over the rights of animals and plants, and eventually this discussion will likely encompass nonliving matter as well. RODERICK NASH, THE RIGHTS OF NATURE, *see e.g.,* 5 (Figure 1) (1989). Has the development of environmental ethics kept pace with the growing ecological crisis?

9. As Lynn White notes, early scientists described their conclusions in the context of religious terms. By the late 18th century, however, "the hypothesis of God became unnecessary to many scientists." Perhaps the most prominent of these post-18th century scientists was Charles Darwin. Darwin's theory of evolution remains controversial to this day because of its implications for the Christian religious tradition. Darwin, himself, was untroubled by this fact: "Man in his arrogance thinks himself a great work worthy the interposition of a deity. More humble, and I believe, true, to consider him created from animals." *Quoted in* E.S. TURNER, ALL HEAVEN IN A RAGE 162 (1965).

10. White doubts "that disastrous ecologic backlash can be avoided simply by applying to our problems more science and more technology." Note that many U.S. environmental laws are designed to promote "technology-forcing;" *i.e.,* the development of better pollution abatement techniques than are available when the law is enacted. Is this a flawed approach? White believes that a change in attitude toward nature would alter the destructive tendencies of technology. Should government play a role? Rene Dubos echoed many (including fellow scientist Barry Commoner) when he wrote of "the social and economic necessity of imposing directions and limitations to many technological developments." So HUMAN AN ANIMAL, *supra* at 11; *see also* BARRY COMMONER, SCIENCE AND SURVIVAL (1966). Other scientists, such as Jacob Bronowski, have argued more broadly that limiting technological developments limits the human search for knowledge and truth. To Bronowski, humans are scientific, rational animals. To impose restrictions on science and technology is to inhibit good human qualities. For Bronowski, science practices the virtues of honesty, integrity, and tolerance of new ideas. Inhibitions on science, therefore, pave the road to social repression because they suppress those virtues and dissent. JACOB BRONOWSKI, A SENSE OF THE FUTURE 196-262 (1977).

11. The technological optimists rely on unfettered technological progress to solve the problems that arise from present uses of technology. They would claim that by limiting science and technology, we trap ourselves in our present problems and preclude a better life. Dubos makes the pessimists' case by arguing that technology endlessly creates new problems as it solves old ones. He further argues that our political and social institutions have been wholly inadequate to "predict [and] control the nefarious consequences of the exploitation of technological developments for economic purposes. So HUMAN AN ANIMAL, *supra*, n. 4 at 185. Professors Krier and Gillette provide a comprehensive discussion of this important debate over the role of technology in environmental policy in *The Uneasy Case for Technological Optimism,* 84 MICH. L. REV. 405 (1985).

12. If White is correct in suggesting that Eastern societies adhere to ethical norms which view the relationship between humans and nature more holistically, why have these societies been unable to avoid their own ecological crises? Yi-Fu Tuan describes serious problems in China with soil erosion and deforestation as far back as the 10th century and argues that "Western intellectuals who look at Chinese culture tend to be overgenerous" in their assessment of Eastern attitudes toward nature. Yi-Fu Tuan, *Our Treatment of the Environment in Ideal and Actuality,* 58 AM. SCIENTIST 244 (1970) at 244, 247-48 (1970). He further argues that one's ethical attitudes toward the environment may have a limited impact on how one treats environmental resources: "A culture's publicized ethos about its environment seldom covers more than a fraction of the total range of its attitudes and practices pertaining to that environment. In the play of forces that govern the world, esthetics and religious ideals rarely have a major role." *Id.* at 244.

13. Roderick Nash analogizes the environmental movement today with the abolition movement of the 1850's and argues that the abolitionists inevitably concluded that coercion was the only viable way to achieve their agenda. RODERICK NASH, THE RIGHTS OF NATURE, *supra* at 207-210. The Civil War resulted. Does an ethical approach to environmental law inevitably suggest coercive violence?

14. Whether or not a comparison with the abolitionist movement is justified, a small but vocal segment of the environmental community appears to accept destruction of property at least as a legitimate tool to accomplish environmental objectives. This tactic was popularized in Edward Abbey's widely-read novel, THE MONKEY WRENCH GANG (1975), which describes the efforts of a small band of environmental activists to blow up the Glen Canyon Dam on the Colorado River. It was further promoted by the environmental group, Earth First!, David Foreman, co-founder of the group, describes "monkey-wrenching" as "the non-violent resistance to the destruction of natural diversity and wildness. It is never directed toward harming human beings or other forms of life. Care is always taken to minimize a possible threat to people, including the monkey wrenchers themselves." DAVID FOREMAN, CONFESSIONS OF AN ECO-WARRIOR 113 (1991); *see also* DAVID FOREMAN & BILL HAYWOOD, ECODEFENSE: A FIELD GUIDE TO MONKEYWRENCHING (2d ed. 1987) which is a detailed manual of monkeywrenching techniques (including, for example, detailed instructions on tree-spiking) prepared, according to the authors, "for entertainment purposes only." Foreman and four others were arrested in 1989 for, among other things, conspiracy to destroy government property. The charges were made after an FBI informant infiltrated the group. *See* Bill McKibben, *Court Jester*, MOTHER JONES, (Nov-Dec 1991) at 20. Foreman's co-defendants all received jail time. Foreman, who was not directly involved in the incident, pled guilty to conspiracy to commit property destruction. Sentencing was postponed for 5 years at which time Foreman would be permitted to change his plea or plead guilty to a misdemeanor. Donna E. Correll, Note, *No Peace For Greens: The Criminal Prosecution of Environmental Activists and the Threat of Organization Liability,* 24 RUTGERS L.J. 773, 788-790 (1993). The terms "ecotage," and the more pejorative "eco-terrorism," have sometimes been used to describe the activities of these groups. Is property destruction ever justified to protect the environment?

15. Non-violent protests and civil disobedience have also played an important role in shaping the environmental debate. Greenpeace International and its local affiliates for example, have long participated in civil disobedience actions, which have included protests against whaling and sealing, and more recently, nuclear testing. *See* RODERICK NASH, THE RIGHTS OF NATURE, 179-181 (1989). Civil disobedience as a vehicle for changing public policy, has generally received favorable treatment from writers and philosophers. *See e.g.*, LEO TOLSTOY, TOLSTOY'S WRITINGS ON CIVIL DISOBEDIENCE AND NON-VIOLENCE (1967); Henry David Thoreau, *On the Duty of Civil Disobedience, in* WALDEN AND CIVIL DISOBEDIENCE 222 (1960); John Rawls, *The Justification of Civil Disobedience, in* EDWARD ALLEN KENT, LAW AND PHILOSOPHY 343 (1970).

The following excerpt from Aldo Leopold's posthumously published collection of essays is probably the most influential statement of ethics in the American environmental movement. In addition to his pioneering work at the U.S. Forest Service to preserve wild tracts of land and at the University of Wisconsin to establish the field of wildlife management, Leopold also helped found The Wilderness Society in 1935.

THE LAND ETHIC
Aldo Leopold
A Sand County Almanac (1949, 1966)*

When God-like Odysseus returned from the wars in Troy, he hanged all on one rope a dozen slave-girls of his household whom he suspected of misbehavior during his absence.

---

* Copyright 1949, 1966 Oxford University Press. Reprinted with permission.

This hanging involved no question of propriety. The girls were property. The disposal of property was then, as now, a matter of expediency, not of right and wrong.

Concepts of right and wrong were not lacking form Odysseus' Greece: witness the fidelity of his wife through the long years before at last his black-prowed galleys clove the wine-dark seas for home. The ethical structure of that day covered wives, but had not yet been extended to human chattels. During the three thousand years which have since elapsed, ethical criteria have been extended to many fields of conduct, with corresponding shrinkages in those judged by expediency only.

THE ETHICAL SEQUENCE

This extension of ethics, so far studied only by philosophers, is actually a process in ecological evolution. Its sequences may be described in ecological as well as in philosophical terms. An ethic, ecologically, is a limitation on freedom of action in the struggle for existence. An ethic, philosophically, is a differentiation of social from anti-social conduct. These are two definitions of one thing. The thing has its origin in the tendency of interdependent individuals or groups to evolve modes of co-operation. The ecologist calls these symbioses. Politics and economics are advanced symbioses in which the original free-for-all competition has been replaced, in part, by co-operative mechanisms with an ethical content.

The complexity of co-operative mechanisms has increased with population density, and with the efficiency of tools. It was simpler, for example, to define the anti-social uses of sticks and stones in the days of the mastodons than of bullets and billboards in the age of motors.

The first ethics dealt with the relation between individuals; the Mosaic Decalogue is an example. Later accretions dealt with the relation between the individual and society. The golden rule tries to integrate the individual to society; democracy to integrate social organization to the individual.

There is as yet no ethic dealing with man's relation to land and to the animals and plants which grow upon it. Land, like Odysseus' slave-girls, is still property. The land-relation is still strictly economic, entailing privileges but not obligations.

The extension of ethics to this third element in human environment is, if I read the evidence correctly, an evolutionary possibility and an ecological necessity. It is the third step in a sequence. The first two have already been taken. Individual thinkers since the days of Ezekiel and Isaiah have asserted that the despoliation of land is not only inexpedient but wrong. Society, however, has not yet affirmed their belief. I regard the present conservation movement as the embryo of such an affirmation.

An ethic may be regarded as a mode of guidance for meeting ecological situations so new or intricate, or involving such deferred reactions, that the path of social expediency is not discernible to the average individual. Animal instincts are modes of guidance for the individual in meeting such situations. Ethics are possibly a kind of community instinct in-the-making.

THE COMMUNITY CONCEPT

All ethics so far evolved rest upon a single premise; that the individual is a member of a community of interdependent parts. His instincts prompt him to compete for his place in the community, but his ethics prompt him also to co-operate (perhaps in order that there may be a place to compete for).

The land ethic simply enlarges the boundaries of the community to include soils, waters, plants, and animals, or collectively: the land.

This sounds simple: do we not already sing our love for and obligation to the land of the free and the home of the brave? Yes, but just what and whom do we love? Certainly not the soil, which we are sending helter-skelter downriver. Certainly not the waters, which we assume have no function except to turn turbines, float barges, and carry off sewage. Certainly not the plants, of which we exterminate whole communities without batting an eye. Certainly not the animals, of which we have already extirpated many of the largest and most beautiful of species. A land ethic of course cannot prevent the alteration, management, and use of the "resources," but it does affirm their right to continued existence, and, at least in spots, their continued existence in a natural state.

In short, a land ethic changes the role of *Homo sapiens* from conqueror of the land-community to plain member and citizen of it. It implies respect for his fellow-members, and also respect for the community as such.

In human history, we have learned (I hope) that the conqueror role is eventually self-defeating. Why? Because it is implicit in such a role that the conqueror knows, *ex cathedra*, just what makes the community clock tick, and just what and who is valuable, and what and who is worthless, in community life. It always turns out that he knows neither, and this is why his conquests eventually defeat themselves.

In the biotic community, a parallel situation exists. Abraham knew exactly what the land was for: it was to drip milk and honey into Abraham's mouth. At the present moment, the assurance with which we regard this assumption is inverse to the degree of our education.

* * *

To sum up: a system of conservation based solely on economic self-interest is hopelessly lopsided. It tends to ignore, and thus eventually to eliminate, many elements in the land community that lack commercial value, but that are (so far as we know) essential to its healthy functioning. It assumes, falsely, I think, that the economic parts of the biotic clock will function without the uneconomic parts. It tends to relegate to government many functions eventually too large, too complex, or too widely dispersed to be performed by government.

An ethical obligation on the part of the private owner is the only visible remedy for these situations.

THE LAND PYRAMID

An ethic to supplement and guide the economic relation to land presupposes the existence of some mental image of land as a biotic mechanism. We can be ethical only in relation to something we can see, feel, understand, love, or otherwise have faith in.

The image commonly employed in conservation education is "the balance of nature." For reasons too lengthy to detail here, this figure of speech fails to describe accurately what little we know about the land mechanism. A much truer image is the one employed in ecology: the biotic pyramid. I shall first sketch the pyramid as a symbol of land, and later develop some of its implications in terms of land-use.

Plants absorb energy from the sun. This energy flows through a circuit called the biota, which may be represented by a pyramid consisting of layers. The bottom layer is the soil.

A plant layer rests on the soil, an insect layer on the plants, a bird and rodent layer on the insects, and so on up through various animal groups to the apex layer, which consists of the larger carnivores.

The species of a layer are alike not in where they came from, or in what they look like, but rather in what they eat. Each successive layer depends on those below it for food and often for other services, and each in turn furnishes food and services to those above. Proceeding upward, each successive layer decreases in numerical abundance. Thus, for every carnivore there are hundreds of his prey, thousands of their prey, millions of insects, uncountable plants. The pyramidal form of the system reflects this numerical progression from apex to base. Man shares an intermediate layer with the bears, raccoons, and squirrels which eat both meat and vegetables.

* * *

Land, then, is not merely soil; it is a fountain of energy flowing through a circuit of soils, plants, and animals. Food chains are the living channels which conduct energy upward; death and decay return it to the soil. The circuit is not closed; some energy is dissipated in decay, some is added by absorption from the air, some is stored in soils, peats, and long-lived forests; but is a sustained circuit, like a slowly augmented revolving fund of life. There is always a net loss by downhill wash, but this is normally small and offset by the decay of rocks. It is deposited in the ocean and, in the course of geological time, raised to form new lands and new pyramids.

* * *

The process of altering the pyramid for human occupation releases stored energy, and this often gives rise, during the pioneering period, to a deceptive exuberance of plant and animal life, both wild and tame. These releases of biotic capital tend to becloud or postpone the penalties of violence.

* * *

THE OUTLOOK

It is inconceivable to me that an ethical relation to land can exist without love, respect, and admiration for land, and a high regard for its value. By value, I of course mean something far broader than mere economic value; I mean value in the philosophical sense.

Perhaps the most serious obstacle impeding the evolution of a land ethic is the fact that our educational and economic system is headed away from, rather than toward, an intense consciousness of land. Your true modern is separated from the land by many middlemen, and by innumerable physical gadgets. He has no vital relation to it; to him it is the space between cities on which crops grow. Turn him loose for a day on the land, and if the spot does not happen to be a golf links or a "scenic" area, he is bored stiff. If crops could be raised by hydroponics instead of farming, it would suit him very well. Synthetic substitutes for wood, leather, wool, and other natural land products suit him better than the originals. In short, land is something he has "outgrown."

Almost equally serious as an obstacle to a land ethic is the attitude of the farmer for whom the land is still an adversary, or a taskmaker that keeps him in slavery. Theoretically, the mechanization of farming ought to cut the farmer's chains, but whether it really does is debatable.

* * *

The case for a land ethic would appear hopeless but for the minority which is in obvious revolt against these "modern" trends.

The "key-log" which must be moved to release the evolutionary process for an ethic is simply this: quit thinking about decent land-use as solely an economic problem. Examine each question in terms of what is ethically and aesthetically right, as well as what is economically expedient. A thing is right when it tends to preserve the integrity, stability, and beauty of the biotic community. It is wrong when it tends otherwise.

* * *

The mechanism of operation is the same for any ethic: social approbation for right actions; disapproval for wrong actions.

By and large, our present problem is one of attitudes and implements. We are remodeling the Alhambra with a steam-shovel, and we are proud of our yardage. We shall hardly relinquish the shovel, which after all has many good points, but we are in need of gentler and more objective criteria for its successful use.

* * *

NOTES

1. What is Leopold's "land ethic"? Does it reflect a realistic goal for modern societies? Some loss to the "integrity, stability and beauty of the biotic community" seems inevitable. Does it offer people sufficient guidance to conduct their affairs? Is Leopold's "land ethic" realistic in accepting this loss? Is hunting compatible with the land ethic?

2. Professor Charles Wilkinson suggests that we need to develop an "ethic of place," a recognition that the environment and its people are equals and are both sacred. Wilkinson sees an ethic of place as a shared community value, resulting in respect for animals, vegetation, water, and air, as well as for the people of the land. *See* Charles Wilkinson, *Law and the American West: The Search for an Ethic of Place,* 59 U. COLO. L. REV. 401, 405 (1988); CHARLES WILKINSON, THE EAGLE BIRD: MAPPING A NEW WEST (1992). Does an ethic of place that accommodates extractive use of natural resources compromise the land ethic? CHARLES WILKINSON, CROSSING THE NEXT MERIDIAN 17 (1992). Is an ethic of place what Leopold had in mind when he described the land ethic as "enlarging the boundaries of the community to include soils, waters, plants and animals?" For another view of the ethic of place, *see* Mark Sagoff, *Settling America or the Concept of Place in Environmental Ethics,* 12 J. ENERGY NAT. RESOURCES & ENVTL. L. 349 (1992).

3. Does Leopold's land ethic ultimately ignore the fact that the human species is a part of the biotic community? If the human species is a part of the biotic community, can all of its supposed transgressions against nature be simply attributed to the natural evolution of the human species? If so, is it even possible that human actions can be "wrong" in a biological sense? In this context, consider the views of Herbert Spencer, the renowned nineteenth century philosopher, on the evolution of the human species:

> The ultimate development of the ideal man is logically certain—as certain as any conclusion in which we place the most implicit faith; for instance that all men will die.* * * Progress, therefore, is not an accident, but a necessity. Instead of civilization being artificial, it is part of nature; all of a piece with the development of the embryo or the unfolding of a flower.

HERBERT SPENCER, SOCIAL STATICS 79-80 (1850), *quoted in* RICHARD HOFSTADTER, SOCIAL DARWINISM IN AMERICAN THOUGHT 40 (Rev. ed. 1955).

4. Leopold asserts that instincts prompt us to compete but that ethics prompt us to cooperate within a community. For an explanation of how cooperation may arise solely from individual self-interest, *see* ROBERT AXELROD, THE EVOLUTION OF COOPERATION (1984).

5. Leopold suggests that the root of our ecological problems lies in our view of land use "as solely an economic problem." In a passage from the forward to A SAND COUNTY ALMANAC, Leopold further explains: "We abuse land because we regard it as a commodity belonging to us. When we see land as a community to which we belong, we may begin to use it with love and respect." A SAND COUNTY ALMANAC x (1949).

6. James Lovelock has taken Leopold's notion of a land ethic a step further by describing the Earth or—as he calls it—the Gaia, as a super organism:

> Gaia theory sees the biota and the rocks, the air and the oceans as existing as a tightly coupled entity. Its evolution is a single process and not several separate processes studied in different buildings of universities.
>
> * * *
>
> * * * I see the world as a living organism of which we are a part; not the owner not the tenant, not even a passenger. To exploit such a world on the scale we do is as foolish as it would be to consider our brains supreme and the cells of other organs expendable. * * *

James E. Lovelock, *The Earth as a Living Organism, reprinted in* E.O. WILSON, BIODIVERSITY 488-89 (1988); *see also,* JAMES E. LOVELOCK, GAIA: A NEW LOOK AT LIFE ON EARTH (1979).

7. Leopold claims that the "land-relation is still strictly economic, entailing privileges but not obligations." Is this true? Professor Carol Rose finds a much more diverse suite of meanings of property, which includes obligations. *See* Carol Rose, *Given-ness and Gift: Property and the Quest for Environmental Ethics,* 24 ENVTL. L. 1 (1994), *infra* at Chapter Four, Part A. Even John Locke, the 17th century philosopher whose work forms the foundation for much of modern property law, might have disagreed with Leopold's description of private property: "* * * [W]hereby anyone unites his person, which was before free, to any common-wealth, by the same he unites his possessions, which were before free, to it also; and they become, both of them, person and possession, subject to the government and dominion of that common-wealth, as long as it hath a being * * * ." JOHN LOCKE, SECOND TREATISE OF GOVERNMENT § 120 (C. B. Macpherson, ed. 1980) (1690).

8. Leopold's land ethic suggests a holistic or biocentric approach toward nature, whereas the Christian values of the Western tradition seem to support an anthropocentric view. Many writers have suggested that the holistic tradition has its roots in Eastern religious philosophy, and in various aboriginal cultures throughout the world, including Native American cultures. For example, Alan Watts, a Zen Buddhist, has described the Buddhist view of the world as a "seamless unity" of which humans are merely one part. ALAN W. WATTS, NATURE, MAN AND WOMAN (1958); and while it is now generally accepted that Chief Seattle never called the earth our mother, or the river our brothers, *see* Paul S. Wilson, *What Chief Seattle Said,* 22 ENVTL. L. 1451 (1992), this fact has not diminished the generally accepted view that many Native American people share Leopold's holistic view. Tom Tso, Chief Justice of the Navajo Nation Supreme Court has eloquently described the Navajo attitude toward nature:

> We refer to the earth and sky as Mother Earth and Father Sky. These are no catchy titles; they represent our understanding of our place. The earth and sky are relatives. Nature communicates with us through the wind and the water and the whispering pines * * * .
>
> Just like our natural mother, our Mother Earth provides for us. It is not wrong to accept the things we need from the earth. It is wrong to treat the earth with disrespect. It is wrong if we fail to protect and defend the earth * * *

Tom Tso, *The Process of Decision Making in Tribal Courts,* 31 ARIZ. L. REV. 225, 233-34 (1989). *See also,* JOHN FIRE LAME DEER, LAME DEER SEEKER OF VISIONS: THE LIFE OF A SIOUX MEDICINE MAN (Richard Erdoes, ed. 1992); N. Scott Momaday, *A First American Views His Land,* 150 NAT'L GEOGRAPHIC 13-18 (July 1976)

9. The Land Ethic has had a profound influence on the evolution of environmental ethics, and has spawned a substantial body of related work. *See e.g.,* J. BAIRD CALLICOTT, IN DEFENSE OF THE LAND ETHIC, (1989), J. BAIRD CALLICOTT, COMPANION TO A SAND COUNTY ALMANAC: INTERPRETIVE AND CRITICAL ESSAYS (1987); Eric T. Freyfogle, *The Land Ethic and Pilgrim Leopold,* 61 U. COLO. L. REV. 217 (1990); James P. Karp, *Aldo Leopold's Land Ethic: Is An Ecological Conscience Arising in Land Development Law?,* 19 ENVTL. L. 737 (1989). The leading biography on Aldo Leopold is CURT MEINE, ALDO LEOPOLD: HIS LIFE AND WORK (1988).

The following article by Professor Christopher Stone was inspired by litigation arising over a proposal by Walt Disney Enterprises to develop a ski resort in the Mineral King Valley, a relatively pristine area of national forest land. As Stone was writing in support of standing for threatened resources, the decision of the U.S. Court of Appeals for the Ninth Circuit denying the Sierra Club standing to sue was pending before the U.S. Supreme Court. In hopes of influencing the Court's decision, Stone and the editors of the Southern California Law Review rushed page proofs to the office of Justice William O. Douglas, the Court's most likely champion of Stone's position. Although Douglas was indeed persuaded by Stone's reasoning, he was not able to command a majority of the Court and the lower court's decision denying standing was affirmed by a majority of the Court. *Sierra Club v. Morton,* 405 U.S. 727 (1972). Justice Douglas's dissent in the *Sierra Club* case, however, has been frequently cited and remains one of the most powerful statements in support of Stone's position. Despite having lost the case, the Sierra Club was ultimately successful in stopping the proposed ski development. In 1978, Congress made the Mineral King Valley part of the Sequoia National Park. National Parks and Recreation Act of 1978, Pub. L. No. 95-625, § 314, 92 Stat. 3467 (*codified* at 16 U.S.C. § 45f (1994)). The background to Stone's article is further described by Roderick Nash in THE RIGHTS OF NATURE 128-31 (1989).

SHOULD TREES HAVE STANDING?—TOWARD LEGAL RIGHTS FOR NATURAL OBJECTS
Christopher D. Stone
45 S. Cal. L. Rev. 450 (1972)*

INTRODUCTION: THE UNTHINKABLE

In *Descent of Man,* Darwin observes that the history of man's moral development has been a continual extension in the objects of his "social instincts and sympathies." Originally each man had regard only for himself and those of a very narrow circle about him; later, he came to regard more and more "not only the welfare, but the happiness of all his fellowmen"; then "his sympathies became more tender and widely diffused, extending to men of all races, to the imbecile, maimed, and other useless members of society, and finally to the lower animals * * * ."

The history of the law suggests a parallel development. Perhaps there never was a pure Hobbesian state of nature, in which no "rights" existed except in the vacant sense of each man's "right to self-defense." But it is not unlikely that so far as the earliest "families" (including extended kinship groups and clans) were concerned, everyone outside the family was suspect, alien, rightless. And even within the family, persons we presently regard as the natural holders of at least some rights had none. Take, for example, children. We know something of the early rights-status of children from the widespread practice of infanticide—especially of the deformed and female.

---

* Reprinted with the permission of the Southern California Law Review.

The legal rights of children have long since been recognized in principle, and are still expanding in practice. And we have done the same, albeit imperfectly some would say, with prisoners, aliens, women (especially of the married variety), the insane, Blacks, foetuses, and Indians.

Nor is it only matter in human form that has come to be recognized as the possessor of rights. The world of the lawyer is peopled with inanimate right-holders: trusts, corporations, joint ventures, municipalities, Subchapter R partnerships, and nation-states, to mention just a few. Ships, still referred to by courts in the feminine gender, have long had an independent jural life, often with striking consequences. We have become so accustomed to the idea of a corporation having "its" own rights, and being a "person" and "citizen" for so many statutory and constitutional purposes, that we forget how jarring the notion was to early jurists. * * *

Throughout legal history, each successive extension of rights to some new entity has been, theretofore, a bit unthinkable. We are inclined to suppose the rightlessness of rightless "things" to be a decree of Nature, not a legal convention acting in support of some status quo. It is thus that we defer considering the choices involved in all their moral, social, and economic dimensions. And so the United States Supreme Court could straight-facedly tell us in *Dred Scott* that Blacks had been denied the rights of citizenship "as a subordinate and inferior class of beings, who had been subjugated by the dominant race * * * ."[19]

In the nineteenth century, the highest court in California explained that Chinese had not the right to testify against white men in criminal matters because they were "a race of people whom nature has marked as inferior, and who are incapable of progress or intellectual development beyond a certain point * * * between whom and ourselves nature has placed an impassable difference."[20] * * * The first woman in Wisconsin who thought she might have a right to practice law was told that she did not, in the following terms:

> The law, of nature destines and qualifies the female sex for the bearing and nurture of the children of our race and for the custody of the homes of the world * * * . [A]ll life-long callings of women, inconsistent with these radical and sacred duties of their sex, as is the profession of the law, are departures from the order of nature; and when voluntary, treason against it * * * . Nature has tempered woman as little for the juridical conflicts of the court room, as for the physical conflicts of the battle field * * * .[23]

The fact is, that each time there is a movement to confer rights onto some new "entity", the proposal is bound to sound odd or frightening or laughable. This is partly because until the rightless thing receives its rights, we cannot see it as anything but a *thing* for the use of "us"—those who are holding rights at the time.

* * *

The reason for this little discourse on the unthinkable, the reader must know by now,

---

[19] Dred Scott v. Sandford, 60 U.S. (19 How.) 396, 404-05 (1856). In Bailey v. Poindexter's Ex'r, 56 Va. (14 Gratt.) 132, 142-43 (1858) a provision in a will that testator's slaves could choose between emancipation and public sale was held void on the ground that slaves have no legal capacity to choose. * * *

[20] People v. Hall, 4 Cal. 399, 405 (1854). * * *

[23] *In re* Goddell, 39 Wisc. 232, 245 (1875). * * *

if only from the title of the paper. I am quite seriously proposing that we give legal rights to forests, oceans, rivers and other so-called "natural objects" in the environment—indeed, to the natural environment as a whole.

As strange as such a notion may sound, it is neither fanciful nor devoid of operational content. In fact, I do not think it would be a misdescription of recent developments in the law to say that we are already on the verge of assigning some such rights, although we have not faced up to what we are doing in those particular terms. We should do so now, and begin to explore the implications such a notion would hold.

TOWARD RIGHTS FOR THE ENVIRONMENT

Now, to say that the natural environment should have rights is not to say anything as silly as that no one should be allowed to cut down a tree. We say human beings have rights, but—at least as of the time of this writing—they can be executed. Corporations have rights, but they cannot plead the fifth amendment. Thus, to say that the environment should have rights is not to say that it should have every right we can imagine, or even the same body of rights as human beings have. Nor is it to say that everything in the environment should have the same rights as every other thing in the environment.

What the granting of rights does involve has two sides to it. The first involves what might be called the legal-operational aspects; the second, the psychic and socio-psychic aspects. I shall deal with these aspects in turn.

THE LEGAL-OPERATIONAL ASPECTS

What it Means to be a Holder of Legal Rights

There is, so far as I know, no generally accepted standard for how one ought to use the term legal rights. Let me indicate how I shall be using it in this piece.

First and most obviously, if the term is to have any content at all, an entity cannot be said to hold a legal right unless and until *some public authoritative body* is prepared to give *some amount of review* to actions that are colorably inconsistent with that "right." For example, if a student can be expelled from a university and cannot get any public official, even a judge or administrative agent at the lowest level, either (i) to require the university to justify its actions (if only to the extent of filling out an affidavit alleging that the expulsion "was not wholly arbitrary and capricious") or (ii) to compel the university to accord the student some procedural safeguards (a hearing, right to counsel, right to have notice of charges), then the minimum requirements for saying that the student has a legal right to his education do not exist.

But for a thing to be *a holder of legal rights*, something more is needed than that some authoritative body will review the actions and processes of those who threaten it. As I shall use the term, "holder of legal rights," each of three additional criteria must be satisfied. All three, one will observe, go towards making a thing *count* jurally—to have a legally recognized worth and dignity in its own right, and not merely to serve as a means to benefit "us" (whoever the contemporary group of rights-holders may be). They are, first, that the thing can institute legal actions *at its behest*; second, that in determining the granting of legal relief, the court must take *injury* to *it* into account; and, third, that relief must run to the *benefit of it*.

The Rightlessness of Natural Objects at Common Law

Consider, for example, the common law's posture toward the pollution of a stream. True, courts have always been able, in some circumstances to issue orders that will stop the pollution * * * . But the stream itself is fundamentally rightless, with implications that deserve careful reconsideration.

The first sense in which the stream is not a rights-holder has to do with standing. The stream itself has none. So far as the common law is concerned, there is in general no way to challenge the polluter's actions save at the behest of a lower riparian—another human being—able to show an invasion of *his* rights. This conception of the riparian as the holder of the right to bring suit has more than theoretical interest. The lower riparians may simply not care about the pollution. They themselves may be polluting, and not wish to stir up legal waters. They may be economically dependent on their polluting neighbor. And, of course, when they discount the value of winning by the costs of bringing suit and the chances of success, the action may not seem worth undertaking.

The second sense in which the common law denies "rights" to natural objects has to do with the way in which the merits are decided in those cases in which someone is competent and willing to establish standing. At its more primitive levels, the system protected the "rights" of the property owning human with minimal weighing of any values: "*Cujus est solum, ejus est usque ad coleum et ad infernos.*"[34] Today we have come more and more to make balances—but only such as will adjust the economic best interests of identifiable humans. For example, continuing with the case of streams, there are commentators who speak of a "general rule" that "a riparian owner is legally entitled to have the stream flow by his land with its quality unimpaired" and observe that "an upper owner has, prima facie, no right to pollute the water."

Such a doctrine, if strictly invoked, would protect the stream absolutely whenever a suit was brought; but obviously, to look around us, the law does not work that way. Almost everywhere there are doctrinal qualifications on riparian "rights" to an unpolluted stream. Although these rules vary from jurisdiction to jurisdiction, and upon whether one is suing for an equitable injunction or for damages, what they all have in common is some sort of balancing. Whether under language of "reasonable use," "reasonable methods of use," "balance of convenience" or "the public interest doctrine," what the courts are balancing, with varying degrees of directness, are the economic hardships on the upper riparian (or dependent community) of abating the pollution vis-á-vis the economic hardships of continued pollution on the lower riparians. What does not weigh in the balance is the damage to the stream, its fish and turtles and "lower" life. So long as the natural environment itself is rightless, these are not matters for judicial cognizance. Thus, we find the highest court of Pennsylvania refusing to stop a coal company from discharging polluted mine water into a tributary of the Lackawana River because a plaintiff's "grievance is for a mere personal inconvenience; and * * * mere private personal inconveniences * * * must yield to the necessities of a great public industry, which although in the hands

---

[34] To whomever the soil belongs, he owns also to the sky and the depths. *See* W. BLACKSTONE, 2 COMMENTARIES *18.

of a private corporation, subserves a great public interest.[38] The stream itself is lost sight of in "a quantitative compromise between *two* conflicting interests."[39]

The third way in which the common law makes natural objects rightless has to do with who is regarded as the beneficiary of a favorable judgment. Here, too, it makes a considerable difference that it is not the natural object that counts in its own right. To illustrate this point, let me begin by observing that it makes perfectly good sense to speak of, and ascertain, the legal damage to a natural object, if only in the sense of "making it whole" with respect to the most obvious factors. The costs of making a forest whole, for example, would include the costs of reseeding, repairing watersheds, restocking wildlife—the sorts of costs the Forest Service undergoes after a fire. Making a polluted stream whole would include the costs of restocking with fish, water-fowl, and other animal and vegetable life, dredging, washing out impurities, establishing natural and/or artificial aerating agents, and so forth. Now, what is important to note is that, under our present system, even if a plaintiff riparian wins a water pollution suit for damages, no money goes to the benefit of the stream itself to repair its damages. This omission has the further effect that, at most, the law confronts a polluter with what it takes to make the plaintiff riparians whole; this may be far less than the damages to the stream, but not so much as to force the polluter to desist. For example, it is easy to imagine a polluter whose activities damage a stream to the extent of $10,000 annually, although the aggregate damage to all the riparian plaintiffs who come into the suit is only $3000. If $3000 is less than the cost to the polluter of shutting down, or making the requisite technological changes, he might prefer to pay off the damages (*i.e.*, the legally cognizable damages) and continue to pollute the stream. * * *

I ought to make clear at this point that the common law as it affects streams and rivers, which I have been using as an example so far, is not exactly the same as the law affecting other environmental objects. Indeed, one would be hard pressed to say that there was a "typical" environmental object, so far as its treatment at the hands of the law is concerned. There are some differences in the law applicable to all the various resources that are held in common: rivers, lakes, oceans, dunes, air, streams (surface and subterranean), beaches, and so forth. And there is an even greater difference as between these traditional communal resources on the one hand, and natural objects on traditionally private land, *e.g.*, the pond on the farmer's field, or the stand of trees on the suburbanite's lawn.

On the other hand, although there be these differences which would make it fatuous to generalize about a law of the natural environment, most of these differences simply underscore the points made in the instance of rivers and streams. None of the natural objects, whether held in common or situated on private land, has any of the three criteria of a rights-holder. They have no standing in their own right; their unique damages do not count in determining outcome; and they are not the beneficiaries of awards. In such fashion, these objects have traditionally been regarded by the common law, and even by all but the most recent legislation, as objects for man to conquer and master and use—in such a way as the law once looked upon "man's" relationships to African Negroes. Even

---

[38] Pennsylvania Coal Co. v. Sanderson, 113 Pa. 125, 149, 6 A. 453, 459 (1886).

[39] Hand, J. in Smith v. Staso Milling Co., 18 F.2d 736, 738 (2d. Cir. 1927) (emphasis added). * * *

where special measures have been taken to conserve them, as by seasons on game and limits on timber cutting, the dominant motive has been to conserve them *for us*—for the greatest good of the greatest number of human beings. Conservationists, so far as I am aware, are generally reluctant to maintain otherwise. As the name implies, they want to conserve and guarantee *our* consumption and *our* enjoyment of these other living things. In their own right, natural objects have counted for little, in law as in popular movements.

Toward Having Standing in its Own Right

It is not inevitable, nor is it wise, that natural objects should have no rights to seek redress in their own behalf. It is no answer to say that streams and forests cannot have standing because streams and forests cannot speak. Corporations cannot speak either; nor can states, estates, infants, incompetents, municipalities or universities. Lawyers speak for them, as they customarily do for the ordinary citizen with legal problems. One ought, I think, to handle the legal problems of natural objects as one does the problems of legal incompetents—human beings who have become vegetable. If a human being shows signs of becoming senile and has affairs that he is de jure incompetent to manage, those concerned with his well being make such a showing to the court, and someone is designated by the court with the authority to manage the incompetent's affairs. The guardian (or "conservator" or committee—the terminology varies) then represents the incompetent in his legal affairs. Courts make similar appointments when a corporation has become "incompetent"—they appoint a trustee in bankruptcy or reorganization to oversee its affairs and speak for it in court when that becomes necessary.

On a parity of reasoning, we should have a system in which, when a friend of a natural object perceives it to be endangered, he can apply to a court for the creation of a guardianship. * * *

The potential "friends" that such a statutory scheme would require will hardly be lacking. The Sierra Club, Environmental Defense Fund, Friends of the Earth, Natural Resources Defense Counsel, and the Izaak Walton League are just some of the many groups which have manifested unflagging dedication to the environment and which are becoming increasingly capable of marshalling the requisite technical experts and lawyers. If, for example, the Environmental Defense Fund should have reason to believe that some company's strip mining operations might be irreparably destroying the ecological balance of large tracts of land, it could, under this procedure, apply to the court in which the lands were situated to be appointed guardian. As guardian, it might be given rights of inspection (or visitation) to determine and bring to the court's attention a fuller finding on the land's condition. If there were indications that under the substantive law some redress might be available on the land's behalf, then the guardian would be entitled to raise the land's rights in the land's name, *i.e.*, without having to make the roundabout and often unavailing demonstration, discussed below, that the "rights" of the club's members were being invaded. Guardians would also be looked to for a host of other protective tasks, *e.g.*, monitoring effluents (and/or monitoring the monitors), and representing their "wards" at legislative and administrative hearings on such matters as the setting of state water quality standards. Procedures exist, and can be strengthened, to move a court for the removal and substitution of guardians, for conflicts of interest or for other reasons, as well as for the termination of the guardianship.

* * *

The guardianship approach would secure an effective voice for the environment even where federal administrative action and public-lands and waters were not involved. It would also allay one of the fears courts * * * have about the extended standing concept: if any ad hoc group can spring up overnight, invoke some "right" as universally claimable as the esthetics and recreational interests of its members and thereby get into court, how can a flood of litigation be prevented? If an ad hoc committee loses a suit brought *sub nom.* Committee to Preserve our Trees, what happens when its very same members reorganize two years later and sue *sub nom.* the Massapequa Sylvan Protection League? Is the new group bound by res judicata? Class action law may be capable of ameliorating some of the more obvious problems. But even so, court economy might be better served by simply designating the guardian de jure representative of the natural object, with rights of discretionary intervention by others, but with the understanding that the natural object is "bound" by an adverse judgment. The guardian concept, too, would provide the endangered natural object with what the trustee in bankruptcy provides the endangered corporation: a continuous supervision over a period of time, with a consequent deeper understanding of a broad range of the ward's problems, not just the problems present in one particular piece of litigation. It would thus assure the courts that the plaintiff has the expertise and genuine adversity in pressing a claim which are the prerequisites of a true "case or controversy."

The guardianship approach, however, is apt to raise two objections, neither of which seem to me to have much force. The first is that a committee or guardian could not judge the needs of the river or forest in its charge; indeed, the very concept of "needs", it might be said, could be used here only in the most metaphorical way. The second objection is that such a system would not be much different from what we now have: is not the Department of Interior already such a guardian for public lands, and do not most states have legislation empowering their attorneys general to seek relief—in a sort of *parens patriae* way—for such injuries as a guardian might concern himself with?

As for the first objection, natural objects *can* communicate their wants (needs) to us, and in ways that are not terribly ambiguous. I am sure I can judge with more certainty and meaningfulness whether and when my lawn wants (needs) water, than the Attorney General can judge whether and when the United States wants (needs) to take an appeal from an adverse judgment by a lower court. The lawn tells me that it wants water by a certain dryness of the blades and soil—immediately obvious to the touch—the appearance of bald spots, yellowing, and a lack of springiness after being walked on; how does "the United States" communicate to the Attorney General? For similar reasons, the guardian-attorney for a smog-endangered stand of pines could venture with more confidence that his client wants the smog stopped, than the directors of a corporation can assert that "the corporation" wants dividends declared. We make decisions on behalf of, and in the purported interests of, others every day; these "others" are often creatures whose wants are far less verifiable, and even far more metaphysical in conception, than the wants of rivers, trees, and land.

As for the second objection, one can indeed find evidence that the Department of Interior was conceived as a sort of guardian of the public lands. But there are two points to keep in mind. First, insofar as the Department already is an adequate guardian it is only with respect to the federal public lands as per Article IV, section 3 of the Constitution. Its guardianship includes neither local public lands nor private lands. Second, to judge from the environmentalist literature and from the cases environmental action groups have been bringing, the Department is itself one of the bogeys of the environmental movement. * * * Whether the various charges be right or wrong, one cannot help but observe that the Department has been charged with several institutional goals (never an easy burden), and is currently looked to for action by quite a variety of interest groups, only one of which is the environmentalists. In this context, a guardian outside the institution becomes especially valuable. Besides, what a person wants, fully to secure his rights, is the ability to retain independent counsel even when, and perhaps especially when, the government is acting "for him" in a beneficent way. I have no reason to doubt, for example, that the Social Security System is being managed "for me"; but I would not want to abdicate my right to challenge its actions as they affect me, should the need arise. I would not ask more trust of national forests, vis-á-vis the Department of Interior. The same considerations apply in the instance of local agencies, such as regional water pollution boards, whose members' expertise in pollution matters is often all too credible.

* * *

Toward Recognition of its Own Injuries

As far as adjudicating the merits of a controversy is concerned, there is also a good case to be made for taking into account harm to the environment—in its own right. As indicated above, the traditional way of deciding whether to issue injunctions in law suits affecting the environment, at least where communal property is involved, has been to strike some sort of balance regarding the economic hardships on *human beings*. Even recently, Mr. Justice Douglas, our jurist most closely associated with conservation sympathies in his private life, was deciding the propriety of a new dam on the basis of, among other things, anticipated lost profits from fish catches, some $12,000,000 annually. Although he decided to delay the project pending further findings, the reasoning seems unnecessarily incomplete and compromising. Why should the environment be of importance only indirectly, as lost profits to someone else? Why not throw into the balance the cost *to the environment*?

* * *

One possible measure of damages, suggested earlier, would be the cost of making the environment whole, just as, when a man is injured in an automobile accident, we impose upon the responsible party the injured man's medical expenses. Comparable expenses to a polluted river would be the costs of dredging, restocking with fish, and so forth.

* * *

To what extent the decision-maker should factor in costs such as the pain and suffering of animals and other sentient natural objects, I cannot say; although I am prepared to do so in principle. Given the conjectural nature of the estimates in all events, and the roughness of the balance of conveniences procedure where that is involved, the practice would be of more interest from the socio-psychic point of view, discussed below, than from the legal-operational.

Toward Being a Beneficiary in its Own Right

As suggested above, one reason for making the environment itself the beneficiary of a judgment is to prevent it from being "sold out" in a negotiation among private litigants who agree not to enforce rights that have been established among themselves. Protection from this will be advanced by making the natural object a party to an injunctive settlement. Even more importantly, we should make it a beneficiary of money awards. * * * Not only should damages go into these funds, but where criminal fines are applied (as against water polluters) it seems to me that the monies (less prosecutorial expenses, perhaps) ought sensibly to go to the fund rather than to the general treasuries. Guardians fees, including legal fees, would then come out of this fund. More importantly, the fund would be available to preserve the natural object as close as possible to its condition at the time the environment was made a rights-holder.

(Incidentally, if "rights" are to be granted to the environment, then for many of the same reasons it might bear liabilities as well—as inanimate objects did anciently. Rivers drown people, and flood over and destroy crops; forests burn, setting fire to contiguous communities. Where trust funds had been established, they could be available for the satisfaction of judgments against the environment, making it bear the costs of some of the harms it imposes on other right holders. In effect, we would be narrowing the claim of Acts of God. The ontological problem would be troublesome here, however; when the Nile overflows, is it the responsibility of the river? the mountains? the snow? the hydrologic cycle?)

* * *

THE PSYCHIC AND SOCIO-PSYCHIC ASPECTS

There are, as we have seen, a number of developments in the law that may reflect a shift from the view that nature exists *for men*. These range from increasingly favorable procedural rulings for environmental action groups—as regards standing and burden of proof requirements, for example—to the enactment of comprehensive legislation such as the National Environmental Policy Act and the thoughtful Michigan Environmental Protection Act of 1970. Of such developments one may say, however, that it is not the environment *per se* that we are prepared to take into account, but that man's increased awareness of possible long range effects on himself militate in the direction of stopping environmental harm in its incipiency. And this is part of the truth, of course. Even the far-reaching National Environmental Policy Act, in its preambulatory "Declaration of National Environmental Policy," comes out both for "restoring and maintaining environmental quality *to the overall welfare and development of man*" as well as for creating and maintaining "conditions under which *man and nature can exist in productive harmony*." Because the health and well-being of mankind depend upon the health of the environment, these goals will often be so mutually supportive that one can avoid deciding whether our rationale is to advance "us" or a new "us" that includes the environment. * * *

But the time is already upon us when we may have to consider subordinating some human claims to those of the environment *per se*. Consider, for example, the disputes over protecting wilderness areas from development that would make them accessible to greater numbers of people. I myself feel disingenuous rationalizing the environmental protectionist's position in terms of a utilitarian calculus, even one that takes future generations into account, and plays fast and loose with its definition of "good." Those who favor development have the stronger argument—they at least hold the protectionist to a standstill—from the point of advancing the greatest good of the greatest number of people. And the same is true regarding arguments to preserve useless species of animals. * * * One *can* say that we never know what is going to prove useful at some future time. In order to protect ourselves, therefore, we ought to be conservative now in our treatment of nature. I agree. But when conservationists argue this way to the exclusion of other arguments, or find themselves speaking in terms of "recreational interests" so continuously as to play up to, and reinforce, homocentrist perspectives, there is something sad about the spectacle. One feels that the arguments lack even their proponent's convictions. I expect they want to say something less egotistic and more emphatic but the prevailing and sanctioned modes of explanation in our society are not quite ready for it. * * *

For my part, I would prefer a frank avowal that even making adjustments for esthetics improvements, what I am proposing is going to cost "us," *i.e.*, reduce our standard of living as measured in terms of our present values.

Yet, this frankness breeds a frank response—one which I hear from my colleagues and which must occur to many a reader. Insofar as the proposal is not just an elaborate legal fiction, but really comes down in the last analysis to a compromise of *our* interests for *theirs*, why should we adopt it? "What is in it for 'us'?"

This is a question I am prepared to answer, but only after permitting myself some observations about how *odd* the question is. It asks for me to justify my position in the very anthropocentric hedonist terms that I am proposing we modify. One is inclined to respond by a counter: "couldn't you (as a white) raise the same questions about compromising your preferred rights-status with Blacks?"; or "couldn't you (as a man) raise the same question about compromising your preferred rights-status with women?" Such counters, unfortunately, seem no more responsive than the question itself. (They have a nagging ring of "yours too" about them.) What the exchange actually points up is a fundamental problem regarding the nature of philosophical argument. Recall that Socrates, whom we remember as an opponent of hedonistic thought, confutes Thrasymachus by arguing that immorality makes one miserably unhappy! Kant, whose moral philosophy was based upon the categorical imperative ("Woe to him who creeps through the serpent windings of Utilitarianism") finds himself justifying, *e.g.*, promise keeping and truth telling, on the most prudential—one might almost say, commercial—grounds. This "philosophic irony" (as Professor Engel calls it) may owe to there being something unique about ethical argument. "Ethics cannot be put into words," Wittgenstein puts it; such matters "make themselves manifest." On the other hand, perhaps the truth is that in any argument which aims at persuading a human being to action (on ethical or any other bases), "logic" is only an instrument for illuminating positions, at best, and in the last analysis it is psychological appeals to the listener's self-interest that hold sway, however "principled" the rhetoric may be.

With this reservation as to the peculiar task of the argument that follows, let me stress that the strongest case can be made from the perspective of human advantage for conferring rights on the environment. Scientists have been warning of the crises the earth and all humans on it face if we do not change our ways—radically—and these crises make the lost "recreational use" of rivers seem absolutely trivial. The earth's very atmosphere is threatened with frightening possibilities: absorption of sunlight, upon which the entire life cycle depends, may be diminished; the oceans may warm (increasing the greenhouse effect of the atmosphere), melting the polar ice caps, and destroying our great coastal cities; the portion of the atmosphere that shields us from dangerous radiation may be destroyed. Testifying before Congress, sea explorer Jacques Cousteau predicted that the oceans (to which we dreamily look to feed our booming populations) are headed toward their own death: "The cycle of life is intricately tied up with the cycle of water * * * the water system has to remain alive if we are to remain alive on earth." We are depleting our energy and our food sources at a rate that takes little account of the needs even of humans now living.

These problems will not be solved easily; they very likely can be solved, if at all, only through a willingness to suspend the rate of increase in the standard of living (by present values) of the earth's "advanced" nations, and by stabilizing the total human population. For some of us this will involve forfeiting material comforts; for others it will involve abandoning the hope someday to obtain comforts long envied. For all of us it will involve giving up the right to have as many offspring as we might wish. Such a program is not impossible of realization, however. Many of our so-called "material comforts" are not only in excess of, but are probably in opposition to, basic biological needs. Further, the "costs" to the advanced nations is not as large as would appear from Gross National Product figures. G.N.P. reflects social gain (of a sort) without discounting for the social *cost* of that gain, *e.g.*, the losses through depletion of resources, pollution, and so forth. As has well been shown, as societies become more and more "advanced," their real marginal gains become less and less for each additional dollar of G.N.P. Thus, to give up "human progress" would not be as costly as might appear on first blush.

How far we are from such a state of affairs, where the law treats "environmental objects" as holders of legal rights, I cannot say. But there is certainly intriguing language in one of Justice Black's last dissents, regarding the Texas Highway Department's plan to run a six-lane expressway through a San Antonio Park. Complaining of the Court's refusal to stay the plan, Black observed that "after today's decision, the people of San Antonio and the birds and animals that make their home in the park will share their quiet retreat with an ugly, smelly stream of traffic * * * . Trees, shrubs, and flowers will be mown down." Elsewhere he speaks of the "burial of public parks," of segments of a highway which "devour parkland," and of the park's heartland. Was he, at the end of his great career, on the verge of saying—just saying—that "nature has 'rights' on its own account"? Would it be so hard to do?

NOTES

1. Is it necessary to confer legal rights on natural objects in order to secure the protection of such objects for their own sake? Could the public trust doctrine—which has been used successfully to protect public rights in stream beds, tidelands and water resources—be extended to encompass all natural objects? *See infra* Chapter Four, Part C. Why might Stone object to use of the public trust doctrine in lieu of granting legal rights to natural objects?

2. Professor Stone suggests two possible objections to the use of guardians to represent natural objects—(1) that the guardian might be incapable of judging the objects' needs; and (2) that the state and federal governments already have the authority to protect natural objects. What other possible objections might be made? Consider the case of the California condor—a species listed as endangered under the federal Endangered Species Act. So tenuous was the condor's chance for survival that the federal government concluded that the species would become extinct unless the government was able to remove all of the remaining birds from the wild and carry out successfully a captive breeding program. Some members from the environmental community supported the captive breeding program; others opposed it on the grounds that the best approach to preserving the species was to minimize human interference. How should a court decide on an appropriate guardian from between these two opposing perspectives? Recent reports suggest that the captive breeding program for the California condor is succeeding. Jeffrey P. Cohn, *The Flight of the California Condor*, 43 BioScience 206 (1993). *See* Bayard Webster, *Should Man Manipulate Animals*, New York Times, July 3, 1984, at C3, col.1.

3. Stone complains that the common law fails to recognize the right of a natural object to be made whole. He notes, for example, that when a person sues for pollution to a stream, she recovers for the damages to her—not for the damage to the stream environment itself. Natural resource damage assessments have become more widely accepted, however, as a result of provisions in three federal laws. The Clean Water Act authorizes recovery of natural resource damages caused by the discharge of oil or hazardous substances into the navigable waters of the United States. 33 U.S.C. § 1321(f)(4). The Oil Pollution Act of 1990 likewise authorizes recovery of such damages from oil spills into navigable waters, adjoining shorelines, and certain ocean waters, for "injury to, destruction of, loss of, or loss of use of natural resources, including the reasonable costs of assessing the damage * * * ." 33 U.S.C. § 2702(b)(2)(A). Finally, the Comprehensive Environmental Response, Compensation and Liability Act (Superfund), authorizes recovery of natural resource damages for releases of hazardous substances which cause response costs to be incurred. 42 U.S.C. § 9607(a)(4)(C). Under rules promulgated by the U.S. Department of the Interior to implement the Clean Water Act and Superfund provisions, the compensable value of the lost or injured resources "includes the value of lost public use of the services provided by the injured resource, plus lost non-use values such as existence and bequest values." 43 CFR § 11.83(c)(1) (1994). The Department's original rules, which would have limited recovery to the lesser of restoration and replacement costs, or diminution of use values, were struck down by the Court of Appeals for the District of Columbia Circuit. *State of Ohio v. U.S. Department of the Interior*, 880 F.2d 432, 459 (D.C. Cir.

1989). The court also rejected the Department's claim that Congress intended to limit recoveries to use values. *Id.* at 464.

Perhaps the most commonly offered reason for protecting our environment and preserving natural systems is our responsibility to future generations. It is not surprising then that one of the principal goals of the National Environmental Policy Act is to make the federal government responsible for improving and coordinating federal programs "to the end that the Nation may—(1) fulfill the responsibilities of each generation as trustee of the environment for succeeding generations." 42 U.S.C. § 4331(b). The following two articles offer different perspectives on this important issue.

DO WE OWE A DUTY TO FUTURE GENERATIONS TO PRESERVE THE GLOBAL ENVIRONMENT?
Anthony D'Amato
84 Am. J. Int'l L. 190 (1990)*

A common assumption underlying nearly every book or essay on the global environment is that the present generation owes a duty to generations yet unborn to preserve the diversity and quality of our planet's life-sustaining environmental resources. This duty is sometimes said to be an emerging norm of customary international law, including the more recently treaty-generated custom of the "common heritage of mankind." Professor Edith Brown Weiss lists three different approaches one might take in response to an asserted environmental obligation to future generations: the "opulent" model, which denies any such obligation and permits present extravagance and waste; the "preservationist" model at the other extreme, which requires the present generation to make substantial sacrifices of denial so as to enhance the environmental legacy; and the "equality" model— favored by Professor Weiss—which says we owe to future generations a global environment in no worse condition than the one we enjoy.[3]

I. PARFIT'S PARADOX OF FUTURE INDIVIDUALS

International law scholars appear to have overlooked the startling thesis put forth by Derek Parfit in 1976.[4] I will state his thesis in a somewhat stronger form than he did. Let us picture the people who will be living 100 years from now: they will be specific, identifiable persons. We can claim that we currently owe an environment-preserving obligation to those particular as-yet-unborn persons. Parfit's paradox arises when we seek to discharge that postulated obligation. Suppose that we undertake a specific environmental act of conservation. For example, we help to pass a law requiring catalytic converters

---

* Reprinted with permission. Copyright by The American Society of International Law.
[3] E. BROWN WEISS, ON FAIRNESS TO FUTURE GENERATIONS: INTERNATIONAL LAW, COMMON PATRIMONY AND INTER-GENERATIONAL EQUITY (1989).
[4] Derek Parfit, *On Doing the Best for Our Children*, in ETHICS AND POPULATION 100 (M. Bayles ed. 1976) * * * .

on all automobiles in our state. We will thus have succeeded in intervening in the environment—making the environment slightly different from the way it would have been but for our action. Our intervention will reduce the amount of air pollution that otherwise would have taken place, and increase the utilization of energy and resources in the manufacture of catalytic converters.

Yet this slight difference resulting from our intervention in the environment will affect the ecosphere in the years subsequent to our intervention. In particular, it will affect the conditions under which human procreation takes place. The particular sperm and egg cells from which any human being develops is a highly precarious fact; the slightest difference in the conditions of conception will probably result in fertilization of the egg by a different sperm. Hence, when the environment is disrupted even a slight amount, a different future person will probably be conceived. According to Parfit's thesis, our intervention in the environment will make a sufficient impact to assure that different sperm cells will probably fertilize the egg cells in all procreations that take place subsequent to our environmental intervention. Different people will be born from those who would have been born if we had not intervened in the environment. To be sure, in the first few years following our environmental intervention, there is very low probability that many subsequent human conceptions will be affected. But as years go by, the effect of our single environmental intervention increases exponentially until it is a virtual certainty that 100 years from now all human conceptions will have been affected a little bit from our single act of environmental intervention, and that this little effect will actually result in fertilization of egg cells by sperm cells different from those that would have fertilized those egg cells in the absence of our act. Parfit's conclusion is that every single person alive 100 years from now will be an entirely different individual from the person he or she would have been had we not intervened in the environment.

This fact creates a paradox in our attempt to discharge our moral obligation to future generations. How can we owe a duty to future persons if the very act of discharging that duty wipes out the very individuals to whom we allegedly owed that duty? Our attempted environmental altruism will prevent the birth of the precise beneficiaries of our altruism.

It is no answer to argue that the entirely new set of individuals who will replace those we wipe out will themselves greatly benefit from our intervention. For although they may be the beneficiaries of our environmental intervention, we could not have owed a duty to them because they were not probable persons at the time we claimed that we had a duty. Any present duty that we have to future generations can only be a duty to particular future persons who are awaiting their turn to be born. If in exercise of such an alleged duty we commit an act of environmental intervention that denies the opportunity to be born to those very individuals, we cannot possibly be making them better off by virtue of our intervention. Thus, we find that any attempted altruism on our part to intervene in the environment to help future persons will make those persons incomparably worse off than if we had not intervened. They would be better off living in a degraded environment 100 years from now—that is, in an environment we did not act to preserve—than not living at all.

Parfit's paradox is uncomfortable and counterintuitive. Is it somehow fallacious? If not, is there any way we can accept Parfit's thesis and still make sense of the notion of "obligation to preserve the environment"?

II. IS PARFIT'S REASONING FAULTY?

People encountering Parfit's thesis for the first time are properly skeptical that a minor intervention in the environment can actually result in entirely different individuals in 100 years from those who would have existed then had there been no such intervention. But the result is scientifically accurate, stemming from the discovery in recent years of chaos theory. In the 1950s, Edward Lorenz, a meteorologist at the Massachusetts Institute of Technology, discovered that a very slight shift in the initial data about weather conditions fed into a computer will result in drastic differences in simulated weather conditions after a number of iterations. The differences, or perturbations, grow exponentially, doubling every 4 days. Lorenz called this the "butterfly effect." An environmental intervention as slight as a butterfly flapping its wings near a weather station will change long-term weather predictions. Although 2 weeks after the butterfly's capricious flight the effect will hardly be felt outside an area 16 times the path of the butterfly, after 1 or 2 years the butterfly's flight could actually be the cause of a major storm that otherwise would not have taken place. A weekly quadrupling rate means that an initial perturbation will increase by 4 to the 52d power after just 1 year—enough to make itself felt anywhere on the planet. By my own rough calculations, after 3 years the number of perturbations will have increased by more than the total number of atoms in the universe. Thus, applying chaos theory in support of Parfit's thesis makes clear that any action we take will affect the environment in such a way as to change the conditions of all acts of human procreation several decades hence. Even minor acts in the present can substantially affect which particular sperm cells succeed in fertilizing humans over 60 years from now.

* * *

Perhaps we can shift the ground of contention to argue that Parfit's thesis should be disregarded because our obligation to act to preserve the environment stems from a generic notion of "future generations" and not because we have any particular future individuals in mind. In other words, can we say that we do not care which persons inherit the earth so long as whoever inherits it inherits a habitable planet in no worse condition than the one we enjoy? Of course we can say all this, and in a rather rough way we probably think it and act upon it. But the argument, upon inspection, simply glosses over the problem. Future generations are not an abstraction; they consist of individuals. The particularity of the individuals is apparent when we consider how lucky it is for anyone to be born. The odds of your being born instead of one of your many potential siblings are comparable to the odds of winning the Pennsylvania Lottery in the recent drawing when the first prize was over $100 million. The point is that the winner of the lottery would not be equally content to have any other person win the lottery; similarly, you and I would not be content if a different person had been born instead of us. We may have been lucky to have been born at all, but we are not ready to relinquish that luck simply on the ground that large numbers and vanishingly small probabilities are involved. The fact that somebody will be born does not mean that the person lucky enough to be born is indifferent about who it is. Future generations cannot be indifferent about whether it is they or other persons who will enjoy the fruits of the earth. If we feel we owe an obligation to them, we, too, cannot be indifferent about the question. We cannot discharge our obligation to them if in the process of doing so we deprive them of life.

III. GIVEN PARFIT'S PARADOX, DO WE HAVE ENVIRONMENTAL OBLIGATIONS?

At first blush, Parfit's thesis appears to set us back. It seems to justify Professor Weiss's "opulent" model in a way that most of us would instinctively find morally repulsive. Although I believe that Parfit's thesis is unassailable, I do not think it is retrogressive. Instead, it may help us to clear the ground of unnecessary conceptual confusion and proceed on a firmer footing.

I suggest that we begin by noticing that the notion of obligation to future generations is typically located within the developing concept of international human rights. The general argument starts with the claim that human rights are more important than any other value in international law, including the rights of states. And it continues by claiming that future generations also have a human right—the right to inherit an environment no worse than the one we enjoy.

The foregoing are relatively uncontroversial assertions. But if we look closely, we see that the entire concept of "human rights" is species chauvinistic. This form of chauvinism is illustrated by the following quotation from Judge Richard Posner: "Animals count, but only insofar as they enhance wealth. The optimal population of sheep is determined not by speculation on their capacity for contentment relative to people, but by the intersection of the marginal product and marginal cost of keeping sheep."[14] Posner purports to derive these conclusions from his principle of wealth maximization, which for him constitutes the bedrock moral justification for all law. He characterizes "wealth" solely in human terms; the sheep's own wealth, of course, is not to be maximized or even taken into account. Since a sheep's own capacity for enjoying life has by definition nothing to do with maximizing human wealth, it becomes for Posner morally and legally irrelevant.

One of the most articulate opponents of "animal rights" is R. G. Frey, whose species chauvinism is explicit when he writes:

> [I]t is the sheer richness of human life, and in what this richness consists, which gives it its superior quality. Some of the things which give life its richness we share with animals; there are other things, however, which can fill our lives but not theirs. For example, falling in love, marrying, and experiencing with someone what life has to offer; having children and watching and helping them to grow up; working and experiencing satisfaction in one's job; listening to music, looking at pictures, reading books * * * . By comparison with animals, our lives are of an incomparably greater texture and richness * * * .[16]

Few persons would quarrel with this statement if Professor Frey has in mind the lowest forms of animal life such as insects and mollusks. But what about whales or chimpanzees? Some whales possess a brain six times bigger than the human brain; Dr. John Lilly has claimed that they are more intelligent than any man or woman.[17] According to Dr. Kenneth Norris, whales see and taste through sounds, and possess many other faculties of which

---

[14] R.A. POSNER, THE ECONOMICS OF JUSTICE 76 (1983).

[16] R.G. FREY, RIGHTS, KILLING, AND SUFFERING, 109-110 (1983).

[17] J. LILLY, MAN AND DOLPHIN (1961).

we are only vaguely aware.[18] Chimpanzees, monkeys and gorillas take obvious pleasure in raising their young, and exhibit the same gamut of emotions in the process as do humans. They seem to understand human sign language and, indeed, their "language ability" seems to increase the more researchers take pains to teach them our language.

Are we bound by a notion of "human rights" to consider that the only things that are valuable in the world are those that directly benefit ourselves? Consider the following thought experiment. Suppose Robinson is the last person on earth. When he dies, the human species will have come to an end. During his lifetime, would he have a moral right to kill animals for sport, even knowing that some of those he would kill are the last survivors of their own species? Posner's principle of maximizing wealth would still apply in Robinson's case; it is not dependent upon the existence of other humans. Under that principle, Robinson has a moral right to do whatever would contribute to his own wealth, including the hunting and termination of various animal species for no other reason than the "sport" of it. And under Frey's view, Robinson can do anything he pleases because his life is incomparably richer than any lives of the animals or animal species that he destroys.

Note, however, that the same result obtains under the traditional international conception, mentioned at the outset of this discussion, of preserving the environment for the benefit of future generations. Since there will be no future generations, Robinson has a moral license under this conception—as well as under Posner's and Frey's views—to engage in hunting for sport even if in so doing he terminates entire animal species.

If this result is uncomfortable, it points to the shortcomings of the species chauvinism that underlies the theories of Posner, Frey and "fairness to future generations." All three are impoverished accounts of our actual sense of moral obligation. They are too dependent upon finding an articulate link to the improvement of the human condition.

It is important to recall that Parfit's thesis only deconstructs the notion of obligation to future generations, and not environmental obligations generally. If we have a choice between committing a wasteful act (such as killing a whale) or committing an environmentally preserving act (such as planting a tree), either act, under Parfit's thesis, will change the identity of future generations. Hence, we cannot assert a moral obligation to future generations to commit or refrain from committing either the wasteful or the conserving act. But that does not necessarily mean that we have no moral obligation at all.

Is there a different sense of moral obligation that could yield a duty to present generations to preserve the environment? Consider Parfit's own thoughts on the subject:

> We need some new principle of beneficence, which is acceptable in all kinds of cases. Though we have not yet found this principle, we know that it cannot take a person-affecting form. It will be about human well-being, and the quality of life, but it will not claim that what is morally most important is whether our acts will affect people for good or bad, better or worse * * * . [N]on-religious moral philosophy is a very young subject. We should not be surprised that much of it is still puzzling.[21]

---

[18] *Cited in* D. DAY, THE WHALE WAR (1987).
[21] Parfit, *Future Generations*, [*Further Problems*, 11 PHIL. & PUB. AFF. 113 (1982)] at 171-72.

I agree with the sentiment of these thoughts but take slight exception to Parfit's search for a moral principle. In fact, I think the search for moral principles and precepts can indirectly support much immoral conduct, because no matter how a principle is stated, it may be interpreted and construed in such a way as apparently to justify immoral behavior. In my view, it is better to begin with our preverbal sense of morality. That sense, I would suggest, tells us that it is somehow wrong to despoil the environment, to act in ways that waste natural resources and wildlife, and to gratify pleasures of the moment at the expense of living creatures who are no threat to us.

What George F. Will said about whales in a sense is true of all acts of environmental preservation: "The campaign to save whales is a rare and refreshing example of intelligence in the service of something other than self-interest."[24] Natural evolution has produced some prey-specific predatory animals that will hunt their prey to extinction, at which point they will become extinct themselves. Presumably if they had developed a greater intelligence, they would exercise restraint. Humans are lucky in that we are blessed with the intelligence to figure out how to survive in an environment where we are not physically the strongest, fastest or best-protected animals. That same intelligence can be stretched to include a world-based empathy for the environment, "beneficent" in Parfit's sense.

We should not limit our actions to those we are able to determine now as directly or indirectly benefiting ourselves or our descendants. Rather, we should cultivate our natural sense of obligation not to act wastefully or wantonly even when we cannot calculate how such acts would make any present or future persons worse off. There is good evidence that customary international law—with various fits and starts and setbacks—is moving generally in this direction, perhaps responding to a deep and inarticulate sense that human beings are not in confrontation with, but rather belong to, their natural environment. That such law is currently given the label "human rights" should not constrict our understanding of what it is or where it is going.

NOTES

1. Consider how Parfit's theorem offers a potential justification to future generations for any human activities, no matter how destructive. One can argue that an individual in a future generation cannot complain about the destructive actions of past generations because but for those actions, that individual would not have been born! Derek Parfit's thesis is described in greater detail in Derek Parfit, *On Doing the Best for Our Children, reprinted in* ETHICS AND POPULATION 100 (M. Bayles ed. 1976).

2. D'Amato is not persuaded by the argument that "Parfit's thesis should be disregarded because our obligation to preserve the environment stems from a generic notion of 'future generations' and not because we have any particular future individuals in mind." Why does he take this position? D'Amato goes on to state: "The point is that the winner of

---

[24] *Quoted in* D. Day, *supra* note 18, at 9 (from Washington Post).

the lottery would not be equally content to have any other person win the lottery; similarly, you and I would not be content if a different person had been born instead of us." Is D'Amato's analogy of being born to winning the lottery sound? Consider that when we talk about obligations to future generations, we are, by analogy, talking not about ourselves winning the lottery or ourselves being born, but rather about someone unknown to us who has accomplished these feats. If we do not know the person, does it really matter to us who wins the lottery or who is born?

3. Mark Sagoff claims that "Parfit's argument does not clear us of moral responsibility with respect to future generations; rather it helps us to understand what our responsibility is." MARK SAGOFF, THE ECONOMY OF THE EARTH 62 (1988). According to Sagoff, we have a responsibility not *to* the future but rather *for* the future. *Id.* at 63. Noting that "our decisions concerning the environment will * * * determine to a large extent, what future people will be like" Sagoff argues:

> Surely, it is morally bad for us to deteriorate into a pack of yahoos who have lost both knowledge of and taste for the things that give value and meaning to life. Future generations, might not complain: A pack of yahoos will *like* a junkyard environment. This is the problem. That kind of future is efficient. It may well be ethical. But it is tragic all the same.

Id. (Emphasis in original.) Is Sagoff's view of our obligation to future generations elitist? To what extent does the present generation have the responsibility or the right to shape the values of future generations?

4. D'Amato asks whether the obligation to future generations extends beyond the human species to certain animals. He quotes Richard Posner for the proposition that wealth maximization of humans is the "bedrock moral justification of all law," and R.G. Frey for the proposition that the superior quality of human life warrants concern only for "human rights." He nonetheless suggests that humans may have obligations toward other creatures—such as whales and chimpanzees—which exhibit "feelings" and have certain cognitive abilities. Does D'Amato go far enough? Several prominent animal rights activists have explored this issue in depth. In THE CASE FOR ANIMAL RIGHTS (1983), Tom Regan shares, what seems to be D'Amato's view, that humans have obligations toward certain creatures which share cognitive and emotional attributes of humans. In ANIMAL LIBERATION: A NEW ETHICS FOR OUR TREATMENT OF ANIMALS (1975), Peter Singer relies on the work of Jeremy Bentham, the renowned Utilitarian, to argue that humans have ethical obligations toward all creatures with a capacity for suffering and enjoyment. *Id.* at 7-8. Aldo Leopold's holistic land ethic goes beyond both Regan and Singer in arguing for a human responsibility to entire biotic systems. But Lynn White takes Leopold's notion even a step further in a remarkable essay which appeared in 1973:

> Do people have ethical obligations toward rocks? * * * To almost all Americans still saturated with ideas historically dominant in Christianity * * * the question makes no sense at all. If the time comes when to any considerable group of

us the question is no longer ridiculous, we may be on the verge of a change of value structures that will make possible measures to cope with the growing ecological crisis. One hopes there is enough time left.

Lynn White, Jr., *Continuing the Debate, in* WESTERN MAN AND ENVIRONMENTAL ETHICS (Ian Barbour, ed. 1973).

OUR RIGHTS AND OBLIGATIONS TO FUTURE GENERATIONS FOR THE ENVIRONMENT
Edith Brown Weiss
84 Am. J. Int'l L. 198 (1990)*

* * *

To define intergenerational equity, it is useful to view the human community as a partnership among all generations. In describing a state as a partnership, Edmund Burke observed that "as the ends of such a partnership cannot be obtained in many generations, it becomes a partnership not only between those who are living but between those who are living, those who are dead, and those who are to be born."[4] The purpose of human society must be to realize and protect the welfare and well-being of every generation. This requires sustaining the life-support systems of the planet, the ecological processes and the environmental conditions necessary for a healthy and decent human environment.

In this partnership, no generation knows beforehand when it will be the living generation, how many members it will have, or even how many generations there will ultimately be. It is useful, then, to take the perspective of a generation that is placed somewhere along the spectrum of time, but does not know in advance where it will be located. Such a generation would want to inherit the earth in at least as good condition as it has been in for any previous generation and to have as good access to it as previous generations. This requires each generation to pass the planet on in no worse condition than it received it in and to provide equitable access to its resources and benefits. Each generation is thus both a trustee for the planet with obligations to care for it and a beneficiary with rights to use it.

Intergenerational equity calls for equality among generations in the sense that each generation is entitled to inherit a robust planet that on balance is at least as good as that of previous generations. This means all generations are entitled to at least the planetary health that the first generation had. In practice, some generations may improve the environment, with the result that later generations will inherit a richer and more diverse natural resource base. In this case, they would be treated better than previous generations. But this extra benefit would be consistent with intergenerational equity, because the minimum level of planetary robustness would be sustained and later generations would not be worse off than previous generations. The converse is also possible, that later generations would

---

* Reprinted with permission. Copyright by The American Society of International Law.

[4] E. Burke, *Reflections on the Revolution in France*, 139-40 (1790), *in* 2 WORKS OF EDMUND BURKE 368 (London, 1854).

receive a badly degraded environment with major loss of species diversity, in which case they would be treated worse than previous generations. This latter case would be contrary to principles of intergenerational equity. Equity among generations provides for a minimum floor for all generations and ensures that each generation has at least that level of planetary resource base as its ancestors. This concept is consistent with the implicit premises of trusteeship, stewardship and tenancy, in which the assets must be conserved, not dissipated, so that they are equally available to those who come after.

The theory of intergenerational equity finds deep roots in international law.[8] The Preamble to the Universal Declaration of Human Rights begins, "Whereas recognition of the inherent dignity and of the equal and inalienable rights of all members of the human family is the foundation of freedom, justice and peace in the world." The reference to all members of the human family has a temporal dimension, which brings all generations within its scope. The reference to equal and inalienable rights affirms the basic equality of these generations in the human family.

The United Nations Charter, the International Covenant on Civil and Political Rights, the Convention on the Prevention and Punishment of the Crime of Genocide, the American Declaration on the Rights and Duties of Man, the Declaration on the Elimination of Discrimination against Women, the Declaration on the Rights of the Child and many other human rights documents protect the dignity of all people and the equality of their rights. The Declaration of the Principles of International Cultural Co-operation provides in Article 1 that "each culture has a dignity and value which must be respected and preserved," and that "all cultures form part of the common heritage belonging to mankind." These instruments reveal a fundamental belief in the dignity of all members of human society and in an equality of rights that extends in time as well as space. Indeed, if we were to license the present generation to exploit our natural and cultural resources at the expense of the well-being of future generations, we would contradict the purposes of the United Nations Charter and international human rights documents.

It is not enough, however, to apply a theory of intergenerational equity only among generations. It also carries an intragenerational dimension. When future generations be-come living generations, they have certain rights and obligations to use and care for the planet that they can enforce against one another. Were it otherwise, members of one generation could allocate the benefits of the world's resources to some communities and the burdens of caring for it to others and still potentially claim on balance to have satisfied principles of equity among generations.

Moreover, the fulfillment of intergenerational obligations requires attention to certain aspects of intragenerational equity. As is well-known, poverty is a primary cause of ecological degradation. Poverty-stricken communities, which by definition have unequal access to resources, are forced to overexploit the resources they do have so as to satisfy their own basic needs. As an ecosystem begins to deteriorate, the poor communities suffer most, because they cannot afford to take the measures necessary to control or adapt to the degradation, or to move to pristine areas.

---

[8] E. BROWN WEISS, [IN FAIRNESS TO FUTURE GENERATIONS: INTERNATIONAL LAW, COMMON PATRIMONY AND INTER-GENERATIONAL EQUITY (1989)] note 1, at 25-26.

Thus, to implement intergenerational equity, countries need to help poor communities to use the natural environment on a sustainable basis, to assist them in gaining equitable access to the economic benefits from our planet, such as potable water, and to help protect them from degraded environmental quality. As beneficiaries of the planetary legacy, all members of the present generation are entitled to equitable access to and use of the legacy. The future nationals of all countries will benefit from efforts of the present generation to protect the general planetary environment for future generations. Conversely, all will suffer if the present generation does not make such efforts.

I have proposed three basic principles of intergenerational equity. First, each generation should be required to conserve the diversity of the natural and cultural resource base, so that it does not unduly restrict the options available to future generations in solving their problems and satisfying their own values, and should also be entitled to diversity compara-ble to that enjoyed by previous generations. This principle is called "conservation of options." Second, each generation should be required to maintain the quality of the planet so that it is passed on in no worse condition than that in which it was received, and should also be entitled to planetary quality comparable to that enjoyed by previous generations. This is the principle of "conservation of quality." Third, each generation should provide its members with equitable rights of access to the legacy of past generations and should conserve this access for future generations. This is the principle of "conservation of access."

* * *

Professor D'Amato in his essay takes issue with the notion of rights of future generations to the planet by invoking Derek Parfit's famous paradox and combining it with the new theory of chaos. He argues that future generations cannot have rights because they are composed of individuals who do not exist yet and every intervention we take today to protect the environment affects the composition of these future individuals, robbing some potential members of future generations of their existence.

It is important to parse this analysis into its two component parts: that future generations cannot have rights because the individuals do not exist yet, and that actions to protect the environment for future generations will destroy the rights of some future individuals because different people will be born as a result of the intervention. The first is that future generations cannot have rights, because rights exist only when there are identifiable interests, which can only happen if we can identify the individuals who have interests to protect. Since we cannot know who the individuals in the future will be, it is not possible for future generations to have rights.

This paradox assumes the traditional conceptual framework of rights as rights of identifiable individuals. The planetary, or intergenerational, rights proposed in *In Fairness to Future Generations* are not rights possessed by individuals. They are, instead, genera-tional rights, which must be conceived of in the temporal context of generations. Genera-tions hold these rights as groups in relation to other generations—past, present and future. This is consistent with other approaches to rights, including the Islamic approach, which treats human rights not only as individual rights, but as "rights of the community of believers as a whole."[14] They can be evaluated by objective criteria and indices applied

---

[14] M. KHADDURI, THE ISLAMIC CONCEPTION OF JUSTICE 233 (1984).

to the planet from one generation to the next. To evaluate whether the interests represented in planetary rights are being adequately protected does not depend upon knowing the number or kinds of individuals that may ultimately exist in any given future generation.

Enforcement of these intergenerational rights is appropriately done by a guardian or representative of future generations as a group, not of future individuals, who are of necessity indeterminate. While the holder of the right may lack the capacity to bring grievances forward and hence depends upon the representative's decision to do so, this inability does not affect the existence of the right or the obligation associated with it.

* * *

The second part to Professor D'Amato's argument is that if we intervene to conserve the environment to protect future generations, we cannot succeed in protecting them because our intervention will cause a different group of individuals to emerge. But since the rights of future generations exist only as generational rights, it does not matter who the individuals are or how many they may be. Only at the point where the individuals are born and by definition become members of the present generation do the generational rights attach to individuals.

Professor D'Amato's response is that "[f]uture generations are not an abstraction; they consist of individuals." But they do not consist of individuals until they are born, and hence it is necessary and appropriate to speak of future generations qua generations as having rights in relation to the planet.

Professor D'Amato correctly points out that the composition of future generations cannot be known in advance, in part because it is affected by actions of the present generation. Indeed, he does not make his own case as strongly as he might. For example, we do not need to limit ourselves to ascribing these effects to subtle changes in the biochemistry of conception, as Professor D'Amato does in his amusing excursion into the dynamics of egg and sperm.

Virtually every policy decision of government and business affects the composition of future generations, whether or not they are taken to ensure their rights under the guidelines enunciated above. Decisions regarding war and peace, economic policy, the relative prosperity of different regions and social groups, transportation, health, education—all influence the demographics and the composition of future generations by affecting the lives and fortunes of the present generation: who will succeed and prosper, who will marry whom, who will have children, and even who will emigrate.

* * *

Professor D'Amato proposes that there is a "preverbal sense of morality" that tells us not to waste resources, degrade the environment or wantonly kill animals. But, if anything, history in the last few centuries suggests that our natural instincts are self-indulgent. We have desecrated environments, wasted resources and slaughtered animals purely for plea-sure or for modest personal gain. It may be that the human species carries both a selfish gene and an altruistic one, as the sociobiologists tell us, but it is hardly sufficient to rely on the generous gene to build a theory of morality to overcome the selfish genes, without more.

In Fairness to Future Generations relies on a fundamental norm of equality among generations of the human species in relation to the care and use of the natural system. But it recognizes that we are part of the natural system and that we, as all other generations, must respect this system. We have a right to use and enjoy the system but no right to destroy its robustness and integrity for those who come after us.

Whether we rely on a beneficent "preverbal sense of morality" toward the planet and its resources or on theories rooted in the welfare of the human condition and the ecological system of which people are a part, there is a shared recognition that the present generation has an obligation to care for the planet and to ensure that all peoples can enjoy its services.

NOTES

1. Weiss argues that "intergenerational equity calls for equality among generations in the sense that each generation is entitled to inherit a robust planet that on balance is at least as good as that of previous generations." But how does one measure whether our planet is more or less robust from generation to generation? Should we look to maximization of human wealth as Posner suggests? What other measures are available? To whom should we leave the task of establishing criteria for assessing the relative health of our planet—economists, ethicists, scientists, or politicians?

2. Weiss proposes three principles of intergenerational equity: (1) conservation of options; (2) conservation of quality; and (3) conservation of access. Obviously, adherence to these principles requires international cooperation. Over the years, the international community has reached agreement on matters which tend to support at least some of these principles. For example, the Convention on Trade in Endangered Species of Wild Fauna and Flora (CITES), 993 U.N.T.S. 243, 27 U.S.T. 1087 (1973), seeks to protect endangered species from extinction by regulation of trade in listed species and species parts. The Convention for the Protection of the World Cultural and Natural Heritage, 27 U.S.T. 40 (1973), fosters international cooperation in the protection of important cultural and natural properties as designated by member states.

A major advance over this piecemeal approach came at the United Nations Conference on Environment and Development, or the "Earth Summit" which met in Rio de Janeiro, Brazil in 1992. The Rio Declaration which came out of that conference proclaims 27 principles for achieving international cooperation and understanding on matters affecting the environment. 31 I.L.M. 874 (1992). Among these is principle 3, which proclaims that "[t]he right to development must be fulfilled so as to equitably meet developmental and environmental needs of present and future generations." In addition to the Rio Declaration, the Earth Summit served as the occasion for signing the Climate Change Convention and the Biodiversity Convention, 31 I.L.M. 818 (1992), and produced a detailed action plan, known as Agenda 21, for addressing environmental problems and achieving sustainable development. The United Nations has since established a Commission on Sustainable

Development whose purpose is "to maintain the momentum and commitment to sustainable development, to transform it into policies and practice, and to give it effective and coordinated organized support." UN Secretary-General Boutros-Boutros Ghali, United Nations General Assembly, (November 2, 1993) *quoted in* S. Jacob Scherr and Jared E. Blumenfeld, *Implementing UNCED, reprinted in* GREENING INTERNATIONAL LAW 236 (Phillippe Sand ed. 1994). While acknowledging the tangible progress that has been made, Scherr and Blumenfeld are skeptical about the international community's current commitment to implementing Agenda 21 and other international obligations which have already been made. *Implementing UNCED, supra.* International issues are addressed in greater detail in Chapter Six, *infra.*

3. Even assuming that intergenerational equity is a worthy goal, complex practical problems arise in trying to achieve it. Perhaps the most fundamental of these problems is reflected in the disagreements between economists and ethicists over the practice of "discounting." Most economists believe that future benefits should be discounted or reduced to reflect the fact that people tend to place a higher value on present assets than on the same dollar value of future assets. Some ethicists argue, however, that when the present and future assets being compared are lives or individual health, discounting makes no sense. Under this way of thinking, a future life is worth just as much as a present life. How should we resolve this dilemma? Should we worry about future lives even if the average well-being of such future lives is better than the average well-being of persons living today? *See* Timothy J. Brennan, *Discounting and the Future: Economics and Ethics*, RESOURCES 3 (Summer, 1995).

4. The World Commission on Environment and Development (WCED) (now the United Nations Commission on Environment and Development (UNCED)) was established by the United Nations General Assembly in 1983 amid "a growing realization * * * that it is impossible to separate economic development issues from environmental issues." OUR COMMON FUTURE 3 (WCED, 1987). The Commission had three objectives: "[1] to re-examine the critical environment and development issues and to formulate realistic proposals for dealing with them; [2] to propose new forms of international co-operation on these issues that will influence policies and events in the direction of needed changes; and [3] to raise the levels of understanding and commitment to action of individuals, voluntary organizations, businesses, institutes, and governments." *Id.* at 3-4. While the Earth Summit in Rio produced a substantial body of work, the Commission's most ambitious and influential study to date might well be a report prepared in 1987 titled OUR COMMON FUTURE. This report, often referenced as the Brundtland Commission report after the Commisssion's chair, Prime Minister Gro Brundtland of Norway, focuses on the need to achieve sustainable development, which it defines as "development which meets the needs of the present without compromising the ability of future generations to meet their own needs." *Id.* at 43. Among the report's most significant contributions was its focus on the interrelationship between poverty and environmental problems. Has not wealth proved to be at least as problematic in contributing to global environmental problems as poverty? If so, wherein lies the answer to addressing these problems?

5. Among the most difficult problems associated with providing a healthy environment for future generations is the high level of scientific uncertainty surrounding environmental problems. In recent years, the international community has begun to embrace the precautionary principle—the idea that lack of scientific certainty should not be used as an excuse to avoid addressing an environmental problem. For example, both the Biodiversity Convention and the Climate Change Convention, 31 I.L.M. 818 (1992), reflect this principle. *See* Phillipe Sands, *The "Greening" of International Law: Emerging Principles and Rules,* 1 IND. J. GLOBAL LEGAL STUD. 293, 297-302 (1994). Given the substantial costs associated with environmental protection, does the precautionary principle reflect sound policy? What problems might arise in trying to use this principle to protect future generations? Consider this question both in the context of the degree of uncertainty surrounding an environmental problem and the trade-offs that are made when we choose to address a particular environmental problem.

In their efforts to protect the environment from unwarranted or unsound development, both government agencies and environmental groups have sometimes lost sight of the fact that minorities and low income people are often asked to bear a disproportionate amount of environmental costs while receiving substantially fewer environmental benefits. Professor Lazarus offers a comprehensive look at the problem of environmental justice and points to possible solutions.

PURSUING "ENVIRONMENTAL JUSTICE": THE DISTRIBUTIONAL EFFECTS OF ENVIRONMENTAL PROTECTION
Richard J. Lazarus
87 Nw. U. L. Rev. 787 (1993)*

I. INTRODUCTION

Environmental protection policy has been almost exclusively concerned with two basic issues during the last several decades: (1) what is an acceptable level of pollution; and (2) what kinds of legal rules would be best suited for reducing pollution to that level. By contrast, policy-makers have paid much less attention to the distributional effects, including the potential for distributional inequities, of environmental protection generally.

To be sure, scholars have engaged in considerable discussion of how the costs of environmental controls affect particular industries, and how these costs place a dispropor-

* Reprinted by special permission of Northwestern University School of Law, *Northwestern University Law Review,* VOLUME 87, ISSUE 3, pp. 787-855 (1993).

tionate burden on new versus existing, and large versus small, industrial sources of pollution. But there has been at best only an ad hoc accounting of how the benefits of environmental protection are spread among groups of persons. And, when the costs of pollution control have been considered, such discussions have been narrowly confined to the economic costs. There has been virtually no accounting of how pollution controls redistribute environmental risks among groups of persons, thereby imposing a cost on some for the benefit of others.

The 1970s marked the heyday of the modern environmental era. Earth Day in 1970 caught the imagination of a nation seeking consensus in the midst of the internal conflict engendered by the Vietnam war. Largely ignored in the celebration that accompanied the passage of a series of ambitious environmental protection laws during this time were those distinct voices within minority communities that questioned the value of environmentalism to their communities. They did not share in the national consensus that these new laws marked a significant movement towards a more socially progressive era. Some minority leaders described environmentalism as "irrelevant" at best and, at worst, "a deliberate attempt by a bigoted and selfish white middle-class society to perpetuate its own values and protect its own life style at the expense of the poor and the underprivileged."[5] Environmentalists were seen as ignoring both the "urban environment" and the needs of the poor in favor of seeking "governmental assistance to avoid the unpleasant externalities of the very system from which they themselves have already benefitted so extensively."[6] As one commentator described, environmentalists "would prefer more wilderness * * * for a more secure enclave in nature from the restlessness of history and the demands of the poor." [7] A prominent black elected official put it even more bluntly: "[T]he nation's concern with the environment has done what George Wallace has been unable to do: distract the nation from the human problems of black and brown Americans."[8]

Neither the United States Environmental Protection Agency (EPA) nor the mainstream environmental groups appear to have paid attention to these charges. Quite possibly, this was because such claims were so unsettling and potentially divisive, particularly to the extent that they implicated the welfare of racial minorities. The environmental movement of the 1970s finds much of its structural roots and moral inspiration in the civil rights movement that preceded it. Hence, for many in the environmental community, the notion that the two social movements could be at odds was very likely too personally obnoxious to be believed or even tolerated.

More recently, however, the number of those suggesting that there may be serious distributional problems in environmental protection policy has significantly increased, and the character of their claims has shifted. Prominent voices in racial minority communi-

---

[5] James N. Smith, *The Coming of Age of Environmentalism in American Society, in* ENVIRONMENTAL QUALITY AND SOCIAL JUSTICE IN URBAN AMERICA 1 (James N. Smith ed., 1974) [hereinafter ENVIRONMENTAL QUALITY AND SOCIAL JUSTICE].

[6] Peter Marcuse, *Conservation for Whom?, in* ENVIRONMENTAL QUALITY AND SOCIAL JUSTICE, *supra* note 5, at 17, 27. * * *

[7] Rev. Richard Neuhaus, *In Defense of People: A Thesis Revisited, in* ENVIRONMENTAL QUALITY AND SOCIAL JUSTICE, *supra* note 5, at 59, 62 (excerpt from conference presentation of Rev. Neuhaus).

[8] Leonard G. Ritt & John M. Ostheimer, *Congressional Voting and Ecological Issues*, 3 ENVTL. AFF. 459, 465 & n.18 (1974) (quoting *The Rise of Anti- Ecology?*, TIME, Aug. 3, 1970, at 42 (*quoting* Richard Hatcher, Mayor of Gary, Indiana)). * * *

ties across the country are now forcefully contending that existing environmental protection laws do not adequately reflect minority interests and, in some instances, even perpetuate racially discriminatory policies. For these individuals, the potential for a regressive distribution of the economic costs associated with pollution control is, while often mentioned, not the principal focus of their concerns. Rather, it is the prevalence of hazardous pollutants in the communities where they live and work that draws the brunt of their attention. One shorthand expression for such claims is "environmental racism," but "environmental justice" (or "equity") appears to have emerged as the more politically attractive expression, presumably because its connotation is more positive and, at the same time, less divisive.

Until very recently, the legal academic community has paid relatively little attention to these emerging issues of "environmental justice." This absence of legal commentary contrasts sharply with a growing literature in other academic and popular periodicals, with the more recent efforts to increase awareness of environmental justice concerns within government, and with the filing of lawsuits derived from such concerns in the context of formal litigation.

The purpose of this Article is to explore the distributional side of environmental protection and, more particularly, to explain the significance of including environmental justice concerns into the fashioning of environmental protection policy. Unlike earlier legal commentary, hazardous waste facility siting is not this Article's dominant focus. It offers a broader, more systemic, examination of environmental protection laws and policies.

The Article is divided into three parts. First, it describes the nature of the problem. This includes a discussion of the varied distributional implications of environmental protection laws, as well as the ways in which racial minorities could receive too few of the benefits, or too many of the burdens, associated with those laws. The second part of the Article accepts (without purporting to verify) the thesis that distributional inequities exist, and seeks to explain such inequities theoretically in terms of the present institutional framework for the fashioning of environmental protection policy and the probable distributional implications of that framework. The final part of the Article outlines how environmental justice concerns might be pursued within present and future environmental protection law and policy.

II. THE BENEFITS AND BURDENS OF ENVIRONMENTAL PROTECTION LAWS

A. The Potential for Distributional Inequity

Environmental protection confers benefits and imposes burdens in several ways. To the extent that the recipients of related benefits and burdens are identical, no problem of discrimination is presented (there may, of course, be other problems with the tradeoff). But identical recipients are rarely, if ever, the result. Hardly any laws provide pareto optimality in the classic sense of making everyone better off and no one worse off. Virtually all laws have distributional consequences, including those laws designed to further a particular conception of the public interest. Problems of discrimination, therefore, may arise in the disparities between the distribution of benefits and their related burdens.

The benefits of environmental protection are obvious and significant. A reduction in pollution decreases the public health risks associated with exposure to pollution. It also enhances public welfare by allowing greater opportunity for enjoyment of the amenities associated with a cleaner natural environment. Many would also contend that environmental protection furthers the human spirit by restoring balance between humankind and the natural environment. More pragmatically, environmental protection laws are the source of new jobs in pollution control industries. EPA recently estimated, for instance, that the recently amended Clean Air Act would result in the creation of 30,000 to 45,000 full-time equivalent positions during 1996-2000.

The burdens of environmental protection range from the obvious to the more subtle. They include the economic costs borne by both the producer and the consumer of goods and services that become more expensive as a result of environmental legislation. For consumers, product and service prices may increase; some may become unavailable because the costs of environmental compliance renders their production unprofitable; while other goods and services may be specifically banned because of their adverse impact on the natural environment. For those persons who produce goods and services made more costly by environmental laws, personal income may decrease, employment opportunities may be reduced or displaced, and certain employment opportunities may be eliminated altogether. Finally, environmental protection requires governmental expenditures, the source of which varies from general personal and corporate income taxes to special environmental taxes. These expenditures necessarily decrease public monies available for other social welfare programs.

The burdens of environmental protection, however, also include the redistribution of the risks that invariably occur with pollution control techniques that treat pollution following its production. For instance, air pollution scrubbers and municipal wastewater treatment facilities reduce air and water pollution, but only by creating a sludge that, when disposed, will likely impose risks on a segment of the population different than the segment which would have been exposed to the initial pollution in the air or water. Additionally, the incineration of hazardous wastes stored in drums and tanks converts a land disposal problem into an air pollution issue (leaving, of course, a sludge residue that presents a different land disposal problem), and thereby may change the identity of those in the general population exposed to the resulting pollution. Just transporting solid and hazardous wastes from one geographic area to another for treatment or storage results in a major redistribution of the risks associated with environmental protection. Indeed, such transportation, and the resulting shift of environmental risks, has been the recent subject of massive litigation, as various jurisdictions have sought to export their wastes or prevent the importation of waste from elsewhere.

Nor does the purported prevention of pollution, as opposed to its treatment, necessarily eliminate the distributional issue. "Pollution prevention" frequently depends upon production processes that reduce one kind of pollution by increasing another. For example, water pollution may increase as air pollution is decreased, or a decrease in the mining of one kind of natural resource may be limited or completely offset by the increase in mining of another. Such shifts in the type of pollution or activity allowed will almost invariably shift those risks arising with the "new" pollution or activity to different persons. Hence, pollution may decrease for society as a whole, yet simultaneously increase for certain subpopulations.

Racial minorities could therefore be disproportionately disadvantaged by environmental laws in a number of ways. For example, with regard to the benefits of environmental protection, the natural environments that are selected for protection may be less accessible, or otherwise less important, to minorities. This may be the result of priorities expressly established by statute, or by agency regulations or enforcement agenda.

Inequities in the ultimate distribution of environmental protection benefits may also result, paradoxically, from environmental improvement itself. A cleaner physical environment may increase property values to such an extent that members of a racial minority with fewer economic resources can no longer afford to live in that community. Indeed, the exclusionary impact of environmental protection can be more than just an incidental effect; it can be the raison d'etre, with environmental quality acting as a socially acceptable facade for attitudes that cannot be broadcast.

Minorities may at the same time incur a share of the burdens of environmental protection that are disproportionate to those benefits that they receive. Higher product and service prices may be regressive, as may some taxes depending on their form. Although whites are poorer in greater absolute numbers than nonwhites, the latter group is disproportionately poorer in terms of population percentages. Minorities may also more likely be the victims of reduced or eliminated job opportunities. Similarly, they may be less likely to enjoy the economic, educational, or personal positions necessary to exploit the new job opportunities that environmental protection creates. Finally, minorities may receive an unfair share of the environmental risks that are redistributed by environmental protection. Elimination of the risks in one location may result in the creation or increase of risks in another location where the exposure to minorities is greater.

B. Evidence of Environmental Inequity

To date, there has been relatively little systematic empirical investigation concerning the extent of inequity in the distribution of the benefits and burdens of environmental protection. The evidence that is available, however, "lend[s] support to the view that, on balance, programs for environmental improvement promote the interests of higher-income groups more than those of the poor; they may well increase the degree of inequality in the distribution of real income."[34]

There are especially few studies, apart from anecdotal accounts, regarding the specific issue that racial minorities are distinctly disadvantaged by environmental protection laws. Those few studies, however, lend substantial credence to the claim that such disadvantages do exist, and suggest some reasons for their occurrence. As summarized in a recent congressional report, "[e]arlier studies conducted by government agencies and non-profit environmental organizations have concluded that disproportionate effects stem from many factors, including racism, inadequate health care, low-quality housing, high-hazard workplace environments, limited access to environmental information, and simple lack of sufficient political power."[35] Without a doubt, the available evidence is not immune from challenge. But for present purposes, it seems enough to suggest the strong possibility that virtually all of the theoretical distributional inequities outlined earlier in this Article are in fact occurring.

---

[34] William J. Baumol & Wallace E. Optes, THE THEORY OF ENVIRONMENTAL POLICY 253 (2d ed. 1988).
[35] H.R. Rep No. 428, 101st Cong., 2d Sess. 41-42 (1990).

1. Benefits Of Environmental Protection.—The reduction of pollution mandated by environmental protection laws is likely to have the greatest potential for a redistribution that is favorable to minority communities. After all, for the same reasons that minorities may disproportionately be the recipients of redistributed environmental risks, they also were more likely subject to greater pollution in the first instance. There is substantial support for the thesis that minorities have historically been more likely to live in closer proximity to polluting industries than nonminorities. There is likewise substantial evidence that minorities occupy significantly more environmentally hazardous jobs and, as a result, suffer a disproportionately higher number of environmentally-related injuries. However, for these same reasons, any across-the-board reduction in pollution (or increase in occupational safety) should confer on minorities a larger benefit commensurate with their historically larger burden.

It is not at all certain, however, that this expected proportional redressing of the past has in fact occurred. Without addressing the factor of race, several empirical studies have suggested that the distribution of benefits from a reduction in pollution is neutral or even regressive. These benefits include federal subsidies to publicly-owned wastewater treatment plants, and the advantages of better air pollution control, including those associated with programs directed at improving urban air quality. A similar conclusion has been drawn regarding the impact of federal occupational health and safety laws.

2. The Burdens of Environmental Protection.—The burdens associated with environmental protection generally take two forms. First, there are the economic costs of pollution control. These are typically imposed on either the government or industry in the first instance, but are ultimately redistributed through taxes and higher prices for consumer goods. They may also be indirectly redistributed through salary cuts and layoffs. Second, as previously described, there are the burdens of environmental risks that are necessarily redistributed by environmental protection laws. Although these laws strive for a net reduction of risks, some discrete populations may suffer a net increase in the process.

The "burden" dimension to environmental protection has received significantly more attention than the "benefit" side. Additionally, until quite recently most studies addressing the distribution of environmental protection burdens have focused on the economic costs associated with such protection. Less attention has been paid to the distribution of environmental risks.

Most of the studies lend considerable support to the thesis that distributional inequities exist insofar as the distribution of burdens may be regressive. Moreover, to the extent that these studies have specifically considered the distributional effects upon racial minorities, preliminary inquiries strongly suggest that inequities exist there as well.

(a) Economic costs.—Economists have occasionally studied how the costs and benefits of pollution control are distributed. These analyses generally suggest that pollution controls are regressive. As one commentator put it fairly early on, "[u]nfortunately, the further one moves towards 'putting a price on pollution' the more regressive the burden generally becomes * * * . [W]hen it comes to cleaning up the environment, policy makers will be confronted with the classical dilemma between distributional fairness and allocative efficiency."[45] * * *

---

[45] DORFMAN & SNOW, *supra* note 44, at 115. [NANCY S. DORFMAN & ARTHUR SNOW, WHO WILL PAY FOR POLLUTION CONTROL?—THE DISTRIBUTION BY INCOME OF THE BURDEN OF THE NATIONAL ENVIRONMENTAL PROTECTION PROGRAM 1972-80, 28 NAT'L TAX J. 101, 101-15 (1975).]

(b) Environmental risks.—Studies addressing the redistribution of environmental risks are far fewer in number than those concerned with economic costs, but race has more frequently been a focus of inquiry in the former. Two studies are no doubt the most widely acknowledged because they advance the thesis that race matters in the distribution of environmental risks and that racial minorities receive a disproportionate amount of those risks.

* * *

III. THE STRUCTURE OF ENVIRONMENTAL INEQUITY

A. General Causes: Racism and the Relative Absence of Minority Economic and Political Power

The structural roots of environmental inequities are very likely the same as those that produce other forms of racially disproportionate impacts. In this regard, environmental protection is yet another expression of a more widespread phenomenon.

The most obvious and common source are racist attitudes—whether in blatant, thinly disguised, or unconscious forms—that pervade decisionmaking. Historically, racial minorities have been persistent victims of racial discrimination in this country. Although de jure discrimination is now forbidden by law, racist attitudes, both consciously and unconsciously held, are plainly widespread.[78] These range from hostility toward racial minorities, to false stereotypical judgments about members of that class. As Alex Aleinikoff recently explained, "[r]ace matters with respect to the people we choose to spend time with or marry, the neighborhoods in which we choose to live, the houses of worship we join, our choice of schools for our children, the people for whom we vote, and the people we allow the state to execute."[79] People routinely make stereotypical judgments about others based on racial identity. While such judgments may appear less threatening than those based on outright racial hostility, their adverse impact may in fact be more potent because of their pervasiveness and masked nature, which makes them so difficult to identify and root out.

Therefore, it is not at all unlikely—and, indeed, it may be probable—that racist attitudes and false stereotypes have influenced various decisions relating to environmental protection. Certainly there is no reason to suppose that environmental protection is somehow immune from actions based on societal attitudes that, while widely condemned, are nevertheless prevalent. For example, the use of environmental quality to support racially exclusionary zoning practices would seem to confirm that suspicion.

* * *

B. Exacerbating Causes: The Structure of Environmental Policymaking

There exist, moreover, factors more endemic to environmental law itself that may exacerbate distributional inequities likely present in the context of any public welfare

---

[78] Thomas A. Aleinikoff, *A Case for Race-Consciousness*, 91 Colum. L. Rev. 1060, 1066-69 (1991); Charles R. Lawrence, III, *The Id, the Ego, and Equal Protection: Reckoning with Unconscious Racism*, 39 Stan. L. Rev. 317 (1987).

[79] Aleinikoff, *supra* note 78, at 1067.

law. These factors suggest more than the disturbing, yet somewhat irresistible thesis, that the distributional dimension of environmental protection policy likely suffers from the same inequities that persist generally in society. They suggest the far more troubling, and even less appealing, proposition that the problems of distributional inequity may in fact be more pervasive in the environmental protection arena than they are in other areas of traditional concern to civil rights organizations, such as education, employment, and housing.

Indeed, it is the absence of that minority involvement so prevalent in the more classic areas of civil rights concern that may render the distributional problem worse for environmental protection. Minority interests have traditionally had little voice in the various points of influence that strike the distributional balances necessary to get environmental protection laws enacted, regulations promulgated, and enforcement actions initiated. The interest groups historically active in the environmental protection area include a variety of mainstream environmental organizations representing a spectrum of interests (conservation, recreation, hunting, wildlife protection, resource protection, human health), as well as a variety of commercial and industrial concerns. Until very recently, if at all, the implications for racial minorities of environmental protection laws have not been a focal point of concern for any of these organizations.

* * *

Likewise, and at the behest of mainstream environmental groups, substantial resources have also been directed to improving air and water quality in nonurban areas. Programs for the prevention of significant deteriorations in air quality, the reduction of "acid rain," and the protection of visibility in national parks and wilderness areas, all require significant financial expenditures. Substantial resources have similarly been expended on improving the quality of water resources that are not as readily accessible to many minorities because of their historical exclusion. Without meaning to suggest that these programs lack merit on their own terms (for the simple reason that they possess great merit), their return in terms of overall public health may be less than pollution control programs directed at improving the environmental quality of urban America's poorer neighborhoods, including many minority communities. Lead poisoning provides an excellent illustration of how redirection of some financial resources may go a long way toward improving the health and welfare of minorities. There seems to be a widespread consensus that black children are disproportionately victims of excessive absorption of lead, a toxic chemical. The Federal Center for Disease Control, Agency for Toxic Substances and Disease Registry (ATSDR), reported in 1988 that percentages of black children with excessive levels of lead exceeded by several orders of magnitude the percentages of white children with such levels. These differential impacts, moreover, could not be explained on economic grounds. According to the ATSDR, black children have a higher incidence of excessive levels of lead at all income levels.

The absence of any systematic consideration of minority interests in environmental protection has also likely affected the implementation of environmental protection laws. * * *

* * *

Similarly, state governments have proven unwilling or unable to commit the resources or efforts to ensure such compliance. And, public interest organizations have never been capable of enlisting those resources necessary to bring the huge number of citizen suit enforcement actions that would be required to fill the enforcement gap. Nor is it clear, given the needs of other competing social welfare programs, that the government's (or public interest organizations') failure to do so is incorrect from either an economic efficiency or social justice perspective. Be that as it may, what remains clear is that the allocation of those resources necessary to ensure actual compliance—whether the enforcer be the federal, state, or local governments, or a public interest organization—is a significant determinant in the distribution of benefits and burdens ultimately realized. Compliance will necessarily be greater in both those substantive and geographic areas where the government decides to allocate its limited investigative and enforcement resources. And, in the absence of such governmental initiative, compliance is more likely where the community members possess the resources necessary to launch an independent, citizen-based, enforcement effort.

* * *

Minorities are likewise underrepresented in those parts of the national government that dominate environmental protection policymaking. The gains minorities have made in obtaining elective office are almost exclusively at the state and local level. However, it is at the national level that environmental protection policy—including the allocation of its benefits and burdens—is largely determined by Congress, by those federal agencies responsible for statutory implementation, and by the federal courts of appeals through judicial review of agency decisions. Very few minorities have been elected to Congress. Until this year, there had been no blacks in the Senate for more than a decade, and only a small number of blacks are elected Representatives in the House. Moreover, almost none of these few representatives has long been a major player in congressional committees and subcommittees with jurisdiction, and thus influence, over environmental protection issues. Until relatively recently, they have not been especially active on environmental issues.

The same pattern of underrepresentation and lack of interest appears to be repeated within the federal agencies principally charged with implementing the federal environmental protection laws. These agencies include the EPA, Department of the Interior, National Oceanic and Atmospheric Administration, and, within the Executive Office of the President itself, the Council on Environmental Quality, Office of Management and Budget, and the Domestic Policy Office. For instance, within EPA there is an Office of Civil Rights, but that Office has traditionally been almost exclusively concerned with personnel issues. It has had virtually no ongoing programmatic responsibility regarding the implementation of any environmental protection laws within the agency's jurisdiction. The number of minorities in policymaking positions at EPA is also reportedly small.

* * *

IV. PURSUING ENVIRONMENTAL JUSTICE

The pursuit of "environmental justice" within the context of environmental law is necessarily problematic because to define the issue exclusively in those terms misapprehends the nature of the problem in the first instance. The distributional inequities that appear to exist in environmental protection are undoubtedly the product of broader social forces. To be sure, features endemic to the ways in which environmental protection laws have historically been fashioned may have exacerbated the problem in the environmental context. But the origins of the resulting distributional disparities do not begin, nor will they end, with reforming either the structure of environmental protection decisionmaking or the substance of environmental law itself.

Hence, while a series of measures within the environmental law arena have the potential for redressing or, at least reducing, the existing distributional inequities, their undertaking cannot be to the exclusion of more broadly directed actions. Distributional inequities are very likely rooted in past and present racial hostility, racial stereotypes, and other forms of race discrimination. The vestiges of past discrimination may be the greatest factor contributing to such disparities because of the self-perpetuating impact of such discrimination on racial minority economic and political power. These vestiges effectively deny minorities the autonomy to choose, either by purchase or through the ballot, the level of environmental quality that they will enjoy or the amount of pollution that they will tolerate.

With that significant, threshold caveat, important reforms can nevertheless be implemented within the existing environmental law framework. These reforms could both ameliorate the inequities currently resulting from those laws and, more importantly, provide a much-needed impetus to those seeking broader social reforms. These reforms include: (1) providing environmental policymakers with a better understanding of the nature and scope of the problem; (2) litigating the associated civil rights issues as civil rights issues; (3) rethinking the substance of environmental law to take better account of distributional concerns; (4) reforming the structure of environmental policymaking to promote minority involvement and interests; and (5) reclaiming the common ground of environmentalism and civil rights. Each reform is discussed below.

A. Providing A Better Understanding

Both those who believe that distributional inequities exist in environmental protection, and those who remain skeptical, should be able to join in one common recommendation: the need for better empirical investigation. To date, there have been relatively few technically rigorous studies addressing the distributional issue. * * *

EPA currently collects massive amounts of information relating to environmental pollution and quality. The agency needs to correlate this data with information already available on race, ethnicity, and socioeconomic status. One obvious source of such data is the toxic release inventory, collected pursuant to the Emergency Planning and Community Right-to-Know Act. This inventory provides an authoritative accounting of all toxic releases throughout the country. By joining this data with existing census information, a nationwide correlation between toxic releases and race, ethnicity, and socioeconomic status should not be difficult to derive. * * *

* * *

B. Litigating The Civil Rights Issue

Litigation provides another medium for addressing the distributional issue. Two basic litigation strategies are available. First, an administrative or judicial complaint could be filed on behalf of a minority group for the purpose of preventing the siting of an unwanted facility in its community, and the basis of the lawsuit could be the facility's noncompliance with an applicable environmental statute. The possibility of distributional inequities would not be directly relevant to the substantive merits of the administrative challenge or lawsuit. It would simply be the reason why the lawsuit was necessary and why, for example, a minority community should be entitled to a greater share of enforcement resources. Alternatively, the distributional inequities could provide the substantive basis for the lawsuit by supporting a civil rights cause of action. In other words, the cause of action would itself derive from the fact that a distributional inequity exists.

To date, minority plaintiffs appear to have favored the civil rights approach. However, virtually none of those suits has been successful. This is largely because existing equal protection doctrine, which has been the focal point of most lawsuits, has not proved hospitable to the kinds of arguments upon which environmental justice claims have depended. For this reason, federal and state environmental laws may offer the best opportunity for minority plaintiffs to ameliorate environmental inequities. Many of these statutes impose a panoply of procedural and substantive limitations on those wishing to site polluting facilities, and many confer private attorney general status on citizens aggrieved by actions that violate applicable statutory limitations. Plaintiff organizations with the necessary resources have consequently been quite successful in resisting environmentally undesirable facilities under these environmental statutes. To the extent that such legal and technical resources are made available to minority communities, those statutes could likewise provide a basis for considerable relief from distributional inequities.

There is nonetheless substantial reason for continued emphasis on civil rights litigation aimed at redressing distributional inequities in environmental protection. Burdens of proof are difficult to overcome under existing doctrine, but if litigation efforts were to receive additional resources, some isolated successes might be achievable. In addition, the cases brought so far have relied on only a few legal theories. Several promising theories have not yet been fully explored and warrant greater attention.

Perhaps more importantly, the real value of these lawsuits extends beyond their ability to obtain a favorable decision in a given case. Indeed, the symbolic value of filing the lawsuit is itself substantial. The mere filing of a formal complaint provides a very powerful and visible statement by minorities regarding their belief that distributional inequities exist in environmental protection. The publicity that frequently surrounds the complaint's filing enhances public awareness of these concerns and thereby serves an important educational function. Should, moreover, a victory on the merits be achieved, the benefits could be tremendous. For many within the minority community it is extremely important that a formal judicial decision be obtained confirming their belief that environmental protection presents its own unique civil rights issues.

1. Equal Protection and the Problem of Discriminatory Intent.—Equal protection claims have been the principal focus of most environmental justice lawsuits brought to date. [The author describes several cases where an equal protection claim was raised unsuccessfully by minority groups in environmental justice litigation.]

2. Title VI of the Civil Rights Act: The Search for Federal Funds to Avoid the Intent Limitation.—One option not yet well explored by civil rights plaintiffs in the environmental context is Title VI of the Civil Rights Act of 1964. Title VI provides that: "No person in the United States shall, on the ground of race, color, or national origin, be excluded from participation in, be denied the benefits of, or be subjected to discrimination under any program or activity receiving Federal financial assistance."

The principal advantage of Title VI over equal protection is that courts have not required a showing of discriminatory intent in the Title VI context; disparate impact has been enough. * * *

There are, however, two limitations to Title VI. Although each is significant, Title VI's reach in the environmental protection arena remains potentially great. The first limitation is that Title VI's nondiscrimination mandate applies only to "any program or activity receiving Federal financial assistance." Thus, while covering all federal agency activities, nonfederal actions are within Title VI's mandate only when a sufficient federal financial nexus can be established. Federal financial assistance for environmental protection is extensive, however, particularly assistance to state governments. Virtually all federal environmental laws, including those dealing with hazardous waste, toxic substances, water pollution control, and clean air provide funding to state programs. These state programs make many of the decisions that, when not initiated by the federal government, effectively determine the distribution of benefits and burdens from environmental protection at the state and local level. * * *

The second Title VI limitation is remedial in nature. Until recently, it appeared fairly well settled that in the absence of a showing of discriminatory intent, equitable relief was the only remedy available to redress a Title VI violation. Just this past Term, however, the U.S. Supreme Court unanimously ruled, in *Franklin v. Gwinnett County Public Schools*, that a damages remedy is available in implied private rights of actions brought under Title IX of the Education Act Amendments of 1972. Because the language of Title IX was expressly modeled after Title VI of the Civil Rights Act, and because the Court has frequently relied on constructions of one in interpreting the other, it would seem fair to assume that a damages remedy is now generally available for Title VI violations, even absent a showing of discriminatory intent.

To date, however, there has been very little reliance on Title VI in any of the litigated cases. EPA has likewise not exploited its Title VI responsibilities as it could to redress distributional inequities. There are a host of ways that EPA could implement Title VI's nondiscrimination mandate in the agency's disbursement of federal pollution control funds. A relatively modest measure would be for EPA to require the recipient of the funds to make a showing that the funds are being disbursed according to racially neutral criteria. A more aggressive approach would be to require a further showing that racial minority groups are proportionately represented among the ultimate beneficiaries of the federal funds. Such a showing could include proof that the "neutral" distribution of federal funds in no manner perpetuated the vestiges of past racial discrimination within the relevant community. For instance, in the case of a federally funded wastewater treatment facility, EPA would need to be satisfied that the community's sewage treatment program provides service to minority communities (e.g., connections to sewage treatment plants) equal to that provided to nonminority communities in the affected area.

* * *

3. Title VIII of the Civil Rights Act and 42 U.S.C. § 1982: The Need to Bridge Housing and the Environment.—Two other potentially useful, but even less explored, civil rights causes of action are Title VIII of the Civil Rights Act of 1968 and 42 U.S.C. § 1982. Title VIII makes it unlawful "[t]o discriminate against any person in the * * * sale or rental of a dwelling, or in the provision of services or facilities in connection therewith, because of race, color, religion, sex, familial status or national origin." Section 1982 provides that all United States citizens "shall have the same right * * * to inherit, purchase, lease, sell, hold, and convey real and personal property."

There are several threshold advantages to Title VIII's nondiscrimination mandate. Like a claim under Title VI of the Civil Rights Act of 1964, and unlike a constitutional equal protection claim, no showing of discriminatory intent is required under Title VIII. An unjustified, racially discriminatory impact may alone be sufficient to establish a Title VIII violation. Furthermore, unlike either Title VI or the equal protection clause, but like Title VII of the Civil Rights Act of 1964, Title VIII applies to some purely private conduct. A showing of federal financial assistance is not, therefore, always necessary. Finally, as under Title VI, the focus of a Title VIII complaint is the provision of governmental services, which seems to be a more favorable context within which to bring a civil rights claim.

The ultimate usefulness of Title VIII's nondiscrimination mandate in redressing environmental inequity largely turns, however, on the meaning of "provision of services or facilities" within Title VIII. In particular, what kinds of "services or facilities," and what types of providers, fall within the statute's scope? The statutory language suggests some potentially significant limitations. For example, it does not purport to bar discrimination in the distribution of services or facilities generally. Instead, Title VIII proscribes only those "dealing with the specific problems of fair housing opportunities" and, even more specifically, the "services or facilities" restricted are those "in connection with [the] sale or rental of a dwelling." Clearly, some issues related to environmental quality would more easily fit within this analytical framework than others.

The significance of Title VIII's command that all federal agencies "administer their programs and activities relating to housing and urban development in a manner affirmatively to further the purposes of [Title VIII]" turns on similar considerations. As with Title VI, EPA has historically adhered to a narrower construction of that command than the United States Commission on Civil Rights. EPA concluded early on that its pollution control programs did not "relat[e] to housing and urban development" within the meaning of Title VIII.[244] Hence, EPA has declined to withhold "treatment works construction grant assistance from communities which are charged with having exclusionary zoning ordinances precluding location of low cost and medium income housing within their jurisdictions."[245] The Civil Rights Commission faulted EPA for failing to apply a "liberal construction of Title VIII" and for failing to recognize that "EPA's program for sewage treatment is essential for the development and maintenance of urban areas, and thus it is clear that even within the strictest meaning of the term 'program relating to housing and urban development,' it is covered by Title VIII."[246]

---

[244] [U.S. COMMISSION ON CIVIL RIGHTS, THE FEDERAL CIVIL RIGHTS ENFORCEMENT EFFORT—1974 (1975)] at 589. * * *

[245] *Id.*

[246] *Id.*

* * *

Finally, 42 U.S.C. § 1982 provides an alternative basis for a civil rights lawsuit based upon interference with property rights. Although Section 1982's proscription is generally less comprehensive than Title VIII, unlike Title VIII, it extends to the mere "hold[ing]" of real and personal property. Section 1982 also applies, although not without debate, to both private and public action. Because, moreover, the U.S. Supreme Court has previously intimated that Section 1982 "might be violated by official action that depreciated the value of property owned by black citizens," it would at least seem to offer a theoretical basis for bringing an environmental justice claim based on a civil rights law.[251] While the issue remains unsettled, Section 1982's primary limitation is that federal courts are likely to require a showing of discriminatory intent under this statute.

C. Rethinking The Substance Of Environmental Law To Take Better Account Of Distributional Concerns

A better accounting of the distributional implications of environmental protection will likely also require substantive reform of the federal environmental laws. This is in part because EPA has historically resisted embracing a distributional mandate in its enforcement of these laws. The agency has consistently viewed "sociological" concerns, such as distributional impacts, as outside the purview of its purely "technical" mandate of establishing technically effective, and economically efficient, pollution control standards.

Notwithstanding EPA's apparent assumption, the agency's failure to take distributional equity into account has not resulted in a neutral distribution of the benefits and burdens of environmental protection. Indeed, the agency's position may instead have facilitated a distributional skewing unfavorable to those persons, such as racial minorities, less able to influence the legislative, regulatory, and enforcement agendas that ultimately determine who will receive the benefits and burdens of a particular legislative initiative.

Two kinds of statutory reforms could address this problem. One possibility would be to require formal agency consideration of the distributional impacts associated with a particular decision. Such consideration could be required where the agency establishes rulemaking agendas, promulgates implementing regulations, and determines enforcement priorities. It could also be required when the agency allocates grant monies and technical assistance. The second, more ambitious, reform would be to establish equitable benchmarks that would provide standards for judging discretionary agency determinations with significant distributional impacts.

Neither substantive reform is as radical a proposal as it might seem. Indeed, there is plenty of applicable precedent for infusing distributional factors into the fashioning of legal standards and agency priorities. For example, environmental impact statements, prepared pursuant to the National Environmental Policy Act, have long included discussions of the socioeconomic effects of certain proposed federal actions. Somewhat ironically, the notion of a more overt distributional inquiry finds precedential support in legislation now pending that would require federal agencies to consider the impact of their actions on private property rights. Whatever the merits of that legislative proposal, which opponents

---

[251] *City of Memphis v. Greene*, 451 U.S. 100, 123 (1981).

fear will chill the promulgation of needed environmental regulation, the racial minority status of a person would certainly seem to be a more compelling trigger for such a particularized distributional accounting of agency environmental decisionmaking.

* * *

In one notable respect, moreover, the nation's natural resources laws take explicit account of their distributional impact on an identifiable minority group: Native American tribes. The Bureau of Indian Affairs within the Department of the Interior is charged, inter alia, with honoring the United States' treaty obligations and general fiduciary duties to Native American tribes. The existence of that formal voice within the executive branch may, in part, explain why some federal environmental protection laws articulate specific exemptions aimed at ameliorating some of the distributional impacts that those laws may have on Native Americans, particularly when those laws adversely affect some of their subsistence ways of life.

* * *

Significant opportunities exist for including such distributional analysis in formal EPA decisionmaking. For example, EPA has not traditionally accounted for equitable considerations in its risk assessment analysis, which has become the linchpin of agency decisionmaking in recent years. Thus, while EPA's practice has resulted in risk minimization in the aggregate, the agency has not generally taken into account how that risk is specifically being spread. The end result may be a policy determination that minimizes the risk to society overall, but which does so at the expense of an identifiable segment of the population that ultimately receives more than its "fair share" of the risks being distributed. Such equitable concerns are a proper and necessary factor to be considered in most EPA policy decisions and rulemakings.

* * *

Finally, because EPA is currently contemplating greater utilization of decentralized approaches, such as market incentives, for the accomplishment of environmental quality objectives, the need for overt distributional inquiry may be all the more pressing. Reliance on market incentives reduces the distributional inequities that result because of the enhanced political access that some enjoy to centralized decisionmakers under a command-and-control regulatory regime. But, rather than eliminate inequities, this approach more likely just shifts the cause for such distributional inequity away from a relative absence of political power at the national level to the relative absence of market power at home. For instance, the distribution of pollution under a market system of transferable pollution rights will tend to replicate existing income and property distributions that, to the extent that such distributions are themselves the product of racial discrimination, will only continue to produce and exacerbate inequitable results. The likely outcome is the further occurrence of pollution "hot spots" in racial minority communities and low income neighborhoods.

This problem could be addressed in a number of ways. One approach would be to impose certain substantive limitations on the market system to guard against the likelihood of inequitable distributions. For instance, there could be fixed limits on the amount of pollution that would be permitted within any one geographic community. Another approach would be to work within the market system by leveling the playing field. Communities identified as lacking in resources might, for example, be allocated vouchers that would allow them to bargain more effectively within the pollution rights market.

D. Reforming The Structure Of Environmental Policymaking To Promote Minority Involvement

Apart from the substance of environmental law, serious consideration should be given to reforming the structure of environmental policymaking so as to enhance minority access to relevant decisionmaking fora. Governmental and nongovernmental organizations that currently dominate the process need to promote minority participation in the dialogue and, even more fundamentally, they need to educate themselves about minority concerns. It is not enough to provide minorities with an opportunity to adequately represent their own interests because correction of distributional equities is not, and should not be, the sole responsibility of racial minorities. Those in positions of authority, whether or not they happen to belong to a racial minority, have an independent responsibility to work toward the fair distribution of environmental benefits and burdens.

Mainstream environmental groups need, therefore, to work towards better representation of minorities within their organizations, both as members and as professional employees. They should likewise lend expertise to local communities in need of financial, legal, and technical assistance, and should also target those communities in their educational programs. There are currently a host of new environmental organizations, more directly involved with environmental issues of special concern to racial minorities, which could greatly benefit from the mainstream groups' sharing of available resources.

* * *

E. Reclaiming The Common Ground Shared By Environmentalists and Civil Rights Advocates

Environmentalists need to do more, however, than simply modify the structure of environmental lawmaking and reform its substance to take better account of distributional concerns. Environmentalists need to return to the roots of modern environmental law, reacquainting themselves with the natural relationship that exists between what is advocated by both environmentalism and civil rights. Much suspicion and resentment currently exists between the two social movements. However, the potential for claiming substantial common ground and shared values still persists, as it did in the late 1960s when the civil rights movement first spawned both the rhetoric and the tactics of modern environmentalists.

Similarities between the two movements, however, run deeper than shared rhetoric or tactics. Both challenge the status quo as a means of promoting and protecting the interests of those with less political power, whether they be racial minorities, future generations of persons, or endangered species. Furthermore, to that end, both movements seek to reform those rules that tend to deny access to the institutions capable of bringing about legal reform.

More substantively, both movements are redistributive in their ultimate focus. Civil rights plainly depends on a redistribution of wealth to achieve its ends. Similarly, environmentalism requires a de-emphasis of existing absolutist notions of private property rights in natural resources, because the unrestrained exercise of such rights can create tremendous environmental degradation. Therefore, both movements tend to view, regardless of their legitimacy, those constitutional provisions aimed at preserving the status quo by protecting the existing distribution of private property rights as significant obstacles to the achievement of their desired ends. Indeed, some civil rights scholars suggest that the Constitution's "giving priority to the protection of property" was intended to protect property in slaves.[310]

Similarly, environmentalists describe how "[t]he law is wedded to a concept of property that gives precedence to a right to change the existing biologic character of the land over increases in the owner's individual wealth. The constitutional shibboleths of the Justices could freeze the fluid stream of property law in the posture of acquisitive individualism."[311]

* * *

Some recent scholarship suggests a possible reclamation of common ground by the environmental and civil rights movements. Commentators have begun to look anew to civil rights discourse for ideas and inspiration for environmental protection law. They point out the relevance in each of notions of community, empathy, egalitarianism, and interconnectedness. For example, "Ecofeminism" embodies this new tradition of cooperation in its effort to apply feminist ideology to environmental protection policy.

It is essential, however, that the common ground that must be seized extend beyond the inspirational or thematical and include pragmatic proposals for joining environmental protection and civil rights objectives in shared endeavors. Mass transit is a simple, yet powerful example. Our society's excessive reliance on private motor vehicles needlessly wastes natural resources and degrades the environment. Such reliance can also create a substantial economic barrier to many career and recreational opportunities. Those with fewer economic resources are less likely to have access to the private transportation required to take advantage of those opportunities. Finally, billions of dollars are spent to construct highways that subsidize the lifestyles of those who choose to live in the more affluent neighborhoods outside major urban areas. For all these reasons, however, promotion of mass transit offers the potential for promoting the interests of both minority and low-income persons and environmental protection. Mass transit, in short, improves the environment while simultaneously redistributing life's amenities more equitably. Environmentalists need to develop and promote other such natural unions between the two movements.

* * *

---

[310] Bell, *supra* note 205, at 6-7. [Derrick A. Bell, Jr., *Foreword: The Civil Rights Chronicles*, 99 Harv. L. Rev. 4 (1985)]

[311] J. Peter Byrne, *Green Property*, 7 Const. Commentary 39, 249 (1990) ("The opinions of Scalia and Rehnquist suggest that a radical transformation of property law to reflect ecological values would encounter judicial resistance. . . . The task of green property law is both to find practical mechanisms for utopian aspirations and to criticize those elements of the legal culture that obstruct urgent reforms.") * * * .

NOTES

1. Professor Lazarus makes a compelling argument that minorities receive fewer of the benefits and bear a disproportionate share of the burdens and risks associated with environmental problems. Among the reasons suggested for this phenomenon is racism. Acknowledging that racism remains prevalent in our society, does it really explain why minority groups are disproportionately disadvantaged by environmental policy? Is it possible, for example, that a minority or low income community might knowingly, willingly, and rationally choose to assume certain environmental risks in exchange for some form of economic development? Is it racist to deny these communities economic development opportunities which may entail some environmental risks on grounds of environmental justice? In this regard, *see* Kevin Gover and Jana L. Walker, *Escaping Environmental Paternalism: One Tribe's Approach to Developing a Commercial Waste Disposal Project in Indian Country,* 63 U.Colo. L. Rev. 933, 942 (1992), wherein the authors conclude:

> For tribes considering developing commercial waste projects on reservations, the major issue they will face will not be an environmental one, but instead one of power and racism. Much of the environmental community seems to assume that, if an Indian community decides to accept such a project, it either does not understand the potential consequences or has been bamboozled by an unprincipled waste company. In either case, the clear implication is that Indians lack the intelligence to balance and protect adequately their own economic and environmental interests. This clearly is a racist assumption * * * .

2. On February 11, 1994, President Clinton signed Executive Order 12,898 relating to "environmental justice." Under this Order, each federal agency is required to—

> conduct its programs, policies and activities that substantially affect human health or the environment, in a manner that ensures that such programs, policies and activities do not have the effect of excluding persons (including populations) from participation in, denying persons (including populations) the benefits of, or subjecting persons (including populations) to discrimination under, such programs, policies and activities because of their race, color, or national origin.

Id. at § 2-2. To implement the Order, each federal agency is required to prepare an environmental justice strategy which "identifies and addresses disproportionately high and adverse human health or environmental effects of its programs, policies, and activities on minority populations and low income populations." *Id.* at §§ 1-1, 1-103(a). Among other things, the strategy must, at a minimum, "(1) promote enforcement of all health and environmental statutes in areas with minority and low income populations; (2) ensure greater public participation; (3) improve research and data collection relating to the health of and environment of minority populations and low income populations; and (4) identify differential patterns of consumption of natural resources among minority populations and low income populations." *Id.* To what extent will Executive Order 12,898 likely ameliorate the problems identified by Professor Lazarus?

3. Environmental justice and environmental racism have only recently become prominent legal issues, but a burgeoning literature has helped propel these issues to the forefront of environmental policy. *See e.g.,* Michael Fischer, *Environmental Racism Claims Brought Under Title VI of the Civil Rights Act*, 25 ENVTL. L. 285 (1995); *Essays of Environmental Justice*, 96 W. VA. L. REV. 1017-1190 (1994) (featuring 12 essays on environmental justice by leading commentators.); Bunyan Bryant & Paul Mohai, *Environmental Injustice: Weighing Race and Class as Factors in the Distribution of Environmental Hazards*, 63 U. COLO. L. REV. 921 (1992). Note also that the issue has an important international as well as national dimension. *See* Katharina Kummer, *The International Regulation of Transboundary Traffic in Hazardous Waste: The 1989 Basel Convention*, 41 INT'L & COMP. L.Q. 530 (1992). How should the law treat environmental injustice claims? Should it be enough to show, for example, that a proposed siting decision may have a disparate impact on low income and minority people? Note that under the Equal Protection Clause of the Constitution, discriminatory intent, not just a disparate impact, must be proved. As a result, claims of environmental injustice have not generally fared well in the courts. Michael Fisher, *Environmental Racism Claims Brought Under Title VI of the Civil Rights Act, supra* at 303-05, nn. 89-95. According to Lazarus, what other authority might offer stronger support for a claim of environmental injustice? What problems and limitations would a litigant face under each of these claims?

Two
Legal Institutions

Environmental law is dominated by legislation. The principal sources of federal environmental law are statutes enacted by Congress, regulations promulgated by the Environmental Protection Agency (EPA) and other administrative agencies, and interpretive decisions handed down by the courts. The statutes articulate national policy, create a framework for regulation, and delegate authority to the administrative agencies to implement and enforce the statutory provisions. The agency regulations add considerable detail to the statutory framework, specifying such matters as the circumstances under which pollution permits are required, the conditions that must be satisfied in order to obtain and operate in compliance with such permits, and the permissible levels of pollutant emissions for different types of facilities. Court decisions construe the meaning or constitutionality of statutory provisions, as well as the consistency of agency regulations with the governing statutory provisions. Thus, all three branches of government play significant roles in the continual shaping and reshaping of environmental law.

This chapter examines the role of each of the three branches of government in the development of environmental law. Because environmental law is an amalgam of statutes, regulations, and case law, and because the three institutions operate not in isolation but in dynamic relation to one another, the division of this chapter into the three institutional units is somewhat artificial. Accordingly, each subchapter contains one article that focuses primarily on the institution in question, as well as others that cut across institutional lines. The objective is to appreciate the unique contributions of Congress, EPA and other administrative agencies, and the courts to the shaping of environmental law.

As the first quarter-century of modern environmental lawmaking draws to a close, one cannot help being impressed, if not overwhelmed, by the sheer volume of environmental law generated by each of the three branches of government. Between 1970 and 1995, dozens of complex regulatory statutes were enacted. In many cases, these statutes were substantially amended throughout this 25-year period. Volumes of new regulations were promulgated. And thousands of cases were litigated. Still, the pace of change has not slowed. Congress is considering rewriting the basic premises of many environmental statutes, and the EPA is attempting to "reinvent" environmental regulation. As one examines the roles of the three branches of government during the first 25 years of environmental lawmaking, consider whether the forces that have thus far driven and challenged each branch will continue to do so, or whether new institutional considerations may supplant the old. Will retrospective articles in 2025 address themes similar to those addressed in this volume?

A. Congress

Inasmuch as environmental law is overwhelmingly statutory, the logical branch to address first is Congress. Congressional activity in the environmental arena can be divided into three periods. From 1970 to 1980, Congress enacted dozens of environmental laws in rapid succession. Some were debated at length; others were passed with little focused attention. Whereas federal law barely addressed environmental protection prior to 1970, a maze of federal statutory provisions dominated the field a decade later. During the 1980s (through 1990), Congress revisited the major federal statutes and substantially amended them. Congress added more stringent standards, more specificity, and more stinging enforcement provisions. Since 1990, Congress has been reviewing the "big picture," and debating whether fundamental changes in the statutory scheme are warranted.

The subchapter opens with an article analyzing the forces that contributed to the initial explosion of environmental lawmaking in 1970. Whereas conventional wisdom focuses on the role of newly-formed or re-energized environmental groups in pressing Congress to enact strong legislation, Donald Elliott, Bruce Ackerman, and John Millian attribute the evolutionary development of environmental statutes to an institutional model based on the "prisoners' dilemma," where parties have incentives to seek less-than-ideal solutions in order to avoid even worse results. Then follow two articles that address, from different perspectives, the landscape of environmental laws that resulted from the legislative explosion of the Seventies. William Rodgers highlights the seven most influential statutory provisions, and finds common explanations for their significance. Adam Babich analyzes the important federalism issues that characterize environmental law, focusing on the area of hazardous waste. Finally, Lakshman Guruswamy looks forward, offering suggestions for integrating the implementation of the numerous and diverse environmental statutory schemes.

The following article was written by a group of authors: Donald Elliott, a former Assistant Administrator and General Counsel of EPA (1989 - 1991); Professor Bruce Ackerman; and practicing attorney John Millian. The authors trace the development of the early environmental laws, ascribing both their enactment and the stringency of their provisions not to the influence of national environmental organizations, but to the forces of a "politicians' dilemma." Their analysis supports the surprising conclusion that environmental laws might be less stringent than they are today had Richard Nixon not been seeking re-election as President in 1972. (The journal in which this article was originally published did not use a footnote format; the footnotes shown here appeared as citations within the text of the original.)

TOWARD A THEORY OF STATUTORY EVOLUTION: THE FEDERALIZATION OF ENVIRONMENTAL LAW

E. Donald Elliott, Bruce A. Ackerman, and John C. Millian

1 J. L. Econ. & Org. 313 (1985)*

INTRODUCTION

* * *

* * * What we are embarked on is an exercise in statutory biography: by tracing the life histories of statutes in the environmental area, we hope to deepen our understanding of the factors that influence the growth and development of statutory law over time.

* * * We will describe in general terms what we have in mind when we say that statutes "evolve" and then illustrate by describing a particularly important period in the history of environmental law. During this period, roughly from 1965 through 1970, strong federal environmental legislation was passed, although environmentalists were not yet well-organized as a conventional interest group in Washington. Thus, the period is interesting in its own right because it seems to contradict the usual wisdom that statutes are passed in response to political activity by well-organized pressure groups.

1. THE EVOLUTION OF STATUTES

By drawing this analogy between the processes by which statutes change and biological evolution, we mean to question the vocabulary that American lawyers typically use to describe statutory and bureaucratic lawmaking. American lawyers talk about statutes as if they were created by a single individual. The personification of lawmaking is built into our language: we speak of Congress "writing" statutes. Court opinions invariably invoke the "intent" of Congress or the "will" of the legislature as if a complex lawmaking system composed of legislative committees, a majority of 535 legislators in two houses, subject to veto by the president, implemented by an administrative agency of several thousand bureaucrats, and subject to review in the courts could be compared usefully to the mind of a single lawgiver.

* * *

The law regulating environmental pollution is not the creation of a single intelligence. We will never understand why it is as it is if we persist in thinking of it as the product of a single, coherent intelligence; environmental law, like other statutory and bureaucratic law, *grows,* like a living thing, in response to forces internal and external to the legal system. * * *

We propose to try to model the conditions and dynamic processes by which environmental law has developed. In adopting evolution as our central metaphor, we do not want to imply either that some mysterious deterministic mechanism is at work or that the interest groups and politicians who constitute the primary actors in our story are not rational, self-conscious beings. On the contrary, we assume that individuals and groups generally act

---

according to what they perceive to be their rational self-interest. Our central point is rather that what constitutes rational, self-interested behavior changes depending upon the structure of the environment in which an individual or group finds itself. The structures of the lawmaking system and the organization and capabilities of various interest groups affect what rational legislators perceive to be in their self-interest. As these structures change, the incentives confronting lawmakers do also.

* * *

Our evolutionary model has six stages, each associated with a distinctive pattern of organization and incentives: Time One, the period of common law ascendancy; Time Two, the period of political cost-externalization; Time Three, the period of pre-emptive federalization; Time Four, the period of aspirational lawmaking; Time Five, the period of legalistic bureaucracy; and Time Six, the period of statutory revisionism. Our analysis of each stage has two related aspects, the first static, the second dynamic. Under the static approach, we analyze the lawmaking institutions characteristic of each period in an effort to describe the distinctive incentives each structure gives those who wish to further their interests through the lawmaking system. Under the dynamic approach, we show how each period's institutional structure carries in it the seeds of its own destruction. We shall argue that each is stable only so long as one or another of the relevant interests fails to solve one or another fundamental organizational problem that confronts it in furthering its self-interest. Once the critical strategic problems are solved, a previously less powerful interest will influence the making of new laws that usher in a new period, with its own distinctive lawmaking institutions, its own decisionmaking incentives, and its own strategic vulnerabilities.

* * *

Time One, the period of common law ascendancy, is characterized by pervasive *dis*organization on behalf of both polluters and environmentalists. During Time One, there are no significant groups organized around pollution issues. The primary lawmaking institution which addresses pollution during Time One—decentralized common law courts which respond to lawsuits brought by individuals or small groups—reflects the organizational environment. A number of factors account for the absence of groups organized around pollution problems, but perhaps the most important is the lack of information connecting individual maladies with pollution. As long as pollution remains invisible, groups cannot be organized and the period of common law ascendancy continues.

A number of factors combine to destabilize common law ascendancy and mark the transition to Time Two, the period of political cost-externalization. As concerned scientists gradually identify the scientific basis of pollution and the harms which it causes, polluters lose their shield of invisibility, and it becomes possible to organize small groups of citizens at the local, and eventually the state, level. The initial organization of environmental groups tends to take place in the context of the lawsuits which are the dominant form of lawmaking then available. Thus, the existing legal structure becomes a kind of seed crystal which helps to shape the form of the organizations which will in turn transform existing lawmaking institutions.

Time Two, the period of political cost-externalization, is characterized by the formation of organized groups of environmentalists at the state and local level. Industry, however, remains passive and disorganized with regard to pollution issues. Politicians respond to the strategic imbalance created by the local organizational successes of environmentalists by passing laws which place the primary costs of pollution control on out-of-state interests—hence, our label, the period of political cost-externalization. Time Three, which we discuss at some length in this paper, is the period of preemptive federalization, when industry groups attempt to counter the organizational successes of environmentalists at the state and local level through preemptive lawmaking at the federal level.

The temporary success of industry at obtaining federal legislation in turn provokes a counter-response by environmentalists, who possess a mass grassroots following but still lack a well-organized institutional structure at the national level to counter industry lobbyists. The final section of the present paper describes the peculiar political dynamics of Time Four, the period of aspirational lawmaking, in which very tough environmental laws are passed by politicians seeking to gain political advancement by appealing to these mobilized, but poorly organized, mass publics.

The laws passed during the period of aspirational lawmaking are responsible for changing the organizational setting and ushering in a new incentive structure, which we call Time Five, the period of legalistic bureaucracy. As a result of the successes of mass environmentalism, a new legal structure is created which is dominated by two new players, the Environmental Protection Agency (EPA) and the national environmental groups which use the courts and the news media to challenge EPA's actions.

Thus, we maintain that the surprisingly strong environmental statutes of the early 1970's were not passed in response to lobbying by well-organized national environmental groups; on the contrary, it is the other way around—the statutes of the early 1970s made it possible to consolidate national environmental groups.

The final stage, the period of statutory revisionism, is only now beginning. It is characterized by effective national counter-organization by industry to deregulate and repeal parts of the legal structure created by the legislative, judicial, and administrative victories won by environmentalists.

* * *

2. PROBLEM: ENVIRONMENTAL STATUTES OF THE 1960s AND 1970s

An extraordinary outburst of lawmaking related to pollution and the environment occurred at the national level during the 1960s and 1970s as a dozen major federal pollution control statutes were enacted. This network of national statutes—together with a much larger body of implementing regulations promulgated by the Environmental Protection Agency—now constitutes one of the most pervasive systems of national regulation known to American law. Today every discharge into the land, water or air—from the smallest smokestack to the largest landfill for the disposal of toxic chemicals—requires direct or indirect permission from the national government.

This comprehensive structure of environmental regulation by the federal government is a curious feature of American law for at least two reasons. First, the effects of industrial pollution on the natural environment had been generally free from regulation by government, except for sporadic nuisance actions under the common law and a few municipal ordinances to control smoke. Second, it is curious that the environmental law of the 1970s was made primarily at the national level, rather than by state or municipal governments which had traditionally had legislative authority over such matters. * * *

The environmental statutes of the 1960s and 1970s are distinctive not only for their number but also for their content. In a variety of ways, they represent a sharp break from the attitudes which preceded them. Consider the approach which the Clean Air Act takes toward economics and technology, for example. For hundreds of years, the common law held that no one had an absolute right to be free from the harmful effects of air pollution. Instead, the basic attitude of the law was one of accommodation and "reasonableness," balancing the harmful effects of air pollution on the one hand against the benefits of industrial activity and the availability and cost of abatement technology on the other.

In the 1970 Clean Air Act, however, Congress staked out a more extreme position. In setting mandatory national air quality standards, EPA is instructed to give no weight whatsoever to economic considerations. Nor is the technical infeasibility of pollution controls admissible as an excuse. In essence, Congress declared that every American, including particularly sensitive groups such as asthmatics, has a statutory right to be protected from "any known or anticipated adverse effects associated with" air pollution, *whatever* the cost.[1]

* * *

3. TWO FAILED HYPOTHESES: PROBLEM-SOLVING AND INTEREST GROUP POLITICS

What accounts for this "dramatic plunge forward"? After decades of incrementalism and accommodation, why did Congress suddenly enact a series of relatively extreme federal environmental statutes in the early 1970s?

3.1 Congress as Problem-Solver

To an environmental lawyer, one answer is immediate and obvious: Congress enacted strong statutes because it recognized that the country faced an environmental crisis.

We do not for a moment deny the seriousness of the problems that the environmental statutes of the late 1960s and early 1970s address. * * * On reflection, however, it should be clear that our typical environmental lawyer's first intuition is really no answer at all.

It is a non sequitur to assert—as lawyers frequently do—that Congress passes statutes "because" policy problems exist. The existence of a real or perceived policy problem may be a necessary condition for the passage of a statute, but the existence of a problem alone does not a statute make; additional conditions must be satisfied, which explains why Congress passes statutes addressed to certain problems while other equally pressing problems go unredressed. Conversely, when the Clean Air Act was passed, at least some air pollution problems were getting better as a result of the gradual substitution of oil for coal during the 1960s.

---

[1] Clean Air Act, §§ 109(b)(1) and (2), 84 Stat. 1679, 1970, 42 U.S.C. §§ 7409(b)(1) and (2), 1980.

* * *

3.2 Interest Group Politics

A lawyer's second thought about how environmental statutes came into being is likely to involve a story about interest group politics.

* * * In its modern versions, the interest group account legislation almost always ends up emphasizing the degree to which one or another group is able to organize for political action more effectively than groups with opposing interests. * * *

It is possible to construct a plausible story about the birth of federal environmental legislation in the late 1960s and early 1970s which is consistent with the standard view of interest group power as directly correlated with degree of organization. In this hypothetical story, persons who want a cleaner environment somehow manage to overcome their free-rider problems to become a well-organized interest group in Washington—thereby earning the title "environmentalists." Industry, on the other hand, remains passive on environmental issues, at least until after the passage of major federal legislation. According to this hypothesis, the "dramatic plunge forward" in federal environmental legislation occurred because environmentalists were a well-organized effective pressure group on environmental issues and industry was not.

* * *

* * * There are, however, two problems with this approach. First, it is untrue, and second, it is not very powerful.

A theory that explains the early federal environmental statutes in terms of conventional interest group politics is untrue in the sense that one can detect no striking imbalance between the organizational presence of environmentalists and industry as lobbying forces in 1970 which might account for the stringent provisions of the Clean Air Act. If anything, industry lobbyists seem to have been more plentiful and better organized in Washington in 1970 than were the environmentalists. * * *

Not only do the facts fail to confirm the standard version of interest group theory, but the theory also lacks power to explain how and why environmentalists suddenly solved their free-rider problems to emerge as a powerful force on the national political scene in the 1970s.

4. COLLECTIVE ACTION AND PRISONERS' DILEMMA

The model of legislative politics as a function of the organization of interest groups fails to account for the fact that strong environmental statutes were passed in the early 1970s without pressure from well-organized environmental advocacy groups at the federal level. It is difficult, moreover, to explain the rise of national environmental groups in terms of prevailing theories of voluntary organization.

* * *

4.1 The Problem of Collective Action

Modern theories of voluntary organization, derived from Mancur Olson,[2] imply that national environmental groups will be difficult, if not impossible, to organize. Large

---

[2] MANCUR OLSON, THE LOGIC OF COLLECTIVE ACTION (1965).

numbers of citizens, each with only a small stake in clean air, will, if they are rational in the narrow economic sense, decline to invest time or money in the cause of cleaning up the environment in the hope that they will be able to "free-ride" on the efforts of others. * * * The paradox, of course, is that everyone ends up worse off than they would have been if they had been able to organize their actions for their collective benefit.

It is a small step from Olson's theory of voluntary organizations to the political corollary that the interest of citizens in a clean environment will be systematically underrepresented in any lawmaking process in which interest group politics plays a significant role. Individual citizens who wish to breathe clean air are a classic example of a large, disorganized population seeking a collective good which will benefit each individual by only a small amount. The costs of environmental regulation, on the other hand, tend to fall heavily on a relatively small number of companies, which are already reasonably well-organized and thus presumably less subject to free-rider problems. According to most popular theories of political influence, well-organized industries would be systematically overrepresented and diffuse environmentalists systematically underrepresented in formulating policy. How, then, is one to explain the passage of strong environmental legislation in the late 1960s and early 1970s and the rise of well-organized environmental groups on the national level?

* * *

4.2 Politicians' Dilemma

The answer * * * can be discovered by considering the problems of environmental organizing and passing environmental legislation as analogous to the game of Prisoners' Dilemma.

Prisoners' Dilemma gets its name from a story about two prisoners who are separately interrogated about a crime. The two were the only witnesses, so if they both refuse to testify, the worst that can happen to them is a one-year conviction for illegal possession of firearms. However, a clever prosecutor approaches each prisoner and offers him a proposition: "If you confess and testify against your partner, he'll get life but you'll go free; the only hitch is that if you both confess, you'll both get a sentence of six years for armed robbery. I should tell you that I'm offering the same deal to your partner." Assuming that the game is played only a single time, and assuming further that the prisoners are rational and motivated only by self-interest, they will both confess—and get six years in jail, rather than keep quiet and get off with only a year. The paradox, of course, is that by pursuing their individual self-interest, the prisoners behave in a way that is contrary to their shared collective interest in shorter sentences. If they could only organize their actions for their common benefit, they would both be better off.

In his recent book on collective action, Russell Hardin has shown that the problems of forming voluntary groups described by Olson are an application of Prisoners' Dilemma.[3] In classic Prisoners' Dilemma, each prisoner confesses in an attempt to exploit his codefendant, and as a result they both end up worse off than they would have been if they had coordinated their actions for the collective benefit. Similarly, a citizen who wants clean

---

[3] RUSSELL HARDIN, COLLECTIVE ACTION 25-30 (1982).

air but refrains from joining an environmental group in the hope she can free-ride on the efforts of others is also playing an exploitative strategy. She will be best off if she gets the benefits of clean air without paying her fair share of the costs for this collective good; her exploitative strategy will not work, however, if everyone plays the same strategy. When everyone, or nearly everyone, tries to free-ride, they all end up worse off than they would have been if they had been able to coordinate their actions to play a cooperative strategy.

* * *

The hidden moral to the story of Prisoners' Dilemma is that forming a voluntary organization for collective benefit is not the only way to organize persons to engage in collective action; it is also possible to coordinate actions by altering the structure of incentives which motivate them. * * * It is this institutional structure * * * that defines the incentives facing the prisoners and explains their otherwise inexplicable actions.

This institutional perspective helps to explain the evolution of environmental law during the late 1960s and early 1970s. Not that the evolving institutional structure technically complied with all the conditions for the game of Prisoners' Dilemma—in contrast to the standard game, our story involves many relevant players, no single subset of which could have coordinated their strategies in a way that guaranteed them an optimal result. Nonetheless, like prisoners, many of the key actors responded to institutional threats of terrible outcomes by rationally choosing strategies that were very far from first-best from their point of view. We shall, then, use the term *Politicians' Dilemma* to describe situations which are analogous to the game of Prisoners' Dilemma in that the structure of incentives facing the players creates a strong incentive for them to pursue a less than ideal outcome in order to avoid an even less desirable result. We believe that institutional structures which create the Politicians' Dilemma are a particularly important feature of our lawmaking system, * * * as groups are forced to abandon their true preferences to coalesce around compromise legislation.

5. POLITICIANS' DILEMMA AND ENVIRONMENTAL STATUTES

The first significant federal statutes regulating air pollution, the Motor Vehicle Pollution Control Act of 1965 and the Air Quality Act of 1967, were not passed because of the political power of environmentalists at the national level but because two well-organized industrial groups, the automobile industry and the soft coal industry, were threatened with a state of affairs even worse from their perspective than federal air pollution legislation— namely, inconsistent and progressively more stringent environmental laws at the state and local level. As a consequence of the structure of our federal lawmaking system, environmentalists were able to organize industry to do their bidding for them. Thus, the first federal legislation regulating air pollution was passed not because environmentalists solved their own organizational problems on the national level but because environmentalists exploited the organizational difficulties of their industrial adversaries at the state and local level.

The auto industry and the soft coal industry undoubtedly would have preferred no government regulation of air pollution rather than federal legislation. When faced with the threat of inconsistent and increasingly rigorous state laws, however, they resolved their Politicians' Dilemma by using their superior organizational capacities in Washington to preempt or control the environmentalists' legislative victories at the state level.

* * *

5.1 Time Two: The Period of Political Cost-Externalization

The existence of states aids environmentalists in three ways. First, and most obvious, the existence of the states makes it possible for environmentalists to seek piecemeal solutions to their organizational difficulties. Not that the effort to transcend their free-ride problems will be easy * * *. Nonetheless, even here, the demands on a variety of resources—from political savvy to hard cash—do not compare with the challenges involved in achieving organizational credibility in a nation of a quarter of a billion. Moreover, environmental groups do not form spontaneously at even the state level. States consist of a hierarchy of smaller governmental units, over 80,000 in total in the United States, which form a kind of lattice around which organizations crystallize. Environmental groups tend to be comprised of coalitions of groups which organized first on a smaller scale, around local problems or narrow interests.

Second, federalism opens up the possibility of a distinctive credit-claiming strategy for aspiring politicians on the state level, which we call *cost-externalization*. Quite simply, dividing the nation into fifty geographic zones makes it almost inevitable that some pollution problems will be generated by out-of-staters. Since midwestern auto workers don't vote on whether California should ban the internal combustion engine to control smog and Appalachian coalminers don't vote on whether New York should ban coal to control sulfur oxides from power plant smoke stacks, these issues promise politicians on the state level the equivalent of a free lunch—"tough" legislation allows them to garner public credit for bringing a benefit to *their* constituents at somebody else's expense.

Finally, as scattered environmental victories begin to appear, this evidence of success will feed efforts in other states. Activists will be prompted to continue the fight, rather than seek out other issues; the media and the public will gradually begin to take greater notice and express increased interest. A bandwagon effect becomes possible: victories in one state may promote the marshalling of the resources necessary for victory in another. Indeed, legislation in one state can stimulate other states to adopt even more stringent laws.

5.2 Time Three: Preemptive Federalization

The Motor Vehicle Air Pollution Control Act of 1965. The first statute which gave the federal government regulatory power over air pollution was the Motor Vehicle Air Pollution Control Act of 1965. The roots of this federal legislation run deep into the California of the 1950s and 1960s. * * * [T]hrough a combination of a cost-externalization strategy by California politicians, auto industry ineptitude, and local environmental organizing, state air pollution legislation had begun to pose a serious threat to the automobile industry by the middle 1960s. * * *

* * * Unlike most other industries, the automobile industry has strong reasons to prefer national legislation over state and local regulation of air pollution. Most manufacturing industries would rather have state and local governments set air pollution standards, because the political and economic costs of controlling their pollution are concentrated at the local level. * * *

The automobile industry is in a very different strategic position, however, because it is geographically concentrated and its product, not its factories, is the main source of its pollution. Local politicians can set strict antipollution standards for motor vehicles without fear of being accused of putting their constituents out of work. It is true that pollution controls tend to increase the price of new cars, but the connection between government action and particular price increases is only dimly perceived by voters. And unlike other industries, Detroit could not credibly threaten to stop selling cars in California or other states which established stringent pollution standards. Moreover, differing or inconsistent air pollution standards set at the state and local level were perceived as a serious threat to Detroit's assembly lines. Finally, the companies feared a kind of political domino effect, in which one state legislature after another would set more and more stringent emission standards without regard to the costs or technical difficulties involved.

Ideally the auto companies would have preferred to remain free of any substantial government regulation of pollution, but if they were going to be regulated, federal legislation was preferable to state legislation—particularly if federal standards were set based on technical presentations to an administrative agency rather than through symbolic appeals to cost-externalizing politicians.

During the early 1960s, the automobile industry successfully opposed federal emission standards for motor vehicles. In mid-1965, however, the industry abruptly reversed its position on the advice of Washington lawyer Lloyd Cutler: provided that the federal standards would be set by an administrative agency, and provided that they would preempt any state standards more stringent than California's, the industry would support federal legislation. As a result, Senator Muskie's pending bill to have the federal government set emission standards for motor vehicles was amended to provide that standards would be set by HEW, rather than in the legislation itself, and legislative history was written to leave no doubt that more stringent state laws were preempted. With auto industry backing, the Motor Vehicle Pollution Control Act of 1965 became the first federal statute regulating air pollution.

The Air Quality Act of 1967. The Air Quality Act of 1967 was the first federal statute to give the federal government a significant role in regulating air pollution from stationary sources such as factories and powerplants. Under the 1967 act, the federal government was to promulgate criteria based on the latest scientific evidence concerning the adverse effects of air pollution. Each state was then to develop its own air pollution control plan based on the federal criteria. If any state failed to adopt a satisfactory plan, the federal government could promulgate one for it.

The story behind the Air Quality Act of 1967 is complicated, but here too the threat of state and local legislation provided the impetus for a crucial industry to acquiesce in federal legislation in the hope that it might dampen local legislative initiatives. Like the automobile industry, the high-sulphur, soft (bituminous) coal industry is geographically concentrated, and its product, not its factories, constitutes the primary source of its air pollution. Soft coal provided a logical target for local politicians anxious to place the blame for pollution on out-of-state sources.

During the mid-1960s, the soft coal industry faced increasingly strict air pollution regulations in the Northeast, which eventually threatened it with the loss of a major market. In 1965, Mayor John Lindsay of New York proposed—and despite strong opposition mounted by the coal industry, the city council eventually passed—a program to ban the use of coal as a heating fuel and to greatly restrict the sulfur content of coals used for other purposes. In 1966, New York, New Jersey, Pennsylvania, and Connecticut announced joint plans to combat air pollution. * * *

Ideally, the soft coal industry, like the automobile industry, probably would have preferred that there be no government regulation of the pollution produced by its product. However, if there was going to be regulation, federal legislation offered distinct advantages to the coal industry over runaway state and local lawmaking. While the 1967 federal Air Quality Act did not forbid states from setting air pollution standards more stringent than those recommended by HEW, as a practical, political matter, the air quality criteria which HEW established based on the latest scientific evidence would tend to restrain state legislation. * * * Moreover, Senator Randolph's amendments placed federal air pollution policy firmly on the road toward seeking technological "fixes" to pollution problems as opposed to encouraging switches to inherently less polluting fuels. This bias in favor of technological solutions still dominates federal pollution policy, although its wisdom is questionable from the standpoint of sensible national policy. From the perspective of the high-sulfur coal industry, however, it is clearly preferable to have a federal EPA force electric utilities to install scrubbers than to sit idly by and watch other cities and states follow New York's lead by banning coal-burning to solve their pollution problems.

The Air Quality Act of 1967, like the Motor Vehicle Air Pollution Control Act of 1965, passed not because environmentalists were a well-organized pressure group at the federal level, but because their efforts, and the actions of local politicians, created a Politicians' Dilemma for a well-organized industry. Faced with the even less desirable alternative of a significant loss of markets through state and local legislation, the soft coal industry strongly supported passage of Senator Muskie's bill "with the addition of the amendments offered by Senator Randolph"[4] which became the Air Quality Act of 1967. * * *

5.3 Time Four: Aspirational Lawmaking

A structurally similar process also accounts for some of the surprisingly stringent provisions of the Clean Air Amendments of 1970. In particular, the requirement that automobile manufacturers reduce their pollution by 90 percent within five years, and the stipulation that EPA ignore economic and technological feasibility, did not result from the success of environmentalists at organizing a strong lobbying presence of their own in Washington. Here too a Politicians' Dilemma was at work. The "prisoners" in this case were politicians, primarily Senator Edmund Muskie and President Richard Nixon. By strategically threatening these political entrepreneurs with the loss of political capital which they had previously worked to build, environmentalists were able to organize them

---

[4] *Air Pollution—1967: Hearings on S. 780 Before the Subcommittee on Air and Water Pollution of the Senate Committee on Public Works,* 90th Cong., 1st Sess. 2026, 1967 [statement of W.V. Hartman, Peabody Coal Co.] (1967).

to pass a statute more stringent than the politicians really wanted. In an ideal world both Nixon and Muskie probably would have preferred a compromise statute less likely to alienate either industry or environmentalists, but as in Prisoners' Dilemma, they were confronted with a situation in which they both had to choose the least-worst situation politically.

The structural feature which creates the Politicians' Dilemma is the fragmentation of the lawmaking system between Congress and the Executive, between House and Senate, between legislative committee and legislative committee. This division of lawmaking authority creates a situation in which various politicians can credibly claim credit for any particular law. * * *

* * *

Throughout the 1960s, Senator Muskie carefully invested his time and legislative effort in the environment, long before the issue achieved great public attention. As the primary drafter of the federal air pollution statutes of 1965 and 1967, as well as several water pollution statutes, Muskie stood to gain from the rapid rise in importance which the voting public attached to environmental issues in the early 1970s. However, because of the separation of the lawmaking function into multiple bodies and the difficulty which the voting public has in monitoring all the lawmaking activities in Washington, Muskie was vulnerable to see "his" issue stolen by other politicians, particularly the one in the White House. In addition, because most voters do not bother to follow the details of what goes on in Washington that closely, Muskie was also vulnerable to charges from the embryonic environmental movement that he was really "Mr. Dirty," not "Mr. Clean."

The divisions of lawmaking authority, coupled with the difficulty of credibly communicating with the voters about the political significance of legislative activities, created a situation in which Nixon and Muskie were caught in a Politicians' Dilemma. The result was the passage of the Clean Air Act of 1970 in a form which was more stringent than either of them would have preferred.

The Clean Air Act of 1970. The Clean Air Amendments of 1970 is a complex statute. There is no denying that a number of strands came together to contribute to its passage. One factor was the realization that the Air Quality Act of 1967 had failed to achieve its goal of cleaning up the air. In addition, by 1970 there had been an enormous increase in popular concern about the environment, fueled in part by the attention which the issue was receiving in the press and on television. Finally, 1970 was different from 1967 in that a "loose coalition" of environmentalists was just beginning to organize on the national level, although environmentalists were still nowhere near a match for even a single auto company's lobbyists, either in terms of numbers or funding.

In this political environment, it would not have been surprising for Congress to pass additional air pollution legislation of an incremental sort—perhaps an increase of funding here, or a realignment of federal and state authority there. In fact, on December 10, 1969, the leading proponent of federal air pollution legislation, Senator Muskie, introduced just such a bill, the Air Quality Improvement Act. * * *

* * *

* * * [O]n February 10, 1970, two months after Muskie had introduced his Air Quality

Improvement bill, President Nixon transmitted his own air pollution proposals to Congress. Nixon's proposals called for major structural changes in existing federal air pollution statutes, including national standards for extremely hazardous air pollutants and a requirement that states develop abatement plans to meet mandatory federal air quality standards within one year.

The next significant event occurred in May 1970, when a Ralph Nader task force published a report harshly criticizing Muskie as being soft on industry. * * * The Nader report went on to claim that Muskie should be "stripped of his title as 'Mr. Pollution Control'" and to demand that he resign his chairmanship of the air and water pollution subcommittee.[5] Muskie was clearly stung by Nader's public criticism.

In August, Muskie's subcommittee reported out a revised air quality bill, which essentially followed the outlines of Nixon's proposal but was tougher at every turn than what the president had proposed: where Nixon's proposal would have allowed states one year to develop their implementation plans, Muskie's bill allowed only nine months; where the administration proposed that the auto companies be given until 1980 to achieve a 90 percent reduction in emissions, Muskie's subcommittee cut the deadline to 1975; where Nixon proposed nationwide federal air quality standards, Muskie's subcommittee added the requirement for an additional "margin of safety" and the protection of especially sensitive groups; where Nixon had proposed that we do what "we can do within the limits of existing technology", Muskie deleted technological or economic feasibility as a constraint.

These surprisingly tough provisions of the Clean Air Act of 1970 did not result from organized lobbying by environmentalists, at least not in the conventional sense. As a result of the Nader report, which threatened Muskie with the loss of his national reputation as "Mr. Clean," both Nixon and Muskie found themselves trapped in a Politicians' Dilemma. Both were forced to support legislation more stringent than either would have preferred.

* * *

Muskie wrote a "tough" pollution statute in 1970, one which ran a serious risk of alienating industry, only when he was threatened with an outcome which was even worse from his perspective—the loss of his reputation with the public as a crusader to clean up the environment; Nixon went along, reluctantly, because the adverse political consequences of vetoing the bill were perceived as greater than those of signing it.

The particular structural feature of the lawmaking system which environmentalists were able to exploit to create the Politicians' Dilemma was the division of lawmaking authority between president and Congress. Because of this division (and other similar divisions, such as between the House and Senate), it is never entirely clear to the voters that a particular politician is responsible for particular legislation. In these circumstances, aspiring politicians have incentives to compete with one another for credit with the public for having passed "strong" environmental legislation. The Nader report was able to compound the pressure on the politicians by exploiting the difficulty that the public has in identifying the politicians who deserve credit for enacting legislation in response to a perceived need.

---

[5] John C. Esposito, Vanishing Air: The Ralph Nader Study Group Report on Air Pollution 290, 292 (1970).

It is important to recognize that the surprisingly strong environmental legislation in 1970 did not result from superior organization by environmentalists. Indeed, it is possible to speculate that if environmentalists had been more tightly organized as a conventional pressure group in 1970, as they later became, the Clean Air Act amendments might have been less, rather than more, stringent. Had there been a well-organized environmental lobby in 1970, Muskie could have deflected Nader's charges by giving in to its demands. And it is quite likely that this lobby would have settled for far less than the Great Leap Forward achieved by the Clean Air Act. In 1970, however, no group yet existed with whom to bargain. In these circumstances, Muskie had no way of knowing how much would be enough. He did about all that he could have done to prove that he was more "pro-environmental" than Nixon: he proposed a bill which was essentially Nixon's, only more so on every point.

NOTES

1. The article suggests that regulated industries supported the rush of unprecedented environmental lawmaking on the federal level in the 1970's because they found uniform, preemptive federal standards preferable to the plethora of varying environmental laws that were being enacted on the state and local levels. In 1995, the conservative-dominated Congress considered a number of proposals to shift substantial authority back to the states in implementing many of the key environmental laws. Why? Did the initial promise of federal preemption prove illusory when most of the federal statutes expressly authorized states to adopt more (but not less) stringent standards? Why might a scheme that encourages, rather than simply allows, state decisionmaking be more palatable to regulated industries? In what circumstances might a federally-dominated scheme be preferable to the regulated community or to environmentalists?

2. Professor Richard Revesz observes that federal environmental legislation is most often justified to prevent states from engaging in a "race to the bottom," whereby each state is presumably enacting increasingly lax standards to entice industry to locate or relocate in the state. Richard L. Revesz, *Rehabilitating Interstate Competition: Rethinking the "Race-to-the-Bottom" Rationale for Federal Environmental Regulation,* 67 N.Y.U. L. REV. 1210 (1992). Although Professor Revesz challenges the validity of the assumption that states would "race to the bottom," he clearly believes that the concern over states adopting excessively weak environmental standards nonetheless played a central role in motivating Congress to enact the comprehensive federal environmental laws that now dominate the landscape.

Professor Revesz also addresses the phenomenon of state standards that exceed comparable federal standards; once the federal floor is in place, states' adoption of more stringent environmental standards is not inconsistent with the assumption that, in the absence of the federal floor, the states might otherwise engage in a race-to-the-bottom. *Id.* at 1227-33. Is the thesis of the Elliott *et al.* article, that Congress enacted comprehensive federal laws largely to create some uniformity out of the diversity of states' approaches to environmental lawmaking, consistent with the belief that Congress enacted federal environmental laws to prevent states from racing to set competitively lower environmental standards? Consider the Surface Mining Control and Reclamation Act of 1977, 30 U.S.C. §§ 1201 *et seq.,* which states among its findings the following:

> [S]urface mining and reclamation standards are essential in order to insure that competition in interstate commerce among sellers of coal produced in different States will not be used to undermine the ability of the several States to improve and maintain adequate standards on coal mining operations within their borders * * *.

30 U.S.C. § 1201(g).

3. Unlike the first wave of comprehensive federal environmental statutes enacted during the 1970's, which created the broad outlines of regulatory programs and authorized the EPA or other administrative agencies to fill in the details, the congressional enactments during the 1980's reflected a different dynamic between Congress and the EPA. The manifestation of this change in the 1984 amendments to RCRA (the Hazardous and Solid Waste Amendments) and in the 1986 amendments to CERCLA (the Superfund Amendments and Reauthorization Act) are described by James Florio, who at the time was Chairman of the House of Representatives committee with jurisdiction over hazardous waste issues, and subsequently served as Governor of New Jersey. James J. Florio, *Congress As Reluctant Regulator: Hazardous Waste Policy in the 1980's,* 3 YALE J. ON REG. 351 (1986). Congressman Florio summarized his analysis as follows:

> In the 1970's Congress established an environmental protection regulatory system by passing laws which, like many preceding regulatory statutes, set relatively broad goals and timetables and left substantial discretion to the implementing agency on how best to achieve those goals. As demonstrated in the recent reauthorizations of the Resource Conservation and Recovery Act (RCRA) and the Comprehensive Environmental Response, Compensation and Liability Act (CERCLA), however, Congress is no longer confident that the Environmental Protection Agency (EPA) will exercise such discretion as intended by Congress. As a result, Congress itself has had to assume the role of regulator, making some of the detailed technical and administrative determinations typically left to the implementing agency. Instead of authorizing EPA to regulate the disposal of chemical wastes, Congress has prescribed the limits. Instead of relying on EPA to meet deadlines, Congress has established self-enforcing standards to be implemented in the absence of agency action. Instead of allowing EPA to establish technical standards of safety, Congress has set minimum requirements that EPA may not reduce.

Ibid. How much regulatory detail ought Congress include in legislation?

In the mid-1990's, Congress is again (or still) unwilling to rely on EPA's technical or policy judgment to enhance the effectiveness of the existing environmental regulatory programs. This time, proposals for change focus less on congressional micromanagement than on statutory restrictions on the agency's powers together with a broader scope of judicial review. H.R. 9, 104th Cong., 1st Sess. (1995).

4. For a more theoretical approach to congressional lawmaking in the environmental arena, see CASS R. SUNSTEIN, AFTER THE RIGHTS REVOLUTION: RECONCEIVING THE REGULATORY STATE (1990), and Daniel A. Farber's review, *Playing the Baseline: Civil Rights, Environmental Law, and Statutory Interpretation*, 91 COLUM. L. REV. 676 (1991).

In the following piece, Professor Rodgers highlights the elements common to what he perceives to be the seven most significant provisions from the dozens of federal environmental laws that Congress has enacted over the years.

THE SEVEN STATUTORY WONDERS OF U.S. ENVIRONMENTAL LAW: ORIGINS AND MORPHOLOGY
William H. Rodgers, Jr.
27 Loy. L.A. L. Rev. 1009 (1994)*

I. INTRODUCTION

Students from around the world often ask my opinion on the most influential or effective of the United States environmental laws. I offer an opinion based on two criteria: What laws have contributed most to protection of the natural world and what laws have been most emulated? * * *

Here are the nominees for the seven great U.S. environmental laws:

(1) section 409 of the Food Additives Amendment of 1958, known popularly as the Delaney Amendment, which states in part that no food additive "shall be deemed to be safe if it is found to induce cancer when ingested by man or animal";[2]

(2) section 2 of the Land and Water Conservation Fund Act of 1965,[3] which established a special fund from certain federal revenues—including receipts from oil and gas leasing on the Outer Continental Shelf—that can be used for the acquisition of parks and conservation lands;

(3) section 2 of the Wilderness Act of 1964 which established the National Wilderness Preservation System and defines wilderness "as an area where the earth and its community of life are untrammeled by man, where man himself is a visitor who does not remain";[5]

---

* Reprinted with permission.
[2] 21 U.S.C. § 348(c)(3)(A) (1988).
[3] * * * 16 U.S.C. § 460l-5 (1988).
[5] 16 U.S.C. § 1131(c) (1988).

(4) section 102 of the National Environmental Policy Act of 1969 (NEPA),[6] which requires that environmental impact statements accompany all actions by federal agencies that may have a significant effect on the human environment;

(5) section 301 of the Federal Water Pollution Control Act Amendments of 1972 (Clean Water Act or CWA),[7] which makes unlawful the discharge of any pollutant by any person;

(6) section 7 of the Endangered Species Act of 1973 (ESA), which states that no federal agency shall take action "likely to jeopardize" the continued existence of a protected species or result in the "destruction or adverse modification" of its habitat;[9] and

(7) section 107 of the Comprehensive Environmental Response, Compensation, and Liability Act of 1980 (CERCLA),[10] which imposes strict and joint and several liability on any person whose disposal of hazardous substances causes the owner of the affected property to incur response costs.

The measures of influence of these extraordinary enactments can be underscored in various ways. And now for my choices, in descending order of significance:

My first-place vote goes to the Land and Water Conservation Fund Act, which, since its inception, has resulted in expenditures of $6.8 billion to maintain, purchase, and acquire parklands, changing the face of urban and rural America for the better.

A close second is the Wilderness Act, which has given rise to a tenfold expansion in protected acreage since 1964—now close to 100 million acres—and coincidentally offers the opportunity to secure advances in the protection of North American biodiversity.

In third place is the Delaney Amendment, which is much more than a low-level, pollutants-in-food law. This statute should be best remembered for bringing down DDT and putting in motion a worldwide social revolution against the serious problem of pesticide pollution. In an irony that may yet be too conspicuous to escape the notice of Congress, the cancer studies that helped ban DDT twenty-five years ago have been supplemented dramatically by recent findings implicating the chemical as an indicator of human breast cancer.

In fourth place is section 7 of the ESA, which is the most protective of all domestic environmental laws and admired throughout the world. Much of section 7's influence is measured in hope and not results. But the U.S. courts have embraced this protective law, which has accounted for no small number of impressive victories for the creatures of the North American continent.

In fifth place is section 102 of NEPA, which has been replicated in rapid fashion throughout the United States and around the world. NEPA is the most frequently copied and most frequently cited of all U.S. domestic environmental laws. It also must be credited with significant gains in environmental quality on many fronts, although there is some disagreement at the margins of this proposition.

My sixth-place finisher is section 301 of the Clean Water Act, which deserves a lion's share of the credit for the significant gains in the quality of U.S. surface waters in the last quarter century.

---

[6] * * * 42 U.S.C.A. § 4332 (West 1985).

[7] * * * 33 U.S.C.A. § 1311(a) (West 1986).

[9] 16 U.S.C. § 1536(a)(2) (1988).

[10] * * * 42 U.S.C. § 9607 (1988 & Supp. III 1991).

In seventh place is section 107 of CERCLA. In thirteen short years, this statute has thoroughly revolutionized commercial property management and exchange in the United States. More than any other single enactment, section 107 has brought environmental law into the blue-ribbon law firms of every major city. In no small way, this statute has transformed the practice of environmental law from fringe novelty to mainstream reality.

Another perspective on the influence of this wondrous seven is to ask whether anybody has noticed. Turned around in this fashion, one is hard put to identify seven more controversial landmarks on the contemporary legal and political landscape. Land acquisitions and wilderness set-asides are under attack by the "wise-use" and other landowner movements. The Delaney "paradox" has tied Congress in knots for the last decade. Section 7 and other features of the ESA are under perpetual reconsideration, with the spotted owl adding new fuel to these flames. Congress has nibbled away at NEPA with sufficient frequency so as to give rise to a separate literature on the subject. Section 301 of the CWA has been exposed as the epitome of a "command and control" statute, a pejorative of no small moment among legal academics who claim to know something about environmental law. As of this writing, the legislative reauthorization process of section 107 of CERCLA is underway and Congress is receiving a barrage of new information about transaction costs, gross unfairness, and the legal springs and traps that haunt this unpopular law.

Most remarkable about this process, though, is that many believe that these seven extraordinary laws have become virtually repeal-proof. According to this view, the details can change; screens, clouds, and shrouds can appear; decelerators and modifiers can emerge; but the central features of these seven statutes will remain unchanged as a kind of functional constitutional law. Whether or not this estimate is accurate, the suggestion encourages a closer look at the common features of these seven impressive laws. What are the ingredients of a great environmental law?

II. COMMON FEATURES OF THE SEVEN STATUTORY WONDERS

Undoubtedly, a host of different theories of congressional behavior, political timing, constituency service, and what-not might be unfurled to explain the striking trajectory of a successful law. This Essay focuses on (1) strong leadership; (2) an inspirational and even radical message; (3) growth and sleeper potential; (4) research implantation; and (5) attentive monitoring.

A. Strong Leadership

One conspicuous feature of the super seven is that these laws were advanced by strong leaders—respected and powerful members of Congress, savvy staffers, influential outsiders—sometimes all three. Entrepreneurial skills, sheer passion, and force of will figured in the outcome. The Delaney Amendment was the product of a crusty New York City congressman who was moved to help a friend who was worried about the long-range effects of the post-World War II pesticides. The name most closely associated with the Land and Water Conservation Fund Act is Stewart Udall, the highly respected Secretary of Interior in the Kennedy Administration, and a card-carrying environmentalist. Although the Wilderness Act was a long time in incubation and boasts a list of sponsors that grows as memories fade, it was written by nonlawyer and nonmember of Congress, Howard Zahniser of the Wilderness Society, which might account for the superior quality of the prose. NEPA came into being with powerful political sponsorship (Henry Jackson), energetic academic support (Lynton Caldwell), and sophisticated staff work (William Van Ness and Grenville Garside). Section 301 of the Clean Water Act was a central page in the distinguished career of Senator Edmund Muskie, with the staff heroics accomplished by Leon Billings and Tom Jorling. Section 7 of the ESA was the creation of John Dingell, with key staff assistance by Frank Potter, and the tale of its enactment is marked by impressive entrepreneurial skills. Superfund's critical features are credited to the skillful opportunism of senior Environmental Protection Agency (EPA) management, including Doug Costle, although more of this story awaits the telling.

The first message, then, is that great laws are the product of great deeds. The process of enactment is chaotic and unpredictable, to be sure, but opportunity is not waiting on every corner. A close analogy, perhaps, is the process of extraordinary scientific discovery, which is filled with enough accidents to be called "serendipity," but comes only to those who created the opportunities and are in a position to seize them.

B. The Inspirational and Radical Message

A second conspicuous and surprising feature of these laws is that they lack the compromised and ambiguous form normally associated with an act of Congress. This bold portrait may be part mirage because trade-offs may be buried elsewhere in what is always a complex legislative picture. Or it may be partly attributed to the entrepreneurial verve that brings these laws into being. But something more seems to be involved. In the first place, these laws successfully make connection with what can best be described as a widely shared human sense of justice and fair dealing. The genius of Delaney is that it hit upon a theme—who would put cancer in our food?—with a universal appeal that continues to stymie the most clever of legislative second guessers. The Land and Water Conservation Fund Act was moved by images of children of many colors coming together in public playgrounds. Recreational opportunities for the poor and underprivileged were a prominent theme of this Act, which became the first and most successful step in what has recently become known as the "environmental justice movement."

The Wilderness Act succeeded in tapping the psychological and emotional roots—some would say religious feelings—that tie humans to the pristine physical environments that are part of our distant evolutionary history. NEPA exploited the popular cautionary principle by identifying government as the culprit at a time when technological blunder and agency boosterism had become empirically unmistakable. Section 7 of the ESA appeals to similar sentiments, not to mention the emotional attachment to other living creatures that is shared by many members of the species of *Homo sapiens*. Again, who could stand up and argue for the entitlement of public officials to kill, maim, or cripple the few members of a species close to the brink of extinction? The Clean Water Act, too, has an inspirational core that challenges the very morality of dumping pollutants into the community water supply. CERCLA expresses the same sort of contempt for polluters and their legally derived refinements of fault that stand in the way of retaliation. The ruling proposition is that the "polluters pay," and behind this proposition is the sentiment that they should pay. After all, they made the earth uninhabitable, we did not. Polluters are perfectly appropriate lightning rods for the moralistic aggression sent their way.

The more interesting part of the story, though, is that the moralism of these laws is unbounded. Protections are relentless, paybacks unforgiving, qualifiers swept away. On this level, these seven great laws are radical, extremist, and absolutist. No cancer-causing substances in the food? Even to the tune of parts per trillion? Natural carcinogens in infinitesimal amounts? And is the march to parkland so irresistible that the park becomes the paradigm and the people the spectators? Does the wilderness really care if a few hammers and nails put in a functional appearance? NEPA extends to *all* federal actions with significant effects. The ESA can stop the project *without* regard to cost. The Clean Water Act says *no* discharge of any pollutants, and it backs this up with the no-discharge goal of subsection 101(a)(1), which simply says that the discharge of pollutants into navigable waters shall be eliminated by 1985. The hypothetical reach of CERCLA liability is often illustrated by the fable of the high school chemistry teacher who makes the mistake of sending a small amount of laboratory waste to the Hanford nuclear reservation for treatment: This individual is jointly and severally liable for the entire fifty billion dollars or so that will be needed to clean up the Hanford facilities.

* * * These are daredevil laws and are much admired for it; audacity is an integral part of the successful package. People can subscribe to the visionary missions of wholesome food, pristine wilderness, and clean water. Nobody takes to the streets in support of marginal cost.

C. Growth and "Sleeper" Potential

A strong leader sometimes can sell generalities with the details to follow. For this reason, many of these great laws did not confront opposition at the moment of enactment. Several of them, moreover, were enacted as "sleepers" in the sense that the full reach and application of the legislative hand were not imagined at the moment of enactment. Like weeds in a field, these great laws suddenly appeared without the usual residue of legislative reflection, give and take, trading and compromise.

That great law is in large measure inadvertent law is a proposition that many might doubt, so let me reinforce the conclusion with a few examples. The conventional account of the expansion in the influence of Delaney is that extraordinary technological developments in our ability to detect chemicals in food since 1958 have rendered obsolete the "zero tolerance" standard that the amendment represents. Thus, according to this view, a law that in 1958 meant to exclude a few offending chemicals from the food supply now threatens our agricultural way of life because of wholly unanticipated technological change. Similar tales of evolutionary change, legislative surprise, and unexpected application attend the other great laws. NEPA, enacted without expectation of lawsuit, has produced thousands of lawsuits. The ESA slipped through for the benefit of a few warm and cuddly mammals, and now section 7 is being unfurled in the interests of plants, mice, and insects. CERCLA emerged at the eleventh hour with limited ambitions, and has become a legal monster. Section 301 of the Clean Water Act was itself not a sleeper; however, the principle it embraced was a reincarnation of the 1899 Refuse Act, which has a "no discharge" ultimatum that is one of the great sleepers of our time.

Obviously, these great laws do not remain "sleepers" for long. Their influence quickly becomes conspicuous and impressive. But the key to success in law, as in other evolutionary systems, is in getting started. The contributions of the leader and the sleeper features help these great laws get started. Their inspirational character assures maintenance and nourishment by enthusiastic constituencies. Other support for these laws is found in their scientific anchorage, discussed in the following section.

D. Research Implantation

While causes and effects are obscure, another feature of the seven great laws is their ability to attract and hold scientific constituencies and to generate scientific questions. This result may be an accidental artifact of the breadth and reach of these laws, a fallout consequence of their spectacular influence, or a necessary ingredient built into the legal structure that contributes to the credibility of the endeavor. All of these laws have a scientific component, and some of them have contributed in no small way to advancing the particular sciences with which they are associated. For example, the entire Clean Water Act has generated a host of questions on subjects such as chemistry, biology, hydrology, and land morphology. The ESA is closely associated with a variety of new work in population and conservation biology, CERCLA with a number of sciences related to groundwater, and the Delaney Amendment with the toxicology, epidemiology, and other sciences brought to bear in the real world of risk assessment. Interestingly, the Wilderness Act came into being with a specific research component, and who would be surprised? The whole idea of setting lands apart in protective status suggests the notion of a "natural" baseline, which has obvious implications for scientific comparisons with properties that might be treated differently. NEPA, of course, is definite in its embrace of the science of ecology, and the central idea of predictive impact statements cries out for follow-up research to validate or contradict the predictions.

It is hard to tell what to make of the scientific connections found in the great environmental laws. Here is one possibility: All of these laws assert bold propositions about humans, nature, and the physical environment—for example, carcinogenic toxics should be excluded from the food supply, pollutants should be banned from the water, and the habitat of endangered species should be absolutely protected. If one puts aside the normative content, what remains are striking scientific hypotheses: Introducing animal carcinogens to human food will produce human cancers; discharging pollutants into water will result in dead fish; endangered species can survive only if their habitats are protected. In an indirect way, the Dingells, Muskies, and Delaneys of the world advance propositions about how nature works that are as challenging as those advanced by Einstein, Hubble, or Turing. Needless to say, scientists will respond to the challenge.

E. Attentive Monitoring

With the exception of the Land and Water Conservation Fund Act, and perhaps the Wilderness Act, all of the great laws are prohibitive, and sweepingly so. This means that there will be compliance problems. How well do these great laws exploit various mechanisms of social control—such as self-monitoring, neighbor monitoring, formal legal sanctions, and market influences—that are identified in the literature? Reasonably well, which leads us to another secret to the success of a great law.

At first glance there appears to be nothing unusual or especially effective about how these laws exploit traditional legal sanctions or market influences. Indeed, these two staples of environmental law enforcement are largely missing from the pages of the great laws. Occasionally, one can find a prosecution for discharging without a permit, the dumping of hazardous waste, or the taking of endangered species. But the numbers are hardly impressive, and it is difficult to believe that one-step-ahead-of-the-prosecutor fears figure, in any meaningful way, in the record of compliance with the great seven laws. Similarly, economic incentives are not prominent on this scene in a practical sense, not to mention the problem that many of these absolutist prohibitions forbid behavior that is expected and encouraged by the underlying economic theory. The "reasonable person" of economic theory does not withhold all discharges into the water, avoid negligible insults in food, or throw away a dam to save a tiny fish. It is also difficult to embrace any scenarios of maniacal enforcement, business reputation, and so on, that encourage reliable compliance as a matter of sound economic choice.

Some progress might be made on the compliance front by recognizing that the inspirational messages of the seven great laws advance the cause of self-monitoring as manifested by the pangs of conscience, accumulated remorse, or even the fears of supernatural retribution. The inspirational tones of Delaney, the Endangered Species Act, and the Clean Water Act obviously can reach observers and sympathizers, but they can also be heard by would-be offenders. The business world is not filled exclusively with people who resist the killing of endangered species or the polluting of food with carcinogens only if benefits are likely to exceed costs.

With this said, the triumph of these laws is that they successfully exploit what I describe as "attentive monitoring." This includes personal activities such as face-to-face observation, emotions such as shame and pride, and group sanctions such as ostracism and citizen lawsuits. Structural legal changes often facilitate this attentive monitoring. The business of federal land acquisition is furthered obviously by an identifiable source of funds, but it is also assisted by a personalized, hands-on lawmaking in the Congress that makes each transaction very much a small-numbers game. Wilderness set-asides create constituency managers and users that are highly motivated and keenly attentive to abusive practices. Both NEPA and the ESA have elaborate consultative arrangements where the proposals of the agencies are displayed to friend and foe alike, criticized and refashioned, and bound up in commitments of various sorts—with varying degrees of credibility—among the principals. Compliance in the early stages is high because everyone is watching. Eventually, compliance breaks down as time, space, and personnel changes displace attentive monitoring with formal monitoring. Section 301 of the Clean Water Act long was backed by a highly effective citizen-suit mechanism that only in recent years has been dismantled by Supreme Court decisions. The genius of section 107 of CERCLA is that it exploits the model of nuisance law by strengthening the legal hand of the owner whose property is polluted; this is the epitome of face-to-face, neighbor-to-neighbor enforcement. Delaney lacks an effective day-to-day system of attentive monitoring, which might help explain its general reputation for being widely violated.

The important point is that great laws cannot stand indefinitely on the reputation of the leader, the inspiration of the message, or the interest of the scientific community. Somehow, the zeal that brought these laws into being must be sustained at the level of monitoring and enforcement.

III. CONCLUSION

The secrets of the seven great environmental laws are simple enough: All that is needed is a messianic leader with a stirring message containing seeds of growth in a sustainable environment. In practice, legal oases of this sort are few and far between.

NOTES

1. Ironically, at least three of the seven statutory provisions that appeared to be "virtually repeal-proof" in 1994 were subject to fierce attack by the 104th Congress (1995-1996). In the case of the Delaney Clause, the EPA's 1988 policy of exempting from the provision pesticides that pose only a "de minimis" or "negligible" risk (*i.e.*, an excess cancer risk of one-in-a-million) was overturned by the Ninth Circuit on the basis of the plain statutory language. *Les v. Reilly*, 968 F.2d 985 (9th Cir. 1992). The EPA and industry have asked Congress to add a negligible risk threshold into the Delaney provision. In the case of the Endangered Species Act, several legislative proposals would substantially undercut the law—by softening the prohibition against actions likely to jeopardize the continued existence of endangered or threatened species, by requiring the consideration of costs in deciding whether to list species as endangered or threatened, and by requiring private party compensation in the event of a regulatory "taking." And in the case of CERCLA, congressional interest in revising the statute has moved from the 1994 objective of trying to make the existing scheme function more effectively and more efficiently to a 1995 interest, expressed by a number of congressional leaders, in rewriting the basic liability rules. Professor Rodgers noted congressional interest in changing these three statutes, and reported without endorsing the belief that changes would be more peripheral than central to the statutory programs. Yet the changes that Congress seriously considered in 1995 targeted the hearts of these programs.

2. It is interesting to note that, although numerous commentators trace the enactment of strong federal legislation to a concern about state lawmaking (regardless of whether the states are perceived to be racing to the ceiling or to the cellar), only one of Professor Rodgers' seven statutory wonders is characterized by a state level counterpart program. That is, only section 301 of the Clean Water Act involves the formal delegation of federal implementation authority to comparably-empowered state programs. Some states have elected to adopt their own versions of NEPA and CERCLA, and some states have their own wilderness preservation and conservation fund schemes, but none of the federal programs in these areas either mandates or is designed to function in harmony with a strong state program.

Thus, federal environmental law appears to have made its biggest mark in areas where there is little or no state role. If the states did not have well-developed regulatory programs under the aegis of the federal Clean Air Act and RCRA, might those statutes have made it into the super seven? Is the presence or absence of a state role relevant to the determination of which laws satisfy Professor Rodgers' two selection criteria of (1) contributing the most to environmental protection and (2) being emulated?

3. What other laws might be considered "statutory wonders"? Consider Title II of the

Clean Air Act, under which lead was phased out and ultimately eliminated from motor vehicle fuels, resulting in a dramatic decline in the atmospheric loading of lead, a proven hazard to human health. What other candidates would you nominate?

4. Conversely, might you challenge the inclusion of any of Professor Rodgers' seven wonders? In terms of "inspirational and radical message," do you agree that NEPA and the Land and Water Conservation Fund Act fit the bill? NEPA is a brief statement of federal policy, applicable in limited situations, and enforceable only as to its procedural, but not its substantive, provisions. Consider also the Wilderness Act, which allowed mining and the location of new mining claims on wilderness lands for another 20 years after its enactment, and which still allows grazing on wilderness lands.

5. How does Rodgers' analysis help us in designing new legislation? How might his principles be applied in drafting a bill to conserve biodiversity or control carbon loading of the atmosphere?

6. For further consideration of the Delaney Clause and the risk management issue more generally, see Alon Rosenthal et al., *Legislating Acceptable Cancer Risk from Exposure to Toxic Chemicals*, 19 ECOLOGY L.Q. 269 (1992) and related notes in Chapter Five of this anthology.

The relationship between federal and state law has already been highlighted as a significant aspect of environmental law. Indeed, the impetus behind the enactment of federal law in this area is explained, at least in part, by the motivation either to prevent states from imposing inconsistent and increasingly-stringent environmental laws, or to prevent states from outbidding one another for economic development by weakening their environmental laws. In either event, the relative roles of federal and state law in this area have always been the subject of some controversy. The following article by Adam Babich, Editor-in-Chief of the *Environmental Law Reporter*, was part of a Symposium on Environmental Federalism, published in 54 MD. L. REV. 1141-1690 (1995).

OUR FEDERALISM, OUR HAZARDOUS WASTE, AND OUR GOOD FORTUNE
Adam Babich
54 Md. L. Rev. 1516 (1995)*

Fate, the saying goes, looks after fools, drunkards, and the United States. One manifestation of this phenomenon is the evolution of "Our Federalism"[1] from a vague limitation

---

* Reprinted with permission.

[1] Younger v. Harris, 401 U.S. 37, 44-45 (1971) ("It should never be forgotten that this slogan, 'Our Federalism,' born in the early struggling days of our Union of States, occupies a highly important place in our Nation's history and its future.").

on the reach of national power into a promising tool for enforcing environmental laws against some of this country's most persistent polluters: federal agencies and state and local governments.

If asked to design an ideal system of government, few people's first impulse would be to create a big sovereign whose jurisdiction overlapped that of many little sovereigns. Even those sold on the checks and balances created by separating the legislative, executive, and judicial branches of government might balk at establishing over fifty such three-part structures to govern one nation. But like much of the Constitution, modern federalism can function in ways that appear to reflect subtle genius. Given the apparent frustration of the framers' original hopes for the doctrine, however, federalism's continuing vitality must be chalked up largely to good fortune.

* * *

I. OUR HAZARDOUS WASTE

A. Regulation and Cleanup

Hazardous waste is a powerful symbol of the need for environmental protection. Disasters like those at Bhopal and Chernobyl, and incidents like those at Love Canal and Times Beach raised legitimate concerns about public exposure to invisible poisons. These concerns, however, have arguably been blown out of proportion as movies and television programs reinforced a popular conception that exposure to hazardous waste is one of the worst fates that one might suffer. Important aspects of Superfund and RCRA seem geared more to responding to these popular fears than reducing actual risks.

For lawyers, "hazardous waste" and "hazardous substances" are terms of art that say more about the legal status of chemicals than about the dangers those chemicals present. Under RCRA, the U.S. Environmental Protection Agency (EPA) imposes stringent and expensive regulation on management of subtitle C hazardous wastes. But, for seemingly arbitrary reasons, EPA exempts equally dangerous chemicals from the system and regulates others hardly at all. This regime may allow government representatives to tell the public that hazardous wastes are carefully regulated, but only because Congress and EPA have defined the term "hazardous waste" to exclude many potentially dangerous materials.

Although broader and more flexible than RCRA subtitle C, the Superfund program for cleanup of "hazardous substances" is now notorious for fostering too much litigation and too little actual cleanup. Superfund's dramatic success in addressing imminent hazards has been overshadowed by misguided attempts to restore contaminated sites to almost pristine conditions. Meanwhile, other sites—which present dangers that are not immediate enough to qualify for "removal action" and score too low on EPA's hazard ranking system for "remedial action"—receive essentially no federal attention under Superfund, even if they pose risks in excess of the Agency's "acceptable" range.

The result under both RCRA and Superfund, is that society spends a disproportionate amount of resources addressing a relatively limited selection of the risks posed by toxic materials. Despite these problems, however, both statutes have dramatically improved environmental protection.

B. Governmental Polluters

The most dangerous hazardous waste sites in the United States generally are those that the federal government created itself. During the Manhattan Project and the cold war that followed, the federal government and its various contractors built a vast infrastructure across the United States for manufacture and storage of nuclear and chemical weapons. This weapons production "came at a price that few . . . could have anticipated": pervasive environmental contamination.[29] Some sites continue to pose risks of explosion and nuclear chain reaction. The government exacerbated many of these problems throughout much of the 1980s by engaging in "[c]rude waste disposal practices that were banned in the private sector."[31]

States and their political subdivisions are also significant polluters, although their contribution to pollution problems is not as well documented as that of federal agencies. One significant problem is that RCRA and the Clean Water Act, working together, have the perverse effect of transforming toxic waste generated by private facilities into toxic discharges from municipal sewage treatment plants. This is because EPA exempts the discharge of industrial waste through sewers to municipal treatment plants from regulation under both RCRA and the Clean Water Act's National Pollution Discharge Elimination System (NPDES). These exemptions reduce the role of federal and state enforcement agencies, leaving the municipal operators of sewage treatment plants responsible for regulating industrial discharges of hazardous materials to municipal plants. The system tends to break down, largely because it is unrealistic to expect municipalities to enforce federal mandates aggressively against companies that make up a good part of the municipalities' tax and employment bases. Industrial pollutants that pass through or interfere with municipal facilities, however, can cause municipalities to violate their NPDES permits. Moreover, the system can also result in releases from municipal plants of pollutants that EPA—or state permitting authorities—failed to anticipate when writing municipalities' NPDES permits.

Governmental sources of pollution—whether federal, state, or local—are generally more difficult to control than their privately owned analogues. This is because, by and large, environmental laws depend on effective enforcement to inspire compliance efforts. Unless the laws are enforced, the natural tendency of any regulated party is to put its resources into achieving its primary mission, whether that mission is to manufacture a product or to provide a governmental service such as police protection or national security. By virtue of its sovereign status, the federal government has developed a number of subtle and not-so-subtle ways to stave off enforcement actions. In contrast, states and local governments are clearly vulnerable to federal enforcement. Nonetheless, enforcement actions against these entities can be politically sensitive.

II. OUR FEDERALISM

The Supreme Court has used the phrase "Our Federalism" to refer to "a proper respect for state functions . . . [and a] belief that the National Government will fare best if the

---

[29] OFFICE OF TECHNOLOGY ASSESSMENT, U.S. CONGRESS, COMPLEX CLEANUP, THE ENVIRONMENTAL LEGACY OF NUCLEAR WEAPONS PRODUCTION (1991). * * *

[31] Matthew L. Wald, *Waste Dumping that U.S. Banned Went on at Its Own Atom Plants,* N.Y. TIMES, Dec. 8, 1988, at A1 * * *.

States and their institutions are left free to perform their separate functions in their separate ways."[43] The Court stressed:

> The concept does not mean blind deference to "States' Rights" any more than it means centralization of control over every important issue in our National Government and its courts. . . . What the concept does represent is a system in which there is *sensitivity to the legitimate interests of both State and National Governments*, and in which the National Government, anxious though it may be to vindicate and protect federal rights and federal interest, always *endeavors to do so in ways that will not unduly interfere* with the legitimate activities of the States.

* * *

Whatever the framers' intent, the very document they drafted doomed from the beginning any dream of a national government with sharply limited powers. For one thing, the framers enumerated federal powers "in language broad enough to allow for the expansion of the Federal Government's role."[47] For another, the Constitution's command that federal law "be the supreme law of the Land"[48] more or less predetermined the legal outcome of any power struggle between the federal government and the states. Most importantly, the framers embedded into the Constitution a great evil—slavery—the lingering effects of which would require the full breadth of the commerce power to battle.

Yet, while the federal government apparently now has the *power* to displace most state regulation, this has not meant the destruction of state sovereignty. As noted by the Supreme Court in *Garcia v. San Antonio Metropolitan Transit Authority*, the "built-in restraints that our system provides through state participation in federal governmental action" provide for a continued role for state sovereignty in the federal system.[53] Although it recently supplemented those restraints in *Lopez v. United States*,[54] to date the Court has left it largely up to Congress to define the respective roles of the federal and state governments. Thus, federalism and state sovereignty are changeable concepts. * * *

III. COOPERATIVE FEDERALISM

The "built-in restraints" protecting the states' primacy in their traditional domains are reflected in Congress's practice of pursuing environmental protection—at least under most modern antipollution laws—through "program[s] of 'cooperative federalism'" which "offer States the choice of regulating . . . according to federal standards or having state law pre-empted by federal regulation."[59] The Supreme Court described Congress's first use of environmental cooperative federalism in the Clean Air Act Amendments of 1970 as

---

[43] Younger v. Harris, 401 U.S. 37, 44 (1971)

[47] New York v. United States, 112 S. Ct. at 2418-19 * * *.

[48] U.S. Const. art. VI, § 2 * * *.

[53] [469 U.S.] 528, 550, 556 [(1985)].

[54] 115 S. Ct. 1624 (1995). * * *

[59] New York v. United States, 112 S. Ct. at 2412; *see also* Mark Squillace, *Cooperative Federalism Under the Surface Mining Control and Reclamation Act: Is This Any Way to Run a Government?*, 15 Envtl. L. Rep. (Envtl. L. Inst.) 10,039, 10,039 (Feb. 1985) * * *.

Congress "taking a stick to the States."[60] That stick (the threat of preemption), however, usually is accompanied by a carrot—federal funding for qualifying state antipollution programs. Although Congress and EPA occasionally have attempted to command that states develop and implement regulatory programs, cooperative federalism, in general, is based on federal *incentives* for state regulation.

* * *

IV. FEDERALISM AND HAZARDOUS WASTE

As illustrated below—primarily through the examples of Superfund and RCRA—Congress and EPA must adhere to five basic principles for cooperative federalism schemes to work well. A program of cooperative federalism should: (1) provide for state implementation; (2) set clear standards; (3) reflect respect for state autonomy; (4) provide mechanisms to police the process; and (5) apply the same rules to government and private parties. But even when Congress and EPA have ignored many of these principles—as they have under Superfund and RCRA—cooperative federalism can improve the regulatory system.

A. Providing for State Implementation

The essence of cooperative federalism is that states take primary responsibility for implementing federal standards, while retaining the freedom to apply their own, more stringent standards. Even when constrained by the need to meet minimum federal standards, every permitting or cleanup decision involves countless judgment calls. How agencies use their discretion to resolve detailed implementation issues can have an enormous impact on whether the public will perceive the overall decision as successful. State regulators usually can be more responsive to the needs and concerns of affected citizens than federal agencies.

With an important exception, RCRA adopts a typical structure for allowing qualified states to implement federal environmental policy. Under Superfund, however, EPA violated this most basic principle of cooperative federalism, failing for over a decade to acknowledge that any state could be trusted to direct the cleanup of released hazardous substances. * * *

On its face, Superfund contains the most flexible statutory provision for cooperative federalism of any environmental law. It allows—but does not require—the federal government to enter into agreements with states to "carry out actions authorized in this section."[72] The agreement "*may* cover a specific facility or specific facilities,"[73] but presumably may also cover states as a whole. For the first thirteen years of the Superfund program, however,

---

[60] Train v. Natural Resources Defense Council, Inc., 421 U.S. 60, 64 (1975) (noting that Congress acted in frustration over states' disappointing response to federal concerns about air pollution). Arguably, modern cooperative federalism was not practical before the late 1960s because

> it was unclear whether the federal government could constitutionally operate air and water pollution programs. The expansion of the commerce clause in support of the federal regulatory power was a long process and was not completed until the Civil Rights Act of 1964. . . . The Supreme Court's vindication of [that Act] opened the door for sweeping environmental health and safety regulation.

J. William Futrell, *The History of Environmental Law, in* Sustainable Environmental Law at 38 [Celia Campbell-Mohn et. al. eds., 1993]. * * *

[72] 42 U.S.C. § 9604(d)(1)(A).

[73] *Id.* § 9604(d)(1)(B) (emphasis added).

EPA refused to delegate *any* remedy-selection decisions to states. Apparently because Congress merely authorized EPA to delegate instead of requiring it to do so, the Agency saw no reason to relinquish any of its turf. In 1993, the D.C. Circuit remanded a portion of the National Contingency Plan (NCP) to EPA because the Agency failed "to offer any reasoned explanation" of its refusal to delegate Superfund remedy-selection and enforcement authorities to states.[76]

Because Congress required Superfund cleanups to meet both state and federal "applicable or relevant and appropriate requirements" (ARARs), EPA often finds itself administering state-promulgated standards. Essentially all cooperative federalism programs allow states to set standards that surpass the federal minimum level of stringency. But, under most federal environmental laws, states that go beyond federal standards are directly responsible for administering their more stringent programs, and thus, for handling whatever practical or political problems arise. In contrast, Superfund relies on threats of financial burdens and waivers of state law to prevent states from imposing standards that EPA deems needlessly stringent. This scheme has pitted EPA against the states in a continuing battle to control the stringency of Superfund cleanups.

B. Setting Clear Standards

Without clear, objective standards, a program of cooperative federalism cannot meet the goal of providing a minimum level of protection for the public and the environment. Minimum federal standards allow federal agencies to restrain state and local tendencies to risk public health and welfare on short-sighted attempts to provide an attractive climate for businesses. But, unless those standards are reasonably clear and objective, federal oversight of state programs will be arbitrary, ineffectual, or both. Although RCRA Subtitle C standards doubtless could be improved and simplified, they are nonetheless capable of reasonably objective application. Under Superfund, however, EPA compounded its failure to delegate implementation by failing to set clear standards for cleanups.

Superfund cleanups are governed by EPA's NCP, which provides for remedy-selection decisions based on evaluation of nine criteria. Although these criteria appear to provide a solid framework for site-by-site common-sense decision-making, EPA clearly did not design them to achieve consistent results. Instead, stakeholders—including states, local governments, potentially liable parties, and, ideally, potentially affected members of the surrounding community—negotiate with the Agency about a separate cleanup plan for each contaminated site. Thus, in its current design, the Superfund program cannot provide citizens with a minimum level of protection regardless of whether the federal government or the states administer it.

C. Respecting State Autonomy

For states to serve as credible implementers of environmental policy, federal oversight must be conducted in a way that affords state laws and institutions some degree of respect. The Superfund program's ARARs process, under which EPA passes judgment on whether states relied on "relevant considerations" when promulgating standards that are more

---

[76] Ohio v. EPA, 997 F.2d at 1542. * * *

stringent than their federal counterparts, is inconsistent with this need for respect. * * * Congress displayed a similar lack of respect for state autonomy in the way that it handled changes to the requirements of the federal RCRA program.

EPA constantly supplements and changes environmental regulations and Congress occasionally changes the statutes. Sovereign states, therefore, require a reasonable period of time for their legislators and agencies to make necessary conforming changes. Moreover, EPA needs additional time to approve the state changes as "consistent" with the federal program. Thus, there will be a necessary lag between adoption of federal policies, and the implementation of those policies by states. Most environmental programs, including those portions of RCRA enacted before its amendment in 1984, provide for a reasonable grace period to allow for continued state implementation.

In 1984, however, Congress became unwilling to accept the inevitable delays associated with cooperative federalism. Thus, when enacting the Hazardous and Solid Waste Amendments of 1984 (HSWA), it created an exception to the authority of EPA-authorized states to regulate in lieu of the federal government. As amended, RCRA requires that each HSWA requirement, and each regulation that implements such a requirement, take effect on the same date in every state. Pending EPA's approval of each state's incorporation of each such requirement into its program, RCRA requires EPA to implement it directly.

As a result, a state can essentially never achieve primacy in RCRA implementation and RCRA implementation has become incredibly confusing. Cooperative federalism under RCRA, therefore, has become an irritant to the regulated community, that—depending on the applicable state—may or may not be justified by the state's willingness to apply greater flexibility to implementation. For states, RCRA's cooperative federalism program is part of a pattern of complexity that has generally prevented them from attempting significant innovations.

D. Policing the Process

Federal regulators should not expect to agree with every decision made by their counterparts in state government. But allowing states to ignore minimum substantive and procedural standards would endanger the credibility of the regulatory system. For cooperative federalism to be effective, the states' commitments to implement federal standards must be enforceable.

Because delegation under Superfund has been so limited, policing state compliance with minimum federal standards has not been a significant issue. * * * Moreover, Superfund provides states with a powerful incentive to follow federal law: It authorizes only states that follow the NCP to recover their response costs from responsible parties.

In contrast, RCRA has a relatively elaborate mechanism for policing state compliance. EPA actively oversees state implementation and requires that states afford it unrestricted access to information. If a state program changes or is interpreted or implemented in a way that fails to meet minimum federal requirements, EPA may withdraw its authorization. EPA reviews, and may terminate, state permits and may suspend or revoke interim status. Moreover, RCRA allows EPA to comment on draft state RCRA permits and then, if the state does not respond to EPA's satisfaction, enforce certain comments as if they were permit conditions. EPA may also issue compliance orders or bring enforcement actions in states with authorized programs after providing notice to the applicable state.

* * *

E. Applying the Same Rules to Government and Private Parties

A basic principle of modern antipollution law is that no entity is above the law. Instead, the laws generally apply equally to every party—whether an individual, a private company, or a government—that engages in regulated conduct. Thus, both Superfund and RCRA— like the Clean Air and Water Acts before them—mandate that federal agencies "be subject to, and comply with" the law "in the same manner and to the same extent, both procedurally and substantively, as any nongovernmental entity."[109] Similarly—like other antipollution laws—both Superfund and RCRA apply to "any person" and define "person" to include states and municipalities.

Although the courts have enforced it inconsistently, the principle that no entity is above the law has enabled Superfund and RCRA to put a dent in the government-generated pollution problem. When this principle is applied to cooperative federalism, no government need be in the position of being the sole regulator of its own conduct (a situation that invites trouble). Moreover, forcing each government to put up with independent oversight can provide a refreshing dose of reality. Thus, for example, before insisting on "gold-plated" cleanups at federal facilities, states must face the question of whether they can afford to meet the same standards at landfills owned and operated by their political subdivisions. And before insisting on extensive cleanups of private Superfund sites, the federal government should be prepared to attain the same standards at federal facilities.

State sovereignty has been an essential tool in the battle to impose regulatory controls on dangerously contaminated federal facilities. Indeed, to date, state sovereignty has proven to be the most effective answer to DOJ's decision to employ its "unitary executive policy" to cripple EPA's ability to police the conduct of federal polluters.[116] The unitary-executive policy is premised on the notion that all executive agencies work for the same sovereign. If one agency were to sue another, according to the policy, the executive branch, in essence, would be suing itself, leaving no case of actual controversy to which Article III jurisdiction could attach. The practical import of the policy is that the same DOJ lawyers represent both polluting federal agencies and federal enforcers. Thus, absent vigorous enforcement by states and citizens, the activities of federal polluters go largely "unchecked by any parties whose interest are in any real sense adverse to those of the [polluters]."[118]

Not surprisingly, given the legal theories that the nation's top enforcers have adopted, the federal government's record of compliance with its own laws is one of "flagrant" violation. Only the principle that no government is above the law—recently reinforced by Congress in the Federal Facilities Compliance Act—has allowed states and citizen

---

[109] 42 U.S.C. § 9620(a)(1) (Superfund); *id.* § 6961 (RCRA); *id.* § 7418(a) (Clean Air Act); 33 U.S.C. § 1323(a) (Clean Water Act).

[116] *See* U.S. ENVTL. PROTECTION AGENCY, FEDERAL FACILITIES COMPLIANCE STRATEGY VI-3, app. H (Nov. 1988) (setting forth DOJ's unitary executive policy in 1987 testimony of F. Henry Habicht); Maine v. United States Dep't of the Navy, 702 F. Supp. 322, 338 n.8 (D. Me. 1988) (magistrate's opinion) ("The United States' position is that EPA has no authority to proceed against the federal government."), *vacated on other grounds*, 973 F.2d 1007 (1st Cir. 1992).

[118] Colorado v. United States Dep't of the Army, 707 F. Supp. 1562, 1570 (D. Colo. 1989). * * *

enforcers to gain a toe-hold in the struggle to force the government to obey its own laws.

The strength of cooperative federalism—that it forces sovereign regulators to function on overlapping turf, regulate one another, and feel the frustration of dealing with independent oversight—is also a source of stress and volatility. Indeed, after championing the principle of equal treatment under the law for decades, Congress recently has taken tentative steps toward eroding it. Recent Superfund reform proposals have included a "cap" on the liability of state and local governmental owners and operators of landfills, and two senators have introduced a bill intended to "serve as a pilot" for exempting federal facilities from federal, state, and local environmental requirements. Also, the Unfunded Mandates Reform Act of 1995 tends to elevate the importance of state and local governmental compliance costs above private compliance costs.

* * *

CONCLUSION

It is tempting to conclude that cooperative federalism in the hazardous waste field has failed. Clearly, Congress and EPA have made fundamental mistakes that have limited the doctrine's utility. Indeed, at one time or another, they have violated each of the five, relatively uncontroversial, principles of cooperative federalism identified in this Article. Nonetheless, cooperative federalism has caused states to build the capacity to grapple with problems posed by hazardous waste on a sophisticated level.

Even in the face of EPA's refusal to delegate under Superfund, most states have accepted the challenge of attempting to clean up contaminated property. The informed comments of state regulators—concerned about the enforceability and effectiveness of their own state programs—have helped shape EPA's development of hazardous waste regulations and Congress's statutory initiatives. The existence of state programs can also serve, at times, to moderate shifts in federal law and to ease the burden on regulated entities. Moreover, minimum federal standards, accompanied by federal oversight of state programs, have produced a relatively consistent and powerful body of law.

But it is as a tool against federally generated pollution that cooperative federalism has been most important. Although the battle to subject federal facilities to independent state oversight may be far from won, it is also far from lost. And, surely, nobody expected it to be easy to force the world's most powerful sovereign to obey its own laws. The progress we have made to date is powerful testimony to both the framers' wisdom in preserving the sovereignty of the several states and the 91st Congress's good sense in adapting the federalist structure to the problem of environmental protection.

In an age when so many of the world's nations are struggling with the effects of pollution from governmental facilities that operate above the law, the United States has been fortunate, indeed, to discover that one of the "happy incidents of the federal system"[141] is that it can cause its various governments to begin to regulate each other.

---

[141] New State Ice Co. v. Liebmann, 285 U.S. 262, 311 (1932) (Brandeis, J., dissenting) ("It is one of the happy incidents of the federal system that a single courageous State may, if its citizens choose, serve as a laboratory; and try novel social and economic experiments without risk to the rest of the country.").

NOTES

1. Consider Babich's discussion of "cooperative federalism" in relation to two other models of environmental federalism outlined by Robert Percival in the lead article in the Symposium, *Environmental Federalism: Historical Roots and Contemporary Models*, 54 MD. L. REV. 1141, 1173-78. One model features federal financial or regulatory incentives to encourage, but not require, states to adopt environmental standards.

> While this approach proved to be largely ineffective at controlling air and water pollution, it is still the principal federal approach to issues such as land-use regulation where political sensitivity to federal regulation is particularly high. Federal law encourages state and local land-use and solid waste management planning under the Coastal Zone Management Act, the Clean Water Act, and Subtitle D of the Resource Conservation and Recovery Act.

Id. at 1173. Another model focuses exclusively on federal implementation of federally-set standards. This approach, which "has been employed sparingly," is evident in the Toxic Substances Control Act, which regulates the introduction of new chemicals into the marketplace, the Federal Insecticide, Fungicide, and Rodenticide Act, which requires federal registration of pesticides, and the provisions of the Clean Air Act governing vehicular emissions. *Id.* at 1176. As to the third model of cooperative federalism, Percival notes that its effectiveness varies with the states' commitment to provide adequate resources to administer and enforce the federal programs.

> As the burden of environmental expenditures increasingly falls on financially-strapped state and local governments, the quality of state administration of federal programs has become even more variable.

Id. at 1175. As federal environmental expenditures are reduced in order to attain a balanced federal budget, that will likely affect cooperative federalism. First, states authorized to administer federal programs typically receive some federal funding to assist their efforts; smaller EPA budgets will presumably translate into smaller cost-sharing with authorized states. Second, the success of the cooperative federalism model depends in part on a strong federal presence in setting minimum standards and in monitoring the states' implementation thereof. Insofar as reduced EPA budgets will weaken the EPA's ability to perform those functions effectively, that will also undermine the cooperative federalism approach.

2. Although the conceptually neat allocation of powers between federal and state governments may satisfy various constitutional and political considerations, it results in a confounding array of requirements facing the regulated community. It is not difficult to find enforcement cases where a regulated entity satisfied the governmental entity with primary regulatory authority, yet was nonetheless sued by the EPA under its residual enforcement powers. *See, e.g., United States v. Chevron U.S.A. Inc.*, 757 F. Supp. 512 (E.D. Pa. 1990); *United States v. Sharon Steel Corp.*, 30 Env't Rep. Cas. (BNA) 1778 (N.D. Ohio 1989).

3. Consider whether the Supreme Court's decision in *United States v. Lopez*, 115 S.Ct. 1624 (1995), holding that a statute prohibiting the knowing possession of a firearm in a school zone went beyond congressional authority under the Commerce Clause, will circumscribe federal authority in the environmental area. Consider also whether the Tenth Amendment materially constrains the development and continual expansion of federal environmental law. *See New York v. United States*, 505 U.S. 144 (1992) (finding violative of the Tenth Amendment a provision in the Low-Level Radioactive Waste Policy Act that required states to accept ownership of low-level radioactive waste or adopt a regulatory program specified by Congress).

To wrap up this subchapter addressing congressional enactments in the environmental area, the following article analyzes their fragmented, medium-specific nature. Providing a convenient segue into the next subchapter, Professor Guruswamy recommends that environmental law be reshaped in an integrated, multimedia manner not by statutory changes but by the EPA's policies and practices in administering existing statutes.

INTEGRATING THOUGHTWAYS: RE-OPENING OF THE ENVIRONMENTAL MIND?
Lakshman Guruswamy
1989 Wis. L. Rev. 463 (1989)*

* * *

I. INTRODUCTION

* * *

The aquatic, atmospheric and terrestrial environments are capable of performing tremendous scavenging, assimilating and dispersing functions. Every modern society has made the fundamental assumption that the environment can and should be used as a medium for disposing of wastes. When, however, the environment is incapable of coping with residuals, or its neutralizing capacity is overburdened, pollution occurs. In general, pollution laws have not absolutely prohibited the disposal of such wastes in the environment. An absolute prohibition would be impossible without banning many of the activities on which Western society is dependent. What the laws have done, except in very special circumstances, is to control only the harmful effects of potentially polluting activities. Under such laws, discharges of harmful residuals have been treated, processed, or redistributed in an effort to remove the undesirable substances or render them harmless.

Unfortunately, the formidable, complicated web of law and policy controlling pollution

* Copyright 1989 by The Board of Regents of the University of Wisconsin System. Reprinted by permission of the Wisconsin Law Review.

in the United States, and in most European industrial countries, leads to a regrettable conclusion. Separate pollution control programs for air, water and land have been established without an adequate appreciation of the interrelated character of the three environmental sectors, a comprehension of the total burden of pollution, or a determination of which method of disposal would cause the least environmental damage overall. The result, in many situations, is that present pollution controls are ineffective and inefficient. * * * This Article will explore the basis and rationale for the fragmentation of law and policy dealing with pollution, and make the case for a more integrated approach. In doing so, the Article will traverse the broader issues of administrative law, policy and politics surrounding integration. * * *

* * *

II. THE FRAGMENTED SYSTEM

A. Defects of Fragmented Controls

* * *

The present fragmentation of the environment by the law, policy and administration (the fragmented approach) fails to provide effective pollution controls for numerous reasons * * *. First, the fragmented approach does not usually consider the part played by inputs in the creation of residuals. The relationship of inputs to residuals can be illustrated by the coal electric industry. In a coal-burning power plant, the combustion of coal to create electricity produces sulfur dioxide (SO_2), oxides of nitrogen (NO_x), particulates, bottom ash, and other unwanted materials. The quantity of SO_2 generated in combustion is a function of the sulfur content of raw coal and the extent, if any, of its removal in coal processing or by washing. The extent to which the sulfur content of the coal (the input) determines the nature of the residuals has been vividly demonstrated. The gains achieved by simple and inexpensive washing techniques used on high-sulfur coal, prior to its use in production, varied from twenty to forty percent, compared to less than fifty percent gained from employing billion-dollar scrubbers. Similarly, the burning of high quality natural gas releases even fewer harmful residues.

Second, the fragmented approach generally does not hold the end product accountable for harmful residuals. Yet, the extent to which the final product influences the residuals discharged is considerable. For example, the production of a highly bright (bleached) white paper requires substantially greater quantities of chemicals, water and energy, resulting in the generation of larger amounts of residuals than an unbleached paper. One study found that the liquid residuals were reduced by eighty-five to ninety percent, while gaseous residuals were reduced by fifty percent, by producing unbleached paper. The same argument applies to a wide variety of end products. Accordingly, certain environmental costs of the bewildering and often unnecessary products that are paraded on the market are often ignored.

Pollution laws, in general, concentrate on end-of-line controls and do not treat input and final products as part of the problem. When regulating end-of-line controls on industrial processes, pollution control laws have set separate standards for air, water and land. Controls applicable to each medium are applied and administered independently of each other. In so doing, congressional laws have ignored the overriding law of nature that "nothing goes away." A basic law of physics states that matter is indestructible. This law dictates that the residuals from a production process cannot be destroyed. Their initial destination may be altered, but ultimately they re-enter the flow of materials within the environment. While limitations on discharges may correct the immediate environmental problem to which they are directed, these restrictions themselves often have impacts in other places. These impacts, known as cross-media or inter-media pollution transfers, could happen either by direct transfers ("trade-offs") or by indirect transfers.

Direct transfers occur when control technologies aimed at achieving specific limits to pollution generate new streams of residuals which have adverse environmental effects on other media. Unfortunately, when limitations on discharges into one medium are imposed, those ordering the limitation sometimes give scant attention or consideration to the parallel impacts. The massive quantities of sludge created by existing pollution controls offer disturbing evidence of this problem. EPA has estimated that between three and six tons of scrubber sludge may be produced for each ton of sulphur dioxide removed from flue gases. Consequently, the problem of sulphur dioxide in the air is replaced by one of sludge disposal. Municipal wastewater treatment and sewage treatment plants also produce large quantities of sludge. Some of this contains toxic substances which are nondegradable and bioaccumulable. In all, it is estimated that over 118 million metric tons of sludge are produced annually.

The troubling question is: Where does the sludge go? It could be spread or buried on land, incinerated, or dumped at sea. But all these solutions have attendant problems. If managed on land, there is a danger either of rain water run-off transferring heavy metal into water, or of organic chemicals leaching into surface and ground water. While sewage sludge may fertilize agricultural land, this could result in heavy metals and organic chemicals being absorbed by plants and entering the food chain. Incineration is possible but very expensive. Moreover, even incinerators capable of cutting emissions by ninety percent still produce ash containing heavy metals and organic chemicals. Burying contaminated ash presents many of the problems of land waste disposal that incineration was intended to avoid. Dumping at sea raises questions similar to those applicable to water pollution.

Direct transfers are only part of the picture. They are compounded by indirect transfers which take place in a number of ways. For example, pollutants discharged into the air can leave the atmosphere through precipitation or can adhere to particles carried by the wind and later be deposited on land. Pollutants on land may erode with soil particles into a stream, leach into groundwater, or volatilize into air. The present fragmented system of controls does not trace the path of a pollutant through its entire ecological chain from source to receptor. Consequently, the fragmented approach does not take sufficient account of indirect cross-media transfers. To be effective, pollution controls need to trace and track every stage of a pollutant's journey, including its origination in a plant, its migration through the environment, and its final sinks or receptors. A proper risk evaluation, revealing where and how a substance is capable of causing harm, should be undertaken. * * *

Finally, the fragmented approach considers each end-of-line source of pollution in isolation. The use of separate technologies to control discharges into a single medium means that the effects of one set of controls upon another are not considered, and that the waste loads produced are not considered simultaneously. Fragmented controls show little thought to the way in which the plant is designed, to the manner of its operation, to the distribution of wastes, and to coordination of efforts to reduce the overall impact of pollution. The wastes or residuals generated by an industrial activity have to go somewhere, yet the first destination of the wastes or residuals generated by an industrial activity is largely predetermined by plant design and pollution control technology. Thus, in order to induce changes in technology that reduce or eliminate some of the pollutants in question, effective pollution controls should target plant design and production methods. Pollution controls should attempt to reach the best balance of residuals. This, however, is not usually the case.

The present approach also lacks economic efficiency. Pollution controls already in place ensure that wastes cannot be discharged or off-loaded onto the environment at a polluter's option. In a case where air pollution controls require a plant to reduce air pollution, the atmospheric gases and dusts created by a plant may be trapped in a spray of water or washed out of filters. The resulting polluted water could be discharged into a river or directly into the sea. The water could also be piped into a lagoon to settle and dry out and then be disposed of on land as solid waste. In this example, the efforts to meet air pollution requirements might lead to water discharges or solid waste disposal problems that cause greater overall damage to the environment than might be the case if the wastes had been distributed differently. It is also possible that other controls applicable to water and land could prevent the wastes resulting from air pollution controls from simply being discharged into water or disposed of as solid waste, without further treatment. Because additional costs are involved, the question becomes whether such costs can be justified.

A more efficient and cost-effective method of pollution control would be to divide the wastes between the three media of water, air and land, thus making optimum use of the environment and of any special or particular assimilative capacity it might possess. Lawmakers must consider whether the present controls make optimal use of the environment as a resource, or whether these controls are too stringent in one place and too lax in another.

B. Reasons for Fragmented Controls

The late 1960s and the early 1970s were a period in which the "policy primeval soup" of environmental policy bubbled with a rich mix of ideas. Ideas based on integration prevailed and gave birth to two notable developments: the National Environmental Policy Act (NEPA) and the Environmental Protection Agency (EPA). These developments marked the high tide of environmentalism, yet two following pieces of legislation flowed in a different direction. Out of the dialectic interaction between fragmentation and integration, fragmentation emerged as the more powerful policy stream.

The predominance of fragmentation is borne out first in the Clean Air Act of 1970, which was signed into law just thirty days after EPA began operations, and the 1972 amendments to the Federal Water Pollution Control Act. Both acts contained provisions dictating clear goals, specific means by which these goals should be achieved, and rigorous timetables for implementing these goals and means. Such provisions overran the integrative thrust of NEPA and EPA. * * *

The greater force of fragmentation is further evidenced by the way in which EPA was exempted from making environmental impact assessments under NEPA. A fundamentally important step towards an integrated approach lies in ascertaining the total environmental impact of an activity. That essential first stage is provided for in NEPA. It requires that all agencies of the federal government make environmental impact assessments where their proposed actions might significantly affect the environment. A plain reading of NEPA leaves no doubt that the making of environmental regulations constitutes an action significantly affecting the environment. It would seem to follow, therefore, that EPA should be legally obliged to make environmental impact assessments when undertaking their regulatory functions. When making environmental impact assessments, EPA would confront the inescapable cross-media impacts of their regulations and be compelled to evaluate both the wisdom and the necessity of an integrated approach.

EPA did not become engaged in this exercise for a number of reasons. To begin with, Senator Edmund Muskie sought to exclude air and water pollution controllers [sic] from the application of NEPA. Additionally, the deadlines in the Clean Air Act relating to the preparation of implementation plans for meeting national ambient standards arguably could have prevented EPA from undertaking the strict and formal environmental assessments required by NEPA. * * *

Finally, the express statutory exemption from NEPA assessments granted under the FWPCA, and later under the Clean Air Act, served to confirm and supply an even firmer foundation to the segmented and discrete approach to pollution control embodied in some of their provisions. * * *

It is useful to understand why Congress legislated in the way it did. * * *

1. Disaffection with the New Deal Idealism

The crucible of ideas in the 1960s gave rise to two different currents of thinking. On the one hand, environmentalism in the late 1960s was rooted in holistic and ecological thinking which found expression in the enactment of NEPA and the creation of EPA. On the other hand, serious doubts about whether the New Deal belief in independent and expert administrative agencies could creatively regulate a complex social problem in the public interest affected the approaches taken to environmental problems. * * *

* * *

One of the central themes present when environmental legislation was being formed, therefore, was that expertise could be an excuse for inaction, and even worse, could be captured by special interests. The remedy suggested by believers in regulation was the enactment of legislation setting forth explicit goals, specific means by which these goals could be attained, and rigorous timetables in which to do so.

2. Pragmatism and Incrementalism

Another compelling policy stream which converged with New Deal dissatisfaction with expert solutions to complicated problems was that of pragmatic incrementalism or "muddling through." * * * With specific reference to environmental policy, Charles Lindblom was skeptical about integrated environmental management. At a conference organized under the auspices of the EPA in 1973, he articulated his doubts about a policy which adopted an holistic approach to the environment. He argued that precisely because everything is interconnected, the environmental problem is beyond our capacity to control in one unified policy. The very enormity of the interconnected environment makes it impossible to treat as a whole. Critical points of intervention (tactically defensible or strategically defensive points of intervention) must be found.[92] According to this argument, a step-by-step approach will solve a problem better than one based upon the necessarily incomplete analysis offered by comprehensive rationality.

The appeal of incrementalism as an approach to environmental protection becomes immediately evident. When faced with a particularly difficult problem of pollution in one medium, the natural response is to solve that problem. An environmental crisis usually manifests itself in one medium, and its linkage with other media is often unknown. * * *

3. The Political Context

A fragmented approach to legislation also arose from the way in which jurisdiction over environmental legislation was carved up between congressional committees. * * *

* * *

4. Bureaucratic Preference

The EPA was created by the Nixon Administration with the specific objective of integrating the various legislative mandates entrusted to it. Nixon's Administration envisioned an EPA that would end much of the fragmentation of environmental policy. Douglas Costle, who later became EPA's administrator, directed the White House task force that handled the transition between congressional approval of the new agency and the actual start of EPA's operations. Costle believed that a reorganization of environmental regulation along functional lines was the desired long-term goal; however, he advocated that an incremental strategy was preferred in the short term.

* * *

There were a number of reasons for Costle's caution in pushing forward with integration. To begin with, the differing policy streams leading to the creation of EPA and the passage of the 1970 Clean Air Act, proceeded along parallel paths. The White House's vision of comprehensive environmental management leading to the creation of EPA was not a vision shared by Congress or embodied in the Clean Air Act of 1970. Consequently, EPA mirrored a curious policy division. On the one hand, it housed those loyal to the original philosophy of NEPA and EPA, while on the other, it was staffed by those committed to a programmatic administration based on fragmented policies. EPA was unprecedented in terms of the number and size of disparate agencies brought under a new organizational roof. In many cases, the agencies had been rivals who enjoyed substantial autonomy. Costle reasoned that there would be resistance and disruption if integration were attempted immediately. Most bureaucrats within EPA had a program perspective. They were tied to specific legislation, functions and appropriations. They took their cues from Congress and reflected the pragmatic, fragmented policies of that body.

Second, Costle feared that the agency would undergo a period of confusion and even chaos while its programmatic inheritance was broken down and rebuilt along functional lines. The resulting confusion would prevent it from meeting the obligations of its legislative mandates and particularly the inflexible demands of the Clean Air Act. * * *

William Ruckelshaus, EPA's first administrator, appeared to be even more apprehensive than Costle. * * * Apart from being nervous about their position and prospects in a new

---

[92] Charles Lindblom, *Incrementalism and Environmentalism*, in MANAGING THE ENVIRONMENT 83 (1973).

organization, the bureaucrats he had inherited from other departments and programs were loyal to specific statutes and programs and were unable to view the environment as a whole. These bureaucrats were familiar with, and committed to, these particular legislative mandates, and feared that concrete directives were in danger of being ignored in the move towards integration. They also had access to senators and representatives of congressional committees who had enacted such legislation and continued to supervise its implementation. Faced with the prospect of bureaucratic resistance and congressional criticism, Ruckelshaus decided to play safe. These initial rumblings of discontent, signifying a bureaucratic preference for fragmentation, led to EPA's plea that it be excluded from NEPA, and set the stage for EPA's virtual rejection of an integrated approach.

* * *

III. AN INTEGRATED APPROACH

A. Towards a Concept of Integration

* * *

1. Strategic Principles

The first principle underlying an integrated approach is that pollution control should be based upon an holistic, rather than a discrete or segmented, view of the environment. The environment should not be artificially divided into separate areas of air, water and land. A necessary corollary of this premise is that administrative structures dealing with environmental protection should be capable of dealing with the environment as a whole.

Secondly, an integrated approach requires that the major deficiencies of a fragmented approach be corrected. Both inputs and final products must be considered, and systematic environmental assessments should be made across all three media—a "longitudinal" analysis. Finally, cross-media pollution controls based on integrated analysis should be adopted. These principles appear attractive and worthy of praise. * * * The real difficulty lies in applying them. * * *

2. Comparative Lessons

The environment in which we live cannot be encapsulated within national boundaries. * * * The difficulties encountered by fragmented controls figure significantly among the shared environmental problems of the international community. A transnational perspective offers a vantage point from which to gain some impression of how others perceive the problems arising out of fragmented controls, as well as the nature of any integrated responses to those problems. In addition to the United Kingdom, the Commission of the European Communities, Sweden and the Netherlands have taken some steps towards integrated pollution controls.

* * *

The concept of integration was introduced to the United Kingdom by the Royal Commission on Environmental Pollution (RCEP) in 1973. Initially, the RCEP addressed only questions of cross-media pollution and argued that pollution or wastes generated by an industrial activity could potentially affect water and land, as well as air. In deciding where pollution should occur, it was sensible that the form and medium of disposal of pollution should be such as to cause the least environmental damage overall. A new integrating concept was mooted. Decisions should be aimed at securing the best practicable environmental option (BPEO). * * * The recommendations of the RCEP have been only partially adopted by the British government.

3. The Integrative Compass

For our purposes, the British formulation of an integrated approach (BPEO) raises two important and interconnected questions that need to be restated before the concept of integration can be satisfactorily implemented. The first concerns the meaning of integration. It is one thing to accept the principle of cross-media pollution, but altogether another to define it. * * * The second question, which to a considerable degree subsumes the first, involves the application of the principle. As a concept that seeks to address the source rather than the effects of pollution, it is possible to conceive of integration as extending from treatment and process to products, and even to grand strategic decisionmaking.

* * * Suppose that the plant and process (a point source) consists of a coal burning electric generator, and that the generator discharges unacceptable levels of sulphur dioxide. The plant management proposes to implement flue gas desulphurization to deal with the problem. One of the desulphurization technologies envisaged is the application of pulverized limestone which results in the creation of gypsum-rich sludge waste. Large quantities of such waste are envisaged. How might the concept of integration be applied in such a situation? At the strictly operational level, an integrated approach would accept the fact of such residuals or wastes, and seek to find the optimal balance for disposing of them, whether to air, land or water, by the use of a coordinated permit. An extended version of the approach would evaluate the decision to undertake flue gas desulphurization within a broader context. Such an inquiry would involve an investigation of the environmental effects of limestone quarrying. What effect would this have on the area from which it is removed, particularly if limestone is found, say, in a national park? * * * Furthermore, what are the effects of transporting limestone across the rural countryside, and what are the environmental consequences of having to store limestone in large quantities? Finally, what is the environmental impact of disposing of the sludge created by this particular technology?

After assessing the environmental impact of the proposed changes, this version of integration would consider whether a case could be made for a different method of desulphurization based on an alternative technology. Although the British government favors the narrow operational approach, the RCEP seems to favor a broader approach. Integration arguably should go further and consider the broader socioeconomic question as to the acceptability of coal fired generators and to balance this against alternative power sources, such as nuclear, solar or wind. Alternatively, it could be asked if generators are necessary at all, when better energy conservation would reduce the need for electric energy. This line of thinking could be extended much further. Most human activities result in the creation of residuals or wastes, and most social and economic activities could, therefore, have environmental and ecological repercussions. From this perspective, anything less than comprehensive planning which totally integrates environmental factors into the decisionmaking and which is based upon environmental considerations, would be inadequate.

* * *

4. Practical Applications

It is essential that difficulties about scope and definition, real though they be, should not be allowed to deflect and delay the implementation of an integrated approach. The question that confronts us at this stage is how to arrive at a starting point from which integrated decisionmaking can commence. * * * Since the seemingly obvious starting points of air, water or land have been rejected, from where does one start? In applying the principles discussed, there is no definitive and preordained point from which to begin, but a promising response is offered by the Conservation Foundation's Draft Environmental Protection Act.[171] The Second Draft divides the sources of pollution into mobile sources, point sources, nonpoint sources and substances and articles. Point sources include the plant and process capable of producing air, water and solid waste pollution which may hitherto have been treated separately under air, water and solid waste laws. For heuristic purposes, point sources offer a good starting point for testing the practicability and applicability of an integrated analysis. First, the point sources could be divided according to type of plant—steel and rolling mills, pulp and paper mills, sugar cane extracting mills, etc. Second, a single permit would be issued for each such point source. This single coordinated permit contrasts with the present practice of issuing different permits for air, water and solid waste. In setting standards, EPA would abide by those standards already established under present legislation, and then try to ensure a balance that would secure the best practicable environmental option.

The RCEP has proposed an insightful and instructive "procedure" for the practical implementation of an integrated approach. * * *

The analysis starts by focusing on the objective of an activity. Since the objective of most industrial activities is the production of goods, it seems sensible to begin with the nature of the final product and raise questions about possible alternatives that might be less polluting. For example, if the activity is coal-fired generation of electricity, questions may be raised about the options to the generation of extra electricity. Does a need for more electricity actually exist where better insulation and more careful use of energy could achieve savings equivalent to the electricity that is to be generated? If the activity is the manufacture of bright paper that causes considerable pollution, the option of manufacturing less bright, non-bleached paper which causes much less pollution should be considered. An obvious constraint that arises in this context is the extent to which pollution control laws allow for inquiries of this kind. If the laws do not, attention would shift to the controlling of process and inputs.

A further objective of an industrial plant or process is the disposal of the residuals. Such an objective is formulated in the light of, and within the limits laid down by legal, technical and economic factors. It is important that further analysis of the objectives pertaining to the method of disposal precede any final decision. * * *

The next stage lies in generating options. Such options would be subject to the existing

---

[171] CONSERVATION FOUNDATION, THE ENVIRONMENTAL PROTECTION ACT, SECOND DRAFT (1988) [hereinafter Second Draft]. This Second Draft is cited for a very limited purpose. It should be distinguished from the Draft Act discussed *infra* ***.

laws controlling pollution. They would arise from the canvassing of technologies, plant designs and methods which create the most environmental benefit at the least cost. For example, the most efficient answer to pollution caused by the generation of liquid residuals containing mercury in the chlor-alkali industry does not lie in the use of end-of-pipe technologies that attempt to remove the mercury from waste water. Instead, it is found in employing a different method of production—a diaphragm, rather than a mercury cell, in the manufacturing process.

The third stage involves an environmental impact assessment of a short list of options generated by stages one and two. * * * [A]ny environmental impact assessment should take the cross-media pollution transfers into account. * * *

During the fourth stage, ways of reducing the environmental impact of the short list of options will be considered. They will involve a consideration, inter alia, of (1) the importance of inputs, (2) the possibilities of reclamation of residuals and recycling, and (3) changes to production process in order to reduce waste. Finally, an overall evaluation of the options is undertaken, and the one best befitting an integrated approach is adopted. The same analysis can be extended to cover input and strategic planning.

B. Integration and Regulatory Reform

To the extent that integrated thinking converges with the criticism of "command and control" regulation by "regulatory reformers," it may be prudent at this juncture to point out that an adventitious convergence of views does not lead to any confluence of conclusions. * * *

To begin with, regulatory reformers often adopt arguments based on an economic analysis which would have the effect of relaxing the present controls and allowing market forces to play a key role in environmental policy. Those arguments contend that the present controls impose billions of dollars in compliance costs and lead to decreases in productivity, technological innovation and market competition. They argue that the present uniform standards governing pollution do not achieve environmental protection at the lowest cost. Some polluters may have lower abatement costs than others because of their technological superiority or their favorable physical and geographical location. These polluters should contribute more towards achieving a required environmental quality because they could do so at the least cost. * * * Further, such standards do not consider the true social cost of environmental legislation. The true social costs will include not only the costs involved in installation, maintenance and management of pollution controls, but also the "opportunity costs" incurred in not deploying the resources required for pollution control in other profitable ventures such as streamlining the plant or extending it. Any opportunities for such beneficial investment are foregone as a result of having to set up pollution controls. * * *

* * *

A central theme common to a number of the reformer proposals appears to coalesce with one which lies at the heart of cross-media pollution control. The regulatory reformers contend that decisionmakers should consider all economic, environmental and control strategies before devising an efficient system. * * * Obtaining such information involves both time and money, and time is not something readily available when there is a need for expeditious action. In many environmental situations, the consequences of postponing action until all information becomes available could be very damaging. Risk assessment is notoriously difficult, and postponing a decision or making no decision for the reason that the issue is indeterminate promotes interests which benefit polluters. * * *

The regulation of pollutants confronts at least four types of uncertainty which stand in the way of scientific certainty or proof. They are data uncertainty, indeterminacy, nonrecurring and nonreplicable events, and transcientific policy questions. Eventually, these uncertainties can be combatted only by policy choices based upon the psychological, political and legal acceptability of a given risk, rather than upon alleged scientific judgment. * * * It is quite clear that an integrated approach does require some form of risk evaluation, but the crucial point that needs emphasis is that such risk evaluation is too important and too uncertain to be left exclusively to risk assessors who hide their policies and politics behind a facade of science.

Accordingly, the integrative analysis of risk advocated in this Article is intended to encourage and induce tighter and more effective environmental controls to remedy the defects of existing regimes. Since it is based on the premise that those controls already in place will remain intact, it is not a vehicle for avoiding or relaxing existing controls, though there is the possibility that the nature and wisdom of some of the existing controls may need to be reconsidered. The integrative analysis advocated here is based upon several grounds. First, the failure scientifically to find or prove an effect cannot lead to the conclusion that there is no effect. * * * Second, risk assessment is as much a political as a scientific evaluation. The primary purpose of a regulatory agency is to achieve the goals set out in its statute, and an agency's mission should not be paralyzed by the complexities of scientific uncertainty. * * *

Unfortunately, the regulatory reformers and economic analysts have succeeded in stealing the mantle of "rationality." By giving decisionmakers supposedly objective numbers derived from markets, and a way of using them in cost-benefit analysis, the economic approach appears to be more rational than the subjective values or judgments of administrators. This Article accepts the need to move from "incrementalism" to "comprehensive rationality," but rejects the view that such a development should be based upon economic analysis. The "comprehensive rationality" advocated in these pages is premised upon the principle that the policymaker must promote only those goals specified by the politically responsible legislature. The objective and purpose of administrative action is to realize these goals in a manner consistent with the publicly articulated purpose of the statute. It is not to re-balance them against the criteria of economic analysis, and emphatically not to substitute the goal of economic efficiency. * * *

* * *

IV. THE NEXT STEPS

* * *

Integrated controls have been advocated by academic commentators, governmental organizations, non-governmental organizations and even by EPA. * * *

* * *

A. The Conservation Foundation Proposal

The Conservation Foundation has been prominent among non-governmental, environmental organizations in making a case for crossmedia pollution control. It has occupied the vanguard in the move towards environmental integration and, together with other commentators, believes that the objective of integration should be embodied in new legislation. Pursuant to a cooperative agreement, the Conservation Foundation has submitted to EPA the final draft of an Environmental Integration and Information Act (Draft Act). [282] * * *

Although there is an unquestionable need for integrating norms that will countervail the effect of the existing norms of fragmentation, the quest of the Conservation Foundation for new legislation is misconceived and futile. It is futile because the difficulties in the way of new legislation are almost insurmountable. It is misconceived because countervailing norms are to be found in existing legislation.

1. New Legislation

* * *

Any legislation seeking overall integration is bound to fail as it runs the gauntlet of the committee system. Because it will impinge on the territories of at least thirty committees, a bill based on the Draft Act cannot succeed. Such an integration bill may be referred to a hostile committee and quietly pigeonholed, or it may never be placed on a committee agenda because of the chairperson's opposition. * * * Given the importance of subcommittee jurisdiction and power, attempts at new legislation may succeed only in aborting any move to implement integration through the administrative process. Any effort to introduce new legislation is therefore misconceived.

2. Countervailing Norms

* * *

The heart of the Draft Act's objective lies in a two-sided provision. One side states that the regulating agency shall consider all significant health and environmental effects of its actions, especially if such effects may affect the ability of other agencies to fulfill their goals. The other side states that no action shall be taken by the agency to control one type of environmental hazard if such action is likely to lead to more than offsetting damage from cross-media transfers. The controlling impact of this provision is offset by a different section which provides that no action taken by the agency should delay the deadlines established in any statute.

B. Integration Through Existing Legislation

The Conservation Foundation's proposal to use integrating goals to counter the sectoral and single medium goals of existing legislation has substantial merit. The argument of this paper is that such goals can be reached through existing legislation. The rightful call

---

[282] Letter from Conservation Foundation to Hank Schilling of EPA (Mar. 13, 1987) (accompanying the final draft of the Environmental Integration and Reformation Act). * * *

in this situation is for an exhaustive and definitive analysis of every statutory provision dealing with pollution control to ascertain if any of these permit or authorize integration. It would then be necessary to ascertain the extent to which these provisions could be woven together to form a pattern of law, policy and administration supporting an integrated approach. * * * An aerial view of the present statutory landscape spanning chemicals offers one good example of a statute, the Toxic Substances Control Act of 1976 (TSCA), that takes an integrated approach. * * * When meshed with the integrating principles already institutionalized by NEPA and EPA, TSCA presents a viable baseline from which to move towards the administrative implementation of an integrated approach. Even provisions of statutes such as the Clean Air Act could be telescoped into TSCA and, consequently, strengthen an integrated approach. * * *

1. The Toxic Substances Control Act of 1976

* * *

The TSCA has three objectives. One objective is to prevent unreasonable risks of injury to health or the environment and to take action on imminent hazards from the specified chemicals without unduly impeding technological innovation. * * *

The second objective of TSCA is to have the industry in question test chemical substances—where there is insufficient data to determine their effects—if the administrator finds that (1) they may present an unreasonable risk of injury to health or the environment, (2) they will be produced in substantial quantities and enter the environment in substantial quantities, or (3) they will be produced in substantial quantities and result in significant or substantial human exposure. The purpose of the testing is to determine whether the manufacture, distribution in commerce, processing, use, or disposal of the substance presents an unreasonable risk of injury to health or the environment. The third objective TSCA required was the establishment of an Interagency Testing Committee, to screen chemicals for potential "significant risk of serious and widespread harm" and to recommend a list of chemicals that should be tested further. TSCA defines the term "environment" to include "water, air, land and the interrelationship which exists among and between water, air and land and all living things." Manufacturers are required to give notice to the administrator of EPA before manufacturing a new chemical substance or putting an old substance to a significant new use. TSCA also empowers the administrator to delay or restrict the manufacture of a new chemical, to adopt rules to prohibit manufacture and processing, and to obtain injunctive relief.

TSCA has institutionalized an integrated approach to the control of chemicals. It embraces the entire environment, together with total human exposure, and is not confined to the usual divisions between air, land and water, or to particular routes of exposure. Integration is crystallized by section 9 of TSCA, dealing with the act's relationship to other laws. When available information leads to the conclusion that there is an unreasonable risk of injury to health or the environment from an activity not controlled by other federal laws, section 9 authorizes the administrator to require other agencies to help abate the activity in question.

Even more significant is the provision of section 9 dealing with laws administered by EPA. * * * The section commands the administrator to coordinate an integrated approach to pollution control established by TSCA with the segmented approaches of the other legislation. The administrator is instructed to consider whether the powers granted under those other acts could be used to control the risks defined in TSCA. If they can, the existing body of pollution control legislation, insofar as it concerned chemicals, would need to be interpreted in the light of the integrating and holistic policies embodied in TSCA. Because the section stipulates that the administrator shall use the powers under those acts rather than TSCA, the case for a reinterpretation of existing legislation is considerably strengthened. In sum, TSCA institutionalizes a countervailing norm of integration. Many of the provisions of apparently single medium statutes can now be interpreted from a different perspective. In the light of TSCA's provisions, it would be very difficult to ignore the applicability of an integrated approach to pollution control in the administration of other legislation.

* * *

V. CONCLUSION

We have seen how ecological streams of thinking based on integration arose at a time of general disillusionment with New Deal idealism. A suspicion of administrative expertise shaped the environmental perspective and resulted in calls for clear, precise and easily followed legislative mandates. Such demands converged with incrementalist models of administration and resulted in the institutionalization of fragmentation. The new confluence of fragmented thought swamped even integrating developments, such as NEPA and EPA, and obstructed the implementation of others, such as TSCA. After some remarkable successes, fragmented policies have resulted in equally conspicuous failures, and these failures call for a review and re-examination of existing policies, and demand fresh initiatives. A re-examination of the foundations of environmental thought, law and policy reveals the extent to which the answers to contemporary problems can be shaped by a rediscovery of existing integrative norms. Existing integrative norms are rendered even more important in the light of a different convergence of thoughtways. Incrementalism is giving way to comprehensive rationality, and comprehensive rationality admirably complements the pursuit of integration. This Article has suggested how the ecological thinking which gave birth to NEPA, EPA and TSCA could be meshed with comprehensive rationality in order to meet the challenge of the 1990s and the twenty-first century.

The most promising way out of the present impasse is for EPA to restructure itself along functional lines, abolish its programmatic divisions, and take a fresh look at the statutes it administers. It may be a difficult undertaking, but it is not anything as exacting as trying to persuade Congress to disengage itself from the existing legislation. Significantly, Administrator Reilly, together with many others within EPA, have acknowledged the critical importance of an integrated approach and the need to change direction. By moving from an incremental, program-based approach to one that is functional and rational, EPA will be reclaiming its integrating mandate, while simultaneously rediscovering its ecological roots. Perhaps there may be a happy ending to the story.

* * *

NOTES

1. Since Professor Guruswamy wrote this article in 1989, both Congress and EPA have addressed pollution prevention and, more generally, an integrated approach to environmental law.

On the legislative front, Congress enacted the Pollution Prevention Act of 1990, which is more hortatory than prescriptive in directing the EPA to encourage industry to undertake more pollution prevention efforts. 42 U.S.C. §§ 13101–13109. Although Congress has neither enacted nor seriously considered legislation that would overhaul and rewrite in an integrated fashion the dozens of environmental laws currently on the books, the 104th Congress has seriously considered (and may pass) "regulatory reform" bills that would cut across the spectrum of environmental laws, imposing uniform standards of risk assessment and cost-benefit analysis on the agencies' efforts to implement those laws. *See, e.g.,* H.R. 9/S.343, 104th Cong., 1st Sess. (1995).

On the administrative front, the EPA has actively promoted pollution prevention, and has undertaken several efforts to implement and enforce the environmental laws in a more integrated, multimedia fashion. In 1991, the EPA published a Pollution Prevention Strategy, 56 Fed. Reg. 7849 (1991), and initiated thereunder several programs to encourage specific industrial sectors to achieve certain pollution prevention goals. The EPA has developed a multimedia enforcement strategy, and has begun to draft regulations that set standards under different statutes for the same industry.

The literature has well documented these and related developments. *See, e.g.,* Robert F. Blomquist, *Government's Role Regarding Industrial Pollution Prevention in the United States*, 29 GA. L. REV. 349 (1995); E. Donald Elliott, *Environmental TQM: Anatomy of a Pollution Control Program That Works!* 92 MICH. L. REV. 1840 (1994); Thomas R. Mounteer, *The Inherent Worthiness of the Struggle: The Emergence of Mandatory Pollution Prevention Planning as an Environmental Regulatory Ethic*, 19 COLUM. J. ENVTL. L. 251 (1994); and Peter J. Fontaine, *EPA's Multimedia Enforcement Strategy: The Struggle to Close the Environmental Compliance Circle*, 18 COLUM. J. ENVTL. L. 31 (1993).

2. With regard to pollution prevention, Barry Commoner contends that the entire regulatory framework is misguided insofar as it addresses the effects, and not the causes, of pollution. He urges that our efforts be refocused toward the root causes—the technology of production. *See* Barry Commoner, *Failure of the Environmental Effort*, 18 Envtl. L. Rep. (Envtl. L. Inst.) 10195 (1988). Professor Eric Orts suggests that "reflexive" environmental law, focusing on internal auditing and self-critical management programs, offers a potentially more effective alternative or supplement to existing regulatory schemes. *See* Eric W. Orts, *Reflexive Environmental Law*, 89 Nw. U. L. REV. 1227 (1995).

3. Professor Guruswamy proposes that the EPA utilize the Toxic Substances Control

Act (TSCA) as a vehicle for administratively integrating the various strands of existing environmental regulation. Is this feasible without amendments to the TSCA statute?

For new chemicals, TSCA allows the EPA only 90 days to screen information about the chemical and its potential environmental consequences. Moreover, the statute does not empower the EPA routinely to require companies to develop information on the environmental impacts of new chemicals before submitting the "premanufacture notification" that starts the 90-day clock running. *See* TSCA §§ 4–5, 15 U.S.C. §§ 2603-2604.

For existing chemicals, it is even more difficult for the EPA to impose regulatory controls. *See* TSCA §§ 6 and 9, 15 U.S.C. §§ 2605 and 2608. The EPA's most prominent attempt to regulate an existing chemical, asbestos, involved a ten-year rulemaking period, followed by an appellate remand of the agency's final rule. *Corrosion Proof Fittings v. EPA*, 947 F.2d 1201 (5th Cir. 1991).

For a critical analysis of the TSCA provision that requires the EPA to *refrain from invoking TSCA* where a problem can be addressed under other provisions, see Cynthia Ruggerio, *Referral of Toxic Chemical Regulation Under the Toxic Substances Control Act: EPA's Administrative Dumping Ground*, 17 B.C. ENVTL. AFF. L. REV. 75 (1989).

Former Congressman Jim Florio, who participated in the enactment of TSCA, states that the law was designed to fill gaps that might exist among the other environmental laws, and that efforts to convert it to an expansive, "umbrella" law, would require statutory amendment. Jim Florio, *Federalism Issues Related to the Probable Emergence of the Toxic Substances Control Act*, 54 MD. L. REV. 1354, 1354-57 (1995).

4. TSCA regulation is based on the concept of unreasonable risk. Although defining and characterizing environmental hazards on the basis of risk would appear to be inherent in setting regulatory priorities and in achieving an integrated approach to environmental regulation, previous attempts to set regulatory standards on the basis of risk have proven to be problematic at best, infeasible at worst. Although both the Clean Air Act and the Clean Water Act set out initially, in 1970 and 1972 respectively, to regulate toxic and hazardous pollutants on the basis of risk, both attempts failed and resulted in statutory overhauls using technology-based standards as the principle means of establishing emission limits. *See, e.g.,* Oliver A. Houck, *The Regulation of Toxic Pollutants Under the Clean Water Act*, 21 ENVTL. L. REP. (Envtl. L. Inst.) 10528 (1991). Is there reason to believe that the TSCA context will enable the EPA to overcome the uncertainties and controversies currently inherent in the application of risk concepts to regulatory decisionmaking? See Chapter Five of this anthology for a thorough discussion of the role of risk concepts in environmental law.

5. Another statute in which Professor Guruswamy sees possibilities of enhanced integration is the National Environmental Policy Act (NEPA). Although NEPA requires that all varieties of environmental impacts be considered prior to undertaking a "major federal action significantly affecting the quality of the human environment," it has inherent limitations. 42 U.S.C. § 4332(2)(C). It does not apply to actions that are not "federal," and it does not apply to actions that do not significantly affect the environment. Moreover, even when it does apply, it requires only that such factors be taken into account; it does not mandate an environmentally-sensitive outcome. *See, e.g., Robertson v. Methow Valley Citizens Council*, 490 U.S. 332 (1989); *Strycker's Bay Neighborhood Council, Inc. v. Karlen*, 444 U.S. 223 (1980).

6. While serving on the First Circuit Court of Appeals—shortly before ascending to the Supreme Court—Justice Breyer authored a book that addresses, from a different perspective, some of the fundamental issues analyzed in Professor Guruswamy's article. STEPHEN BREYER, BREAKING THE VICIOUS CIRCLE: TOWARD EFFECTIVE RISK REGULATION (1993). An excerpt from this book and a discussion of the issues surrounding decisionmaking by somewhat insulated "experts" are included in Chapter Five, *infra*.

B. The Environmental Protection Agency

Regardless of how insightfully conceived, carefully designed, and clearly written an environmental statute may be, its success ultimately depends upon how effectively it is administered by the executive branch. Because most of the principal environmental laws delegate implementation powers to the Environmental Protection Agency, this subchapter will focus on the efforts and role of the EPA in the implementation of the nation's environmental statutes. Since its creation in 1970—just when Congress was beginning the fast and furious process of drafting dozens of environmental statutes—the EPA has played a pivotal as well as controversial role in the shaping of environmental law. The EPA promulgates regulations that further define and make much more specific the general requirements prescribed in the environmental statutes. For example, the Clean Water Act states that all point source dischargers of pollutants to the waters of the United States must have permits, and that the permits are to reflect, at a minimum, technology-based effluent limitations. The EPA then publishes regulations that specify how permits may be obtained, other regulations that dictate what conditions will be imposed on permit holders, and yet other regulations that translate the concept of various different technology-based standards into numerical (or other) limitations on the concentrations of pollutants in industrial effluent. The EPA is also responsible for enforcing the statute and regulations, through reporting requirements, inspections, and the pursuit of administrative and judicial enforcement actions against violators. Where the statutory programs involve substantial state roles, such as under the Clean Water Act, Clean Air Act, and the Resource Conservation and Recovery Act, the EPA defines the parameters of the states' participation in implementing the federal program, oversees the states' administration of the programs, and occasionally brings superseding enforcement actions. Going beyond the responsibilities expressly delegated to the EPA under the environmental statutes, the agency also undertakes policy initiatives, devising innovative means of interpreting and implementing the environmental laws. For example, although considerable consensus developed in 1994 concerning legislative changes to the Superfund law (the Comprehensive Environmental Response, Compensation, and Liability Act), Congress did not complete the process of enacting statutory amendments by the close of the 103rd Congress. The EPA then stepped in and announced several policy initiatives designed to implement administratively various aspects of the proposed changes. *Superfund Administrative Reform Update Documents Released May 25 by EPA,* 26 Env't Rep. (BNA) 288 (June 2, 1995); *Materials on EPA Initiative on Administrative Reforms to Superfund,* 1995 Daily Env't Rep. (BNA) 33 (Feb. 17, 1995). In addition, the EPA engages in and funds research pertaining to the technical and scientific issues surrounding the various environmental programs.

Given this wide range of activities, there is plenty of opportunity for critique and controversy. This subchapter contains two articles concerning the role of the EPA in shaping environmental law. Professor Howard Latin presents eight "laws" that describe agency behavior in implementing statutory programs, and suggests that statutes be written with greater appreciation of the incentives that shape administrative behavior. He uses the Clean Air Act for illustrative purposes. Professor Richard Lazarus surveys the first two decades of the EPA's existence, and analyzes the "tragedy of distrust" that has clouded the agency's performance.

REGULATORY FAILURE, ADMINISTRATIVE INCENTIVES, AND THE NEW CLEAN AIR ACT
Howard Latin
21 Envtl. L. 1647 (1991)*

I. INTRODUCTION

A central theme in this Article is the adage that those who fail to learn from history are compelled to repeat it. Congress has enacted dozens of ambitious environmental protection programs in the past quarter-century, but regulatory implementation has seldom conformed to legislative expectations and rarely if ever achieved the desired degree of protection. Indeed, the gap between the text and implementation of environmental laws has grown so wide that most regulatory practices cannot be understood by studying the applicable legislation. The central lesson of this history is that good implementation, not good legislative intentions, is the key to effective environmental protection.

* * *

This Article * * * emphasizes the critical importance of implementation, but it develops a different thesis: *There are inherent limits to legislative control of regulatory behavior, and effective implementation consequently requires more careful attention to the institutional incentives of agencies and to the professional and personal incentives of regulators than Congress has recognized.*

Regulatory failure is a complex phenomenon with many causes and manifestations. In contrast to the prevailing administrative law focus on imperfect legislation and judicial review, I believe the seeds of regulatory failure are most often grounded in the intrinsic characteristics of regulatory processes. Society asks regulators to do impossible things; we ask them to do difficult things under impossible time and resource constraints; we ask them to behave decisively, selflessly, heroically in ways that are incompatible with normal modes of human behavior. We may be disappointed when regulation falls short of legislative ideals, but we should not be surprised—for regulatory agencies remain imperfect human institutions and administrators are human beings no better or worse than most. * * *

Can Congress expect regulatory agencies to make politically controversial choices if the legislature itself will not provide clear direction? Can Congress insist that administrators develop a comprehensive, consistent, proactive approach to all regulatory issues? Can Congress ask agencies to resolve disputed scientific issues despite the absence of a reasonable scientific consensus? Can Congress tell regulators to achieve the best possible

---

* Reprinted with permission.

results under severe resource constraints, or will agencies tend to allocate budgets and attention in whichever ways are likely to create the appearance of bureaucratic competence? Can Congress demand that agency officials ignore constant criticism and other forms of negative feedback from regulated parties? Can Congress force regulators to act expeditiously when they must consider all facets of remarkably complicated problems and when any major decision may be challenged in appellate proceedings? The history of environmental protection demonstrates that the answer to these questions must be "No" in the great majority of regulatory contexts, irrespective of how artfully the organic statutes are drafted. Yet, these kinds of heroic requirements were imposed by most environmental laws, and agencies predictably tried to evade such mandates or to refashion them into more manageable, if less meaningful, missions.

From the perspective of implementation and administrative incentives, the Clean Air Act Amendments of 1990 (1990 Amendments) largely represent legislative "business as usual." Congress has tried to rectify past failures of the Clean Air Act (CAA) by mandating a plethora of specific regulatory strategies—some patterned after existing approaches under various environmental laws and others intended to be innovative departures from current practices. The 1990 Amendments present a bewildering array of pollution control details and yet, with the exception of a few provisions, the statute does not reflect a sufficient recognition of the need to devise effective administrative incentives. * * *

* * *

Other analysts may disagree with my predictions about the 1990 Amendments' failures, but I believe my central conclusion is unarguable: Congress cannot command agencies or administrators to disregard diverse political, economic, and professional factors that affect the implementation burdens and popularity of regulatory programs. Legislators must instead learn to create agency and bureaucratic incentives that may indirectly encourage desired regulatory behavior. High-level administrators similarly cannot compel bureaucrats to ignore various professional and personal considerations. Agency managers must therefore also learn to develop incentive systems that will induce better regulatory performance. I do not contend that attention to administrative incentives can solve all regulatory problems, but I believe Congress will continue to repeat past mistakes until it recognizes that the discrepancy between environmental goals and implementation cannot be remedied simply by drafting more and more detailed statutes. A realistic assessment of implementation constraints and related incentives is essential if legislators are to revitalize existing environmental protection programs and develop effective new ones.

II. EIGHT "LAWS" OF ADMINISTRATIVE BEHAVIOR

The gap between environmental laws and implementation can be explained partly by budget and personnel constraints, shifts in American economic circumstances, and the Reagan Administration's overt hostility to government regulation. If these were the main causes of ineffective environmental control programs, regulation could be improved simply by allocating more resources to "better" bureaucrats. I believe, however, that inaction and inefficient action were predictable results of the difficult implementation problems confronting all environmental regulators. Yet, most environmental statutes devoted little attention to how agencies and their staff would function under severe implementation constraints.

For heuristic purposes, I have chosen to describe agency and bureaucratic responses to implementation constraints in terms of several "laws" of administrative behavior. These are not laws in a Newtonian sense; they describe customary modes of regulatory behavior, and occasional counter-examples would not invalidate them. If agencies *usually* obey these laws regardless of the content of particular organic statutes, a better understanding of administrative incentives and the limits of legislative control is necessary for the development of effective environmental protection programs.

A. In Conflicts Between Political Considerations and Technocratic Requirements, Politics Usually Prevails

In a seminal article published nearly two decades ago, Louis Jaffe contended that agencies cannot function absent widespread political support, regardless of how much authority the regulatory statutes appear to provide.[8] Experience with many environmental programs confirms Professor Jaffe's generalization, or at least shows that administrators themselves believe it. Environmental regulation is an expensive and controversial enterprise that may impact on innumerable activities. It cannot be surprising, then, that agencies often respond to political and social circumstances not enumerated, and sometimes clearly excluded, in the applicable legislation.

In the past twenty years, EPA distributed tens of billions of dollars for construction of publicly-owned sewage treatment works (POTWs) under the Clean Water Act (CWA) and cleanup of hazardous waste sites under the Comprehensive Environmental Response Compensation and Liability Act's "Superfund" program. What strategy should EPA have adopted for allocation of these funds: Should the agency have provided the greatest financial assistance to states with the worst pollution problems? Should EPA have expended most funds where the competence and commitment of regional officials ensured the best pollution control returns for the money? Should EPA have spread funds across many areas to promote the appearance that all states derive worthwhile benefits from these programs? In practice, EPA adopted a mix of these strategies but allocated the majority of funds on a proportional basis to all states, whatever their relative need or expertise, in order to secure widespread legislative and public support. Thus, EPA's desire to widen its political support often superseded explicit statutory program objectives.

Subchapter II of the CWA imposes an elaborate structure for sewage treatment planning: river basin and state plans at the highest level; section 208 "areawide" plans for areas with substantial water quality problems; and section 201 "facility" plans for each POTW and related sewage-feeder lines. This program incorporated a top-down technocratic theory of planning in that facility plans must be consistent with the applicable basin, state, and areawide plans. * * * Congress's emphasis on areawide planning reflected its recognition that ecological biosystems, pollution dispersion patterns, and water quality problems cut across the boundaries of existing political jurisdictions.

In reality, this top-down technocratic planning structure has been turned completely on its head. Local governments have made most major decisions on which types of POTWs would be built and where they would be located; facility plans have consequently been

---

[8] Jaffe, *The Illusion of the Ideal Administration,* 86 HARV. L. REV. 1183, 1198 (1973).

based primarily on local political and economic conditions; and higher-level plans have become little more than unintegrated compendiums of local plans. * * *

This administrative inversion of the CWA planning process appears inefficient from a technocratic perspective, but reflects realistic political judgments. Neither EPA nor state agencies viewed the CWA as a congressional mandate for comprehensive land-use regulation and restriction of the traditional prerogatives of localities to control patterns of development. Any community that strenuously objected to a section 208 areawide plan could delay POTW construction for years through recourse to judicial review and political lobbying, which would impede the statutory and EPA goal of achieving rapid water pollution control progress. If EPA found areawide or state plans inadequate, its only enforcement sanction was to withhold federal grants, which would delay pollution control progress and would not penalize the communities that resisted construction of large-scale POTWs. State governors and agencies were reluctant to intervene when adjacent localities could not agree on a common areawide plan, because the political cost of imposing POTW facilities and increased tax burdens on unwilling citizens outweighed the political benefits. In short, communities joined together to build and operate facilities when they wanted to cooperate, and developed separate treatment plans if no consensus was present. Local political considerations came to dominate ecological circumstances and technocratic rationality in sewage treatment planning, and thereby deprived most areawide plans of any significant meaning.

* * *

B. Agencies Avoid Making Regulatory Decisions that Would Create Severe Social or Economic Dislocation

The CWA lists technological and economic criteria that EPA must use to develop water pollution controls and requires that uniform standards be issued on a nationwide basis for "classes or categories" of pollution sources. The statute and legislative history reflect Congress's recognition that some old or relatively unprofitable dischargers could not afford to comply and would therefore have to cease operations. EPA nevertheless tried to exempt marginal steel plants in Ohio's Mahoning Valley because imposition of the costly national standards would entail severe economic impacts and social dislocation in the rust-belt area.

EPA issued a rule in 1981 that, if states could not attain the national ambient air quality standards (NAAQS) by 1987, they must identify "all possible measures" that would "result in attainment as quickly as possible."[20] EPA argued that this approach to mandated State Implementation Plans (SIPs) would be better than encouraging the submission of "artificial SIPs that appeared to demonstrate attainment through control measures the state never intended to implement."[21] In 1990, the U.S. Court of Appeals for the Ninth Circuit relied on EPA's statement to force the Agency to impose stringent controls in nonattainment

---

[20] EPA, State Implementation Plans; Approval of 1982 Ozone and Carbon Monoxide Plan Revisions for Areas Needing an Attainment Extension, 46 Fed. Reg. 7182, 7188 (1981).

[21] EPA, State Implementation Plans; Approval of Post-1987 Ozone and Carbon Monoxide Plan Revisions; Policy Clarification, 55 Fed. Reg. 38,326, 38,327 (1990).

areas. EPA promptly revoked its "all possible measures" rule to avoid "severely disruptive socioeconomic impacts" from "draconian control measures."[23] EPA contended that "[t]he statute does not require measures that are absurd, unenforceable, or impracticable," and the Agency then refused "to impose severely disruptive measures calculated to produce immediate attainment."[24]

The Mahoning Valley and "all possible measures" examples show EPA's great reluctance to cause serious social dislocation, even if that result appears clearly mandated by the statute. In a similar vein, EPA has seldom been willing to impose environmental standards that adversely affect the relative economic positions of states or regions, even when a statute requires controls that may have disproportionate effects. One example has been EPA's reluctance to limit acid rain precursors, which would impose greater burdens on states that rely on high-sulfur coal and correspondingly benefits states near clean coal deposits. EPA arguably had statutory authority under the CAA to control Midwestern acid rain sources, but it repeatedly refused to act absent a national consensus on which control measures were appropriate and which regions or groups ought to pay for them. The legislative histories of the CAA and other statutes expressed a congressional policy against creating competitive disadvantages among states or regions, and EPA consistently has adopted the same policy even if particular statutory provisions appeared to require the opposite result.

* * *

C. Agencies Avoid Resolving Disputed Issues Unless They Can Render Scientifically Credible Judgments

Virtually all pollution control regulations fall under one of three distinctive approaches:

Harm-Based Standards: Regulatory agencies must determine what level of emissions is "acceptably" safe and then transform that general finding into specific emissions limits for each pollutant and each discharger. This approach requires agencies to identify adverse health and ecological degradation from particular levels of each regulated pollutant. * * *

Individualized Cost-Benefit Analysis: Agencies must identify and balance pollution risks, exposure levels, control costs, indirect economic effects, possible social dislocation, and other relevant concerns to select the most appropriate emissions limit for each regulated pollutant. This requires harm-based determinations to identify the potential benefits of alternative emissions control levels, technology-based assessments to identify the costs of alternative control measures, and policy assessments of whether the benefits justify the economic and social costs of regulation. Cost-benefit analysis also entails inconsistencies arising from the individualized nature of the determinations and differing values of various administrators.

Technology-Based Standards: Agencies must determine the "best available" control technologies that are economically feasible for each regulated industry.

---

[23] *Id.*
[24] *Id.*

The primary issue is not what level of risk is created by each pollution discharge, but rather what types of control measures disparate industries can afford to install. Agencies must therefore address varied technological and economic uncertainties, but need not identify pollution harms with any degree of specificity.

The history of American pollution controls, including the 1990 Amendments, reflects a continuing shift from harm-based and cost-benefit strategies to reliance on technology-based standards. For example, water pollution limits prior to 1972 were based on a water quality approach administered by state agencies. This harm-based program required states to classify bodies of water in terms of desired uses, issue water quality criteria that ensured ambient pollution would not interfere with designated uses, and impose waste-load allocations limiting discharges from specific pollution sources. After hearings in 1971, Congress determined that this approach was not working: nearly half of the states had not issued water quality standards approved by EPA; water quality criteria had not been developed for many pollutants; most states did not impose strict controls because they feared competitive disadvantages and resulting outmigration of industries; many states also lacked the manpower and expertise needed to administer effective programs. In response to the problems with water quality regulation, Congress chose to adopt technology-based controls as the centerpiece of the new CWA. In the same manner, Congress in 1977 adopted a technology-based approach to control toxic water pollutants and required all air polluters to install "reasonably available control technology" (RACT). The 1990 Amendments similarly impose the "maximum available control technology" requirements on major sources of 189 hazardous air pollutants.

* * * Technology-based standards normally impose end-of-the-pipe controls that may not promote pollution prevention and cannot ensure that any given level of ecological purity will be maintained. Technology-based regulations are complicated, expensive, and often fail to achieve benefits that justify the high regulatory costs. Technology-based standards may stifle technical innovation and would allow high levels of emissions to continue from relatively unprofitable dischargers. Given these serious conceptual and practical deficiencies, why has Congress chosen to mandate technology-based controls in one regulatory program after another?

The most plausible explanation is that different regulatory strategies require different kinds of information and introduce different implementation problems that agencies must resolve. Technology-based controls may be inflexible, costly, and partly ineffective, but at least agencies can draw reasonably credible and defensible conclusions on the characteristic issues presented under this regulatory approach. In contrast, most harm-based approaches require agencies to resolve health and toxicity issues beyond the boundaries of scientific knowledge. * * *

* * *

If one examines administrative behavior realistically, there are numerous reasons why regulators would resist any statutory prescription to "guess." EPA and other agencies must function in a setting where every factual finding, scientific inference, and policy choice is vigorously contested by affected parties. Agency judgments must also survive intensive judicial review in which regulators normally bear the burden of proving regulatory decisions are rational and supported by substantial evidence. If agencies concede they have had to guess, their decisions may become fair game for interest-group and media ridicule; yet, a realistic administrator would not expect much legislative support if the wolves begin howling. Environmental protection programs often entail high regulatory costs that agencies may be reluctant to impose on the basis of speculation, but that is precisely the effect of regulation under uncertainty. Finally, but not least important, officials responsible for complex technical decisions will often try to protect their image of professional competence by complying with norms of the disciplines in which they are trained. Good scientists are often unwilling to guess about indeterminate issues, even if good regulators should not be.

In light of these circumstances, legislators and high-level administrators must be sensitive to whether specified regulatory strategies raise issues that cannot be resolved in a reasonably reliable manner. If policy makers cannot compel bureaucrats to guess about unanswerable questions, environmental statutes should never adopt regulatory strategies that are likely to depend upon agency speculation. From the perspective of the credibility of agency judgments, technology-based standards have proven far more administrable than harm-based strategies and administrators have consequently been much less reluctant to implement them. * * * Congress has chosen to rely on technology-based strategies after concluding that imperfect regulation is better than virtually no regulation under harm-based approaches * * *.

* * *

D. Agencies Will Not Meet Statutory Deadlines If Budget Appropriations, Personnel, Information, or Other Resources Are Inadequate

* * * No matter how precise and emphatic the deadlines prescribed in environmental statutes may be, agencies will not meet target dates unless they can support regulatory determinations with credible scientific, economic, or political rationales. When agencies lack adequate information, personnel, budget allocations, or other essential resources, inaction and further "study" will generally be more attractive bureaucratic options than imposing expensive control requirements on the basis of superficial analyses—analyses that are likely to be the subject of extensive criticism by affected interest groups and politicians.

As one illustration, the technology-based approach mandated by the CWA required EPA to promulgate national control standards for many discrete categories and classes of pollution sources. These uniform standards imposed discharge limits derived from the best feasible control measures that EPA could identify for each source category. The implementation process was supposed to occur in two phases, "best practicable control technology" (BPT) and "best available control technology" (BAT). The 1972 CWA also required EPA or state agencies to issue discharge permits incorporating the BPT and BAT limits specified in the category of standards applicable to each polluter. Technology-based controls do not require any showing that a pollutant causes unacceptable harm, but the agency must make findings on many other uncertain issues including the kind of control measures suitable in each industry, the probable costs of those controls, and the economic capacity of each industry to bear the regulatory burdens. Despite the novelty and complexity of this approach, the CWA instructed EPA to issue all required BPT standards in one year, a timetable that proved wildly optimistic.

EPA found that technological and economic variations among industrial pollution sources necessitated development of about 560 separate sets of categorical standards applicable to common water pollutants. The Agency initially lacked adequate knowledge and expertise on technology-based issues—in 1972 most Agency staff had expertise on water quality issues, not control technologies. Yet, EPA needed to provide strong evidentiary support for every set of technology-based standards because many were challenged in court by industry and environmental groups with contradictory objectives. As a result of these implementation constraints, a process Congress envisioned would be completed in less than one year took more than a decade for BPT regulations and is still continuing for BAT limits. This example of noncompliance with legislatively-imposed deadlines has special import for the 1990 Amendments because they also require implementation of diverse technology-based standards on a statutory timetable that is very likely to be violated.

A 1991 investigative report found that "the EPA considers drinking water pollution one of the four greatest environmental risks facing Americans, causing as many as 1,000 cancer cases a year and stunting the mental development of as many as 240,000 children."[53] The Safe Drinking Water Act Amendments of 1986 directed EPA to regulate eighty-three specified contaminants within three years. Two years after the statutory deadline expired, EPA had not issued standards for forty percent of listed toxics. Many thousands of violations of existing drinking water standards also occurred in the years from 1988-1990, but only a few resulted in EPA or state enforcement actions. Public utilities frequently failed to test water supplies on a regular basis, as the statute requires; one Washington utility went seven years without the necessary measurements. In short, EPA failed to implement or enforce virtually every statutory requirement in the drinking water program. Administrator Reilly contended that "many of the agency's lapses stem from unrealistic statutory deadlines, inadequate staff and scientific uncertainties."[58] * * *

* * *

My point is not that regulatory agencies are always remiss for their failures to meet legislative timetables. Congress has enacted many target dates with little concern for administrative burdens and other implementation problems. Rather, the theme here is that legislatures cannot compel agencies to act on complicated issues absent adequate personnel, information, resources, time, and expertise. * * *

E. Regulators Are Influenced by Disciplinary Norms That May Conflict with Statutory Mandates

In an insightful 1972 essay that deserves to be more widely read, Ned Bayley described several reasons for the reluctance of regulators in the 1960s to respond to problems raised by Rachel Carson's *Silent Spring* and growing political concern about the environmental

---

[53] Weisskopf, *EPA Falls Far Short in Enforcing Drinking Water Laws,* Wash. Post, May 20, 1991, at A1, col. 2, 5.

[58] *Id.* at A4, col. 1.

effects of pesticide usage.[67] Bayley noted that the U.S. Department of Agriculture's (USDA) pesticide division, which he directed, was placed within the agency's research office and was dominated by a scientific viewpoint. This scientific orientation led USDA bureaucrats to emphasize the weakness of some of Carson's evidence, to dismiss harmful effects not proven with reasonable scientific certainty, to request more funding for long-term pesticide research than for regulation, to adopt the extended timeframe typical of scientific research, and to underestimate the political clout of the nascent environmental movement. Bayley concluded: "Although scientific data are essential to decisionmaking on pesticide regulations, I believe (as a scientist who has had to modify his thinking drastically as an administrator) that having a regulatory function operate under a science-dominated administration is a mistake."[69]

In 1980, Congress created the National Acid Precipitation Assessment Program (NA-PAP) to develop an independent scientific and policy-oriented understanding of the causes of acid rain and the potential benefits of remedial measures. This $500 million study was dominated by a pure-science orientation and contributed little to the political debate that culminated in the acid rain provisions of the 1990 Amendments.[70] A NAPAP participant noted that "NAPAP became obsessed by the need to have the best science, but the best science and the best models aren't always the best way to get answers to the things that matter most for policy."[71] * * * The last NAPAP director agreed that it made scientific contributions "at the expense of greater policy relevance" and he rationalized this result by claiming: "I had the sense that if we tried to do both, we would have failed at both."[73] Yet Congress created the NAPAP study to produce policy-oriented guidance, not science for its own sake. Several NAPAP experts cautioned that this "scenario is already repeating itself in the new federal climate change program," which "is driven too much by raw science."[74]

* * *

F. Bureaucrats Are Conditioned by Criticism or Other Forms of Negative Feedback

I have found little evidence that EPA and other agencies are "captured" by regulated interests as a result of bribes or career opportunities for bureaucrats who adopt pro-industry policies. More subtle influences, however, often do condition the behavior of administrators in favor of regulated interests. Agency officials, like most human beings, prefer to avoid criticism and controversy whenever possible. Industry representatives appear regularly in agency proceedings and can usually afford to offer detailed comments and criticisms on possible agency decisions, while environmental groups intervene on an intermittent basis and the unorganized public seldom participates at all. This routine asymmetry will increase agency responsiveness to industry criticisms. No matter how

---

[67] See Bayley, *Memoirs of a Fox,* 2 ENVTL. AFF. 332 (1972-1973). * * *

[69] *Id.* at 335. * * *

[70] See Roberts, *Learning from an Acid Rain Program,* 251 SCIENCE 1302, 1304-05 (1991).

[71] *Id.* at 1302 (quoting Professor Edward Rubin of Carnegie-Mellon University). * * *

[73] [*Id.*] at 1305 (quoting Dr. James Mahoney).

[74] *Id.* at 1305 (quoting Dr. Mahoney).

sincere and public-spirited officials are when appointed, a process of negative feedback will produce shifts toward the positions espoused by regulated parties. * * *

* * *

Another important conditioning factor is that agency staff and industry representatives must work together on a continuing basis to implement environmental control programs. Whatever the effects of environmentalists on federal policy making, they cannot participate in the thousands of day-to-day activities that shape such issues as permit compliance, site inspections, or contamination of food by pesticides. At the least, continuous contacts with regulated parties are likely to sensitize agency personnel to the problems and priorities of industry employees. This familiarity is surely desirable to some extent, but it may also lead to an "us against them" reluctance of regulators to obey legislative or high-level agency directives that further burden the people with whom they must work. * * *

Regulators also commonly exhibit a reluctance to engage in intra-agency or interagency criticism. Regulatory bureaucracies are never monolithic institutions and disagreements often arise among different departments or officials. * * * Bureaucrats are often unwilling to present disagreements and mutual criticism at the highest level of agency policy making or to disclose them outside the Administration because they must continue to function with other administrators on an ongoing basis. Public criticism may interfere with operations that require intra-agency cooperation and may jeopardize career advancement of dissenters. The antipathy of bureaucracies to "whistle blowers" represents an extreme form of this problem.

* * *

G. Agency Behavior is Partly Conditioned by Manipulative Tactics of Regulated Parties

Industry often has large economic interests at stake and may be willing to expend commensurate efforts in agency proceedings to weaken or delay prospective environmental controls. Agencies are, moreover, required by administrative law and judicial review to consider in detail most industry evidence and arguments. When agencies find the mandated consideration creates a severe drain on their resources or otherwise prevents them from making timely progress, they may reach a "compromise" position that industry accepts precisely because it is relatively lenient. Manipulative behavior by affected interests is the regulatory norm rather than the exception. * * *

* * *

H. Administrators of Multiple-Purpose Statutes Usually "Simplify" the Decisional Process to Emphasize Only One or Two Statutory Goals

* * *

In context after context, the emergence of environmentalism forced regulators to shift from relatively well-defined missions to attainment of disparate objectives for which there was no common metric or unifying principle. The Federal Power Commission had to begin considering recreation and conservation as well as technical and economic aspects of electricity generation. Bureau of Land Management range managers could no longer limit their attention to livestock grazing effects. Forest Service officials were not supposed to emphasize timber production, a traditional priority, without equal concern for environmental preservation, watershed management, wildlife protection, and wilderness recreation. The Army Corps of Engineers was now expected to protect wetlands areas in addition to its historical mission of constructing as many dams and canals as possible. Congress enacted the National Environmental Policy Act of 1970 and amended many organic statutes to impose environmental protection responsibilities on federal agencies, but new legislative mandates did not invariably or rapidly alter agency priorities.

There are numerous reasons why regulatory agencies prefer to emphasize a limited set of goals even when the applicable statute mandates balancing of many competing considerations. An agency's staff may have expertise in some areas and not in others required by environmental protection missions. Any requirement to examine and balance a multitude of criteria will increase budget and time demands, and may detract from an agency's ability to perform the functions it has traditionally managed. The more objectives an agency must consider, the more certain it becomes that regulators will be subjected to constant criticism and lobbying activities by diverse affected parties. Organized groups representing some statutory objectives will normally be able to maintain closer contact with agency staff and provide more effective criticism than adherents of competing interests who may interact with regulators on only an intermittent basis. Organized interest groups may also attain more political leverage on specific issues through their ability to generate campaign funds for politicians at all levels of government. Agency officials who live among the constituents most directly affected by the economic impacts of regulatory decisions, such as ranchers or lumberjacks, may come to share the values and priorities of people with whom they have daily contact. Local officials may be especially sensitive to the social and economic dislocation resulting from environmental protection policies in areas dependent upon resource exploitation industries for jobs and taxes.

Aside from these various external influences, agencies may choose to focus on only a few statutory goals in response to pressures exerted by their own regulatory culture. Organizations require criteria on which to evaluate their performance and that of their staff, but some objectives are more amenable than others to the development of clear and consistent performance standards. * * *

* * *

I considered including two more "laws" of administrative behavior: *Short-term "crises" come to dominate most regulatory processes, while problems that require long-range commitments of agency resources are underemphasized*; and *The "squeaky wheel" gets the regulatory grease*. However, these tendencies for the most part appear to be consequences of previously identified behavioral factors, including budgetary and personnel constraints, agency concern for political support, and bureaucratic aversion to criticism. Other commentators might produce a different set of behavioral "laws" and could doubtless cite many other agency decisions to illustrate my list of generalized rules. The number and arrangement of "laws" is not important—the central point is that congressional control of agency behavior is limited in many intractable ways, and legislators must therefore learn to create administrative incentives that will indirectly promote regulatory activities or attitudes they cannot simply mandate. Legislators and other policy makers cannot simply identify the social goals, priorities, and procedures they want implemented. They must also devote close attention to the kinds of questions that regulatory agencies are expected to resolve and to professional and personal motivations that influence the behavior of agency officials.

* * *

IV. CONCLUSION

Legislators and high-level administrators cannot simply identify the social goals, policies, priorities, and procedures they want implemented. They must also devote careful attention to the kinds of issues that agencies are asked to resolve and to professional and personal incentives that influence the behavior of agency officials. The central thesis of this Article is that legislators, administrators, and legal commentators can neither understand nor hope to remedy regulatory failures unless they begin to assess realistically the incentives of the people who must make regulatory programs work. * * *

* * *

If there are any solutions to problems arising from agency aversion to criticism and vulnerability to "capture," they lie in development of bureaucratic incentives that may counterbalance the effects of negative feedback. The legislature could provide funds to facilitate participation by underrepresented groups in administrative proceedings and could also appoint some form of ombudsman to represent unorganized public interests. Legislators could allocate agency resources based on performance criteria; for example, agencies would be more willing to bring enforcement actions if they retained a portion of the fines collected. The legislature might require that agency personnel be rotated to different offices or areas on a regular basis, like magistrates in Imperial China, which would increase bureaucratic independence but sacrifice benefits arising from familiarity with the issues and players in environmental disputes. The legislature or an agency manager could make particular officials responsible for guarding against "sweetheart deals" in a program, and assess their job performance in terms of that criterion. These proposals only serve to illustrate a general theme: *Modifying the rewards and penalties associated with bureaucratic behavior may be far more effective in improving performance than any amendment of formal laws could be.*

This list of incentive-based reforms is far from complete and each suggestion has disadvantages that must be evaluated in the context of particular regulatory goals and circumstances. My point is that critical implementation problems frequently cannot be remedied by substantive changes in environmental laws and are better addressed through influencing the motivations and behavior of officials who administer the laws. * * *

NOTES

1. If Congress agreed wholeheartedly with Professor Latin's analysis of the significance of behavioral incentives affecting agency actions, what steps might it take to enhance the effective implementation of statutory goals? The few suggestions that Latin floated in his penultimate paragraph are, as he conceded, problematic. For example, public funding of underrepresented groups in administrative proceedings would raise a host of concerns, such as who decides which groups to fund, how such decisions are made, under what circumstances the funding might or should be terminated prior to the natural conclusion of the administrative proceeding, whether the spokespeople of the funded groups are truly representative, and whether the groups for whom they speak are truly underrepresented. Starting where Latin leaves off, develop and refine some feasible recommendations for behavioral incentives to improve the EPA's implementation of environmental statutes.

2. Are there constitutional limits on the means employed by Congress to ensure the effective implementation of statutory objectives? Would some of Latin's suggestions, or other behavioral incentives, raise separation of powers concerns? Consider *Immigration and Naturalization Service v. Chadha*, 462 U.S. 919 (1983), holding unconstitutional a provision in the Immigration and Nationality Act authorizing one house of Congress to veto an Executive Branch decision allowing a deportable alien to remain in the U.S. The Court held that the congressional veto was a legislative act, and therefore required the approval of both houses and presentation to the President.

3. In arguing that agencies avoid resolving disputes where scientific or technical uncertainties require "guessing," Latin states that agency judgments must "survive intensive judicial review in which regulators normally bear the burden of proving regulatory decisions are rational *and supported by substantial evidence*." (emphasis added) Based on your study of environmental cases, do you agree with this description of the normal scope of judicial review? When does the Administrative Procedure Act authorize a reviewing court to determine whether a challenged agency action is based on substantial evidence? *See* 5 U.S.C. § 706(2)(E).

4. Latin discusses the problems Congress has experienced in attempting to force the EPA to meet statutory deadlines. In the 1984 Amendments to RCRA—formally the Hazardous and Solid Waste Amendments of 1984, Congress included a "hammer" provision to attempt to ensure the timely implementation of the new "land ban" program, requiring the treatment of hazardous waste prior to its disposal by land. Congress was concerned that the EPA would not meet the statutorily-prescribed deadlines for promulgating land disposal treatment standards. The hammer provision flatly prohibited the land disposal of any hazardous waste for which a treatment standard was required to have been, but was not, established. 42 U.S.C. § 6924(g)(6)(C). With both the regulated and the environmental communities supporting the EPA's efforts to develop the treatment standards in a timely fashion, the EPA satisfied the deadlines—and the hammer never fell.

Does the success of the land ban hammer provision in forcing the EPA to meet statutory deadlines undermine Latin's fourth law of agency behavior, that agencies will not meet statutory deadlines if budget appropriations, personnel, information, or other resources are inadequate? In light of such inevitable resource limitations, do hammer provisions compromise the quality of regulations promulgated thereunder? Whereas challenges to the early land ban treatment standards were generally upheld, the last rulemaking—the one associated with the flat ban on land disposal of wastes lacking treatment standards—was substantially vacated on grounds that ultimately lead the EPA to a new approach to setting land ban treatment standards. *See Chemical Waste Management, Inc. v. EPA*, 976 F.2d 2 (D.C. Cir. 1992), *cert. denied*, 113 S. Ct. 1961 (1993); and 59 Fed. Reg. 47982 (1994) (promulgation of new "universal treatment standards").

5. The relationship between Congress and the EPA in the shaping of environmental law and policy is as complex as it is controversial. The role of the EPA, including its relationship with Congress, was explored at a 1990 symposium at Duke Law School commemorating the twentieth anniversary of the creation of the agency. The papers presented at the symposium are compiled in Symposium, *Assessing the Environmental Protection Agency After Twenty Years: Law, Politics, and Economics,* 54 LAW & CONTEMP. PROBS. 1 (1991).

Two of the articles in the symposium focus on congressional oversight, an aspect of the relationship between Congress and the EPA that goes beyond the issues of statutory structure and direction addressed in Professor Latin's preceding article. Professor Richard Lazarus states:

> * * * Commentators have mistakenly defined EPA's relationship with Congress almost exclusively in terms of the statutory provisions that Congress has passed and placed within EPA's jurisdiction. Those laws, however, are just the more prominent strands in a profoundly detailed web of congressional efforts to oversee EPA's work that has profoundly affected the agency and the development of federal environmental protection policy.
>
> The amount and character of congressional oversight of EPA are both remarkable. Congress appears to engage in more intense and pervasive oversight of EPA than it does of other agencies. In addition, the character of congressional oversight of EPA appears to be consistently adversarial and negative. * * *

* * *

Congressional supervision of EPA each year includes lengthy and rigorous appropriations hearings on the agency's budget, numerous appearances by EPA officials at hearings, between 100 and 150 congressionally commanded EPA reports to Congress, approximately 5,000 congressional inquiries to the agency, and doubtless even more frequent, less formal ency contacts. It also includes as many as forty GAO reports to Congress about EPA and its programs, and, when presidential appointments are made to the agency, confirmation hearings on those nominations. Finally, the Office of the Inspector General at the EPA (which was created in 1978) has played an active oversight function within the agency; EPA inspector generals' reports have frequently triggered, or otherwise been the subject of, formal congressional oversight.

Richard J. Lazarus, *The Neglected Question of Congressional Oversight of EPA:* Quis Custodiet Ipsos Custodes *(Who Shall Watch the Watchers Themselves)?*, 54 LAW & CONTEMP. PROBS. 205, 206, 211-12 (1991). Lazarus finds both advantages and disadvantages in such intense congressional oversight, and recommends some limitations on congressional oversight in order to reduce the adverse impacts. In response, Steven Shimberg, then Minority Staff Director and Chief Counsel of the Senate Committee on Environment and Public Works, finds the effects of congressional oversight to be overstated, particularly in light of the detailed statutory provisions whereby Congress directs the EPA in the implementation of environmental law.

Whatever the shortcomings of federal environmental legislation, congressional "oversight" in the form of hearings, press conferences, meetings, and letters is not the cause of EPA's problems. Rather, oversight is a mirror reflecting problems that exist independently. The reflection may intensity, magnify, or distort the image, but it does not create the image.

The real question that needs to be answered is whether Congress has the institutional capability to engage in *effective, constructive* oversight that can produce *significant* changes in EPA's implementation of federal environmental policy. For several reasons, the answer is "no."

First, oversight work is detailed, complex, and tedious. * * * Micromanaging the technical work of EPA is the last thing members of Congress want to do.

Second, Congress is not a single entity. It has 535 separate voices. * * *

Third, other than threatening to cut off funds or passing new legislation, what sort of oversight powers does Congress have? * * *

* * *

With respect to the hundreds or thousands of relatively minor decisions confronting EPA, congressional oversight, or the mere threat of oversight, can be used to alter agency behavior and to change decisions. With respect to the major policy decisions, however—decisions that shape federal environmental policy—traditional forms of congressional oversight have limited effect. Behavior may be altered, but rarely are decisions altered solely as a result of congressional oversight. When a major policy question is working its way through the system (first within EPA and then within the executive branch as a whole), the voices heard from Congress in the name of "oversight" are treated just like those from any other interest group.

Over the past twenty years, it has become apparent to members of Congress who want to influence major policy decisions at EPA that the most effective form of oversight is detailed, prescriptive legislation. For example, the original 1970 Clean Air Act was reportedly only thirty-five pages long. The 1990 amendments to the Clean Air Act include more than 350 pages of specific legislative directives to EPA, a tenfold increase.

Steven Shimberg, *Checks and Balance: Limitations on the Power of Congressional Oversight,* 54 LAW & CONTEMP. PROBS. 241, 245-47 (1991).

A second symposium article by Professor Lazarus takes a more detailed look at the variety of pressures on the EPA and seeks to explore the causes of "regulatory failure."

THE TRAGEDY OF DISTRUST IN THE IMPLEMENTATION OF FEDERAL ENVIRONMENTAL LAW
Richard J. Lazarus
54 Law & Contemp. Probs. 311 (1991)*

I. INTRODUCTION

* * *

* * * EPA commenced operations on December 2, 1970, amidst much fanfare and congressional good wishes. EPA's tenure has nonetheless been marked by * * * crisis and controversy * * *. What should seem to be unlikely combinations of institutional forces have in fact seriously frustrated from the outset the agency's development and implementation of federal environmental protection policy.

Congress has repeatedly demanded that the agency perform impossible tasks under unrealistic deadlines. Courts have rejected many of the agency's efforts to provide itself with more leeway in their implementation, while the White House, OMB, and congressional appropriation committees have simultaneously resisted subsequent agency efforts to comply with strict judicial mandates. The agency spends much of its limited resources defending its decisions in court, negotiating with OMB and the White House, and justifying its decisions to multiple congressional committees. A virtual state of siege and a crisis mentality have persisted at the agency for much of its existence as Congress has responded to each EPA failure by passing even more restrictive deadline legislation that the agency again fails to meet.

In short, a pathological cycle has emerged: agency distrust has begotten failure, breeding further distrust and further failure. The destructive cycle is not simply a product of personality or partisan politics. * * *

The cycle results from the way in which our governmental institutions have responded

---

* Reprinted with permission.

to persistent public schizophrenia concerning environmental protection policy. Public aspirations for environmental quality are relatively uniform and strongly held. But those aspirations contrast sharply with the public's understanding of their implications and its demonstrated unwillingness to take the steps necessary to have those aspirations realized. There is an appearance of harmony underlain by much actual disharmony.

Our governmental institutions have exacerbated rather than redressed the discrepancy. These institutions are founded on deep-seated skepticism of those who wield governmental authority, and they seek, through the checks and balances embraced by our tripartite system, to curb potential governmental overreaching and any branch's abuse of the public trust. In the case of EPA, the illusion of harmony suggested agency abuse of its public trust as public aspirations have gone unrealized. At the same time, the various interests that are in disharmony have exploited to their own advantage the institutional forces of distrust within the government to guard against adverse EPA actions. The upshot has been a pattern of agency crisis and controversy and, as described, a cycle of regulatory failure.

The cycle must now be reversed. The need to reduce dramatically the strain we place on the natural environment is simultaneously immediate and long-term. Our domestic laws reflect that understanding and express a symbolic commitment to that goal. Those laws have achieved, moreover, significant improvement in discrete areas and, in some others, have managed to resist further environmental degradation in the face of a growing economy. For that reason, they warrant great praise. The past twenty years nevertheless reveal that those same laws decline to undertake the concomitant modification of our governmental institutions, and the way we think about them, which is necessary for a fuller realization of our environmental goals. * * * A retrospective on EPA illustrates the causes and effects of the cycle of distrust that has plagued the agency since its inception. More importantly, the inquiry lays the foundation for a more positive discussion of how to avoid repeating the cycle and how instead to facilitate the type of social and institutional innovation necessary for protection of the natural environment.

II. THE ORIGINS OF EPA AND ITS EARLY YEARS: AGENCY CAPTURE AND THE SEEDS OF DISTRUST

Historically, the creation of EPA in 1970 was a modest step in the wake of decades of debate concerning how best to institutionalize natural resource planning and environmental protection within the federal government. * * * President Nixon * * * proposed only the creation of a noncabinet-level federal agency that consolidated the federal pollution standard setting functions then located in fifteen offices within four agencies and one interagency council. The reorganization transferred to EPA only nine of approximately fifty federal programs then pertaining to the environment.

* * *

Simply put, EPA was not trusted. Myriad interest groups were potentially affected by a federal agency responsible for environmental protection. Some favored the agency's establishment and its mandate; many others, however, were threatened by both. All recognized that the agency would face tremendous pressures in its effort to fashion and implement federal environmental protection laws. Each therefore sought to prevent "agency capture," meaning EPA's domination by an adverse competing interest.

In particular, three variants of agency capture theory have predominated and strongly influenced EPA's institutional development. The first hypothesis, identified with the works of Professor Marver Bernstein,[16] concerns the tendency of administrative agencies to ally themselves, over time, with the community they regulate. At the time of EPA's creation, Ralph Nader's organization had published a series of books, relying on Bernstein's thesis, that accused various federal agencies (including the Department of Agriculture's pesticides program) of being in a state of agency capture.[17]

The second thesis, most thoughtfully articulated by Professor Joseph Sax, concerns the tendency of agency personnel to bargain away environmental values as part of the political process.[18] According to Sax, agency officials are simply incapable of providing natural resources with long-term protection from persistent and influential economic interests. The constant demands on the bureaucracy for compromise are too great.

Finally, there are those who fear the agency's capture by its own bureaucracy. Unlike the other two theories, the primary proponents of this view are concerned with the agency paying too *little* attention to the needs of the regulated. * * *

EPA's creation and the manner in which it was initially received within the executive branch, by Congress, and the courts can largely be traced to these three different capture theories. These theories affected EPA's organization within the executive branch, its internal structure, the structure and focus of the federal environmental laws under its jurisdiction, and the amount and character of judicial review of its actions.

A. Executive Branch

Within the Executive Office of the President and Cabinet in 1970, there were two competing philosophies regarding environmental regulation. Those sympathetic to an active federal pollution control program were opposed to its inclusion in a cabinet agency along with the government's traditional natural resource management programs. The historically pro-development bias of those natural resource programs, it was feared, would dominate the agency and undermine pollution control efforts. Conversely, those in the executive branch, including President Nixon, who were concerned about the possible adverse economic impact of environmental protection on existing federal programs, sought to limit the new agency's jurisdiction and maintain presidential control over the agency's decisions.

The final presidential proposal reflected a compromise of these forces. The agency was independent in the sense that it was placed outside the formal jurisdiction of any other agency, but unlike a truly independent agency, its administrator and assistant administrators were to serve at the President's pleasure and formally report to the President

---

[16] See, for example, Marver Bernstein, *Regulating Business by Independent Commission* 79-94 (Princeton U. Press, 1955). * * *

[17] See generally Robert C. Fellmeth, Edward F. Cox & John E. Schulz, *The Nader Report on the Federal Trade Commission* (R.W. Baron, 1969); James S. Turner, *The Chemical Feast: The Ralph Nader Study Group Report on Food Protection and the FDA* (Grossman, 1970); Robert C. Fellmeth, *The Interstate Commerce Commission: The Ralph Nader Study Group Report on the Interstate Commerce Commission and Transportation* (Grossman, 1970); John C. Esposito, *Vanishing Air: The Ralph Nader Study Group Report on Air Pollution* (Grossman, 1970); David Zwick, *Water Wasteland: The Ralph Nader Study Group Report on Water Pollution* (Grossman, 1971). * * *

[18] See generally Joseph L. Sax, *Defending the Environment* (Knopf, 1970).

through OMB. The agency's pollution control jurisdiction was not combined with any of the federal government's natural resource management authority, but neither was the pollution control dimension of that management authority surrendered to the new agency. * * *

In addition, at the same time that the President proposed the creation of EPA, he counterbalanced it with the creation of the National Oceanic and Atmospheric Administration ("NOAA") and National Industrial Pollution Control Council ("NIPCC") within the Department of Commerce. Commerce's pro-business perspective, the President believed, would minimize the chance of NOAA impeding economic activity within the coastal zone. NIPCC was made up of senior officials of major domestic corporations and trade associations and was designed to provide an authoritative source within the government on the adverse economic impact of pollution control. Working with OMB, NIPCC was intended to provide the President with an institutional mechanism for maintaining control over EPA.

Finally, the internal structure of EPA reflected competing agency capture concerns. The Ash Council contemplated that, like the Defense Department, EPA would be organized by function (for example, by abatement, monitoring, enforcement, standard setting, and research). Such a structure would allow the agency to approach the environment as an interrelated system * * *, rather than as a series of discrete media (for example, air, water, and land). There were many perceived advantages to a cross-media approach, including avoidance of the tendency of media-specific programs to ignore their impact on other media.

EPA's first administrator, William Ruckelshaus, however, never fully adopted the contemplated functional, integrated organization. He was not persuaded of the importance of organization in the first instance, and he anticipated objections from members of Congress and the environmental community who, because they were themselves organized by media, would be concerned about the adverse impact of such an organizational scheme on their respective abilities to influence agency policy. The final agency structure was a compromise that still persists today under which EPA is simultaneously organized both by media and by function.

B. Congress

EPA's initial reception in Congress reflects the same tension between different philosophies and agency capture theories. There were those in Congress concerned about EPA's possible capture by the regulated community and about the bureaucratic tendency to give in to the political forces that can be wielded in the executive branch by powerful economic interests opposed to expensive pollution control measures. There were also members of Congress concerned about the dangers of a runaway bureaucracy imposing excessive costs on the nation's economy.

* * *

Congressional committees dominated by those favoring a strong federal pollution control effort secured passage of statutes specifically designed to minimize the possibility of bureaucratic neglect and compromise and of agency capture by regulated industry. Those in Congress who were more wary of the economic costs of pollution control also sought to oversee and influence EPA's work. Neither side favored consolidation of environmental jurisdiction in a few committees. Each wanted to avoid any reduction in leverage over the agency that might result from any loss of committee jurisdiction. As a result, there was great resistance to many of the early efforts to achieve a congressional reorganization of environmental jurisdiction that was similar to that which was occurring within the executive branch.

C. Courts

Finally, the initial relationship between EPA and the courts was likewise heavily influenced by various forms of the capture theory. * * * [T]he courts' opinions reflected two different views of the agency. Some courts viewed the agency's work as the product of an overzealous bureaucracy that acted without proper regard for economic concerns; others "pictured the EPA as a marginally competent but occasionally careless agency that from time to time needs to be reminded of the importance of its statutory goals and warned against bowing to demands from the White House and industry."[40] The effect was the spawning of the so-called "hard look" doctrine and modern administrative law of the 1970s, much of which was fashioned in the context of environmental litigation.

III. THE COLLISION OF INSTITUTIONAL FORCES: THE BREEDING OF REGULATORY FAILURE AND CONTROVERSY

* * *

A. The Breeding of Regulatory Failure

Congress responded to the perception of a national consensus in environmental protection by passing a series of laws in the 1970s that set the stage for institutional conflict and agency failure. * * *

1. From Public Aspiration to Statutory Mandate.

The federal environmental statutes of the early 1970s were dramatic, sweeping, and uncompromising, consistent with the nation's spiritual and moral resolution of the issue. The laws also reflected skepticism and distrust of agency implementation of statutory mandates, consistent with agency capture theory and the general political ill will then existing between the executive and legislative branches. The statutes imposed hundreds of stringent deadlines on the agency and removed much of the agency's substantive discretion in accomplishing them. * * * According to EPA's current administrator, William Reilly, Congress and the courts had imposed 800 deadlines on the agency through 1989.[51] Congress made no effort to bridge the gap between the nation's aspirations for environmental protection and its understanding of the underlying issues and its own capacity for change.

The result was a seemingly never-ending onslaught of impossible agency tasks. * * *

---

[40] [R. Shep] Melnick, *Regulation and the Courts: The Case of the Clean Air Act*, at 371 [Brookings Inst., 1983].

[51] See William K. Reilly, *The Turning Point: An Environmental Vision for the 1990s* (Marshall Lecture at the Natural Resources Defense Council, Nov. 27, 1989), reprinted in 20 Env't Rep. Curr. Dev (BNA) 1386, 1389 (Dec. 8, 1989).

EPA was "told to eliminate water pollution, and all risk from air pollution, prevent hazardous waste from reaching ground water, establish standards for all toxic drinking water contaminants, and register all pesticides."[53] To date, EPA has met only about 14 percent of the congressional deadlines imposed and has had 80 to 85 percent of its major regulations challenged in court.[54]

a. Air Pollution

In the Clean Air Act Amendments of 1970, Congress mandated the achievement by 1975 of national ambient air quality standards ("NAAQS") necessary for the protection of public health (primary standard) and public welfare (secondary standard). Congress also instructed EPA to publish an initial listing of "hazardous" air pollutants within ninety days and then, within 180 days of its listing, to publish for each such pollutant a proposed "emission standard" for the protection of public health. The deadline for final emission standard regulations was 180 days later. Congress established a similarly rigid schedule for EPA's listing of categories of stationary sources that "may contribute significantly to air pollution which causes or contributes to the endangerment of public health or welfare" (ninety days), and an even tighter schedule for promulgation of regulations for new sources (120 days after inclusion as a secondary source for proposal; ninety days after proposal for final promulgation). The Clean Air Act also mandated that the administrator achieve a 90 percent reduction in existing automotive pollutant levels by 1975 (hydrocarbons and carbon monoxide) and 1976 (nitrogen oxides), with a narrow provision for a possible one-year extension.

The administrative task was enormous. It required strict regulation of 20,000 to 40,000 major stationary sources of air pollution, millions of cars and trucks being driven by average citizens, and 275 toxic air pollutants (sixty of which are known or suspected carcinogens), many of which were emitted by industries vital to local economies. In short, the Act challenged not only "business as usual" but "life as usual" in the United States and demanded that EPA immediately seek dramatic change in both. The short time scale necessarily precluded prolonged attention to the tremendous scientific uncertainty associated with the complex mechanics of air pollution. It also did not allow for much serious agency consideration of the relative costs and benefits of air pollution reduction. Neither the NAAQS nor the toxic emission standards allowed for any significant consideration of their economic costs.

Not surprisingly, fewer than 15 percent of the Clean Air Act's deadlines were met. * * * Twenty years later, many areas of the nation still have not met the NAAQS. Both EPA and Congress have given the auto companies numerous extensions of the deadline for meeting 90 percent reduction in emissions of hydrocarbons, carbon monoxide, and nitrogen oxides, and, twenty years later, the companies have still not reduced nitrogen oxides by 90 percent. * * *

---

[53] Council on Environmental Quality, *Sixteenth Annual Report* 14 (U.S. Govt Printing Office, 1985) * * *.

[54] EESI, *Statutory Deadlines [in Environmental Legislation: Necessary But Need Improvement]* at ii, 12 [(Envir. & Energy Study Inst. and Envtl. L. Inst., 1985)] (14% compliance refers to all environmental statutory deadlines, 86% of which apply to EPA) * * *.

b. Water Pollution

The Federal Water Pollution Control Act Amendments of 1972 took a similar approach. The 1972 enactment sought fishable and swimmable waters everywhere by 1983 and zero discharge of pollutants by 1985, and it made unlawful any discharge of pollutants into navigable waters absent a permit issued by EPA. The act instructed EPA to require through the permitting process that industry secure the "best practicable control technology currently available" ("BPT") by 1977 and "best available technology economically achievable" ("BAT") by 1984. Section 306 of the Act compelled EPA to require new sources of water pollution to achieve effluent reduction "achievable through the application of the best available demonstrated control technology" ("BDT"). EPA was supposed to promulgate effluent guidelines by October 1973 and permit limitations by December 1974.

The required administrative undertaking was no less daunting than that posed by the Clean Air Act. There are at least 68,000 point sources of water pollution requiring federal permits and probably thousands more. * * * The zero discharge goal was plainly impossible and the fishable/swimmable mandate could not, in any event, be met by the strict technology-based effluent reduction requirements of the permit program; the large amount of nonpoint pollution not covered by the Act's permitting program was sufficient, by itself, to prevent EPA's success. By 1985, only 18 percent of the deadlines established by federal water pollution legislation had been met. As with the Clean Air Act, none of the deadlines for compliance with environmental quality standards was met.

c. Pesticides, Toxic Substances, and Hazardous Waste

In the 1972 amendments to the Federal Insecticide, Fungicide, and Rodenticide Act ("FIFRA"), Congress gave EPA just four years to review approximately 50,000 pesticides that had previously been registered under far more permissive statutory requirements. For registration, EPA had to determine that the pesticide's intended use would not cause "unreasonable adverse effects on the environment" when used "in accordance with widespread and commonly recognized practice." The 1976 deadline, like others, proved impossible. * * * Before recent changes in the pesticides law, EPA's rate of re-registration suggested that the agency would not complete the re-registration process until 2024.

The Toxic Substances Control Act ("TSCA"), which became law in 1976, asked EPA to review approximately 50,000 to 55,000 chemicals then in commerce as well as each of the 1,000 new chemicals introduced each year to determine if they "may present an unreasonable risk of injury to health or the environment." By 1985, EPA had performed the necessary health assessments on fewer than 100 of the chemicals in commerce.

Finally, congressional dictates to EPA regarding the regulation and cleanup of hazardous wastes were no less overwhelming. In the Resource Conservation and Recovery Act of 1976 ("RCRA"), enacted just ten days after TSCA, Congress gave EPA only eighteen months to promulgate regulations regarding the identification, generation, transportation, treatment, storage, and disposal of hazardous wastes. In the Comprehensive Environmental Response Compensation and Liability Act ("CERCLA"), enacted in 1980, Congress authorized EPA to take action to clean up inactive and abandoned hazardous waste sites either by filing lawsuits against those who contributed to the sites to force them to clean up the sites themselves, or by arranging for government cleanup, followed by lawsuits for reimbursement from contributors.

These mandates on hazardous waste control and cleanup may have proved the most difficult to achieve. There are approximately 650,000 generators of hazardous wastes producing 250 million metric tons of such waste each year. There are 5,000 facilities authorized to treat, store, or dispose of hazardous waste and approximately 27,000 abandoned hazardous waste sites, 2,000 of which will require federal action. The Office of Technology Assessment estimates that there are also about 600,000 active or former solid waste disposal facilities, 10,000 of which may require federal action. EPA did not meet any of the 1978 RCRA deadlines and as of 1989 had completed cleanup at fewer than fifty abandoned sites.

2. The Coalition for Failure

These series of impossible tasks did more than guarantee repeated agency failure; they triggered a chain of events that profoundly influenced EPA's institutional development and the evolution of federal environmental law. Those who supported these statutory mandates sought judicial review and enlisted some in Congress to oversee EPA's implementation. Their aim was to guard against EPA's abdication of its statutory responsibilities. At the same time, those who were opposed to the statutory mandates but who were unable to muster the political capital to defeat their passage, were nonetheless quite successful in enlisting others in Congress, the executive branch, and some courts to impede EPA's implementation of the mandates.

a. Agency Funding

Forces within Congress were able to secure passage of various environmental statutes that reflected the nation's aspirations for environmental quality, but a very different set of institutional forces was responsible for appropriating funds for the implementation of those laws. Members of the appropriations committees typically did not share the environmental zeal of those on the committees who drafted the laws. * * * Such congressional skeptics were joined in their efforts by those in the executive branch, especially in the White House and OMB, who shared their policy outlook and who, accordingly, routinely requested less funding for EPA than Congress ultimately provided. This coalition for modest EPA funding proved virtually unbeatable.

* * *

Of course, during this same period, Congress dramatically increased the scope of EPA's statutory responsibilities. * * * [F]ollowing the passage of air and water pollution legislation in the early 1970s, Congress added FIFRA to EPA's mandate in 1973, the Safe Drinking Water Act in 1974, and TSCA and RCRA in 1976. Further programmatic expansions were called for by the 1977 Clean Air Act amendments, the 1977 Clean Water Act, and CERCLA, passed in 1980. Finally, amendments to RCRA in 1984 and to CERCLA in 1986 further exacerbated the gap between statutory responsibilities and agency funding by imposing even greater and more rigid statutory responsibilities on the agency.

* * *

Hence, Congress has spoken with two different voices to EPA. Each voice reflected the distinct legislative path followed by the authorization and appropriation processes within Congress. Legislators demanded immediate action requiring a massive agency undertaking. At the same time, however, they never provided a remotely commensurate level of agency funding. Ironically, therefore, while Congress was willing to ask American business and the public to curtail pollution, regardless of the cost, in order to ensure public health, Congress itself refused to fund the level of agency activity necessary for even a good faith effort to implement such an ambitious program.

b. Executive Branch Oversight

OMB was naturally hostile to the federal environmental statutes of the 1970s because those laws took little account of their economic impact. The White House exhibited a similar bias, perhaps because of its enhanced sensitivity to those national economic indicators that are often utilized to measure the relative success of an administration. Such concerns likely prompted the White House's and OMB's persistent requests for low funding of EPA's environmental programs.

* * *

The OMB review process began, not coincidentally, just a few months after EPA commenced operations, and has gradually and inexorably increased in significance ever since. Under President Nixon, the process was dubbed the "Quality of Life Review" and focused primarily on the economic impact of EPA rules.[119] Under President Ford, EPA was required to submit an inflation impact statement along with every proposed major regulation or rule.[120] President Carter issued an executive order requiring each agency to prepare a regulatory analysis for every proposed regulation that either would cost the economy more than $100 million or threatened to cause a major price increase.[121] The executive order directed OMB to oversee the order's implementation. Under all three presidents, frequent and significant confrontations resulted between OMB and EPA concerning proposed EPA rules.

* * *

* * * During 1985, 1986, and 1987, EPA revised 74.5, 66.2, and 66.2 percent, respectively, of agency rules reviewed by OMB. When disagreements between EPA and OMB have arisen, OMB has invariably won.[136] * * *

* * *

c. Judicial Oversight

Partly to prevent agency capture, Congress encouraged judicial oversight of EPA by including citizen suit and judicial review provisions in each of the environmental statutes and by requiring EPA to follow decisionmaking procedures more rigorous than those normally employed in informal notice and comment rulemaking. The citizen suit provisions routinely allowed successful plaintiffs to recover their attorneys' fees. Both environmental organizations and industry took advantage of the increased judicial access and together challenged between 80 and 85 percent of EPA's major decisions.

---

[119] See [Stanley] Bach, *Governmental Constraints* [*in Environmental Regulation,* in Nat'l Res. Council, ed.] at 168-171, 173-74, 178-81 * * *.

[120] See Exec. Order 11821, 3 C.F.R. 926 (1971-1975), amended by Exec. Order 11949, 3 CFR 161 (1977).

[121] Exec. Order 12044, 3 C.F.R. 152 (1979).

[136] See *OMB Said to Have Influenced About One-Third of Regulations Proposed by EPA in 1986,* 17 Env't Rep. (BNA) 1616 (Jan. 1987).

The deadlines and mandatory duties contained in the various federal laws, along with their carefully crafted legislative histories, provided environmentalists with enormous leverage over EPA through litigation, which they used as their dominant tool to influence agency decisions. Whenever EPA failed to meet a deadline, or otherwise to satisfy a statutory obligation, which was inevitably often, environmentalists used litigation to compel EPA to negotiate with them in drafting a consent decree. Environmentalists utilized the consent decree and the threat of contempt sanctions to control the agency's future actions. The filing of lawsuits also provided environmentalists with media events that provided publicity for their cause and incidentally aided fundraising efforts. The media was naturally receptive to accusations of agency malfeasance, and the result was a steady stream of negative articles about EPA in the national press.

There were likewise those who have had tremendous economic incentives to use litigation to challenge EPA decisions. EPA's regulations impose huge costs on a wide segment of economic activity; indeed, no significant economic activity has been unaffected. * * *

* * * [T]he judiciary did not shy away from careful examination of EPA's actions. Especially during EPA's early years, courts of appeals frequently rejected the agency's efforts to relax the statutory mandates through "loose" construction of their terms. The courts also often remanded agency rulemaking for further proceedings based on perceived inadequacies in the rulemaking record. Environmentalists benefitted from many of the courts' more expansive constructions of the federal environmental laws. Industry, however, benefitted from many of the judicial remands of agency rules. * * *

In addition, even when industry plaintiffs fared poorly in their initial efforts to persuade courts of appeals to require or permit EPA's consideration of the adverse economic impact of its rules on business, individual industry defendants in EPA enforcement actions appear to have been more successful in their efforts to have trial courts fashion remedies in response to economic factors. One explanation for the disparity is the differing perspectives of the district courts and the courts of appeals: courts of appeals are possibly more influenced by academic theories of agency capture than are district courts; district courts, unlike courts of appeals, are closer to the impact on local economics of applying the law according to its strict terms.

d. Congressional Oversight

Perhaps the most important (and most often overlooked) of the institutional forces that have buffeted EPA has been the operation of congressional oversight, long referred to as Congress's "neglected" function. Congress did not quietly disappear following its passage of the federal environmental protection laws under EPA's jurisdiction. It has actively overseen the agency's implementation of those laws through informal agency contacts, General Accounting Office and Office of Technology Assessment investigations, agency reporting requirements, formal oversight hearings, confirmation hearings, appropriation hearings, appropriation riders, inspector general reports, and amendments of the laws themselves.

* * * EPA's exposure to congressional criticism has been especially great because of the structure (or lack thereof) of congressional oversight. EPA's jurisdiction is so sweeping, and therefore important to so many interest groups, that the demand for its

oversight has grown commensurately among the committees and subcommittees in Congress. Most committees can find some nexus between their assigned jurisdiction and some aspect of EPA's work.

* * *

e. Congressional Prescription

Congress has not confined itself to overseeing EPA's work. In the aftermath of repeated regulatory failures, Congress has favored passing increasingly detailed environmental statutes to guard against agency dereliction in the first instance. Oversight therefore has been supplemented with prescription.

Amendments to the Clean Air Act and Clean Water Act in 1977, to the Clean Water Act, CERCLA, FIFRA, RCRA, the Safe Drinking Water Act, and TSCA during the 1980s, and to the Clean Air Act in 1990, all exhibit the same trend. Each eliminated substantial EPA discretion, imposed more deadlines, and included more prescription. * * *

* * *

IV. THE TRAGEDY OF DISTRUST: THE STIFLING OF ENVIRONMENTAL PROTECTION

EPA is plainly in a dilemma. The agency strives to be responsive to both the environmentalists' vision and the regulated community's pragmatism, but ultimately satisfies neither. EPA is also a pawn in an ongoing struggle between the executive and legislative branches for control over national policy. Finally, EPA is pushed in one direction by public aspirations and pulled in the other direction by the absence of public willingness to change and by the public's proven incapacity for self-sacrifice.

To be sure, EPA is itself responsible for some of its failures and for the generation of some of its controversies; it is not solely a victim of historical and institutional circumstances. As with other federal agencies, there have been many instances of mismanagement and poor decisionmaking for which agency officials deserve to be held accountable. But placed in proper perspective, most of EPA's reported failures and controversies seem more justly viewed as the product of institutional conflict and public schizophrenia than as the result of systematic EPA dereliction or incompetence.

EPA's dilemma could nonetheless be viewed positively as a small price to pay in the United States' first effort to reshape its relationship with its natural environment. Certainly this nation's accomplishments in seeking to produce a legal regime for environmental protection have been extraordinary. In relatively few years, the nation's laws have been dramatically rewritten. Viewed from this perspective, repeated regulatory failure could be seen as the necessary cost of our attempt to address pressing environmental problems in the face of scientific uncertainty. * * *

The conflict and controversy surrounding EPA during the last twenty years could be similarly viewed as a necessary evil, as the inevitable consequence of administrative agency implementation of fundamental social change in our system of government, which heavily depends on the actions of each branch being overseen by the others. Isolated excesses may have resulted, and there may have been cases of overreaching, but the advantages of intense oversight have been overwhelming.

* * *

Close judicial and congressional scrutiny of EPA has clearly also had significant benefits. It is likely that an active judiciary improved the quality of EPA decisionmaking in some cases. And, as was the case in Congress's exposure of EPA's initial mishandling of the Superfund program, persistent congressional examination of EPA can be credited for having revealed instances of agency neglect and corruption and of OMB over-reaching. * * *

There is also some advantage to the public in the way environmental laws have evolved in response to repeated agency failure. The statutes allow for less agency discretion while arguably reflecting greater congressional assumption of responsibility for making public policy. Congress was faulted for unfairly (and improperly) passing the buck to EPA in the environmental statutes of the 1970s. In the more prescriptive environmental statutes, Congress is now making many of the difficult policy determinations necessary to fashion environmental quality standards.

* * *

Appreciation of the benefits of the current institutional regime does not, however, mean that its adverse effects are insubstantial. Nor does it mean that significant reform is unnecessary. * * * There is a growing consensus that fundamental changes in approach will be necessary for the country to reach acceptable levels of environmental protection while maintaining a high standard of living. A detailed accounting of the ways in which existing institutional forces have impeded federal environmental protection efforts over the last twenty years strongly suggests, moreover, that institutional reform will be required for such fundamental change to be achieved.

A. Loss of Public Confidence and Agency Self-Esteem

Included among the most immediate and persistent impacts of the current institutional scheme are loss of public confidence in EPA and loss of the agency's confidence in itself. EPA's repeated regulatory failures and frequent controversies created a public image of an incompetent, neglectful, and at times even corrupt agency. A myth of scientific incompetence resulted, which EPA can ill afford, but which others may have an incentive to perpetuate.

The level of distrust in EPA, moreover, is inconsistent with the needs of an administrative agency responsible for the implementation of federal environmental laws. An important lesson of the last twenty years is that EPA simply cannot do its job effectively without greater public confidence in the agency. * * *

* * *

[T]he absence of public confidence has exacerbated the gap between the public's and the agency's perception of risk, undermining the validity of the agency's efforts to manage risk. EPA's Science Advisory Board recently concluded that "the remaining and emerging environmental risks considered most serious by the general public today are different from those considered most serious by the technical professionals charged with reducing environmental risk."[260] Not only does the public fail to accept EPA's assessment of the

---

[260] EPA Science Advisory Board, *Reducing Risk* [*: Setting Priorities and Strategies for Environmental Protection*] at 12 [(Sept. 1990)].

relative risks of various hazards, but EPA, too, fails to appreciate the public's distinct assessment. * * *

* * *

B. Polarization of Debate and Proliferation of Litigation

Another significant adverse effect of the current scheme is its tendency to polarize the debate on environmental issues and to encourage litigation. Environmentalists, the regulated community, Congress, and even EPA repeatedly rely on extreme allegations in seeking public support for their respective positions. * * *

* * *

One harmful result of such issue polarization is excessive reliance on litigation to resolve conflicts. Indeed, agency decisionmaking becomes a mere prelude to litigation. * * *

C. Wasted Resources and Misdirected Priorities

The legacy of distrust created by the current institutional scheme also creates tremendous delay and poorly allocates the limited agency resources among competing priorities. The combination of impossible statutory mandates and increased judicial access has created a situation in which more than 80 percent of EPA's major decisions are finally decided by formal negotiated settlement or court decision. EPA officials are compelled to spend as much as 90 percent of their time defending their actions in court and in congressional hearings. They are left little time to make thoughtful, considered determinations and are forced to spend excessive time on a few issues in order to satisfy the various overseers.

* * *

Another adverse effect of excessive oversight of EPA is that it has caused the agency to go "underground" in its lawmaking. To avoid overseers, EPA has increasingly resorted to less formal means of announcing agency policy determinations. Instead of promulgating rules pursuant to the Administrative Procedure Act, EPA now frequently issues guidance memoranda and directives. Also, many important agency rulings are not reflected in generic rulemaking, but in individual permit decisions. OMB oversight is thereby avoided, and judicial review of agency action is limited.

Excessive congressional, OMB, and judicial oversight also has resulted in poor allocation of agency resources and skewed national environmental priorities. Each overseer can use his or her leverage (that is, power to delay or reduce appropriations, hold up confirmation of agency appointments, create bad publicity, eliminate agency discretion, or impose appropriations riders to redefine agency priorities), but the end result is unlikely to reflect any broad or thoughtful determination of environmental priorities. In fact, quite the opposite is true.

* * *

The competence of congressional staff to draft environmental legislation containing increasingly detailed prescriptions can also be questioned. Because authority among congressional committees is so fragmented, it is extremely difficult, if not impossible, for any one committee to undertake a broad, coordinated look at a complex problem. * * *

Finally, there is also some reason for questioning the wisdom of exacting judicial review of EPA decisions. * * * Some question the extent to which judicial review prompted process changes within the agency that may have improved its decisions. Other commentators question the competency of the courts to second-guess the policy judgments and complex technical determinations underlying EPA's major regulatory decisions. * * * Finally, because courts are not in a position to make a considered judgment concerning how the agency might best allocate its limited resources among competing priorities, court orders force agency choices that may misallocate those resources.

For all of these reasons, EPA's statutory priorities are diverging from the agency's own perception of the relative risks presented by various environmental hazards. Agency staff believe that too little attention has been paid to certain hazards and, at least in relative terms, too much to others. In addition, the demands for immediate results and agency action made by Congress and the courts have left EPA with little room for long-term planning, which, as noted above, is an essential aspect of environmental protection.

D. Chilling of Innovation

The worst result of the current administrative scheme is that it has undermined environmental protection by chilling agency and congressional innovation. Increased statutory prescription comes at the expense of agency discretion and flexibility. Intense agency oversight, repeated regulatory failure, and frequent controversy likewise discourage agency initiative.

EPA officials have long recognized the need for administrative experimentation and reorganization. Congress, however, has increasingly denied the agency the option of exercising administrative innovation. Moreover, even when the opportunity remains, EPA officials have often shied away from innovation because of actual and anticipated objections from those elsewhere in the executive branch, the regulated community, Congress, and environmental organizations who are suspicious of the agency's motives.

* * *

V. CONCLUSION: REVERSING THE CYCLE: INSTILLING TRUST AND PROMOTING INNOVATION

Reversing the current pathological cycle of regulatory failure, crisis, and controversy will not be easy. * * *

* * * The issues are complicated and perhaps too complex for many members of the public to grasp. Moreover, because the benefits of environmental controls are realized over generations while the cost to society is immediate, few politicians are likely to have the electoral incentives necessary to embrace the kinds of societal changes now needed. Finally, interest group politics, which have rooted themselves deeply into modern democratic political processes, exacerbate the problem by promoting incremental, fragmented decisionmaking.

* * *

One * * * reform would be to reduce the level of distrust directed at EPA by other governmental institutions. Much of the distrust is derived from an intellectual mistake concerning the possibility of EPA's capture. Second, some of the unintended organizational mistakes of the past need to be redressed. With the benefit of hindsight, we can better organize the federal environmental protection agency, reducing conflict and facilitating environmental decisionmaking by the government. Finally, the existing gap between public aspirations for environmental quality and public understanding of the issues needs to be bridged, as does the gulf between public and agency perceptions concerning the nature of environmental risk.

A. Dispelling the Myth of Agency Capture

Much of the momentum behind the constant clashes that have marked EPA's existence originates in concerns about agency capture. These concerns have been needlessly destructive of effective environmental protection. There is good reason to believe that the risk of agency capture would be slight, even without the intense oversight mechanisms that various competing factions have utilized to prevent capture. Indeed, the only plausible justification for the intensity of each of those mechanisms is the threat now presented by the excesses of the others. * * *

No single interest group is likely to capture an agency with characteristics similar to those of EPA. Unlike the agencies considered by the original agency capture theorists, EPA has a "social mission"; and unlike agencies such as the Interstate Commerce Commission, EPA does not manage a distinct kind of economic activity. EPA is subject to a complex set of constituencies. There is no single dominant interest that threatens to capture the agency.

Contrary to the assumption of agency capture theory, public interest in environmental issues has not been fleeting. National environmental organizations have enjoyed sustained public support. Technological advances have greatly enhanced the ability of such citizen groups to marshall public support and to influence agency decisionmaking. And, conversely, the agency is itself capable of avoiding decay and capture by enlisting the environmental organizations in support of controversial agency actions.

In the case of environmental protection, the regulated community or industry does not speak with one voice, as agency capture theory assumes. Because environmental protection laws sweep so broadly, those affected are an exceedingly diverse group. Accordingly, their interests frequently conflict, making capture improbable. Companies that have already invested substantial sums in pollution control are less likely, for instance, to support the relaxation of restrictions that would result in their competitors avoiding similar expenditures. Such companies generally desire regulatory stability. The manufacturers of pollution control equipment, a sizeable industry in itself, resist deregulatory efforts, as do states and localities, which have become dependent on federal largesse in aiding their own pollution control efforts.

In addition, because employees of agencies like EPA tend to share the agency's social mission, the agency staff is less susceptible to ideological conversion by those regulated. Indeed, quite the opposite might be true. The greater risk could be their tendency to discount the needs of the regulated, which serve as a useful counterweight to the inherent difficulty of evaluating environmental benefits. Nor, contrary to agency capture theory, does there appear to be any significant threat of agency corruption presented by the lure of career opportunities in the private sector. Past experience indicates that agency employees enhance their employment prospects by engaging in more aggressive action, rather than by appearing to coddle future employers.

* * *

It is nevertheless difficult to be optimistic that oversight of EPA will become less intense or adversarial in the near future. To be sure, the judiciary already appears to have cut back on the degree of its scrutiny of agency decisionmaking. And there is reason to believe that Congress may succeed in reducing OMB's excesses, which may have the incidental effect of reducing Congress's incentive to engage in an unhealthy escalating competition with OMB for agency control.

The more likely result, however, is that Congress will prove to be a much tougher nut to crack. A shift in judicial philosophy has resulted because of the power of presidential appointment of federal judges. And if a change occurs with regard to OMB oversight, it will be because of Congress's great power over the purse strings. Realistically, there is currently no such countervailing authority in a position to compel Congress to change its ways.

* * *

B. Reorganizing the Institutional Framework for Federal Environmental Protection to Eliminate the Vestiges of Distrust

The practical hurdles that may prevent congressional reorganization of its own decisionmaking processes with regard to federal environmental policy need not preclude Congress and the White House from now revisiting how best to organize and structure a federal environmental agency. * * *

* * * As members of both parties now appear to recognize, EPA should be elevated to cabinet status. Contrary to what some might think, EPA's elevation would not be mere window dressing. It could provide a meaningful opportunity for agency renewal and a fitting occasion for reversing the pathological cycle of distrust that has plagued the agency over the last twenty years.

For example, the endorsement of the agency's mission implicit in such an elevation in status would likely reinvigorate the agency. Agency morale could significantly improve, which would in turn enhance employee retention and recruitment. It would also have the added benefit of ameliorating some of the agency's historical problems. The agency's leverage within the executive branch would be greater, making it theoretically less subject to OMB's influence and providing the agency head with more ready access to the President when controversies arise. In addition, because EPA's elevation would increase the prestige and visibility of a presidential appointment at the new agency, the reorganization might make it more likely that those nominated and confirmed to top positions are reasonably capable.

The creation of a cabinet-level EPA would be one important step, but more would be necessary to redress the institutional vestiges of past political compromises. In particular, fragmentation of environmental protection authority within the executive branch needs to be reduced. To be sure, fragmentation probably can never be eliminated, given the huge scope of activities affecting environmental quality. But the degree of fragmentation can be substantially lessened, with a concomitant increase in integration and decrease in interagency conflict.

To that end, serious consideration should now be given to transferring to the new department the various pollution control activities that have remained in agencies other than EPA. The National Oceanic and Atmospheric Agency ("NOAA") is a good example.

NOAA is currently within the Department of Commerce largely as a byproduct of President Nixon's 1970 compromise with Commerce Secretary Maurice Stans, who was concerned about Nixon's creation of EPA. It would seem sensible to combine EPA's and NOAA's two jurisdictions in one cabinet department. A strong argument can likewise be made in favor of merging into that same department another relic of past political compromise: the Army Corps of Engineers' jurisdiction over wetland pollution. Other areas of federal environmental protection jurisdiction whose transfer to a Department of Environmental Protection could achieve greater integration and reduce conflict include: surface mining control at the Office of Surface Mining in the Department of the Interior, endangered species protection at the Fish and Wildlife Service in Interior, remaining parts of the pesticides program still at Agriculture and elsewhere, and pollution control aspects of scattered programs within the Department of Energy and the Nuclear Regulatory Commission. Greater consolidation of authority is needed if the new department is going to fulfill its stated mission of being responsible for fashioning pollution control standards, including those ultimately applicable to federal as well as private activities.

Within the existing agency, a shift in perspective may now be in order. While the current media-specific, command and control approach has certainly achieved much success, the returns are diminishing. The current system is very inefficient, at times counterproductive, and ultimately defended as the most we can do in a "second-best" world. The perceived advantages of organizing the agency by function to facilitate a cross-media approach may be substantial; and, even if overstated, they are promising enough to be worthy of greater emphasis and experimentation.

* * *

Another change needed within the agency itself is greater emphasis on long-term planning. * * *

Finally, the institutional framework within the Executive Office of the President warrants modification. OMB has been the lead unit within the EOP during EPA's twenty years, while the president's Council on Environmental Quality ("CEQ") has had a diminishing voice. As a result, one perspective dominates the dialogue with EPA; because of OMB's basic opposition to the precepts underlying the federal environmental laws, the upshot has been an unhealthy, escalating competition with Congress for agency control.

* * * There is, at bottom, a pressing need for an "environmental policy decisionmaking unit" within EOP to serve the clearinghouse function that OMB has served, but with a broader outlook. There needs to be an office within EOP with the clout of the Council of Economic Advisors or even the National Security Council that is in a position to give thoughtful consideration to the many environmental protection issues that cut across important questions of national policy. Environmental protection must become fully integrated in the workings of the entire federal government—ranging throughout the implementation of federal tax, energy, agriculture, and international policies—which is a task beyond the capability of any one agency outside the EOP. * * *

* * *

C. Bridging the Gap Between Public Aspirations and Understanding and Public and Agency Perception of Environmental Risk

Only public education, including a sustained effort to promote environmental literacy in the public, will bridge the gap that has persisted between public aspirations for environmental quality and public understanding of the complexity of the associated trade-offs. Only bilateral education of both the public and EPA will bridge the recent gap that has developed between agency and public perception of the nature of environmental risk and of environmental protection priorities.

A revolution has taken place in this nation's environmental laws over the last twenty years. No accompanying revolution occurred, however, in the nation's classrooms to enhance the public's appreciation of the underpinnings of the environmental laws and their ramifications. More environmental educators and fewer environmental lawyers are now necessary. Creative environmental curricula need to be developed and made a regular part of secondary school education. The subject matter warrants intensive coverage as an independent course in every student's curriculum.

Public education will also do much to bridge the gap between public and agency perceptions of environmental risks and priorities, but more than that will be necessary. The gap finds its roots in the very different perspective each brings to the pollution problem. Much of the public starts with the premise that pollution is morally and culturally unacceptable; by contrast, the agency professional seeks to determine the optimal level of pollution for a specific human activity at a particular location. Little common ground exists at the outset, and whatever there might have been is quickly lost in the aftermath of repeated agency regulatory failure and its repeated denunciation by elected representatives, environmentalists, and industry.

To bridge the existing chasm, EPA must supplement formal public education with candid explanations of the competing factors, including the scientific uncertainty underlying its decisions. In addition, EPA must not view the dialogue with the public as a one-way street, with the "expert" agency having the responsibility to educate the "ignorant" public. The success of a program of public risk management depends on its acceptance by the public. EPA therefore must educate itself about public perception of risk at the same time that it seeks to enhance the public's understanding of the agency's perspective. Risk assessment is not simply a technical matter. It also depends on value judgments that turn on basic notions of justice and equity. Both EPA and the public therefore have much to learn from each other. Moreover, when EPA ignores the public's distinct perception of risk, the agency's resolution of acceptable levels of risk and relative agency priorities will find little acceptance where the agency needs it most: in the public. If nothing else, the last twenty years make clear that EPA cannot afford the tragedy associated with that result.

NOTES

1. One of Professor Lazarus's suggestions for breaking the vicious circle of EPA failure and distrust is the elevation of EPA to a cabinet-level department. Indeed, he observed when he wrote the foregoing article in 1991 that "Congress seemed close to passing the needed legislation." 54 LAW & CONTEMP. PROBS. at 368, n.357. Although the legislation was not enacted at that time, it was considered in the next Congress and was again close to enactment in 1994. It was killed, however, in the crossfire over "regulatory reform" when an amendment regarding risk assessment was grafted onto the bill. *Risk Assessment: Compromise Risk Language From USDA Bill Not Enough to Revive EPA Cabinet Legislation,* 18 Chem. Reg. Rep. (BNA) 892 (Oct. 7, 1994). Prospects for enactment of the necessary legislation remained dim as of this publication in 1996.

2. Lazarus's suggestion for internal EPA reorganization along functional lines has fared somewhat better. The agency has undertaken a reorganization designed to promote multimedia considerations in the implementation of environmental law. Insofar as the statutory scheme remains fragmented, however, the agency's medium-specific structure remains largely intact. *See generally* EPA, ENFORCEMENT AND COMPLIANCE ASSURANCE ACCOMPLISHMENTS REPORT—FY 1994, EPA 300-R-95-004 (1995).

3. His third suggestion—a shift in perspective within the Executive Office of the President—has been largely satisfied during the Clinton Administration. The Office of Management and Budget no longer plays such an adversarial role vis-a-vis the EPA, and although the Council on Environmental Quality also has a somewhat diminished role in environmental policy, the newly-created White House Office of Environmental Policy has occupied a prominent position within the Executive Office regarding environmental matters. *See General Policy: Administration's Proposal on Policy Office Should Be Dropped, Senators Tell White House,* 25 Env't Rep. (BNA) 631 (Aug. 5, 1994).

4. The relationship between the President (and his Executive Office) and the EPA raises several interesting issues. Although the EPA is technically part of the executive branch of government, there has historically been sufficient tension between the President (and his Executive Office) and administrative agencies—including but by no means limited to the EPA—that the agencies are often referred to as "the fourth branch." *See generally Symposium on Administrative Law: "The Uneasy Constitutional Status of the Administrative Agencies," April 4, 1986: Part II: Presidential Oversight of Regulatory Decisionmaking,* 36 AM. U. L. REV. 443 (1987).

5. For further reading on the subject of the EPA, see MARC K. LANDY ET AL., THE ENVIRONMENTAL PROTECTION AGENCY: ASKING THE WRONG QUESTIONS (1990). Using the case study approach, the authors attribute the shortcomings in the EPA's performance to its "penchant for asking the wrong questions," and suggest how the agency might instead ask "good questions." *See also* JONATHAN LASH, SEASON OF SPOILS: THE REAGAN ADMINISTRATION'S ATTACK ON THE ENVIRONMENT (1984) (regarding the Gorsuch period).

C. The Courts

The judicial branch has played a significant role in the development of environmental law. In the late 1960s and early 1970s, federal courts began according private citizens fairly broad standing rights to challenge agency action. *See, e.g., Sierra Club v. Morton,* 405 U.S. 727 (1972), and *Citizens to Preserve Overton Park v. Volpe,* 401 U.S. 402 (1971). These precedents made the courts an attractive forum for citizens to press environmental claims, including newly-conceived claims under existing statutes. In addition, more than 2,000 suits challenging environmentally-sensitive projects have been brought under the National Environmental Policy Act which, because it made no provision for administrative agency enforcement, placed the courts squarely in the center of numerous environmental disputes. Furthermore, the newly-enacted pollution control statutes triggered an explosion of environmental litigation—citizen suits against the EPA to force the agency to implement the newly-enacted provisions, suits by both regulated entities and environmental interests challenging the EPA's newly-promulgated regulations, enforcement actions by the EPA against regulated entities, and newly-authorized citizen suits against regulated entities for alleged violations of the new environmental statutes and regulations.

This subchapter focuses on three aspects of the complex role of the courts in shaping environmental law. The first selection analyzes the impact of judicial decisions on the EPA's programs and policies. The second article examines the phenomenon of citizen suits under the environmental statutes. The third addresses environmental litigation outside of the statutory context—common law "toxic tort" suits alleging personal injury due to exposure to chemicals or pollutants.

The following article was written by Rosemary O'Leary, a lawyer and political scientist. She presents empirical findings of her examination of the impact of federal court litigation—including cases filed but not adjudicated—on the EPA. While she detects both positive and negative impacts, Professor O'Leary highlights the ad hoc method by which federal litigation has redirected the agency's priorities.

THE IMPACT OF FEDERAL COURT DECISIONS ON THE POLICIES AND ADMINISTRATION OF THE U.S. ENVIRONMENTAL PROTECTION AGENCY
Rosemary O'Leary
41 Admin. L. Rev. 549 (1989)*

* * *

This work presents the findings of a recently completed three-year study of the impact

---

* Reprinted with permission.

of federal court decisions on the policies and administration of the United States Environmental Protection Agency (EPA) in all seven of its major statutory areas.[1] * * * *

* * *

DATA SOURCES AND ANALYSIS

Using the LEXIS and WESTLAW legal databases, all cases in which the EPA was either a plaintiff or defendant, from the inception of the agency in 1970 through 1988 in each of its seven major statutory areas, were generated. These data were verified, and at times supplemented by environmental reporters published by the Bureau of National Affairs and the Environmental Law Institute, as well as by EPA records. Settlement agreements were derived from the EPA, the Department of Justice, and the courts. Over 2,000 federal court decisions were read and analyzed. Nine key components of each case were examined: (1) the laws involved, (2) the plaintiffs, (3) the defendants, (4) the subject matter, (5) the outcome of case, (6) judicial actions, (7) the court order(s), (8) the response of the EPA, and (9) follow-up actions by the court and the parties to the suit. These cases were augmented by interviews of over three dozen EPA officials, as well as interviews with staff from the Office of Management and Budget (OMB) and the Congressional Budget Office (CBO).

* * *

FINDINGS OF STUDY

A major conclusion of this study is that federal courts have had a significant effect on the policies and administration of the EPA. The following sections describe first, how federal courts have affected the EPA. Second, the policy and administrative consequences of such judicial agency interaction are explained.

Patterns of Judicial Intervention

Judicial intervention into disputes concerning the EPA were categorized into five groups * * *. Those groups are: (1) cases in which the mere filing of a lawsuit, without judicial action, has evoked a change in the EPA; (2) cases in which courts have upheld the agency's position completely, without yielding changes in the agency's policies and administration; (3) cases in which judges, who have been passive and unwilling to intervene in the affairs of the EPA, have issued decisions that nonetheless have affected the agency's policies and administration; (4) cases in which judges have legitimately used their discretionary powers deliberately to affect agency actions; and (5) cases in which judges have gone beyond the normal limits of judicial activism to evoke change in the agency.

* * * Thus, the courts have been neither entirely passive nor totally aggressive. Instead,

---

[1] The EPA's seven major statutes are: the Clean Air Act (CAA); the Comprehensive Environmental Response, Compensation and Liability Act (CERCLA); the Federal Insecticide, Fungicide, and Rodenticide Act (FIFRA); the Federal Water Pollution Control Act (FWPCA or "Clean Water Act'"); the Resource Conservation and Recovery Act (RCRA); the Safe Drinking Water Act (SDWA); and the Toxic Substances Control Act (TSCA).

the actions of judges are seen to fall along a continuum. A discussion of each major group of cases along that continuum follows.

Filing of Lawsuits Prompts Changes

At one end of the judicial intervention spectrum are cases in which the mere filing of a lawsuit, without judicial action, has evoked a change in the EPA's policies and administration. In this context, the federal courts have been used as tools by plaintiffs to get the agency's attention and to impress upon the EPA the seriousness of the plaintiff's grievances. In one case, for example, the EPA reversed what EPA career staff referred to as a "purely political decision"[9] not to regulate the chemical formaldehyde in response to the filing of a lawsuit.[10] In another instance, the mere filing of a lawsuit prompted an EPA policy reversal concerning liquids in landfills. Subsequent lawsuits coupled with political pressures yielded a second "liquids in landfills" policy reversal.[11]

Courts Uphold EPA

Second, in hundreds of cases, federal courts have given legal approval to EPA decisions without yielding changes in the agency's policies and administration. Examples can be found in judicial interpretations of the Superfund statute during its early years when courts agreed with virtually every interpretation of the act by the EPA. Other examples can be found in the EPA's implementation of its Clean Water Act (CWA) National Municipal Policy in which judges and the EPA have banded together to force municipal compliance with the CWA, to establish pro-EPA precedents, to assess penalties, and to schedule corrective actions. In both sets of cases, judicial support of EPA's statutory interpretations served to confirm and strengthen government policy. * * *

Passive Judicial Review Affects EPA

Third, federal courts have had an impact on the policies and administration of the EPA simply because of the nature of judicial review. In these instances, even the most passive judges, at times, have affected the discretion and autonomy of the agency. A typical example is a case in which the EPA was sued for not meeting a statutory deadline for regulation promulgation under the Resource Conservation and Recovery Act. By straightforwardly interpreting the statute, finding that the EPA had missed the deadline, and issuing an ongoing, affirmative decree, the judge prompted an acceleration of the pace of EPA actions.[14] * * *

Use of Discretionary Judicial Powers to Prompt Action

In a fourth set of circumstances, judges have used their discretion and authority to push the agency in a specific direction. Included in this group are judicial efforts to manage the agency's response to a court order, judicial denial of agency requests during

---

[9] Interviews with EPA staff, EPA headquarters, Washington, D.C., week of May 15, 1988. * * *

[10] Natural Resources Defense Council (NRDC) v. Gorsuch. There was no court decision in this case since the EPA reversed its actions soon after the filing of the lawsuit.

[11] Shell Oil v. EPA. *See EPA Suspends Ban on Liquids in Landfills, Proposes Alternative Rule; Lawsuit Filed,* 12 Env't Rep. (BNA) No. 45 at 1387 (March 5, 1982).

[14] Illinois v. Gorsuch[I], 532 F. Supp. 337 (D.D.C. 1981). This case was originally filed as Illinois v. Costle.

and after litigation, and judicial efforts to force the EPA to take a second look at its actions. In one case, for example, the court read into a statute an implied time frame of "reasonableness" within which the agency was to develop final regulations, even though no such time limit was imposed by the statute. The court then ordered the EPA to meet with the plaintiff environmental group to develop a compliance schedule. The case involved an ongoing, affirmative decree and detailed judicial supervision. * * *

Active, Aggressive Judicial Actions Affect EPA

Finally, in some instances judges have actively and aggressively intervened in the administration and policies of the EPA. This group includes cases in which judges have overstepped their statutory bounds, have questioned the scientific and policy expertise of EPA staff, and have aggressively pushed the EPA into action. In one toxics case, for example, after refusing to defer to the scientific expertise of EPA administrators, the judge ordered the plaintiff environmental group to enforce the court order by commencing a new action should the EPA not comply with the court mandate.[20] To facilitate the filing of a new lawsuit against the EPA, the judge waived a congressionally mandated sixty days' notice provision, in direct violation of the statute. In this instance, the judge coupled detailed judicial supervision of the agency through an ongoing affirmative decree with supervision by the plaintiffs. * * *

THE IMPACT OF FEDERAL COURT DECISIONS ON EPA'S POLICIES

In all five of the categories just discussed, the major impact of federal court decisions on the EPA has been policy related. From a "macro" or agency-wide perspective, compliance with court orders has become the agency's top priority, at times overtaking congressional mandates. The courts have dictated which issues get attention at the EPA. In an atmosphere of limited resources, coupled with unrealistic and numerous statutory mandates, the EPA has been forced to make decisions among competing priorities. With few exceptions, court orders have been the "winners" in this competition.

From a "micro" or individual organizational unit perspective, compliance with court orders also has become the top priority of EPA divisions. For example, in nearly every case examined, EPA staff reported concentrating the majority of their efforts on implementing the court decree. Other programs and priorities became secondary or were dropped. Moreover, EPA staff developed specific programmatic policies and changed regulations in response to court decisions.

Such judicial dominance over EPA policy formulation has grave ramifications in two respects. First, * * * courts by their very nature are narrowly focused on the issues presented in a case. Yet those narrow court-generated issues have become EPA's highest priorities. As a consequence, the most pressing environmental problems are not necessarily those addressed by our nation's environmental agency. Matters suitable for litigation are the "squeaky wheels that get the grease," while other important environmental problems fall by the wayside. Huge amounts of resources have been dedicated to meeting court decisions, when the environmental and health benefits, at times, have been marginal. As

---

[20] Natural Resources Defense Council v. Costle. 10 ENVTL. L. REP. (Envtl. L. Inst.) 20274 (S.D.N.Y. 1980). *See also* 11 ENVTL. L. REP. (Envtl. L. Inst.) 20202 (S.D.N.Y. 1981).

an example, in one Clean Air Act radionuclides case, $7.6 million and 150 staff work years were spent over a six-year period to develop regulations that would prevent one cancer death every thirteen years.[23]

Second, from a representative democracy perspective, judicial dominance over EPA policies is problematic. Court orders can differ from the mandates of our elected congressional representatives. Moreover, judicial dominance of agency policy makes it difficult for those not a party to a lawsuit to participate in the EPA regulatory process. In one Clean Water Act case, for example, the EPA carried out programs and processes ordered by a court-modified consent decree that were beyond those mandated by Congress. Congress reacted by amending the CWA to adopt the provisions of the consent decree.[26] * * *

THE IMPACT OF FEDERAL COURT DECISIONS ON THE ADMINISTRATION OF THE EPA

Federal court decisions have affected the administration of the EPA in several ways. First, court decisions have prompted a redistribution of budgetary and staff resources within the EPA. Second, court decisions have reduced the discretion and autonomy of EPA administrators as a whole. Third, court decisions have increased the power of the EPA legal staff. Fourth, court decisions have decreased the power and authority of EPA scientists. Finally, court decisions have selectively empowered certain organizational units within the EPA.

Negative Effects

Federal court decisions have served to redistribute resources within the EPA. * * *

With one exception, the EPA has not received additional staff or funds from Congress to enable it to comply with court decisions. There are several reasons for this fact. First, the EPA's budget and planning cycles are two to three years ahead of the current fiscal year. The implementation of most EPA court orders does not exceed that length of time. Therefore, when a court decision mandating EPA action is issued, there is usually no opportunity to include requests for additional agency resources for court order compliance in the budget.

Second, in this time of fiscal austerity, there is very little "extra" money in the federal budget. This has caused the process for review of requests for additional funds to become very strict and cumbersome.* * * Very few requests make it through the process. * * *

* * *

* * * When former EPA Administrator Anne Gorsuch attempted to cut the EPA budget by 30 to 40 percent, she began by listing agency priorities: court decisions were at the top of the list, followed by statutory mandates. All other programs and priorities dropped to the bottom and were subject to budgetary cuts.

Reprogramming

* * *

---

[23] Sierra Club v. Ruckelshaus, 602 F. Supp. 892 (N.D. Cal. 1984). * * *

[26] The case was the Clean Water Act "Flannery Decision," Natural Resources Defense Council v. Train, 8 Env't Rep. Cas. (BNA) 2121 (D.D.C. 1976).

EPA staff reported relying more often on consulting firms to perform work necessary to comply with court orders because of the lack of specialized internal resources readily available for such a task. There are several consequences of this increased use of consultants. On one hand, it is an expeditious way to meet rapid change in the agency without greatly disturbing the status quo. On the other hand, as use of consultants has grown, there has been a gradual erosion of EPA's in-house expertise. In hiring new staff, EPA managers now look "less for technical geniuses" and more for generalists who can oversee and communicate with technical consultants. This has affected morale, as EPA technical staff at times resent not being able to use their expertise.

* * *

Reduction in Discretion and Autonomy

From an administrative perspective, courts have reduced the discretion, autonomy, power, and authority of EPA administrators. * * * First, oftentimes new programs are never implemented because resources are devoted to meeting court demands. Next, court decisions affect EPA planning activities.* * * Finally, court decisions can be broad and vague, affecting more than they need to. An example is a case concerning trade secrets and the Federal Insecticide, Fungicide and Rodenticide Act (FIFRA).[39] In that instance, a judge held that the statute was unconstitutional because Congress had exceeded its regulatory authority and violated the Fifth Amendment's prohibition against the taking of property without just compensation. The court issued a permanent injunction barring the EPA from carrying out four provisions of the statute. EPA attorneys agreed that the court could have reached the same conclusion without nullifying all four statutory sections.

Increased Power of Legal Staff

In addition, the proliferation of court decisions has forced what one EPA staff member called "non-user-friendly" regulations.[41] According to EPA technical staff, the Office of General Counsel often rewrites regulations, notices, and proposals in anticipation that a lawsuit is imminent. Lawyers have the last word in most EPA actions. * * *

Decreased Power and Authority of Scientists

From a scientific perspective, the effect of court decisions on the EPA has grave ramifications. * * * Certain actions must build on other actions before final products can be issued. For example, scientific studies must be completed, data must be collected, and then the data must be analyzed prior to technical regulations being developed. There is a need for peer scientific review. Oftentimes the EPA either cannot comply with the court decision because these foundation steps have not been completed, or it skips needed steps and issues poorly conceived standards. Time constraints are exacerbated.

An example can be found in the case of *Sierra Club v. Ruckelshaus* [602 F.Supp. 892 (N.D.Cal. 1984)] in which the EPA was ordered by a court to issue regulations under the Clean Air Act to regulate radionuclides. The EPA requested nine years to develop a

---

[39] Monsanto v. Acting Administrator, 564 F. Supp. 522 (1983). The case was later reversed by the Supreme Court in Ruckelshaus v. Monsanto, 463 U.S. 1315 (1983).

[41] Interviews with EPA staff, EPA headquarters, week of May 15, 1988. * * *

scientific basis for the regulations; instead a judge gave the agency 180 days. The agency issued the regulations, bypassing the typical review by its Science Advisory Board (SAB). When the SAB finally reviewed the regulations, it found them scientifically flawed. The EPA Administrator responded by withdrawing the regulations and was held in contempt of court. In order to purge itself from the contempt of court citation, the agency issued "sham" regulations which conformed with the letter of the court's order, but, in fact, liberalized the amount of radionuclides which could be emitted into the atmosphere.

* * *

Positive Impacts on EPA Administration

Despite these negative effects of federal court decisions, most EPA staff within program offices involved in court cases reported several positive consequences of court decisions from a "micro" or individual organizational unit perspective. The positive attributes included the following:

(1) *An increase in power for program offices within the EPA.* A court mandate always gets the attention of upper echelon managers at the EPA. Offices that usually find their ideas concerning programmatic changes lost in the bureaucratic maze find that their ideas are listened to if tied to the implementation of a court decision.

(2) *An increase in resources for certain program offices, almost always derived from reprogramming.* As funds are needed to implement a court order, they usually are taken from other programs and offices within the EPA. The EPA program charged with implementing a court order is the beneficiary in this budgetary redistribution process.

(3) *An increase in staff motivation and morale.* As workers band together to accomplish the goal of court order compliance, they become more focused and directed. Staff expressed great pride in implementing a court order in a timely fashion.

(4) *A lifting of administrative burdens and prolonged OMB review.* Internal agency approval procedures are streamlined in an effort to expeditiously comply with court mandates. * * *

(5) *An increase in external power, authority and discretion for EPA as a whole.* As pro-EPA precedents are decided, the EPA gains legitimacy. The agency's power over the entities it regulates, as well as other federal agencies, has increased.

Three examples of these five positive effects merit attention. First, in a Clean Water Act case concerning the regulation of toxic chemicals, EPA staff reported that the court-approved program was administratively more efficient and environmentally more sound than the agency's previous program. Moreover, the court order sparked positive interest in Congress, yielding both an increase in agency resources and a codification of the judicially mandated changes. (It should be noted, however, that this 1977 example is cited by EPA staff as the only instance in which Congress provided additional funds for implementation of a court order involving the EPA.) The case was heralded by EPA staff as a way to "focus on getting something done." With the pressures and the resources the court order brought, "people were motivated better; consequently the final product was better."[43]

---

[43] Interviews with EPA staff, EPA headquarters, week of May 15, 1988. * * *. The case was the Clean Water Act "Flannery Decision."

Second, in a Superfund case in which a judge ordered the EPA to release the names of alleged polluters to a reporter, the agency complied by changing both its policy and procedure on the subject. The result was a streamlined agency operation.[44]

Third, in a Resource Conservation and Recovery Act (RCRA) and Clean Water Act (CWA) case concerning EPA regulation of Department of Energy (DOE) facilities, a judge ordered DOE to apply for EPA permits. Although the EPA was neither a plaintiff nor a defendant in the suit, the decision had a positive effect on the EPA's policies and administration, increasing EPA's power and authority over DOE. Moreover, according to a General Accounting Office (GAO) study, the decision had unanticipated positive effects as the EPA acquired further leverage over other DOE facilities, yielding greater DOE compliance with EPA statutes and regulations.[45]

CONCLUSION

* * * [T]he impact of federal court decisions on the policies and administration of the United States Environmental Protection Agency has been multifaceted and complex. The actions of courts have been neither entirely positive nor totally negative. Rather, the actions of judges fall along a continuum, ranging from confirming and legitimizing the actions of the EPA to evoking change in the agency's policies and administration, both positive and negative.

From an agency-wide policy perspective, however, the impact of court decisions on the EPA is problematic. Compliance with court orders has become the agency's top priority, at times overtaking congressional mandates and threatening representative democracy. Clearly litigation is not the best way to formulate environmental policy or to set our nation's environmental priorities.

The problems lie primarily with the judicial system, with certain judges themselves, and with Congress. First, there are obvious institutional influences that come into play including the fact that judges are "chained" to the issues developed by attorneys representing their clients' narrow interests. The judicial system generally is not designed to allow a full analysis of the public policy implications of specific court decisions.

On the other hand, individual judicial personalities are partially responsible for the negative effects of federal court decisions on the EPA. In some instances judges have overstepped their statutory bounds to force change in the agency. In other instances judges with no scientific background have questioned the scientific expertise of EPA staff. In yet other instances, judges have aggressively pushed the EPA in a specific direction seemingly based on their own personal biases.

Finally, much of the responsibility for the negative effect of court decisions on the development of environmental policy within the EPA must lie with Congress. Congress created the EPA's statutes which allow the agency to be second-guessed by outside groups. Congress set the numerous and unrealistic statutory deadlines making the EPA an "easy mark" for litigation. And Congress created incentives for abundant incremental litigation

---

[44] Interviews with EPA staff, EPA headquarters, week of May 15, 1988. * * *. The case was Cohen v. EPA, 19 Envir. Rep. Cas. 1377 (1983).

[45] Leaf v. Hodel, 586 F. Supp. 1165 (1984); General Accounting Office Report No. GAO/RCED-85-23, "Department of Energy Acting to Control Hazardous Wastes at Its Savannah River Nuclear Facilities."

against the EPA by liberally allowing and rewarding narrowly focused citizen suits.

In short, Congress and the legal profession have done a poor job of assessing the public policy implications of such statutory provisions. The laws should be reexamined and refined. Clearly the judicial-administrative "partnership" will continue to significantly affect our nation's environmental policies and the administration of our nation's most important environmental protection agency.

NOTES

1. Is it surprising that litigation has had a policy impact on the EPA? Is that an inherent feature of our three branch, checks-and-balances government? Should changes be made to minimize and/or alter the impact of litigation on the EPA? Even if you agree with Professor O'Leary that litigation is not the best way to formulate environmental policy, do courts nonetheless play an important role in modifying the EPA's priorities and policies?

2. Whereas many of the policy impacts detected by O'Leary are passive effects of litigation, other commentators have found a policy agenda imbedded in court—particularly Supreme Court—decisions in the environmental area. *See* Richard E. Levy and Robert L. Glicksman, *Judicial Activism and Restraint in the Supreme Court's Environmental Law Decisions*, 42 VAND. L. REV. 343 (1989).

> * * * [A] consistent pro-development pattern has prevailed in the Supreme Court's environmental law decisions since 1976. Although the Court exercised institutional restraint in the majority of its environmental law decisions, the pro-development results are not explainable solely as the product of a neutral exercise of institutional restraint; these decisions reflect policy activism by the Court. In a number of significant decisions the Court abandoned the principles of institutional restraint in order to reach a pro-development result. Moreover, in many cases the Court's exercise of institutional restraint seems inconsistent with statutory language or legislative history. * * *
>
> In particular, the Supreme Court has elevated economic efficiency to a level of importance not shared by Congress and has virtually ignored the legislative desire to force improvements in pollution control technology. This policy activism has pervaded the Court's substantive review of administrative decisions. * * * [T]he Court has used its characterization of legislative intent to defer to administrative decisions that accommodated economic efficiency at the expense of environmental protection. * * * [W]hen the Court believed that agencies had gone too far in protecting environmental interests, * * * it invoked constitutional principles reminiscent of substantive economic due process to block the agency's action. Similarly, the Court has employed its perception of the congressional desire to balance environmental protection and economic efficiency to

reject supplemental remedies in the face of strong evidence of congressional intent to preserve and foster such remedies. Indeed, the Court has taken virtually every opportunity to discourage supplemental remedies, whether by exercising institutional restraint to reject federal remedies * * *, or by exercising activism to strike down remedies created under state law * * *. Similarly, the Court has run roughshod over Congress's desire to facilitate such remedies through the reimbursement of attorney's fees. * * *

Id., 42 VAND. L. REV. at 421-22.

Karin Sheldon, who served as counsel for environmental interests before becoming a law professor, found that in twelve NEPA cases decided over a twenty-year period, the Supreme Court ruled against environmentalists' claims on every occasion. Karin P. Sheldon, *NEPA in the Supreme Court,* 25 LAND & WATER L. REV. 83 (1990).

3. O'Leary takes aim at Congress for "liberally allowing and rewarding narrowly focused citizen suits" under the environmental statutes. While her article focuses on the substantive aspects of environmental litigation, procedural issues have played an increasingly prominent role, particularly with respect to citizen suits. In two recent cases, the Supreme Court substantially narrowed the scope of standing opportunities for environmental plaintiffs.

In *Lujan v. National Wildlife Federation,* 497 U.S. 871 (1990) (*Lujan I*), the Court held that the National Wildlife Federation lacked standing to challenge the Interior Department's program under the Federal Land Policy and Management Act of reviewing and reconsidering the classification of public lands concerning the uses to which they might be put (i.e., limited to recreation or wilderness preservation or available for mining and other development activities). To establish the organization's standing, two members of the National Wildlife Federation had submitted affidavits stating that they hiked and made visits in the vicinity of one tract that might be opened up for mining. The Court found that the affidavits did not satisfy the standing test that the plaintiff suffer "injury in fact" from the contested action. The plaintiff's allegations were too generalized to survive a motion for summary judgment on the ground that plaintiff lacked standing:

> [The summary judgment rule] is assuredly not satisfied by averments which state only that one of respondent's members uses unspecified portions of an immense tract of territory, on some portions of which mining activity has occurred or probably will occur by virtue of the government action. It will not do to "presume" the missing facts because without them the affidavits would not establish the injury that they generally allege.

Id. at 889.

The Court utilized the standing doctrine to limit the policymaking function of the courts, in comparison with the two other branches of government:

> Respondent alleges that violation of the law is rampant within this program * * *. Perhaps so. But respondent cannot seek wholesale improvement of this program by court decree, rather than in the offices of the Department or the halls of Congress, where programmatic improvements are normally made.

Id. at 891.

Two years later, in a second *Lujan* case, the Court underscored the critical significance of the "injury in fact" element of standing. In *Lujan v. Defenders of Wildlife*, 504 U.S. 555 (1992) (*Lujan II*), the Court held that the Defenders of Wildlife lacked standing to challenge Interior Department regulations limiting the application of the Endangered Species Act to actions within the United States (or on the high seas). As in *Lujan I*, affidavits of two of the organization's members were deemed to be too generalized to establish standing. The affidavits alleged that the Defenders' members had traveled overseas to observe endangered species (or their habitat) and intended to return to do so again. The Defenders of Wildlife described certain American-supported projects in these overseas areas that would harm species protected under the Endangered Species Act.

> We shall assume for the sake of argument that these affidavits contain facts showing that certain agency-funded projects threaten listed species—though that is questionable. They plainly contain no facts, however, showing how damage to the species will produce "imminent" injury to Mss. Kelly and Skilbred. That the women "had visited" the areas of the projects before the projects commenced proves nothing. * * * And the affiants' profession of an "intent[t]" to return to the places they had visited before—where they will presumably, this time, be deprived of the opportunity to observe animals of the endangered species—is simply not enough. Such "some day" intentions— without any description of concrete plans, or indeed even any specification of *when* the some day will be—do not support a finding of the "actual or imminent" injury that our cases require.

Id. at 564. Although the Defenders also sought standing by virtue of "procedural injury," insofar as the Interior Department regulation deprived them of the interagency consultation procedures that apply under the Endangered Species Act, the Court also rejected this standing claim.

> * * * The question presented here is whether the public interest in proper administration of the laws (specifically, in agencies' observance of a particular, statutorily prescribed procedure) can be converted into an individual right by a statute that denominates it as such, and that permits all citizens (or, for that matter, a subclass of citizens who suffer no distinctive concrete harm) to sue. If the concrete injury requirement has the separation-of-powers significance we have always said, the answer must be obvious: To permit Congress to convert the undifferentiated public interest in executive officers' compliance with the law into an "individual right" vindicable in the courts is to permit Congress to transfer from the President to the courts the Chief Executive's most important constitutional duty, to "take Care that the Laws be faithfully executed," Art. II, §3. It would enable the courts, with the permission of Congress, "to assume a position of authority over the governmental acts of another and co-equal department," * * * and to become "'virtually continuing

monitors of the wisdom and soundness of Executive action.'" We have always rejected that vision of our role.

Id. at 576-77.

For an analysis of both *Lujan* decisions, see Cass R. Sunstein, *What's Standing After Lujan? Of Citizen Suits, "Injuries," and Article III*, 91 MICH. L. REV. 163 (1992).

4. O'Leary notes that court orders may require the EPA to act before scientists can confirm research methods or results. On the other hand, the threat of searching judicial review may spur the Agency to invest more resources and power in staff scientists in order to ensure that a regulation being developed will withstand challenge in court. Is O'Leary suggesting that the relative distribution of power within the EPA between lawyers and scientists is skewed? How much power should scientists have in making regulatory decisions?

Citizen suits are the focus of the following article by Michael Greve, Executive Director of the Center for Individual Rights. As you read this, consider whether Dr. Greve is challenging the concept of citizen suits, or their present manifestation.

THE PRIVATE ENFORCEMENT OF ENVIRONMENTAL LAW
Michael S. Greve
65 Tul. L. Rev. 339 (1990)*

I. INTRODUCTION

Since the beginning of the 1970s, Congress has increasingly come to rely upon private law enforcement as a means of attaining public objectives.[1] * * * Virtually all federal environmental statutes contain a citizen suit provision that, typically, allows "any person" to sue private parties for noncompliance with statutory provisions or with standards and regulations issued under the statute. Groups and individuals suing under these provisions have sustained no injury or, at most, a minimal injury-in-fact. They act not as victims who redress a wrong done to them but as "private attorneys general."

Over the past two decades, Congress has repeatedly strengthened and expanded environmental citizen suit provisions. Congress views these provisions as an efficient policy instrument and as a participatory, democratic mechanism that allows "concerned citizens" to redress environmental pollution. This assessment is shared by a large majority of legal scholars and by environmental advocates. This Article, in contrast, argues that the history of sustained legislative support has little to do with whatever substantive merits citizen

---

* Reprinted with permission.
[1] Throughout this Article, the term "private (law) enforcement" shall refer only to the private enforcement of public purposes, and not to the private enforcement of private rights by individual victims of illegal conduct. * * *

suits may have. Congressional support for private environmental law enforcement is an outgrowth of interest group politics. In purpose and effect, citizen suit provisions are an off-budget entitlement program for the environmental movement.

To summarize the basic argument, environmental citizen-plaintiffs are supposed to be altruists. Citizen suit provisions offer no rewards because private enforcers are supposed to be guided exclusively by the public benefits to be gained from righting environmental wrongs, and not by the personal benefits of a reward. This injunction against rewards notwithstanding, citizen suit provisions do permit environmental groups to solicit transfer payments from alleged polluters. But, the provisions make enforcement financially attractive for almost no one *except* environmental advocacy groups. They thus create what amounts to an environmentalist enforcement cartel. This system of enforcement is unsupported by any plausible economic or environmental rationale. Congress has failed to contemplate potentially more efficient private enforcement mechanisms because no other system would lend itself equally as well to the purpose of subsidizing the environmental movement.

* * *

III. PRIVATE ENVIRONMENTAL LAW ENFORCEMENT: PATTERN AND PRACTICE

When it first included citizen suit provisions in environmental statutes, Congress expected that citizen suits against alleged polluters would usually be brought by individual "concerned citizens," not by nationally organized environmental advocacy groups. However, enforcement by "concerned citizens" without organized support has turned out to be a rare phenomenon. The vast majority of private enforcement actions has been brought by environmental advocacy groups such as the Natural Resources Defense Council (NRDC). In contrast to unorganized individuals, these groups possess sufficient expertise and resources to monitor the EPA's administration of environmental statutes and to take legal action when they consider it necessary.

Prior to 1982, even environmental organizations filed very few citizen suits directly against alleged violators, preferring instead to bring suit against the EPA to force it to adopt tougher standards vis-a-vis regulated industries. This litigation pattern also contravened the initial expectations of Congress. Yet, it is easily explained. Cases brought and won against the EPA generally have a broader policy impact than cases against individual polluters. There are too many enterprises to sue a significant number of them. The deterrent value of a few lawsuits is very limited, because every firm may assume that it will not be next in line. Moreover, proving ongoing, site-specific violations of environmental standards is ordinarily very difficult and costly. It often requires the alleged or suspected violator's cooperation, which is rarely forthcoming.

However, in late 1982 the number of citizen suits and notices of intent to sue filed with the EPA began to increase dramatically, due almost entirely to a surge of enforcement activity under the Clean Water Act. * * *

This burst of activity resulted from a concerted enforcement program that was designed by the NRDC. Having monitored the EPA's administration of the effluent guidelines program under the Clean Water Act, the NRDC concluded that the program would be ineffective without stringent enforcement. With a seed grant that helped to fund initial citizen suits, the NRDC established a self-sustaining Act enforcement program, using attorneys' fees recovered in one case to fund future cases. A coalition of advocacy groups, including the Sierra Club Legal Defense Fund, Friends of the Earth, the Student Public Interest Research Group of New Jersey (SPIRG), the Atlantic States Legal Foundation, and the Connecticut Fund for the Environment, joined the NRDC's campaign. * * *

* * *

Companies requiring NPDES permits must file Discharge Monitoring Reports (DMRs) with regional EPA offices. By the early 1980s, this requirement had created a record-keeping system that documented each individual polluter's specific violations of regulatory standards and permit conditions. The reports, which are available to any interested person upon request, make NPDES permit violations easily discernible even to laymen. It takes less than a half-day for environmental organizations to train student volunteers to scan DMRs and identify infractions. Staff attorneys review the results of these investigations. Depending on the severity and frequency of violations and a number of other factors, environmental groups file notices of intent to sue, usually offering to discuss the matter with the alleged violator. Unless the case is dropped because of prior or ongoing government enforcement, or the alleged violator agrees to enter into settlement negotiations, environmental groups file a complaint. * * *

In the early phase of the Clean Water Act enforcement campaign, corporations relatively often refused to settle cases brought by private enforcers, preferring instead to litigate the matter. But virtually all defenses raised by alleged polluters—including challenges to the constitutionality of citizen suit provisions—have been rejected by the courts. The few Clean Water Act private enforcement cases that still find their way into court concern marginal legal problems and unique factual circumstances; the basic legal questions have been adjudicated and resolved. For many years now, most notices of intent to sue have led not to litigation but to negotiations and, relatively quickly, to settlements and consent decrees.

Settlements typically contain four elements: A fine payable to the general Treasury; provisions for achieving compliance with NPDES permit limits, which often stipulate the installation of additional pollution control equipment, a schedule of fines for future violations, and the periodic submission of DMRs to environmental plaintiff-groups; payment of attorneys' fees and litigation costs to the plaintiff-group or its counsel; and, finally, so-called "mitigation" or "credit" programs, to be instituted or paid for by the alleged violator in addition to fines or in lieu of a portion of the fines.

Substantial portions of such settlements constitute direct transfer payments to environmental groups. First, environmental groups can and do insist on obtaining above-cost attorneys' fees in settlements, since that is what they would get at trial. Courts have held that the "market rate" at which public interest attorneys are to be reimbursed is the average rate charged for similar work by for-profit attorneys in the community. This rate usually far exceeds the salary of public interest lawyers and the actual costs incurred by environmental organizations during the course of a citizen suit under the Clean Water Act. Second, payments for credit projects agreed upon in private settlements almost always go to environmental organizations, although normally not to the organization bringing the enforcement action.

* * *

Alleged violators assent to demands for transfer payments in lieu of penalties because this is cheaper than either a trial or dealing with EPA enforcement. The alleged violators know that the enforcers will "trade" even very substantial Treasury fines for private rewards in the form of attorneys' fees and credit projects, and they can, therefore, obtain a heavy discount to the amount of fines that could be assessed. The price of credit projects to the violator is further reduced because in contrast to penalties paid to the Treasury, payments for credit projects are often tax deductible. And at least some credit projects have a positive public relations value.

Private enforcers, on the other hand, stand to gain by "converting" Treasury fines into attorneys' fees. A review of consent orders entered in 1983 revealed that "an amount equivalent to about 400 percent of the penalties paid to the federal Treasury was paid to reimburse environmental groups for their attorneys [sic] fees."[82] Similarly, civil fines are "converted" into credit projects. Whereas the government accepts credit projects in lieu of penalties only under exceptional circumstances, almost every private settlement includes a credit project. Virtually every such project involves payments to environmental groups for research, "outreach" and education, or land acquisition. These payments, which sometimes amount to millions of dollars,[84] far exceed the level of fines assessed. More than ninety percent of "penalties" that industry paid in response to citizen suits under the Clean Water Act in 1983 went to environmental organizations, not to the Treasury.[85] * * *

IV. PRIVATE ENFORCEMENT: MOTIVES AND EFFECTS

Settlements of private enforcement actions under the Clean Water Act have triggered a spirited debate about the motives of private enforcers. Industry representatives have denounced private enforcement actions of the Clean Water Act as "hold-up operations" and "extortion," undertaken for the private benefit of environmental advocacy groups. Fearing that this perception might gain currency, environmental organizations have sought to avoid the appearance of illicit motives. Payments for credit projects are usually made to environmental organizations other than the group bringing the enforcement action. In order to facilitate these transactions, environmental groups have created institutional "shells" such as the Open Space Institute, which was specifically "created as a repository for cash settlements in Clean Water Act permit violation suits."[91] Predictably, though, transfers of settlement awards to such third parties have done little to dispel the concerns

---

[82] Lewis, [*Environmentalists' Authority to Sue Industry for Civil Penalties is Unconstitutional Under Separation of Powers Doctrine*, 16 Envtl. L. Rep. (Envtl. L. Inst.) 10,101,] 10,102 [(1986)]. * * *

[84] *Cf.* Wall St. J., Feb. 23, 1990, at B-2, col. 4 (Sierra Club Legal Defense Fund's CWA citizen suit against Unocal settled for $5,500,000, with about half of the amount payable to the Trust for Public Land, an environmental group); Washington Post, Feb. 17, 1987, at B-1 ($1,500,000 settlement between Bethlehem Steel and NRDC and Chesapeake Bay Foundation); N.Y. Times, Dec. 31, 1986, at A-12, col. 5; Brief of *Amicus Curiae* for the Connecticut Business and Industry Association, at 34-40, Gwaltney of Smithfield v. Chesapeake Bay Found., 484 U.S. 49 (1987) (No. 86-473).

[85] Lewis, [*Environmentalists' Authority to Sue Industry for Civil Penalties is Unconstitutional Under Separation of Powers Doctrine*, 16 Envtl. L. Rep. (Envtl. L. Inst.) 10,101] at 10,102 [(1986)].

[91] Stever, *Environmental Penalties and Environmental Trusts—Constraints on New Sources of Funding for Environmental Preservation*, 17 Envtl. L. Rep. (Envtl. L. Inst.) 10,356, 10,361 (1987).

of critics who have argued that, in any event, cash settlements do benefit the environmental movement at large.

From the parties' point of view, this preoccupation with motives may be understandable. But it misses the larger problem of private environmental law enforcement: The pattern of enforcement—its scope and direction—is determined not, as intended, by public benefits but by private economic rewards. It cannot be otherwise.

The dominant role of economic incentives in private environmental law enforcement has been widely acknowledged. Most commentators have concluded that the post-1982 surge of enforcement under the Clean Water Act cannot be ascribed to the ideological commitments or accidental preferences of environmental groups, a sudden deterioration of water quality or the perception of such deterioration, or a slackening of government enforcement, but that it was triggered by the uniquely favorable incentives provided by the Act and its regulatory progeny. By 1982, when the record-keeping system was firmly established, the Clean Water Act and its regulatory apparatus had made it much easier and cheaper for litigants to bring, prove, and win cases than under any other environmental statute. The NPDES system reduced search and detection costs to the point where an organized, self-sustaining, remunerative enforcement project became a viable option. At the same time, the fact that the Clean Water Act (in contrast to most other environmental statutes) authorizes private plaintiffs to enforce civil fines meant that private actions had an "extraction value," leading to negotiated transfer payments. In short, environmental organizations systematically capture the "spread" between enforcement costs and rewards. The fact that this spread is larger under the Clean Water Act than under any other environmental statute accounts for the high level of enforcement of the Act.

This interpretation of private environmental law enforcement is confirmed by an examination of the cases and targets selected by environmental organizations. For example, professional enforcers of the Clean Water Act tend to proceed against corporate entities whose DMRs show numerous violations, reaching into the recent past. While sensible, this strategy is not based upon careful calculations of the social and environmental costs and benefits of enforcement, for such calculations are conjectural and very expensive. * * * Rather, the focus on recent and repeat offenders results from the incentive structure set up by the Clean Water Act and its regulatory progeny. Isolated, accidental permit violations may be discounted as nonpunishable "upsets." Moreover, the courts have held that citizen-plaintiffs must make a good faith allegation of an *ongoing* violation. Since private enforcers have an interest in keeping enforcement costs low, they seek to avoid lengthy and complicated factual disputes over particular violations and the time of their occurrence. And of course, settlement awards are likely to increase with the number of alleged violations.

The systematic effort to maximize expected rewards also accounts for the fact that environmental organizations almost always proceed against private industry, and almost never against government entities. * * * This pronounced preference for proceeding against private industry cannot be explained by environmental considerations—municipal facilities cause far more water pollution than private industry, and violate their NPDES permits far more frequently. Rather, this preference is explained by economic calculations. A private corporation's greater capacity for fast, authoritative decisionmaking makes settlement negotiations less complicated and expensive than negotiations with a bureaucratized government body that worries about the legality of settlements and about its accountability to the electorate.

It would be erroneous, though, to attribute this strategy of maximizing expected economic rewards (as opposed to estimated environmental benefits) to the *motives* of advocacy groups. Environmental groups are highly professional and dedicated. They are not "in it for the money" but organize and operate primarily for noneconomic reasons. * * * The problem lies elsewhere: Ideological organizations, no less than economically motivated actors, face cost constraints. They have to allocate scarce resources and choose among alternative strategies. In doing so, altruistic, ideological organizations *must* react primarily to private economic incentives. * * *

* * *

The incentives provided by environmental law and by the Clean Water Act in particular have only rarely and coincidentally generated enforcement choices close to those that would result from an impartial, disinterested assessment of the public environmental benefits to be gained from enforcement. As previously mentioned, environmental groups tend to proceed against recent and repeat violators of NPDES permits. This incentive-induced effect is desirable, inasmuch as numerous violations are grounds for suspecting both that the damage is considerable, and that the violations occurred through ill will or negligence rather than through accidental circumstances. But this congruity of private and public benefits is the exception, not the rule. An enforcer who considered nothing but the public environmental benefits of alternative enforcement strategies would scarcely focus virtually all his energies upon the Clean Water Act and the NPDES permit program. Nor would the public benefits of enforcement appear to justify the pronounced anticorporate bias of professional private law enforcement of the Clean Water Act. * * * To mention a final example of disparity between private rewards and public benefits, the violations that are easiest to prove, and, therefore, attract the particular attention of private enforcers, often turn out to be paperwork violations rather than substantive violations. Enforcement proceedings brought for violations of the voluminous paperwork requirements of the Clean Water Act generate tens of thousands of dollars in attorneys' fees but no discernible environmental benefits.

* * *

V. CITIZEN SUITS: CONFLICTS AND CONTRADICTIONS

* * * [C]itizen suit provisions differ from traditional bounty-hunter provisions in three respects. First, citizen-plaintiffs are supposed to be altruists. Second, citizen suits have certain attributes of a private, remedial lawsuit. Third, private enforcers are not strictly subordinate to the executive; they act as independent "private attorneys general." This Section examines these features and their underlying rationales in light of the preceding discussion of the inevitably reward-oriented nature of private enforcement. * * * What explanations might Congress (or anyone else) offer in defense of constructing environmental citizen suits in their present form, as opposed to alternative arrangements? It turns out that all plausible rationales and rationalizations of citizen suits are untenable. Ultimately, citizen suit provisions, as currently written, are based upon inconsistent and incompatible rationales, and fall far short of promoting the purposes they are ostensibly intended to serve.

A. Incompatible Conceptions of Private Enforcement

Two propositions about the nature and purpose of environmental citizen suits are virtually uncontested: Private environmental law enforcers should have no incentive for litigation other than public, environmental benefits; and, citizen suit provisions should be widely utilized. These presumptions reflect the express intent of Congress, and they are practically undisputed in the legal literature. However, they are exceptionally hard to reconcile. Any effort to do so will undermine crucial rationales for citizen enforcement.

The experience of two decades has shown that the mere prospect of being reimbursed for attorneys' fees and litigation costs draws no more than a few private enforcers into the market. Private enforcement entails search and detection costs, which have to be paid up front. As long as recovery is uncertain and, at best, compensates plaintiffs for their litigation costs, environmental organizations prefer to sue the Administrator. Concerned citizens, who band together in order to increase their leverage and to overcome free-rider problems, incur significant and nonrecoverable transaction costs. Hence, they will rarely bring enforcement actions.

Against this background, the present policy of permitting credit projects and above-cost attorneys' fees can be interpreted as a compromise aimed at producing citizen enforcement that is both extensive and "altruistic." Having found that an absolute prohibition upon rewards would practically eliminate private actions against alleged polluters, Congress has decided to tolerate rewards *as long as the rewards are not "profits."* It is no longer the *lack* of rewards but the *form* of rewards that is supposed to ensure the enforcers' altruistic motivation.

This approach, quite naturally, raises the specter of abuse. If private enforcement becomes remunerative, there is no longer a guarantee that it will be undertaken only by altruistic enforcers and for altruistic reasons. * * * In practice, though, this problem has proven insignificant. A large portion of the available transfer payments consists of credit projects, a currency valued almost exclusively by environmental organizations. This is one of the major reasons why few enforcers with the "wrong motivation"—that is, a desire for profits—have engaged in enforcement.

The real problem lies not in the enforcers' motives but in the fact that permitting transfer payments undermines the central rationale for altruism—namely, its purpose of ensuring that private enforcers pursue nothing but public benefits. Tolerating credit projects and windfalls (while prohibiting profits) would make sense if the form of rewards—anything but profits—made a crucial difference in terms of case selection and deterrence levels. But this is not the case. "Altruistic" environmental enforcers, no less than bounty hunters, seek to maximize the return on their investment in enforcement activities. They assign some positive value to the payments they extract. The level of enforcement and the choice of enforcement targets depend on the difference between that value and the amount of search and enforcement costs, and not upon the use to which the payment is put or the reasons for which it is solicited. In short, the "proper" motives cannot be shown to produce environmental benefits that could not also be produced through profitable law enforcement. If the prospect of profits poses a danger of excessive or misguided enforcement, so do cash settlements and attorneys' fees.

* * *

The "private" citizen suit model suggests that environmental plaintiffs should ordinarily be "concerned citizens." But this has never been so, and it cannot be so. The predominant force in private environmental law enforcement has always been, and will always be, highly organized, professional advocacy and litigation groups. These organizations have already paid the transaction costs that unorganized citizens still have to overcome, and they possess superior resources and expertise. To structure financial incentives in such a way as to produce a large number of "concerned citizen" actions without triggering an organized environmentalist enforcement campaign is practically impossible. As long as enforcement costs are high and no rewards can be had, organized and unorganized enforcers alike will, to a large extent, refrain from enforcement. Positive financial incentives, on the other hand, exacerbate the natural differences between concerned citizens and environmental organizations. While the reduction of search and detection costs (brought about by the DMR system) and increased leverage (brought about by the private enforceability of civil fines) did raise the number of enforcement actions filed by unorganized or locally organized citizens, they simultaneously raised the activity of organized environmental groups at a much greater rate. The NRDC's Clean Water Act enforcement campaign was designed largely by an attorney with extensive experience in government and in public-interest law practice. The campaign was further facilitated by a philanthropic start-up grant to the NRDC. These resources are beyond the reach of ordinary private citizens.

The dominant role of environmental organizations in private enforcement is not a problem in and of itself, and may even have certain advantages. It does, however, call into question the presumptive rationales behind the "private" citizen suit model. According to that model, "concerned citizens" exercise their own rights and remedy an injury done to them. A defense of environmental citizen suit provisions on these grounds implies a division of labor between private and public enforcers. It assigns the task of designing and implementing a coherent and efficient enforcement scheme to public officials, and it directs "concerned citizens" to fill the "gaps" in the government's enforcement scheme. Enforcement by citizen-plaintiffs should increase the likelihood of detection and apprehension of alleged violators by addressing violations that are so recent or so limited in locale that they have yet to come to the EPA's attention.

Obviously, though, the national advocacy groups that dominate private enforcement are no more attuned to local conditions than the EPA. The overriding objective of these groups is to change environmental policy. Their primary addressee is the federal government. And their perspective is entirely different from that of ordinary citizens who seek to remedy local problems that fail to register on the EPA's radar screen. Moreover, environmental groups seek to minimize the costs of detecting violators, which means that they usually spring into action only when the government and private industry have already paid a substantial portion of those costs. They direct their energies not toward the violations that tend to escape the EPA, nor toward the expensive discovery and abatement of ongoing violations, but toward the punishment of known violations. This requires only record scanning. * * * Private enforcement will either be directed toward the "gaps" in public enforcement, in which case it will be rare, or it will be utilized to surpass the current level of public enforcement, in which case it will no longer satisfy the rationales advanced for the quasi-private attributes of citizen suit provisions.

* * *

B. Broad-Based Private Environmental Law Enforcement: Rationales and Irrationalities

* * * The most common and most plausible rationale for encouraging the broad use of citizen suit provisions is to compensate for the government's underenforcement of environmental laws. Thus, it is often argued that the government does not possess, and can never possess, sufficient resources to enforce environmental laws to their full extent. Private enforcers can compensate for this deficiency without burdening the public Treasury. Unlike the "private" conception, this explanation implies that citizen suits serve the same purposes as government enforcement. The purpose of private enforcement, thus understood, is not "participation" but efficiency; its thrust is not remedial but deterrence oriented.

* * * Ideally, private enforcement is to be extensive, while stopping short of impinging upon the executive's inherent discretion to implement the law. This is why previous or ongoing government enforcement precludes citizen suits. However, citizen suit provisions do not permit the government to preserve its discretion or a coherent enforcement scheme by terminating private actions or by unilaterally adjusting or withholding private rewards. If the government wants to prevent private enforcement, it has to initiate its own "diligent" prosecution. Furthermore, attorneys' fees awards are placed in the judiciary's hands, not the executive's.

This scheme of coordination (or lack thereof) has been recognized as potentially problematic even by supporters of citizen suit provisions.[152] Specifically, the scheme poses a danger of overenforcement *and underenforcement*. Since the government cannot stop citizen suits by any means short of instituting its own proceedings, private parties can force the government into enforcement actions, including pointless or counterproductive ones. This is bound to lead to excessive enforcement. Conversely, the fact that private settlements may be heavily discounted raises the specter of underenforcement. This in turn, has forced the Department of Justice (DOJ) to insist that citizen suits and private settlements do not bar the government from bringing its own suit over the same violations. If it did not so insist, the DOJ could not remedy inadequate private settlements or effectively ensure that at least a portion of the assessed penalties goes to the Treasury (as opposed to being converted into credit projects). Given the DOJ's position, however, violators are confronted with the possibility of what amounts to the civil equivalent of double jeopardy. At the same time, the government's position reinforces the threat of inadequate enforcement by weakening the bargaining leverage of those who step into its shoes. Since a settlement with private enforcers may subsequently be upset by the government, it is worth less to an alleged polluter than a final disposition of the charges; as a result, settlements are reduced.

Although we lack solid empirical data concerning the effects of citizen enforcement, there is no reason to believe that this system of coordinating public and private enforcement generates optimal results. And, quite obviously, its coordination problems would not arise if no private enforcement action could go forward without government participation, and

---

[152] The scheme is primarily criticized for posing awkward, though manageable, problems of coordination. *See, e.g.*, Miller, *Private Enforcement* [*of Federal Pollution Control Laws*] *III*, [14 Envtl. L. Rep. (Envtl. L. Inst.) 10,407 (1984)] at 10,424-28; Boyer & Meidinger, [*Privatizing Regulatory Enforcement*, 34 BUFFALO L. REV. 833 (1985)] at 839 *passim* (coordination between private and public enforcement one of the key problems of citizen suits).

if the government could structure private settlements and rewards. This raises the question of *why* citizen suit provisions fail to subordinate private enforcers more clearly to executive control, as was clearly the case with traditional bounty hunters. Several explanations can be and have been proffered.

One line of argument is based on the citizen-plaintiff's distinctive characteristics: Altruistic law enforcers need not be subject to government control to the same extent as bounty hunters. Whatever merits this argument may have in the context of strictly altruistic law enforcement, it clearly does not apply to the existing system of selective rewards, which induces altruistic enforcers to act and calculate like bounty hunters. For reasons discussed above, the reliance upon motives as a safeguard against excessive and erratic enforcement is misplaced.

* * *

A second, very different line of argument for limiting executive control over private enforcers is based upon the distinctive characteristics of environmental law. * * *

Environmental statutes mandate very ambitious goals and standards, which the EPA often fails to attain. This is not surprising, considering the specific demands of these statutes. Some environmental statutes mandate goals that are unattainable even in theory. The Clean Water Act, which since its enactment in 1972 has called for fishable and swimmable waters by 1983 and zero discharge of pollutants anywhere by 1985, is perhaps the best known example of such an "absolutist" statute. Other objectives required by environmental law, even if desirable and attainable, could be achieved only at enormous costs. Many environmental statutes do not even mention the values that compete and conflict with maximum enforcement, such as economic growth and preventing the dislocation of industry and workers. At some point in the regulatory and enforcement process, the EPA will take these factors into consideration. The result will be a performance record which falls short of the statutorily prescribed performance standards.

Some scholars have criticized absolutist statutory goals as counterproductive[163] and demagogic.[164] Others, however, have argued that the EPA's frequent failure to attain statutorily mandated goals constitutes strong evidence of underenforcement. In light of the discrepancy between promise and performance, additional enforcement resources (including, presumably, those of private enforcers) are clearly needed. As long as statutory environmental goals have not been reached, the argument goes, enforcement—by public or private parties—cannot be excessive. The government need not be granted the authority to terminate private enforcement actions because any actions taken over and above the existing level of enforcement constitute an improvement, and, barring frivolous litigation, none are excessive.

When measured by the yardstick of legislatively determined environmental goals, underenforcement is indeed rampant. But this line of argument has a strangely disembodied character inasmuch as it "determines" the adequate level of enforcement without reference

---

[163] *Cf.* Aman, *Administrative Law in a Global Era: Progress, Deregulatory Change, and the Rise of the American Presidency,* 73 CORNELL L. REV. 1101, 1135-36 (1988) (discussing legal literature on the point).

[164] *See generally* Melnick, *Pollution Deadlines and the Coalition for Failure,* 75 PUB. INTEREST 123 (1984).

to anything in the real world, including economic costs and even environmental quality. The Clean Water Act illustrates the problematic nature of this approach.

In mandating the total elimination of discharges, Congress deliberately sidestepped what one would believe to be the central question of water pollution regulation: the link between discharges and water quality. The "official" congressional response to the question, how much pollution is too much, was that *any* pollution was too much, regardless of its effects. From this approach flowed a system of technology-based regulatory standards that make no systematic reference to water quality. * * * Technology-based standards, while too lax to ensure the integrity of relatively pure streams, impose extravagantly strict and expensive requirements to prevent discharges that have no discernible effect upon water quality. At the same time, the regulatory regime establishes a strong bias towards regulation of and enforcement against "point sources" of pollution, such as municipal sewers and especially industrial plants. These are easy to regulate, but they account for a much smaller part of water pollution than nonpoint pollution (such as runoff from agricultural fields, construction sites, and roads). The economic and environmental results of this regulatory regime are sobering. According to the EPA, the country spent about $200 billion dollars on water pollution control between 1970 and 1984. Yet, "the best of admittedly poor statistics show essentially no change in water quality"[172] since 1972.

These considerations do not permit a definitive assessment of the actual economic and environmental effects of the private Clean Water Act enforcement campaign. They do, however, cast considerable doubt on both the utility of that campaign and, more generally, on the crucial assumptions behind the rationalization of citizen suits as a remedy for "underenforcement." As shown previously, environmental groups have directed Clean Water Act citizen suits almost exclusively against industrial point sources, which account for less than one-tenth of all water pollution. In light of the unimpressive cost-benefit ratio of water pollution control, one must assume that the marginal environmental gains from enforcement in this area are quite small and that they are bought at enormous costs. If so, "underenforcement" would be a rational way of preventing or at least reducing expensive treatment for treatment's sake. The private enforcement campaign under the Clean Water Act may have merely exacerbated the already strong legislative and regulatory bias of targeting easily regulated industrial point sources. There is evidence that the targets, faced with a punitive regulatory and enforcement regime, have responded in ways that have cancelled whatever environmental gains may have been generated by the citizen suit campaign.

* * * Absolutist statutory goals and standards are a strong indication that Congress has failed to make necessary and inevitable trade-offs between environmental and economic objectives. Having failed to make trade-offs at the legislative stage, Congress must make them in the enforcement process, and a "lack of resources" is the most basic and most effective way of doing so. By much the same token, absolutist standards are not an argument for releasing private enforcers from executive control. They are an argument for *stricter* control. Unless one wishes to argue that everything (and hence nothing) should be a priority, or that public priorities should be selected by private parties—a proposition

---

[172] Pedersen, [*Turning the Tide on Water Quality*, 15 ECOLOGY L.Q. 69 (1988)]; *see id.* at 69-70 n.4 * * *

explicitly disavowed by Congress—the lack of specific legislative directives increases the need for executive oversight.

Advocates of citizen suits, in discussing arguments and evidence pointing toward excessive environmental enforcement, have continued to insist that Congress has left no room for considerations of cost, efficiency, or effects.[179] By providing that any amount of water pollution is too much, Congress is said to have mandated full enforcement at any cost. * * * But this insistence is misplaced. In the first instance, Congress could remedy underenforcement by raising the fines available under environmental statutes, by increasing the EPA's enforcement budget, or by doing both. This would be easier and more effective than the authorization of private attorneys general, whose decisions are hard to predict and even harder to control and correct. Second, and more importantly, the claim that Congress has mandated full enforcement at any cost is incompatible with the restrictions Congress has placed upon citizen suits—in particular, the injunction against profitable private enforcement. For why should enforcers not turn a profit, and why should their motives matter, if we know that every additional enforcement proceeding generates environmental benefits? The prohibition on profitable private enforcement shows that Congress does not assume that more enforcement is always better enforcement. Hence, that assumption cannot serve as a rationale for the lack of government control over citizen-enforcers.

* * *

VI. THE POLITICS OF PRIVATE ENFORCEMENT

* * *

* * *[E]nvironmental citizen suit provisions incorporate an amalgam of competing, conflicting, and mutually exclusive policies and purposes. One might want to attribute this phenomenon to conceptual confusion or political compromise, but the evidence suggests otherwise. The features that distinguish citizen suits from traditional bounty-hunter provisions have the effect of subsidizing the environmental movement. No other system of incentives and institutional arrangements would have the same effect. The most plausible inference is that the subsidization of the environmental movement is the *intended* effect of citizen suit provisions.

The most obvious case in point is the policy of permitting rewards in the forms of above-cost attorneys' fees and credit and mitigation projects. These rewards draw environmental organizations into the enforcement market. At the same time, the prohibition on profits erects a barrier to market entry. The result is an enforcement cartel, consisting principally of the environmental movement. Under no alternative incentive system would environmental advocacy groups fare equally as well.

A similar argument applies to what this Article has called the "private" elements of citizen suits. * * * [C]itizen suit provisions are suffused with the language and some of the elements of a private right of action. Private enforcers are not *quite* like the government. They have their own rights at stake. In practice, this ensures that citizen suits are not, as

---

[179] *See* van Putten & Jackson, [*Dilution of the Clean Water Act*, 19 U. MICH. J. L. REF. 863 (1986)] at 865-73; *see also* Terris, *Environmentalists' Citizen Suits*, 17 Envtl. L. Rep. (Envtl. Law Inst.) 10,254, 10,255-56 (1987).

were bounty-hunter provisions, a discretionary payment-for-services program that is open to all comers. Citizen suit provisions are an off-budget entitlement program for a particular political constituency. Obviously, this is advantageous for the intended beneficiaries. Entitlement programs are less vulnerable to executive discretion and budget cuts than are discretionary programs, and are not immediately discernible as subsidies.

* * *

The creation of an environmentalist enforcement cartel may not have been the original purpose of citizen suit provisions. The first environmental statute to permit private enforcement, the 1970 Clean Air Act, was passed in a great hurry and in a very emotional atmosphere. Its citizen suit provision was inserted at the last minute and maneuvered past congressional committees by Senator Muskie, the main sponsor of the Act. Nearly identical provisions were later written into almost every environmental statute, with mechanical regularity and without much deliberation. In 1970, Congress may have believed that enforcement proceedings would ordinarily be brought by individual citizens or neighborhood associations, and not by environmental advocacy groups (most of which were very young and small at the time and less numerous than they are today). However, Congress now knows, and has known for some time, that citizen suits serve as an entitlement program for environmental organizations. * * * [C]ongress is well aware that private enforcers do not bring the types of cases they were ostensibly supposed to bring; that private suits are normally brought not by "concerned citizens" but by professional lobbying and litigation groups; and that private enforcement usually results in private settlements containing substantial payments to environmental groups. Yet, Congress has done nothing to bring private enforcement more closely in line with the enforcement pattern it purportedly sought to achieve. In fact, far from being confused about the implications of citizen suit provisions, Congress has been very deliberate in straddling the conflicts and contradictions of private environmental law enforcement, and in maintaining the conditions that support the environmentalist enforcement cartel.

The 1987 amendments to the Clean Water Act provide the clearest example of the congressional awareness of the problems associated with private enforcement. The flood of private actions under the Clean Water Act had raised concerns in the EPA and the Department of Justice. Executive officials warned that private enforcement was coming dangerously close to producing a result which the congressional authors of environmental legislation ostensibly sought to prevent—namely, a shift of control over enforcement from the government to private parties. DOJ officials also argued that the frequent substitution of credit projects created a potential for abuse. They raised these concerns in congressional hearings and in public. Congress responded to these concerns by expanding government oversight of private settlements. As a result, proposed private settlements under the Clean Water Act must now be submitted to the Department of Justice, which may comment upon the settlements within forty-five days.

Although this provision was intended to preserve the government's primacy in environmental law enforcement, it falls short of doing so. Considering the sheer number and the complexity of proposed settlements, as well as the fact that the DOJ can devote only limited resources to the oversight process, forty-five days is an insufficient amount of time in which to exercise more than passing scrutiny upon most proposed settlements.

* * * The executive still is not permitted to *terminate* private actions or to void private settlements. In other words, Congress stopped short of transferring control over the enforcement process to the government. It did just enough to address the government's concerns and to correct the impression that citizen suits might be subject to "abuse," while failing to address the structural problems of private environmental law enforcement.

The deliberate, sustained congressional support for a "cartellized" enforcement process is explained by a number of mutually reinforcing factors. To an extent, private enforcement is a convenient mechanism to support favored political constituencies. Congress has come to utilize this mechanism extensively. Although environmental law, with few exceptions, has been the only field where private enforcement has taken the specific form of citizen suit provisions, private rights to sue, to object, to complain, and to comment have proliferated in many policy areas in which advocacy groups are active. * * *

* * *

This sprawling system of compulsory philanthropy has a partisan aspect: its beneficiaries—environmentalists, consumer groups, civil rights groups, community activists, among others—are uniformly constituencies of the Democratic Party. This is not surprising, since the Democrats have dominated the Congress for the entire period during which private enforcement provisions have proliferated. Still, the fact that Congress could attain the objective of supporting advocacy constituencies in a more direct and targeted form— namely, through grants and subsidies—indicates that more than mere partisanship is at work. Most obviously, direct grants would burden the federal budget, whereas the authorization of coerced wealth transfers does not. More importantly, though, constituency-based law enforcement comports with congressional, institutional interests and incentives far better than the available alternatives. As long as the law is enforced by the government or by bounty hunters, Congress can prevent undesired results only through a legislative selection of priorities—that is to say, by means of legislation or appropriations. For legislators, these processes are inconvenient at best and painful at worst. *Ex ante*, they involve unpopular trade-offs and the resolution of conflicts among a multitude of interest groups. *Ex post*, they entail responsibility for results. Hence, legislators are persistently inclined to make difficult regulatory choices look easy and to avoid responsibility. The current system permits them to do so. Congress legislates demands for zero pollution, facilitates the enforcement of that objective by the constituencies who demanded it, and disavows responsibility for the results. Enforcement cartels and coerced wealth transfers are an integral part of this technique of reducing the costs and increasing the benefits of doing legislative business.

The prevention of such a unilateral reduction of legislative transaction costs was the point of the separation of powers. As long as Congress cannot enforce the laws it produces, it will pass laws only if it is reasonably certain that they will be beneficial even when enforced by a president with a different political constituency and different institutional ambitions. Of course, Congress has always influenced law enforcement through appropriations, oversight, and other means. But, the separation of powers keeps Congress, at least, a step removed from the actual process of law enforcement. It preserves the crucial difference between governing and doing favors, and thwarts some of the more brazen attempts to aid political constituencies in the guise of advancing the public interest.

Once Congress manages to confer law enforcement powers upon its constituencies, public administration mirrors its worst institutional proclivities—a diffusion of responsibility, a relentless orientation toward procuring economic rents instead of public benefits, and an utter inability to distinguish between the implementation of public purposes and the conferral of benefits to "regulatory beneficiaries." There is perhaps no better illustration of this inability than the ambivalent status of "citizen-plaintiffs" between private actor and public authority.

It is almost certainly too late in the day to change environmental citizen suits in a fundamental way, to separate the exercise of public authority more clearly from interest group politics. The provisions, as currently written, enjoy enormous support among members of Congress and among members of the enforcement cartel. They are an integral part of the legislative and political scheme through which Congress has chosen to regulate environmental risk. Nonetheless, serious thought about the nature and purpose of citizen suits is worthwhile. The extensive use of environmental citizen suits by Congress may be attributed, at least in part, to the widely held view that the environment has a unique claim to judicial protection and citizen participation. But, as environmental law has become something of a paradigm for administrative law and social regulation in general, Congress has begun to "transfer" heretofore unique elements of environmental regulation, including citizen suit provisions, into other areas of the law. Before this process advances any further, citizen suit provisions deserve more careful scrutiny. If, as this Article has argued, the real purpose and effect of citizen suits is not efficient law enforcement but the subsidization of political constituencies, they are best treated not as an appropriate paradigm but as a peculiar feature of environmental law and policy.

NOTES

1. Dr. Greve's principal complaint is with the plethora of citizen suits filed under the Clean Water Act for violations discovered in Discharge Monitoring Reports (DMRs). DMRs describe the amount of pollutants actually discharged each month by the permittee. When compared with the permit, specifying the amount of pollutants authorized to be discharged, the DMRs make it fairly easy to determine whether the permittee has been violating its permit. If violations are in fact occurring, what is wrong with facilitating citizen suits to correct these violations?

2. Greve pays scant attention to the limitations on citizen suits. Prior notice must be provided to the EPA and, in suits to enforce alleged violations, to the state and the alleged violator. Governmental enforcement actions preclude overlapping citizen suits. See, *e.g.,* 33 U.S.C. § 1365(b) for the Clean Water Act language. Similar provisions appear in the other principal environmental statutes.

In addition, at least in Clean Water Act cases, citizen suits may not be brought seeking penalties for wholly-past violations. *Gwaltney of Smithfield, Ltd. v. Chesapeake Bay Foundation*, 484 U.S. 49 (1987). Furthermore, once a governmental agency issues a pollution permit, citizens may not sue the permittee for emitting pollutants not authorized by the permit. The permit provides a shield in that case, emphasizing the primacy of the regulatory agency and the supplementary role of the citizen suit. *See Atlantic States Legal Foundation v. Eastman Kodak, Inc.*, 12 F.3d 353 (2d Cir. 1994), *cert. denied,* 115 S. Ct. 62 (1994), and 33 U.S.C. § 1342(k) (Clean Water Act); 42 U.S.C. § 7661c(f) (Clean Air Act).

3. On the other hand, both Congress and the courts have expanded the availability of environmental citizen suits since Greve wrote the foregoing article in 1990.

When Congress enacted the Clean Air Act Amendments of 1990, it included a far-reaching set of provisions requiring operating permits for virtually all significant sources of air pollution. The new "Title V" permits, like the long-required NPDES permits under the Clean Water Act, require operators to submit regular reports describing their actual emissions. These reports can be readily compared with permit limits to spot (and prove) permit violations. Once the Title V permit program is in operation, the 1980s explosion of Clean Water Act citizen suits described by Greve may be replicated in the Clean Air Act context. *See* 42 U.S.C. §§ 7661-7661f (new Title V) and § 7604 (preexisting citizen suit provision, as amended in 1990).

The Ninth Circuit has recognized a new variety of the "endangerment" actions that citizens may pursue under the Resource Conservation and Recovery Act, 42 U.S.C. § 6972(a)(1)(B). In *KFC Western, Inc. v. Meghrig*, 49 F.3d 518 (9th Cir. 1995), *cert. granted,* 116 S. Ct. 41 (1995), the court held that not only could a citizen plaintiff obtain injunctive relief to abate an imminent or substantial endangerment as authorized under the cited section, but a citizen suit could also seek restitution of abatement costs that the plaintiff had incurred. *Contra Furrer v. Brown*, 62 F.3d 1092 (8th Cir. 1995) (holding that restitution or private cost recovery not authorized under the RCRA endangerment citizen suit). Because these cases involve the leakage of petroleum from an underground storage tank, a common occurrence, a Supreme Court decision upholding the Ninth Circuit could have far-reaching implications.

In the Clean Water Act context, a Supreme Court decision has already served to expand the scope of citizen suits. In *Northwest Environmental Advocates v. City of Portland,* 56 F.3d 979 (9th Cir. 1995), the Ninth Circuit vacated its initial decision and held that a citizen suit could allege the violation of a Clean Water Act permit condition prohibiting discharges in violation of applicable water quality standards, even where such standards were not specifically reflected in effluent limitations. In changing its initial ruling, the Ninth Circuit relied expressly on the Supreme Court's decision in *PUD No. 1 of Jefferson County v. Washington Department of Ecology,* 114 S. Ct. 1900 (1994), which held that states could exercise their certification authority under § 401 of the Clean Water Act, 33 U.S.C. § 1341, to protect designated water uses independent of the ultimate water quality standards derived from such designated uses.

4. One type of private action—for reimbursement of cleanup costs under the Comprehensive Environmental Response, Compensation, and Liability Act—has suffered a setback since 1990. In *Key Tronic Corp. v. United States,* 114 S. Ct. 1960 (1994), the Court held that parties pursuing private cost recovery claims under 42 U.S.C. § 9607 may not recover attorneys' fees incurred in the litigation. This decision does not affect the prototypical citizen suit, brought not for monetary recovery but to enforce a statutory provision against either the EPA or a regulated entity. Such citizen suits are separately authorized under CERCLA, which expressly allows for the award of attorneys' fees to prevailing or substantially prevailing parties, subject to the court's discretion. 42 U.S.C. § 9659.

5. Greve notes that many settlements of private enforcement actions involve a "credit project," whereby the defendant contributes funds to an environmental or community organization for purposes such as environmental research, education, or land acquisition. Greve contrasts the frequent inclusion of credit projects in private enforcement actions with their use only in "exceptional circumstances" in settlements of government-initiated enforcement actions. Greve cites (in a footnote omitted from the foregoing excerpt) the EPA's 1984 Civil Penalty Policy. In the decade since that policy, however, anecdotal evidence suggests that the EPA has been including credit projects in its settlements with greater frequency. For example, a routine EPA Press Release issued June 9, 1995 reported the settlement of an administrative enforcement action brought by EPA against Formosa Plastics for failure to report several releases in violation of the Emergency Planning Community Right-to-Know Act and the reporting provisions of CERCLA. In addition to paying a $50,000 civil penalty and installing a $1.68 million containment system to prevent future releases, Formosa also agreed to perform a $10,000 community benefit project and to contribute $35,000 to the local emergency planning committee. EPA, Press Release: Formosa Plastics Agrees to Compliance Package (June 9, 1995).

6. Since Greve's article was published in 1990, "supplemental environmental projects" have become important items in both government and citizen suit settlements. These projects typically commit the alleged violator to undertake pollution prevention activities that are not otherwise required by law. As of 1995, the Department of Justice seeks—through its review of citizen suit settlement agreements—a provision requiring reports to the court describing how the supplemental project money is being spent. *DOJ Says Prosecution Unlikely If Company 'Reasonably' Relies on State Interpretation,* 26 Env't Rep. (BNA) 180 (May 12, 1995).

7. Near the close of his article, Greve opines that the statutory sanctioning of private enforcement is politically-inspired, insofar as the groups that seek to utilize citizen suits are supporters of the Democratic Party and the statutory provisions were enacted by Democrat-majority Congresses. With the Republican assumption of majority control of Congress in 1995, will Congress seek to restrict or preclude private enforcement of environmental laws? Should it? What effects would that have on compliance? Might a reduction in citizen suits occasion a reduction in government enforcement?

8. Greve's article underscores the significance of environmental organizations in the shaping of environmental law. More generally, "nongovernmental organizations" (known to acronym aficionados as NGOs) affect lawmaking at the congressional level (*see* Elliott article in subpart A of this chapter), the administrative level (*see* Lazarus article in subpart B of this chapter), and the judicial level (*see* the foregoing Greve article). *See also* Richard B. Stewart, *The Reformation of American Administrative Law,* 88 HARV. L. REV. 1667 (1975).

9. Is it appropriate to criticize citizen suit enforcement by comparing it to "impartial, disinterested assessment of the public environmental benefits to be gained by enforcement"? Does the federal government engage in this impartial disinterested assessment? Note that in 1982, when the Natural Resources Defense Council began its citizen suit initiative, the EPA was demoralized by a substantial roll-back in enforcement and controversial settlements with industry under then-Administrator Gorsuch. *See* JONATHAN LASH, SEASON OF SPOILS: THE REAGAN ADMINISTRATION'S ATTACK ON THE ENVIRONMENT 45-53 (1984).

10. Would an old-fashioned bounty provision support better citizen enforcement of environmental laws? If Congress enacted a law allowing citizen suit plaintiffs to keep ninety percent of any penalty award otherwise payable to the U.S. Treasury, would that alter the current set of incentives in the "enforcement cartel"? At least one commentator has proposed enacting bounty provisions in environmental law to bolster citizen standing post-*Lujan.* Cass R. Sunstein, *What's Standing After* Lujan*? Of Citizen Suits, "Injuries," and Article III,* 91 MICH. L. REV. 163, 232-34 (1992).

In the Clean Air Act Amendments of 1990, Congress provided a bounty provision, although not one tied to citizen suits. Any person who furnishes information or services which lead to a criminal conviction or a civil penalty for a Clean Air Act violation may earn an award of up to $10,000 from the EPA. 42 U.S.C. § 7413(f).

11. One of the important matters addressed only tangentially in this chapter is governmental enforcement of environmental laws, referring principally to administrative and judicial enforcement actions, civil and criminal, initiated by administrative agencies such as the EPA (with legal representation, for judicial enforcement purposes, by the Department of Justice).

In the context of civil enforcement, additional sources include Leroy C. Paddock, *Environmental Enforcement at the Turn of the Century,* 21 ENVTL. L. 1509 (1991) (addressing the change in enforcement emphasis from fewer, larger pollution sources to more, and smaller, regulated entities); Peter J. Fontaine, *EPA's Multimedia Enforcement Strategy: The Struggle to Close the Environmental Compliance Circle,* 18 COLUM. J. ENVTL. L. 31

(1993) (discussing EPA's ongoing attempt to integrate the enforcement efforts under different statutes applicable to the same facility).

In the context of criminal enforcement, Congress in 1990 spurred the already-growing use of criminal sanctions to punish violations of the environmental laws. The Pollution Prosecution Act of 1990 directs the EPA to hire specified numbers of criminal investigators (as well as civil investigators), and to establish a National Enforcement Training Institute to train civil and criminal enforcement personnel. Each year, the EPA reports new record numbers of criminal prosecutions, of prison sentences meted out, and of monetary fines imposed. ENVIRONMENTAL PROTECTION AGENCY, ENFORCEMENT AND COMPLIANCE ASSURANCE ACCOMPLISHMENTS REPORT FY 1994 (EPA 300-R-95-004) (May 1995).

12. Perhaps the single most notable aspect of the criminal enforcement case law is the courts' construction of the knowledge element of environmental crimes. For example, most of the circuits that have addressed the issue have held that, in order for the government to obtain a criminal conviction under RCRA for knowingly treating, storing, or disposing of hazardous waste without a RCRA permit, 42 U.S.C. § 6928(d)(2)(A), the government need only demonstrate that the defendant knew that he or she was treating, storing, or disposing of hazardous waste; it need not prove that the defendant knew that a permit was required or that such permit was lacking. *See, e.g., United States v. Laughlin*, 10 F.3d 961 (2d Cir. 1993), *cert. denied sub nom. Goldman v. U.S.*, 114 S. Ct. 1649 (1994); *United States v. Goldsmith*, 978 F.2d 643 (11th Cir. 1992); and *U.S. v. Dean*, 969 F.2d 187 (6th Cir. 1992), *cert. denied*, 113 S. Ct. 1852 (1993). *But see United States v. Speach*, 968 F.2d 795 (9th Cir. 1992) (regarding 42 U.S.C. § 6928(d)(1)).

In a comprehensive and critical analysis of the development of environmental criminal law, Professor Lazarus finds that the principles of criminal law have not been effectively integrated into the environmental statutory framework.

> All three branches of government did not, in their respective spheres of responsibility, consider the nature, aims, and limits of criminal law and how they relate
> to the underlying substantive offenses defined in the environmental statutes.

Richard J. Lazarus, *Meeting the Demands of Integration in the Evolution of Environmental Law: Reforming Environmental Criminal Law,* 83 GEO. L. J. 2407, 2412 (1995). For other scholarly analyses of the environmental crimes area, *see* Christopher H. Schroeder, *Cool Analysis Versus Moral Outrage in the Development of Federal Environmental Criminal Law,* 35 WM. & MARY L. REV. 251 (1993); and Helen J. Brunner, *Environmental Criminal Enforcement: A Retrospective View,* 22 ENVTL. L. 1315 (1992).

The final selection in this chapter addresses a significant aspect of "environmental" litigation that is outside the scope of the statutory scheme on which the rest of this chapter is so heavily focused—toxic tort actions. Notwithstanding the complex array of seemingly-comprehensive statutes, none of the federal environmental laws authorizes a private action for personal injury or property damage associated with polluting activities, even when tnose activities involve statutory violations. In contrast to the strict liability rules that govern in statutory enforcement actions, toxic tort claims require proof of causation. That has been a substantial obstacle to the successful litigation of many toxic tort cases, and is the subject of Professor Farber's article below.

Toxic Causation
Daniel A. Farber
71 Minn. L. Rev. 1219 (1987)*

Since 1970, legal attention to the risks created by toxic substances has increased dramatically. Congress has passed numerous regulatory statutes aimed at preventing future problems or cleaning up current hazards. In the meantime, courts have been faced with an increasing number of tort actions seeking damages for injuries allegedly caused by toxic substances. These cases have presented the legal system with a wide range of novel issues, and have sometimes strained the system to its limits. One of the most intriguing of these toxic tort issues involves causation. Proof that a toxic substance is harmful often involves evidence on the frontiers of science. In many cases, the most that can be said is that exposure to a substance increased the risk that the plaintiff would contract a disease. Epidemiological evidence often can indicate only the probability that the plaintiff's injury was caused by the defendant. The difficult problem of how to handle these cases has given rise to extensive scholarly debate.

At present, something of a scholarly consensus exists in favor of making recoveries proportional to the probability of causation. For instance, if there was a thirty percent likelihood that the defendant caused the plaintiff's cancer, the plaintiff would receive thirty percent of his total damages. Proportional recovery spreads compensation over all possible victims, fully compensating no one but paying something even on the weakest claims.

This Article argues that proportional recovery is valid only under limited circumstances. It proposes a new theory (called the MLV or "most likely victim" approach) that is generally more appropriate. Under MLV, those plaintiffs whose injuries were least likely to have been caused by the defendant receive nothing, while those with the highest causation probabilities get full compensation. MLV has the advantage of focusing compensation on those who were most clearly injured by the defendant, while denying compensation to those whose claims are the most speculative. Even where MLV is not directly applicable, the theory illuminates the proper handling of other varieties of toxic tort cases.

* * *

I. THE EMERGING LAW OF TOXIC CAUSATION

Understanding the causation issue requires some background. This issue arises in the context of toxic tort litigation, which in itself is a new and rapidly changing field. Courts have had more occasion to think about causation in the related field of toxics regulation.

---

* Reprinted with permission.

In the last few years, however, a substantial number of toxic tort opinions have come out of the lower federal courts. These opinions are useful not only because of what they may indicate about the direction of legal development, but also because they illuminate the diverse factual settings in which the toxic causation issue arises.

A. Toxic Torts In A Nutshell

The plaintiff's first problem is to establish that the defendant's conduct met the requisite liability standard. Although many toxic tort plaintiffs have brought actions under products liability theories holding manufacturers strictly liable for defective products, the liability standard is less clear in cases not involving manufacturers. The generally accepted liability test for hazardous waste releases is stated in the Second Restatement of Torts. Under this test, liability exists despite the exercise of due care if an activity was "abnormally dangerous." To determine whether an activity is abnormally dangerous, a court must weigh the probability and severity of foreseeable harm, whether the activity is unusual or is in an inappropriate location, and other factors. Thus, fault plays a role in the Restatement assessment. A few courts have rejected this fault element, however, and have begun to move beyond the abnormally dangerous test. In *State v. Ventron Corp.*, the New Jersey Supreme Court imposed strict liability for harm caused by toxic substances escaping from a landowner's property.[21]

Even if the defendant's conduct meets the requisite legal standard for liability, several possible barriers may prevent recovery. Statutes of limitations can create major difficulties in some states. * * *

Another problem is establishing a link between the defendant and the release of the substance. For example, many hazardous waste generators may have shipped similar materials to the site in question. It may be quite difficult to establish whose containers leaked or in what quantities. A similar issue can arise in products liability cases. In *Sindell v. Abbott Laboratories*, the plaintiff's mother was administered the drug diethylstilbesterol (DES) during pregnancy. Although DES was routinely given to prevent miscarriage, it is now known to cause a rare form of cancer in some daughters of women who took the drug. After developing such cancer, the plaintiff sued eleven of the more than two hundred manufacturers of DES. Although the plaintiff was unable to identify the manufacturer of the particular DES which her mother took, the court held that she had stated a cause of action against manufacturers of the drug using an identical formula. * * * The *Sindell* court then adopted a novel theory of liability by making each defendant liable for a share of the plaintiff's damages, based on its share of the DES market. Assuming that the *Sindell* theory or one of its variants becomes the norm in products liability litigation, it could be readily adapted to hazardous waste litigation.

B. The Causation Problem

Sindell and related theories address the problem of linking the defendant to the chemical exposure. An even more difficult problem is that of linking the exposure to the plaintiff's injury. It is a commonplace that toxic chemical regulation involves matters at the boundaries

---

[21] [94 N.J. 473, 468 A.2d 150 (1983)] at 491, 468 A.2d at 159-60. * * *

of scientific knowledge. This scientific uncertainty causes severe problems for government regulators, but even more serious problems result for private plaintiffs who must establish a defendant's liability by a preponderance of the evidence.

In considering compensation, it is important to keep in mind that there are really two causation problems. One is the problem of establishing that the chemical involved is capable of causing the type of harm from which the plaintiff suffers. This is often difficult because the causation of diseases like cancer is so poorly understood. For this reason, medical theory is relatively unhelpful in filling in gaps in the factual picture. Facts themselves are hard to come by. Many toxic substances are relatively novel, and, given the long latency periods associated with cancer, sufficient evidence concerning health effects is not likely to be available for the foreseeable future. Animal studies, although useful, generally involve much higher doses that are difficult to extrapolate to low doses over prolonged periods; there is also the question of whether extrapolation of results between species is valid. Epidemiological studies are also helpful but often inconclusive regarding the level of risk created by a toxic substance.

The other problem relating to proof of causation is that of establishing, given that the toxic substance in question can cause harm of the type suffered by the plaintiff, that the plaintiff's harm did in fact result from such exposure. A chemical may increase the prevalence of a disease enough to leave no doubt that some members of the exposed population were injured by that chemical. Others, however, may have suffered injuries from independent sources, and the two groups may be impossible to distinguish. The statistical association between exposure and illness may be too weak to justify a finding that a particular plaintiff's disease is causally linked to an exposure to a hazardous substance.

1. Causation in the Regulatory Context

Toxic chemicals are regulated under a number of federal statutes. A recurring problem has been the difficulty of establishing, given the limits of present scientific knowledge, that a particular substance is indeed a health hazard and therefore subject to regulation.

The leading case on the problem of scientific uncertainty in this context is *Reserve Mining Co. v. EPA*.[42] Reserve Mining discharged huge amounts of mining byproducts containing asbestos into Lake Superior, thereby contaminating Duluth's drinking water. In considering the question of risk, the Eighth Circuit was handicapped by a lack of scientific evidence on the danger of ingesting (as opposed to inhaling) asbestos. The plaintiffs' only significant evidence was that workers exposed to asbestos dust suffered from a moderate increase in gastro-intestinal cancer. One possible explanation, according to expert witnesses, was that asbestos workers first inhaled the asbestos dust and then coughed up and swallowed the asbestos particles. The most the court could conclude was that public exposure to asbestos fibers "gives rise to a reasonable medical concern for the public health."[45] The court was unable to conclude, however, that "the probability of harm is more likely than not."[46] Nevertheless, given the potential seriousness of the threat

---

[42] 514 F.2d 492 (8th Cir. 1975). * * *
[45] [514 F.2d 492] at 520 [(8th Cir. 1975)].
[46] *Id.*

to public health, the Eighth Circuit found the evidence sufficient to justify an order requiring Reserve Mining to eliminate the discharge expeditiously.

The Supreme Court's first encounter with the problem of toxic chemicals was in *Industrial Union Department, AFL-CIO v. American Petroleum Institute*, generally known as the "benzene case." The case involved an occupational safety regulation governing benzene, a carcinogen for which a safe level of exposure is not known to exist. The Secretary of Labor had set the permissible exposure level for workers at one part per million (ppm), which he considered the lowest economically feasible level that industries could achieve. * * * According to the plurality opinion, the Secretary must make a threshold finding of a "significant risk of harm" before issuing any regulation.[51] The plurality went to some lengths to rebut the dissent's charge that this approach would prevent effective regulation until deaths had actually occurred. First, the plurality stated that what constitutes a "significant" risk was a judgment for the agency to make and plainly involved policy considerations. Second, the plurality noted that the agency's findings need not be supported by "anything approaching scientific certainty." Thus, the plurality concluded that "so long as they are supported by a body of reputable scientific thought, the Agency is free to use conservative assumptions in interpreting the data with respect to carcinogens, risking error on the side of overprotection rather than underprotection."[54]

* * *

The courts' relatively liberal attitude toward proof of harm in the regulatory context might appear to argue strongly for a similar attitude in the compensation context. In the regulatory cases, however, the issue is one of prevention. If society can prevent possible injuries in the future by taking sensible preventive action today, clearly society ought to do so even if no one can be sure that any injuries would otherwise occur. Wearing a seat belt makes sense even though you do not know in advance that you will ever be in an accident. Moreover, prevention does not require that the particular victims be identified. Compensation is a different matter. We do not impose liability on a driver who *might* have been involved in a car crash but who was more likely in a different city on the day of the accident. Prevention is always linked to the possibility of a future accident. Compensation, although serving some deterrent purpose, is primarily based on the existence of a past accident. Thus, the regulatory cases have only limited relevance to the compensation problem.

2. Tort Litigation

Despite the novelty of tort litigation over toxic causation, clear patterns have already evolved in some areas. * * *

Litigation about Agent Orange, a defoliant and herbicide used by American forces in the Vietnam War, has provided the most extensive judicial discussion of toxic causation. Numerous lawsuits were filed against the manufacturers by veterans, their families, and others who contended that Agent Orange had caused various illnesses. Ultimately, the litigation was consolidated in Judge Weinstein's court in the Eastern District of New

---

[51] [448 U.S. 607] at 642 [(1980)]. * * *
[54] *Id.* [at 656].

York. The weakness of the plaintiffs' causation evidence persuaded Judge Weinstein to approve a $180 million settlement, which was considered highly favorable to the defendants.

As Judge Weinstein explained, the evidence concerning the possible dangers from Agent Orange would have been enough for a court to uphold an administrative order limiting its use. Emphasizing the distinction between preventive regulatory measures and compensatory legal actions, however, Judge Weinstein noted that "[i]n the latter [case], a far higher probability (greater than 50%) is required since the law believes it unfair to require an individual to pay for another's tragedy unless it is shown that it is more likely than not that he caused it."[70] The key flaw in the plaintiffs' case was that government epidemiological studies showed no statistical link between Agent Orange exposure and significant health effects. * * *

In companion cases, involving opt-outs or individuals never included in the class, Judge Weinstein was forced to rule on the merits of the plaintiffs' claims. In these cases, he granted summary judgment for the defendants despite the plaintiffs' tender of expert testimony linking Agent Orange with health effects. The epidemiological studies played a key role in these decisions. "The numerous epidemiological studies . . . are sufficient to shift the burden to plaintiffs of showing that a material fact exists as to causation."[74] Judge Weinstein ruled the plaintiffs' expert testimony inadmissible, and then granted summary judgment because the plaintiffs had no admissible evidence to counter the defendants' epidemiological studies.

* * * The D.C. Circuit, however, has permitted recovery solely on the basis of expert clinical assessments despite a lack of statistical evidence. In *Ferebee v. Chevron Chemical Co.*, the court stated:

> Thus, a cause-effect relationship need not be clearly established by animal or epidemiological studies before a doctor can testify that, in his opinion, such a relationship exists. As long as the basic methodology employed to reach such a conclusion is sound, such as use of tissue samples, standard tests, and patient examination, products liability law does not preclude recovery until a "statistically significant" number of people have been injured or until science has had the time and resources to complete sophisticated laboratory studies of the chemical. In a courtroom, the test for allowing a plaintiff to recover in a tort suit of this type is not scientific certainty but legal sufficiency. . . .[79]

This language, while not inconsistent with Judge Weinstein's rulings, seems more favorable toward the admission of expert testimony.

Although a few courts have followed *Ferebee's* broader view of admissibility, the law of toxic causation is just beginning to receive judicial attention. Clearly, a "Restatement of the Law of Toxic Torts" would be premature. It is not too early, however, to look for patterns in the cases and to begin to undertake a theoretical analysis of the causation issue.

---

[70] [*In re "Agent Orange" Prods. Liab. Litig.*, 597 F. Supp. 740] at 781 [(E.D.N.Y. 1984)].

[74] *In re "Agent Orange" Prods. Liab. Litig.*, 611 F. Supp. at 1259.

[79] [736 F.2d 1529] at 1535-36 [(D.C. Cir.), *cert. denied*, 469 U.S. 1062 (1984)].

II. THEORETICAL PERSPECTIVES ON TOXIC CAUSATION

* * *

A. The Scholarly Debate On Proportional Recovery

Much of the causation debate has revolved around a single paradigm case. In this paradigm case, a chemical is known to have raised the death rate by some specified amount over the background rate for a particular disease. For example, suppose the normal rate of some variety of cancer among the unexposed public is ten cases per 100,000; among the exposed population, the rate is fifteen per 100,000. Under the "preponderance of the evidence" standard, none of the fifteen cancer victims could recover, because two-thirds of them probably would have gotten the disease anyway (although we do not know which two-thirds). Yet, it seems unjust to relieve the defendant of liability, because the defendant very likely did cause five cancer cases.

Several scholars have argued that these plaintiffs should receive a recovery proportional to the probability that they were harmed by the defendant. * * * Regardless of the mechanics, the result is to expand compensation beyond the plaintiffs who actually got cancer from the chemical while correspondingly reducing each plaintiff's recovery.

Powerful arguments have been made in favor of proportional recovery. *Sindell* has already established that a plaintiff may recover without proving a particular defendant was the cause of the injury. Proportional recovery inverts *Sindell*, allowing recovery where the uncertainty concerns the identity of the injured party rather than that of the defendant. A general consensus seems to exist in favor of blurring the causation requirement in the *Sindell* situation of the "indeterminate defendant." It seems but a small additional step to do so here for the "indeterminate plaintiff." Another point in favor of proportional recovery is that it guarantees that the defendant pays the plaintiffs as a class for the full amount of injury done by the chemical. The defendant is thus given a powerful economic incentive to avoid imposing this harm. Without proportional recovery, the defendant would often escape liability altogether because of the causation problems. Economic theory indicates that requiring defendants to "internalize" these costs increases economic efficiency. Finally, imposing liability serves the goal of "loss spreading" by shifting some of the loss from individuals to firms that can often pass on the cost of insurance to their customers. * * *

* * *

Thus, although proportional recovery is a substantial deviation from current practice, the theoretical arguments against it are unpersuasive. A more serious question is how often the factual assumptions underlying proportional recovery are valid. The key assumption—the paradigm case—is that the only evidence of causation is a single statistic expressing the increased rate of disease (or death) among the exposed population. As it turns out, this assumption is often false. Normally, at least some additional information is available, and a different solution becomes appropriate.

B. The MLV Remedy: Compensating The Most Likely Victims

Generally, all of those exposed to a toxic chemical are not equally at risk. Although the exact relationship between doses and disease rates is often poorly understood, the risk of disease is normally related to the amount of exposure. The timing of exposure may also be significant; for example, exposure to DES early in pregnancy seems to have been much more dangerous than exposure late in pregnancy. Thus, the assumption of a uniform increase above the background rate is generally unrealistic.

Similarly, the assumption of a uniform background rate is valid only when nothing except the link to chemical exposure is known about a disease. Often, however, at least some knowledge of other risk factors exists. For instance, cigarette smokers are more likely to get lung cancer than nonsmokers, and the difference is even greater among asbestos workers.

Thus, given two individuals who have become ill after exposure to a chemical, some basis often exists for believing that the chemical was more likely to have caused one case than the other. Using a single statistic for the entire group as a basis for proportional recovery thus overcompensates some plaintiffs and undercompensates others. * * *

One possible solution would be to divide the group into subgroups composed of individuals with comparable risks. As a practical matter, the data may not allow such fine-tuning. There may exist only a qualitative knowledge about the distribution of risk within the group, rather than the quantitative information needed to make each subgroup's recovery proportional to that subgroup's risk. * * *

To understand the proper treatment of these cases, it is helpful to begin with a somewhat simplified example. Suppose we have a single defendant D and a group of N exposed individuals, $X_1, X_2, \ldots X_N$. Each individual has suffered one unit of damage due to cancer. For the individual X_i, the probability that the defendant caused the individual's cancer is p_i, with $p_1 > p_2 > \ldots p_N$. The total amount of damage actually caused by the defendant is M, with $M <$ than N.

The first question is how much D should pay in damages. For much the same reasons advanced in favor of proportional recovery, the answer would seem to be M, the total amount of damage caused by the defendant. This amount provides the proper economic deterrent to D's behavior. Even if we do not count depriving D of these funds as an affirmative good, D has very little ground for complaint so long as the damages are not greater than the actual injury. * * *

* * *

A more difficult question is presented by the argument that individuals should be compensated for exposure to risk, not merely for the harm that results in some instances. As one of the commentators who argues for risk-based compensation admits, this is a substantial deviation from normal tort law:

> [I]t is difficult to conceive as a practical matter how one could have an action for the risk of an automobile accident. Either plaintiff has been in an accident or he has not; if he has not it seems queer to think of bringing suit against a negligent driver for a harm that might have occurred but did not.[117]

The only real difference between the automobile case and the toxics case is that better information is available about the events in the automobile case whereas the relevant biological events in the toxics case are unobservable. If some method did exist of determin-

---

[117] Robinson, [*Probabilistic Causation and Compensation for Tortious Risk,* 14 J. LEGAL STUD. 779] at 797 [(1985)].

ing the cause of a particular plaintiff's cancer, courts would presumably follow the normal rules of tort law and award damages only to plaintiffs who could show actual causation. Imperfect information prevents us from implementing this rule, but the compensation scheme should attempt to approximate the result as much as possible.

Assume, then, that the goal is to compensate those whose injuries were actually caused by the defendant so that each dollar going to such a plaintiff is counted as a success. We may not begrudge the other plaintiffs their money (after all, they have suffered a serious illness), but we would prefer that the money went to D's "actual victims." If we let S be the amount of money successfully distributed to D's actual victims, then the statistically expected value of S is simply $p_1z_i + \ldots p_Nz_N$, where z_i, is the amount of damages received by the ith victim. Presumably, we do not wish to give any plaintiff more than his actual damages (set at one unit). This gives us the simple mathematical problem of maximizing the expected value of S.

The solution is to give the M units of damages to the M plaintiffs with the highest probabilities of being actual victims, giving nothing to the remaining plaintiffs. * * * The basic reason * * * is fairly obvious. If we take a dollar from a plaintiff high on the probability list and give it to one lower down the list, the odds are less that the new recipient is an actual victim. So we can maximize the odds that the money will go to actual victims by loading as much as possible high on the list. Because the only constraint is that no victim should receive more than a unit of damages, we give one unit to the victim with the highest probability and keep going down the list until we run out of money with victim $M + 1$. This is the MLV or "most likely victim" approach to compensation.

Obviously, literally ranking all victims is impractical in actual litigation. The MLV solution can be approximated, however, by putting the victims in subgroups, going down the list of subgroups, paying full compensation to each subgroup, until the defendant's total damages have been exhausted. Implementing MLV is more difficult if each plaintiff brings a separate case but the problems do not seem insurmountable * * *.

An example may help clarify the differences between the various methods of compensation. Suppose we have a group of fifty-one people who have developed cancer after exposure to a drug. Based on the amount of exposure and the individuals' other risk characteristics, we have determined the probability that each individual's cancer was caused by the drug. The first individual has a fifty-one percent probability of causation, the second individual has a fifty percent probability, the third has a forty-nine percent probability, all the way down to the fifty-first person, who has a probability of only one percent. The average probability of causation is twenty-six percent. Each individual has suffered one million dollars in damages. This means that we can expect that the drug caused about thirteen cases of cancer (twenty-six percent of fifty-one individuals), or thirteen million dollars in damages.

Under the traditional preponderance standard, only one individual (the highest person on the list) can show that the drug "more likely than not" caused her disease. Hence, she receives one million dollars and the defendant is relieved of any liability for the remaining twelve million dollars of damages caused by the drug. This is an unjustifiable windfall to the defendant.

Under proportional recovery, each individual receives a percentage of his damages. This avoids any windfall to the defendant, but distributes the fund poorly. For example, the individual with a one percent probability of causation gets one percent of his damages, or $10,000. The odds are overwhelming (ninety-nine to one) that this money is going to someone who is not actually a victim of the drug. If we transferred the payment to the top person on the list, we would have better than even odds that the recipient would be an actual victim.

MLV does a better job of targeting victims. Under MLV, we start at the top of the list and pay off the claims in full until we run out of money. This means that the top thirteen people on the list get full compensation; those with causation probabilities below thirty-eight percent get nothing. If we were to move a dollar from the top group to the bottom group, we would necessarily lower the odds that the money was going to an actual victim. Under MLV, the defendant pays out a total of thirteen million dollars, thus avoiding any windfall, and as much as possible of the money is directed to actual victims.

Thus, the MLV approach maximizes the amount of money going to plaintiffs whose injuries were actually caused by the defendant. It has some other advantages over proportional recovery. Plaintiffs who are low on the probability list may not really be even "possible victims" of the defendant, let alone actual victims. Probability information is unlikely to be perfectly reliable; the lower the probability assigned a given plaintiff, the more likely that the true probability is zero. Also, applying proportional recovery to a heterogenous group requires reliable quantitative information about subgroups. To apply proportional recovery, we must know not only that members of subgroup *A* had higher risks than those in subgroup *B*, but also the precise amount of the difference in risk in order to calculate the recovery percentages. In contrast, MLV requires only a qualitative ranking of subgroups. Epidemiological knowledge is expensive, hard to obtain, and often imprecise. The less we need to demand of the epidemiologists, the better.

* * *

* * * Admittedly, MLV does not achieve equity between groups of victims, because some groups known to contain some victims receive no compensation. Unfortunately, any attempt to achieve intergroup equity necessarily increases the amount of money going to individuals whose injuries were not in reality caused by the defendant. Thus, greater equity between groups can only be purchased at the expense of less fairness to individuals.

* * *

III. A TAXONOMY OF TOXIC CAUSATION CASES

Current understanding of toxic torts is as yet fairly limited. What is clear is that toxics cases come in many forms. * * *

A. Conclusive Evidence On Causation: "Signature Disease" And "No Causation" Cases

The scholarly literature might easily give the impression that toxic causation is invariably mysterious. In many cases, however, the causation issue is quite clear-cut.

One group of cases involves so-called "signature" diseases. These are diseases that are extremely rare in the general population but far more prevalent among those exposed to a particular substance; the disease in a sense bears the signature of the substance. A classic example is mesothelioma, an unusual, lethal form of cancer. Most cases are associated with exposure to asbestos. The odds of contracting mesothelioma are roughly seventy times greater for asbestos workers than for members of the general population. This means that when an asbestos worker gets mesothelioma, it is almost certainly caused by asbestos.

We might, following the proportional recovery theory, reduce the damages paid each worker by a small fraction to represent the remote possibility that the mesothelioma might not be asbestos-induced. Given the inevitable crudeness of the tort system, such fine-tuning seems somewhat inappropriate, rather like putting velvet gloves on the proverbial bull in the china shop. * * * Rather, the proper approach would seem to be an irrebuttable presumption of causation in mesothelioma cases.

* * *

The MLV approach strengthens the argument for an irrebuttable presumption of causation. Victims of "signature diseases" are clearly in the category of "most likely victims." Hence, MLV theory indicates that their claims should be paid in full, while cutting off speculative claims at the other end of the spectrum.

Causation also poses no great conceptual problem in another set of cases. These are the cases in which the evidence affirmatively disproves the possibility of a causal link. To date, the most important example is found in the Agent Orange cases, in which Judge Weinstein found no admissible evidence of causation and powerful epidemiological evidence disproving causation. Although the correctness of his admissibility ruling may be debatable, Judge Weinstein's opinion makes it clear that the weight of the evidence was strongly against the plaintiffs. Apparently, Agent Orange simply did not pose long-term risks to its users. These "no causation" cases may involve difficult matters of proof and may raise real concerns about jury control, but they do not require any conceptual inquiry into the role of causation in tort law.

B. "Purely Statistical" and "Statistics Plus" Cases

* * * [P]roportional recovery is normally the proper remedy if our only information is a uniform increase in a uniform background rate. It is rather difficult, however, to find any examples of this situation.

The "statistics plus" cases are much more common. In these cases, we have statistics demonstrating an overall increase in the incidence of a disease, as well as information indicating varying degrees of increased risk within the exposed group. For example, the risk of lung cancer among asbestos workers is apparently affected by the type of asbestos used in an industry, the length and degree of exposure, and cigarette smoking (even taking into account the direct effect of smoking on lung cancer). In these cases, the proper solution is the MLV remedy. We should pay full compensation to those with the highest risks attributable to asbestos, for example, cigarette smokers with high asbestos exposure in high-risk industries, and no compensation to those with the lowest risks, for example, nonsmokers with low exposure in low-risk industries.

* * *

C. Diffuse Risks

Another category of cases involves very small increases to existing widespread risks. For example, some estimates indicate that carcinogens in drinking water may cause roughly a thousand cases of cancer nationwide annually. Such information may provide a sufficiently reliable basis for government regulation. For three reasons, however, compensation for such diffuse risks, whether administered by courts or administrative agencies, is far more problematic.

First, because of the difficulties of conducting epidemiological studies of these diffuse risks, the estimates of risk are extremely unreliable. * * * Even when the estimates are available at the time of a chemical's release, their extraordinary unreliability would make it extremely difficult for the discharger to foresee the extent of future liability. This makes any deterrent effect highly speculative at best.

Further, because the level of risk is often quite low in these cases, even under a proportional liability scheme the individual recoveries could be very small—perhaps on the order of one to ten percent of an individual's damages. Thus, compensation for diffuse risks often would not substantially serve the goal of loss spreading. Moreover, in cases involving extremely low-risk levels, the vast majority of recipients would be individuals who were not in fact harmed by the chemicals. Thus, in these cases, compensation has little to recommend it even from the "victim's perspective."

Finally, for many diffuse risks, any compensation scheme would involve high transaction costs. To take the example of drinking water, the cost of compensation would have to be somehow allocated among thousands of municipalities and industrial sources. Some method would have to be devised for distributing the proceeds among the enormous group of cancer patients in this country. The entire proceeding would be complicated still more, of course, by the high degree of uncertainty about the total risk and how it is distributed among the populations, what chemicals create the greatest part of the risk, which individuals are most affected, and so forth. * * *

As information about particular toxic substances expands, some risks may be well enough understood to allow the creation of a sensible compensation system based on the MLV theory. At present, however, most diffuse risks cannot be meaningfully made the subject of compensation. * * * Although compensation rules can be adapted to deal with less than certain knowledge of causation, there comes a point at which uncertainty becomes overwhelming. Any attempt to press compensation beyond that point is counterproductive.

D. Clinical Proof Cases

Some toxics cases do not fit the statistical mold of the cases we have discussed so far. Rather than relying on statistical evidence, the plaintiff may simply present the testimony of experts familiar with the facts of the case, giving their opinion that toxic exposure was the cause of the injury. If they contradict more rigorous epidemiological evidence, these clinical assessments should be given little weight. Often, however, more reliable information is unavailable.

* * *

Although MLV theory is not directly applicable to these cases (given the lack of statistical data), MLV is nevertheless relevant. The goal still should be to compensate the most likely victims. Even where quantitative information is not available, this goal can still be implemented. Among the class of potential plaintiffs exposed to a hazard, successful plaintiffs should be those with the relatively strongest claims. Thus, they should have relatively high exposures and should not exhibit other risk factors that would tend to explain the disease.

CONCLUSION

The most intriguing of the causation cases involve statistical proof that the plaintiffs' injuries may be due to the defendant, but at a level of probability well below certainty. For these cases, previous writers have suggested some form of proportional recovery. Proportional recovery is actually appropriate, however, only when the risk is uniform across the class of plaintiffs.

This Article proposes a new approach to cases involving nonuniform risks. When different plaintiffs have different probabilities of having been injured by the defendant, the MLV ("most likely victim") approach is more appropriate than proportional recovery. This approach allocates the total damages the defendant has caused to a subset of plaintiffs, those whose injuries were the most likely to have been caused by the defendant.

Perhaps the most striking characteristic of toxic causation cases is their diversity. In some, the defendant's responsibility for the plaintiff's injury is nearly indisputable; in others, defendants may be clearly innocent of causal responsibility. Some cases involve individual plaintiffs who were exposed to rare chemicals; others involve thousands of plaintiffs and imperil the financial stability of entire industries. It is the beginning of wisdom to realize that no one approach can do justice under such diverse circumstances.

NOTES

1. Does Professor Farber convince you that providing damages to some (more likely) victims but not to others is fair? Under the problem he hypothesizes (part II.B. of the article), the person with a causation probability of thirty-nine percent would obtain full recovery, yet the person with a causation probability of thirty-eight percent would be denied any recovery. Is this fair, particularly when considering the high degree of uncertainty surrounding the calculation of causation probabilities? Might Farber's MLV approach be modified to achieve his objectives without denying recovery altogether to those who fall just below the full recovery line?

2. Troyen Brennan, Professor of Law and Public Health at the Harvard School of Public Health, has contributed a thorough analysis of the development of toxic tort litigation. After a detailed evaluation of the reasons for and impact of toxic tort litigation during the 1970s and 1980s, Professor Brennan concludes as follows:

> For now, the incidence of environmental tort litigation is simply too low to support any empirical analysis. Instead we must rely on the kind of conjecture that has characterized the normative theory of environmental torts discussed here. This Article's tentative conclusion is that more litigation, incorporating some of the caveats noted above, is advisable from a deterrence point of view.

Given the failure of regulation and the theoretical benefits of common-law litigation, any other course seems to sanction the status quo of morbidity and mortality from environmental pollution.

Troyen A. Brennan, *Environmental Torts,* 46 VAND. L. REV. 1, 73 (1993).

3. Causation is but one of the complex issues that frequently arise in toxic tort cases. Another is whether the plaintiff's common law claim has been expressly or implicitly preempted by the federal statutes regulating the emission of pollutants or the manufacture and sale of chemicals and pesticides. *See* Robert L. Glicksman, *Federal Preemption and Private Legal Remedies for Pollution*, 134 U. PA. L. REV. 121 (1985).

4. Another difficult issue in toxic tort cases is whether novel scientific evidence is admissible at trial. Although the Supreme Court rarely addresses toxic tort matters, as they are grounded in state common law, the Court in 1993 decided a case concerning scientific evidence admissibility. In *Daubert v. Merrell Dow Pharmaceuticals, Inc.,* 113 S. Ct. 2786 (1993), the Court held that the Federal Rules of Evidence had supplanted the common law rule of admissibility, originally articulated in *Frye v. United States,* 293 F. 1013 (D.C. Cir. 1923), which required that novel scientific evidence meet the rigorous test of "general acceptance" in the scientific community in order to be admissible. The Court held that admissibility is now governed by the Federal Rules of Evidence, principally Rule 702:

> * * * [U]nder the Rules the trial judge must ensure that any and all scientific testimony or evidence admitted is not only relevant, but reliable.
>
> * * * The subject of an expert's testimony must be "scientific . . . knowledge." The adjective "scientific" implies a grounding in the methods and procedures of science. Similarly, the word "knowledge" connotes more than subjective belief or unsupported speculation. * * * Of course, it would be unreasonable to conclude that the subject of scientific testimony must be "known" to a certainty; arguably, there are no certainties in science. * * * But, in order to qualify as "scientific knowledge," an inference or assertion must be derived by the scientific method. Proposed testimony must be supported by appropriate validation—i.e., "good grounds," based on what is known. In short, the requirement that an expert's testimony pertain to "scientific knowledge" establishes a standard of evidentiary reliability.
>
> Rule 702 further requires that the evidence or testimony "assist the trier of fact to understand the evidence or to determine a fact in issue." This condition goes primarily to relevance. * * * Rule 702's "helpfulness" standard requires a valid scientific connection to the pertinent inquiry as a precondition to admissibility.

Daubert v. Merrell Dow Pharmaceuticals, Inc., 113 S. Ct. at 2795-96.

Although toxic tort cases are of an entirely different species than statutory environmental law cases, at bottom in both are issues of scientific uncertainty, and the challenges of determining when and how to make use of new and often-imperfect approaches to complex issues involving human health and the environment.

Three
Economics

Economic issues have always been important to the study of environmental law, but those issues have taken on a new urgency, as government decision-makers struggle to find more efficient and effective ways of addressing environmental problems. Chapter Three offers a historical perspective on the role of economic theory in environmental policy-making as well as a look at contemporary economic solutions to environmental problems. It begins with Kenneth Boulding's classic metaphor of the earth as a spaceship—a closed system which destroys its assets only at its future peril. Robert Repetto then describes how market systems can help to provide appropriate incentives to protect and preserve a nation's resource base.

Following these introductory articles, we begin a review of the extensive literature describing how various microeconomic theories can be used to address particular environmental problems. Along the way, we step back to ponder whether economic theory, by itself, offers a sufficient basis for addressing environmental concerns.

In an obituary written upon Kenneth Boulding's death in 1993, the Chicago Tribune described him as "an unorthodox economist, social scientist, philosopher, poet and peace activist." CHICAGO TRIBUNE, March 21, 1993, at 8. He was also the author of three dozen books, three volumes of poetry and about 800 articles. *Id.* Boulding's prescient warning in 1966 about society's need to plan for the coming "spaceship economy" is perhaps his most famous work, and may be even more compelling today than when written three decades ago. What does Boulding's essay say about the ability of conventional economic theory to address long-term environmental problems?

THE ECONOMICS OF THE COMING SPACESHIP EARTH
Kenneth E. Boulding
Environmental Quality in a Growing Economy (1966)*

We are now in the middle of a long process of transition in the nature of the image which man has of himself and his environment. Primitive men, and to a large extent also men of the early civilizations, imagined themselves to be living on a virtually illimitable plane. There was almost always somewhere beyond the known limits of human habitation, and over a very large part of the time that man has been on earth, there has been something like a frontier. That is, there was always some place else to go when things got too difficult, either by reason of the deterioration of the natural environment or a deterioration of the social structure in places where people happened to live. The image of the frontier is probably one of the oldest images of mankind, and it is not surprising that we find it hard to get rid of.

Gradually, however, man has been accustoming himself to the notion of the spherical earth and a closed sphere of human activity. A few unusual spirits among the ancient Greeks perceived that the earth was a sphere. It was only with the circumnavigations and the geographical explorations of the fifteenth and sixteenth centuries, however, that the fact that the earth was a sphere became at all widely known and accepted. Even in the nineteenth century, the commonest map was Mercator's projection, which visualizes the earth as an illimitable cylinder, essentially a plane wrapped around the globe, and it was not until the Second World War and the development of the air age that the global nature of the planet really entered the popular imagination. Even now we are very far from having made the moral, political, and psychological adjustments which are implied in this transition from the illimitable plane to the closed sphere.

Economists in particular, for the most part, have failed to come to grips with the ultimate consequences of the transition from the open to the closed earth. One hesitates to use the terms "open" and "closed" in this connection, as they have been used with so many different shades of meaning. Nevertheless, it is hard to find equivalents. The open system implies that some kind of structure is maintained in the midst of a throughput from inputs to outputs. In a closed system, the outputs of all parts of the system are linked to the inputs of other parts. There are no inputs from outside and no outputs to the outside; indeed, there is no outside at all. Closed systems, in fact, are very rare in human experience, in fact almost by definition unknowable, for if there are genuinely closed systems around us, we have no way of getting information into them or out of them; and hence if they are really closed, we would be quite unaware of their existence. We can only find out about a closed system if we participate in it. Some isolated primitive societies may have approximated to this, but even these had to take inputs from the environment and give outputs to it. All living organisms, including man himself, are open systems. They have to receive inputs in the shape of air, food, water, and give off outputs in the form of effluvia and excrement. Deprivation of input of air, even for a few minutes, is fatal. Deprivation of the ability to obtain any input or to dispose of any output is fatal in a relatively short time. All human societies have likewise been open systems. They receive inputs from the earth, the atmosphere, and the waters, and they give outputs into these reservoirs; they also produce inputs internally in the shape of babies and outputs in the shape of corpses. Given a capacity to draw upon inputs and to get rid of outputs, an open system of this kind can persist indefinitely.

* * *

Systems may be open or closed in respect to a number of inputs and outputs. Three important classes are matter, energy, and information. The present world economy is open in regard to all three. We can think of the world economy or "econosphere" as a subset of the "world set," which is the set of all objects of possible discourse in the world. We then think of the state of the econosphere at any one moment as being the total capital stock, that is, the set of all objects, people, organizations, and so on, which are interesting from the point of view of the system of exchange. This total stock of capital is clearly an open system in the sense that it has inputs and outputs, inputs being production which adds to the capital stock, outputs being consumption which subtracts from it. From a material point of view, we see objects passing from the noneconomic into the economic set in the process of production, and we similarly see products passing out of the economic set as their value becomes zero. Thus we see the econosphere as a material process involving the discovery and mining of fossil fuels, ores, etc., and at the other end a process by which the effluents of the system are passed out into noneconomic reservoirs-for instance, the atmosphere and the oceans-which are not appropriated and do not enter into the exchange system.

From the point of view of the energy system, the econosphere involves inputs of available energy in the form, say, of water power, fossil fuels, or sunlight, which are necessary in order to create the material throughput and to move matter from the noneconomic set into the economic set or even out of it again; and energy itself is given off by the system in a less available form, mostly in the form of heat. These inputs of available energy must come either from the sun (the energy supplied by other stars being assumed to be negligible) or it may come from the earth itself, either through its internal heat or through its energy of rotation or other motions, which generate, for instance, the energy of the tides. Agriculture, a few solar machines, and water power use the current available energy income. In advanced societies this is supplemented very extensively by the use of fossil fuels, which represent, as it were, a capital stock of stored-up sunshine. Because of this capital stock of energy, we have been able to maintain an energy input into the system, particularly over the last two centuries, much larger than we would have been able to do with existing techniques if we had had to rely on the current input of available energy from the sun or the earth itself. This supplementary input, however, is by its very nature exhaustible.

The inputs and outputs of information are more subtle and harder to trace, but also represent an open system, related to, but not wholly dependent on, the transformation of matter and energy. * * *

From the human point of view, knowledge, or information, is by far the most important of the three systems. Matter only acquires significance and only enters the sociosphere or the econosphere insofar as it becomes an object of human knowledge. We can think of capital, indeed, as frozen knowledge or knowledge imposed on the material world in the form of improbable arrangements. A machine, for instance, originates in the mind of man, and both its construction and its use involve information processes imposed on the material world by man himself. The cumulation of knowledge, that is, the excess of its production over its consumption, is the key to human development of all kinds, especially to economic development. We can see this preeminence of knowledge very clearly in the experiences of countries where the material capital has been destroyed by a war, as in Japan and Germany. The knowledge of the people was not destroyed, and it did not take long, therefore, certainly not more than ten years, for most of the material capital to be reestablished again. In a country such as Indonesia, however, where the knowledge did not exist, the material capital did not come into being either. By "knowledge" here I mean, of course, the whole cognitive structure, which includes valuations and motivations as well as images of the factual world.

The concept of entropy, used in a somewhat loose sense, can be applied to all three of these open systems. In material systems, we can distinguish between entropic processes, which take concentrated materials and diffuse them through the oceans or over the earth's surface or into the atmosphere, and antientropic processes, which take diffuse materials and concentrate them. Material entropy can be taken as a measure of the uniformity of the distribution of elements and, more uncertainly, compounds and other structures on the earth's surface. There is, fortunately, no law of increasing material entropy, as there is in the corresponding case of energy, as it is quite possible to concentrate diffused materials if energy inputs are allowed. Thus the processes for fixation of nitrogen from the air, processes for the extraction of magnesium or other elements from the sea, and processes for the desalinization of sea water are antientropic in the material sense, though the reduction of material entropy has to be paid for by inputs of energy and also inputs of information, or at least a stock of information in the system. In regard to matter, therefore, a closed system is conceivable, that is, a system in which there is neither increase nor decrease in material entropy. In such a system all outputs from consumption would constantly be recycled to become inputs for production, as for instance, nitrogen in the nitrogen cycle of the natural ecosystem.

In the energy system there is, unfortunately, no escape from the grim second law of thermodynamics; and if there were no energy inputs into the earth, any evolutionary or developmental process would be impossible. The large energy inputs which we have obtained from fossil fuels are strictly temporary. Even the most optimistic predictions expect the easily available supply of fossil fuels to be exhausted in a mere matter of centuries at present rates of use. If the rest of the world were to rise to American standards of power consumption, and still more if world population continues to increase, the exhaustion of fossil fuels would be even more rapid. The development of nuclear energy has improved this picture, but not fundamentally altered it, at least in present technologies, for fissionable material is still relatively scarce. If we should achieve the economic use of energy through fusion, of course, a much larger source of energy materials would be available, which would expand the time horizons of supplementary energy input into an open social system by perhaps tens to hundreds of thousands of years. Failing this, however, the time is not very far distant, historically speaking, when man will once more have to retreat to his current energy input from the sun, even though with increased knowledge this could be used much more effectively than in the past. Up to now, certainly, we have not got very far with the technology of using current solar energy, but the possibility of substantial improvements in the future is certainly high. It may be, indeed, that the biological revolution which is just beginning will produce a solution to this problem, as we develop artificial organisms which are capable of much more efficient transformation of solar energy into easily available forms than any that we now have. * * *

The question of whether there is anything corresponding to entropy in the information system is a puzzling one, though of great interest. There are certainly many examples of social systems and cultures which have lost knowledge, especially in transition from one generation to the next, and in which the culture has therefore degenerated. One only has to look at the folk culture of Appalachian migrants to American cities to see a culture which started out as a fairly rich European folk culture in Elizabethan times and which seems to have lost skills, adaptability, folk tales, songs, and almost everything that goes up to make richness and complexity in a culture, in the course of about ten generations. The American Indians on reservations provide another example of such degradation of the information and knowledge system. On the other hand, over a great part of human history, the growth of knowledge in the earth as a whole seems to have been almost continuous, even though there have been times of relatively slow growth and times of rapid growth. As it is knowledge of certain kinds that produces the growth of knowledge in general, we have here a very subtle and complicated system, and it is hard to put one's finger on the particular elements in a culture which make knowledge grow more or less rapidly, or even which make it decline. One of the great puzzles in this connection, for instance, is why the takeoff into science, which represents an "acceleration," or an increase in the rate of growth of knowledge in European society in the sixteenth century, did not take place in China, which at that time (about 1600) was unquestionably ahead of Europe, and one would think even more ready for the breakthrough. This is perhaps the most crucial question in the theory of social development, yet we must confess that it is very little understood. * * *

The closed earth of the future requires economic principles which are somewhat different from those of the open earth of the past. For the sake of picturesqueness, I am tempted to call the open economy the "cowboy economy," the cowboy being symbolic of the illimitable plains and also associated with reckless, exploitative, romantic, and violent behavior, which is characteristic of open societies. The closed economy of the future might similarly be called the "spaceman" economy, in which the earth has become a single spaceship, without unlimited reservoirs of anything, either for extraction or for pollution, and in which, therefore, man must find his place in a cyclical ecological system which is capable of continuous reproduction of material form even though it cannot escape having inputs of energy. The difference between the two types of economy becomes most apparent in the attitude towards consumption. In the cowboy economy, consumption is regarded as a good thing and production likewise; and the success of the economy is measured by the amount of the throughput from the "factors of production," a part of which, at any rate, is extracted from the reservoirs of raw materials and noneconomic objects, and another part of which is output into the reservoirs of pollution. If there are infinite reservoirs from which material can be obtained and into which effluvia can be deposited, then the throughput is at least a plausible measure of the success of the economy. The Gross National Product is a rough measure of this total throughput. It should be possible, however, to distinguish that part of the GNP which is derived from exhaustible and that which is derived from reproducible resources, as well as that part of consumption which represents effluvia and that which represents input into the productive system again. Nobody, as far as I know, has ever attempted to break down the GNP in this way, although it would be an interesting and extremely important exercise, which is unfortunately beyond the scope of this paper.

By contrast, in the spaceman economy, throughput is by no means a desideratum, and is indeed to be regarded as something to be minimized rather than maximized. The essential measure of the success of the economy is not production and consumption at all, but the nature, extent, quality, and complexity of the total capital stock, including in this the state of the human bodies and minds included in the system. In the spaceman economy, what we are primarily concerned with is stock maintenance, and any technological change which results in the maintenance of a given total stock with a lessened throughout (that is, less production and consumption) is clearly a gain. This idea that both production and consumption are bad things rather than good things is very strange to economists, who have been obsessed with the income-flow concepts to the exclusion, almost, of capital-stock concepts.

* * *

It may be said, of course, why worry about all this when the spaceman economy is still a good way off (at least beyond the lifetimes of any now living), so let us eat, drink, spend, extract and pollute, and be as merry as we can, and let posterity worry about the spaceship earth. It is always a little hard to find a convincing answer to the man who says, "What has posterity ever done for me?" and the conservationist has always had to fall back on rather vague ethical principles postulating identity of the individual with some human community or society which extends not only back into the past but forward into the future. Unless the individual identifies with some community of this kind, conservation is obviously "irrational." * * *

* * *

All these considerations add some credence to the point of view which says that we should not worry about the spaceman economy at all, and that we should just go on increasing the GNP and indeed the Gross World Product, or GWP, in the expectation that the problems of the future can be left to the future, that when scarcities arise, whether of raw materials or of pollutable reservoirs, the needs of the then present will determine the solutions of the then present, and there is no use giving ourselves ulcers by worrying about problems that we really do not have to solve. There is even high ethical authority for this point of view in the New Testament, which advocates that we should take no thought for tomorrow and let the dead bury their dead. There has always been something rather refreshing in the view that we should live like the birds, and perhaps posterity is for the birds in more senses than one; so perhaps we should all call it a day and go out and pollute something cheerfully. As an old taker of thought for the morrow, however, I cannot quite accept this solution; and I would argue, furthermore, that tomorrow is not only very close, but in many respects it is already here. The shadow of the future spaceship, indeed, is already falling over our spendthrift merriment. Oddly enough, it seems to be in pollution rather than in exhaustion that the problem is first becoming salient. Los Angeles has run out of air, Lake Erie has become a cesspool, the oceans are getting full of lead and DDT, and the atmosphere may become man's major problem in another generation, at the rate at which we are filling it up with gunk. It is, of course, true that at least on a microscale, things have been worse at times in the past. The cities of today, with all their foul air and polluted waterways, are probably not as bad as the filthy cities of the pretechnical age. Nevertheless, that fouling of the nest which has been typical of man's activity in the past on a local scale now seems to be extending to the whole world society; and one certainly cannot view with equanimity the present rate of pollution of any of the natural reservoirs, whether the atmosphere, the lakes, or even the oceans.

* * *

The problems which I have been raising in this paper are of larger scale and perhaps much harder to solve than the more practical and immediate problems * * *. Our success in dealing with the larger problems, however, is not unrelated to the development of skill in the solution of the more immediate and perhaps less difficult problems. One can hope, therefore, that as a succession of mounting crises, especially in pollution, arouse public opinion and mobilize support for the solution of the immediate problems, a learning process will be set in motion which will eventually lead to an appreciation of and perhaps solutions for the larger ones. My neglect of the immediate problems, therefore, is in no way intended to deny their importance, for unless we make at least a beginning on a process for solving the immediate problems we will not have much chance of solving the larger ones. On the other hand, it may also be true that a long-run vision, as it were, of the deep crisis which faces mankind may predispose people to taking more interest in the immediate problems and to devote more effort for their solution. This may sound like a rather modest optimism, but perhaps a modest optimism is better than no optimism at all.

NOTES

1. Kenneth Boulding's description of the coming "spaceship earth" suggests a fundamentally different view of economic questions, particularly as they impact the environment. Is a "spaceman economy" inevitable, as Boulding suggests? If it is inevitable how should we prepare for it?

2. Robert Hahn has noted that Boulding's spaceship earth analogy "should not be taken too far * * *, since the earth is not a closed system with respect to energy." Robert W. Hahn, *Toward a New Environmental Paradigm,* 102 YALE L. J. 1719, 1744, n.139 (1993). Is Hahn right? Would Boulding agree with Hahn's assessment? Does the advent of space travel challenge Boulding's fundamental assumption about the closed system of the earth? Would mining asteroids or planets alleviate constraints on consumption? Can we use deep space as a sink for excess waste and pollution? What ethical issues are likely to arise if we choose to go beyond the Earth to overcome its finite resources?

3. Boulding's concern about the limited resource base of the earth is shared by other resource economists, including for example Paul Erhlich, Herman Daly, Robert Costanza and Donella Meadows. *See e.g.,* Paul Erhlich, *Ecological Economics and the Carrying Capacity of the Earth*, and Robert Costanza, *Three General Policies to Achieve Sustainability, in* A. JANSSON, M. HAMMER, C. FOLKE & R. COSTANZA, INVESTING IN NATURAL CAPITAL: THE ECOLOGICAL ECONOMICS APPROACH TO SUSTAINABILITY 38 and 392 (1994); Herman E. Daly, *Sustainable Growth: An Impossibility Theorem, in* HERMAN E. DALY & KENNETH N. TOWNSEND, VALUING THE EARTH: ECONOMICS, ECOLOGY, ETHICS 267; DONELLA H. MEAD-

OWS, BEYOND THE LIMITS: CONFRONTING GLOBAL COLLAPSE (1992). Yet others, including some most closely identified with the conservation point of view, have argued that economic growth is sustainable: "Ecological economists are unable to point to a single scarcity of natural resources that knowledge and ingenuity are unlikely to alleviate." Mark Sagoff, *Carrying Capacity and Ecological Economics*, 45 BIOSCIENCE 610, 618 (1995). Should we rely on human creativity and technological advances to overcome the physical constraints of the planet? Even assuming that resource scarcity is not a sufficient reason for conserving resources, what ethical reasons might justify such a response?

4. The "grim second law of thermodynamics" states in one of its many permutations that "the total *quantity* of energy must be *conserved* in any process * * * ." P.W. ATKINS, THE SECOND LAW 9 (1984) (emphasis in original). Thus, as Boulding suggests, the laws of physics make us dependent on the finite energy inputs to the earth. Also important to Boulding's thesis is another aspect of the second law—"that the entropy, or the disorder of an isolated system always increases; once an egg falls to the floor and breaks, it is not likely ever to reform into its original shape." STEPHEN HAWKING, A BRIEF HISTORY OF TIME, A READERS COMPANION 93 (1992). What does this principle teach us about managing our "spaceman" economy?

5. Does our current system of assessing economic performance and success reflect a bias favoring a "cowboy economy" or a "spaceman economy"? Is a "spaceman economy" compatible with capitalism? Consider these questions in the context of the following article by Robert Repetto, an economist with the World Resources Institute.

WASTING ASSETS: THE NEED FOR NATIONAL RESOURCE ACCOUNTING
Robert Repetto
Technology Review (January 1990)*

National income accounts, which provide the framework for analyzing the performance of an economy, are one of the most significant social inventions of the twentieth century. Their political and economic impact can scarcely be overestimated. Consider the most famous component of these statistics, gross national product (GNP). When quarterly GNP figures emerge, policymakers stir. Should the numbers be lower, even marginally, than those of the preceding three months, a recession is declared, the strategies and competence of the administration are impugned, and public debate ensues.

The current system, first published in 1942, reflects the Keynesian model that dominated

---

* Reprinted with permission.

macroeconomic thought at the time. It carefully defines and measures the great aggregate concepts of Keynesian analysis—consumption, savings, investment, and government expenditures. But Keynes and his contemporaries were preoccupied with the Great Depression and the business cycle—they wanted to explain why an economy could remain at less than full employment for such a long time. The least of their worries was a scarcity of natural resources.

Just as Keynesian analysis largely ignores the productive role of these resources, so does the United Nations system of national accounts, which most countries follow closely. As a result, a nation could exhaust its mineral reserves, cut down its forests, erode its soils, pollute its aquifers, and hunt its wildlife to extinction—all without affecting measured income.

The difference in the treatment of natural resources and other tangible assets provides false signals to both economists and politicians. It reinforces a false dichotomy between the economy and the environment that leads them to ignore or destroy the latter in the name of development. It confuses the depletion of valuable assets with the generation of income. And it promotes and validates the idea that rapid economic growth can be achieved and sustained by exploiting the resource base.

The consequences can be illusory gains in income and permanent losses in wealth. The situation is especially serious for low-income countries, which are typically heavily dependent on natural resources for employment, revenues, and foreign exchange. As long as these governments use a system for national accounting and macroeconomic analysis that almost completely ignores their principal assets, their future is in jeopardy.

NO FREE GIFTS

National income accounts have become so much a part of our life that it is hard to remember they are scarcely 50 years old. It is no coincidence that this half-century has been one in which the governments of most countries have taken responsibility for the growth and stability of their economies.

Before the mid-1800s, classical economists regarded income as the return on three kinds of assets: natural resources, human resources, and invested capital—land, labor, and capital, in their vocabulary. However, natural-resource scarcity played little part in neoclassical economics, from which most contemporary economic theories derive. In nineteenth-century Europe, steamships and railroads were markedly lowering transportation costs, while grains and raw materials were flooding in from North and South America, Australia, Russia, and the imperial colonies. What mattered to England and other industrializing nations was the pace of investment and technological change. Thus, neoclassical models concentrated almost exclusively on labor and invested capital.

The result is a dangerous asymmetry in the way we think about and measure the value of natural resources versus other assets. Buildings and equipment, for example, count as productive capital, and their depreciation is subtracted from the value of production. Consumption that diminishes the stock of capital is seen to reduce the sustainable level of income. But natural-resource assets are not so valued, so their loss entails no debit that would suggest a decrease in future production.

Should a farmer cut and sell timber to pay for a new barn, the farm's private accounts would reflect the acquisition of one asset—the barn—and the loss of another—the timber.

The farmer is better off only if the barn is worth more to him or her than the timber. In national accounts, on the other hand, income and investment would rise as the barn was built *and* as the wood was cut. Nothing would reflect the loss of a valuable asset.

Such anomalies come from the implicit, and inappropriate, assumption that natural resources are so abundant that a small loss has no economic cost. But natural resources make important contributions to economic productivity and face increasing pressure from human activities. Strictly speaking, they are economic assets.

Natural resources are also assumed to be "free gifts of nature," entailing no investment costs to be written off. However, the real value of an asset is its income potential, not its investment cost. For example, brilliant ideas are the principal assets of companies worth billions of dollars. The Polaroid camera, the Apple computer, and the Lotus spreadsheet are worth vastly more than what their inventors spent to develop them.

It is important to remember that the common formulas for depreciating investment costs are just convenient rules of thumb and, in many cases, artifacts of tax legislation. The true measure of depreciation is the amount that future income will decline as an asset decays or becomes obsolete. Just as machines depreciate as they age, soils depreciate when their fertility diminishes.

The fundamental definition of income does, in fact, encompass the notion of sustainability.

Accounting and economics textbooks alike say that income is the amount someone can consume now without reducing future consumption. Business income is the dividend a firm can pay without reducing net worth. Depreciation recognizes that unless physical assets are maintained, future consumption will decline. The failure to extend this concept to natural-resource assets is a major inconsistency.

* * *

REVISING THE ACCOUNTS

Fortunately, a large and growing body of experts has recognized the need to reform the national accounting systems. For example, in 1985, the Organization for Economic Cooperation and Development (OECD) issued its report, *Declaration on Environment: Resources for the Future*, which endorses steps to ensure "long-term environmental and economic sustainability" and commits OECD nations to developing "more accurate resource accounts." Similarly, *Our Common Future*, the 1987 study by the U.N.-sponsored World Commission on Environment and Development, observes that "in all countries, rich or poor, economic development must take full account in its measurement of growth of the improvement or deterioration in the stock of natural resources."

Some developed countries have already established environmental accounting systems. In both Norway and France, extensive resource accounts supplement the national economic accounts. The West German government recently announced that it will include resource and environmental degradation in its national income accounts. These systems reflect two types of approach to natural-resource accounting.

On the one hand, planners can register the stocks of natural resources—and changes in those stocks—in physical units. Opening stocks *plus* all additions *less* all reductions *equals* closing stocks. Consider, for example, timber resources. Additions to the timber stock can originate from growth and regeneration of the initial supply, from reforestation, and from planting new forest. Production (harvesting), natural degradation (for instance, fire), and deforestation by humans would reduce the stock. Separate accounts might be established for categories such as virgin production forests, logged (secondary) forests, protected forests, and plantations. In temperate forests, which have relatively few tree types, stocks could be further classified by species. In each case, cubic meters of available wood is probably the most important measure, since a substantial part of a nation's standing timber cannot be profitably harvested with current technology or sold under today's market conditions.

However, physical accounting by itself has considerable shortcomings. First of all, it does not lend itself to amassing many different accounts into a single useful number. Combining the cubic meters of various tree types obscures wide variations in the economic value of different species. Similarly, aggregating total mineral reserves in tons obscures the vast differences that grade and recovery costs make in the value of deposits. But maintaining physical accounts in fine detail yields a mountain of hard-to-manage statistics.

Further, physical accounts must be expressed in monetary terms before planners can directly integrate them into economic decisions—presumably the point of the exercise. (The necessary calculations rely on the concept of economic rent, which is broadly equivalent to the net price. For example, if a barrel of crude oil can be sold for $10 and costs a total of $6 to discover, extract, and market, each barrel has a rent of $4. Natural-resource rents arise from factors such as the scarcity and location of particular stocks.)

Like physical accounts, monetary valuation has its limits, set mainly by how tightly a resource is tied to the market economy. Some resources, such as many minerals, are relatively easy to value in monetary terms, but others, such as noncommercial wild species, can be valued only through quite roundabout methods involving numerous, somewhat questionable assumptions.

Thus, Norway's resource accounts are tabulated in physical units, such as tons or cubic feet, and are not directly integrated with the national income accounts. Norway compiles accounts for "material" resources such as fossil fuels and other minerals, "biotic" resources such as forests and fisheries, and "environmental" resources such as land, water, and air. However, the Central Bureau of Statistics does express some important resource accounts, especially those for petroleum and gas, in monetary terms for macroeconomic planning and projection models.

France's "natural patrimony accounts" have been designed to provide a comprehensive framework for monitoring changes in all resources that can be affected by human activity. Since 1971, French statisticians have been developing the methodology for these accounts and compiling empirical estimates of the stocks of specific resources. The patrimony accounts now cover the same range of resources as Norway's: nonrenewables, the physical environment, and living organisms. As in Norway, the basic accounting units are physical, with monetary values for resources that are sold or contribute directly to producing marketable goods.

Some developing countries, recognizing their dependence on natural resources, have also become interested in a better accounting framework. The World Resources Institute is working on pilot studies with government researchers and statistical agencies in Indonesia, Costa Rica, and the People's Republic of China. The Philippines' government has recently begun compiling resource accounts, and the World Bank and the U.N. Environment

Programme are planning to carry out limited experimental studies in Thailand, the Ivory Coast, Argentina, and possibly some other countries.

THE ROLE OF THE UNITED NATIONS

Since most developing countries must think of natural resources as productive assets, the first priority is to document these reserves in a way that gives due emphasis to the costs as they disappear. Here, the U.N. Statistical Office has an important role to play. Its system of national accounts (SNA), which includes privately owned assets used in the commercial production of goods and services, supplies as standard that most countries follow closely, at least in its main accounts. The Statistical Office is also a worldwide source of economic expertise and guidance in designing and using national accounts.

Already, the SNA is more complete with respect to natural-resource accounting than the systems most nations derive from it. The framework provides for "reconciliation accounts"—corrections to the main balance sheets that cover changes in the value of natural-resource stocks due to both price shifts and material alterations, such as growth, discoveries, depletion, and extraction. Reconciliation accounts cover not only reproducible assets, such as farmland and subsoil minerals.

But dissatisfaction with SNA stems from its many inconsistencies and omissions. For example, it largely fails to look at goods and services outside the market sector, notably those that households produce. Thus, when a person buys an apple pie at the supermarket instead of baking it, national income rises. Also, the SNA ignores important capital assets, such as education and workforce training. Furthermore, it only imperfectly measures goods and services that governments create. It treats as income-generating many activities undertaken only to avert or remedy the disadvantages of modern industrial society, such as pollution.

These and many other deficiencies have led to a long agenda of suggested improvements, and the U.N. Statistical Commission, advised by a number of expert working groups, is preparing to modify the SNA, as it does once every 20 years or so. However, the commission has evidently already decided to make no fundamental changes, even though deliberations will continue until 1991. Rather, the expert committees have proposed encouraging countries to link natural-resource accounts to conventional national-income measures through "satellite accounts." In other words, natural-resource depletion would simply be an addendum to the main tables.

In a sense, the U.N.'s existing methodology is protected by its very inadequacy: wholesale reform is a massive task, and improvement limited to some aspects is hard to justify when so many other problems would remain. At both the national and international level, statisticians, who are typically short on staff, money, and raw data, resist changes, especially since so much is yet to be done to implement the existing SNA.

Nonetheless, events of the past decade—such as coastal pollution, tropical deforestation, and the accumulation of greenhouse gases—demonstrate the importance of bringing natural-resource considerations into the main national income accounts as early as possible. Certainly another 20 years is too long to wait for reforms that are already overdue. Only when the basic measures of economic performance, codified in an official framework, conform to a valid definition of income will economic policies be influenced toward sustainability. While virtually all countries calculate national income accounts, few have implemented past U.N. recommendations with respect to satellite tables because, with limited resources, they have "stuck to the basics." Moreover, politicians, journalists, and sophisticated economists continue to treat the GNP as the prime measure of economic performance. Even the "basic indicators" table that leads off the World Bank's annual *World Development Report* cites GDP [gross domestic product], GDP growth per capita, and rate of inflation, but no net figures.

* * *

There is ample time before the U.N. Statistical Office announces a revised SNA to fully explore the implications of extending the concept of depreciation to natural-resource assets. That office should use this time to prepare for a change in the main accounts. Certainly the reforms could be put in place within three to five years.

At the same time, key international economic institutions—including the World Bank, the International Monetary Fund, and the OECD—need to begin to compile, use and publish figures for net national product and income. And these institutions should ready themselves to assist the growing number of national statistical offices that are deciding to make and use such estimates themselves.

NOTES

1. To what extent does Repetto's proposal that countries account for natural resources in the national income accounts solve the problem of the "cowboy economy" posed by Boulding?

2. Commentators have noted two distinct categories which are not generally considered in national accounting systems: depletion of non-renewable resources and environmental degradation. Which of these will likely be more difficult to measure? Assuming they can be measured accurately, how should depleted resources and environmental degradation be valued? *See* RAYMOND PRINCE & PATRICE GORDON, GREENING THE NATIONAL ACCOUNTS (1994).

3. In EARTH IN THE BALANCE, then-Senator Al Gore offered a simple, but convincing argument in support of Repetto's proposal:

> The hard truth is that our economic system is partially blind. It "sees" some things and not others. It carefully measures and keeps track of the value of those things most important to buyers and sellers, such as food, clothing, manufactured goods, work, and, indeed, money itself. But its intricate calculations often completely ignore the value of other things that are harder to buy and sell: fresh water, clean air, the beauty of the mountains, the rich diversity of life in the forest, just to name a few. In fact, the partial blindness of our

current economic system is the single most powerful force behind what seem to be irrational decisions about the global environment.

* * *

This partial blindness in the way we account for the impact of our decisions on the natural world is * * * a major obstacle to our efforts to formulate sensible responses to the strategic threats now facing the environment. Typically, we cite hugely inflated estimates of the expense involved in changing our current policies, with no analysis whatsoever of the expense associated with the impact of the changes that will occur if we do nothing.

For example, the loss of 75 percent of California's annual moisture has long been predicted by some climatologists as a consequence of global warming. Yet because the scale of the problem is so large, no one seems to even consider including the cost of the water shortage in California in our calculation of the benefits of an aggressive program to counter global warming. We should also calculate the costs of doing nothing, because the consequences of the seven-year drought are already staggering and may get worse.

AL GORE, EARTH IN THE BALANCE: ECOLOGY AND THE HUMAN SPIRIT 182-92 (1992).

4. Compare Repetto's approach with that of economist E. F. Schumacher. In an essay supporting "Buddhist economics" over "modern economics," Schumacher writes:

Modern economics does not distinguish between renewable and nonrenewable materials, as its very method is to equalize and quantify everything by means of a money price. Thus, taking various alternative fuels, like coal, oil, wood, or water power: the only difference between them recognized by modern economics is relative cost per equivalent unit. The cheapest is automatically the one to be preferred, as to do otherwise would be irrational and "uneconomic." From a Buddhist point of view, of course, this will not do; the essential difference between nonrenewable fuels like coal and oil on the one hand and the renewable fuels like wood and waterpower on the other cannot be simply overlooked. Nonrenewable goods must be used only if they are indispensable, and then only with the greatest care and the most meticulous concern for conservation. To use them heedlessly or extravagantly is an act of violence, and while complete nonviolence may not be attainable on this earth, there is nonetheless an ineluctable duty on man to aim at the idea of nonviolence in all he does.

Just as a modern European economist would not consider it a great economic achievement if all European art treasures were sold to America at attractive prices, so the Buddhist economist would insist that a population basing its economic life on nonrenewable fuels is living parasitically, on capital instead of income. Such a way of life could have no permanence and could therefore be justified only as a purely temporary expedient. As the world's resources

of nonrenewable fuels—coal, oil, and natural gas—are exceedingly unevenly distributed over the globe and undoubtedly limited in quantity, it is clear that their exploitation at an ever increasing rate is an act of violence against nature which must almost inevitably lead to violence between men.
E. F. Schumacher, *Buddhist Economics*, 11 RESURGENCE 1 (1968), *reprinted in* HERMAN E. DALY & KENNETH N. TOWNSEND, VALUING THE EARTH 159, 179 (1993).

5. As Kenneth Boulding suggested, the broad economic policy questions described in the foregoing materials may ultimately be more intractable than more immediate problems such as control of pollution. It should come as no surprise then that most of the literature in this field has focused on microeconomic theory, or solving particular environmental problems. The materials which follow offer some insights into how economists have addressed these problems.

In 1991, University of Chicago economist, Ronald Coase won the Nobel Prize in economics for his contributions to the field. By that time his ideas had become so ingrained in economic thought that they now seem unexceptional. It was not always that way. In 1960, Coase attended a dinner party at which his views on free markets and privatization were discussed. As the evening began, the guests voted 20 to 1 against Coase's theories— Coase himself being the lone dissenter. By the end of the evening, however, Coase had won over all of them. According to two of those guests, they all "stumbled out in a state of shock mumbling to each other that they had witnessed intellectual history." DAVID WARSH, ECONOMIC PRINCIPALS: THE MASTERS AND MAVERICKS OF MODERN ECONOMICS 114-15 (1993).

THE PROBLEM OF SOCIAL COST
R.H. Coase
3 J. L. & Econ. 1 (1960)*

This paper is concerned with those actions of business firms which have harmful effects on others. The standard example is that of a factory the smoke from which has harmful effects on those occupying neighboring properties. The economic analysis of such a situation has usually proceeded in terms of a divergence between the private and social product of the factory, in which economists have largely followed the treatment of Pigou in *The Economics of Welfare*. The conclusions to which this kind of analysis seems to have led most economists is that it would be desirable to make the owner of the factory liable for the damage caused to those injured by the smoke, or alternatively, to place a tax on the factory owner varying with the amount of smoke produced and equivalent in money to the damage it would cause, or finally, to exclude the factory from residential

---

* Reprinted with permission.

districts (and presumably from other areas in which the emission of smoke would have harmful effects on others). It is my contention that the suggested courses of action are inappropriate, in that they lead to results which are not necessarily, or even usually, desirable.

The traditional approach has tended to obscure the nature of the choice that has to be made. The question is commonly thought of as one in which A inflicts harm on B and what has to be decided is: how should we restrain A? But this is wrong. We are dealing with a problem of a reciprocal nature. To avoid the harm to B would inflict harm on A. The real question that has to be decided is: should A be allowed to harm B or should B be allowed to harm A? The problem is to avoid the more serious harm. I instanced in my previous article the case of a confectioner the noise and vibrations from whose machinery disturbed a doctor in his work. To avoid harming the doctor would inflict harm on the confectioner. The problem posed by this case was essentially whether it was worth while, as a result of restricting the methods of production which could be used by the confectioner, to secure more doctoring at the cost of a reduced supply of confectionery products. Another example is afforded by the problem of straying cattle which destroy crops on neighboring land. If it is inevitable that some cattle will stray, an increase in the supply of meat can only be obtained at the expense of a decrease in the supply of crops. The nature of the choice is clear: meat or crops. What answer should be given is, of course, not clear unless we know the value of what is obtained as well as the value of what is sacrificed to obtain it. To give another example, Professor George J. Stigler instances the contamination of a stream. If we assume that the harmful effect of the pollution is that it kills the fish, the question to be decided is: is the value of the fish lost greater or less than the value of the product which the contamination of the stream makes possible? It goes without saying that this problem has to be looked at in total *and* at the margin.

* * *

NOTES

1. Note that however property rights or pollution rights are assigned among competing users of resources, Coase's theorem posits that, assuming a free market, and absent transaction costs, the most cost-efficient result should obtain. On the basis of this theorem, some have described a world free of transaction costs as a "Coasian world." Coase, however, has distanced himself from any suggestion that such a world exists: "The world of zero transaction costs has often been described as a Coasian world. Nothing could be further from the truth. It is the world of modern economic theory, one which I was hoping to persuade economists to leave." RONALD COASE, THE FIRM, THE MARKET AND THE LAW 174 (1988). Indeed, as Judge Richard Posner has suggested, Coase's theorem will likely work to achieve the most efficient result only where "the transaction cost is less than the value of the transaction to the parties." RICHARD A. POSNER, ECONOMIC ANALYSIS OF LAW 51 (4th Ed. 1992).

2. Where many people are affected by the resolution of a particular problem, the transaction costs associated with negotiating a solution to that problem are likely to be high, and the utility of the Coase theorem correspondingly low. Does this circumstance suggest that government regulation may be the most efficient mechanism for resolving such problems? *See* Joseph Farrell, *Information and the Coase Theorem*, 1 ECON. PERSPECTIVES 113, 114 (1987).

3. What role does information play in the operation of the Coase theorem? Are negotiations typically entered with all parties having full access to all of the information available to the other side, or do parties typically withhold information in an effort to strengthen their bargaining position? Joseph Farrell argues that negotiations are typically characterized by the latter situation, and that the efficient outcomes contemplated by the Coase theorem are thus unlikely to be achieved. Joseph Farrell, *Information and the Coase Theorem*, 1 ECON. PERSPECTIVES, 113, 115 (1987). How does the lack of full access to information impede efficient negotiations?

4. What does the problem of transaction costs tell us about the likelihood that commodities like marketable pollution rights will reach the most efficient user? What does it say about the need to assign those rights with care in the first instance? *See* Robert C. Ellickson, *The Case for Coase and Against "Coasianism"*, 99 YALE L. J. 611, 625-26 (1989).

5. What does it mean to say that a transaction is efficient? Most economists employ the Kaldor-Hicks test. Judge Guido Calabresi has described this test as follows: "[A] move is efficient whenever the winners win more than the losers lose, in the sense that, if the winners compensated the losers to their satisfaction, the winners would still be better off before the change." Guido Calebresi, *The Pointlessness of Pareto: Carrying Coase Further*, 100 YALE L. J. 1211, 1221 (1991); *see also* RICHARD A. POSNER, ECONOMIC ANALYSIS OF LAW, *supra*, n. 1, 13-16.

6. Related to Kalder-Hicks efficiency, and the chief subject of Judge Calebresi's article noted above, is the problem of "Pareto optimality." This principle states that "society is not in its optimal position if there exists at least one change which would make someone in that society better off and no one in it worse off." Guido Calebresi, *The Pointlessness of Pareto: Carrying Coase Further*, 100 YALE L. J. 1211, 1215 (1991). Calebresi makes a compelling argument, however, that "the set of Pareto superior changes. . .[is] a void set." How might he reach this conclusion? As you think about this question, consider the role that transaction costs play in impeding otherwise optimal changes, and consider also that the cost of acquiring the knowledge that a change is Pareto superior may itself be substantial.

7. Professor Mark Kelman argues that, irrespective of transaction costs, "[c]onsumers do not behave in a way such that the [Coase] Theorem holds true." Mark Kelman, *Consumption Theory, Production Theory, and Ideology in the Coase Theorem*, 52 S. CAL. L. REV. 669, 678 (1979). Kelman explains his thesis through examples which suggest that consumers treat lost opportunity income as different from, and less valuable than, realized income. So, for example, a person who pays $5 for a bottle of wine, which appreciates in value, might rationally choose to refuse an offer to sell the bottle for $100, even though he would never pay $100 for a bottle of wine. *Id.* at 678-79. Likewise, "a person will probably feel worse when he loses a fifty-dollar bill than when he fails to walk from one store to the next to save fifty dollars in the purchase of a washing machine." *Id.* at 689. If Kelman is right in describing consumer behavior, what problems does this create for valuing the environment? While Kelman's theory may hold true for individual consumers, is it likely to hold true for rational, profit-maximizing business entities?

As society gropes for better solutions to complex environmental problems, benefit-cost analysis has come to the fore. Some have argued that administrative agencies should be allowed to adopt only those rules where the benefits exceed the costs and where no more cost-effective alternatives are available. Legislation which would impose such limits on the authority of all federal agencies was passed by the U.S. House of Representatives. *See* H. R. 9, 104th Cong., 2d Sess. (Risk Assessment and Cost Benefit Act of 1995, § 3201). The following three articles address some of the difficulties associated with the use of benefit-cost analysis as a tool for environmental decision-making.

BENEFIT-COST ANALYSIS AND THE COMMON SENSE OF ENVIRONMENTAL POLICY
Arthur P. Hurter, Jr., George S. Tolley, and Robert G. Fabian
reprinted in
D. Swartzman, R. A. Liroff, K. G. Croke, ed.
Cost-Benefit Analysis and Environmental Regulations: Politics, Ethics and Methods (1982)*

Much of the controversy over environmental policies can be attributed to the fact that some people emphasize the benefits and minimize the disadvantages of a particular policy while others do just the opposite. Although this is due partly to a difference in priorities and values, it is also due partly to the problems involved in determining advantages and disadvantages, a process that requires expertise from many diverse fields. * * *

Once the effects of an environmental regulation have been estimated, a crucial problem remains: how can the various effects of a regulation be compared with one another? What

---

* Reprinted with permission.

kind of framework can be used to compare the improved health of residents in a cleaned-up area with the increased cost of goods and services? * * *

AGREEING ON A FRAMEWORK

Economic analysis is one tool or framework that can be used to compare the various effects of environmental regulations. But many object to the use of economic analysis, stating that various effects of environmental actions are noncommensurate and consequently should not be compared. When formulating environmental policy, however, these effects must be compared either explicitly or implicitly. In fact, comparison of seemingly noncommensurate things is not only common but inevitable. For example, everyday decisions involve comparing such seemingly noncommensurate items as the nutritional value and culinary delight of food with increased self-confidence and social advancement associated with being thin and wearing stylish clothing. Weighing such trade-offs is inevitable as long as there is more than one commodity people wish to consume.

These trade-offs, made by individuals in personal decisions, also are made in group or public decisions, for example, in decisions formulating environmental policy. Thus, when considering actions to control environmental pollution, advantages must be weighed against disadvantages and trade-offs between apparently noncommensurate items must be made.

The problem of estimating weights for different, seemingly incomparable effects requires going beyond qualitative into quantitative assessment. If only one effect were important, then analysis could be limited to a qualitative comparison of this single dimension, for example, human health. But when considering alternative environmental polices with varying costs, analyzing only a single dimension is inadequate and potentially misleading. For example, one action that may only minimally improve the environment and human health could be considered desirable because its costs would be relatively small. Another action that may be expected to produce sizable improvements could be considered undesirable because its costs would be relatively large.

As seen above, creating sound environmental policy requires two related steps: (1) establishing a framework for making comparisons, and (2) making quantitative estimates within that framework. The framework suggested by economists—benefit-cost analysis—although used to some extent, is not universally accepted for a variety of reasons. One reason is that the quantitative estimates have been suspect, a problem occasionally exacerbated by the practice of according results a numerical precision that is not justified. Particularly troublesome can be the instances in which a single number representing benefits is compared with a single number representing costs without any recognition of the uncertainty that may surround both. However, this criticism of benefit-cost analysis has been overdone. In many and perhaps most cases, either the benefits exceed the costs by a wide margin or visa versa. In these cases, the ranges or outcomes are not large enough to affect the comparison appreciably.

* * *

MEASUREMENT PROBLEMS

When comparing the effects of any environmental policy, two types of uncertainty or error may be distinguished. One is error in estimating physical effects, e.g., the improvement in human health associated with cleaner air. The second is error in estimating the weights to be attached to the physical effects, for example, the weights, often expressed in dollars, associated with an improvement in human health. A common view is that the estimates of physical effects, determined by physical scientists, are "hard" evidence and are inherently more accurate than are the "soft" estimates of human behavior made by economists or other social scientists. As the formulation of environmental policy grows more sophisticated and as the uncertainty involved in estimation is examined more extensively, it may well become apparent that the estimates from social scientists are "harder" than the scientific evidence of the physical effects of pollution. For instance, although it is difficult to determine how much "less sickness" is worth, the range of uncertainly about this economic question is far less than the uncertainty concerning the physical effects of air pollution on sickness.

ESTABLISHING TRADE-OFFS

The weights attached to the physical effects of an environmental policy specify the trade-offs that people are willing to make between one physical effect and another. But who should make the comparisons? Whose trade-offs should be considered? The relevant trade-offs should be those made by the people affected by the environmental policy. Accordingly, the weights on the benefits of an environmental policy are the trade-offs that the people affected are willing to make between a cleaner environment and other goals. Similarly, the weights on the costs of producing a cleaner environment are the trade-offs that the people incurring the costs are willing to make.

It is important to clarify whose trade-offs are being considered, since some discussions imply that trade-offs by those other than the individuals affected are relevant to a decision. For example, some suggest that the trade-offs should be made by a policy maker or by some wise person other than those affected by the particular policy. In our view, the opinions of a journalist in Boston who feels that the carbon monoxide content of the air should be lower in St. Louis should be of little interest to the decision maker concerned with the trade-offs that the people in St. Louis are willing to make. The relevant trade-offs are those of the people receiving the consequent advantages and disadvantages of an environmental policy.

* * *

CONVENIENCE OF MEASURING IN DOLLARS

Economists usually express weights, whether they represent trade-offs of different physical effects or of distributional effects, in dollar terms. This practice has been labeled as shallow, incomplete, and callous and has produced a tendency, in some forums, to attempt to preclude economics from the formulation of environmental policy. Such a view reflects a lack of understanding about the criteria used to make choices.

When weights are given in dollar terms, it does not imply that it is the dollars themselves that matter; dollars merely are a convenient unit in which to express people's trade-offs. Units other than dollars can be used to express weights or trade-offs. The use of clams, oil, or miles of visibility instead of dollars would make inescapable the fact that people are willing to give up one worthwhile thing for another; it can be difficult, however, to make comparisons when different units are used simultaneously.

* * *

SOURCES OF UNCERTAINTY

Having discussed the framework that can be used to compare the benefits and costs of environmental programs and regulations, we proceed to a discussion of the potential sources of uncertainty, bias, and error in assessing these benefits and costs. We detail these sources of uncertainty to help decision makers reduce these shortcomings and to help them interpret the results of benefit-cost analysis performed with currently available methods and data.

Benefits, Costs, and Market Prices

Benefits and costs would be relatively easy to measure if they were the result of transactions that indicated clearly individuals' willingness to pay for marketed goods. But since public goods such as national defense or clean air are not traded in a marketplace, the analyst must infer the affected individuals' willingness to pay for them. For example, the aesthetic quality of a clean lake can be assigned a monetary value, but the procedures necessary for such a valuation are indirect. Economic theory is a useful guide to benefit estimation primarily because it provides ways of measuring willingness to pay when market information is unavailable. Private benefits from government actions usually are evaluated using the market prices for the flow of goods and services from a specific project or the changes in these flows associated with a particular regulation. Market prices do not always convey accurate information about willingness to pay, however, because of market distortions.

* * *

* * * Markets may be distorted in various ways, causing prices to reflect individual valuations inaccurately. Taxes are an important example of a market distortion that the analyst must consider carefully in benefit-cost analysis. Product or productive input pricing, which reflects the presence of monopoly, is also relevant. In addition, the distinction between monetary outlays and the true opportunity costs must be considered by the benefit-cost analyst. * * *

* * *

Real Benefits and Distributional Effects

When conducting benefit-cost analysis, real benefits should be distinguished from distributional effects. Real benefits are those effects of a project characterized by increases in satisfaction and/or decreases in the total amount of resources required to produce goods and services. For example, the real benefits of increased water quality may be approximated by the amount people are willing to pay for the additional enjoyment of fishing, swimming, and boating. Distributional effects are changes that occur in the well-being of one group of individuals at the expense of another group. For example, increased fishing due to improved water quality might increase the price of fishing equipment, thus increasing the profit of the merchants. Improved water quality might also result in increased motel facilities. If there were relatively full employment, any resources used for motel construction would have to be diverted from other productive activities. These effects are transfers from one set of purchasers and sellers to another, rather than increases in productive activity. They are not project benefits, although one group or region might benefit at the expense of another. Benefit-cost analysis should include the real benefits but not the distributional effects.

Estimating Costs

Three basic approaches for estimating the costs of pollution control strategies are often used: (1) the survey technique, (2) engineering estimation, and (3) statistical estimation. The *survey method* relies on the polluter to provide information on emissions and control costs and assumes that the respondent is both knowledgeable and honest. The *engineering approach* relies extensively on technical analysis for cost estimates. Knowledge of the type and quantity of outputs as well as the underlying technical processes enables the analyst to estimate both uncontrolled pollutant levels and expenditures relating to the most efficient (least cost) methods of achieving various target levels of control. The analyst must assume that the polluter uses a "typical" production technology, must determine the control strategy being used, and then must estimate current emission levels. The analyst must forecast the method that the polluter will choose to attain further control levels and then must estimate the cost of the selected technology. This approach is likely to be very costly and requires the analyst to have an adequate level of technological expertise. The *statistical approach* requires that the analyst use statistical methods to discover the specific relationship between inputs and output. Cost functions then are derived from the statistical "production function." A limitation of the statistical approach is that once new control techniques are developed, adequate historical data for a statistical analysis are not likely to exist.

* * *

Survey Methods

Benefits and costs usually can be measured by using market prices of goods, services, and productive inputs. Sometimes market prices must be adjusted for distortions such as taxes or monopoly influences. Sometimes the market provides prices only indirectly indicative of willingness to pay; for example, property value differentials as a measure of pollution damage. In all of these uses of price, the market is yielding information about people's valuations based on actual decisions they have made. Occasionally, however, benefit-cost analysts use questionnaire surveys to get direct information on willingness to pay.

Questionnaire surveys must be designed to elicit information as accurately as possible. Questions must be expressed in a way that avoids leading the respondent in a particular direction. It is especially important to structure a questionnaire situation so that the respondent is able to focus on the issues clearly. Extraneous influences, such as the tendency for a respondent to give the answer he or she thinks the interviewer desires, need to be avoided. Ideally, questionnaire surveys should be used to corroborate market information, in which preferences are revealed through actual decisions. Even the most skillfully designed survey, however, cannot create a situation in which the respondent can make a genuine willingness-to-pay decision.

Option Value and Irreversible Decisions

Measured willingness to pay for the benefits of a project or regulation is likely to underestimate the true benefits of a project when the future demand for some related product is uncertain. For example, consider additional or better recreational facilities. Suppose that if the project or regulation is not undertaken now, it will be impossible to provide these facilities at a later date. Thus, the current decision is irreversible. Under these circumstances, the benefits of the project or regulation can be separated into two parts: (1) the present and future benefits to those who are certain to use the facility, and (2) the benefits to those who are not sure they will use the facility but who support its establishment because they feel it is important to keep their options and those of future generations open. This second class of benefits, often called "option values" is potentially important when irreversibility exists and is not fully captured by the usual willingness-to-pay measures.

Discounting Benefits and Costs to Present Value

The effects of environmental projects and regulations extend many years into the future. For any given project, the time profile of benefits is likely to differ from the time profile of costs; frequently costs are concentrated in the near future while significant benefits do not appear for a number of years. In addition, different projects, perhaps competing for scarce resources for environmental improvement, have different time profiles of benefits. In order to compare the expected effects of various regulations over time, the anticipated costs and benefits must be discounted to present value. For example, $1,000 of costs imposed by a project 10 years from now will be valued less than $1,000 of costs that must be borne immediately. How much to discount deferred costs and benefits is a problem the analyst must solve in order to evaluate and compare projects. Once a discount rate has been determined, the analyst can calculate the net present value of projects, and costs and benefits can be compared in terms of these equivalent values to society today. The net present value of projects is sensitive to the value of the discount rate. Analysts frequently employ alternative discount rates to establish a range of measures of benefits and costs.

Professional and Political Bias

In view of the uncertainty surrounding the measurement of costs and benefits, subjectivity can color analyses. Unconsciously, the personal biases of an investigator may creep in. Within any agency, unconscious pressures exist for an analyst to make assumptions favorable to the agency's purpose. In political forums, there can be a tendency to take advocacy positions wherein the name of the game is to deliberately choose assumptions as favorable as possible to one's position. The analyst must resist such pressures, however subtly they may be manifested. The influences can sometimes be countered by having analyses conducted by agencies or organizations with conflicting vested interests or viewpoints.

STRATEGIES FOR AIDING DECISION MAKERS

Given the unavoidable existence of some uncertainty, error, and bias—even if the best efforts are made to eliminate them—can adequate procedures be devised for dealing with these factors? The answer to this is complex and provides the grist for further work aimed at improved public decision making. If the consequences of environmental actions are to be compared systematically, the issue is not whether to undertake benefit-cost analysis but rather how to make it as useful as possible. Efforts must be allocated intelligently, results must not appear more precise than they actually are, and decision makers must be given a basis for understanding the results so that they can evaluate them thoughtfully. We offer the following suggestions for meeting these challenges.

Analyze Several Alternatives

To provide decision makers with sufficient information to analyze a proposal, a number of policy alternatives should be assessed. Policy alternatives are defined here as a collection of assumptions about the nature of a regulation. These include factors such as the stringency of a regulation, its comprehensiveness, and its compliance schedule.

How many policy alternatives should be analyzed? One viewpoint is simply to evaluate the benefits and costs of the proposed regulation. If the proposal is altered during the public-decision process, then these alterations would have to be evaluated at a later date or in a different set of hearings.

A second procedure is to evaluate both the proposed regulation and minor modifications of it in order to assess the effect that small changes would have on the costs and benefits of the regulation. For example, if a maximum lead standard were proposed at X parts per million, analysts could consider the costs and benefits of the proposal, together with the costs and benefits of hypothetical proposals that set the standard at 90 percent and at 110 percent of the proposed standard.

A third option is to assess the proposed regulation and one "challenger" proposal developed after discussions with groups likely to oppose the proposed regulation. Thus, if the Environmental Protection Agency proposes a lead standard at X parts per million, industrial groups may help develop a challenger proposal involving a standard of Y parts per million that may find much greater acceptance in industrial circles. The evaluation of the original proposal and one challenger would tend to crystallize those issues that would be brought before a pollution control board during formal hearings on the proposal.

A fourth option is to evaluate a broad range of proposals in order to generate a benefit-cost relation showing the effect of wide variations in the stringency of the proposed regulation. Such an approach implicitly assumes that policy makers will not only assess small changes to the regulation or changes proposed by groups having challenging positions but also may take the initiative in making and promulgating a regulation that is significantly different from the one proposed.

The choice among these alternatives will depend upon the situation and context of the particular proposal being made. The cost of the analysis will increase, of course, as the range of alternative proposals being evaluated increases. The analyst should have a clear understanding in the initial stages of the investigation about the extent of the regulatory alternatives to be evaluated.

Choose Aggregation Carefully

The level of aggregation used to assess benefits and costs varies widely, depending partly on the factors being studied and the objectives of the assessment. If a regulation affects relatively few emission sources, then the analyst may decide to do a very detailed study of each pollution source in order to determine compliance behavior and control costs. An example of this would be a sulfur dioxide regulation that affects only major power plants outside metropolitan areas. Because relatively few sources are affected and because each source may incur a significant control cost, the analyst is justified in extensively examining each generating plant. In other cases, such as the control of hydrocarbon sources, thousands of individual pollution control sources may be involved. In such cases the analyst will be forced to aggregate sources into source categories and to study the cost and control options available to each source category. This type of aggregation can lead to situations in which a pollution control source within a certain category has been assumed to adopt a pollution control strategy or technology that, in fact, it would not be capable of using. Therefore, such aggregation assumptions will be open to question by decision makers.

* * *

Deal Explicitly with Uncertainty, Error and Bias

All of the sources of uncertainty, error and bias identified influence the estimates of proposed regulation's effects and, as noted, will remain at least to some degree in spite of an analyst's best efforts. To summarize, one source of uncertainty is related to assumptions about parameters such as the discount rate. Such parameters are fraught with some degree of uncertainty stemming not from randomness in the data but from difficulties in determining the appropriate conceptual basis for these parameters. Another source of ambiguity is related to uncertainty in prices and costs because of data errors. This would include such examples as randomness in plume models used to translate emissions into ambient air quality, per unit costs of pieces of equipment, and increases in prices because increased costs that are likely to be charged. Statistical and other cost-estimation techniques yield further uncertainty. The technique chosen to estimate costs and benefits should be related to the data and the problem at hand but often the method used depends on the training and bias of the investigator and would not necessarily be related to the regulation itself.

* * *

Of all the ways of handling uncertainty, error, and bias, sensitivity tests to specified changes in data and procedures have the most to recommend them. The decision maker can relate the cause of change in the estimate to the reason for the change (altered data and procedures) and can judge the likelihood of the change occurring. Some sensitivity tests can be reported in fair detail in the text of a report to a decision maker. Another useful procedure is to report briefly on the outcome of a number of sensitivity tests, so that the decision maker will know that these tests are carried out and will know the sensitivity of results without being overwhelmed by a barrage of numbers pertaining to sensitivity. Test data should be included as an appendix.

Even with very thorough sensitivity tests, there are usually more variables than can be tested. The factors affecting the reliability of estimates should be highlighted in such a way that the decision maker can understand the ranges involved without the benefit of actual numerical comparisons.

CONCLUSION

We have emphasized that benefit-cost analysis is simply an approach to comparing the results of environmental regulation in terms of the values of all the individuals who are affected by it. Costs are a measure of what must be given up to implement regulation; benefits are the effects received in exchange. Since benefits and costs are incommensurate in physical terms, benefit-cost analysts seek to make the comparison easier by expressing the effects in commensurate terms. Expressing effects in dollar terms whenever possible facilitates estimates of the trade-off between benefits or costs and other goods and services that are desired—trade-offs that are inevitable.

The tools of benefit-cost analysis have been drawn from economic analysis over the past 45 years or so and have been applied and refined in hundreds, if not thousands, of studies. While some of the procedures are technical, they are all aimed at discovering as accurately as possible the weights that people attach to what they receive versus what they give up. Benefit-cost analysts make the same kinds of comparisons people make in their everyday life. The past contribution of benefit-cost analysis—and more than ever its usefulness in the future—is based upon the assistance it gives in organizing individual valuations into a coherent and comprehensible way of thinking about environmental actions.

NOTES

1. The authors acknowledge that measurement problems frequently arise in benefit-cost analysis. Robert Dorfman uses sulfur oxide regulation to show the complexities that can arise:

> To appreciate how demanding B-CA's [benefit-cost analysis's] data requirements are, consider the task of estimating the monetary value of the health benefits of a regulation intended to reduce emissions of sulphur oxide into the atmosphere. Among the data required are:
>
> 1. The amount by which power plant and other emitting sources will actually reduce their discharges in response to the regulation,
>
> 2. Given the amount of reduction at the sources, the amount by which the concentrations of sulphur oxide and its chemical products will be reduced at various places in the city,
>
> 3. Given the amount of reduction at different places in the city, the numbers of people who are exposed to various concentrations for various lengths of time,

4. Given the numbers of people exposed to different concentrations and durations, the reductions in the number of days of illness (perhaps distinguished by severity) and in medical expenses,

5. Given the reduction in days of illness, the social value to attach to it.

All this for one item in the table. Particularly difficult are steps 2 (because the process of the diffusion of pollutants in the atmosphere is complicated and not well understood), 4 (because the health effects of exposure to airborne and waterborne pollutants, technically called the "dosage-response curves," are known only very roughly), and 5 (because of the difficulty of attaching monetary values to nonmonetary consequences).

Robert Dorfman, *An Introduction to Benefit-Cost Analysis, in* ECONOMICS OF THE ENVIRONMENT (3d ed. 1993). Chapter Five of this anthology reviews in detail the problems associated with estimating the health risks posed by pollution, and the costs associated with abating that pollution.

2. The National Environmental Policy Act (NEPA) requires federal agencies to prepare an environmental impact statement (EIS) for all "major federal actions which significantly affect the quality of the human environment." 42 U.S.C. § 4332(2)(C). The primary purpose behind this EIS requirement is to promote better decisions by helping the agency understand the environmental consequences of the various alternative courses of action open to it. 40 C.F.R. § 1500.1(c). The regulations implementing NEPA do not require that an EIS include a benefit-cost analysis; but where an agency chooses independently to prepare a benefit-cost analysis it must be incorporated into the EIS to aid in evaluating the environmental consequences. Even in this circumstance, however, the rules caution that "the weighing of the merits and drawbacks of various alternatives need not be displayed in a monetary cost-benefit analysis, and should not be when there are important qualitative considerations." 40 C.F.R. § 1502.23.

3. One of the techniques which the authors recommend as an aid to decision-making is an analysis of alternatives. Where NEPA applies, federal agencies are expressly required to analyze all reasonable alternatives to a proposed action. 42 U.S.C. § 4332(2)(C)(iii) and (2)(E); *see also*, 40 C.F.R. § 1502.14 (1994). In what way does the alternatives analysis help refine the benefit-cost analysis?

4. Some federal agencies use benefit-cost analysis routinely to guide their decisions. For example, in the preparation of forest plans, the Forest Service requires that the interdisciplinary team "formulate a broad range of reasonable alternatives." 36 C.F.R. § 219.12(f). "The primary goal in formulating alternatives, besides complying with NEPA procedures, is to provide an adequate basis for identifying the alternative that comes nearest to maximizing net public benefits * * * ." *Id.* The plans that result from this process "shall provide for multiple use and sustained yield * * * in a way that maximizes long-term net public benefits in an environmentally sound matter." 36 C.F.R. § 219.1(a).

Likewise, the U.S. Army Corps of Engineers conducts a public interest review for various permits which it issues for discharges into the navigable waters of the United States. Pursuant to this public interest review, the Corps' rules require that the Corps balance "the benefits which reasonably may be expected to accrue from the proposal * * * against its reasonably foreseeable detriments." 33 C.F.R. § 320.4(a). Are the rules of the Corps and the Forest Service consistent with the rules implementing NEPA? Can you see any risks associated with the use of benefit-cost analysis to aid decision-making? Consider this question as you read the following article.

While most economists and many politicians promote economically efficient results, Mark Sagoff argues that efficiency should not be our only goal. Sagoff is the former Director of the Center for Philosophy and Public Policy at the University of Maryland and continues his association with the Center. His writings bridge the fields of environmental economics, environmental ethics, and environmental law.

ECONOMIC THEORY AND ENVIRONMENTAL LAW
Mark Sagoff
79 Mich. L. Rev. 1393 (1981)*

Many economists take the view that environmental problems are economic problems. They believe that market failure causes these problems: private and social costs diverge; profit-maximizing decisions, therefore, are socially inefficient. Economists would correct this market failure by requiring private decision makers to internalize externalities, that is, to make the price of goods reflect all the economic and social costs of producing them, including the pollution costs. When this is done, they argue, pollution will be controlled, endangered species will be saved, and pristine areas will be preserved, but only to the extent that the benefits therefrom exceed the costs. Any increase in environmental protection from an "optimal" level "would cost more than it is worth," while any decrease would "reduce benefits more than it would save in costs."

Although this economic approach purports to allow us to choose the best among available policies, in fact it makes economic efficiency our only goal. Economic efficiency has traditionally been understood to require the maximum satisfaction of the preferences that markets reveal. These are typically self-regarding or self-interested preferences, that is, preferences that reflect a person's idea of his or her individual welfare. Preferences of this sort may be contrasted with preferences that express what the individual believes is in the public interest or in the interest of a group or community to which he or she belongs. Political activity is supposed, in theory at least, to provide a vehicle for airing, criticizing, and settling upon interests or opinions of this group-related kind.

The search for economic efficiency might take us to the best public policies if we were

---

* Reprinted with permission.

a nation of individuals competing each for his or her own welfare with no regard for or conception of the collective good. Then an efficient market might lead us to satisfy as well as possible all of our interests. In such a situation, government might best be conceived as a prophylactic on markets, and public policies might be considered irrational if they could not be construed as reasonable responses to market failures. But we are not simply a group of consumers, nor are we bent on satisfying only self-regarding preferences. Many of us advocate ideals and have a vision of what we should do or be like as a nation. And we would sacrifice some of our private interests for those public ends.

There may be individuals who believe that our nation as a whole should dedicate itself entirely to the interests that individuals pursue as individuals. This belief comes into question, however, when we distinguish what people want for themselves and what they think is best for the community. Why should we believe that the right policy goal is the one that satisfies only the self-interested preferences of consumers? Why should we not take into account the community-regarding values that individuals seek through the political process as well?

In Part I of this essay, I argue that environmental legislation, at least during the past twenty years, fails to make economic "common sense," that is, it fails to maximize the satisfaction of consumer demand over the long run. Laws like the Endangered Species Act flout this conception of economic efficiency. This is how most Americans would have it: most Americans reject the notion that the natural environment should be made over to serve the wants of the self-interested consumer. Part II describes the way that economists have attempted to take account of citizen or community-regarding preferences. I suggest that they do this primarily by giving these convictions and beliefs shadow or surrogate prices as if they were market externalities. In Part II, I argue briefly that this shadow pricing of political, moral, and cultural convictions vitiates cost-benefit analysis. Shadow pricing allows the analyst to justify virtually any policy by assigning the appropriate prices to the opinions of the political constituency that favors it. There is, then, no popular public policy that cannot then be justified on "economic" grounds.

In Part III of this essay, I extend my criticism of cost-benefit analysis to show that it confuses statements of principle or opinion with wants and interests of the kind that are properly revealed in and satisfied by markets. I argue that it is a mistake to treat views or convictions that merit the dignity of a hearing as if they were only wants or interests deserving of a price. I conclude that attempts to base environmental law on economic theory must fail.

I

Anyone who believes that government ought to be primarily interested in correcting market failure must find puzzling much of our environmental legislation. Environmentalist groups, not famous for their economic "common sense," successfully backed much of this legislation in the 1970s. It is not surprising, therefore, that environmental protection goes beyond the mere correction of market deficiencies. Congress designed the Clean Air and Clean Water Acts to improve the quality of our air and water. It passed the Endangered Species Act to protect threatened species, even if the economic costs of protection outweigh the benefits. Similarly, the Occupational Safety and Health Act seeks to make the workplace safe and healthful, a goal that is not always consistent with market efficiency. These laws attempt to correct perceived environmental, rather than economic, problems. Congress did not limit itself to providing economically optimal solutions.

Consider, for example, the 1977 Clean Air Act Amendments, which designated all national parks and wilderness areas as Class I lands to protect them from significant deterioration of air quality. This insistence upon preserving air quality in pristine areas does not rest upon an economic calculation. It is justified, rather, by a national sense of responsibility. What kind of nation would turn magnificent wilderness areas into polluted fens in order to make energy cheaper and therefore easier to waste? Questions like this have led many Americans to believe that the preservation of wilderness from pollution is what national dignity and self-respect minimally require. This belief has little to do with economic "common sense." Those of us who approve of the amended Clean Air Act are not necessarily likely to use the wilderness areas that these laws protect. We are more likely to consume the energy that would be produced by polluting these lands. Cost-benefit analysis, insofar as it reflects what consumers buy rather than what citizens respect, would lead to a policy directly opposed to the Act.

* * *

One reason for these laws is that Americans have moral convictions about the environment that have nothing to do with economic "common sense." A majority of Americans strongly prefer environmental laws that are not economically efficient. The Endangered Species Act remains popular, even though people must recognize that the benefits of preserving Lange's metalmark, the snail darter, or the furbish lousewort may not equal the costs. We choose to save the metalmark to prove to ourselves that we are not motivated solely by economic self-interest. Rather, we act upon moral values and a sense of national responsibility to the land that we inhabit.

* * *

Although economic approaches to public policy may purport to weigh both consumer and citizen values, we may, as citizens, believe that certain public values or collective goals (e.g., that an innocent person not be convicted) supersede the values that we pursue as self-seeking individuals (e.g. security from crime). Moreover, we might decide to sacrifice economic optimality for cleaner air and water. Once legislatures, responding to political pressure, have made this choice, is it defensible for economists to insist that our policymaking process include the very consumer values that we have decided to sacrifice? Shall economic analysts, rather than legislatures, determine the balance to be struck between our preferences as consumers and our opinions as citizens? To ask the question in this fashion is to answer it. Before we draw any final conclusions, we should examine more closely the decision making apparatus that the economists advocate. Part II attempts such an examination.

II

Economists understand, of course, that environmental legislation may be founded on different values than consumers reveal in the marketplace. They recognize the importance of "public" as well as "private" wants. Related distinctions are sometimes drawn between "ideal-regarding" and "want-regarding" preferences, and between "external" and "personal" preferences. * * * [I]t is not the individual but the situation—or the way that a question is put—that determines whether public or private wants enter materially into his or her response. Does the individual act in a political context, for example, by answering a survey or casting a vote? If so, he or she is likely to express or reveal citizen preferences. If it is a market situation instead, then he or she will probably choose as a consumer. The role that the individual plays depends upon the way that the stage is set. The question, then is how can a neutral balance be struck between values revealed in market and in nonmarket transactions? Since people usually find themselves making consumer choices, the preferences that they are likely to express will be self-regarding rather than group-regarding. An individual may buy a vacation home even if he or she disapproves of the vacation home industry because it destroys wilderness. What we do as consumers—the choices that we make and may feel constrained to make within markets—may dismay us as citizens. How can we avoid these citizen "costs" unless we vote against our consumer interests? That we may reject consumer sovereignty in our role as citizens does not mean that all economic approaches to public policy are futile. It only implies that economists must develop a convincing way to take into account citizen "costs" or "externalities" (if that is what they are).

Economists typically accomplish this by assigning prices to public wants or citizen preferences. These are swept together with "merit wants," and "ideal-regarding" preferences (which include ethical principles) to form what economists generally refer to as "fragile," "soft," or "intangible" variables. Once they are priced, these values are integrated with ordinary self-interested consumer wants on a single social preference-schedule.

Thus, economists may ask what you are willing to pay for the knowledge that your nation preserves beautiful environments and rare species. What is it worth to you to have a clear conscience about these matters, insofar as you think of yourself as a responsible member of the national community? They may determine, by aggregating the individual amounts, that even the metalmark and the lousewort have considerable shadow prices. In this way, economists argue that they have found a value-neutral mechanism that takes into account all of our values, and indicates the optimal decision.

Economists have used this method to justify seemingly inefficient environmental legislation. In 1975, the Environmental Protection Agency, implementing the Clean Air Act, directed the states to "prevent significant deterioration" in areas where air quality exceeds national secondary standards. The regulation, in other words seeks to keep clean air clean. The "prevention of significant deterioration" (PSD) doctrine may appeal to us on aesthetic or on ethical grounds, but its goal potentially conflicts with plans to locate a network of power plants in the Southwest, where both clean air and coal are abundant. Because PSD ignores many economic facts, the EPA's regulations appear to be inconsistent with economic "common sense." In a recent article, "An Experiment on the Economic Value of Visibility," three University of Wyoming economists attempt to explain and justify the PSD requirements in economic terms. "Aesthetics," the authors said, "will play a major role. The PSD regulations amount to formal governmental admission that aesthetics, at least as embodied in atmospheric visibility, is a 'good' that might have a positive value."

In order to put a price on aesthetic preferences for visibility, the authors showed a number of individuals photographs of scenes of the Southwest. In some of the pictures, the visibility was better than in others. They then asked the participants how much they would pay to preserve the visibility portrayed in the clearer photographs. The answers allowed the economists to establish a surrogate market in which they could price aesthetic benefits.

* * *

The economist's solution is to internalize the externality by giving preservation benefits and other noninstrumental uses a fair market price. Heller suggests that we determine how much preservationists will pay for an "increase in the industry output of preservation services." This would measure the economic surplus that preservationist policies produce. That surplus represents the "difference between what preservationists would be willing to pay and what they do pay for the preservation use of the resources." This surplus could then be balanced, together with the other costs, against the benefits of vacation home development.

The outcome of such a cost-benefit analysis will depend upon which views the analyst deems worthy of pricing. If the analyst is an environmentalist, he or she may give the citizen preferences of environmentalists a high price; an economist working for industry may set a lower price. Other technical problems arise. How can the analyst tell whether an individual speaks the truth in response to a questionnaire when the individual knows that his response is likely to influence public policy? It would make more sense for the individual to overstate his willingness to pay for a policy that he approves since he will not be required actually to pay that much money. Likewise, the individual may lie on a questionnaire because it threatens his or her "cherished illusion" that elected officials and not bureaucrats should make public policy. These and other theoretical problems vex efforts to extend cost-benefit analysis beyond values for which markets exist and are appropriate.

Cost-benefit analysis, nevertheless, may play a useful role in supplementing or informing political decision making. Some economists go one step further, however, and suggest that their method provides a better framework for decision making than can be found within the political process. These economists argue that cost-benefit analysis provides a better measure of both our "private" and "public" wants than does political argument. The political process, they argue, is less precise and less able to take into account all of our relevant desires. Some economists may suggest then, that they are better able than legislators to define the national will.

I shall be concerned, in the rest of this essay, with the idea that economic analysis can replace political argument and decision. I shall be particularly concerned with the notion that economists can take account of "public" wants by pricing them. I argue that Congress, and not cost-benefit analysts, should reflect public values and convictions in legislation, and that environmental legislation must do something more than merely correct market deficiencies. * * *

III

Economic methods cannot supply the information necessary to justify public policy. Economics can measure the intensity with which we hold our beliefs; it cannot evaluate those beliefs on their merits. Yet such evaluation is essential to political decision making. This is my greatest single criticism of cost-benefit analysis. The many problems involved in applying the concept of shadow pricing are secondary, because the concept itself rests on a mistake.

To recognize this mistake, we must first understand what it is that economists attempt to measure. If they measure consumer interests, market data are appropriate and relevant. The pricing mechanism can suggest when resources used to satisfy certain wants might be more efficiently employed to satisfy others. When economists approach issues that concern us as citizens, however, they do not, as they should, abandon the pricing mechanism. They believe that they can account for citizen-preferences as well as consumer-preferences by determining their dollar value. They do this, for example, by asking citizens what they would pay for a certain level of environmental protection. But this attempt to measure the convictions of values of citizens by pricing them as market externalities confuses what the individual wants as an individual and what he or she, as a citizen, believes is best for the community.

This confusion involves what logicians call a category-mistake. One makes a category-mistake by treating facts or concepts as if they belong to one logical type or category, when they actually belong to another. Several examples are illustrative. It is logically correct to predicate whiteness of snow or even of coal. (It may not be true, but it is intelligible.) To say that the square root of four is white, however, makes no sense because it is impossible meaningfully to predicate color of a number. When two concepts are in different categories, one cannot measure the first by methods that are appropriate only to the second. * * *

Private and public preferences also belong to different logical categories. Public "preferences" do not involve desires or wants, but opinions or beliefs. They state what a person believes is best or right for the community or group as a whole. These opinions or beliefs may be true or false, and we may meaningfully ask the individual for the reasons that he or she holds them. But an economist who asks how much citizens would pay for opinions that they advocate through political association commits a category-mistake. The economist asks of objective beliefs a question that is appropriate only to subjective wants.

When an environmentalist argues that we ought to preserve wilderness areas because of their cultural importance and symbolic meaning, he or she states a *conviction and not a desire*. When an economist asserts that we ought to attain efficient levels of pollution, he or she, too, states a belief. Both beliefs are to be supported by arguments, not by money. One cannot establish the validity of these beliefs by pricing them, nor can that mechanism measure their importance to society as a whole. One can judge how strongly people hold their beliefs by asking how much they would pay to see them implemented, but that is how we make policy decisions. Those who think that Creationism should be taught in the public schools, for example, are able to raise a lot of money. But the amount of money that partisans raise does not demonstrate the merit of their position. A person who wants his or her child taught a particular doctrine is free to pay for that; willingness to pay may correctly measure the strength of that desire. When a person advocates a policy as being right or appropriate for society as a whole, however, the intensity of the desire is no longer relevant. Rather, advocates must present arguments that convince the public or its representatives to adopt a policy. Political decision makers judge ideas on their merits, and make decisions based on what is good for us all. These policymakers may consider economic factors, but they should not use the economic method to evaluate competing beliefs.

The distinction between public and private interests is indispensable to the study of political philosophy. "To abolish the distinction," as one commentator has written, "is to make a shambles of political science by treating things that are different as if they were alike." Markets are the appropriate arena for the competition of private interests. This competition may best be understood and regulated in terms of individual willingness to pay. When one advocates not a special or private interest but what one describes as the public interest or the interest of all, however, the framework of debate completely changes. Public discussion must then be carried on in public terms. The issue is no longer to measure the stake that the individual has in his proposal; indeed, the larger the individual's private stake, the more suspect is his public pretension. What matters is whether the argument that he or she offers is sound.

This is not to say that economic data are irrelevant in public decision making. It is to argue that the satisfaction of revealed preferences is only one goal among others that policymakers must take into account. And willingness to pay, as opposed to ability to argue, is not a method for making this choice. Costs and benefits, of course, are important—there are economic constraints. But this does not show that cost-benefit analysis provides an appropriate framework for testing the legitimacy of law.

* * *

This might seem grossly inefficient to economists, and perhaps it is, but it is what democratic government is all about. An alternative—technocracy—quarantines or localizes conflict so that it may be resolved by the application of some mechanical rule or decision procedure. Cost-benefit approaches to public policy, if taken to their extreme, would do this, and thus they would make useless the institutions of democratic government. Cost-benefit analysis localizes conflict among affected individuals and prevents it from breaking open into the public realm. This suggests that the reason that industry favors economic approaches to public policy is not necessarily the obvious one, namely, that cost-benefit analysis is sensitive to the costs of regulation. The deeper reason may be that cost-benefit analysis defines a framework for conflict that keeps the public *qua* public and the citizen *qua* citizen out.

Once we recognize the logical difference between wants and beliefs, it becomes clear that cost-benefit analysis can measure only the former. To conduct such an analysis, the economist asks how much we would pay for certain policies. How much would you pay to save Lange's metalmark? How much would you pay to preserve the quality of the air in the Southwest? Our responses indicate only the degree to which we care about the issues. If the analyst prices these views by willingness-to-pay criteria, or makes any similar economic trade-off, he tests neither the validity of the views nor the reasons for them, but only the intensity with which they are held.

* * *

What many economists do not understand is that efficiency is one value among many and is not a meta-value that comprehends all others. Economists as a rule do recognize one other value, namely, justice or equality, and they speak, therefore, of a "trade-off" between efficiency and equality. They do not speak, as they should, however, about the trade-off between efficiency and our aesthetic moral values. What about the trade-off between efficiency and dignity, efficiency and self-respect, efficiency and the magnificence of our natural heritage, efficiency and the quality of life? These are the trade-offs that are important in setting environmental policy.

If we were to pursue efficiency as our goal in environmental policy, I believe that we would quickly turn all of our natural beauty into commercial blight. This is what happens when self-fueling and irreversible consumer markets have their way. To forestall this result by "pricing" beliefs, values, and ideals as if they were consumer benefits, I have argued, is to commit a category-mistake. Cost-benefit analysis, at that point, disintegrates into storytelling; it becomes a bad exercise in *ad hoc* justification.

I do not pretend to assess the merits of the arguments that I have made here. I only want to point out that it *is* an attempt at argument. I did not treat the position that economists defend as if it were merely their private preference. I did not survey economists to find out how much they were willing to pay to have their views implemented. Why, then do economists survey environmentalists to find out how much they would pay to keep a vista clear or a river pure? Why do economists believe that opinions that oppose theirs deserve a price and not a reply?

NOTES

1. Sagoff expands on his theories in MARK SAGOFF, THE ECONOMY OF THE EARTH (1988). Note, for example, his extended criticism of cost-benefit analysis—

> Cost-benefit analysis does not, because it cannot, judge opinions and beliefs on these merits but asks instead how much might be paid for them, as if a conflict of views could be settled in the same way as a conflict of interests. Analysts who take this approach, of course, tend to confuse views with interests. They do this by giving political, ethical and cultural convictions technical names—"bequest values," "existence values," "intangibles," "fragile values," or "soft variables"—as if by the nomenclature they could transform beliefs that have carried the day before legislatures into the data of economic methodology * * *.
>
> [W]hen cost-benefited analysis attempts to do the work of ethical and political judgment, it loses whatever objectivity it might have had and becomes a tool of partisan politics * * * . [W]hen cost-benefit analysis assigns "shadow" prices to "amenity," "option," "bequest," and other citizens beliefs and values, theoretical "breakthroughs" replace sound judgment and common sense. At that point, economic analysis deteriorates into storytelling and hand-waving likely to convince no one except those partisans who agree with—and possibly have paid for—its results.

Id. at 38-39.

2. Under Sagoff's view, what role, if any, should economic theory play in environmental decision-making? Is the problem simply that natural resource economics has traditionally focused on microeconomic issues, even when macroeconomic concerns are at least as important? *Compare* Mark Sagoff, *Environmental Economics: An Epitaph, with* Raymond J. Kopp, *Environmental Economics: Not Dead but Thriving*, RESOURCES 2, 7 (Spring 1993).

COST-BENEFIT ANALYSIS: AN ETHICAL CRITIQUE
Steven Kelman
Regulation 33 (Jan./Feb. 1981)*

At the broadest and vaguest level, cost-benefit analysis may be regarded simply as systematic thinking about decision-making. Who can oppose, economists sometimes ask, efforts to think in a systematic way about the consequences of different courses of action? The alternative, it would appear, is unexamined decision-making. But defining cost-benefit analysis so simply leaves it with few implications for actual regulatory decision-making. Presumably, therefore, those who urge regulators to make greater use of the technique have a more extensive prescription in mind. I assume here that their prescription includes the following views:

(1) There exists a strong presumption that an act should not be undertaken unless its benefits outweigh its costs.

(2) In order to determine whether benefits outweigh costs, it is desirable to attempt to express all benefits and costs in a common scale or denominator, so that they can be compared with each other, even when some benefits and costs are not traded on markets and hence have no established dollar values.

(3) Getting decision-makers to make more use of cost-benefit techniques is important enough to warrant both the expense required to gather the data for improved cost-benefit estimation and the political efforts needed to give the activity higher priority compared to other activities, also valuable in and of themselves.

My focus is on cost-benefit analysis as applied to environmental, safety, and health regulation. In that context, I examine each of the above propositions from the perspective of formal ethical theory, that is, the study of what actions it is morally right to undertake. My conclusions are:

(1) In areas of environmental, safety, and health regulation, there may be many instances where a certain decision might be right even though its benefits do not outweigh its costs.

(2) There are good reasons to oppose efforts to put dollar values on non-marketed benefits and costs.

(3) Given the relative frequency of occasions in the areas of environmental, safety, and health regulation where one would not wish to use a benefits-outweigh-costs test as a decision rule, and given the reasons to oppose the monetizing of non-marketed benefits or costs that is a prerequisite for cost-benefit analysis, it is not justifiable to devote major resources to the generation of data for cost-benefit calculations or to undertake efforts to "spread the gospel" of cost-benefit analysis further.

---

* Reprinted with the permission of The American Enterprise Institute for Public Policy Research, Washington, D.C.

I

How do we decide whether a given action is morally right or wrong and hence, assuming the desire to act morally, why it should be undertaken or refrained from? Like the Moliere character who spoke prose without knowing it, economists who advocate use of cost-benefit analysis for public decisions are philosophers without knowing it: the answer given by cost-benefit analysis, that actions should be undertaken so as to maximize net benefits, represents one of the classic answers given by moral philosophers—that given by utilitarians. To determine whether an action is right or wrong, utilitarians tote up all the positive consequences of the action in terms of human satisfaction. The act that maximizes attainment of satisfaction under the circumstances is the right act. That the economists' answer is also the answer of one school of philosophers should not be surprising. Early on, economics was a branch of moral philosophy, and only later did it become an independent discipline.

* * *

Utilitarianism is an important and powerful moral doctrine. But it is probably a minority position among contemporary moral philosophers. It is amazing that economists can proceed in unanimous endorsement of cost-benefit analysis as if unaware that their conceptual framework is highly controversial in the discipline from which it arose—moral philosophy.

Let us explore the critique of utilitarianism.

* * *

Imagine the case of an old man in Nazi Germany who is hostile to the regime. He is wondering whether he should speak out against Hitler. If he speaks out, he will lose his pension. And his action will have done nothing to increase the chances that the Nazi regime will be overthrown: he is regarded as somewhat eccentric by those around him, and nobody has ever consulted his views on political questions. Recall that one cannot add to the benefits of speaking out any satisfaction from doing "the right thing," because the purpose of the exercise is to determine whether speaking out *is* the right thing. How would the utilitarian calculation go? The benefits of the old man's speaking out would, as the example is presented, be nil, while the costs would be his loss of his pension. So the costs of the action would outweigh the benefits. By the utilitarians' cost-benefit calculation, it would be *morally wrong* for the man to speak out.

Another example: two very close friends are on an Arctic expedition together. One of them falls very sick in the snow and bitter cold, and sinks quickly before anything can be done to help him. As he is dying, he asks his friend one thing, "Please, make me a solemn promise that ten years from today you will come back to this spot and place a lighted candle here to remember me." The friend solemnly promises to do so, but does not tell a soul. Now, ten years later, the friend must decide whether to keep his promise. It would be inconvenient for him to make the long trip. Since he told nobody, his failure to go will not affect the general social faith in promise-keeping. And the incident was unique enough so that it is safe to assume that his failure to go will not encourage him to break other promises. Again, the costs of the act outweigh the benefits. A utilitarian would need to believe that it would be *morally wrong* to travel to the Arctic to travel to the Arctic to light the candle.

* * *

To those who believe that it would not be morally wrong for the old man to speak out in Nazi Germany or for the explorer to return to the Arctic to light a candle for his deceased friend, * * * utilitarianism is insufficient as a moral view. We believe that some acts whose costs are greater than their benefits may be morally right and, contrariwise, some acts whose benefits are greater than their costs may be morally wrong.

This does not mean that the question whether benefits are greater than costs is morally irrelevant. Few would claim such. Indeed, for a broad range of individual and social decisions, whether an act's benefits outweigh its costs is a sufficient question to ask. But not for all such decisions. These may involve situations where certain duties—duties not to lie, break promises, or kill, for example—make an act wrong, even if it would result in an excess of benefits over costs. Or they may involve instances where people's rights are at stake. We would not permit rape even if it could be demonstrated that the rapist derived enormous happiness from his act, while the victim experienced only minor displeasure. We do not do cost-benefit analyses of freedom of speech or trial by jury.

* * *

The notion of human rights involves the idea that people may make certain claims to be allowed to act in certain ways or to be treated in certain ways, even if the sum of benefits achieved thereby does not outweigh the sum of costs.

* * *

In the most convincing versions of non-utilitarian ethics, various duties or rights are not absolute. But each has a *prima facie* moral validity so that, if duties or rights do not conflict, the morally right act is the act that reflects a duty or respects a right. If duties or rights do conflict, a moral judgment, based on conscious deliberation, must be made. Since one of the duties non-utilitarian philosophers enumerate is the duty of beneficence (the duty to maximize happiness), which in effect incorporates all of utilitarianism by reference, a non-utilitarian who is faced with conflicts between the results of cost-benefit analysis and non-utility-based considerations will need to undertake such deliberation. But in that deliberation, additional elements, which cannot be reduced to a question of whether benefits outweigh costs, have been introduced. Indeed, depending on the moral importance we attach to the right or duty involved, cost-benefit questions may, within wide ranges, become irrelevant to the outcome of the moral judgment.

In addition to questions involving duties and rights, there is a final sort of question where, in my view, the issue of whether benefits outweigh costs should not govern moral judgment. I noted earlier that, for the common run of questions facing individuals and societies, it is possible to begin and end our judgment simply by finding out if the benefits of the contemplated act outweighs the costs. This very fact means that one way to show the great importance, or value, attached to an area is to say that decisions involving that area should not be determined by cost-benefit calculations. This applies, I think, to the view many environmentalists have of decisions involving our natural environment. When officials are deciding what level of pollution will harm certain vulnerable people—such as asthmatics or the elderly—while not harming others, one issue involved may be the right of those people not to be sacrificed on the altar of somewhat higher living standards for the rest of us. But more broadly than this, many environmentalists fear that subjecting decisions about clean air or water to the cost-benefit tests that determine the general run of decisions removes those matters from the realm of specially valued things.

II

In order for cost-benefit calculations to be performed the way they are supposed to be, all costs and benefits must be expressed in a common measure, typically dollars, including things not normally bought and sold on markets, and to which dollar prices are therefore not attached. The most dramatic example of such things is human life itself; but many of the other benefits achieved or preserved by environmental policy—such as peace and quiet, fresh-smelling air, swimmable rivers, spectacular vistas—are not traded on markets either.

Economists who do cost-benefit analysis regard the quest after dollar values for nonmarket things as a difficult challenge—but one to be met with relish. They have tried to develop methods for imputing a person's "willingness to pay" for such things, their approach generally involving a search for bundled goods that are traded on markets and that vary as to whether they include a feature that is, *by itself,* not marketed. Thus, fresh air is not marketed, but houses in different parts of Los Angeles that are similar except for the degree of smog are. Peace and quiet is not marketed, but similar houses inside and outside airport flight paths are. The risk of death is not marketed, but similar jobs that have different levels of risk are. Economists have produced many often ingenious efforts to impute dollar prices to non-marketed things by observing the premiums accorded homes in clean air areas over similar homes in dirty areas or the premiums paid for risky jobs over similar nonrisky jobs.

* * *

[I]f we have already decided we value something highly, one way of stamping it with a cachet affirming its high value is to announce that it is "not for sale." Such an announcement does more however, than just reflect a preexisting high valuation. It signals a thing's distinctive value to others and helps us persuade them to value the thing more highly than they otherwise might. It also expresses our resolution to safeguard that distinctive value. To state that something is not for sale is thus also a source of value for that thing, since if a thing's value is easy to affirm or protect, it will be worth more than an otherwise similar thing without such attributes.

If we proclaim that something is not for sale, we make a once-and-for-all judgment of its special value. When something is priced, the issue of its perceived value is constantly coming up, as a standing invitation to reconsider that original judgment. Were people constantly faced with questions such as "how much money could get you to give up your freedom of speech?" or "how much would you sell your vote for if you could?," the perceived value of the freedom to speak or the right to vote would soon become devastated as, in moments of weakness, people started saying "maybe it's not worth *so much* after all." Better not to be faced with the constant questioning in the first place. Something similar did in fact occur when the slogan "better red than dead" was launched by some pacifists during the Cold War. Critics pointed out that the very posing of this stark choice—in effect, "would you really be willing to give up your life in exchange for not living under communism?"—reduced the value people attached to freedom and thus diminished resistance to attacks on freedom.

Finally, of some things valued very highly it is stated that they are "priceless" or that they have "infinite value." Such expressions are reserved for a subset of things not for sale, such as life or health. Economists tend to scoff at talk of pricelessness. For them, saying that something is priceless is to state a willingness to trade off an infinite quantity of all other goods for one unit of the priceless good, a situation that empirically appears highly unlikely. For most people, however, the word priceless is pregnant with meaning. Its value-affirming and value-protecting functions cannot be bestowed on expressions that merely denote a determinate, albeit high, valuation. John Kennedy in his inaugural address proclaimed that the nation was ready to "pay any price [and] bear any burden * * * to assure the survival and the success of liberty." Had he said instead that we were willing to "pay a high price" or "bear a large burden" for liberty, the statement would have rung hollow.

III

An objection that advocates of cost-benefit analysis might well make to the preceding argument should be considered. I noted earlier that, in cases where various non-utility-based duties or rights conflict with the maximization of utility, it is necessary to make a deliberative judgment about what act is finally right. I also argued earlier that the search for commensurability might not always be a desirable one, that the attempt to go beyond expressing benefits in terms of (say) lives saved and costs in terms of dollars is not something devoutly to be wished.

In situations involving things that are not expressed in a common measure, advocates of cost-benefit analysis argue that people making judgments "in effect" perform cost-benefit calculations anyway. If government regulators promulgate a regulation that saves 100 lives at a cost of $1 billion, they are "in effect" valuing a life at (a minimum of) $10 million, whether or not they say that they are willing to place a dollar value on a human life. Since, in this view, cost-benefit analysis "in effect" is inevitable, it might as well be made specific.

This argument misconstrues the real difference in the reasoning processes involved. In cost-benefit analysis, equivalencies are established in *advance* as one of the raw materials for the calculation. One determines costs and benefits, one determines equivalencies (to be able to put various costs and benefits into a common measure), and then one sets to toting things up—waiting, as it were, with bated breath for the results of the calculation to come out. The outcome is determined by the arithmetic; if the outcome is a close call or if one is not good at long division, one does not know how it will turn out until the calculation is finished. In the kind of deliberative judgment that is performed without a common measure, no establishment of equivalencies occurs in advance. Equivalencies are not aids to the decision process. In fact, the decision-maker might not even be aware of what the "in effect" equivalencies were, at least before they are revealed to him afterwards by someone pointing out what he had "in effect" done. The decision-maker would see himself as simply having made a deliberative judgment; the "in effect" equivalency number did not play a causal role in the decision but at most merely reflects it. Given this, the argument against making the process explicit is the one discussed earlier in the discussion of problems with putting specific quantified values on things that are not normally quantified—that the very act of doing so may serve to reduce the value of those things.

My own judgment is that modest efforts to assess levels of benefits and costs are justified, although I do not believe that government agencies ought to sponsor efforts to put dollar prices on non-market things. I also do not believe that the cry for more cost-benefit analysis in regulation is, on the whole, justified. If regulatory officials were so insensitive about regulatory costs that they did not provide accept able raw material for deliberative judgments (even if not of a strictly cost-benefit nature), my conclusion might be different. But a good deal of research into costs and benefits already occurs—actually, far more in the U.S. regulatory process than in that of any other industrial society. The danger now would seem to come more from the other side.

NOTES

1. What problems does Kelman see with the use of benefit-cost analysis in decisions regarding environmental protection? To what extent does Kelman support the use of such analysis in decision-making?

2. "Contingent valuation" is a phrase commonly used to describe the process for ascertaining "willingness to pay" values. *See* R. G. CUMMINGS, D. S. BROOKSHIRE, & W. D. SCHULZE, VALUING ENVIRONMENTAL GOODS: AN ASSESSMENT OF THE CONTINGENT VALUATION METHOD (1986). Typically, such values are determined through the use of surveys. Assuming the contingent valuation is an appropriate economic tool, what problems might you foresee with the reliability of surveys?

3. How can or should benefit-cost analysis account for future values. Suppose, for example, that the United States Forest Service is considering two alternatives for managing a large, intact, primitive area of the forest. Under one proposal, the agency would allow extensive logging which would destroy the primitive character of the land. Under the other proposal, it would set aside the land for wilderness preservation. A benefit-cost analysis (including contingent valuation surveys) might be performed to assist the decision-makers, but how do they account for the potential future value of the land? The future value for logging might be reasonably ascertained by looking at the regeneration rates in similar forests. But what about the value of wilderness land 50 or 100 years from now, when far less wilderness remains? Is it possible to predict the value of such land? Consider that many people value wilderness even though they have no plans to enjoy it personally. How should such "existence" values be measured for both present and future generations? It is reasonable to take such values into account?

4. Kelman's reluctance to apply benefit-cost analysis to environmental problems has been criticized by Stephen Edwards. Edwards argues that "[m]onetization of non-market values by individuals is relevant and appropriate when a person's preferences are based on self-interest and on indifference between amounts of things that provide equal satisfaction." Stephen Edwards, *In Defense of Environmental Ethics*, 9 ENVTL. ETHICS 73, 84 (1987). He further notes that "[m]ethodologies that are used to assess these values, including the contingent valuation method, are also relevant, being limited only by empirical problems in some applications." *Id.* With whom do you agree more?

Perhaps the simplest and most promising use of economic theory to help solve environmental problems involves the application of market principles. In the following article, Robert Stavins and Bradley Whitehead offer a broad overview of the market mechanisms that are available to solve environmental problems. As you review these materials be sure to consider the kinds of problems for which market mechanisms may work, as well as those for which they may not.

DEALING WITH POLLUTION: MARKET-BASED INCENTIVES FOR ENVIRONMENTAL PROTECTION
Robert N. Stavins and Bradley W. Whitehead
Environment, Sept. 1992, at 7*

As the United States prepares to address the environmental challenges of the 1990s, it faces an economic and political context fundamentally different from that of the 1970s, when the first environmental measures were enacted. More than a decade of large budget deficits, sluggish productivity growth, and intensified foreign competition has spurred interest in environmental approaches that lower compliance and administrative burdens for industry and government. Public restiveness over the size of government expenditures also has heightened interest in environmental approaches that require less bureaucracy and governmental intrusion into business and household decisions. These forces for change have led to a quest for innovative environmental policy instruments.

NEW CHALLENGES FOR ENVIRONMENTAL POLICY

Many environmentalists in the 1970s and early 1980s viewed the market as villainous because it drove businesses to pursue profits without regard for environmental consequences. According to this view, the government should make decisions concerning appropriate technologies and emissions levels in light of the "externalities"—social costs created by business but borne by others in society—that the business world ignores. Furthermore, the government should not merely specify policy goals but also intervene in decisions about the production process itself. The explicit goal of some legislation during this period was to maximize the benefits of environmental protection regardless of the costs. Indeed, some statutes and regulations explicitly forbade the consideration of costs in setting standards. For example, when the ambient standards for criteria air pollutants

---

* Reprinted with permission of the Helen Dwight Reid Educational Foundation. Published by Heldref Publications, 1319 Eighteenth St., N.W., Washington, D.C. 20036-1802. Copyright 1992.

are set under the Clean Air Act, the costs of meeting the standards may not, according to law, be taken into consideration.

This philosophy has driven much of the environmental progress over the last two decades, and in many places, the environment is cleaner now than it was before. But the United States and the world continue to face major environmental challenges, including such ongoing problems as urban smog, groundwater pollution, and acid rain and other, newly recognized problems, such as global climate change and indoor air pollution. Moreover, the economic and political contexts in which environmental policy is formulated have changed significantly. The challenge for policymakers today is to devise policies that harness rather than obstruct market forces.

THE NEED FOR COST-EFFECTIVENESS

The days have ended when the United States could afford to consider environmental protection in isolation from costs. The U.S. Environmental Protection Agency (EPA) estimates that the nation now spends more than $100 billion annually to comply with federal environmental laws and regulations, and there is heightened concern over the impact of these regulations on the strength of the economy and its ability to compete in international markets. As a result, policymakers are increasingly cautious about the degree and type of regulatory burdens placed on businesses and individuals.

The existence of federal, state, and local budget deficits makes it difficult for the United States to increase environmental protection simply by spending more money on programs and policies already in place. A new sensitivity to private costs exists, as well. U.S. citizens and policymakers have not lost sight of the benefits of environmental protection, but they are giving increased attention to cost-effective environmental policies. To some people, the concern over cost effectiveness means getting more environmental protection for the same level of expenditures; to others, it means getting the same level of protection for less money. To both, however, it means making the most of scarce resources and maximizing returns on the resources invested—business costs, regulatory effort, political capital, and taxes—to improve the quality of the environment.

HARNESS MARKET FORCES

An indicator of the presence of such concerns was the adoption of a market-based approach to the control of acid rain in the 1990 Clean Air Act Amendments—tradable "pollution reduction credits." The adoption of this approach suggests that some political leaders recognize that market forces are not only part of the problem but also a potential part of the solution. By dictating behavior and removing profit opportunities, past environmental regulation has placed unnecessary burdens on the economy and stifled the development of new, more effective environmental technologies. Furthermore, such policies have helped engender an adversarial relationship among regulators, environmentalists, and private industry. As a result, excessive economic resources often have been used for litigation and other forms of conflict among concerned parties.

Policies are needed to mobilize and harness the power of market forces for the environment and to make economic and environmental interests compatible and mutually supportive. Policymakers must begin to link the twin forces of government and industry, without extravagant investment.

POLICIES FOR ENVIRONMENTAL PROTECTION

There are two steps to formulating environmental policy: choosing the overall goal and selecting a means to achieve that goal. Market-based environmental policies that focus on the means of achieving policy goals are largely neutral with respect to the selected goals and provide cost-effective methods for reaching those goals. Before investigating market incentives, in general, and pollution charges, in particular, it is useful to review the regulatory approach most frequently used—command and control.

COMMAND-AND-CONTROL REGULATORY APPROACH

Command-and-control regulations tend to force all businesses to adopt the same measures and practices for pollution control and thus shoulder identical shares of the pollution control burden regardless of their relative impacts. Government regulations typically set uniform standards—mostly technology- or performance-based—for all businesses. As the name suggests, technology-based standards specify the method and, sometimes, the equipment that businesses must use to comply with a regulation. Usually, regulations do not specify the technology but establish standards on the basis of a particular technology. In situations where monitoring problems are particularly severe, however, technologies are specified. For instance, all businesses in an industry are sometimes required to use the "best available technology" to control water pollution, or, in a more extreme example, electric utilities may be required to utilize a specific technology, such as electrostatic precipitators, to remove particulates. Performance standards, on the other hand, set a uniform control target for each business but allow some latitude in how to meet it. Such a standard might set the maximum allowable units of pollutant per time period but remain neutral with respect to the means by which each business reaches the goal.

Holding all businesses under the same target can be both expensive and counterproductive. Although uniform standards can sometimes be effective in limiting emissions of pollutants, they typically do so at relatively high costs to society. Specifically, uniform standards can force some business to use unduly expensive means of controlling pollution because the costs of controlling emissions can vary greatly between and even within businesses, and the right technology in one situation may be wrong in another. For example, in a survey of eight empirical studies of air-pollution control, the ratio of actual, aggregate costs of the conventional, command-and-control approach to the aggregate costs of least-cost benchmarks ranged from 1.07 for sulfate emissions in Los Angeles, California, to 22.0 for hydrocarbon emissions at all U.S. Du Pont plants. Indeed, the cost of controlling a given pollutant may vary by a factor of 100 or more among sources, depending upon the age and location of plants and the available technologies.

The command-and-control approach also tends to freeze the development of technologies that could provide greater levels of control. Little or no financial incentive exists for businesses to exceed their control targets, and both types of standards contain a bias against experimentation with new technologies. A business's reward for trying a new technology may be that it will subsequently be held to a higher standard of performance, without significant opportunity to benefit financially from its investment. As a result, money that could be invested in technology development is diverted to legal battles over defining acceptable technologies and standards of performance.

MARKET-BASED POLICIES

Unlike command-and-control policies, which seek to regulate the individual polluter, market-based policies train their sights on the overall pollution in a given area. What is important to most people, after all, is not how many particulates the local widget factory emits but the quality of the air they breathe while walking downtown or sitting in their back yards. Thus, under a market-based approach, the government establishes financial incentives so that the costs imposed on businesses drive an entire industry or region to reduce its aggregate level of pollution to a desired level. Then, as in any regulatory system, the government monitors and enforces compliance.

In terms of policy, a market-based approach achieves the same aggregate level of control as might be set under a command-and-control approach, but it permits the burden of pollution control to be shared more efficiently among businesses. In economic terms, market-based policies equalize the level of marginal costs of control among businesses rather than the level of control. (The marginal costs of pollution control are the additional or incremental costs of achieving an additional unit of pollution reduction.) As a result, market-based polices provide a monetary incentive for the greatest reductions in pollution by the businesses that can do so most cheaply. The result is that fewer total economic resources are used to achieve the same level of pollution control, or more pollution control is obtained for the same level of resources.

Theoretically, the government could achieve such a cost-effective solution by setting different standards for each business and equating the marginal costs of control. However, such a task requires detailed information about the costs each company faces—information that the government clearly lacks and could obtain only at great cost, if at all. Market-based policies provide a way out of this impasse because they lead directly to the cost-effective allocation of the pollution control burden among businesses. By forcing businesses to factor environmental costs into their decisionmaking, market-based policies create powerful incentives for firms to find cleaner production technologies.

Market-based incentives also clarify the environmental debate for the general public because they focus on environmental goals rather than on the difficult technical problems of reaching those goals. One of the reasons market-based systems are not more widely used, however, is that many technical experts have sought to retain the complexity and excluded the public from such debates.

Market-based incentive systems do not represent a laissez-faire, free-market approach. Rather, the inability of a system of private markets to provide certain goods and services at the most desirable level is typically at the core of pollution problems in which the decisions of businesses and consumers do not take into account the consequences of their decisions for society. At the same time, an incentive-based policy rejects the notion that such market failures justify abandoning the market and allowing the government to dictate the behavior of businesses or consumers. Instead, market-based incentives provide freedom of choice for businesses and consumers to determine the best way to reduce pollution. By ensuring that environmental costs are factored into each company's or individual's decisionmaking process, incentive based policies harness rather than impede market forces and channel them to achieve environmental goals at the lowest possible cost to society.

At the broadest level, market-based incentive systems fall into four categories:

• **Pollution charges.** Under this approach, polluters are charged a fee on the amount of pollution they generate. In one category of pollution charges, called deposit-refund systems, all or a part of some initial charge is rebated if the individual performs certain actions.

• **Tradable permit systems.** Under this mechanism, which was used in the 1990 Clean Air Act Amendments for acid rain control, the government establishes an overall level of allowable air pollution and then allocates permits to businesses in the relevant geographic area so that each is allowed to emit some fraction of the overall total. Companies that keep their emissions below the allocated level may sell or lease their surplus permits to other firms or use them to offset excess emissions in other parts of their own facilities.

• **Removal of market barriers.** In some cases, substantial gains can be made in environmental protection by removing existing government-mandated barriers to market activity. For example, measures that facilitate the voluntary exchange of water rights can promote more efficient allocation and use of scarce water supplies while curbing the need for expensive and environmentally disruptive new water-supply projects.

• **Eliminating government subsidies.** Many existing subsidies promote economically inefficient and environmentally unsound development. For example, the U.S. Forest Service subsidizes below-cost timber sales, which recover less money than is spent on making timber available. These subsidies encourage excessive timber cutting which leads to habitat loss and damage to watersheds.

Different mechanisms will be appropriate for different environmental problems, and no single approach is a panacea for all problems. Neither market-based policies nor conventional, command-and-control regulations hold all the answers. Furthermore, when market-based approaches are appropriate, specific circumstances will dictate which of the above categories is best * * *.

MARKET-BASED ENVIRONMENTAL POLICIES

The use of market forces to protect the environment is not a new idea. Economists have called for market-based environmental policies for the past 25 years. Only recently, however, has the broader policy community begun to regard market instruments favorably. For instance, both U.S. President Lyndon Johnson's proposal for effluent fees and President Richard Nixon's recommendations for a tax on leaded gasoline and a fee on sulfur dioxide emissions were dismissed with little consideration.

It is important to understand what political forces have prevented broader acceptance of market-based environmental regulation over the years because these forces are likely to resist further use of such approaches beyond the new Clean Air Act Amendments. Four such forces have been most powerful. The first of these forces is the adversarial attitude that characterized the beginning of the environmental movement. Throughout much of the 1960's and 1970's, environmentalists typically characterized pollution more as a moral failing of corporate and political leaders than as a by-product of modern civilization that can be regulated and reduced but not eliminated. Although that character-ization may have been necessary and successful from a political standpoint, it resulted in wide-spread antagonism toward corporations and a suspicion that anything supported by the business world was probably bad for the environment. Thus, for many years, market-based incentives were characterized by environmentalists not only as impractical but also as "licenses to pollute." Over time, environmental groups have frequently applied a different and more rigorous standard in measuring market-based systems against command-and-control policies, possibly because of the belief that market-based systems legitimize pollution by purporting to sell the right to pollute. This suspicion probably continues among many rank-and-file environmentalists.

A second source of resistance to market-based approaches has been the environmental bureaucracy whose work, organizational power, or even existence might be threatened by a market-based approach. Within EPA, for example, market-based policies for controlling acid rain would not require the service of agency engineers whose task in the current policy regime is to evaluate technologies for disparate sources of emissions across the country. Instead, decisions to select particular air-pollution control technologies would be left up to individual firms. In addition, there has been resistance from some staff in environmental agencies who are simply skeptical about new approaches that have not yet been applied on a large scale.

Third, resistance to market-based approaches has come from lobbyists who, having learned to influence a command-and-control regulatory system, are understandably reluctant to allow any major changes in the rules of the game. Thus, some lobbyists for both environmental organizations and the private sector, as well as some legislators, resist market-based approaches in part to protect the value of their expertise. The resistance by some industry lobbyists to putting these ideas into practice is especially notable given that the business community has long endorsed the theory of cost-effective, market-oriented approaches to environmental protection.

Finally, market-based approaches—pollution charges in particular—are problematic because they involve new taxes, which have been a controversial and often forbidden subject for much of the last decade. Although "compensating reductions" in other taxes—tax cuts that result in unchanged government revenues—can make pollution charges revenue-neutral and can improve the economic efficiency of the overall tax code, many elected officials are wary of embracing such approaches because voters and pundits might doubt that government would rebate revenues once they have been collected.

* * *

Over the past several years, however, a number of factors have combined to overcome some of the older sources of resistance to market-based incentives for environmental protection, including strong interest within the Executive Office of the President, aggressive participation by some segments of the environmental community, notably the Environmental Defense Fund, and the December 1988 release of the bipartisan Project 88 report and the follow-up effort two years later by Senator Timothy Wirth (D-Colo.) and the late Senator John Heinz (R-Penn.). * * *

Market-based systems are gaining an increasingly broad array of political supporters. In March 1991, EPA administrator William K. Reilly established the Economic Incentives Task Force to identify new areas in which to apply market-based approaches. Congress also shows both increasing interest in and a willingness to debate economic incentives. In fact, the phrase "market-oriented environmental policy" may itself be assuming some political value.

Congressional opportunities for adopting market-based schemes have recently been enhanced by the evolving support of major environmental advocacy organizations. An increasing number of these environmental groups now support market-based environmental reforms. First, and foremost, EDF, an early supporter of market-based environmental policies, is an enthusiastic and effective proponent of such ideas. Furthermore, EDF was a major participant in the Project 88 effort, and EDF economist Daniel Dudek worked closely with the Bush administration to develop the Clean Air Act proposal. Other environmental groups, including the Wilderness Society, the National Wildlife Federation, the National Audubon Society, the Sierra Club, and the Natural Resources Defense Council, now support at least selective use of market-based instruments.

The ability of market-based policies to economize scarce resources, combined with a variety of other factors, has brought these policies to center stage in environmental policy debates within Congress. Debate at the federal level has focused mainly on the potential of tradable permits. The most important application to date has been the acid rain provisions of the 1990 amendments to the Clean Air Act. Tradable-permit systems have also been part of other federal environmental policies, including EPA's emissions trading program for local air quality and the nationwide phase out of lead in automotive fuel. Although state impediments and uncertainty about the future course of the emissions trading program have sharply limited trading by firms, the trading that has occurred has saved more than $4 billion with no adverse effect on air quality. According to EPA, the lead program, which has inspired much more trading among firms, reduced overall compliance costs by approximately 20 percent, or about $200 million annually. Tradable-permit systems, including international trading in greenhouse gases, recycling targets combined with tradable permits, and point- and nonpoint-source water pollution control, are now being proposed for a host of environmental problems.

Although permit systems command the attention of the federal government, state and local governments have expressed interest in other market-based environmental policies. "Bottle bills," a well-known type of deposit-refund system intended to reduce litter and promote recycling, have been particularly popular. Also, the removal of market barriers to voluntary water transfers has been an increasingly important policy innovation in the western United States. Water transfers alleviate water supply problems and increase efficiency by creating incentives for water conservation. The most notable transfer plan to date is the $223-million agreement signed in 1988 between the Imperial Irrigation District (IID) of California and the Metropolitan Water District (MWD) of Los Angeles. Under the agreement, MWD will finance the improvements of IID's water system in exchange for the use of IID's water stores. Finally, Congress has reduced government subsidies that cause economic distortions and environmental damage, such as the federal subsidies given to the U.S. Army Corps of Engineer's flood-control projects, which provide incentives for individual landowners to convert forested wetlands to croplands.

Not surprisingly, the business community continues to support cost-effective, market-oriented approaches to environmental protection. General Motors, for instance, has endorsed the adoption of a broad-based carbon fee to limit emissions of greenhouse gases. Other major corporations have expressed support for incentives, at least in principle. The net result of this surge of interest in market-based incentives is increased awareness of the many options open to policymakers at both the federal and local levels. Furthermore, the political and bureaucratic sources of opposition to these approaches may be growing weaker.

Unfortunately, a wide range of market-based initiatives has been largely ignored. In particular, the potential of pollution charge systems has received scant attention compared to other market-based instruments, possibly as a result of the same forces that for years impeded adoption of tradable permits and similar approaches, or because the concepts involved are perceived as too complex. In either case, this lack of attention should now be remedied because pollution charges have several distinct advantages over other policy instruments, especially for certain categories of environmental problems.

THE MECHANICS OF POLLUTION CHARGES

Pollution charge systems are designed to reduce polluting behavior by imposing a fee or tax on polluters. Ideally, the fee should be based on the amount of pollution generated rather than on the level of pollution-generating activities. For example, an electric utility might be charged a tax per unit of sulfur dioxide emitted rather than per unit of electricity generated. The choice of whether to tax pollution quantities, activities preceding discharge, inputs to those activities, or actual damages depends upon tradeoffs between costs of abatement, mitigation, damages, and program administration, including monitoring and enforcement. In some cases, a fee may be based on the expected or potential quantity of pollution. The Organization for Economic Cooperation and Development distinguishes five types of pollution charges: effluent charges based on the quantity of discharges; user charges, which are payments for public treatment facilities; production charges based on the potential pollution by a product; administration charges, which are payments for such government services as registration of chemicals; and tax differentiation, which provides more favorable prices for "green" products. A true pollution charge provides incentives to businesses or consumers to reduce emissions when that action is less expensive than is continuing to pollute. Pollution charges can be applied either to producers to affect their production decisions or to consumers to affect their consumption and disposal behavior.

Although pollution poses real costs to society—for example, health effects, property damage, and aesthetic impacts—businesses typically do not have to pay for these damages and hence, face little or no incentive to take them into account in production decisions. A business that chooses unilaterally to consider such external costs in its production decisions would be penalized by the market, through reduced cost-competitiveness. Pollution charges force businesses to pay for the external costs of pollution and to incorporate those added costs into their daily decisions.

Pollution charges also provide strong incentives for businesses to develop and adopt improved control technologies. Under a command-and-control system, businesses have no financial incentive to perform better than the regulatory standard demands. Pollution charges, however, do not specify a technology or a fixed standard. Instead, charges are incurred for each increment of pollution rather than only for pollution above a given standard. Thus, businesses are constantly motivated to improve their financial performance by developing technologies that allow them to reduce their output of pollutants.

By charging polluters a fee or tax on the amount of pollution they generate and not on their pollution-generating activities, the government gives businesses an incentive to reduce pollution up to the point at which their marginal control costs are equal to their pollution tax rates. As a result, businesses will control their pollution to different degrees, with polluters for whom control is very expensive controlling less and polluters for whom control is relatively cheap controlling more. The challenge for policymakers is to identify the desirable charge level. If the charge is too high, production may be curtailed excessively; if the charge is too low, insufficient environmental protection will result. An effective charge system thus minimizes the aggregate costs of pollution control and enables the public to pursue other environmental quality actions that might have seemed unaffordable under less efficient approaches, such as command-and-control regulations.

* * *

OTHER POTENTIAL APPLICATION

Pollution charges and user fees can be used for combatting many contemporary environmental problems. For example, a charge placed on the sale of pesticides and other agricultural chemicals could encourage farmers to use chemicals more efficiently and manufacturers to find less environmentally harmful substitutes. Such a charge also could help address the difficult problem of non-point source water pollution.

Similarly, the United States could follow the example of Germany and impose efficient charges on water pollution. Such charges could encourage businesses to reduce emissions below levels currently allowed by discharge permits. Emissions charges also could be used to control air pollution, even where standards are already in place. For example, the EPA Economic Incentives Task Force proposed fees on major stationary sources of volatile organic compounds, which are precursors of urban smog.

A set of related policies could help address environmental problems associated with automobile use in major cities. In particular, "congestion pricing" could be used to charge drivers a fee for rush-hour trips. Other approaches that could reduce the total miles traveled in automobiles and, therefore, air pollution include employee parking charges, increased charges for public parking, and smog taxes.

Establishing user fees for U.S. national parks and forests could improve resource management. Such schemes may be critical in weaning forest managers away from their dependence on timber revenues. Although 41 percent of gross U.S. Forest Service forest value is related to recreational uses, recreation generates only 3 percent of Forest Service revenues. Clearly, users of publicly owned natural resources should pay for a portion of the benefits they receive.

POLLUTION CHARGES IN THE POLITICAL ARENA

No single policy mechanism—neither incentive-based policies in general nor pollution charges in particular—can be an environmental panacea. Pollution charges, however, promise to provide cost-effective solutions for some pressing environmental problems while spurring technological advances.

Good ideas are not self-adopting, however. Even if the new Clean Air Act provisions have signaled the beginning of a new era of environmental policy, resistance to market-based approaches has not disappeared. In addition to opposition from those who simply oppose environmental protection, pollution charges will have to overcome the same combination of self-interest and suspicion from those within the environmental protection process who have obstructed market-based approaches for decades.

Initially, it may be practical to apply pollution charges to new problems for which policy mechanisms are not already in place. Such an approach could minimize disruptions to industry and consumers, reduce the chance that regulations will work at cross purposes, and challenge the authority of fewer vested interests. If pollution charges turn out to be effective, they could serve as alternatives to environmental regulations in place today that are deemed to be ineffective or that achieve their objectives only at extremely high costs to society. Furthermore, a growing array of state and local initiatives may help pollution charges overcome public dislike for taxes, reduce the costs of environmental protection, and stimulate technological development.

In fact, pollution charges could make the process of environmental policy formulation more explicit to the U.S. population, which has always been shielded from the very real trade-offs involved in establishing environmental goals and standards. As a result, policy discussions could move away from a narrow focus on technical specifications to a broader consideration of goals and strategies. The public could become involved in constructive debates regarding the desirable level of environmental protection and could recapture the critical decisions of environmental goal-setting from bureaucrats, technicians, and special-interest groups. As new environmental policies arise and old ones persist, the limited resources of government agencies and society at large will be stretched further and further. Pollution charges and other incentive-based instruments may eventually be the only feasible courses of action to sustain or improve environmental quality while maintaining economic well-being. With the necessary political leadership, it may be possible to begin moving in the right direction now.

NOTES

1. In a section from this article not included in this excerpt, the authors note and discuss at length "four particularly promising areas [for pollution charges] that need immediate action: greenhouse gas reduction; motor vehicle fuel efficiency; solid waste reduction; and hazardous waste management." How might pollution charges be used to address these problems? What difficulties would you foresee in achieving an effective program for each of these problems?

2. Stavins and Whitehead briefly mention the tradeable permit program established under the acid deposition control provisions of Clean Air Act Amendments of 1990. Under this program, which is being implemented in two phases, national SO_2 emissions from electric utilities are expected to be cut by 10 million tons/year by the year 2000. 42 U.S.C. § 7651(b). Even before the program became effective on January 1, 1995, the EPA reported substantial reductions of 1994 SO_2 emissions from sources covered by Phase I of the program, from approximately 9.3 million tons/year to about 7 million tons/year. Acid Rain Program, Update No. 2 (EPA, July, 1995). Moreover, significant trading activity in SO₂ "allowances" (each allowance gives its holder the right to emit one ton of SO_2 into the atmosphere) is occurring, and the average price of allowances is well below analysts' original estimates. Nonetheless, some have argued that the full benefits of the allowance trading program are not being realized because individual states and utilities are biased in favor of fuel switching and scrubbing rather than allowance trading. Douglas R. Bohi, *Benefits of Allowance Trading Are Going Unrealized*, COMPLIANCE STRATEGIES REVIEW, Expert Opinion Supplement (January 2, 1994). Why would states and utilities engage in such "inefficient" behavior? While acknowledging that the program "probably will not achieve its full potential for reducing costs to industry," Richard Price argues nonetheless that "the program is a dramatic improvement over previous command-and-control legislation." He further notes:

> Despite the deviations from economic models of emissions trading—deviations which are in part due to real-world imperfections, and partly to imperfections in the models—the implementation of Title IV [the Acid Deposition Program] must be considered a qualified success, and even greater success is likely to ensue once the second, more inclusive phase begins and real demand for allowances arises. The Acid Rain Program is an excellent illustration of the value of an approach to environmental protection based on sound economic principles, and even mistakes made in its implementation have provided useful lessons for future legislation on the control of similar pollutants.

Richard Price, *Judging the Success of Title IV*, COMPLIANCE STRATEGIES REVIEW, Expert Opinion Supplement (July 18, 1994).

3. Stavins and Whitehead distinguish between using economics to establish environmental goals, and using it as a tool for implementing goals which have previously been established. Their work focuses on the implementation phase. Even Mark Sagoff has recognized the utility of using market mechanisms to achieve politically-determined, environmental goals:

> Markets in pollution "rights," offsets, and similar schemes do not necessarily replace ethical thinking with economic thinking, moral norms with economic principles. Rather, they may help us build toward our ethical objectives from the means available to accomplish them * * * .

MARK SAGOFF, THE ECONOMY OF THE EARTH 210 (1988). Some economists argue, however, that economics can and should be used to set environmental goals in the first instance. For example, Anderson and Leal would have polluters bargain with the persons who bear the costs of pollution so that an "efficient" judgment can be made about how much pollution should be allowed? TERRY ANDERSON & DONALD LEAL, FREE MARKET ENVIRON-MENTALISM 17-23 (1991). What practical problems might you foresee in negotiating such a transaction? What objection would Sagoff likely make to using this approach in the first instance? Chapter Four, Part B offers a more detailed review of Anderson and Leal's arguments for "privatizing" environmental resources and decisions relating to their use.

4. An earlier article that addresses the U.S. experience with incentive-based environmental policies, and suggests growing support for them, is Hahn & Stavins, *Inventive-Based Environmental Regulation: A New Era from an Old Idea*, 18 ECOLOGY L.Q. 1 (1991).

5. Project 88, which is referenced briefly in the preceding article, was "a bipartisan effort to find innovative solutions to major environmental and natural resource problems." Robert N. Stavins, *Harnessing Market Forces to Protect the Environment*, ENVIRONMENT, Jan./Feb. 1989, at 5. The report identified 13 major environmental and natural resource problems where market forces might be used, including greenhouse gas emissions, stratospheric ozone depletion, wetlands protection, and energy efficiency. Robert Stavins was staff director for the project.

6. In discussing pollution charge systems, the authors state that "[i]deally, the fee should be based on the amount of pollution generated rather than on the level of pollution generating activities." As an example, they suggest that an electric utility should be charged for each unit of SO_2 emitted, rather than for each unit of electricity generated. Why is a charge on emissions preferable?

7. One important limitation on the utility of tradeable pollution rights is the requirement that such rights be essentially fungible within a given airshed, watershed or geographic region. Why? What kinds of pollutants are more likely to be fungible—hazardous pollutants or conventional pollutants? Note that while many commentators have supported expanding trade in water rights, these efforts have met with only marginal success. How might "fungibility" pose problems for establishing efficient trading in water rights? *See* BONNIE COLBY SALIBA & DAVID B. BUSH, WATER MARKETS IN THEORY AND PRACTICE (1987).

The two articles which follow offer markedly different views about the advantages and disadvantages of conventional pollution regulation regimes as compared with market systems. As you read these materials consider their relevance to specific problems such as—(1) carbon monoxide air emissions in an urban area which currently exceeds health standards by 20% and where 90% of the emissions come from automobiles; (2) carbon dioxide emissions from burning fossil fuels which contribute substantially to global warming; (3) toxic pollutants which are emitted from a single source along an otherwise pristine river; and (4) reclamation of lands mined by a single company.

IDEAL VERSUS REAL REGULATORY EFFICIENCY: IMPLEMENTATION OF UNIFORM STANDARDS AND "FINE-TUNING" REGULATORY REFORMS
Howard Latin
37 Stan. L. Rev. 1267 (1985)*

Many environmental, public health, and safety statutes place primary emphasis on the implementation of uniform regulatory standards. In return for benefits that are often

---

difficult to assess, "command-and-control" standards[2] promulgated under such statutes as the Clean Air Act (CAA), Occupational Safety and Health Act (OSH Act), and Federal Water Pollution Control Act (FWPCA) impose billions of dollars in annual compliance costs on society and also entail significant indirect costs including decreases in productivity, technological innovation, and market competition. As these costs have become increasingly evident, prominent legal scholars such as Bruce Ackerman, Steven Breyer, and Richard Stewart have concluded that command-and-control regulation is inefficient and should be replaced by more flexible strategies. Their principal criticisms may be summarized as follows: Uniform standards do not reflect the opportunity costs of environmental protection, they disregard the individual circumstances of diverse conflicts, they do not achieve environmental protection on a "lowest-cost" basis, and they fail to provide adequate incentives for improved performance.

In response to these alleged deficiencies in the present system, advocates of "regulatory reform" argue that environmental controls should be tailored to particularized ecological and economic circumstances, regulatory benefits weighed against the costs of environmental protection, and increased reliance placed on economic incentive mechanisms, such as taxes on environmentally destructive activities or transferable pollution rights. Professor Stewart, for example, recently advocated "more individualized or 'fine-tuning' approach to regulation." Critics of command-and-control standards differ on suggested "fine-tuning" prescriptions, but there is widespread agreement that some alternative must be preferable to the current regulatory system.

This article contends that the academic literature on "regulatory reform" reflects an excessive preoccupation with theoretical efficiency, while it places inadequate emphasis on actual decisionmaking costs and implementation constraints. Any system for environmental regulation must function despite the presence of pervasive uncertainty, high decisionmaking costs, and manipulative strategic behavior resulting from conflicting private and public interests. Under these conditions, the indisputable fact that uniform standards are inefficient does not prove that any other approach would necessarily perform better. In a "second-best" world, the critical issue is not which regulatory system aspires to ideal "efficiency" but which is most likely to prove effective.[19]

In recognition of severe implementation constraints on environmental regulation, this article identifies numerous advantages of uniform standards in comparison with more particularized and flexible regulatory strategies. These advantages include decreased information collection and evaluation costs, greater consistency and predictability of results,

---

[2] The phrase "command-and-control regulation" is used to describe "measures that require or proscribe specific conduct by regulated firms." Stewart, *Regulation, Innovation, and Administrative Law: A Conceptual Framework,* 69 Calif. L. Rev. 1256, 1264 (1981). Command-and-control regulation is usually contrasted with economic incentive systems that use price mechanisms to encourage regulated parties to attain desired goals. *See id.;* Breyer, *Analyzing Regulatory Failure: Mismatches, Less Restrictive Alternatives, and Reform,* 92 Harv. L. Rev. 547, 595-97 (1979).

[19] There are numerous formal economic definitions of efficiency. *See, e.g.,* Coleman, *Efficiency, Exchange, and Auction: Philosophic Aspects of the Economic Approach to Law,* 68 Calif. L. Rev. 221 (1980); Latin, *Environmental Deregulation and Consumer Decisionmaking Under Uncertainty,* 6 Harv. Envtl. L. Rev. 187, 191 n.26 (1982). For purposes of this article, the important contrast is between an emphasis on ideal or optimal decisionmaking, which is denoted below by the label "efficiency," and an emphasis on "effective" decisionmaking, which means the achievement of a reasonable congruence between regulatory accomplishments and desired legislative objectives.

greater accessibility of decisions to public scrutiny and participation, increased likelihood that regulations will withstand judicial review, reduced opportunities for manipulative behavior by agencies in response to political or bureaucratic pressures, reduced opportunities for obstructive behavior by regulated parties, and decreased likelihood of social dislocation and "forum shopping" resulting from competitive disadvantages between geographical regions or between firms in regulated industries. A realistic implementation analysis indicates that "fine-tuning" would prove infeasible in many important environmental contexts; indeed, the effectiveness of environmental regulation could often be improved by reducing even the degree of "fine-tuning" that is currently attempted.

There is more at stake here than academic disagreement and the possible miseducation of a generation of students. When the Reagan Administration took office, it was explicit about its desire for widespread deregulation. After Congress proved generally unwilling to repeal regulatory legislation, the Administration changed its approach and argued that environmental control programs should be made more "efficient." In a letter to the New York Times, for example, an Environmental Protection Agency (EPA) Assistant Administrator claimed that the agency was committed to "clean water," but that the EPA intended to improve regulatory efficiency by: (1) expanding reliance on "cost/benefit analysis"; (2) basing standards on "scientific evidence and not on rumor and soothsaying"; (3) employing "site-specific data"; (4) providing "more flexibility to local governments"; and (5) not imposing regulatory costs unless "a designated [water quality] use is attainable." These are all proposals for increased "fine-tuning." The letter mentioned nothing about Administration initiatives that reduced EPA budgets and manpower, or about information scarcity and "site-specific" collection costs, or about inadequate scientific understanding of many water quality-related problems. Well-intentioned scholars often recommend "fine-tuning" because they focus on ideal efficiency, while Administration officials may advocate "fine-tuning" precisely because they believe it will seldom work in practice and would therefore accomplish sub rosa deregulation. Intemperate academic criticisms of command-and-control standards combined with support of unrealistic "fine-tuning" strategies may lend an aura of intellectual credibility to political initiatives designed to achieve less regulation, not better regulation.

Part I of this article criticizes the prevailing focus on ideal efficiency and questions the efficacy of conventional academic solutions for uncertainty and other decisionmaking constraints. The primary purpose of this critique is to show that a comparison between the demonstrated inefficiencies of uniform standards and the theoretical advantages of "fine-tuning" cannot lead to the development of a wise regulatory policy. Part II examines the ramifications of uncertainty, high decisionmaking costs, and strategic behavior for different regulatory approaches. These constraints would degrade the performance of any environmental protection program, but competing strategies are not all subject to the same kinds of imponderables, expenses, and manipulation, nor are they all vulnerable to the same degree. The central theme developed in this part is that the most "efficient" strategies in theory will frequently be the least effective in practice. Moreover, many commentators espouse variations of approaches that have already been tried and found unsatisfactory. Part II contends that the implementation problems which subverted these approaches in the past remain essentially unchanged, and consequently that most "fine-tuning" proposals reflect wishful thinking rather than a realistic appraisal of present environmental knowledge and regulatory capabilities. Despite its imperfections, command-and-control regulation has fostered significant improvements in environmental quality at a societal cost that has not proved prohibitive.[25] Critics of uniform standards should therefore be required to demonstrate with reasonable assurance that "fine-tuning" approaches can be successfully implemented, and will actually perform better, before the current regulatory system is "reformed."

I. UTOPIAN CRITICISMS AND ENVIRONMENTAL REALITY

The environment is a mosaic of millions of interrelated ecological features and systems. Because ecosystems are numerous, complex, interdependent, unique in some respects, and change continuously through natural and man-made processes, vast quantities of information are required to understand ecological processes and the environmental ramifications of human activities. Yet ecology is a relatively new science, and society generally lacks adequate data on long-term environmental conditions and changes. Millions of industrial and consumption activities engender health risks or environmental degradation. Regulatory agencies are frequently unable to correlate gross environmental changes with the marginal consequences of particular activities. Science often lacks adequate data and risk assessment methodologies for environmental dangers. Even when current risks can be estimated with some precision, the nature and dimensions of harmful activities change very rapidly in comparison with the limited adaptive capacity of ecological systems and with our ability to assess long-term environmental impacts. Thus, intrinsic characteristics of ecological systems, human health effects, and potentially harmful activities ensure that environmental decision-making costs must be high and that many important effects cannot feasibly be determined.

Nevertheless, numerous legal and economic commentaries dogmatically maintain that decisionmakers must evaluate all relevant ecological circumstances, human impacts, and regulatory costs to identify the "optimal" level of environmental protection in particular controversies or locations. Part I draws on prominent examples from the literature on environmental regulation to illustrate analytical distortions that arise from this preoccupation with ideal efficiency.

A. The Limits of Technocratic Rationality

Regulatory critics often portray environmental conflicts as technical problems that can be "solved" in an "efficient" manner if decisionmakers are insulated from political pressures and are forced to consider all relevant circumstances. This assumption is clearly reflected, for example, in Bruce Ackerman's studies of environmental regulation. In *The Uncertain Search for Environmental Quality*, Professor Ackerman criticized the scientific underpinnings of the uniform water quality standards adopted in the Delaware River Basin. The regulations were partly based on a pioneering Public Health Service study of effluent

---

[25] *See* Costle, *Environmental Regulation and Regulatory Reform*, 57 WASH. L. REV. 409, 416 (1982) (estimating that pollution control requirements imposed regulatory costs of about 3.3% of GNP and about 3.1% of total industry expenditures on plants and equipment in 1981. Costle does admit, however, that "the effects [of environmentory costs] on specific industries can be substantial." *Id.*). Critics of command-and-control regulation contend that current programs "waste" billions of dollars, not that society is incapable of absorbing the aggregate costs if necessary.* * *

levels and ecological effects in the four-state region. Despite years of effort at substantial expense, the scientific analysis incorporated many unrealistic simplifying assumptions. In conjunction with each technical criticism, Ackerman stressed the need for more complex and comprehensive scientific evaluations: In order to determine the benefits of alternative levels of pollution control, the agency should have assessed the aggregate impacts of all pollutants, of all significant ecological interdependencies, and of dynamic changes in natural conditions and pollutant discharge rates. Ackerman ridiculed the decision to implement uniform standards throughout the Delaware basin on the grounds that stringent controls would produce few if any tangible benefits in heavily polluted stretches of the river. He argued that society, rather than wasting multimillion dollar expenditures in the pursuit of illusory improvements, should adopt a cost-benefit balancing approach tailored to local circumstances and should impose strict pollution control only in smaller environmental enclaves with high-quality conditions.

In *Clean Coal/Dirty Air*, Ackerman and William Hassler criticized the 1979 New Source Performance Standard (NSPS) for sulfur dioxide (SO_2) discharges from coal-burning power plants. The nationally uniform NSPS limits SO_2 emissions to 1.2 lbs/MBtu and also requires new plants to reduce discharges between 70 and 90 percent in comparison with emissions from combustion of untreated coal. Given the current state of control technology, compliance with the percentage-reduction provision requires all newly constructed plants to install some form of flue gas desulfurization ("scrubbing") equipment, although not to implement "full scrubbing" as Ackerman and Hassler contended. The authors repeatedly criticized the EPA for its failure "to develop a full-blown analysis of the costs and benefits of NSPS in general and of scrubbing in particular." Ackerman and Hassler characterized the EPA's reliance on technological controls as a "mindless" decision that served no purpose other than to create an inefficient subsidy for producers of high-sulfur coal. They argued that it would be relatively easy to design a more efficient approach than the current NSPS. The authors recommended that utilities be allowed to meet the 1.2 lbs/MBtu emissions limit by burning untreated low-sulfur coal, while secondary reliance should be placed on localized strategies such as "coal washing" techniques, siting of new plants in rural areas to minimize health effects, reducing smokestack height to decrease geographical dispersion of pollutants, reliance on more stringent regulation of existing SO_2 sources, implementation of a marketable pollution rights scheme, and deferral of regulation pending additional research and development of more cost-effective control methods.

The central theme in *The Uncertain Search* and *Clean Coal/Dirty Air* is the same: Decisionmakers should consider all environmental conditions, all economic circumstances, and all possible control strategies in order to devise "efficient" regulatory systems. As an ideal, this degree of analytical sophistication is surely desirable. But regulators can seldom approach it in practice. In both critiques Ackerman emphasized environmental complexity and uncertainty to attack the basis for the promulgated regulations, but he never acknowledged that those constraints, together with budgetary and time restrictions, severely limit the ability of agencies to develop technocratic solutions for environmental problems. In *The Uncertain Search*, Ackerman did not attempt to demonstrate that existing scientific knowledge was sufficient for protection of his proposed environmental enclaves. He also failed to consider the cumulative decisionmaking costs and extended time requirements associated with comprehensive scientific analyses of many "high-quality" regions possessing dissimilar characteristics. Instead, Ackerman presented his preferred strategy, reliance on marketable pollution rights, in an idealized manner without any discussion of the environmental complexities he emphasized in his criticisms of the Delaware River study.

In *Clean Coal/Dirty Air*, Ackerman again presented his proposed alternatives in an idealized form without a balanced consideration of the legal, political, and implementation constraints that would prevent their introduction or degrade their performance. In contradiction to his dismissive characterization of "mindless" EPA decisionmaking, another discussion of the rulemaking proceeding noted that: "The NSPS process included the most extensive national impacts analysis EPA has performed for a new standard." When the Court of Appeals for the District of Columbia Circuit approved the NSPS in all respects, the decision emphasized the breadth and detail of the agency's analysis. Although the Court identified some analytical imperfections, Judge Wald described the NSPS as reasonable in light of several factors: the "terrible complexity" of the issues; the "extraordinarily technical and often confusing" evidence and "obfuscation" introduced by parties representing "conflicting interests"; the large areas of scientific, technological, and economic uncertainty; the EPA's responsibility to reach an accommodation among the partly incompatible goals of the CAA; the congressional insistence on "speedy decisionmaking"; and the need for "finality" in administrative rulemaking. Ackerman and other proponents of technocratic decisionmaking consistently underestimate these constraints in their attempts to identify "efficient" regulatory solutions. When inherently complex and controversial environmental problems are considered, the development of even moderately effective control strategies can never be a simple undertaking.

Ackerman and many other scholars maintain that regulators, when faced with environmental complexity and uncertainty, limited budgets, and pressing timetables, should nevertheless try to do a comprehensive analysis. For example, Ackerman and Hassler contended:

> If EPA had been required to justify its decision in terms of environmental benefits, Administrator Costle would have had to call on agency modelers specializing in long-distance transport of sulfates rather than on agency experts in frontier technologies. Doubtless the models produced would have been imperfect, requiring innumerable guesses before the link between midwestern smokestacks and eastern ill health could be elucidated. Doubtless the coal companies and Senator Byrd would have protested. At least, though, they would have been openly arguing about the right questions: how serious is the risk to human health? Are eastern lakes being irreversibly damaged by acid rain? If we are to spend billions, should they be spent on new plants or old ones?[71]

Doubtless agency decisionmakers and affected parties would still be "openly arguing" about those questions with no NSPS standard on the horizon, because science is not yet able to link particular SO_2 discharges with particular manifestations of harm. Agencies have strong incentives to promulgate technically and politically defensible standards, or none at all. If officials do not believe they can answer the "right questions" with a

---

[71] B. ACKERMAN & W. HASSLER, [CLEAN COAL/DIRTY AIR] at 103 [(1981)].

sufficient degree of reliability to insulate themselves from criticism, insisting that they must nonetheless do so will not lead to "efficient" regulation. This demand will instead produce very little regulation. Moreover, the delay created by legal requirements that agencies must "answer" complex and uncertain questions would frequently entail serious irreversible consequences: People's exposure to toxic substances would continue during the interim, as would depletion of natural resources and threats to endangered species. Effective environmental protection may require agencies to treat some scientifically and economically relevant, but currently unresolvable, issues as legally irrelevant; that is precisely what command-and-control standards frequently do.

* * *

B. Multiplicity of Statutory Goals

The utility of any regulatory approach must be measured in terms of its ability to achieve desired social objectives. The major environmental statutes encompass many goals that conflict to some degree—for example, protection of the environment, provision of recreational opportunities, avoidance of social dislocation resulting from imposition of expensive regulatory controls, and promotion of economic growth. Critics of command-and-control standards have often argued that "fine-tuning" strategies would be more "efficient," without assessing the impacts of their proposals on the full range of congressional objectives. A distorted portrayal of regulatory purposes may lead to a distorted analysis of the relative effectiveness of competing control strategies. This problem is illustrated in recent regulatory critiques by Ackerman and Stewart.

1. NSPS goals.

In *Clean Coal/Dirty Air*, Ackerman emphasized a single statutory objective— "To endow our point with the dignity of a platitude: *the basic purpose of the Clean Air Act is to clean the air*."[82] He noted that the ecological effects of each pound of SO_2 are the same whether the emissions result from combustion of untreated low-sulfur coal or of high-sulfur coal used in conjunction with scrubbers. Ackerman therefore argued that utilities should be allowed to choose low-sulfur coal as a compliance method whenever that strategy would be less expensive than installation of scrubbers. In contrast, the Court of Appeals opinion cited the agreement of all 92 petitioners and respondents in *Sierra Club v. Costle* that the 1977 CAA Amendments reflect six congressional objectives:

> 1. The standards must not give a competitive advantage to one state over another in attracting industry.
> 2. The standards must maximize the potential for long-term economic growth by reducing emissions as much as practicable. This would increase the amount of industrial growth possible within the limits set by air quality standards.
> 3. The standards must to the extent practical force the installation of all the control technology that will ever be necessary on new plants at the time of construction when it is cheaper to install, thereby minimizing the need for retrofit in the future when air quality standards begin to set limits to growth.

---

[82] B. Ackerman & W. Hassler, *supra* note 7, at 109 (emphasis in original).

4 and 5. The standards to the extent practical must force new sources to burn high-sulfur fuel thus freeing low-sulfur fuel for use in existing sources where it is harder to control emissions and where low-sulfur fuel is needed for compliance. This will (1) allow old sources to operate longer and (2) expand environmentally acceptable energy supplies.

6. The standards should be stringent in order to force the development of improved technology.[85]

In 1971 the original NSPS imposed a 1.2 lbs/MBTU emissions limit but no percentage-reduction requirement. The EPA based that standard on its estimate of the level of pollution control possible through scrubbing. In practice, however, many new plants met the standard exclusively through combustion of untreated low-sulfur coal. In other words, before Congress amended the CAA in 1977, utilities adopted the precise strategy that Ackerman later recommended in his critique of the 1979 NSPS. Because the 1977 legislative history explicitly rejected reliance on untreated coal, Ackerman tried to argue that committee statements did not reflect the congressional intent. Yet he never explained why Congress felt the need for a new NSPS was so urgent that the 1977 Act directed the EPA to promulgate a revised standard within one year. In arguing for unrestricted use of low-sulfur coal, Ackerman removed NSPS from the general legislative approach to regulation of new pollution sources and treated the standard as a wholly independent regulatory initiative. In the CAA and the FWPCA, Congress instituted a technology-based regulatory strategy that generally required new dischargers in all industries to implement the best available technological control methods. Yet, prior to 1977, new coal-burning power plants were often constructed with no engineering controls designed to reduce SO_2 emissions.

The reliance of utilities on low-sulfur fuel from 1971-1977 entailed several consequences that Congress found unacceptable: Thousands of mining jobs were lost in states with high-sulfur coal deposits, resulting in significant social dislocation. The access of utilities in some states to nearby supplies of low-sulfur coal created competitive disadvantages for other areas, thereby encouraging the outmigration of industries with attendant social dislocation. The increased contention for low-sulfur fuel raised the cost of power generation for existing plants that had no alternative except to burn low-sulfur coal in order to meet ambient air quality standards. And the reluctance of new plants to use high-sulfur coal together with scrubbers reduced usable energy resources at a time when "energy independence" had become a high national priority.

* * *

2. Environmental protection and innovation.

In a recent critique of command-and-control standards, Richard Stewart correctly observed that environmental health and safety regulation has retarded social and market innovation. Although he conceded that regulation has not been the major cause of a "lag" in productivity, Professor Stewart advocated restructuring environmental protection programs to promote greater innovation. He noted, for example, that the relatively short "lead times" and frequent revisions of current standards produce a "moving target" effect

---

[85] Sierra Club v. Costle, 657 F.2d 298, 325 (D.C. Cir, 1981), *citing*, 44 Fed. Reg. 33,580, 33,581-82 (1979). * * *

that impedes development of the "stable market" necessary for creation of innovative technologies. He contended that the "moving target" problem could be remedied if Congress and government agencies would establish regulatory standards further in advance, allowing industry greater time to achieve compliance. Stewart criticized the imposition of stricter controls on new sources of environmental degradation than on existing sources. He argued that "[i]ncreased turnover of capital stock" is vital to improved innovation, but current regulations often delay this "turnover" by making construction of new plants and development of new products more expensive than continued use of old ones. Stewart presented an extended discussion of economic incentive mechanisms as potential alternatives to command-and-control regulation. Although most of his treatment pertained to the serious implementation problems raised by these proposals, he nevertheless concluded that "[t]he greatest promise for promoting both market and social innovation lies in decentralized incentive systems, such as fees and transferable permits." Stewart also argued that "formalized" standard-setting procedures impose excessive costs and uncertainty on the regulatory process. He recommended the adoption of a negotiated rulemaking system that would provide greater flexibility and incentives for industrial innovation.

Throughout this critique, Stewart treated the goal of increasing innovation as if it should take precedence over all incompatible objectives. His proposal for longer lead times and less frequent revisions of standards would delay the diffusion of available control methods and would prevent agencies from responding promptly to new environmental and technological knowledge. Stewart recognized these social costs, but his article implies that the benefits of creating a "stable market" generally outweigh the disadvantages. Yet he never provided a quantitative or qualitative argument to support that conclusion. Stewart similarly acknowledged that his proposal for negotiated rulemaking would increase the *ability* of affected parties to impede regulation through obstructive behavior in the negotiations process, but he failed to emphasize their strong *motivation* to do so. With regard to his recommendation for increased reliance on economic incentive mechanisms, he observed that:

> Different regulatory tools or strategies will allocate the burden of uncertainty and change in different ways. For example, under a command-and-control system, unexpectedly high control costs will be borne by the industry unless the stringency of regulations is relaxed. Under a fee system, these costs will result in lower levels of control unless fees are increased. In the first case, the risk of unexpectedly high control costs is imposed on firms; in the second, it is imposed on the environment and those exposed to pollution, health, and safety risks.[118]

Stewart has stressed in other essays that uncertainty and change are pervasive aspects of environmental decisionmaking. Yet he never explained in this critique why the asserted ability of economic incentive mechanisms to promote innovation should outweigh the propensity of those strategies to decrease environmental protection under conditions of uncertainty. Moreover, to the extent that market incentive programs can be adjusted

---

[118] Stewart, [*Regulation, Innovation, and Administrative Law: A Conceptual Framework*, 69 CALIF. L. REV. 1256], at 1270.

flexibly in response to changing knowledge and social priorities, they would produce the same "moving target" effect Stewart criticized in conjunction with command-and-control regulation.

* * *

The critical point is that efficiency depends upon which specific objectives the legislature intends to achieve. Regulatory critics often use the term "efficiency" in a malleable manner: In some passages they mean that "fine-tuning" reforms can achieve specified legislative goals in a more cost-effective way than at present; in other instances they mean that current goals are "bad" goals or that Congress has not adequately considered some important social objectives. If commentators employ "efficiency" in the latter sense, as Stewart did with his emphasis on innovation effects, they should make explicit their disagreement with the values and priorities embodied in existing regulatory programs. A contention that "fine-tuning" approaches will perform better than command-and-control standards ought to be clearly distinguished from a contention that the legislature should have reached a different balance between competing interests. In either context, "fine-tuning" control strategies must be capable of implementation before they can increase the real efficiency of environmental regulation.

* * *

E. Idealized Regulatory Proposals

The regulatory critiques previously discussed illustrate the central assumption challenged in Part I of this article: that alternative regulatory strategies must perform better because the current system works badly. As another example, in 1979 Steven Breyer criticized pollution control standards because they are "difficult to administer, can cause serious anticompetitive harm, and can freeze existing technology." He then argued that economic incentive mechanisms would put "a price tag upon pollution" and would induce dischargers to achieve pollution control on a lowest-cost basis. Breyer expanded this analysis in *Regulation and Its Reform*, where he recognized that identifying the correct price level would be virtually impossible and that market incentive mechanisms are more difficult to administer and enforce than his initial discussion suggested. He nevertheless observed:

> [A]dvocates of incentive systems do not rest their claims of superiority on an ability to deal with the [information and implementation] problems just mentioned. Rather, they claim that taxes or marketable rights are not significantly worse than standards in this regard and that they are likely to be significantly more effective and efficient in several other respects.[170]

Despite this comparative claim, Breyer usually did not contrast incentive systems with the dominant form of regulatory controls in current use. He instead envisioned a regulatory approach in which agencies would impose particularized controls on the basis of ecological conditions, harmful effects, and abatement costs unique to individual dischargers. He then compared implementation constraints on this individualized regulatory system with the

---

[170] [S. Breyer, Regulation and its Reform (1982)] at 271-84.

constraints on incentive systems. In other words, Breyer contrasted an ostensibly "efficient" particularized regulatory program against a theoretically "efficient" economic incentive mechanism.

Congress, however, often has adopted a "second-best" strategy that requires categories of polluters to install the best practicable or best available controls without regard to particularized costs and benefits. This technology-based approach is applied to new air pollution sources, existing and new water pollution dischargers, and toxic substances standards promulgated under the OSH Act. If all regulatory approaches depended equally on establishing a close correlation between marginal causes and marginal environmental effects, as any ideal system must, then perhaps the implementation costs of incentive systems would not be "significantly worse" than the costs of direct regulation. Yet, Congress specifically introduced the technology-based standards approach in order to decouple pollution control from the need to link particular pollutants with particular manifestations of harm. Given this deliberate "inefficiency" of technology-based standards, there is no reason to suppose that the decisionmaking and administrative constraints associated with the present system resemble the implementation problems of market incentive mechanism.

A useful analysis of competing regulatory approaches must include an accurate description of how the current system works, with its distinctive advantages and drawbacks, as well as a realistic prediction of how "fine-tuning" strategies would perform in practice. Breyer compared one idealized control strategy against another, with little recognition that both might prove impracticable under real implementation constraints. Ackerman and Stewart, among many others, compared the actual deficiencies of command-and-control standards against the theoretical advantages of "fine-tuning" approaches. Neither of these modes of utopian regulatory criticism is likely to produce an effective environmental policy. The choice between more "fine-tuning" and greater uniformity cannot be made on the basis of abstract theory alone, but the idealized regulatory analyses criticized in Part I of this article have not addressed implementation problems and party motivations in a realistic manner.

II. "EFFICIENT" VERSUS EFFECTIVE REGULATION

The central tenets in the literature on "fine-tuning" are that costs should be compared against regulatory benefits, and that particularized ecological, technological, and economic circumstances should be considered to a greater degree than at present. The literature on regulatory reform has, however, been long on theory and short on empiricism. Part II describes past experiences with regulatory programs that may serve as approximate analogues for recent "fine-tuning" proposals. Two primary themes are developed. First, theoretically "efficient" regulatory strategies require more data, more sophisticated scientific and economic analyses, more agency expertise and resources, and more cooperation from regulated parties. These requirements ensure that "fine-tuning" strategies cannot be implemented effectively in many environmental protection contexts. Second, past attempts at partial "fine-tuning" often have failed and typically have been superseded by precisely the crude but administrable approaches that academic commentators have attacked as "inefficient." Thus, both implementation theory and implementation experience suggest that "fine-tuning" regulatory reforms should be regarded with great skepticism.

A. Experience with Marginal Harm-Based Approaches

Some command-and-control strategies and most incentive mechanisms require, at a minimum, that agencies identify tolerable levels of ecological degradation and health risk associated with different activities. In other words, these regulatory strategies are predicated on the avoidance of unacceptable levels of harm. Other regulatory approaches replace "harm-based" determinations with alternative decisionmaking criteria. For example, industries may be required to achieve the greatest feasible degree of protection, or they may be prohibited from significantly exceeding current pollutant discharge levels. These strategies are also intended to improve or preserve environmental conditions, but they do not depend on proof of a correlation between specific activities and specific ecological or health effects. It is important to stress that the competing regulatory approaches described in Part II require different kinds of information, raise different types of issues, and present different implementation problems.

* * *

2. Toxic and hazardous pollutant standards.

Section 307(a) of the FWPCA directed the EPA to identify especially harmful pollutants. For each designated toxic pollutant, the 1972 Act commanded the agency to impose an effluent standard or prohibition sufficient to assure an "ample margin of safety." Thus, the EPA was to regulate toxic pollutants under an approach that assumed the agency could make legally defensible harm-based determinations.

In 1973 the EPA issued proposed standards for an initial list of nine toxic water pollutants. During the next four years, however, the EPA failed to promulgate binding regulations for these pollutants "due to the Agency's belief that the record developed at the hearings would not support final standards." Thomas Jorling, the Assistant Administrator for Water and Hazardous Materials, testified before Congress that section 307(a) was "technically impractical" because of the requirement "to demonstrate the cause and effect relationship between pollutants and public health." A 1977 legislative report on toxic pollutant regulation observed: "Without exception, witnesses testified to the overall lack of data for setting standards for either water quality or for individual chemicals, and to there being less data available than estimated at the time the FWPCA was enacted." Witnesses also agreed that reliable harm-based determinations were difficult to make and that the EPA possessed insufficient resources to identify safe exposure levels for most toxic substances. EPA Administrator Douglas Costle testified that "while he could not say EPA's resources were adequate, neither could he say what would be adequate."

Environmental groups brought several suits challenging the EPA's failure to issue final toxic standards for the nine designated pollutants and to include many other substances on the toxic water pollutant list. The agency argued in defense that lack of adequate data and resources precluded these discretionary actions, but that other potentially toxic substances were under study. After the Court of Appeals for the District of Columbia Circuit ordered the EPA to disclose all of the technical information and administrative considerations on which it relied to justify its regulatory inaction, the litigants entered into a settlement agreement. The decree stipulated that the EPA would issue standards for 65 toxic water pollutants by imposing the best available control technology as promptly as possible. In subsequent testimony before Congress, Administrator Costle argued that "experience with the alternative approaches* * *offered by Section 307(a) on one hand and technology-based limitations on the other leave us firmly convinced that for the bulk of known or suspected toxins of concern, technology-based standards established on an industry-by-industry basis are by far the most feasible to implement and administer." The Clean Water Act of 1977 specifically authorized EPA reliance on technology-based standards to control toxic pollutants. Although this Act also allowed the agency to promulgate more stringent water quality standards for toxins when sufficient information is available, no water quality-related standards beyond the original nine listed pollutants have been issued.

* * *

B. Experience with Individualized Decisionmaking

Proponents of "fine-tuning" contend that regulators should consider particularized ecological, technological, and economic circumstances to a substantially greater extent than is required under current control programs. Past experience, however, indicates that attempts to implement regulatory systems dependent on individualized decisionmaking frequently prove ineffective.

1. Technological and economic variances.

Under the FWPCA technology-based regulatory program for industrial dischargers, the EPA must devise five separate sets of categorical standards tailored to the technological and economic characteristics of several hundred subcategories of polluting industries. The EPA must also analyze the costs of technology-based regulations: Three types of standards employ a feasibility test while the other two incorporate a limited cost-benefit comparison on a categorical basis. The cost-benefit test for determination of the best practicable control technology (BPT) was not, however, intended to impose on the EPA "any requirement to consider the location of sources within a category or to ascertain water quality impact of effluent controls, or to determine the economic impact of controls on any individual plant in a single community." Thus, Congress explicitly rejected the notion that technology-based standards must be adapted to particularized circumstances.

Because pollution sources rarely possess identical technological and economic characteristics, the creation of regulatory subcategories and the placement of individual facilities within them required the EPA to make many debatable judgments. Dischargers frequently challenged these agency decisions in appellate litigation. In *E.I. du Pont Nemours & Co. v. Train*, industry petitioners argued that each set of regulations should identify a range of possible effluent limitations and that specific discharge limits must be imposed by decentralized permit-issuing authorities on the basis of individualized circumstances.[231] The Supreme Court rejected this contention on several grounds: Expert agencies are entitled to deference in the interpretation of their statutory mandates; Congress emphasized the need for uniformity in the treatment of comparable dischargers; Congress intended all facilities within each subcategory to achieve the performance of the best plants in

---

[231] *See* E. I. du Pont Nemours & Co. v. Train, 430 U.S. 112, 123-25 (1977).

that subcategory; and "[t]he petitioners' view of the Act would place an impossible [administrative] burden on EPA."

Despite the arguments it cited in favor of uniform treatments, the Court approved the EPA's creation of an individualized "fundamentally different factors" (FDF) variance that allows a firm to demonstrate either significantly different engineering and technical constraints or significantly different compliance costs from those used to establish the categorical limits. In *EPA v. National Crushed Stone Ass'n*, the Supreme Court approved the EPA's decision to exclude consideration in FDF proceedings of each facility's financial capacity to absorb the required compliance costs.[234] Justice White correctly reasoned that FDF variances based on claims by individual dischargers of financial incapacity would frustrate the statutory intent to upgrade the level of industrial pollution control efforts. The Supreme Court again stressed the congressional insistence on uniformity within categories of dischargers:

> [T]he approach of giving variances to pollution controls based on economic grounds has long ago shown itself to be a risky course: All too often, the variances became a tool used by powerful political interests to obtain so many exemptions for pollution control standards and timetables on the filmsiest [sic] of pretenses that they become meaningless. In short, with variances, exceptions to pollution cleanup can become the rule, meaning further tragic delay in stopping the destruction of our environment.[236]

Unfortunately, the Court failed to recognize that an individualized variance procedure for differences in technical characteristics and compliance costs presents a similar potential for abuse. The regulations at issue covered about 4,800 crushed stone and 6,000 coal facilities. Under the current FDF treatment, state or EPA regional administrators determine whether any of those dischargers should be granted particularized variances, and there is no mechanism for assuring that facilities with comparable characteristics will receive comparable emissions limits. Some form of administrative flexibility was undoubtedly necessary in light of the informational deficiencies, budget restrictions, and pressing time constraints under which the EPA had to develop BPT categorical standards. But should this flexibility take the form of an individualized variance procedure or a mechanism for the development of additional subcategories of regulations that treat "fundamental" differences consistently? One critic of the FDF variance program observed that "special treatment might place those plants that do not comply with the category limitations in an advantageous economic position and thereby increase the resistance to regulation of those plants that could otherwise be expected to comply without substantial difficulty."[239] A requirement that agency attempts to grant an FDF variance should trigger a new categorical rulemaking proceeding would reduce the possibility of inconsistencies and competitive disadvantages among equivalent dischargers, and would also encourage meaningful public

---

[234] EPA v. National Crushed Stone Ass'n, 449 U.S. 64, 75-81 (1980).

[236] *Id.* at 81 * * * .

[239] Kalur, [*Will Judicial Error Allow Industrial Point Sources to Avoid BPT and Perhaps BAT Later? A Story of Good Intentions, Bad Dictum and Ugly Consequence*, 7 ECOLOGY L. Q. 955] note 233 at 977. [(1979)]. For an example of the problem, see Georgia-Pacific Corp. v. EPA, 671 F.2d 1235 (9th Cir. 1982).

disclosure and participation before exceptions are authorized from technology-based regulations.

Few FDF variances have been granted to date, but this experience may stem from the failure of the EPA to incorporate in most permits the control levels specified in the categorical regulations. A critique of FDF implementation noted that roughly 20 percent of major industrial dischargers have contested interim permit conditions, and the author of the critique predicted that many of these firms would apply for FDF variances once their initial permits expire. He concluded: "Industrial dischargers that have sought or will seek BPT variances often are the most serious violators of limits . . . and they are the major pressure upon a bureaucracy assigned the task of discretionary enforcement."[245] An empirical study of requests for hearings on permits issued by EPA Region 10 found that approximately 37 percent of all permits had been contested. Some of these challenges resulted from applications for FDF variances. The authors determined that "[n]early all of the challenges were initiated by the dischargers, and over half of the challenges resulted in modifications of permit conditions or other changes that were favorable to the dischargers." There was "minimal citizen involvement in the hearing process," and the little that occurred was "limited to highly visible dischargers." The large number of requests for hearings "strained" EPA resources. Over one-half of the challenges "required more than one year for resolution, and over one-third have taken more than two years." The study concluded that industry challenges to permit terms have been "accompanied by the exercise of discretion on the part of the EPA to a degree that significantly compromises the congressionally mandated requirements of the FWPCA." There is no reason to doubt that industry applications for FDF variances will present similar problems.

* * *

Individualized variances, whether based on ecological conditions or technological and economic factors, generally entail agency reliance on data submitted by the applicants and require administrators to review those data in detail before imposing discharge limits. In these respects, variance proceedings are similar to programs in which regulators must issue individualized water pollution permits to thousands of dischargers. A recent General Accounting Office (GAO) study of industry compliance with permit terms indicated that the EPA and the states made little attempt to identify the many polluters who did not even apply for permits, and that the agencies had not processed tens of thousands of existing permit applications in a timely manner. The GAO and the EPA itself attributed these deficiencies to the lack of administrative resources. The permit-issuing agencies depend almost entirely on monitoring and self-reporting by dischargers to identify violations of permit terms; yet the GAO study determined that over 40 percent of the polluters examined failed to submit discharge monitoring reports or failed to provide all required data. A different study of permit challenges in EPA Region 10 found that some polluters had deliberately falsified data. Despite the EPA's recognition that an enforcement system predicated on self-reporting requires "careful and continuous oversight," the GAO study concluded that agency resources and inspection programs were inadequate to maintain

---

[245] Kalur, [*Will Judicial Error Allow Industrial Point Sources to Avoid BPT and Perhaps BAT Later? A Story of Good Intentions, Bad Dictum and Ugly Consequence*, 7 ECOLOGY L. Q. 955] at 987-88 [(1979)].

the necessary supervision. These experiences with individualized permit programs provide little reason for confidence about the accuracy of information in variance applications, or about the ability of agencies to review those applications in a careful and timely fashion.

The implementation of variances based on individualized circumstances raises numerous problems: high decisionmaking costs, frequent litigation, inconsistent results, persistent delays, increased opportunities for manipulative behavior by applicants or administrators, and inadequate public participation. These deficiencies are not restricted to pollution control variances; similar types of problems have long been recognized in conjunction with variances from zoning ordinances. Yet "fine-tuning" proposals for individualized decisionmaking present equal, or worse, possibilities for abuse. At least in the case of variance applications, the burdens of production and proof are typically placed on those who seek exceptions from general standards, and the standards themselves provide some limits on the exercise of administrative discretion. Neither moderating factor would exist in "fine-tuning" regulatory programs dependent on particularized opportunity-cost balancing or on the prevention of significant adverse effects in particular locations.

* * *

Any requirement that environmental regulation must be based on "good science" is not a neutral principle in areas where information scarcity is endemic and no reasonable scientific consensus exists. The notion that regulators must always attempt to consider individualized circumstances and should make "innumerable guesses" in order to "openly argue" about the "right questions"—to repeat Ackerman's phrases—is a classic example of a "second-best" fallacy. The dogmatic insistence of "fine-tuning" proponents that decisionmakers must always address the "right questions" will not improve the real efficiency of environmental regulation when those questions cannot be reliably answered. If society decides to protect its citizens against potentially severe but currently indeterminate risks, regulators may have no recourse other than to adopt relatively crude decisionmaking criteria that make some logically relevant issues legally irrelevant—exactly the effect of technology-based standards and antidegradation policies as well as qualitative risk assessments of possible carcinogens. The proposition that agencies should wait until particular marginal risks can be identified with assurance is certainly a tenable social policy. But this value judgment has seldom been incorporated in current law and is not patently desirable as a matter of logic or equity.

Proponents of individualized decisionmaking have no difficulty pointing to instances where uniform standards produce "inefficient" results, where agencies do not consider all material factors, and where scientific or economic issues have not been resolved in a reliable fashion. Yet regulatory critics seldom question whether these agency efforts can be distinguished in a principled manner from thousands of other conflicts, whether individualized decisionmaking would increase cumulative regulatory costs and delays to an unacceptable degree, whether particularized approaches would preclude meaningful public participation in most cases, and whether "fine-tuning" would expand opportunities for strategic behavior and intrusive judicial review. In light of the inefficiencies associated with command-and-control standards, one could not conclude that uniform treatments are invariably superior to individualized decisionmaking, but that the opposite generalization is equally untenable. The regulatory experiences described in this article indicate that particularized control strategies often prove ineffective.

* * *

NOTES

1. In Part II of his article, Professor Latin states that "most incentive mechanisms require, at a minimum, that agencies identify tolerable levels of ecological degradation and health risk associated with different activities. In other words, these regulatory strategies are predicated on avoidance of unacceptable levels of harm." In the context of this comment, consider the four market mechanisms described by Stavins and Whitehead: (1) pollution charges; (2) tradeable permits systems; (3) removal of market barriers; and (4) eliminating government subsidies. Does application of any of these mechanisms require identification of "tolerable levels of ecological degradation" any more than would a command-and-control system? Is it not possible (and perhaps inevitable), for example, that pollution charges will be based largely on a rough estimate of an amount which the regulating authority determines will achieve an adequate reduction of pollution levels at an acceptable cost to the regulated community? Likewise, is it not likely that the number of tradeable pollution rights which are made available will roughly approximate the level that the regulating authority considers fair and attainable?

2. Whether or not it is fair to equate harm-based mechanisms with market mechanisms, Professor Latin's observations regarding the difficulties associated with "harm-based" regulations seem unassailable. Another example offering support for his claim is the program established under the Clean Air Act for regulating hazardous air pollutants. Under the 1977 Amendments to the Clean Air Act, Congress had mandated that the EPA establish standards for hazardous air pollutants "at the level which in his judgment provides an ample margin of safety to protect the public health." 42 U.S.C. §7412(b)(1)(B) (1978). Faced with many "non-threshold pollutants" for which there presumably exists no safe level of exposure, the EPA balked at promulgating any standards for most hazardous air pollutants out of fear that entire industries might be forced to close. In the 1990 Clean Air Act Amendments, Congress bowed to practical realities in opting for a new hazardous air pollution program which requires that standards be set, at least initially, on the basis of maximum achievable control technology. 42 U.S.C. §7412(d).

3. Why is it easier for an agency to set technology-based standards than harm-based standards? How does "fine tuning" through the use of variances complicate the problem for the agency, and weaken the effectiveness of the regulatory program? What is the value of affording a variance opportunity?

4. The Clean Air Act establishes a program for "prevention of significant deterioration" of air quality. Under this program, major new stationary sources of air pollution may not be permitted in regions of the country which meet or exceed ambient air quality standards if those sources would emit certain regulated air pollutants in excess of defined increments. This prohibition applies even if the additional air pollution would not adversely affect the public health or public welfare. How might an economist view the merits of such a provision? How might Professor Latin view it? *See* Latin, *supra,* at text accompanying notes 207-23. Why might the Congress choose to impose regulatory restrictions on future air pollution if no adverse health or welfare impacts can be identified?

Professors Ackerman and Stewart have written extensively about economic reforms that might improve environmental law. *See e.g.* Bruce Ackerman & Richard Stewart, *Reforming Environmental Law: The Democratic Case for Market Incentives*, 13 COLUM. J. ENVTL. L. 171 (1988). As you might expect, they take issue with Professor Latin's defense of the current regulatory regime. As you read the following comment on Professor Latin's article keep in mind that the references to BAT are somewhat misleading. In most cases of so-called "command-and-control" regulation, BAT requirements are *not* actually requirements that facilities employ a particular pollution control technology. Rather they are "emission standards" which are set on the basis of the degree of emission control which can be achieved by using the best available technology. Generally, then, if a company is able to achieve the applicable emission standard by using a different technology, the company is free to do so.

REFORMING ENVIRONMENTAL LAW
Bruce A. Ackerman and Richard B. Stewart
37 Stan. L. Rev. 1333 (1985)*

In 1971, Ezra Mishan brilliantly satirized the views of a Dr. Pangloss, who argued that a world of largely unregulated pollution was "optimal" because cleanup would involve enormous transaction costs.[1] Less than 15 years later, Professor Latin uses the same Panglossian argument to rationalize the current regulatory status quo.[2] He not only accepts but endorses our extraordinarily crude, costly, litigious and counterproductive system of technology-based environmental controls. Like Mishan's Pangloss, he seems to believe that if it were possible to have a better world, it would exist. Since it does not, the

---

[1] Mishan, *Pangloss on Pollution*, 73 SWED. J. ECON. 1 (1971). While tempted to emulate Mishan, we have (recognizing our comparative disadvantage) eschewed satire and have chosen to present an affirmative program for reform.
[2] Latin, *Ideal Versus Real Regulatory Efficiency: Implementation of Uniform Standards and "Fine-Tuning" Regulatory Reform*, 37 STAN. L. REV. 1267 (1985).

transaction costs involved in regulatory improvement must exceed the benefits. Proposals for basic change accordingly are dismissed as naive utopianism.

What explains this celebration of the regulatory status quo? As critics of the present system, we believe this question to be of more than academic interest. The present regulatory system wastes tens of billions of dollars every year, misdirects resources, stifles innovation, and spawns massive and often counterproductive litigation. There is a variety of fundamental but practical changes that could be made to improve its environmental and economic performance. Why have such changes not been adopted? Powerful organized interests have a vested stake in the status quo. The congressional committees, government bureaucracies, and industry and environmental groups that have helped to shape the present system want to see it perpetuated. But the current system is also bolstered by an often inarticulate sense that, however cumbersome, it "works," and that complexity and limited information make major improvements infeasible.

Professor Latin has performed an important service in providing an articulate, informed, and sophisticated exposition of this view. By developing and making transparent the arguments that might justify the status quo, he has made it easier to assess their merits. If, as we believe, those arguments lack merit, his sophisticated defense of the status quo may ultimately serve to hasten its demise.

We will not respond to all of the groundless charges that Professor Latin levels at the critics of the current system, ourselves included. We focus instead on the major flaws in his defense of existing law and policy. First, Latin's view is based on a Panglossian interpretation of the status quo. The current system does not in fact "work" and its malfunctions, like those of Soviet-style central planning, will become progressively more serious as the economy grows and changes and our knowledge of environmental problems develops.

Second, Latin mistakenly treats economic incentive systems as a form of regulatory "fine-tuning," rather than recognizing them as fundamental alternatives to our current reliance on centralized regulatory commands to implement environmental goals. Moreover, he completely ignores experience showing that economic incentive systems are feasible and effective.

Third, Latin ignores the increasingly urgent need to improve the process by which Congress, the agencies, and the courts set environmental goals. He is mesmerized by decisionmaking costs, ignoring the great social benefits flowing from a more intelligent and democratically accountable dialogue on environmental policy. We deal with each of these points in turn.

I. THE EXISTING SYSTEM

The existing system of pollution regulation, which is the focus of Latin's defense, is primarily based on a Best Available Technology (BAT) strategy. If an industrial process or product generates some nontrivial risk, the responsible plant or industry must install whatever technology is available to reduce or eliminate this risk, so long as the costs of doing so will not cause a shutdown of the plant or industry. BAT requirements are largely determined through uniform federal regulations. Under the Clean Water Act's BAT strategy, the EPA adapts nationally uniform effluent limitations for some 500 different industries. A similar BAT strategy is deployed under the Clean Air Act for new industrial sources of air pollution, new automobiles, and industrial sources of toxic air pollutants. BAT strategies are also widely used in many fields of environmental regulation other than air and water pollution, which are the focus of Latin's analysis.

BAT was embraced by Congress and administrators in the early 1970s in order to impose immediate, readily enforceable federal controls on a relatively few widespread pollutants, while avoiding widespread industrial shutdowns. Subsequent experience and analysis has demonstrated:

1. Uniform BAT requirements waste many billions of dollars annually by ignoring variations among plants and industries in the cost of reducing pollution and by ignoring geographic variations in pollution effects. A more cost-effective strategy of risk reduction could free enormous resources for additional pollution reduction or other purposes.

2. BAT controls, and the litigation they provoke, impose disproportionate penalties on new products and processes. A BAT strategy typically imposes far more stringent controls on new sources because there is no risk of shutdown. Also, new plants and products must run the gauntlet of lengthy regulatory and legal proceedings to win approval; the resulting uncertainty and delay discourage new investment. By contrast, existing sources can use the delays and costs of the legal process to burden regulators and postpone or "water-down" compliance. BAT strategies also impose disproportionate burdens on more productive and profitable industries because these industries can "afford" more stringent controls. This "soak the rich" approach penalizes growth and international competitiveness.

3. BAT controls can ensure that established control technologies are installed. They do not, however, provide strong incentives for the development of new, environmentally superior strategies, and may actually discourage their development. Such innovations are essential for maintaining long-term economic growth without simultaneously increasing pollution and other forms of environmental degradation.

4. BAT involves the centralized determination of complex scientific, engineering, and economic issues regarding the feasibility of controls on hundreds of thousands of pollution sources. Such determinations impose massive information-gathering burdens on administrators, and provide a fertile ground for complex litigation in the form of massive adversary rulemaking proceedings and protracted judicial review. Given the high costs of regulatory compliance and the potential gains from litigation brought to defeat or delay regulatory requirements, it is often more cost-effective for industry to "invest" in such litigation rather than to comply.

5. A BAT strategy is inconsistent with intelligent priority setting. Simply regulating to the hilt whatever pollutants happen to get on the regulatory agenda may preclude an agency from dealing adequately with more serious problems that come to scientific attention later. BAT also tends to reinforce regulatory inertia. Foreseeing that "all or nothing" regulation of a given substance under BAT will involve large administrative and compliance costs, and recognizing that resources are limited, agencies often seek to limit sharply the number of substances on the agenda for regulatory action.

This indictment is not idle speculation, but the product of years of patient study by lawyers, economists, and political scientists. There are, for example, no fewer than 15 careful efforts to estimate the extra cost burden generated by a wide range of traditional legalistic BAT systems used to control a variety of air and water pollutants in different parts of the country. Of the twelve studies of different air pollutants from particulates to chlorofluorocarbons—seven indicated that traditional forms of regulation were more than 400% more expensive than the least-cost solution; four revealed that they were about 75% more expensive; one suggested a modest cost-overrun of 7%. Three studies of water pollution control in five different watersheds also indicate the serious inefficiency of traditional forms of command-and-control regulation. These careful studies of selected problems cannot be used to estimate precisely the total amount traditional forms of regulation are annually costing the American people. Nonetheless, very large magnitudes are at stake. Even if a reformed system could cut costs by "only" one-third, it could save more than $15 billion a year from the nation's annual expenditure of $50 billion on air and water pollution control alone.[16]

While Latin entirely fails to address this evidence, he does not seriously contest the economic wastefulness of the current system's excessive compliance costs and penalties on new investment. He simply ignores the last three points in our indictment, even though they have been well developed in the literature. Instead, Latin spends all his time castigating all reform proposals as unrealistic. In his view, reformers characteristically propose utopian efforts at administrative "fine-tuning" that would in practice lead to a bureaucratic nightmare, making the present system seem benign by comparison.

We do not accept this despairing view. To explain why, however, we must correct an analytic deficiency in Latin's critique. The various reforms rejected in his article have little in common with one another—except that they all represent departures from BAT. Indeed, it is a sign of Latin's deep commitment to the status quo that, simply because they depart from BAT, he thinks of them as if they were all variations on the problem of "fine-tuning" that he decries. But "fine-tuning" is much too diffuse a notion on which to base an analysis of the reform agenda. Some of our proposals involve reform of the criteria and procedures which Congress, agencies, and the courts use in setting environmental goals; others involve reform of the means by which the goals (whatever they may be) are implemented in the real world. Latin's indiscriminate condemnation of "fine-tuning" fails to distinguish systematically between these two types of proposals. In this, as in so much else, his critique is faithful to the BAT system, which also conflates means and ends, preventing the intelligent assessment of either. If, however, we are to move beyond the status quo, it is best to treat these two different kinds of structural reform separately, beginning with the implementation problem and concluding with the question of goal-setting.

II. IMPLEMENTATION

A BAT system has an implicit environmental goal: achievement of the environmental quality level that would result if all sources installed BAT controls on their discharges. The usual means for implementing this goal are centralized, industry-uniform regulations that command specific amounts of cleanup from specific polluters. When a polluter receives an air or water permit under existing law, the piece of paper does not content

---

[16] See OFFICE OF POLICY PLANNING AND EVALUATION, U.S. EPA, THE COST OF CLEAN AIR AND WATER (1984) (estimating expenditures to comply with federal air and water pollution control expenditures in the ten years 1981-1990 at $525 billion (in constant 1981 dollars)). Moreover, we also think that our reforms are applicable to many other kinds of pollution as well. See notes 39-40 infra and accompanying text.

itself, in the manner of Polonius, with the vague advice that he "use the best available technology." Instead, the permit tries to be as quantitatively precise as possible, telling each discharger how much of the regulated pollutants he may discharge.

Although Latin condemns us as unrealistic, our reforms build upon, rather than abandon, this basic permit system. Indeed, we have only two, albeit far-reaching, objections to the existing permit mechanism. First, existing permits are free. This is bad because it gives the polluter no incentive to reduce his wastes below the permitted amount. Second, they are non-transferable. This is bad because polluter A is obliged to cut back his own wastes even if it is cheaper for him to pay his neighbor B to undertake the extra cleanup instead.

Our basic reform would respond to these deficiencies by allowing polluters to buy and sell each other's permits—thereby creating a powerful financial incentive for those who can clean up most cheaply to sell their permits to those whose treatment costs are highest. This reform will, at one stroke, cure many of the basic flaws of the existing command-and-control regulatory systems discussed earlier.

A system of tradeable rights will tend to bring about a least-cost allocation of control burdens, saving many billions of dollars annually. It will eliminate the disproportionate burdens that BAT imposes on new and more productive industries by treating all sources of the same pollutant on the same basis. It will provide positive economic rewards for polluters who develop environmentally superior products and processes. It will, as we show below, reduce the incentives for litigation, simplify the issues in controversy, and facilitate more intelligent setting of priorities.

Would allowing the sale of permits lead to a bureaucratic nightmare? Before proceeding to the new administrative burdens marketability will generate, it is wise to pause, as Latin does not, to consider marketability's great administrative advantages.

First, marketability would immediately eliminate most of the information-processing tasks that are presently overwhelming the federal and state bureaucracies. No longer would the EPA be required to conduct endless adversary proceedings to determine the best available control technologies in each major industry of the United States, and to defend its determinations before the courts; nor would federal and state officials be required to spend vast amounts of time and energy in adapting these changing national guidelines to the particular conditions of every important pollution source in the United States. Instead of giving the job of economic and technological assessment to bureaucrats, the marketable rights mechanism would put the information-processing burden precisely where it belongs: upon business managers and engineers who are in the best position to figure out how to cut back on their plants' pollution costs. If the managers operating plant A think they can clean up a pollutant more cheaply than those in charge of plant B, they should be expected to sell some of their pollution rights to B at a mutually advantageous price; cleanup will occur at the least cost without the need for constant bureaucratic decisions about the best available technology. Latin seriously misleads when he describes a marketable permit system as one involving administrative "fine-tuning." To the contrary, it is the existing system of command-and-control regulation that envisions inevitably ill-informed bureaucrats continually "fine-tuning" technological and economic decisions best made by the people operating the plants.

Second, marketable permits would open up enormous financial resources for effective and informed regulation. While polluters would have the right to trade their permits among themselves during the *n* years they are valid, they would be obliged to buy new ones when their permits expired at an auction held by the EPA in each watershed and air quality control region. These auctions would raise substantial sums of money for the government on a continuing basis. While no study has yet attempted to make global estimates for the United States as a whole, existing work suggests that auction revenues could well equal the amount polluters would spend in cost-minimizing control activities. Even if revenues turned out to be a third of this amount, the government would still be collecting more than $6-10 billion a year. Moreover, it seems reasonable to suppose that Congress would allow the EPA (and associated state agencies) to retain a substantial share of these revenues. Since the current EPA operating budget is $1.3 billion, using even a fraction of the auction fund to improve regulatory analyses, research, and monitoring would allow a great leap forward in the sophistication of the regulatory effort—something Latin says he supports, but is unable to find any practical way of achieving. Given its revenue-raising potential, environmental reform is hardly a politically unrealistic pipe dream. To the contrary, it is only a matter of time before the enormous federal deficit forces Congress and the President to consider the revenue-raising potential of an auction scheme.

Third, the auction system would help correct one of the worst weaknesses of the present system: the egregious failure of the EPA and associated state agencies to enforce the laws on the books in a timely and effective way. Part of the problem stems from the ability of existing polluters to delay regulatory implementation by using legal proceedings to challenge the economic and engineering bases of BAT regulations and permit conditions. But agencies also invest so little in monitoring that they must rely on polluters for the bulk of their data on discharges. Since polluters are predictably reluctant to report their own violations, the current system perpetuates a Panglossian view of regulatory reality. For example, a General Accounting Office investigation of 921 major air polluters officially considered to be in compliance revealed 200, or 22%, to be violating their permits; in one region, the number not complying was 52%. Even when illegal polluters are identified, they are not effectively sanctioned: The EPA's Inspector General in 1984 found that it was a common practice for water pollution officials to respond to violations by issuing administrative orders that effectively legitimized excess discharges. Thus, while the system may, after protracted litigation, eventually "work" to force the slow installation of expensive control machinery, there is no reason to think this machinery will run well when eventually installed. Although there are many reasons for this appalling weakness in enforcement, one stands out above all others: The present system does not put pressure on agency policymakers to make the large investments in monitoring and personnel that are required to make the tedious and unending work of credible enforcement a bureaucratic reality.

The auction system would change existing compliance incentives dramatically. It would reduce the opportunity and incentive of polluters to use the legal system for delay and obstruction by finessing the complex BAT issues, and it would limit dispute to the question of whether a source's discharges exceeded its permits. It would also eliminate the possibility of using the legal system to postpone implementation of regulatory requirements by requiring the polluter that lost its legal challenge to pay for the permits it would have been obliged to buy during the entire intervening period of noncompliance (plus interest).

The marketable permit system would also provide much stronger incentives for effective monitoring and enforcement. If polluters did not expect rigorous enforcement during the term of their permits, this fact would show up at the auction in dramatically lower bids: Why pay a lot for the right to pollute legally when one can pollute illegally without serious risk of detection? Under a marketable permit approach, this problem would be at the center of bureaucratic attention. For if, as we envisage, the size of the budget available to the EPA and state agencies would depend on total auction revenues, the bureaucracy's failure to invest adequately in enforcement would soon show up in a potentially dramatic drop in auction income available for the next budgetary period. This is not a prospect that top EPA administrators will take lightly. Monitoring and enforcement will become agency priorities of the first importance. Moreover, permit holders may themselves support strong enforcement in order to ensure that cheating by others does not depreciate the value of the permit holders' investments.

A system of marketable permits, then, not only promises to save Americans many billions of dollars a year, to reward innovative improvements in existing clean-up techniques, and to eliminate the BAT system's penalty on new, productive investment. It also offers formidable administrative advantages. It relieves agencies of the enormous information-processing burdens that overwhelm them under the BAT system; it greatly reduces litigation and delay; it offers a rich source of budgetary revenue in a period of general budgetary stringency; and it forces agencies to give new importance to the critical business of enforcing the law in a way that America's polluters will take seriously. Despite his emphasis on administrative realities, Latin has failed to take any of these advantages seriously. Instead, he speaks forebodingly of the dangers of "fine-tuning" that the market reform entails. What precisely are these dangers?

The reformed system we have described involves the execution of four bureaucratic tasks. First, the agency must estimate how much pollution presently is permitted by law in each watershed and air quality region. Second, it must run a system of fair and efficient auctions in which polluters can regularly buy rights for limited terms. Third, it must run an efficient title registry in each region that will allow buyers and sellers to transfer rights in a legally effective way. Fourth, it must consistently penalize polluters who discharge more than their permitted amounts.

And that's that. So far as the fourth bureaucratic task is concerned, we have already given reasons to believe that the EPA would enforce the law far more effectively under the new regime than it does at present. So far as the first three management functions are concerned, we think that they are, in the aggregate, far less demanding than those they displace under the BAT system.

Taking the three functions in reverse order, we assume that Professor Latin would agree that a system of title registration is within the range of bureaucratic possibility. In contrast, the second task—running fair and efficient auctions—is a complicated affair, and it is easy to imagine such a system run incompetently or corruptly. Nonetheless, other agencies seem to have done similar jobs in satisfactory fashions: If the Department of Interior can auction off oil and gas leases competently, we see no reason the EPA could not do the same for pollution rights. Finally, there remains the task of estimating the total allowable wasteload permitted under existing law in each watershed and air control region. If the BAT system functioned properly, these numbers would be easy to obtain. EPA's regional administrators would simply have to add up the allowed amounts appearing in the permits that are in their filing cabinets. * * *

Would a system of marketable rights preclude improvement of environmental quality? By no means. The initial stock of rights can be amortized on a fixed schedule in order to reach a targeted goal, or the government may decide not to reissue existing rights after they expire. Any such reductions will increase the price of rights by reducing supply. Prices will also automatically tend to rise over time as the economy grows and the demand for rights increases. Under a BAT approach, by contrast, regulators must consistently undertake new, difficult, and unpopular initiatives to impose ever more stringent BAT controls on existing sources in order to accommodate economic growth without increased pollution. The prospect of steady increases in the price of rights will be a powerful incentive—far more powerful than the patchwork efforts at "technology forcing" under the BAT system—for businesses to develop cleaner products and processes.

A more serious objection to our proposal is that it ignores the problem of defining the region within which trades are permitted. The short answer is that the EPA and the States have already divided the nation into several hundred air quality control regions; similarly, the states have delineated the watershed boundaries for pollution control and other water management purposes. Rather than starting from scratch, our proposal can proceed on the basis of these existing boundaries. Especially in the area of air pollution, however, we have no doubt that existing regional lines have been drawn in a way that is extremely insensitive to ecological realities. We strongly recommend, therefore, that a reformed statute provide a mechanism for the orderly reexamination of existing regional boundaries—although it may well be wiser to defer this question for five or ten years to allow the EPA to concentrate on the challenges involved in managing the transition to a marketable permit system.

Latin is on stronger ground, we believe, in emphasizing that a reformed implementation system would not easily solve all foreseeable regulatory problems. In particular, the market system we have described could allow the creation of relatively high concentrations of particular pollutants in small areas within the larger pollution control region. In tolerating "hot spots," of course, our reform proposal shares the defects of the existing BAT system, which also generates risk of "hot spots" by imposing the same controls on sources regardless of their location, the size of the human population affected by their discharges, and the nature and vulnerability of affected ecosystems. Nonetheless, the blindness of both systems to intraregional variation is a serious source of concern. The extensive literature on marketable permits—almost entirely ignored by Latin—points to a variety of feasible means for dealing with the hot spot problem. We believe that a long-run strategy for institutional reform should strive to take advantage of these more sophisticated market solutions to the problem of intraregional variation. For the present, it will be enough to emphasize our agreement with Latin's caution that administrative feasibility is an important constraint on the degree of sophistication that we may reasonably expect.

* * *

We entirely agree with Latin, however, that an immediate statutory embrace of regional variation would be premature at the present time. Before taking such a step, we must first construct stronger regional institutions than now exist in the overcentralized federal system.

We look forward to a day when we might go to any region in the country and find a serious professional staff that could both describe the existing environmental data and models and explain how they propose to improve them over the next five or ten years. Without such an ongoing system of data collection and analysis, there can be little hope of designing regulatory systems which are sensitive to regional ecological and economic realities. Rather than conceiving the construction of such ongoing regional centers as a bit of "fine-tuning," we think that their absence constitutes one of the principal failures of the present system. Indeed, if an effort at regional institution-building had been inaugurated 15 years ago with the enactment of the Clean Air and Water Acts, Professor Latin's assertions about the abysmal state of our ignorance would, by now, have less justification.

It is wrong, moreover, to assume that our failure to construct the requisite regional infrastructure is simply a result of tight EPA budgets. The agency, after all, has spent plenty of time and money engaging in factfinding inquiry regarding the state of the best available technology. The reason for the infrastructural failure is that ongoing careful region-by-region study is irrelevant to the regulatory effort as defined by the present BAT system. To change agency incentives, our reformed law would expressly contemplate a more sophisticated form of auction to commence at some future point in time, say 10 or 15 years after enactment. Under these second-generation actions, different regions of the country could be allowed to cut back permitted quantities by different amounts on the basis of a thoughtful cost-effectiveness analysis; similarly, each regional authority would be allowed to vary cutbacks within its region to account for special conditions. At no point, however, would we endorse unfettered technocratic cost-benefit analysis. Congress would continue to decide the overall magnitude of natural cleanup and to stipulate an allowable range of variation that could be justified through regional analysis and decision.

C. Priority-Setting

Our final set of proposals seeks to correct serious deficiencies in the process by which the current BAT system sets priorities in the light of changing information about environmental realities. BAT discourages intelligent priority-setting for two related reasons. First, the EPA is so overwhelmed by factfinding tasks required to implement a technology-based approach that it has relatively few resources left for exploration of risks posed by new pollutants. Second, BAT imposes heavy bureaucratic costs on the EPA every time it recognizes a new threat to the environment. Once a new pollutant has been identified, BAT requires the agency to exhaust itself with yet another series of never-ending inquiries into the state of control technology in each of the industries that have been discharging the "newly discovered" pollutant and to establish an elaborate set of new industry-by-industry standards. Finally, once a pollutant has been targeted for regulation, BAT automatically requires the imposition of controls to the full extent of available technology—a potentially enormous commitment of compliance resources that may not be justified by the benefits achieved and that is likely to be strongly opposed by industry through protracted litigation. It should be no surprise, then, that the EPA has, in fact, been reluctant to expand the number of its pollution targets.

The administrative inertia generated by BAT was, perhaps, of secondary concern so long as one could believe that environmental degradation was the product of a few widespread pollutants, each of which should be controlled to the greatest extent feasible within a period of years. After a decade's practical experience with environmental regulation, however, it should be clear that there are thousands of substances that pose at least some risk and that we cannot deal with all of them simultaneously or impose BAT on all of them within the near future. The defect of the BAT system is that it tends to select, more or less arbitrarily, a relatively few pollutants and devotes enormous administrative and control resources to regulating them to the hilt.

The reforms we have already advocated will create new incentives for the innovative priority-setting that is needed in today's world. First, a statute whose control variables were pollution-based, rather than technology-based, would encourage a more focused discussion of whether the goals set for different pollutants reflect sensible priorities. Indeed, it is not fanciful to suppose that a risk portfolio strategy eventually might emerge that would explicitly attempt to rank the comparative risks confronted by an EPA or an OSHA and then use cost-effectiveness analysis to determine how available administrative and control resources might best be devoted to minimizing overall risk in a given time period. Such a strategy need not be limited to conventional air and water pollutants. It could also be used, for example, to manage the risks posed by pesticides, chemicals, or hazardous wastes.

Second, the adoption of a marketable permit scheme would dramatically change bureaucratic incentives involved in a decision to target a new pollutant. Rather than ignoring new problems in an effort to avoid BAT burdens, the EPA may well gain additional bureaucratic resources by altering its regulatory priorities, since our proposed statutory reform would reward the agency with a share of any auction revenues that any newly regulated pollutant might generate. Indeed, given their budgetary rewards, a critic might fear that our proposals would generate an equal and opposite danger from the one prevailing under the current regime: Why wouldn't the EPA be transformed into a hyperactive agency, eager to maximize its budgetary revenues by expanding its concern to "pollutants" that do not in fact threaten any serious risk to ecological or human values?

While hyperactivity is a danger, its seriousness should not be exaggerated. After all, every large bureaucratic organization experiences a great deal of difficulty redefining its priorities. Given the reality of bureaucratic inertia, and the fact that industry will continue to resist new initiatives (particularly when it must pay for the right to pollute), we believe that it is wiser to offer budgetary rewards for innovative priority-setting rather than allow BAT to reinforce bureaucratic reluctance to take changing environmental realities into account.

Our proposed shift in bureaucratic incentives, however, does reinforce the need for a regulatory structure that endorses thoughtful cost-effectiveness analysis in the priority-setting process. Up to the present time, legislators have been able to indulge in apparently absolute statutory prohibitions of all harmful pollutants. This was possible because legislators could count on regulatory lethargy and covert consideration of costs by administrators in defining BAT to blunt statutory calls for an all-out war on pollution. Once a reformed statute has changed the balance of incentives for bureaucratic innovation, we should insist on thoughtful cost-effectiveness analysis before a new pollutant is made the subject of a marketable permit auction. The critical question, in each case, should be whether available administrative and compliance resources will achieve more reduction in environmental risks if they are used to control the new pollutant rather than being used to deal with other pollutants. (For these purposes, costs—like benefits—should not be measured in any mechanical way, and will inevitably involve major social judgments.) If so, the "new" pollutant should be regulated on the basis of the same pollution-based principles that we have elaborated previously; if not, it should not be regulated. Of course, even if an agency refused to list a new pollutant, Congress would be free to force the agency to change its mind the next time the governing statute is reappraised. Once again, cost-benefit analysis would be subordinated to democratic decision.

Finally, we do not believe that all steps toward more intelligent priority-setting should be delayed until the adoption of some of the more far-reaching reforms we have advanced. It should be emphasized that analysis of costs and benefits is not, as some environmentalists too easily suppose, a code word for regulatory passivity. A stunning counterexample is the EPA's recent decision substantially to eliminate lead additives in gasoline. The key to this decision was an economic analysis performed in the EPA's Office of Planning and Policy Evaluation showing that the move would achieve major health benefits at little or no net cost. Critics like Latin, moreover, underestimate the amount of information which does exist, but which is ignored by regulators who refuse to confront ecological and economic realities. The EPA, for example, routinely develops information relating each industry's costs of control to the amount of pollution or risk the industry's investment can be expected to eliminate. It simply fails to use this available information to make the allocation of burdens among industries more cost-effective or to target enforcement resources to the highest-priority problems. Recent changes in the EPA's approach—again, ignored by Latin—show that such steps are feasible. For example, the EPA recently decided not to regulate emissions of acrylonitrile and other toxic emissions under section 112 of the Clean Air Act when analysis suggested that the risks involved were relatively low compared to the more serious problems posed by chromium emissions—which it did decide to regulate. Such examples show that it is feasible to do a better job of goal-setting—by introducing cost-effectiveness considerations in evaluating control options for different risks and setting priorities more intelligently—even within the existing BAT system.

Steps such as these will not necessarily impose greater burdens on administrators than those that prevail under the BAT approach. Even when they do involve additional burdens for administrators, however, this fact alone should not condemn them. The question is whether increased administrative costs are outweighed by greater benefits for society as a whole. The EPA's development of the bubble and tradeoff policies required additional information-gathering, analysis, and other effort. But the payoff has been enormous. The bubble alone has saved over $700 million and stimulated new ways of cleaning up pollution. To focus on administrative costs, without considering the societal benefits of more intelligent regulation, produces penny-wise and pound-foolish public policies. Such myopia is understandable, if not excusable, in politicians. It should not be encouraged by academics who ignore solid evidence that reform can and has worked.

CONCLUSION

In urging the fundamental reform of environmental law, we do not mean to disparage the very great accomplishments of the generation that enacted sweeping federal legislation in the late 1960s and early 1970s. Apart from the many unambiguous achievements of this statutory revolution, even the embrace of a BAT approach made some sense as a crude first-generation strategy. During the early days of federal environmental concern, perhaps it was plausible for politicians and other policymakers to suppose that only a few pollution problems were out of hand and that these problems could be "solved" in a short time by an all out war against "pollution." From this perspective, it could seem reasonable to try to force everyone to adopt the best available technology everywhere.

Our complaint is not with the statutory draftsmen of the early 1970s, but with lawyers of the 1980s who fail to put these early statutes in historical perspective. Experience with more than a decade of intensive regulation emphasizes that the environmental risks we confront are numerous and vary widely in seriousness. Our strategies for managing these risks must set intelligent priorities, make maximum use of the resources devoted to improving environmental quality, encourage environmentally superior technologies, and avoid unneeded penalties on innovation and investment. Rather than wringing our hands helplessly before these complexities, the challenge is to incorporate maturing perceptions about our regulatory problems into the evolving legal structure—and help our fellow Americans build a system that will not only save many billions of dollars a year, but make environmental law more democratically accountable and bureaucratically effective. It is time for environmental lawyers to stop celebrating the statutory revolution of the 1970s and to start building a statutory structure worthy of the year 2000.

NOTES

1. One of Professors Ackerman and Stewart's criticisms of a "best available technology" (BAT) strategy for pollution control is that it "typically imposes far more stringent controls on new sources * * * [which] penalizes growth and international competitiveness." Is this problem peculiar to this *particular* BAT strategy as opposed to the use of BAT generally? How might an agency structure a BAT policy to encourage growth and competitiveness without risking the untimely demise of large, pre-existing facilities?

2. Ackerman and Stewart strongly advocate a tradeable permit system, whereby individual polluters could buy and sell pollution rights from among a limited number which might be made available by the regulatory agency. How should the initial allocation of such rights be made? What environmental problems might remain following the implementation of such a system? Consider, for example, what might happen if a single company were to purchase a substantial percentage of the pollution rights available for discharge into a discrete river segment or an air shed. How might the system be set up to avoid such problems? To what extent might toxic pollutants pose particular problems for market regulations? Consider that toxic pollutants can pose a substantial risk to public health and welfare even in extremely small concentrations.

3. How does enforcement change under a system of tradeable pollution rights? Consider, for example, a permittee under a traditional command-and-control approach who is violating BAT standards established by the permit. What is involved in taking successful enforcement action against such a permittee? Is there any significant difference in taking enforcement action against a permittee who lacks sufficient pollution rights to cover actual emissions? Have the incentives for compliance changed? Are Ackerman and Stewart justified in their claim that "compliance incentives [will change] dramatically" under a tradeable pollution rights system?

4. The "reformed system" proposed by Ackerman and Stewart has four components:
First, the agency must estimate how much pollution presently is permitted by law in each watershed and air quality region. Second, it must run a system of fair and efficient auctions in which polluters can regularly buy rights for limited terms. Third, it must run an efficient title registry in each region that will allow buyers and sellers to transfer rights in a legally effective way. Fourth, it must consistently penalize polluters who discharge more than their permitted amounts.

Suppose that the regulatory agency decides that the amount of pollution presently permitted is too much. How should the agency decide the level of pollution to allow? Does the process of making such a decision entail the same information obstacles that Ackerman and Stewart would like to avoid? How would an auction system be limited in circumstances where one or two large pollutants dominate the pollution load in a given airshed or watershed? Is the regulatory scheme offered by Ackerman and Stewart as simple and as effective as they suggest? If not, is it nonetheless a better prescription for regulation than that established under the traditional regime endorsed by Latin?

Four
The Environment as Property

This chapter views environmental issues through the lens of property. Property concepts have played an influential role in the philosophy, economic theory, and jurisprudence of environmental law. More practically, many of the media and resources that constitute the environment are capable of ownership and thus within reach of property law. Furthermore, environmental law imposes restrictions on environmentally sensitive uses of property.

Subchapter A describes how the commons concept characterizes many environmental problems. This perspective locates the root cause of environmental problems in the ownership characteristics of a commons. This commons subchapter draws on property law to describe the problems and suggest solutions to important issues in environmental management. Subchapter B focuses on a particular approach to environmental issues: creating private property rights in resources that can be traded in markets. This privatization subchapter considers the case for eliminating publicly owned or unowned parts of the environment. An important part of the privatization debate concerns the legitimacy of collective, public values as distinct from the aggregate of private preferences capable of expression through markets. Subchapter C samples the debate over the public trust concept, which has been influential in shaping the rights discourse for some resources, especially water. The public trust is an assertion of a communal interest in some aspects of property use that is otherwise privately controlled. Finally, subchapter D considers, from an environmental perspective, constitutional limits on governmental interference with private use of property. Takings law prescribes when (and how much) the government must compensate owners who suffer diminution in the value of their property.

Although this chapter divides into subject categories (the commons, privatization, public trust, and takings), all of the material focuses on the same fundamental question: where should we draw the boundary between public and private realms of decisionmaking with respect to the environment?

A. The Commons

The subchapter begins with an excerpt from Professor Hardin's classic article describing the tragedy of the commons in natural resources management. The tragedy of the commons has become a powerful fable in characterizing environmental problems. Hardin briefly surveys two choices for avoiding the tragedy in his article. Professor Ostrom is a political scientist who expands on the options available for people sharing common pool resources to avoid over-exploitation. Her empirical work considers informal as well as formal, legal rules for allocating scarce resources. Professor Rose looks behind property doctrines to explore assumptions about the role of the environment in law and society. She discusses how attitudes about property can be harnessed to protect environmental goods.

The following article, by the biologist Garrett Hardin, appeared in the journal SCIENCE in 1968, before environmental law emerged as a field of specialty. This short theoretical work has become one of the most cited articles in SCIENCE, provoking research and policy analysis in several disciplines that explore environmental issues. Although Hardin was primarily concerned with population, his description of the tragedy of the commons resonated with many scholars who were puzzling over environmental problems. Garrett Hardin continues to participate in debates over environmental management. *See* LIVING WITHIN LIMITS: ECOLOGY, ECONOMICS AND POPULATION TABOOS (1993); FILTERS AGAINST FOLLY: HOW TO SURVIVE DESPITE ECONOMISTS, ECOLOGISTS AND THE MERELY ELOQUENT (1986).

THE TRAGEDY OF THE COMMONS
Garrett Hardin
162 Science 1243 (1968)*

* * *

The tragedy of the commons develops in this way. Picture a pasture open to all. It is to be expected that each herdsman will try to keep as many cattle as possible on the commons. Such an arrangement may work reasonably satisfactorily for centuries because tribal wars, poaching, and disease keep the numbers of both man and beast well below the carrying capacity of the land. Finally, however, comes the day of reckoning, that is, the day when the long-desired goal of social stability becomes a reality. At this point, the inherent logic of the commons remorselessly generates tragedy.

As a rational being, each herdsman seeks to maximize his gain. Explicitly or implicitly, more or less consciously, he asks: "What is the utility *to me* of adding one more animal to my herd?" This utility has one negative and one positive component.

1) The positive component is a function of the increment of one animal. Since the

---

herdsman receives all the proceeds from the sale of the additional animal, the positive utility is nearly +1.

2) The negative component is a function of the additional overgrazing, created by one more animal. Since, however, the effects of overgrazing are shared by all the herdsmen, the negative utility for any particular decisionmaking herdsman is only a fraction of -1.

Adding together the component partial utilities, the rational herdsman concludes that the only sensible course for him to pursue is to add another animal to his herd. And another; and another . . . . But this is the conclusion reached by each and every rational herdsman sharing a commons. Therein is the tragedy. Each man is locked into a system that compels him to increase his herd without limit—in a world that is limited. Ruin is the destination toward which all men rush, each pursuing his own best interest in a society that believes in the freedom of the commons. Freedom in a commons brings ruin to all.

Some would say that this is a platitude. Would that it were! In a sense, it was learned thousands of years ago, but natural selection favors the forces of psychological denial. The individual benefits as an individual from his ability to deny the truth even though society as a whole, of which he is a part, suffers. Education can counteract the natural tendency to do the wrong thing, but the inexorable succession of generations requires that the basis for this knowledge be constantly refreshed.

* * *

POLLUTION

In a reverse way, the tragedy of the commons reappears in problems of pollution. Here it is not a question of taking something out of the commons, but of putting something in—sewage, or radioactive chemicals, and heat wastes into water; noxious and dangerous fumes into the air; and distracting and unpleasant advertising signs into the line of sight. The calculations of utility are much the same as before. The rational man finds that his share of the cost of the wastes he discharges into the commons is less than the cost of purifying his wastes before releasing them. Since this is true for everyone, we are locked into a system of "fouling our own nest," so long as we behave only as independent, rational, free-enterprisers.

The tragedy of the commons as a food basket is averted by private property, or something formally like it. But the air and waters surrounding us cannot readily be fenced, and so the tragedy of the commons as a cesspool must be prevented by different means, by coercive laws or taxing devices that make it cheaper for the polluter to treat his pollutants than to discharge them untreated. We have not progressed as far with the solution of this problem as we have with the first. Indeed, our particular concept of private property, which deters us from exhausting the positive resources of the earth, favors pollution. The owner of a factory on the bank of a stream—whose property extends to the middle of the stream—often has difficulty seeing why it is not his natural right to muddy the waters flowing past his door. The law, always behind the times, requires elaborate stitching and fitting to adapt it to this newly perceived aspect of the commons.

* * *

MUTUAL COERCION MUTUALLY AGREED UPON

The social arrangements that produce responsibility are arrangements that create coercion of some sort. Consider bank-robbing. The man who takes money from a bank acts as if the bank were a commons. How do we prevent such action? Certainly not by trying to control his behavior solely by a verbal appeal to his sense of responsibility. Rather than rely on propaganda we *** insist that a bank is not a commons; we seek the definite social arrangements that will keep it from becoming a commons. That we thereby infringe on the freedom of would-be robbers we neither deny nor regret.

The morality of bank-robbing is particularly easy to understand because we accept complete prohibition of this activity. We are willing to say "Thou shalt not rob banks," without providing for exceptions. But temperance also can be created by coercion. Taxing is a good coercive device. To keep downtown shoppers temperate in their use of parking space we introduce parking meters for short periods, and traffic fines for longer ones. We need not actually forbid a citizen to park as long as he wants to; we need merely make it increasingly expensive for him to do so. Not prohibition, but carefully biased options are what we offer him. A Madison Avenue man might call this persuasion; I prefer the greater candor of the word coercion.

Coercion is a dirty word to most liberals now, but it need not forever be so. As with the four-letter words, its dirtiness can be cleansed away by exposure to the light, by saying it over and over without apology or embarrassment. To many, the word coercion implies arbitrary decisions of distant and irresponsible bureaucrats; but this is not a necessary part of its meaning. The only kind of coercion I recommend is mutual coercion, mutually agreed upon by the majority of the people affected.

To say that we mutually agree to coercion is not to say that we are required to enjoy it, or even to pretend we enjoy it. Who enjoys taxes? We all grumble about them. But we accept compulsory taxes because we recognize that voluntary taxes would favor the conscienceless. We institute and (grumblingly) support taxes and other coercive devices to escape the horror of the commons.

An alternative to the commons need not be perfectly just to be preferable. With real estate and other material goods, the alternative we have chosen is the institution of private property coupled with legal inheritance. Is this system perfectly just? As a genetically trained biologist I deny that it is. It seems to me that, if there are to be differences in individual inheritance, legal possession should be perfectly correlated with biological inheritance—that those who are biologically more fit to be the custodians of property and power should legally inherit more. But genetic recombination continually makes a mockery of the doctrine of "like father, like son" implicit in our laws of legal inheritance. An idiot can inherit millions, and a trust fund can keep his estate intact. We must admit that our legal system of private property plus inheritance is unjust—but we put up with it because we are not convinced, at the moment, that anyone has invented a better system. The alternative of the commons is too horrifying to contemplate. Injustice is preferable to total ruin.

* * *

NOTES

1. Hardin's allegory has had a profound influence on environmental law. *See, e.g.,* *Hendler v. United States*, 952 F.2d 1364, 1375 (Fed. Cir. 1991); *NRDC v. Costle*, 568

F.2d 1369, 1378 (D.C. Cir. 1977); Jeffrey L. Dunoff, *Reconciling International Trade with Preservation of the Global Commons: Can we Prospect and Protect?*, 49 Wash. & Lee L. Rev. 1407 (1992); James E. Krier, *Tragedy of the Commons, Part Two*, 15 Harv. J.L. & Pub. Pol'y 334 (1992); Paula Smith, *Coercion and Groundwater Management: Three Case Studies and a "Market" Approach*, 16 Envtl. L. 797 (1986).

2. What conditions set the stage for the tragedy of the commons? Are most environmental resources "commons"? One necessary condition is a nonexclusive resource. Economists often distinguish between nonexclusive and nonrival goods. A nonexclusive good is one which everyone can use. A nonrival good is one for which no additional costs are imposed for increased use; one person's consumption of a nonrival good does not subtract from the resource base. Radio reception, for example, is both nonexclusive and nonrival. Hardin's commons are nonexclusive but rival. That is, there is no agreed upon or institutional mechanism for limiting use and, after a certain point, increased use imposes costs by degrading or depleting the common resource.

3. The tragedy of the commons as Hardin describes it assumes that those using the commons are primarily or exclusively motivated by self-interest. As rational actors, it makes logical sense to maximize one's own use of the commons. What other motivations or rationales might guide behavior to forestall the tragedy? Are there sources in religion, ethics, social norms, political cultures (*e.g.,* communitarian *vs.* individualistic societies) that can sustain a commons? Why or why not?

Environmental ethics has been promoted by many as the long term solution to such commons problems. *See, e.g.*, Lynton Keith Caldwell, *Land and the Law: Problems in Legal Philosophy*, 1986 U. Ill. L. Rev. 319 (1986); Eric T. Freyfogle, *The Land Ethic and Pilgrim Leopold*, 61 U. Colo. L. Rev. 217 (1990). Hardin, however, claims that appeals to conscience are doomed to failure. He sees the main problem as overpopulation and projects that those practicing altruistic behavior (which would mean voluntarily limiting one's family size) would literally be bred out of existence by those who continue to multiply. Do you agree? How might the law be used to resolve this dilemma? Chapter One of this anthology explores environmental ethics in detail.

4. In addition to characterizing environmental problems, Hardin also advocates the solution of mutual coercion, mutually agreed upon. Do most environmental laws fit Hardin's model solution? Hardin distinguishes between prohibition and coercion. Are polluters more like bank robbers or parking violators?

5. Hardin mentions only briefly the political basis for mutual coercion, relying on what is "mutually agreed upon by the majority of the people affected." He admits that such a system might not be "perfectly just," but prefers injustice to "total ruin." How are injustices minimized in a system of majoritarian rule? What kinds of assurances might you want to provide to minority interests in the use of the commons? Should individual rights trump a scheme of mutual/majoritarian/state coercion for protection of the commons? Which rights?

6. Another way out of the tragedy is what Hardin calls a technical solution. Approaches such as employing ever-improving abatement technology on point sources of pollution or developing substitutes (such as for ozone-depleting chemicals) are popular options. Reliance on scientific and technological innovation rather than change in the social order to deal with commons problems has been termed "technological optimism." James E. Krier and Clayton R. Gillette, *The Un-Easy Case for Technological Optimism*, 84 MICH. L. REV. 405, 407 (1985) (Technological optimism takes the position "that exponential technological growth will allow us to expand resources ahead of exponentially increasing demands." (*citing* WILLIAM OPHULS, ECOLOGY AND THE POLITICS OF SCARCITY 116 (1977))). Hardin himself rejects a technical solution to the commons problem. Krier and Gillette also find reliance on technological optimism misplaced to manage environmental problems:

> Technological optimism is an article of faith as well as a term of art. Simply put, the optimists believe in unending human ingenuity, or at least human ingenuity with no foreseeable limit. They must believe this, because human ingenuity is a necessary, though not a sufficient, condition of technological advance.

* * *

> It is easy enough to see why the debate between the optimists and the pessimists reached a dead end. Repeated assertions of unprovable propositions—that knowledge and its technological products will (will not) continue on their exponential way into the future—don't make for fruitful argument. More promising ground might be opened up by granting the optimists their major premise and assuming exponential technological growth. It hardly follows that the optimistic outlook is then justified. To the contrary, a heady rate of technological growth could aggravate some of the very problems the optimists count on technological advance to solve. Technology is, after all, a mixed blessing, demonstratively capable of producing undesirable as well as desirable consequences. While the optimists concede this point readily enough, they display remarkably little curiosity about what the mixed consequences of technological development are likely to be. Yet this is the obvious and crucially important question that arises from their concession. (It is also a question that becomes more critical the more technological advance entails risks with catastrophic potential.) And it is a question about which exponential technological growth says absolutely nothing.
> Other considerations might at least hint at an answer. There are reasons—having to do with individual incentives and with institutional structure—to suppose that the forces behind technological development are systematically biased in the direction of generating and neglecting certain kinds of undesirable consequences, pollution chief among them. In this light, exponential technological growth takes on an equivocal character. Problems as well as solutions can

accumulate rapidly, hardly what the technological optimists have in mind. Krier and Gillette at 409, 413, 426. The technological optimists are well represented in THE RESOURCEFUL EARTH: A RESPONSE TO GLOBAL 2000 (Julian L. Simon and Herman Kahn, eds., 1984). For an overview of this debate and additional perspectives, see ROBERT PAEHLKE, ENVIRONMENTALISM AND THE FUTURE OF PROGRESSIVE POLITICS (1989).

7. Many commentators propose to prevent a tragedy of the commons by changing the initial condition of nonexclusivity of the commons. This can be accomplished through state regulation (*e.g.* permitting). Or, it can be accomplished through "privatization"—vesting in a single owner a property right to exclude other users of the commons and letting markets manage the trading of rights. Privatization is a solution explored in some detail in subchapter B. The next excerpt discusses problems with both of these approaches.

The following excerpt from Elinor Ostrom's book, GOVERNING THE COMMONS, explores commons management from the point of view of a political scientist who has examined a large number of case studies involving allocation of scarce, non-exclusive resources. Her work is representative of the "new institutionalism" school, which seeks alternatives to exclusively state-centered or private market solutions to the commons problem. The emphasis is on self-generated rules of organization and property rights systems. Consider the role of law in her discussion.

GOVERNING THE COMMONS
Elinor Ostrom
(1990)*

* * *

A * * * view of the difficulty of getting individuals to pursue their joint welfare, as contrasted to individual welfare, was developed by Mancur Olson (1965) in *The Logic of Collective Action*. Olson specifically set out to challenge the grand optimism expressed in group theory; that individuals with common interests would voluntarily act so as to try to further those interests. On the first page of his book, Olson summarized that accepted view:

> The idea that groups tend to act in support of their group interests is supposed to follow logically from this widely accepted premise of rational, self-interested behavior. In other words, if the members of some group have a common interest or object, and if they would all be better off if that objective were achieved, it has been thought to follow logically that the individuals in that group would, if they were rational and self-interested, act to achieve that objective.[a]

---

* Reprinted with the permission of Cambridge University Press.
[a] Olson, M. 1965. THE LOGIC OF COLLECTIVE ACTION. PUBLIC GOODS AND THE THEORY OF GROUPS. Cambridge, Mass.: Harvard University Press. [at 1]

Olson challenged the presumption that the possibility of a benefit for a group would be sufficient to generate collective action to achieve that benefit. In the most frequently quoted passage of his book, Olson argued that

> unless the number of individuals is quite small, or unless there is coercion or some other special device to make individuals act in their common interest, *rational, self-interested individuals will not act to achieve their common or group interests.*[b]

Olson's argument rests largely on the premise that one who cannot be excluded from obtaining the benefits of a collective good once the good is produced has little incentive to contribute voluntarily to the provision of that good. His book is less pessimistic than it is asserted to be by many who cite this famous passage. Olson considers it an open question whether intermediate-size groups will or will not voluntarily provide collective benefits. His definition of an intermediate-size group depends not on the number of actors involved but on how noticeable each person's actions are.

The tragedy of the commons, the prisoner's dilemma, and the logic of collective action are closely related concepts in the models that have defined the accepted way of viewing many problems that individuals face when attempting to achieve collective benefits. At the heart of each of these models is the free-rider problem. Whenever one person cannot be excluded from the benefits that others provide, each person is motivated not to contribute to the joint effort, but to free-ride on the efforts of others. If all participants choose to free-ride, the collective benefit will not be produced. The temptation to free-ride, however, may dominate the decision process, and thus all will end up where no one wanted to be. Alternatively, some may provide while others free-ride, leading to less than the optimal level of provision of the collective benefit. These models are thus extremely useful for explaining how perfectly rational individuals can produce, under some circumstances, outcomes that are not "rational" when viewed from the perspective of all those involved.

What makes these models so interesting and so powerful is that they capture important aspects of many different problems that occur in diverse settings in all parts of the world. What makes these models so dangerous—when they are used metaphorically as the foundation for policy—is that the constraints that are assumed to be fixed for the purpose of analysis are taken on faith as being fixed in empirical settings, unless external authorities change them. The prisoners in the famous dilemma cannot change the constraints imposed on them by the district attorney; they are in jail. Not all users of natural resources are similarly incapable of changing their constraints. As long as individuals are viewed as prisoners, policy prescriptions will address this metaphor. I would rather address the question of how to enhance the capabilities of those involved to change the constraining rules of the game to lead to outcomes other than remorseless tragedies.

* * *

CURRENT POLICY PRESCRIPTIONS

Leviathan as the "Only" Way

Ophuls argued, for example, that "because of the tragedy of the commons, environmental problems cannot be solved through cooperation . . . and the rationale for government with

---

[b] *Id.* [at 2]

major coercive powers is overwhelming."[c] Ophuls concluded that "even if we avoid the tragedy of the commons, it will *only* be by recourse to the tragic necessity of Leviathan."[d] Garrett Hardin argued a decade after his earlier article that we are enveloped in a "cloud of ignorance" about "the true nature of the fundamental political systems and the effect of each on the preservation of the environment."[e] The "cloud of ignorance" did not, however, prevent him from presuming that the only alternatives to the commons dilemma were what he called "a private enterprise system," on the one hand, or "socialism" on the other.[f] With the assurance of one convinced that "the alternative of the commons is too horrifying to contemplate,"[g] Hardin indicated that change would have to be instituted with "whatever force may be required to make the change stick."[h] In other words, "if ruin is to be avoided in a crowded world, people must be responsive to a coercive force outside their individual psyches, a 'Leviathan,' to use Hobbes's term."[i]

The presumption that an external Leviathan is necessary to avoid tragedies of the commons leads to recommendations that central governments control most natural resource systems. Heilbroner (1974)[j] opined that "iron governments," perhaps military governments, would be necessary to achieve control over ecological problems. In a less draconian view, Ehrenfeld (1972, p. 322)[k] suggested that if "private interests cannot be expected to protect the public domain then external regulation by public agencies, governments, or international authorities is needed." In an analysis of the problems involved in water resource management in developing countries, Carruthers and Stoner (1981, p. 29)[l] argued that without public control, "overgrazing and soil erosion of communal pastures, or less fish at higher average cost," would result. They concluded that "common property resources *require* public control if economic efficiency is to result from their development" (1981, p. 29; emphasis added).[m] The policy advice to centralize the control and regulation of natural resources, such as grazing lands, forests, and fisheries, has been followed extensively, particularly in Third World countries.

* * *

Privatization as the "Only" Way

Other policy analysts, influenced by the same models, have used equally strong terms in calling for the imposition of private property rights whenever resources are owned in common. "Both the economic analysis of common property resources and Hardin's treat-

---

[c] Ophuls, W. 1973. Leviathan or Oblivion. In *Toward a Steady State Economy*, ed. H.E. Daly, pp. 215-30. San Francisco, Freeman.

[d] *Id.* at 228.

[e] Hardin, G. 1978. Political Requirements for Preserving our Common Heritage. *In Wildlife and America*, ed. H.P. Bokaw, p. 310. Washington, D.C.: Council on Environmental Quality.

[f] *Id.* at 314.

[g] G. Hardin, The Tragedy of the Commons, 162 *Science* 1243, 1247.

[h] Hardin (1978) at 314.

[i] *Id.*

[j] Heilbronor, R.L. 1974. *An Inquiry Into the Human Prospect*. New York: Norton.

[k] Ehrenfield, D.W. 1972. *Conserving Life on Earth*. Oxford University Press.

[l] Carruthers, I., and R. Stoner. 1981. Economic Aspects and Policy Issues in Groundwater Development. World Bank staff working paper No. 496, Washington, D.C.

[m] *Id.*

ment of the tragedy of the commons" led Robert J. Smith (1981, p. 467)[n] to suggest that "the *only* way to avoid the tragedy of the commons in natural resources and wildlife is to end the common-property system by creating a system of private property rights" (emphasis added). Smith stressed that it is "by treating a resource as a common property that we become locked in its inexorable destruction" (1981, p. 465).[o] Welch advocated the creation of full private rights to a commons when he asserted that "the establishment of full property rights is necessary to avoid the inefficiency of overgrazing" (1983, p. 171).[p] He asserted that privatization of the commons was the optimal solution for all common-pool problems. His major concern was how to impose private ownership when those currently using a commons were unwilling to change to a set of private rights to the commons.

Those recommending the imposition of privatization on the herders would divide the meadow in half and assign half of the meadow to one herder and the other half to the second herder. Now each herder will be playing a *game against nature* in a smaller terrain, rather than a game against another player in a larger terrain. The herders now will need to invest in fences and their maintenance, as well as in monitoring and sanctioning activities to enforce their division of the grazing area. * * *

* * *

It is difficult to know exactly what analysts mean when they refer to the necessity of developing private rights to some common-pool resources (CPRs). It is clear that when they refer to land, they mean to divide the land into separate parcels and assign individual rights to hold, use, and transfer these parcels as individual owners desire (subject to the general regulations of a jurisdiction regarding the use and transfer of land). In regard to nonstationary resources, such as water and fisheries, it is unclear what the establishment of private rights means. As Colin Clark has pointed out, the "'tragedy of the commons' has proved particularly difficult to counteract in the case of marine fishery resources where the establishment of individual property rights is virtually out of the question" (1980, p. 117).[q] In regard to a fugitive resource, a diversity of rights may be established giving individuals rights to use particular types of equipment, to use the resource system at a particular time and place, or to withdraw a particular quantity of resource units (if they can be found). But even when particular rights are unitized, quantified, and salable, the resource *system* is still likely to be owned in common rather than individually. Again, referring to fisheries Clark has argued that "common ownership is the fundamental fact affecting almost every regime of fishery management" (1980, p. 117).[r]

---

[n] Smith, R.J. 1981. Resolving the Tragedy of the Commons by Creating Private Property Rights in Wildlife. *CATO Journal* 1:439-68.

[o] *Id.* at 465.

[p] Welch, W.P. 1983. The Political Feasibility of Full Ownership Property Rights: The Cases of Pollution and Fisheries. *Policy Sciences* 16:165-80.

[q] Clark, C.W. 1980. Restricted Access to Common-Property Fishery Resources: A Game-Theoretic Analysis. In *Dynamic Optimization and Mathematical Economics*, ed. P.T. Liu, pp. 117-32. New York: Plenum Press.

[r] *Id.*

The "Only" Way?

Analysts who find an empirical situation with a structure presumed to be a commons dilemma often call for the imposition of a solution by an external actor: The "only way" to solve a commons dilemma is by doing X. Underlying such a claim is the belief that X is necessary and sufficient to solve the commons dilemma. But the content of X could hardly be more variable. One set of advocates presumes that a central authority must assume continuing responsibility to make unitary decisions for a particular resource. The other presumes that a central authority should parcel out ownership rights to the resource and then allow individuals to pursue their own self-interests within a set of well-defined property rights. Both centralization advocates and privatization advocates accept as a central tenet that institutional change must come from outside and be imposed on the individuals affected. Despite sharing a faith in the necessity and efficacy of "the state" to change institutions so as to increase efficiency, the institutional changes they recommend could hardly be further apart.

If one recommendation is correct, the other cannot be. Contradictory positions cannot both be right. I do not argue for either of these positions. Rather, I argue that both are too sweeping in their claims. Instead of there being a single solution to a single problem, I argue that many solutions exist to cope with many different problems. Instead of presuming that optimal institutional solutions can be designed easily and imposed at low cost by external authorities, I argue that "getting the institutions right" is a difficult, time-consuming, conflict-invoking process. It is a process that requires reliable information about time and place variables as well as a broad repertoire of culturally acceptable rules. New institutional arrangements do not work in the field as they do in abstract models unless the models are well specified and empirically valid and the participants in a field setting understand how to make the new rules work.

Instead of presuming that the individuals sharing a commons are inevitably caught in a trap from which they cannot escape, I argue that the capacity of individuals to extricate themselves from various types of dilemma situations *varies* from situation to situation. The cases to be discussed in this book illustrate both successful and unsuccessful efforts to escape tragic outcomes. Instead of basing policy on the presumption that the individuals involved are helpless, I wish to learn more from the experience of individuals in field settings. Why have some efforts to solve commons problems failed, while others have succeeded? What can we learn from experience that will help stimulate the development and use of a better theory of collective action—one that will identify the key variables that can enhance or detract from the capabilities of individuals to solve problems?

Institutions are rarely either private or public—"the market" or "the state." Many successful CPR institutions are rich mixtures of "private-like" and "public-like" institutions defying classification in a sterile dichotomy. By "successful," I mean institutions that enable individuals to achieve productive outcomes in situations where temptations to free-ride and shirk are ever present. A competitive market—the epitome of private institutions—is itself a public good. Once a competitive market is provided individuals can enter and exit freely whether or not they contribute to the cost of providing and maintaining the market. No market can exist for long without underlying public institutions to support it. In field settings, public and private institutions frequently are intermeshed and depend on one another, rather than existing in isolated worlds.

* * *

An Empirical Alternative

* * * Let us now briefly consider a solution devised by participants in a field setting—Alanya, Turkey—that cannot be characterized as either central regulation or privatization. The inshore fishery at Alanya, as described by Fikret Berkes (1968b),[s] is a relatively small operation. Many of the approximately 100 local fishers operate in two- or three-person boats using various types of nets. Half of the fishers belong to a local producers' cooperative. According to Berkes, the early 1970s were the "dark ages" for Alanya. The economic viability of the fishery was threatened by two factors: First, unrestrained use of the fishery had led to hostility and, at times, violent conflict among the users. Second, competition among fishers for the better fishing spots had increased production costs, as well as the level of uncertainty regarding the harvest potential of any particular boat.

Early in the 1970s, members of the local cooperative began experimenting with an ingenious system for allotting fishing sites to local fishers. After more than a decade of trial-and-error efforts, the rules used by the Alanya inshore fishers are as follows:

- Each September, a list of eligible fishers is prepared, consisting of all licensed fishers in Alanya, regardless of co-op membership.
- Within the area normally used by Alanya fishers, all usable fishing locations are named and listed. These sites are spaced so that the nets set in one site will not block the fish that should be available at the adjacent sites.
- These named fishing locations and their assignments are in effect from September to May.
- In September, the eligible fishers draw lots and are assigned to the named fishing locations.
- From September to January, each day each fisher moves east to the next location. After January, the fishers move west. This gives the fishers equal opportunities at the stocks that migrate from east to west between September and January and reverse their migration through the area from January to May.

The system has the effect of spacing the fishers far enough apart on the fishing grounds that the production capabilities at each site are optimized. All fishing boats also have equal chances to fish at the best spots. Resources are not wasted searching for or fighting over a site. No signs of overcapitalization are apparent.

The list of fishing locations is endorsed by each fisher and deposited with the mayor and local gendarme once a year at the time of the lottery. The process of monitoring and enforcing the system is, however, accomplished by the fishers themselves as a by-product of the incentive created by the rotation system. On a day when a given fisher is assigned one of the more productive spots, that fisher will exercise that option with certainty (leaving aside last-minute breakdowns in equipment). All other fishers can expect that the assigned fisher will be at the spot bright and early. Consequently, an effort to cheat on the system by traveling to a good spot on a day when one is assigned to a poor spot

---

[s] Berkes, F. 1986b. Marine Inshore Fishery Management in Turkey. In *Proceedings of the Conference on Common Property Resource Management,* National Research Council, pp. 63-83. Washington, D.C.: National Academy Press.

has little chance of remaining undetected. Cheating on the system will be observed by the very fishers who have rights to be in the best spots and will be willing to defend their rights using physical means if necessary. Their rights will be supported by everyone else in the system. The others will want to ensure that their own rights will not be usurped on the days when they are assigned good sites. The few infractions that have occurred have been handled easily by the fishers at the local coffeehouse.

Although this is not a private-property system, rights to use fishing sites and duties to respect these rights are well defined. And though it is not a centralized system, national legislation that has given such cooperatives jurisdiction over "local arrangements" has been used by cooperative officials to legitimize their role in helping to devise a workable set of rules. That local officials accept the signed agreement each year also enhances legitimacy. The actual monitoring and enforcing of the rules, however, are left to the fishers.

* * *

The case of the Alanya inshore fishery is only one empirical example of the many institutional arrangements that have been devised, modified, monitored, and sustained by the users of renewable CPRs to constrain individual behavior that would, if unconstrained, reduce joint returns to the community of users. * * *

* * * [S]uccessfully governed CPRs provide theoretical and empirical alternatives to the assertion that those involved cannot extricate themselves from the problems faced when multiple individuals use a given resource. The key to my argument is that some individuals have broken out of the trap inherent in the commons dilemma, whereas others continue remorsefully trapped into destroying their own resources. This leads me to ask what differences exist between those who have broken the shackles of a commons dilemma and those who have not. The differences may have to do with factors *internal* to a given group. The participants may simply have no capacity to communicate with one another, no way to develop trust, and no sense that they must share a common future. Alternatively, powerful individuals who stand to gain from the current situation, while others lose, may block efforts by the less powerful to change the rules of the game. Such groups may need some form of external assistance to break out of the perverse logic of their situation.

The differences between those who have and those who have not extricated themselves from commons dilemmas may also have to do with factors *outside* the domain of those affected. Some participants do not have the autonomy to change their own institutional structures and are prevented from making constructive changes by external authorities who are indifferent to the perversities of the commons dilemma, or may even stand to gain from it. Also, there is the possibility that external changes may sweep rapidly over a group, giving them insufficient time to adjust their internal structures to avoid the suboptimal outcomes. Some groups suffer from perverse incentive systems that are themselves the results of policies pursued by central authorities. Many potential answers spring to mind regarding the question why some individuals do not achieve collective benefits for themselves, whereas others do. However, as long as analysts presume that individuals cannot change such situations themselves, they do not ask what internal or external variables can enhance or impede the efforts of communities of individuals to deal creatively and constructively with perverse problems such as the tragedy of the commons.

Policy Prescriptions as Metaphors

Policy analysts who would recommend a single prescription for commons problems have paid little attention to how diverse institutional arrangements operate in practice. The centrists presume that unified authorities will operate in the field as they have been designed to do in the textbooks—determining the best policies to be adopted for a resource based on valid scientific theories and adequate information. Implementation of these policies without error is assumed. Monitoring and sanctioning activities are viewed as routine and nonproblematic.

Those advocating the private-property approach presume that the most efficient use patterns for CPRs will actually result from dividing the rights to access and control such resources. Systematic empirical studies have shown that private organization of firms dealing in goods such as electricity, transport, and medical services tends to be more efficient than governmental organization of such firms. Whether private or public forms are more efficient in industries in which certain potential beneficiaries cannot be excluded is, however, a different question. We are concerned with the types of institutions that will be most efficient for governing and managing diverse CPRs for which at least some potential beneficiaries cannot be excluded. Privatizing the ownership of CPRs need not have the same positive results as privatizing the ownership of an airline. Further, privatizing may not mean "dividing up" at all. Privatization can also mean assigning the exclusive right to harvest from a resource system to a single individual or firm.

Many policy prescriptions are themselves no more than metaphors. Both the centralizers and the privatizers frequently advocate oversimplified, idealized institutions—paradoxically, almost "institution-free" institutions. An assertion that central regulation is necessary tells us nothing about the way a central agency should be constituted, what authority it should have, how the limits on its authority should be maintained, how it will obtain information, or how its agents should be selected, motivated to do their work, and have their performances monitored and rewarded or sanctioned. An assertion that the imposition of private property rights is necessary tells us nothing about how that bundle of rights is to be defined, how the various attributes of the goods involved will be measured, who will pay for the costs of excluding nonowners from access, how conflicts over rights will be adjudicated, or how the residual interests of the right-holders in the resource system itself will be organized.

An important lesson that one learns by carefully studying the growing number of systematic studies by scholars associated with "the new institutionalism" is that these "institutional details" are important. Whether or not any equilibria are possible and whether or not an equilibrium would be an improvement for the individuals involved (or for others who are in turn affected by these individuals) will depend on the particular structures of the institutions. In the most general sense, all institutional arrangements can be thought of as games in extensive form. As such, the particular options available, the sequencing of those options, the information provided, and the relative rewards and punishments assigned to different sequences of moves can all change the pattern of outcomes achieved. Further, the particular structure of the physical environment involved also will have a major impact on the structure of the game and its results. Thus, a set of rules used in one physical environment may have vastly different consequences if used in a different physical environment.

Policies Based on Metaphors Can Be Harmful

Relying on metaphors as the foundation for policy advice can lead to results substantially different from those presumed to be likely. Nationalizing the ownership of forests in Third World countries, for example, has been advocated on the grounds that local villagers cannot manage forests so as to sustain their productivity and their value in reducing soil erosion. In countries where small villages had owned and regulated their local communal forests for generations, nationalization meant expropriation. In such localities, villagers had earlier exercised considerable restraint over the rate and manner of harvesting forest products. In some of these countries, national agencies issued elaborate regulations concerning the use of forests, but were unable to employ sufficient numbers of foresters to enforce those regulations. The foresters who were employed were paid such low salaries that accepting bribes became a common means of supplementing their income. The consequence was that nationalization created *open-access resources* where limited-access *common-property resources* had previously existed. The disastrous effects of nationalizing formerly communal forests have been well documented for Thailand, Niger, Nepal, and India. Similar problems occurred in regard to inshore fisheries when national agencies presumed that they had exclusive jurisdiction over all coastal waters.

A CHALLENGE

An important challenge facing policy scientists is to develop theories of human organization based on realistic assessment of human capabilities and limitations in dealing with a variety of situations that initially share some or all aspects of a tragedy of the commons. * * *

* * *

What is missing from the policy analyst's tool kit—and from the set of accepted, well-developed theories of human organization—is an adequately specified theory of collective action whereby a group of principals can organize themselves voluntarily to retain the residuals of their own efforts. Examples of self-organized enterprises abound. Most law firms are obvious examples: A group of lawyers will pool their assets to purchase a library and pay for joint secretarial and research assistance. They will develop their own internal governance mechanisms and formulas for allocating costs and benefits to the partners. Most cooperatives are also examples. * * * But until a theoretical explanation—based on human choice—for self-organized and self-governed enterprises is fully developed and accepted, major policy decisions will continue to be undertaken with a presumption that individuals cannot organize themselves and always need to be organized by external authorities.

Further, all organizational arrangements are subject to stress, weakness, and failure. Without an adequate theory of self-organized collective action, one cannot predict or explain when individuals will be unable to solve a common problem through self-organization alone, nor can one begin to ascertain which of many intervention strategies might be effective in helping to solve particular problems. * * * [T]here is a considerable difference between the presumption that a regulatory agency should be established and the presumption that a reliable court system is needed to monitor and enforce self-negotiated contracts. If the theories being used in a policy science do not include the possibility of self-organized collective action, then the importance of a court system that can be used by self-organizing groups to monitor and enforce contracts will not be recognized.

* * *

NOTES

1. Ostrom argues that empirical studies show that a group of people sharing a common resource can self-organize to avoid tragic outcomes. Is this evidence necessarily inconsistent with Hardin or Olson (cited in the beginning of the Ostrom excerpt)? Specifically, what does Ostrom claim to be the flaw in Hardin's and Olson's theory?

2. From what Ostrom tells us about Mancur Olson's view of collective action problems, Olson appears to see scale as a critical factor in the ability of groups to handle the free-rider problem and manage sustainable commons. Short of external coercion, the collective pursuit of joint welfare will be successful only in small communities or intermediate-sized groups where people's actions (particularly their shirking or free-riding on the common resource) will be noticed by others. What is it about the size of a group or the noticeability of individual action that changes the odds in favor of self-management? Some environmentalists advocate decentralization along bioregional lines; *see, e.g.,* KIRKPATRICK SALE, DWELLERS IN THE LAND (1985). Could the environment be regulated on a small enough scale to benefit from collective self-management?

3. Could the self-initiated model of fisheries management illustrated in the Alanya, Turkey example apply to larger, trans-boundary resources such as the Pacific salmon fishery or the global ozone layer? In the Alanya fishery, all of the parties concerned were interested in having the environment produce the same good: fish. How would "users" organize to manage a resource for multiple objectives, such as the Ohio River, which is used for drinking water, recreation, navigation, waste assimilation, and the maintenance of aquatic ecosystems?

In this excerpt, Ostrom mentions some of the internal and external factors that seem to be critical for successful management of common-pool resources. In her book she reviews several cases around the globe and compares those that appear to have worked over long periods of time with those that have failed. What internal group factors might be necessary for successful management? What external factors might play a key role?

4. Would you foresee any problems with the contract theory of enforcement of self-organized agreements that Ostrom mentions at the end of her excerpt? Ostrom appears to favor the use of central government primarily through its courts as enforcers of self-negotiated contracts. She prefers self-regulation schemes to those established by an external regulatory authority. How does her approach differ from current U.S. environmental law? How is it similar?

5. In a subsequent article, Ostrom observes that "common-pool resource" is a broad category that encompasses many different situations, including property owned by the state, property owned by no one, and property owned and defended by a community of resource users. Edella Schlager and Elinor Ostrom, *Property-Rights Regimes and Natural Resources: A Conceptual Analysis*, 68 LAND ECON. 249 (1992). She distinguishes commons on the basis of a variety of rights stakeholders may have, including access, management, exclusion, and alienation. Why might these attributes that distinguish among commons be important in addressing environmental concerns? Consider, for example, public lands which are accessible to persons who wish to graze cattle, extract minerals, enjoy recreational resources, and obtain rights-of-way across the land for electrical transmission or water conveyance. How will this multiplicity of purposes complicate management of this common-pool resource? What problems might arise if a private property solution were imposed on the prospective users of these lands?

Robert C. Ellickson, in *Property in Land*, 102 YALE L.J. 1315 (1993), also breaks down the common ownership concept into component attributes and illustrates his ideas with a number of case illustrations, including American pioneer settlements, Israeli *kibbutzim*, and Mexican *ejidos*. He uses the cases to show "the major advantages in private ownership of land, but * * * [also the] desirable attributes of group-owned property that may be decisive in some contexts." *Id.* at 1321.

6. Professor Ostrom's most recent book is RULES, GAMES AND COMMON POOL RESOURCES (1994).

The following excerpt provides yet another perspective on solutions to the commons problem. Professor Rose, a law professor who has written extensively on environmental and property issues, suggests an environmental ethic based on a broader understanding of property concepts.

GIVEN-NESS AND GIFT: PROPERTY AND THE QUEST FOR ENVIRONMENTAL ETHICS
Carol M. Rose
24 Envtl. L. 1 (1994)*

* * *

This article is about some important ways in which property relates to the environment.

---

* Reprinted with permission.

The most obvious and noticeable point is that in many ways, the relationship between property and the environment is one of opposites. Property is about things that are under our control; in fact, having control of something is a way to prove that you own it. Even our ordinary adages make this point: everyone knows the saying, "possession is nine-tenths of the law," meaning that if you control something, the law is very likely to say that you own it.

On the other hand, the word "environment" in ordinary language often designates something that is not under anyone's control at all, something that is a given, or as we often say, "just a given." We talk, for example, about a business environment or a cultural environment: a set of amorphous surroundings that are just "out there," and that we cannot do very much about.

When we talk about "the environment" without any modifiers, we are usually talking about aspects of our physical surroundings, such as air and water. But these physical surroundings, too, are almost by definition "out of control," and hence outside the comfortable range of property. The elements of the unmodified environment are wild things, and the wilderness habitat of wild things, and include the figuratively "wild" resources like underground fluids that our law calls *ferae naturae*, by analogy to untamed animals on the loose.

Historically, we have had quite mixed emotions about this quality of uncontrolled "given-ness". There are many stories and myths about wilderness, for example, and quite a number of these fall into one of two quite striking categories of horror stories. Both categories revolve about the unowned, property-less character of the wild, and about what happens when wild things are transformed into property. One type of horror story is exemplified by some comments that Jeremy Bentham made in a very forceful argument that prosperity depends on security of property. For Bentham, the North American wilderness presented a decidedly bleak picture. "The interior of that immense region," he wrote, "offers only a frightful solitude, impenetrable forests or sterile plains, stagnant waters and impure vapours; such is the earth when left to itself."[3] He commented on the "fierce tribes" that wandered about in the forests and plains, animated chiefly by the "implacable rivalries" that led them to make constant war on each other: "The beasts of the forests are not so dangerous to man as he is to himself."[4] But Bentham thought that the lands of the settlers, with their secure property, offered a particularly instructive comparison. The settlers had reduced the dangerous and gloomy wildness to property. They enjoyed smiling fields, well-built and populous towns, bustling harbors, and in general presented a picture of "peace and abundance."[5]

Bentham's horror story is thus one in which wilderness is a dark and frightening chaos that becomes sunny and happy only as it vanishes, ceding to property. But there is a counter-horror story too, comprised of many of the narratives we know about the transformation of the wilderness to property. These are stories that begin in innocence and splendor, a pure state that is then subjected to a storm of rampage and heedlessness. Perhaps the most

---

[3] [*Jeremy Bentham, Analysis of the Evils which result from Attacks upon Property, in* THE THEORY OF LEGISLATION (Oceana ed. 1975)] at 72.
[4] *Id.*
[5] *Id.*

dazzling epiphany of this sort of narrative involved a particularly eerie moment on the Great Plains in the fall of 1883. It was the outset of a buffalo hunting season that, it was thought, would repeat the fabled slaughters of the decade before. But the buffalo hunters, fully outfitted and ready for another riotous orgy of killing, stepped off the train to find only the silence of an empty plain.

We all know both these types of stories at some level and in some version. These archetypical narratives exemplify two different views of wilderness, and indeed two different views of the uncontrolled environment in general. The first story, the one that Bentham told, is a vision of the given-ness of nature, and it tells us how deeply problematic that given-ness is. Bentham's story points to the malevolence of those things that are out of control—they are miasmic, shadowy, and filled with sudden violence. This story has a moral too, as many stories do: it tells us that the "given" environment should be reduced to tame and placid property as rapidly as possible.

The second archetypical horror story rests on a vision of the environment that is not just a given, but a gift. Stories of this type are tales of bitter malevolence too, but here the malevolence is the human interaction with the great gifts of nature. It is an interaction that despoils and ravages, that treats with contempt and callousness the things that should be revered, at least in part because they are somehow gifts.

II. ENVIRONMENT AND THE ECONOMICS OF THE COMMONS

* * *

* * * The normal way to establish property rights in completely unowned things, like seashells or abandoned umbrellas, is simply to take them, and to act as if they are subject to one's control. A much-used example of the creation of property is the taking of wild animals: the animal is made into property by "reducing it to dominion," under what is called the Rule of Capture.

But with environmental resources, these normal ways of establishing property rights do not work very well. In fact, they lead to a great deal of destruction, because the goods that we consider environmental usually belong to a kind of natural commons. Environmental resources are difficult to compartmentalize into individual chunks that can be taken without affecting other chunks. In using up air, for example, a factory can scarcely confine the smoke it gives off to a manageable little cube of space; instead, the factory's smoke may get into the air hundreds of miles away. Even when these resources look as if they can be taken in individual chunks, they may actually be part of some larger-scale renewable stocks, and the continued existence and value of these stocks entails leaving behind (or artificially replenishing) an unused reservoir from which the resource can regenerate. Thus, for example, individual fish may be taken from a fish stock, or individual animals may be taken from a wildlife stock. But in either case, enough must be left behind to repopulate the larger wild stock; otherwise the population will eventually decline or even crash, and future fishers and hunters may not get any at all. Similarly, but in a more complicated fashion, the multitudinous plants of the Amazon rain forest appear to nourish one another in a complex energy and water exchange that is disrupted by massive burn offs or cuttings, whose impact cannot be easily isolated.

It is for these reasons that our usual property-defining act, the unregulated rule of capture, turns into a horror story for these great natural commons. These great commons need to be managed as wholes. But because they are so large, no one in particular can acquire them as wholes, and so sometimes no one manages them or reinvests in them at all. Instead, everyone just uses them or takes from them at will. Their great vast wildness seems infinitely exploitable, and puts no bounds on human acquisitiveness. And so sometimes human acquisitiveness itself goes wild: each human actor, fearing to be last in the race to capture the vast wild things, vies with all the others to take while the taking is free.

Through a series of small decisions, the larger environmental resource is wasted, even though it might be in the collective best interest to preserve it. Air gets polluted, fisheries get fished out, forests get felled, bird populations get depleted, and aquifers get pumped dry. In general, people seem to vie to get the most for themselves, while investing the least. All too often, people leave behind a wasteland, where the resources are exhausted to a point that they cannot renew themselves.

From the perspective of any individual, of course, it is entirely sensible to use as much as possible for one's self from common resources: if any one person invests in replenishment, or refrains from polluting, everyone else can take advantage of him or her. Nice guys finish last in this logic; what they replenish or leave in place is simply snatched up by someone else. And so it does not make a lot of sense to be nice in the first place. The well-known name for this process, in which everyone takes and no one gives, is the "tragedy of the commons."[17] The logic of the "tragedy" is to give everyone what the economists call a "high discount rate," in which the prospect of current income outweighs considerations of future well-being. Resources that could be profitably renewed are instead exploited to the hilt now, and thus they are transformed into wasting assets. What is perhaps most tragic of all is that even well-intentioned people—people who know better and would like to do better—can hardly avoid the ruthlessly destructive logic of self interest.

III. SELF-INTEREST, POLITICS, NORMATIVITY: FROM GIVEN-NESS TO GIFT

We know in a general way what needs to be done about environmental resources that we want to use but also want to preserve: we need to devise some way whereby people can take some of the resource, but also leave some behind or contribute to restoration, confident that what is left will not be snatched by others but will instead be used as a replenishment stock. But how can we arrange this? Bentham's successors have noticed the problem, but can they tell us how we might prevent the well-known tragedy? Can they tell us how to preserve these resources, like the oceans or the air or the habitats and stocks of wild things, that we cannot easily turn into private property?

Well, yes and no. One standard answer is to turn the great commons into a kind of great big property, usually owned by a government. When governments become the unified owners of these great resources, they will supposedly maximize the value of the commons

---

[17] The name comes from Garrett Hardin, *The Tragedy of the Commons,* 162 SCIENCE 1243 (1968); the original modern analysis of this problem was Scott Gordon's article on fishing, [*The Economic Theory of a Common-Property Resource: The Fishery,* 62 J. POL. ECON. 124 (1954)].

by restraining individual use to amounts whereby the resources can restore themselves at their value-maximizing levels.

Unfortunately, this is not a smooth or costless enterprise. A variety of regulatory strategies exist to restrain individual use, but these strategies are costly to institute and police—and ever more costly as we need to exercise more and more control to preserve environmental resources like clean air or water or currently undeveloped land. In addition, environmental controls may involve highly technical decisions that are beyond most people's grasp. We may have to hire expensive experts to make these decisions for us, and we do not really know which experts to believe, if any. Then too, if environmental controls succeed in restraining individual use, they will make environmental goods harder to obtain, and this is bound to be reflected in the higher prices of any products that contain them. The increased prices of, for example, porpoise-protective tuna fish or environmentally safe paper products may create strong incentives to cheat, both on the part of producers of fish products and paper and on the part of those who buy these products. The problem of policing cheaters then adds even more to the cost of environmental controls. Many people may not care enough to pay the price, here and now, for environmental protection that is only noticeable later and maybe someplace else, even though the wider and longer-term costs of degradation may be much higher.

Finally, even if many people are indeed willing to pay the price, regulation itself does not always run easily toward desired ends. Regulatory agencies themselves sometimes become the battlefields where the resource users vie to establish their dominance; in effect, the commons problem in resource use turns into a commons problem in access to the regulatory agencies. The tendency of democratic regulatory institutions may be that intensely interested groups dominate the regulatory commons, a tendency that is not likely to benefit the diffuse interests of environmental protection.

For these reasons, it may be thought that a democracy left to itself is incapable of the self-regulation that environmental well-being requires. * * *

All this presents a quite unattractive set of options. In effect, because of the great difficulty of managing the large and diffuse commons of the environment, we could be left with a choice between environmental well-being and democracy. If we are to have environmental good things and democracy at the same time, we need to exercise some self-restraint. This point, incidentally, would have been no great secret to the founders of the republic, who were interested both in Adam Smith's free-market economics and in the notions of republican virtue. In a sense, environmentalism is only a particularly pointed example of a recurring problem in free and democratic governments: the importance of self-imposed citizen restraints for the sake of a common good.

Recent work in political economy has brought us back to this issue, suggesting that a system of norms and conventions may enable us to overcome some commons problems at relatively low perceived costs. The chief problem of the commons is that individually rational strategies undermine a collective good. The individually rational strategy of cheating while others cooperate leads everyone to cheat, and can decimate the things that would make us collectively better off.

But if we suppose that most people value the opinions of others, and if we suppose that most people are perceived to have a good opinion of behavior that corresponds to some particular norms or conventional practices, then commons problems may be overcome relatively painlessly. Under those circumstances, individuals may follow a norm of self-restraint even at some personal cost, in order to gain and hold the approbation of their fellows. Thus, if environmental problems are commons problems, certain kinds of norms about the environment might be a way of lessening the very high costs of environmental protection. Environmental norms could permit us to take some modicum of a given resource, while voluntarily restraining ourselves before we exhaust the underlying common resource.

It is at this point, of course, where the "given-ness" version of the environment arrives at a dead end. When we think about environmental resources as "just a given," we are regarding their use as normatively neutral, ethically up for grabs. And because we have no moral qualms about "givens," nothing except coercion will hold us back from grabbing all we can. The problem, of course, is that it may be very costly to institute the coercion necessary to restrain environmental grabbing. It is technically costly because of the high price of monitoring and policing those who cheat, and politically costly because of the sacrifice of free action and democratic decision making. If we are to have less costly methods, we will have to rely on voluntary self-restraint; but voluntary self-restraint depends on norms.

* * *

Does the "gift" vision help? Well, once again, yes and no. There is scarcely any question that the idea of gift may contain a strong normative element. * * *

With respect to the environment, the gift-vision has a certain spiritual quality. The spiritualism of the "gift" underlies some of the strongest impulses of modern environmentalism, most notably the aesthetic sensibilities so strongly stirred by Ansel Adams's haunting photographs of Yosemite or John Muir's deeply sensitive depictions of his wilderness travels. In our laws, too, we see a certain effort to recognize spiritual values, most notably in our laws about wilderness and wild creatures. For example, the Endangered Species Act, the Marine Mammal Protection Act, and the National Wild and Scenic Rivers Act have sometimes been discussed in the language of utilitarian preservation of a diverse gene pool; but they still seem to be animated by a much more emotional sense of the "gift" of our wild areas, and a sympathetic concern for their loss.

The problem is that in the environmental context, this vision of nature-as-gift may be too *strong* to be an appropriate norm of restraint. The spiritual overtone of the gift may make this vision incompatible with even a restrained rational use of resources. No doubt this spiritualism can be a useful antidote to the narrow self-interest that leads us to the well-known tragedy of the commons in our use of environmental resources. But as a day-to-day matter, the rhetoric of environment-as-gift may take us too far in the direction of restraint. What we need is not a complete hands-off attitude, but rather a norm of use-with-restraint. Thus if the rhetoric of "given-ness" makes us normatively insensitive, we might have to worry that the rhetoric of "gift" makes us normatively oversensitive.

* * *

IV. THREE SOURCES OF ENVIRONMENTAL ETHICS

[In Part IV, Professor Rose turns to a comparison of three general sources of environmental norms, asking whether and to what degree each might help solve commons problems.

She begins with the environmental ethics of indigenous peoples; then considers norms from "biologic rights," including animal rights; and finally takes up the norms implicit in property, as follows:]

* * *

C. Nature's Gift as Common Property

Although environmental good things seem to defy the idea of property, there is a striking amount of property language in modern environmentalism. Even the notion of gift is a property concept, and there are a good many more property metaphors in environmental discussions. Take for example the slogan that appears from time to time in environmental campaigns: the environment is not something we inherit from our ancestors, it is said, but something we borrow from our children. Or the words of Marjorie Kinnan Rawlings about a special place, Cross Creek:

> It seems to me that the earth may be borrowed but not bought. It may be used, but not owned. It gives itself in response to love and tending, offers its flowering and fruiting. But we are tenants and not possessors, lovers and not masters. Cross Creek belongs to the wind and the rain, to the sun and the seasons, to the cosmic secrecy of seed and beyond all, to time.[85]

Much more prosaically, the National Environmental Policy Act uses another trope from property, that of trusteeship and the obligations among generations.

These typical metaphors have some common elements. First is the notion that resources are shared, and that the holders of resources have some usufruct of these resources rather than exclusive ownership. Second, they include a notion that this shared usufruct is temporary to any given holder, a tenancy to be held over time and then relinquished to the next holder. Third is the notion that there is some core or center of the resource that is to be maintained in its integrity for the others who will become its tenants and use its fruits as well.

Those of us who teach property know that tenancy, trusteeship, and usufructory rights are all forms of ownership; but they are forms of shared ownership, often for limited periods, in which current users have responsibilities to others, especially others in the future. Current tenants may not "waste" the property—that is, they may take some of its product, but they may not do so in ways that are disproportionate, or in ways that would destroy the productive thing itself and its usefulness to later successors. Some quite similar notions appear in the law of trusts, in which ownership is split between legal holders and the beneficiaries of the trust property. The legal holder or "trustee" is generally supposed to devise ways to secure the income or product for the beneficiary, but also to behave prudently so as to preserve the core property that produces that income, the *res* of the trust.

In recent years a number of somewhat truculent commentators have criticized what they consider the merely alleged "tragedy of the commons," noting that there are many successful examples of common property. In these examples, the holders have devised quite

---

[85] Marjorie K. Rawlings, CROSS CREEK 368 (1942), *quoted in* Charles L. Siemon, *Who Owns Cross Creek,* 5 J. OF LAND USE & ENVTL L. 323 (1990).

sophisticated devices for permitting limited individual uses of common property—uses that, taken together, do not destroy but rather tend to preserve the whole. These devices are typically enforced by customs and norms. Fishing norms are a common example, as are agricultural practices such as the very widespread and long-lived practice of "stinting" the livestock that any individual peasant may allow to roam on a common field.

These common-property arrangements have been used to manage a great variety of resources. Common law courts have often adopted the customary patterns through which people regulate their own behavior, and the common law thus often reflects these common-property practices. During the years in which our own great Eastern rivers were used for water power, for example, owners of mills were expected to use the streamflow "reasonably."[92] While they could drive their mills with the power of the river waters, they were expected to do so in such a way as to preserve the bulk of the water volume as it flowed past successive mills on the way to the sea.

Thus, some of Bentham's successors may have been thinking about property too narrowly, as individual property exclusively at the disposal of the individual owner. That is only one of our forms of property, and while it is important, forms of common property are important as well. There are great bodies of law about common property, and they revolve around an ethic of moderation, proportionality, prudence, and responsibility to the others who are entitled to share in the common resource. Indeed, even individual property revolves around these normative characteristics. The individual property-holder relies in great part on the recognition and acquiescence of others, and individual property law assumes a large measure of neighborliness and attentiveness to the needs of others in the use of one's own "exclusive" property.

Property thus includes a normative "deep structure" that may be of use in an environmental ethic. The norms that lurk in property go beyond the wondrous power of exclusion that so awed Blackstone in the case of individual property. They include as well the qualities of restraint and responsibility that characterize common or shared property. Property law is most visible when it deals with breakdowns of these norms of restraint and responsibility, but on the whole, property law assumes that these norms do exist and predominate in our behavior. Hence, it is no accident that environmental metaphors are often metaphors of property—shared tenancy, trusteeship, stewardship, and even gift.

Modern environmentalism needs to build on the normative metaphors of property. Of late, there has been a considerable attentiveness to ways property devices might be used to control environmental resources, including everything from abating air pollution by creating tradeable emission rights for electrical utilities to conserving rain forests by recognizing local countries' property rights in the forests' wild genetic resources. A substantial portion of the environmental community has resisted such forays into property concepts, perhaps because they are presented as appeals to self-interest, and involve the classical economic move of harnessing private interest to the general wealth.

The appeal to self-interest is indeed a significant aspect of these property devices, but it is important to observe that there are other normative opportunities in these property-based devices. The rhetoric of property can easily encompass appeals to thrift and care-

---

[92] *See* Elliot v. Fitchburg R.R. Co., 64 Mass. (10 Cush.) 191, 193-95 (1852).

fulness, attentiveness to overuse, and maintenance of a common stock. These normative appeals can apply to new forms of environmental property as well. To be sure, an important facet of such devices as transferable emission permits, for example, is that an individual factory may buy and use such pollution entitlements at will. But an even more important aspect of these permits is that they constitute a very restrained entitlement, allowing the consumption of only a very limited portion of a larger common property, that is, a common property in the air itself. These devices are the modern equivalent of the individual peasant's stint of livestock on the common fields. The peasant indeed had his individual entitlement, but he had to use it carefully and with due regard to the preservation of the larger commonly-held resource. The same may be said of the modern factory's entitlement to consume a small modicum of clean air, while leaving the bulk untouched as a renewable stock.

* * *

We can use the concepts of property, and especially common property, to derive norms of responsibility and carefulness about a shared trust that we want to last. Property concepts do indeed make us understand ourselves to be the gardeners and zookeepers of what we call the wilderness, but they are also compatible with an understanding that the resources of the great commons are not simply "givens" that can be completely tamed and turned to our pleasure. The qualities of the rain and the soil, the majesty of the beasts and the mountains—these are qualities that most people value in thinking of the environment. Property rhetoric can treat these good things as gifts that people should hand along intact, precisely because people have some feel for their otherness as well as for their responsiveness to human management. That combination of respect for the thing itself, together with care for other users, is what it means to have a "gift" that comes to us from beyond our control—a gift that we pass along as yet another gift to those who follow.

NOTES

1. Professor Rose observes that commons problems may be resolved by property rules without the need to privatize. How would concepts of tenancy, trusteeship, and usufructuary rights prevent a tragedy of the commons?

2. Rose states that property rules themselves shape the two essential conditions of the tragedy of the commons: nonexclusivity and rational, self-interested behavior of individuals. One way out of the tragedy of the commons, Rose argues, is through a system of social norms and conventions that would foster self-restraint toward our use of environmental resources. Individually rational strategies would then include regard for others, particularly others' opinions. Is the appeal to an environmental ethic based on a "norm of use-with-restraint" a necessary condition for resolving our commons problem? Is it a sufficient condition? Can current property law concepts provide a foundation for a norm of self-restraint? Is this too ambitious a claim for the metaphorical value of law? Professor Eric Freyfogle is less sanguine than Rose about the ecological messages of legal concepts of ownership. Eric T. Freyfogle, *Ownership and Ecology*, 43 CASE W. RES. L. REV. 1269 (1993).

3. To what extent have public opinion and behavioral norms shaped and/or been shaped by environmental law? Consider the issues of wetlands protection, or cigarette smoking.

4. Note the parallels between the property themes of given-ness and gift and the theological alternative relationships with nature of dominance and stewardship. These relationships are discussed in detail in Chapter One in Professor White's article and the related notes.

5. Both Ostrom and Rose are seeking rules for cooperative problem solving whether through choices of self-governance or ethical norms. They are both building on what Herbert Simon first called "bounded rationality." THE SCIENCES OF THE ARTIFICIAL (1969). This concept derives from criticism of the rational choice model which assumes individuals are driven primarily to optimize their own self-interest. Bounded rationality assumes that the complexity of the world is well beyond our knowledge and computational abilities. Our decisionmaking processes are thus limited by conditions of uncertainty and ignorance, as well as by other factors such as social norms that constrain individual choice, enable cooperation, and accept satisfactory, though not necessarily optimal, solutions.

6. In another article, Rose applies property theory to explain under what circumstances rights vest communally in the public. *Custom, Commerce and Inherently Public Property*, 53 U. CHI. L. REV. 711 (1986). *See also* Carol M. Rose, *Rethinking Environmental Controls: Management Strategies for Common Resources*, 1991 DUKE L.J. 1 (1991) (using property concepts to differentiate environmental problems and describing appropriate management strategies).

7. What does Rose mean by the "deep structure" of property that would inform a new environmental ethic? As you read the next subchapter on privatization, consider how Rose's "deep structure" differs from the concepts of property on which free market environmentalists draw. Are these different constructs mutually exclusive?

B. Privatization

[E]very Man has a *Property* in his own *Person*. This no Body has any Right to but himself. The *Labour* of his Body, and the *Work* of his Hands, we may say, are properly his. Whatsoever then he removes out of the State that Nature hath provided, and left it in, he hath mixed his *Labour* with, and joyned to it something that is his own, and thereby makes it his *Property*. It being by him removed from the common state Nature placed it in, hath by this *labour* something annexed to it, that excludes the common right of other Men.

JOHN LOCKE, SECOND TREATISE OF GOVERNMENT § 27 (Peter Laslett ed. 1960) (1698).

The materials in this subchapter discuss the privatization response to the commons problem in environmental law. Anderson and Leal argue in favor of free market solutions to environmental problems. They believe that creating and vesting private property rights in the environment will best promote liberal political ideals and result in better environmental management. Blumm and Menell criticize the free market approach on a number of grounds. In particular, they highlight the shortcomings of markets and the salutary effects of government regulation on both markets and the environment. Sax makes the case for public management to promote collective values that cannot be realized through private markets.

Beginning with the "sagebrush rebellion" (a political attempt by some western interests to wrest control of federal natural resources) and the presidential election in 1980, libertarian calls for privatization of natural resources as a solution to environmental problems have received renewed attention. Originally called "new resource economics," the private property approach is now often called "free market environmentalism." The following excerpt articulates the rationale for relying on the private sector to allocate both environmental goods (such as minerals or wilderness) and harms (such as pollution).

FREE MARKET ENVIRONMENTALISM
Terry L. Anderson and Donald R. Leal
(1991)*

* * *

At the heart of free market environmentalism is a system of well-specified property rights to natural resources. Whether these rights are held by individuals, corporations, non-profit environmental groups, or communal groups, a discipline is imposed on resource users because the wealth of the owner of the property right is at stake if bad decisions are made. Of course, the further a decision maker is removed from this discipline—as

---

* Reprinted by permission of Westview Press, Boulder, Colorado.

he is when there is political control—the less likely it is that good resource stewardship will result. Moreover, if well-specified property rights are transferable, owners must not only consider their own values, they must also consider what others are willing to pay.

The Nature Conservancy's private land management program offers an excellent example of how free market environmentalism works. When the Conservancy obtains title to a parcel of land, the group's wealth, defined in terms of preserving habitat for a rare or endangered species, depends on good stewardship. When The Wisconsin Nature Conservancy was given title to forty acres of beachfront property on St. Croix, Virgin Islands, some may have thought that the group would protect that pristine beach at all costs. But the Conservancy traded the property (with covenants) for a larger parcel of rocky hillside in northern Wisconsin. The trade allowed the Conservancy to protect an entire watershed containing many endangered plant species. To be sure, tradeoffs were made, but through the exchange of well-defined and enforced property rights—that is, markets—The Nature Conservancy's wealth in the form of environmental amenities was enhanced.

Free market environmentalism emphasizes an important role for government in the enforcement of property rights. With clearly specified titles—obtained from land recording systems, strict liability rules, and adjudication of disrupted property rights in courts—market processes can encourage good resource stewardship. It is when rights are unclear and not well enforced that over-exploitation occurs.

* * *

The theory of free market environmentalism is founded on certain visions regarding human nature, knowledge, and processes. A consideration of these visions helps explain why some people accept this way of thinking as the only alternative to bureaucratic control and why others reject it as a contradiction in terms.

Human nature. Free market environmentalism views man as self-interested. This self-interest may be enlightened to the extent that people are capable of setting aside their own well-being for close relatives and friends or that they may be conditioned by moral principles. But beyond this, good intentions will not suffice to produce good results. Developing an environmental ethic may be desirable, but it is unlikely to change basic human nature. Instead of intentions, good resource stewardship depends on how well social institutions harness self-interest through individual incentives.

Knowledge. In addition to incentives, good resource stewardship depends on the information available to self-interested individuals. Free market environmentalism views this information or knowledge as diffuse rather than concentrated. Because ecosystems depend on the interaction of many different natural forces, they cannot be "managed" from afar. The information necessary for good management varies significantly from time to time and from place to place, and resource management requires knowledge that can only be obtained "on the ground." Therefore, knowledge cannot be gathered into a single mind or group of minds that can then capably manage all of society's natural resources.

The difference between perceptions of knowledge under centralized, political resource management and free market environmentalism centers on the distribution of knowledge among individuals. In visions of centralized, political control, the distribution has a low mean with a high variance. That is, the common man is not perceived as knowing much about the environment, and what he does know (including knowledge of his own value) is incorrect; the high variance means that experts can manage for the good of the masses.

Free market environmentalism sees a much smaller knowledge gap between the experts and the average individual. In this view, individual property owners, who are in a position and have an incentive to obtain time- and place-specific information about their resource endowments, are better suited than centralized bureaucracies to manage resources.

Processes or solutions. These visions of human nature and knowledge combine to make free market environmentalism a study of process rather than a prescription for solutions. If man can rise above self-interest and if knowledge can be concentrated, then the possibility for solutions through political control is more likely. But if there are self-interested individuals with diffuse knowledge, then processes must generate a multitude of solutions conditioned by the checks and balances implicit in the process. By linking wealth to good stewardship through private ownership, the market process generates many individual experiments; and those that are successful will be copied. The question is not whether the right solution has been achieved but whether the relevant trade-offs are being considered in the process.

These three elements of free market environmentalism also characterize the interaction of organisms in ecosystems. Since Charles Darwin's revolutionary study of evolution, most scientific approaches have implicitly assumed that self-interest dominates behavior for higher as well as lower forms of life. Individual members of a species may act in "altruistic" ways and may cooperate with other species, but species survival depends on adjustments to changing parameters in ways that enhance the probability of survival. To assume that man is not self-interested or that he can rise above self-interest because he is part of a political process requires heroic assumptions about homo sapiens vis-a-vis other species.

Ecology also emphasizes the importance of time- and place-specific information in nature. Because the parameters to which species respond vary considerably within ecosystems, each member of a species must respond to time- and place-specific characteristics with the knowledge that each possesses. These parameters can vary widely, so it is imperative for survival that responses utilize the diffuse knowledge. Of course, the higher the level of communication among members of a species, the easier it is to accumulate and concentrate time- and place-specific knowledge. Again, however, it requires a giant leap of faith to assume that man's ability to accumulate and assimilate knowledge is so refined that he can centrally manage the economy or the environment for himself and for all other species. Recent evidence from Eastern Europe underscores the environmental problems that can arise with centralized management.

Ecology is also the study of processes and interaction among species; it is not a scientific prescription for solutions to environmental changes. Like free market environmentalism, ecology focuses on the information and incentives that reach the members of a species. When a niche in an ecosystem is left open, a species can "profit" from filling that niche and other species can benefit as well. If an elk herd grows, there is additional food for bears and wolves and the number of predators will expand as they take advantage of this "profit" opportunity. Individual elk will suffer at the expense of predators, but elk numbers will be controlled. In the process, plant species will survive and other vertebrates will retain their place in the ecosystem. No central planner knows the best solution for filling niches; it is the individualistic process that rewards the efficient use of time- and place-specific information.

Comparing free market environmentalism with ecosystems serves to emphasize how market processes can be compatible with good resource stewardship and environmental quality. As survival rewards species that successfully fill a niche, increased wealth rewards owners who efficiently manage their resources. Profits link self-interest with good resource management by attracting entrepreneurs to open niches. If bad decisions are being made, then a niche will be open. Whether an entrepreneur sees the opportunity and acts on it will depend on his ability to assess time- and place-specific information and act on his assessment. As with an ecosystem, however, the diffuse nature of this information makes it impossible for a central planner to determine which niches are open and how they should be filled. If the link between self-interest and good resource stewardship is broken because good stewards cannot reap the benefits, do not bear the costs of their decisions, or receive distorted information through political intervention, then the efficacy of free market environmentalism will be impaired in the same way that the efficacy of an ecosystem would be impaired by centralized planning.

* * *

Most natural resource and environmental policy has been premised on the assumption that markets are responsible for resource misallocation and environmental degradation and that centralized, political processes can correct these problems. In general, the failure of markets is attributed to private decision makers who do not take into account all costs and benefits, to the unequal availability of information to all buyers and sellers, or to monopolies distorting prices and outputs. In essence, market failure is blamed on the lack of information, inappropriate incentives, or both. To counter market failures, centralized planning is seen as a way of aggregating information about social costs and social benefits in order to maximize the value of natural resources. Decisions based on this aggregated information are to be made by disinterested resource managers whose goal is to maximize social welfare.

Economic analysis in general and natural resource economics in particular have approached resource policy as if there is a "socially efficient" allocation of resources that will be reached when scientific managers understand the relevant trade-offs and act to achieve the efficient solution. For example, forest resources are supposed to be managed to achieve the "greatest good for the greatest number" through "multiple use management" undertaken by an "elite corps of professionals." When problems with management are recognized, they are attributed to "bad people in government" and the solution is to replace them with better trained, better financed managers.

But there is a more realistic way of thinking about natural resource and environmental policy. This alternative recognizes and emphasizes the costs of coordinating human actions. There is no assumption that costs of engaging in a transaction are zero or that there is perfect competition. To the contrary, understanding alternative policies requires that we specify coordination costs and discover why and where competitive forces may not be working.

This analytical framework applies equally to markets and politics. If all people lived alone on remote islands, there would be no costs of coordination; but in a complex society where people gain from trade, interacting individuals must measure and monitor the actions of one another. In the marketplace, consumers must signal to suppliers what quantity and quality of products they demand at what prices; suppliers must determine which products to produce and which input combinations to use. Both demanders and suppliers must monitor one another to ensure that products are delivered and paid for. To the extent that actions can be effectively measured and monitored, demanders and suppliers will internalize costs and benefits, profits will be made, and efficient resource allocation will be a by-product.

Similarly, citizens who demand goods and services from government must monitor the politicians and bureaucrats who supply them. Like a consumer displeased with food purchased from the supermarket, a citizen who is unhappy with the actions of his political representative has experienced the cost of measuring and monitoring supplier performance. Outcomes do not always reflect citizens' desires; the political process may supply too many of goods like nuclear arms or too little of goods like quality education. As with market analysis, policy analysis must focus on how well the political process internalizes costs and benefits to citizens and their political agents so that resources will not be squandered.

In rethinking natural resource and environmental policy, two facts must be recognized. First, *incentives matter to all human behavior*. No matter how well intended professional resources managers are, incentives affect their behavior. Like it or not, individuals will undertake more of an activity if the costs of that activity are reduced; this holds as much for bureaucrats as it does for profit-maximizing owners of firms. Everyone accepts that managers in the private sector would dump production wastes into a nearby stream if they did not have to pay for the cost of their action. Too often, however, we fail to recognize the same elements at work in the political arena. If a politician is not personally accountable for allowing oil development on federal lands or for permitting an agency to dump hazardous wastes into the environment, then we can expect too much development or too much dumping. Moreover, when the beneficiaries of these policies do not have to pay the full cost, they will demand more of each from political representatives.

Second, *information costs are positive in both the private and political sectors*. In a world of scarcity, both private and political resource managers must obtain information about the relative values of alternative uses. When one resource use rivals another, trade-offs must be made. Resource managers can only make these trade-offs based on the information coming to them or on their own values. If they believe lumber is more valuable than wildlife habitat, trees will be cut. Timber managers may know how fast trees grow under certain conditions, but they cannot know what the value of the growth is without incurring some cost in obtaining that information. The lumber market provides information on timber value as a commodity but information about the value of wildlife habitat and environmental amenities is more costly because those markets are less developed. Private timber managers for International Paper, for example, are being forced to consider wildlife habitat in their timber production decisions because prices tell them that consumers are willing to pay increasingly more for hunting, camping, and recreation. Political managers who "give away" recreational services from political lands lack this price information and have less incentive to react to changing values.

When incentives matter and information is costly, resource management is complicated so that it is not sufficient to rely on good intentions. Even if the superintendent of national parks believes that grizzly bear habitat is more valuable than more campsites, his good intentions will not necessarily yield more grizzly bear habitat. In a political setting where camping interests have more influence over a bureaucrat's budget, his peace and quiet, or his future promotion, intentions will have to override incentives if grizzly bear habitat is to prevail. But if a private resource owner believes that grizzly bear habitat is more valuable and can capitalize on that value, then politics will not matter. Moreover, if those who demand grizzly habitat are willing to pay more than those who demand campsites, then incentives and information reinforce one another. Management simply cannot be adequately analyzed without careful attention to the information and incentives that actors face under alternative institutional arrangements.

SCIENTIFIC MANAGEMENT OR ECONOMICS WITHOUT PRICES

For years economists have tried to use computer modeling techniques to simulate the market allocation of natural resources. The U.S. Forest Service, for example, developed FORPLAN, a forest simulation model, to specify the necessary conditions for efficient national forest use. The rationale of such models is simply that if the additional or marginal value of one resource use is greater than another, then allocation will be improved if the resource is reallocated from the latter to the former. This form of analysis teaches us that there are many margins for adjustment and that few decisions have all-or-nothing consequences. When water is allocated for fish or irrigation, trade-offs must be made; it is not an either-or decision. Put simply, neither demand nor supply is unresponsive to price changes. If prices rise, then demanders will make marginal adjustments by shifting consumption to the nearest substitutes; suppliers will adjust by substituting among resources and technologies.

The logic of this analysis combined with models and computers that can simulate resource use can lure policy analysts into believing that the maximization of resource value is a simple matter. Unfortunately, in this case logic and simplicity are not good guides because they mask the information costs and incentives. Consider the case of multiple use management of the national forests, where the scientific manager is supposed to trade off timber production, wildlife habitat, aesthetic values, water quality, recreation, and other uses to maximize the value of the forest. Because the managers are not supposed to be motivated by profit or self-interest, it is assumed that they will impartially apply economic theory and quantitative methods to accomplish efficient resource allocation. The scientific manager, armed with the economic concepts of marginal analysis, is supposed to be "always analytical. . . . Always, the economist's reasoning, his analytical framework . . ., and his conclusions are exposed forthrightly to the examination and criticism of others. In these ways, *scientific objectivity* is actively sought."[3]

To apply marginal analysis to multiple use, decision makers must attach values to the relevant margins. Scientific management assumes that these values are known and, therefore, that there is an efficient solution. The decision maker must only acquire the "correct" information about resource values in alternative uses and reallocate those resources until marginal equalities hold. Management is simply the process of finding the socially optimal allocation. * * *

* * *

As analytical tools, economic models focus on the importance of marginal adjustments, but they cannot instruct managers in which trade-offs to make or which values to place

---

[3] Alan Randall, *Resource Economics* (Columbus, Ohio: Grid Publishing Company, 1981), 36.

on a resource. In the absence of subjective individual evaluations, the marginal solutions derived by sophisticated efficiency maximization models are unachievable ideals. Unfortunately, these models have been used as guides to tell resource managers how to achieve efficient allocation; in fact, they can only provide a way of thinking about trade-offs. Managers argue that these models have added sophistication and authority to political management efforts, allowing shadow prices (that is, prices that are not real but images of what would exist if there was a market) to be derived and used in lieu of actual market processes. The Forest Service and the Bureau of Land Management, enamored with these models, assume that with sufficient data and large enough computers it is possible to produce wise and efficient management plans. Forest economist Richard Behan stated that the planning acts that guide the Forest Service mandate "with the force of law that forest plans can be rational, comprehensive, and essentially perfect."[6] But no matter how rational or comprehensive they may be, models built on marginal analysis will always be constrained by information requirements.

The market process generates information on the subjective values that humans place on alternative resource use as individuals engage in voluntary trades. The decentralized decisions made in markets are crucial, because "practically every individual has some advantage over all others in that he possesses unique information of which beneficial use might be made, but of which use can be made only if the decisions depending on it are left to him or are made with his active cooperation." Once we understand that most knowledge is fragmented and dispersed, then "systemic coordination among the many supersedes the special wisdom of the few." Traditional economic analysis has failed to recognize this fundamental point. The information necessary for "efficient" resource allocation depends on the knowledge of the special circumstance of time and place.

The idea of scientific management has also misguided public policy because it ignores the incentives of decision makers in the political sector. The economic analysis of markets focuses on incentives in the form of prices that determine the benefits and costs that decision makers face. Market failure is said to result when any benefits are not captured or costs are not borne by decision makers. The existence of these externalities or third-party effects means that either too little of a good is produced in the case of uncaptured benefits or too much in the case of unborne costs. A system of private water allocation, for example may not provide a sufficient supply of instream flows for wildlife habitat and environmental quality because owners of water cannot easily charge recreationalists and environmentalists who benefit from free-flowing water. And too much pollution exists because firms do not have to pay the full costs of waste disposal, so they "overuse" the air or water as a garbage dump. Such under- or over-production is often taken as a sufficient condition for taking political control of resource allocation.

There is, however, an asymmetry in the analysis of market and political processes because of a failure to recognize that the *political sector operates by externalizing costs*. Consider the reasoning that political agents apply to scientific management. When land is diverted from timber production to wilderness, there is an opportunity cost associated with the reallocation. Private landowners interested in maximizing the value of the resource must take this cost into account in the "price" of wilderness. The bureaucratic manager

---

[6] Richard W. Behan, "RPA/NFMA-Time to Punt," *Journal of Forestry* 79 (1981): 802.

or politician who does not own the land, however, does not face all the opportunity costs of his decisions. He will take the values forgone [*sic*] into account only if the political process makes him do so. If we assume that the political process worked perfectly (which is the equivalent of *assuming* that markets work perfectly), then the countervailing powers of the opposing sides would internalize the benefits and costs for the decision maker.

But there is little reason to believe that the political process works perfectly or even tolerably well. Because politicians and bureaucrats are rewarded for responding to political pressure groups, there is no guarantee that the values of unorganized interests will be taken into account *even if* they constitute a majority of the population. For example, most Americans will pay marginally higher prices for petroleum products if oil production is not allowed in the Arctic National Wildlife Refuge. Because this cost to each individual is low and the costs of information and action are high relative to the benefits, each person will remain rationally ignorant; that is, he will not become informed on the issue. But organized groups that favor preserving wildlife habitat in the pristine tundra can gain by stopping drilling in the refuge. To the extent that those who benefit from wildlife preservation do not have to pay the opportunity costs of forgone [*sic*] energy production, they will demand "too much" wildlife habitat. In the absence of a perfect political process, we must depend on good intentions to overpower the special interest incentives built into the imperfect system. This takes a giant leap of faith.

Traditional thinking about natural resource and environmental policy ignores the most basic economic tenet: *incentives matter.* * * *

* * *

Because traditional thinking about resource and environmental policy pays little attention to the institutions that structure and provide information and incentives in the political sector, practitioners often seem surprised and puzzled that efficiency implications from their models are ignored in the policy arena. In the private sector, efficiency matters because it influences profits; in the political sector, prices and incentives are often very different. Political resource managers make trade-offs in terms of political currencies measured in terms of special interest support; at best, this unit of account provides imprecise measures of the subjective values of citizens.

The incentive structure in the political sector is complicated because the bottom line depends on the electoral process where votes matter, not efficiency. Because voters are rationally ignorant, because benefits can be concentrated and costs diffused, and because individual voters seldom (and probably never) influence the outcome of elections, there is little reason to expect that elections will link political decisions to efficiency in the same way that private ownership does in the market process.

Under private ownership, profits and losses are the measure of how well decision makers are managing. Even where shareholders in a large company have little effect on actual decisions, they can observe stockprices and annual reports as a measure of management's performance. In other words, private ownership gives owners both the information and the incentive to measure performance. In the political sector, however, both information and incentives are lacking. Annual budget figures offer information about overall expenditures and outlays, but it is not clear who is responsible and whether larger budgets are good or bad. Even when responsibility can be determined, there is no easy way for a citizen to "buy and sell shares" in the government. Therefore, citizens remain rationally ignorant about most aspects of political resource allocation and rationally informed about issues that directly affect them. The rewards for political resource managers depend not on maximizing net resource values but on providing politically active constituents with what they want with little regard for cost. Although it may not be possible to state precisely what is maximized by politicians and bureaucrats, it is clear that efficiency is not the main goal. * * *

* * *

The key, therefore, to effective markets in general and free market environmentalism in particular is the establishment of well-specified and transferable property rights. When a conservation group purchases a conservation easement on a parcel of land, the exchange requires that property rights be well defined, enforced, and transferable. The physical attributes of the resources must be specified in a clear and concise manner; they must be measurable. For example, the rectangular survey system allows us to define ownership rights over land and clarifies disputes over ownership. The system may also help us define ownership to the airspace over land, but more questions arise here because of the fluidity of air and the infinite vertical third dimension above the ground. If property rights to resources cannot be defined, then they obviously cannot be exchanged for other property rights.

Property rights also must be defendable. A rectangular survey may define surface rights to land, but conflicts are inevitable if there is no way to defend the boundaries and prevent other incompatible uses. Barbed wire provided an inexpensive way to defend property rights on the western frontier; locks and chains do the same for parked bicycles. But enforcing one's rights to peace and quiet by "fencing out" sound waves may be much more difficult, as will keeping other people's hazardous wastes out of a groundwater supply. Whenever the use of property cannot be monitored or enforced, conflicts are inevitable and trades are impossible.

Finally, property rights must be transferable. In contrast to the costs of measuring and monitoring resource uses, which are mainly determined by the physical nature of the property and technology, the ability to exchange is determined largely by the legal environment. Although well-defined and enforced rights allow the owner to enjoy the benefits of using his property, legal restrictions on the sale of that property preclude the potential for gains from trade. Suppose that a group of fishermen values water for fish habitat more highly than farmers value the same water for irrigation. If the fishermen are prohibited from renting or purchasing the water from the farmers, then gains from trade will not be realized and potential wealth will not be created. Moreover, the farmer will have less incentive to leave the water in the stream.

In sum, free market environmentalism presupposes well-specified rights to take actions with respect to specific resources. If those rights cannot be measured, monitored, and marketed, then there is little possibility for exchange. Garbage disposal through the air, for example, is more of a problem than solid waste disposal in the ground because property rights to the Earth's surface are better defined than property rights to the atmosphere. Private ownership of land works quite well for producing timber, but measuring, monitoring, and marketing the land for endangered species habitat requires entrepreneurial imagination.

* * *

NOTES

1. After describing the rationale for private property solutions to environmental problems in the excerpt above, Anderson and Leal apply their approach to a wide range of concerns, including energy policy, water allocation, ocean fisheries management, and solid waste disposal. For instance, to manage fisheries, Anderson and Leal praise the Australian and New Zealand method of establishing individual tradable quotas (ITQs).

> An individual quota entitles the holder to catch a specified percentage of the total allowable catch. This system is attractive for several reasons. First, each quota holder faces greater certainty that his share of the catch will not be taken by someone else. Under the current system, total allowable catch is established, but the share is determined by who is best at capturing the fugitive resources. With ITQs, holders do not compete for the shares, so there is less incentive to race other fishermen. Second, transferability allows quotas to end up in the hands of the most efficient fishermen—that is those with the lowest costs and who can pay the hightest price for the ITQs. * * * This is in marked contrast to the current regulatory system, which encourages over-investment in the race for fugitive resources.

ANDERSON & LEAL at 130-131.

How does this ITQ approach compare with the solution described in the Commons subchapter by Elinor Ostrom for management of fisheries in Alanya, Turkey? What, if anything, would be lost if ITQs were established for the Alanya fishery?

Other sources that argue for privatization and apply it to particular environmental issues include: BUREAUCRACY VS. ENVIRONMENT: THE ENVIRONMENTAL COSTS OF BUREAUCRATIC GOVERNANCE (John Baden and Richard L. Stroup eds., 1981); RICHARD L. STROUP AND JOHN A. BADEN, NATURAL RESOURCES: BUREAUCRATIC MYTHS AND ENVIRONMENTAL MANAGEMENT (1983); and *Symposium on Privatization*, 7 J. CONTEMP. STUD., Spr. 1984.

2. The use of market-based incentives as cost-effective tools for distributing pre-determined levels of environmental quality is becoming broadly accepted. *See* Chapter Three of this anthology. Anderson and Leal, however, go further in proposing that markets should also set the levels of environmental protection. How would one use markets to accomplish this goal? Is consumer behavior in markets the best way to arrive at the amount of wilderness to preserve, the level of water pollution to allow in rivers, and the degree to which hazardous waste sites should be cleaned up? Mark Sagoff contends that a person's consumer preferences may not accurately reflect the value that a person places on resources as a citizen:

> Each of us recognizes that he or she acts in different ways and expresses different thoughts in different roles and situations[.] * * * As a *citizen*, I am concerned with the public interest, rather than my own interest; with the good

of the community, rather than simply the well-being of my family. Thus, as a citizen, I might oppose a foreign adventure, like the Vietnam War, because I think it is tragic from the point of view of the nation as a whole. As a consumer or producer of goods and services, however, I might at the same time look at the war as a good thing for me if, for example, neither I nor my children must serve and I have a lot of investments in war-related industry.

* * *

In my role as a *consumer*, in other words, I concern myself with personal or self-regarding wants and interests; I pursue the goals I have as an individual. I put aside the community-regarding values I take seriously as a citizen, and I look out for Number One instead. I act upon those preferences on which my personal welfare depends; I may ignore the values that are mine only insofar as I consider myself a member of the community, that is, as *one of us*.

* * * [S]ocial regulation should reflect the community-regarding values we express through the political process and not simply or primarily the self-regarding preferences we seek to satisfy in markets. * * *[G]oals, or preferences we entertain as citizens with respect to social regulation, moreover, differ *logically* from those we seek to satisfy as individuals.

MARK SAGOFF, THE ECONOMY OF THE EARTH: PHILOSOPHY, LAW, AND THE ENVIRONMENT 7-8 (1988). Do you agree that we pursue different goals as voters than we do as purchasers? Does the boycott as a political tool present a problem for Sagoff?

3. Anderson and Leal criticize public environmental management because it makes "trade-offs in terms of political currencies measured in terms of special interest support." Political pluralists might argue that this is precisely the kind of considerations that ought to be balanced in environmental policy. The challenge is to ensure that all the competing interests are fairly represented when weighing the environmental, economic and social implications of environmental management strategies. *See* JAMES Q. WILSON, THE POLITICS OF REGULATION (1980) (documenting the ways in which industries are able to "capture" the agencies designed to regulate them). The environmental regulations that emerged in the 1970s were designed in part to increase the opportunities for all special interest groups to participate in the policy making process. *See* R. SHEP MELNICK, REGULATION AND THE COURTS: THE CASE OF THE CLEAN AIR ACT (1983) (discussing the kinds of measures developed to counter the potential for industry capture of environmental regulations). Anderson and Leal suggest that environmental regulation has now been captured by environmentalists and that the private interests of landowners, business and industry are underrepresented. Do you agree? How did the reversal of political majorities in the 104th Congress change the incentives for regulators?

4. Anderson and Leal criticize centralized public management. To what extent do their arguments apply to decentralized public management? Suppose each national forest were individually accountable to Congress or to states. Would that alleviate some of the information problems that Anderson and Leal highlight? Note that the U.S. Forest Service historically was one of the most decentralized agencies. HERBERT KAUFMAN, THE FOREST RANGER: A STUDY IN ADMINISTRATIVE BEHAVIOR (1960). The trend toward centralization in recent years has been largely driven by the perception that local, commodity-development interests "capture" rangers (field decisionmakers) to the detriment of the national interest in environmental quality and multiple use, sustained yield management. *See* CHARLES F. WILKINSON AND H. MICHAEL ANDERSON, LAND AND RESOURCE PLANNING IN THE NATIONAL FORESTS (1987) (describing modern federal central planning and environmental constraints imposed on the Forest Service).

5. Anderson and Leal do not see environmental ethics as likely to change the self-interested nature of human beings. How would Carol Rose, excerpted in the Commons subchapter, or Mark Sagoff, excerpted in note 2, respond to that position? In discussing parallels between human organization and ecosystems, Anderson and Leal indicate that altruism and cooperative strategies in general are not essential determinants of species survival. What do you think of the use of these parallels between ecological systems and societal arrangements? Anderson and Leal are not alone in noting the parallels between Charles Darwin's natural selection and Adam Smith's economic theory. *See* STEPHEN JAY GOULD, THE INDIVIDUAL IN DARWIN'S WORLD 20 (1990) (arguing that Darwin drew "upon the laissez-faire system of Adam Smith to construct his theory").

6. Much of the privatization debate has focused on forest management. *See, e.g.,* RANDAL O'TOOLE, REFORMING THE FOREST SERVICE (1988); Robert Fischman and Richard Nagle, *Implementing Forest Management Reform in New Zealand*, 16 ECOLOGY L.Q. 719 (1989). Privatizers and conventional environmentalists have allied in efforts to eliminate federal timber sales where the costs to the federal government to conduct the sales exceed the revenues. However, the two groups might part ways in the Pacific Northwest where timber sales are quite profitable in the ancient forests environmentalists seek to preserve. Under what conditions should environmental groups be allowed to bid against logging companies for national forest timber in order to preserve trees? Would an auction where environmentalists seeking to preserve trees and logging companies seeking to cut trees bid against each other be an appropriate way to allocate forest resources?

7. When Anderson and Leal contrast public and private ownership, they focus on the incentives that private owners-managers have to consider both present and future interests in order to protect their investment This contrasts with the bureaucratic structure, which does not provide an analogous incentive to maximize the social utility of natural resources. Which incentive structure best models *corporate* management? Anderson and Leal claim that "even where shareholders in a large company have little effect on actual decisions," they respond to stock prices and annual reports. Do corporate managers seek to maximize stock prices? Are short-term profits valued more than long-term gain in stock prices? Are some of the incentives that shape corporate behavior more similar to the public model of decisionmaking than the private one described by Anderson and Leal? Consider lobbying by powerful stock holders, the desire not be ousted by a hostile takeover, and the potential for personal gain from "golden parachutes." *See* Michael C. Jenson & William H. Meckling,

Theory of the Firm: Managerial Behavior, Agency Lasts and Ownership Structure, 3 J.
FIN. ECON. 305 (1976).

8. Anderson and Leal describe the importance of time- and place-specific knowledge
to the operation of the free market system. Suppose, however, as is often the case with
environmental problems, that the available knowledge about an ecosystem, or the toxicity
of a pollutant, is substantially in error or in doubt. How does free market environmentalism
cope with this problem? How should the cost of gathering information affect the free
marketeer's choice?

9. Consider that some public resources retain most of their value for certain purposes
even when divided into small parts. For example, mineral resources spread over a 20,000
acre parcel of land may retain much of their value if divided into ten 2,000 acre parcels.
By contrast, those same lands would lose much of their value for other purposes once
divided. Ten separate 2,000 acre parcels of wilderness, for example, would likely have
far less value than a 20,000 acre wilderness area. How is this fact relevant to free market
environmentalism?

The following two criticisms of Anderson and Leal were contributions to Symposium—*Free Market Environmentalism*, 15 HARV. J.L. & PUB. POL'Y 297 (1992). The
symposium contains a number of other thoughtful commentaries on privatization.

THE FALLACIES OF FREE MARKET ENVIRONMENTALISM
Michael C. Blumm
15 Harv. J. L. & Pub. Pol'y 371 (1992)*

* * *

I. MARKET FAILURE, ENVIRONMENTAL PROTECTION,
AND THE PRIVATEERS

The new environmental Privateers are the intellectual progeny of Ronald Coase, father
of the law and economics movement. According to the Coase Theorem, absent transaction
costs, the market will produce efficient results through private bargains. The Theorem
suggests that government regulation, on the other hand, is unlikely to produce efficiently
because resources will be allocated by fallible administrators subject to political pressures,
and because general regulations are likely to be inappropriately applied to specific situations. Coase thus added consideration of "government failure" to the concept of market
failure in deciding whether to regulate. Coase himself recognized that his Theorem might
break down in the presence of transaction costs. Subsequent studies challenge Coasian
assumptions about the capability of bargaining to produce efficient results, and the irrele-

---

vance of the initial assignment of rights to efficiency. Nevertheless, Coasian disciples like the Privateers overlook these market limitations, while extolling the virtues of free markets and denouncing the vices of government regulation.

Environmental Privateers may be willing to overlook the market's shortcomings because of their conviction regarding the pernicious consequences of regulation. A new group of scholars, subscribing to what has become known as Public Choice theory, shares their skepticism of governmental solutions. Public Choice theorists bring economic theory to political science through models that view the political process as a system by which individuals and groups may further their own interests. Their assumption is that political participants use government intervention in the economy to further the welfare of the politically influential. This essentially selfish, "rent-seeking" view of the political process (and human nature) views legislators as corrupt, available to the highest bidding interest group, a vision that corresponds with the Coasian perspective that resources ought to flow to the highest bidder. The Privateers may be the descendants of Coase, but they are surely siblings of Public Choice theorists.

The fusion of Coasian principles and Public Choice theory in environmental thought produces books, like *Free Market Environmentalism*, which completely ignore the failures of the marketplace; failures that produced the environmental regulatory scheme they find objectionable. Market failure is not a seldom-seen phenomenon in the environmental area—it is pervasive. A number of critical assumptions of an efficiently functioning free market invariably are absent in environmental decisionmaking, such as complete information, fully internalized prices, and rational, wealth-maximizing bargaining. The pervasive failure of markets to produce reliable information about risks, costs, and benefits of alternative courses of action makes efficiency at least as unlikely in marketplace ordering of environmental resources as in public decisionmaking.

Even if there were perfect environmental information, markets would fail to allocate environmental resources efficiently because of external cost and collective goods problems. The market does not ensure that resource developers bear the full costs of air pollution, old growth forest liquidation, or water diversions. Developers do not pay these "external" costs, which means that the marketplace overvalues polluting activities and resource consumption, producing economic inefficiency. The inefficient market may be corrected by government regulation or taxation, or by liability rules if good environmental information were not so persistently unavailable. But, unfortunately for the libertarian-minded, the market is not able to correct itself.

Markets also fail to produce efficient results because of collective goods problems. A clean airshed, a free-flowing river, and a spectacular view are collective goods. The benefits from these goods are impossible to price accurately because they are shared by all; they cannot be effectively fenced. "Free riders" may share in these goods as well as the developers who pay their costs. Developers as a result undervalue them, and therefore will not produce them. Moreover, some collective goods need to be experienced to be desired; a lack of demand for a resource today may not be a reflection of its value tomorrow. Yet today's decisions may foreclose tomorrow's options.

All of this means that markets are not necessarily efficient and, in the environmental area, are extremely unlikely to be so. Marketplace allocation of environmental resources is also offensive on grounds of equity. Efficiency's "willingness to pay" criterion is objectionable to those who do not believe that the existing distribution of wealth is fair. Transforming dollars into votes ensures a monopoly by the wealthy and the few. Markets are also preference-shaping. All preferences are a function of experience. And the cultural consequences of preference-shaping by markets include acquisitiveness, selfishness, and quick response. We may justifiably reject the intrusion of 1980s Wall Street upon the culture of the Twenty-First Century.

Further, markets require enforcement; they are not self-executing. A system of environmental protection based exclusively on markets would be an expensive system to enforce. The market relies on common law liability rules like nuisance to enforce private rights. Nuisance showed itself to be a spectacular failure in confronting the environmental problems of the Nineteenth and Twentieth Centuries. An argument premised on the belief that the Twenty-First Century will be different ought to explain with some precision how the pertinent causation, burden of proof, and remedy problems can be overcome. The Privateers proffer none of this. They substitute an analysis of "how it is going to be different this time" with narratives about how the government failed to regulate a particular resource in an optimal manner. Because optimal markets are not readily identifiable, it is not enough to show that a particular regulation is suboptimal.

The market's track record in environmental resource allocation is one that shows high costs involuntarily imposed on receptors of air and water pollution and hazardous waste generation. If the Privateers' argument is premised on the idea that markets will perform differently in the future than they have in the past, they ought to endeavor to explain how and why. * * *

* * *

B. Trashing Government Intervention

If Anderson and Leal are unreasonably optimistic about the results their market experimentation would produce, they are misleading and pejorative in their description of government intervention. They assume that the government's response to market failure is limited to Kremlin-like "centralized planning."[51] Actually, government intervention may take a number of forms in addition to regulation, including taxes, subsidies, and changed liability rules. Non-regulatory mechanisms are increasingly married to regulatory techniques in modern environmental legislation. This marriage will almost certainly be solidified in the future, because as environmental controls affect a wider segment of the population, the costs of regulation and its enforcement become prohibitive.

Strangely, especially for a book whose central contribution is that incentives matter, *Free Market Environmentalism* does not enthusiastically endorse the marriage, because marketable pollution permits, for example, "still require a political determination of the level of pollution that will be allowed."[54] Anderson and Leal want the amount of permissible pollution to be left exclusively to individual bargains between polluters and receptors. Thus, they object to

---

[51] [TERRY ANDERSON AND DONALD LEAL, FREE MARKET ENVIRONMENTALISM (1991)] at 9 ("To counter market failures, centralized planning is seen as a way of aggregating information about social costs and social benefits in order to maximize the value of natural resources. Decisions based on this aggregated information are to be made by disinterested resource managers whose goal is to maximize social welfare.").

[54] *Id.* at 147.

transferable pollution rights where the level of environmental quality is left to the government. In their marketplace, environmental improvements would be a function, not of evolving government standards, but of the wealth of those who wished to purchase those rights and devote them to non-polluting uses. Presumably, the authors' aversion to government intervention forecloses pollution taxes, subsidies for development of resources undervalued by the current market, and transferable land development rights as variances from zoning controls. This sort of "market purity" disables *Free Market Environmentalism* and prevents it from exploring how market incentives might serve to increase regulatory effectiveness.

Not unexpectedly, Anderson and Leal disapprove of federal ownership of public lands. They initially cannot quite bring themselves to advocate selling off the public land "for reasons of political feasibility."[57] But later, sounding like latter-day Sagebrush disciples of James Watt, they suggest it as the only solution to solve the nation's energy problems. They blame "massive reservations of land as public domain" for halting the privatization of land and for "often subsidiz[ing] environmental destruction."[60] There is of course some truth in the latter proposition, but just as much in its converse: Public land management undeniably (if somewhat unpredictably) produces environmental protection. For example, nearly all of the remaining Northern Spotted Owl habitat in the Pacific Northwest is on federal lands where the last vestige of the Pacific forest's old growth timber endures. Virtually all of the old growth on private lands has been logged because the market attributed no value to preservation of old growth ecosystems.

Multiple use is a particularly difficult concept for *Free Market Environmentalism*, for it requires that "decisionmakers have information on the value of alternative uses," which is not possible for the government because of "the absence of market information."[63] The authors' solution is to create a market by selling the public lands to the highest bidders, which, they are careful to point out, might include environmental groups, alleged by Anderson and Leal to be quite wealthy.

Such an auction would create fragmented land management on a myriad of dominant-use parcels, increased spillover costs from incompatible parcels, inestimable difficulties in managing transboundary resources, and would leave ultimate decisionmaking authority in the hands of members of various boards of directors of oil, timber, and mining companies and environmental groups alike. This was, of course, the chief intellectual contribution of the Sagebrush Rebellion that helped usher Secretary Watt to office. The authors of *Free Market Environmentalism* mean to keep the old Sagebrush Rebels agitated.

Anderson and Leal indict government controls for failing to produce information necessary for efficient resource use. Their criticisms of government techniques of supplying prices for unpriced commodities, such as shadow pricing and economic models based on adequate marginal analysis, are on the mark, but they fail to acknowledge that the same information problems disable markets as well. There is almost never good information on health costs, let alone risks, so the market has no way of rationally producing efficient results, of internalizing costs. Anderson and Leal make an unconvincing attempt to explain how cost internalization is possible based on some obscure reasoning about the benefits

---

[57] [*Id.*] at 75.
[60] [*Id.*] at 7.
[63] [*Id.*] at 92.

of pricing, the costs of monitoring and measurement, and the availability of alternative suppliers in a market system. None of this responds effectively to the charge that markets persistently fail to ensure that private bargains internalize environmental costs, risks, and benefits. Moreover, markets measure only existing preferences, objectionable to those who cling to the traditional American belief in progress.

* * *

III. THE HIDDEN COSTS OF PRIVATIZATION

In addition to overestimating the benefits of markets and misunderstanding the premises of governmental intervention, Anderson and Leal fail to examine all the costs associated with privatizing environmental decisionmaking. Private rights are expensive to define and enforce, requiring individual case-by-case adjudications under common law liability rules. The modern regulatory state abandoned heavy reliance on adjudications in favor of notice and comment rulemaking to lower transaction costs and promote expeditious action. A resort to heavy reliance on common law liability rules would drastically increase transaction costs. The result might augment business for lawyers, but increasing billable hours hardly seems to be an intention of Anderson and Leal (neither of whom are attorneys).

There is a further, hidden cost of abandoning regulation in favor of marketplace ordering of environmental resources. Regulation carries with it what Carol Rose has referred to as a "rhetoric of responsibility," a kind of moral suasion or exhortation that appeals to the public's sense of good will or duty. This normative component is diminished in property rights regimes whose message is that environmental degradation is an entitlement if it is in an individual's self-interest. While exhortation alone may be an ineffective response to most environmental problems, when combined with the rhetoric of responsibility employed by the regulatory state, exhortation may be an important (and relatively cheap) means of establishing norms and influencing behavior.

INSTITUTIONAL FANTASYLANDS: FROM SCIENTIFIC MANAGEMENT TO FREE MARKET ENVIRONMENTALISM
Peter S. Menell
15 Harv. J.L. & Pub. Pol'y 489 (1992)*

* * *

A. THE MODEL OF HUMAN NATURE

As a basis for their analysis, Anderson and Leal employ the standard economic model of human nature: Human beings are self-interested, rational actors who seek to maximize their utility. Although this model is a useful predictor of human behavior, it compromises accuracy in order to increase tractability. Convenience alone, however, does not justify uncritical invocation of such simplifications, especially where there is good reason to believe that these assumptions introduce significant biases into the analysis. Since the limitations of the standard economic model of human nature are explored generally elsewhere, I focus here upon * * * shortcomings of special relevance to natural resource and environmental issues * * *.

Failure to Consider the Endogeneity of Preferences

Within the standard economic model of human nature, a person's preferences are determined exogenously (that is, are innate to the individual) and are assumed to be fixed. To *Homo Economicus*, the environment represents simply an array of resources to be consumed or otherwise enjoyed. This assumption is critical to Anderson and Leal's contention that only privately mutually-beneficial trades can improve social welfare.

For many private consumption decisions, the assumption of exogenous and fixed preferences seems reasonable. It is unlikely that the quality of running shoes, the comfort of a chair, or the taste of a good wine will influence one's character in deep and integral ways. Major resource decisions, however, particularly those affecting the range of environmental experiences available, can have a more profound effect on human nature. A completely private economy might generate greater homogeneity of environmental experiences, such as more theme parks and fewer pristine valleys, than a mixed economy, because of the desire to maximize appropriable return on investment in the development of resources. In view of the uniqueness of some environmental resources and the effective irreversibility of their development, such a diminution in the range of opportunities for formative experiences would no doubt alter individuals' developmental processes. The effect of wilderness experience on human development is a principal theme in the writings of generations of American naturalists. The growing concern for the environment has been significantly influenced by the opportunities for a broad range of nature experiences as well as the rich tradition of naturalist writers inspired by such experiences. Thus, human appreciation of the environment is more aptly viewed as an outgrowth of a diversity of environmental opportunities, rather than an exogenous set of tastes.

It is possible, of course, that a market could capture some of the value inherent in a range of resource opportunities, although this type of value, because of its intangible quality, might be particularly difficult to appropriate through markets. For example, the Sierra Club might purchase Yosemite Valley and preserve it in its natural state. This does not mean, however, that the "private" preferences of Sierra Club members as manifested in the collective decisions of the Sierra Club will necessarily reflect the full potential value of such resources since human appreciation of nature may be inchoate. Because preferences may be undeveloped, futures markets for such resources might be particularly difficult to establish. The threshold question is whether public institutions have a role in ensuring a diversity of physical environments. Admittedly, any such decision process invites the abuses of public institutions detailed by public choice theory. Nonetheless, the potential for endogenous preference change raises serious questions about the choice and roles of institutional structures. This set of concerns is clearly relevant to a liberal society's development and enrichment, yet remains outside the reach of the standard economic model of human nature.

* * *

Endowment Effects Associated with Allocation of Ownership

A third shortcoming of Anderson and Leal's analytical framework relates to the potential role of public ownership in the valuation and enjoyment of resources. Substantial empirical evidence indicates a significant divergence between consumers' willingness to pay for resources and their willingness to accept compensation for the loss of such resources. This phenomenon, often referred to as the endowment effect, suggests that the utility people derive from the use of resources depends upon their perception of ownership of such resources. One survey found that hunters were willing to pay an average of $247 to preserve a wetland hunting area but would require more than four times that amount to give up an entitlement to that same area. Holding resources in the public domain may create a broader group of perceived "owners," even though the degree of ownership in terms of exclusive rights is diminished. It is an empirical question whether the value attached to public ownership of a national park in which there are 250 million owners with limited rights, such as access and protection against certain uses, exceeds the value of the same land held by one or a few owners with a more complete bundle of property rights. Anderson and Leal ignore these issues by implicitly assuming that the choice is between no ownership and private ownership.

The endowment effect may also suggest that the experience of using one's own resources, for example, hiking in a "public" park, might be more enjoyable even if a user fee is charged than the experience of renting comparable resources (for example, hiking in a similar "private" park charging the same user fee). This does not necessarily mean that the best public policy is a preference for public rather than private ownership in all circumstances. As Anderson and Leal have highlighted, private parks might be better maintained than public parks. Furthermore, the empirical significance of this effect is a limiting factor. Nonetheless, this phenomenon suggests an additional trade-off between public and private institutions that is not captured by Anderson and Leal's analytical framework.

The Role of Culture in Guiding Human Behavior

A fourth oversimplified assumption of the standard economic model of human nature is the atomistic quality of human decisionmaking. While this assumption is a useful first approximation of human behavior, it obscures the important role of culture and norms in determining behavior in many natural resource and environmental settings. Numerous examples from history and current societies suggest that the commons will not automatically be overgrazed. The decisions of individuals depend upon context, community structure, and shared values, concepts not easily incorporated within an atomistic framework of human behavior.

When market regulation of external effects is costly, for example, because of the high costs of fencing or monitoring use, the fostering of cooperative norms and other social control devices might prove a more effective institutional structure than complete reliance on the market. Yet a framework built entirely on atomistic action will exclude such possibilities. The norms among backpackers of carrying out refuse and not "relieving themselves" near streams are examples where non-market control systems might regulate externalities effectively. Of course, the market is not irrelevant to addressing the problems of overuse. User fees can be an effective means of addressing some overuse and congestion problems in scenic areas. Nonetheless, comprehensive institutional analysis should consider the potential for non-market systems of allocating resources, a task that requires a more sophisticated model of human behavior than that which Anderson and Leal employ.

This discussion of particular shortcomings of the standard economic model of human nature is by no means intended as a complete rejection of Anderson and Leal's analysis. Rather, the purpose of these observations is to highlight some significant, although admittedly less tangible, factors that are obscured by their framework, yet remain relevant to a full comparative analysis of institutions for natural resource and environmental policy. The principal limitations of their analysis lie in their simplistic characterization of market, legal, and public institutions.

* * *

NOTES

1. Many of Blumm's criticisms of Anderson and Leal focus on the failure of markets to achieve efficient outcomes. How far do these criticisms go in challenging the basic libertarian notion that people should be free to decide for themselves whether to contribute to an environmentalist vision of the "good life"? Of the "good nation"? Is efficiency or liberty more important to the "Privateers"?

2. Do Anderson and Leal create a false dichotomy between markets and political control? Blumm criticizes Anderson and Leal for failing to endorse recent reforms in environmental statutes that incorporate market mechanisms. Anderson and Leal view these intermediate steps to incorporate market tools as inadequate because political processes would continue to be employed in setting environmental standards. Is there a bright line separating market decisionmaking from political decisionmaking? Cass R. Sunstein suggests that critics of governmental regulation overlook the affirmative role of government to protect life, liberty and property. AFTER THE RIGHTS REVOLUTION: RECONCEIVING THE REGULATORY STATE (1990). The social contract underlying our constitutional democracy is not only to protect individual freedom from the interference of government, but also to secure the conditions for free and equitable interaction among individuals through affirmative controls of the marketplace. This function originally resided in the common law courts and their development of principles of property, tort and contract. Increasingly, with the market failures described by Blumm, statutory controls and administrative regulation have come to play this affirmative role. How are statutory and administrative tools different from the common law tools endorsed by Anderson and Leal? Are common law courts agents of political control?

3. For a criticism of privatization from an economic perspective, see Carlisle Ford Runge, *The Fallacy of "Privatization"*, 7 J. CONTEMP. STUD., Wint. 1984, at 3.

4. Blumm objects to privatization on grounds of equity. The wealthy will be able to purchase more environmental resources, so more of their preferences will be realized than of those who are poor. How far does this argument go? Would Blumm allocate other essential goods such as food, housing, and medicine through public agencies?

5. How might transaction costs affect the efficient allocation of resources under the Anderson and Leal model? Suppose, for example, that the federal government decides to sell Jellystone National Park to the highest bidder. In a prospectus, the government notes that the Park is valuable for two incompatible purposes. On the one hand, the Park could be used for recreational purposes, with a maximum net income of ten million dollars per year. On the other hand, the Park could be used to mine precious minerals. The net value of minerals in the Park is known to exceed one hundred million dollars. Who are the likely bidders in this scenario? Which of these bidders will likely face the highest transaction costs? Are those transaction costs likely to be sufficiently high to change the outcome of the proposed sale? What is the best economic use of the Park?

6. How does the Anderson and Leal model account for future values of non-market resources? Consider this problem in the context of wilderness land management. Many wilderness areas have substantial value today as recreational areas, and as sanctuaries for ecosystems which are largely unaffected by humans. Suppose that the U.S. Forest Service is facing a choice whether to designate a tract of national forest land as wilderness or to open the land to logging. Suppose further that the government's decision will be designed to maximize the net public benefits from the land. At the time that the Forest Service is making the decision, 10 percent of the land in that particular national forest has been designated wilderness and an additional 25 percent has similar ecological values and remains available and suitable for wilderness designation. Assume that in 100 years no significant tracts of land will remain suitable for wilderness designation and that unless additional lands are designated now, the portion of designated wilderness in the forest will remain at 10 percent. What would likely happen to the value of the tract in question if it were designated as wilderness? If it were available for logging? (Assume that the trees in this forest are suitable for harvesting on a 100-year cycle.) How should the agency assess future values?

Perhaps the most important intellectual challenge privatizers pose to other environmentalists is the notion that there is no public interest apart from the aggregate preferences of individuals in society. If the privatizers are right, then their case for using markets to account for those preferences is significantly strengthened. Menell briefly addresses the issue of using democratic processes to express preferences as his second point of criticism of Anderson and Leal in a portion of his article deleted from the excerpt in this book. Consider the following, more developed defense of public interest and public ownership.

THE CLAIM FOR RETENTION OF THE PUBLIC LANDS
Joseph L. Sax
from Rethinking the Federal Lands (Sterling Brubaker ed., 1984)*

In the spring of 1982, a proposal put forward by the Reagan administration to sell a substantial fraction of the federally owned lands (some 35 million acres was the figure most commonly mentioned) attracted considerable attention. By midsummer, the issue had become a leading news item, reaching the first page of the *New York Times* and the cover of *Time* magazine. As summer waned, so did the land sale proposal. Its principal proponent in the White House, Steve Hanke, had gone back to his academic post after strong reservations to the proposal had been expressed by numerous spokesmen for western public land states; and journalists began to turn their attention to other, more newsworthy issues.

There are sufficient practical and political reasons to make it unlikely that any large-scale sale of federal lands is in the offing. But the issue is a perennial in American political discourse because some profound issues of public policy are raised by substantial public land ownership and management in a nation deeply committed to private proprietorship of major resources and industries. * * *

* * *

* * * It is simply the fact that the existing arrangements for use of the public domain reflect decades of political and economic bargaining under which many interest groups of any consequence have obtained benefits that suit them and to which they have adapted. The existing system, however imperfect it may appear from the perspective of economic efficiency or resource management, is, after all, a "mature" system that incorporates some highly developed expectations. Changes that unsettle long-held expectations are, simply by virtue of that fact, costly. This is not to assert that change should never be made; it is to say only that change imposes its own costs, and that it is unrealistic to expect people to respond to any ideas proposed for an established system as if they were being written on a blank slate. Water may be sold from federal projects at excessively low prices, stockmen may have indefensible advantages on federal grazing lands, inefficient timber management may be supporting marginal mills, but existing communities and industries have grown up around these practices.

Again, there is an irony here. Those who favor disposal tend to sympathize with the claims of property owners, and are wary of government-imposed disruption of their expectations. Should the expectations of those who have had long-standing benefits from

---

* Reprinted with permission.

traditional uses of the public domain be discounted simply because they are not—from a lawyer's perspective—formally cognizable property rights? There is a powerful tension here that suggests the imposition of prudential restraints on any program that threatens sharply destabilizing changes imposed over a very short period of time. It well may be that the result of the current system of political decision making, with all its inconsistencies so maddening to theorists, is more acutely sensitive to the real interests of the various constituencies that comprise the American public than appears to distant critics.

This leads to my final preliminary observation. Ownership, although it is the focus of the current debate over the future of the federal lands, is, in fact, a poor measure of the real relationship that exists between government control and private market decision making on the public lands. For example, nothing in the fact of government ownership itself prevents the government from managing its lands precisely as a private entrepreneur would do. Following the same model of behavior that the proprietor of an office building uses in leasing space in a skyscraper, the federal government could lease lands for mineral or timber production to maximize economic efficiency. By the same token, government could sell off all its lands and subsequently impose through regulation any of a variety of constraints that would impair the economically efficient use of the property. Both such models of behavior, and many in between, can be found somewhere in the vast recesses of the federal government. To those who yearn for economic efficiency as the governing principle, it need only be said that public ownership does not negate its possibility any more than private ownership in a regulatory milieu assures it.

It is often said that government bureaucrats are poor managers or that public ownership is excessively influenced by powerful interest groups, and there is evidence to support those observations. Selling the public lands will not cause those problems to disappear, for to the extent that the government as a proprietor is a source of mischief, there is little reason to believe that the government as regulator will be less mischievous.

* * *

The debate over ownership of the public lands is basically part of a much larger controversy over the legitimacy of collective versus individualistic values. In essence, the argument in principle for disposal of the public lands is this: Each person knows best what is best for him or her, and, therefore, the best system is one that permits the real preference of individuals to be revealed and implemented. With rare exceptions, the ideal mechanism for implementing these preferences is a private marketplace where each individual expresses his or her desires through bidding. Private ownership advances this goal, and public ownership impedes it. If, for example, I want to use land for hiking and you want to use it for timber harvesting, public ownership which sets it aside for hiking permits me to get what I want without paying its true cost, since the losses engendered by prohibiting timber harvesting will be spread throughout the tax-paying population and will not be borne by me. The outcome, unlike that which would be achieved by market bidding between the hikers and the loggers, will thus be imperfect.

It can be seen immediately that the problem thus suggested is not limited to ownership. It also is present in government regulation of privately owned land. If government regulates timber harvesting to advantage recreational users, the recreationists benefit without having to reveal their true preferences, that is, without being willing to pay for the losses generated by the regulation. It is not ownership alone that raises the problem of "distorted preferences," but control through government. * * *

The real issue that divides advocates of sale (or "marketeers") from those who seek retention (or "regulators") is found in the unstated assumption that underlies discussion of "preferences." The marketeers assume that the only real or legitimate preferences are those that are expressed by individuals behaving atomistically. Thus, if an outcome differs from that which would have occurred through the expression of individual preference (the sort that occurs in market transactions), *ipso facto* it must be wrong (except in those relatively rare instances where the market does not reveal true preferences). The regulators believe that individuals have more than one kind of preference, and that because individual behavior in the market reveals only one species of preference, it therefore is incomplete. There is, they say, a kind of preference that people hold solely in their capacity as members of collectivities, and for which only collectivities speak. One such collectivity is the political community, or the government. When the government regulates, or controls use as owner, it is expressing a collective preference.

Thus, for example, if the government restrains timber harvesting to the advantage of hikers, it is expressing a preference no less real or legitimate than the preference I express if I decide to keep my land as a rose garden rather than to sell it to a timber company at a given price. To be sure, that decision may differ from that which any individual or group, acting *as* individuals would have made, but that is simply because the political community as a collectivity has some interests which differ from those of any individual or group. The outcome is not "wrong" because it differs from that which individual action in the market would have produced. Nor is it wrong because somehow the collectivity does not "pay" for its preferences. If the government owns a tract of land and decides to forgo the potential benefits from timber harvesting in order to maintain recreational use, that decision is no different from the one I make in forgoing a large cash payment to maintain my rose garden. Of course, the way in which that willingness to pay is felt differs in a collectivity—it is more indirect, for example, and more diffuse—but that is the only way a collectivity can operate. To characterize its behavior as inappropriate, illegitimate, or inefficient is simply to deny the possibility of a collective value.

* * *

* * * Stated most starkly, the concern is that, as collective values increase, individual autonomy declines. And the corollary premise is that the maintenance of individual autonomy is the premier virtue, so important and so obvious that it barely needs to be defended. That premise often underlies the rhetorical question, What makes you think that the state or some bureaucrat knows better than I do what is best for me?

It is, however, far from clear that the maintenance of individual autonomy is the primary goal of most people most of the time. Indeed, there is a great deal of evidence to suggest that one of our strongest urges is to identify ourselves with a source of moral authority, and to subordinate our autonomy to it; that we draw strength from values external to our purely personal convictions; and that we draw values from collective solidarity. * * *

* * *

Imagine an average individual happily using a tract of land he owns as a rose garden. Another offers him $1,000 for the land, intending to use it to build a house. The owner makes a counteroffer to sell at $2,000, and settles with the builder for $1,500. This individual is operating in the realm of pure preference.

This average individual may well decide to give the tract to the church as an annual contribution—not an unprecedented thing to do. The church then refuses the highest offer made—$1,500—and determines to maintain the rose garden as a senior citizen project. Assume, further, that the outcome differs from that which would have occurred in any individual transaction. The church, as an entity, has different "preferences" than the original owner, or any sum of church members, acting as individuals, would have revealed. And assume finally that the original donor and his co-members of the church are perfectly happy with the result, though it diverges from what any of them would have done had they retained ownership of the property.

What has happened here? Why would someone give up autonomy over the land and permit it to be used this way? Why is it, in short, that people often choose not to express their interests individually, but through the medium of a collectivity?

One possibility is that some collectivities are administratively efficient units which, by summing the property of a number of owners, can more effectively achieve the result each individual wants than would have been possible were each participant to act individually.

Another possibility is that, since information is not costless, the collectivity can obtain information that the individual needs but cannot obtain. The collectivity, once informed, will make the decision each individual would have made if he or she had access to the information.

Still another possibility is that he or she wants the collectivity to help formulate his or her preferences. The individual might believe that he or she should do something about charitable contributions and, to this end, is willing to pay part of an advisor's salary in order to learn how much to contribute on an annual basis both for the present and in the future. A further possibility is that he or she endows some collectivities because of feelings of mutual obligation and duty and to that extent, wants the collectivity to go beyond the advisory role and to shape, intensify, or change preferences held previously. Certainly some collectivities, like churches, behave as if that were their mandate.

One might say that nothing very interesting is revealed by all this since such collectivities are voluntary, allowing any member to resign at any time that the organization does not fully reflect what is desired. Thus the collective decision, whatever it may be, is nothing more than the sum of the then preferences of its members; and the "different" decision of the collectivity is no different than the preferences an individual might express at two different points, depending on what information is available. Thus, the atomistic model still holds.

Yet—whatever the precise mechanism by which collectivities operate—the very decision to give resources to a specific collectivity has consequences. Even if the collectivity does nothing more than provide information that shapes the individual preference, it is not the same information that was available to the individual before he or she had made the endowment. The decision whether to resign subsequently is inevitably affected by the information, or advice, provided to the individual.

This is why action by "voluntary" collectivities cannot be dismissed as simply the implementation of the purely individual decision of each of the members, where the member's nonresignation is treated as a sort of subsequent ratification. The critical period is not the moment after the collective decision is made (at which time one decides whether to resign) but the period between entry into the organization and the moment the decision is made. That is, what happens up until the decision is made—which may be viewed as the information flow from the collectivity to the individual member—will itself change the person (by supplying new data) and will thus itself affect the decision whether to resign. At the very least, one who joins an organization yields autonomy in the sense that individual authority is transferred to another to obtain information that will inform subsequent decisions.

To give but one example of the shaping power of collective action, assume that a group of individuals get together voluntarily to establish an organization to meet their recreational needs, and that organization in turn establishes Central Park. After the park has existed for some time, each member then asks what he or she thinks about such parks. It seems inevitable that the individual's response will be affected by the mere fact that Central Park has existed up to the point that the evaluation takes place. It also will be affected by how much time passes before such an evaluation is made. Whatever the precise answer in a given case, the individual to some extent will have given up some autonomy to the collectivity, by letting the collectivity shape his or her knowledge and experience. * * *

* * *

* * * [I]n organizing governments the public routinely (perhaps uniformly) yields to them more than the absolutely necessary minimum. The so-called night watchman, or minimal, state is in fact more a theoretical construct than a reality. Everywhere one looks, now and in the past, states take on functions such as the promotion of national solidarity by building monuments, supporting the arts, promoting historic consciousness, and advancing education. In short, communities build monuments to what they value, and history is replete with evidence that they often value commitments to solidarity more than mere single-minded devotion to individual autonomy. Perhaps this is only evidence of the sort that simply asserts the importance of something because people have found it important over long periods of time. But do those who think the maintenance of untrammeled autonomy is the central good to be achieved have any evidence *more* compelling to support their conclusion?

To assert the legitimacy, and even the desirability, of collective action by the state does not, of course, reject the importance of the individual; nor does it suggest that every collective value that can obtain a majority should, *ipso facto*, prevail over the claims of a dissenting individual. An intermediate position between the totally autonomous individual and the totally dominating state is what has most often commended itself to every society that takes account of the individual's importance. Rather than saying it is the duty of society to maximize personal autonomy to the greatest extent possible, they have said that *some* elements of personal autonomy are too important to be exposed to collective coercion. At least in the broad sense, those elements are eminently familiar: for example, freedom of speech, association, belief, and religion.

The distinction thus made between carving out a range of personal rights immune from collective coercion and prohibiting coercion everywhere except in a very few essential areas (such as taxing for a police force) serves as a recognition that (1) maximization of autonomy of every kind is not the sole or always dominant social value; (2) that expression of collective values is very important, even though some autonomy is thereby sacrificed; and (3) that the collective values of the political community can be deemed essential, even though the community is wholly involuntary.

* * *

I suggest that there plainly are [collective] values, which I shall try to illustrate with the following example. Imagine a country resembling France having a strong sense of nationhood and a strong interest in what the people call their patrimony. Suppose the country has a large number of historic chateaus—oozing with historical importance and greatly in need of restoration—situated at places that make them prime targets for commercial development. There are a considerable number of people who are interested in both visiting and preserving the chateaus, and though they are willing voluntarily to pay a good deal to purchase them, in general they cannot outbid commercial interests.

Deeply discouraged, they are ready to abandon the effort, believing that their bids represent the true value of preservation, which is, lamentably, less than the value of the chateaus for commercialization, when one of their number makes the following observation.

The interest in preserving these chateaus has been miscalculated up to this point. The preservation value consists not only in the opportunity afforded to us (and others like us) who will visit the places, and who obtain gratification from such preservation; but the entire nation will benefit if patriotism is affirmed and a sense of nationhood engendered and sustained by the maintenance of these buildings. There is no reason why we should pay, or be expected to pay, for values beyond those which flow to us directly because of our special interests. Nor should we pay for those which flow to us as part (but not the whole) of the nation that will benefit by increased national solidarity. We have lost out in the bidding because the true value of preservation is greater than what we bid, or what (acting as individuals) we should bid. It is perfectly possible that if the nation itself bid for the properties, it would outbid the commercial developers.

Still, one may ask, are we not able to generate voluntary contributions that equal the totality of these benefits? The answer is clearly no, for some well-recognized reasons. If one of the benefits of preservation is the strengthening of national solidarity, then preservation will automatically benefit every citizen. Even those who do not contribute voluntarily will nonetheless reap the benefits; this is what is familiarly called the "free-rider" problem. Moreover, *this* benefit (as contrasted to the benefits we reap as individual visitors, for example) will not exist unless and until the nation acting *as* a nation recognizes it. * * *

* * *

Another complaint frequently made by "marketeers" is what might broadly be called the "corruption" of the governmental process. It is suggested, for example, that bureaucrats have dominant control over public programs and that they act selfishly to promote their own well-being rather than the public interest. I do not see how anyone could deny the existence of such a problem, but it must be recognized that this problem exists with any organization employing intermediaries. The tension between corporate managers (who have interests of their own) and stockholders is a staple of the business literature. Every private, collective entity—the churches, the universities, labor unions—are prey to this problem.

It also has been emphasized that the state may be, and often is, at the mercy of powerful interest groups who turn government to their own limited interests. Again, there is no doubt that this is a problem, and a serious one. It is likewise true that elected officials are far from perfectly accountable to their constituents. Some are fond of noting how few Americans even know the name of their representative in Congress, and even if they do, how difficult it is to make a periodic vote reflect any constituent's view of the legislator's vote on the myriad of issues on which he will express himself in the interim between elections. Of course, all these are common, and familiar, failures of politics. No sensible person denies them; no knowledgeable person can dispute them. It is not the existence of the problem that is in controversy, but the solution suggested.

The answer in effect given by the marketeers is to give up on politics, to view it as irredeemable. The suggested response is abolition, rather than reform; or, to put it rather more modestly, to remove from government as much power as possible to do mischief, by limiting its functions to the minimum possible level. Again, I concede that this is a legitimate philosophical view, but I must emphasize that it incorporates a very controversial assumption: That most of the things government seeks to do—the sort of things that are distinctively the product of collective values held by the political community—are relatively unimportant. Thus, in the view of these critics, to give up most collective values is to lose little or nothing. The critique reduces to the proposition that only those values which we hold as individuals, acting atomistically, are worthy values. There simply *is* nothing beyond personal preference. If one is persuaded by such a view, of course there is no point in working at reform of public decision making. My goal here has been to suggest that the assumptions underlying such a position are far from obvious. * * *

* * *

* * * What possible distinctive interest could the national political community have in the hundreds of million acres of publicly owned land, mostly in the western United States, and largely valuable primarily for commodity production, that would induce it to maintain ownership? * * *

I think the answer to the question of the political community's possible interest in the public domain lies in a much more general relationship between public values and the use of land. Without hoping to be exhaustive, let me sketch briefly the transition I see taking place in that relationship, of which the debate over the public domain is only one modest element.

I must begin with the trite observation that there is always some link between the rights that individuals are permitted to obtain in property and some public notion of the public interest. Perhaps the point is most easily illustrated by a very old issue, the right of inheritance. At the outset it is always the political community that decides what interest people may, and may not, obtain in property. To permit individuals to acquire the right to transmit their property to their heirs through inheritance demonstrates a social value. Laws that prohibit or impair the transmission of wealth through inheritance embody quite different collective values. Every rule of property, including rules about what rights of use, or sale, or inheritance, are adopted, begins with some social value.

* * *

As traditional values feel the stress of change, the institutions that grew out of those values will be reexamined, as, indeed, they have been. One might also expect significant changes regarding a shifting relationship between the rights of owners and the scope of public regulation. And we have seen—particularly in recent decades—some very dramatic changes.

To put the matter simply, we have seen increasing regulation constraining traditional ownership—regulation that implements skepticism about the desirability of largely untrammeled economic growth. The most obvious examples, of course, are conventional air and water pollution laws, constraints on hazardous substances like pesticides, and controls over the management and disposition of wastes. All these laws are, as industrialists are fond of pointing out, limitations on economic development. So they are. It might be said that these laws are simply modern examples of the sort of control over harmful externalities that can be traced back centuries to the law of nuisance. So they can, though the balance of interests has certainly shifted away from the traditional encouragement of industrialization that made nuisance a quite limited legal remedy.

But there is also a wide range of controls on property that have no obvious antecedents and which underline sharply the growing idea that nonuse, or preservation, rather than development and exploitation, may well be the highest and best use of property. One example is the recent growth of historic preservation laws, which are remarkable when considered from a traditional perspective. Owners who have done nothing "wrong," who cannot in any ordinary way be said to be imposing harm on others, are nonetheless often required to leave their property as it is, because it is believed that retention of historical structures is a more valuable use of the property than any developmental changes would be. Suburban growth-control ordinances are another example of the same phenomenon; however controversial such laws may be, they are revealing of a sharply changed notion. Communities that traditionally encouraged development, and measured their success by how rapidly they were growing, now often seek to slow or even end growth, because they view maintenance of their rural character, or their quietude, as of the highest importance. Open-space ordinances in towns, and wilderness designation in the country, illustrate a similar principle: Doing nothing is viewed as the highest and best use of the land.

These are only a few of the best-known examples of the kind of change that is occurring to some degree everywhere in America. The change reveals itself in increased regulation because the "new value" is not one that is likely to be implemented by private owners pursuing their own interests. This is simply one more way of saying that traditional private property rights (which will lead to development and use) are becoming increasingly divergent from public values about property. Development and use, to the extent that it fails to promote what is viewed as "progress," sets the public and the private owner on different courses. The likely result is a change in the definition and content of property. And that is what the above examples all illustrate.

From the perspective I have just identified, the controversy over the public lands begins to come into focus. There is resistance to sale, because public ownership is seen as a means (and perhaps the most effective means) of control. Control is seen as necessary—more necessary than ever—because public values are more than ever divergent from the interests of private owners. Private uses are still thought appropriate, of course, and they may and often will still dominate the public lands. But those uses are increasingly constrained, just as urban uses are constrained, by zoning, growth control, environmental legislation, historic preservation, architectural controls, open-space regulation, and a host of other elements of the "new idea of progress." Retention of the public lands is really just another version of what occurs by regulation elsewhere.

To retain public lands only where they now exist—principally in the West—and to leave the rest of the country in private ownership is not as "inconsistent" as it may seem at first glance. It is control in favor of civic values—rather than proprietorship—that counts; and that control is moving toward a national equilibrium, as I have just noted above. In practice, there are doubtless some sensible reasons to treat the public land areas differently. They are, by and large, less developed already and are thus more likely to be affected by greater regulation than is the urbanized East; people in the rural West are less accepting of regulation by zoning, and thus—as I noted earlier—regulation by ownership may be a more effective way of achieving the same goals; some public values—such as wilderness preservation, wildlife habitat, and "open" public recreation—can only be pursued effectively in the West, and such goals are most likely to conflict with conventional private ownership.

The important point, however, is not proprietorship as such, whether in the West or the East, but the conflict between collective and private values, for the movement to sell the public domain lands is ultimately a symbolic one. From that perspective, sale of the lands (assuming it would lead to less regulation than now exists, a disputable assumption but not an obviously erroneous one, * * *) would in fact be a step backwards from the new balance that is everywhere being struck between the claims of privatism and of public values.

NOTES

1. In the introduction to his article, Professor Blumm claims that "setting environmental policy is fundamentally about arriving at collective values—how much economic growth must be sacrificed for a clean airshed, for example. While markets may accurately measure individual consumer preferences, they are incapable of reflecting collective environmental values because most environmental resources are incapable of being accurately priced." Michael C. Blumm, *The Fallacies of Free Market Environmentalism*, 15 HARV. J.L. & PUB. POL'Y 371, 372 (1992). Is there a set of collective environmental values in the heterogeneous, multi-cultural United States? Does the political process accurately reflect collective environmental values? Or just the majority's values? Or just the values of an influential, elite green lobby?

2. According to Sax, public values about land and natural resource protection are diverging from established private interests; and consequently, private interests must adjust their expectations. Is this fair? Is it possible to extend Sax's argument, which focuses on resource preservation, to the pollution policy debate?

3. Professor Sax and many other critics of privatization recognize that the government plays an active regulatory role in managing markets. Professor Krier poses the question: "Why will the government not fail in setting up and overseeing the new natural resource markets, just as it fails, and for the same reasons, in setting up and overseeing regulatory programs?" James E. Krier, *The Tragedy of the Commons, Part Two*, 15 HARV. J.L. & PUB. POL'Y 325, 341-42 (1992).

4. Richard Stroup argues:

> Another related point has been missed entirely by Sax: private speculators provide the only link that future citizens have with resource decisions in the present. Presently, as voters, future citizens have no clout at all. Politicians who hurt today's voters to help those of tomorrow harm their election-day prospects. That simply is not a survival trait for politicians. But speculators who correctly forecast price trends can buy today, taking off the current market a resource (development land, for example), and preserving it for the future. Eventually they will gain by selling it when others have begun to recognize the increased scarcity, and the price increases. The speculator who is even one or two years ahead of the market in his knowledge or expectations can cash in as soon as others jump in, by buying claims to that asset. Note also that a similarly farsighted BLM director or secretary of the interior cannot gain personally by guessing right and "swimming against the tide," sacrificing current benefits to preserve when most people do not see the reason for it. Further, only the generosity of voters permits preservation, even when the majority knows it is good for the future. With private property, charitable instincts are reinforced by future gains in property values, as both speculators and conservation organizations have realized.

Richard L. Stroup, *Weaknesses in the Case for Retention*, *in* RETHINKING THE FEDERAL LANDS 149, 152 (Sterling Brubaker ed., 1984). How do you think Sax would respond? Would there be a difference in the way a conservation group would speculate on the future value of an area as wilderness, and the way a mining company would speculate on the future value of the area's precious minerals?

C. The Public Trust Doctrine

> [I]n *Land* that is *common* in *England,* or any other country, * * * no one can inclose or appropriate any part, without the consent of his Fellow-Commoners: Because this is left common by Compact, *i.e.* by the Law of the Land. * * * Besides, the remainder, after such inclosure, would not be as good to the rest of the Commoners as the whole was, when they could all make use of the whole.

JOHN LOCKE, SECOND TREATISE OF GOVERNMENT § 3 (Peter Laslett ed. 1960) (1698).

The public trust doctrine describes a set of public property rights that are so important to society that the government lacks its traditional authority to dispose of these rights. Most commonly, the doctrine applies to property rights associated with water, such as ownership and use of tidelands, lake beds, and water rights themselves. The doctrine has attracted the attention of many commentators, however, because of its potential application to a wide range of other public property rights, including public lands. Professor Sax's articles lay out the theoretical contours of the public trust. Professor Lazarus describes how courts have used the doctrine and argues that it has outlived its usefulness as a tool for environmental protection. Professor Huffman describes and criticizes many of the conceptual categories in which scholars have placed the doctrine. Huffman argues for a public trust doctrine limited by the law of easements.

Professor Joseph L. Sax's 1970 article describing the public trust doctrine is probably the most frequently cited law review article on an environmental subject. Sax's theories have played an important role in the development of environmental law, particularly in the areas of resource preservation and citizen participation in agency decisionmaking. The first excerpt, from the original 1970 article, describes the doctrine's roots in water law and draws the contours for a public trust doctrine that might encompass other aspects of the environment. The second excerpt, from a 1980 elaboration of ideas justifying a strong public trust doctrine, discusses the importance of public expectations as a basis for judicial recognition of citizens' rights to prevent destabilizing changes in the environment.

THE PUBLIC TRUST DOCTRINE IN NATURAL RESOURCE LAW: EFFECTIVE JUDICIAL INTERVENTION
Joseph L. Sax
68 Mich. L. Rev. 473 (1970)*

* * *

Of all the concepts known to American law, only the public trust doctrine seems to

---

* Reprinted with permission.

have the breadth and substantive content which might make it useful as a tool of general application for citizens seeking to develop a comprehensive legal approach to resource management problems. If that doctrine is to provide a satisfactory tool, it must meet three criteria. It must contain some concept of a legal right in the general public; it must be enforceable against the government; and it must be capable of an interpretation consistent with contemporary concerns for environmental quality.

* * *

Other than the rather dubious notion that the general public should be viewed as a property holder, there is no well-conceived doctrinal basis that supports a theory under which some interests are entitled to special judicial attention and protection. Rather, there is a mixture of ideas which have floated rather freely in and out of American public trust law. The ideas are of several kinds, and they have received inconsistent treatment in the law.

The approach with the greatest historical support holds that certain interests are so intrinsically important to every citizen that their free availability tends to mark the society as one of citizens rather than of serfs. It is thought that, to protect those rights, it is necessary to be especially wary lest any particular individual or group acquire the power to control them. The historic public rights of fishery and navigation reflect this feeling; and while the particular English experience which gave rise to the controversy over those interests was not duplicated in America, the underlying concept was readily adopted. Thus, American law courts held it "inconceivable" that any person should claim a private property interest in the navigable waters of the United States. It was from the same concept that some of the language of the Northwest Ordinance was taken:

> [T]he navigable waters leading into the Mississippi and St. Lawrence and the carrying places between the same, shall be common highways, and forever free, as well to the inhabitants of the said territory as to the citizens of the United States . . . without any tax, impost, or duty therefor.[43]

An allied principle holds that certain interests are so particularly the gifts of nature's bounty that they ought to be reserved for the whole of the populace. From this concept came the laws of early New England reserving "great ponds" of any consequence for general use and assuring everyone free and equal access. Later this same principle led to the creation of national parks built around unique natural wonders and set aside as natural national museums.

Finally, there is often a recognition, albeit one that has been irregularly perceived in legal doctrine, that certain uses have a peculiarly public nature that makes their adaptation to private use inappropriate. The best known example is found in the rule of water law that one does not own a property right in water in the same way he owns his watch or his shoes, but that he owns only an usufruct—an interest that incorporates the needs of others. It is thus thought to be incumbent upon the government to regulate water uses for the general benefit of the community and to take account thereby of the public nature and the interdependency which the physical quality of the resource implies.

Of all existing doctrines, none comes as close as does the public trust concept to

---

[43] Act of July 13, 1787, art. IV, 1 Stat. 51.

providing a point of intersection for the three important interests noted above. Certainly the phrase "public trust" does not contain any magic such that special obligations can be said to arise merely from its incantation; and only the most manipulative of historical readers could extract much binding precedent from what happened a few centuries ago in England. But that the doctrine contains the seeds of ideas whose importance is only beginning to be perceived, and that the doctrine might usefully promote needed legal development, can hardly be doubted.

* * *

LIBERATING THE PUBLIC TRUST DOCTRINE FROM ITS HISTORICAL SHACKLES
Joseph L. Sax
14 U.C. Davis L. Rev. 185 (1980)*

At a superficial level, the shape of the public trust doctrine is easy enough to discern. It draws upon the Roman Law idea of common properties (*res communis*) and on certain provisions of Magna Carta. It deals with lands beneath navigable waters, with constraints on alienation by the sovereign and with an affirmative protective duty of government—a fiduciary obligation—in dealing with certain properties held publicly. Yet to restate these commonplace observations is not to begin to penetrate the core of this unusual legal doctrine.

* * *

It is unreasonable to view the public trust as simply a problem of alienation of publicly owned property into private hands, since many—if not most—of the depredations of public resources are brought about by public authorities who have received the permission of the state to proceed with their schemes. On the other hand, it is inconceivable that the trust doctrine should be viewed as a rigid prohibition preventing all dispositions of trust property or utterly freezing as of a given moment the uses to which those properties have traditionally been put. It can hardly be the basis for any sensible legal doctrine that change itself is illegitimate.

At its heart, the public trust doctrine is not just a set of rules about tidelands, a restraint on alienation by the government or an historical inquiry into the circumstances of long-forgotten grants. And neither Roman Law nor the English experience with lands underlying tidal waters is the place to search for the core of the trust idea.

The essence of property law is respect for reasonable expectations. The idea of justice at the root of private property protection calls for identification of those expectations which the legal system ought to recognize. We all appreciate the importance of expectations as an idea of justice, but our concern for expectations has traditionally been confined to private owners. We have tied the *legal* concern with expectations to private proprietorship and to formal title; and while we recognize that mere title is not enough to sustain every claim of expectation that is made under it, it is hard to imagine legally enforceable expectations unconnected to formal title. At the same time we know that, insofar as expectations underlie strong and deeply held legal-ethical ideals, they are not limited to title ownership.

In *"The New Property,"* Professor Charles Reich[9] introduced the notion that many things lacking traditional status as formal property—things like television or liquor licenses—in fact generate expectations quite like those that attach to traditional forms of property. Even interests that don't at all resemble ordinary property give rise to important values and expectations that cry for recognition, and sometimes get it. Much of the recent controversy over the federal highway program, and over urban renewal, was engendered by the prospect of the destruction of established communities. Similar problems are arising today with the inundation of established western communities by energy development projects. The root values that inhere in the maintenance of an established community have much in common with the established expectations that underlie the recognition of private property rights.

To put the idea of expectations in a broader context, one might say that stability, and the protection of stable relationships, is one of the most basic and persistent concerns of the legal system. Stability in ownership is what we protect with property rights; stability within a community is a major part of the business of the criminal law. Of course, stability does not mean the absence of change, nor does it mean political or legal reaction. It does mean a commitment to evolutionary rather than revolutionary change, for the rate of change and the capacity it provided for transition are precisely what separate continuity and adaptation from crisis and collapse.

Precisely the same point might be made from a biological perspective. The focus of environmental problems is *not*, as is sometimes suggested, the mere *fact* of change, which it is said environmental zealots cannot accommodate, but rather a rate of change so destabilizing as to provoke crises—social, biological and (as we see in the context of energy prices) economic. The disappearance of various species from the earth in the natural, evolutionary process is totally different from the disappearance of species over a short time. The key difference is not the *fact* of change, but the *rate* of change. The essence of the problem raised by public trust litigation is the imposition of destabilizing forces that prevent effective adaptation.

The central idea of the public trust is preventing the destabilizing disappointment of expectations held in common but without formal recognition such as title. The function of the public trust as a legal doctrine is to protect such public expectations against destabilizing changes, just as we protect conventional private property from such changes. So conceived, the trust doctrine would serve not only to embrace a much wider range of things than private ownership, but would also make clear that the legal system is pursuing a substantive goal identical to that for the management of natural resources. Concepts like renewability and sustained yield, so familiar to us in fisheries and forest management, are designed precisely to prevent the sort of sudden decline in stocks that is destabilizing and crisis-provoking. The legal system incorporates parallel concerns in protecting expecta-

---

[9] 73 YALE L.J. 733 (1964).

tions, and it remains only to assure the legal principle's application more comprehensively.

* * *

* * * [T]he public trust doctrine should be employed to help us reach the real issues—expectations and destabilization—whether the expectations are those of private property ownership, of a diffuse public benefit from ecosystem protection or of a community's water supply. The historical lesson of customary law is that the *fact* of expectations rather than some formality is central. Of course, title is not irrelevant where ownership is actually a surrogate for reliance and expectation and where non-recognition of title would in fact be destabilizing. Conversely, where title and expectations are not congruent, title should carry less weight. We do sometimes overtly recognize this point, as in the California cases of 1970 dealing with implied dedication of land permitting access to the sea.

Our task is to identify the trustee's obligation with an eye toward insulating those expectations that support social, economic and ecological systems from avoidable destabilization and disruption. Less acute intrusions should be selected where feasible. In dealing with projects proposed for bottomlands, for example, the trustee should ask whether they need to be water-based. Where the alternatives include a solution which will sustain yields and support long-established human uses or biological communities, that approach should be required. Where traditional expectations must give way to new techniques or new needs, the transition should be as evolutionary—rather than revolutionary—as the new needs permit.

In our legal system there is always a question of separation of powers underlying substantive questions. In considering the rights of private property owners and their rightful expectations, we endow the courts with the final word. Since expectations so diffusely held are not explicitly recognized in the Constitution, courts have been less willing to take ultimate responsibility for public trust claims. Some courts have nonetheless found the trust responsibility to be a constitutional mandate to legislatures, based on the requirement that legislative acts be for a public purpose. For these courts, a failure to recognize, or at least to consider and deal with, expectations in ways that minimize destabilization of expectations could represent a failure to act for a public purpose.

But however appealing such interpretations may be, sharp confrontations between courts and legislatures should be avoided wherever possible. The courts can do much to provoke a search for less disruptive alternatives below the constitutional level. They can assure that decisions made by mere administrative bodies are not allowed to impair trust interests in the absence of explicit, fully considered legislative judgments. Under the rubric of the legislative remand, courts can also press a legislature to fortify its decisions with a full consideration of less disruptive solutions. Finally, the courts can reduce the pressures that claims of private ownership put on public trust resources by looking to the history of common rights. The courts should recognize that mere unutilized title, however ancient, does not generate the sort of expectations central to the justness of property claims, and that long-standing public uses have an important place in the analysis.

With such an approach fully in operation, we could integrate legal doctrine and fundamental principles of intelligent resource management, instead of treating basic social decisions as if they were merely the province of a title examiner. We could draw sustenance from history, rather than viewing it as a sterile, manipulative game.

NOTES

1. In a few celebrated cases, courts have applied the public trust doctrine advocated by Sax to protect the environment. These modern cases extend the public trust in two ways. First, courts augment the traditional public trust rights of navigation and fishing to include other interests, such as recreation and environmental protection. Second, courts broaden the area subject to the trust beyond tidal waters to embrace dry sand beaches, freshwater wetlands, or other natural resources.

In *National Audubon Society v. Superior Court of Alpine County*, 658 P.2d 709 (Cal.), *cert. denied sub nom. City of Los Angeles Dept. of Water and Power v. National Audubon Society*, 464 U.S. 977 (1983), the California Supreme Court found that persons holding state water rights hold those rights subject to a public trust in favor of protecting the people's common heritage of streams, lakes, marshlands and tidelands. The *National Audubon Society* decision is striking because the Court recognized a state duty to reconsider prior grants of water rights in order to protect public trust values. The Court required the state agency that permits water diversions to account for and plan to minimize the aesthetic and ecological harms to saline Mono Lake that result from diversion of its tributary streams.

In *Matthews v. Bay Head Improvement Ass'n*, 471 A.2d 355 (N.J.), *cert. denied*, 469 U.S. 821 (1984), the New Jersey Supreme Court found that the public trust includes the use of the dry sand beach above the high water mark of the sea, extending to the vegetation line. The public may use the dry sand beach not just for access to the tideland, but also "to sunbathe and generally enjoy recreational activities." *Id*. at 364.

2. The key to understanding Sax's idea of the public trust is that all private property owners take title subject to the pre-existing rights of the public. Doesn't this lock in place antiquated expectations about environmental protection? How can the public trust doctrine account for modern concerns for preservation of ecosystems?

3. Sax argues that the public trust doctrine should be employed to prevent the destabilizing disappointment of expectations held in common but not in title. Why should anyone have a reasonable expectation to something not specified in private title? Sax would reply that the fact of the expectation, not the formal recordation, is important. But still, what makes an expectation reasonable if not a formal recordation or clear common law rule? How can courts determine what public expectations are? Who speaks for the public? Legislators? Can the public gain public trust rights through prescription? That is, can use of property by the public at the sufferance of a private landowner ripen into a public trust right? If so, does that create an incentive for private property owners to deprive the public of as much of its diffuse interests as possible?

4. What role should courts play in enforcing the public trust? Should (may) courts find rights that have not been formally recognized by legislatures?

The public trust doctrine is a very appealing concept, particularly in justifying permanent protection of vulnerable or exemplary natural resources (*e.g.* barrier beaches or Yellowstone National Park). Yet Sax goes to great lengths in his article to deny the absolute permanence of such public trusts. At the end of his 1970 article, Sax states that the "fundamental function of courts in the public trust area is one of democratization." Not only must the court cast broadly to assure that the diffusely held interests are adequately represented, but decisions made in previous generations must be open to reconsideration by future generations. Would this doctrine satisfy the demands of preservationists? Are preservationists' ideals founded on elitist, anti-democratic principles?

5. What happens when the special obligation that governments have as trustee of certain natural resources conflicts with other governmental duties to act for the public benefit? These conflicts are not always as dramatic in contrast as chopping down the last redwoods to provide timber, or damming the Grand Canyon to produce electricity. These days, for example, the preservation of wetlands must compete with job security, economic development and needed affordable housing. Is Sax suggesting some hierarchy of governmental functions or some set of decision rules for resolving the tensions between the multiple roles that government plays (which we have come to expect)? Should he?

6. Elsewhere in his 1980 article, Sax supports the "root values" of established communities and the legitimacy of unrecorded public expectations. Does Sax's reasoning support the now widespread NIMBY (Not-In-My-Backyard) reaction to new development of any kind? If the public trust doctrine is to protect against destabilizing valid public expectations, how should the court distinguish between enduring local expectations and parochial but popular resistance to any change in the status quo?

7. Professor Richard Delgado criticizes the public trust doctrine on a number of grounds:

My first reservation with the public trust approach is that the model is inherently antagonistic to the promotion of innovative environmental thought. A trust is, by its nature, conservative—its purpose is to protect a corpus and put it to some use. The idea is to protect what one has, to reduce the risk of improvidence or improper expenditure. Trusts are established to serve an already defined purpose, not to prompt consideration of what that purpose should be. One establishes a trust for a child's college education, for example, once one has decided the child should attend college, not to prompt the child to reflect about his or her future, or about whether he or she should attend college, much less about whether college education, as currently constituted, is good or ideal.

In this view, the trust theory arrived on the scene too early in our debate about the environment. It was adopted before we had explored adequately humanity's relationship with the environment. In short, the fit between it and the stage of social dialogue was poor. Yet something about it attracted us and made us adopt it—made us seize it before we knew precisely what we were protecting and to what extent. The trust theory froze thinking on our relationship to nature in the form in which it was articulated in the early 1970s. Serious reflection on environmental questions continued, of course, but it was marginalized and confined to the pages of fringe journals and the books of the radical environmental movement. It was no longer center stage as it was during the period just prior to the advent of Sax's theory.

My second reservation with the public trust theory is that it is poorly suited to advance natural values. The approach places protection of the environment in the hands of a trustee, generally some agent of the sovereign, who is issued a set of instructions and told to protect the environment accordingly. Unfortunately, the trustee in whose hands the environment is placed is not in the classical position of trustee. Typically a government agency, it will be in no better position to understand how the environment is to be protected than we are.

* * *

In the environmental revolution, th[e] savior was Joseph Sax, whose trust theory, *Mountains Without Handrails*, and other landmark works established his credentials as a serious reformer and condemnor of the old order. At the same time, his public trust article dealt the coup de grace to legal scholars and environmentalists who were pushing for a radical transformation in consciousness. His theory, then, was in some ways forward-looking, an imaginative, pragmatic—even gallant—effort to save the environment from further deterioration. Yet the theory won wide support largely because it did not promise farreaching environmental protection. It offered exactly what society needs during the middle and late stages of a revolution—a way of confining change to a manageable level.

Sax's public trust doctrine was attractive because it offered protection from our base instincts. It enabled us to tell ourselves that we no longer needed to worry about the dark sides of our natures. It enabled us to tell ourselves and each other that we had finally done something about the environmental problem. Yet by placing control over natural resources and wilderness areas in government agencies run by people like us, we could feel confident that familiar, comfortable values would shape and restrain environmental decisionmaking. The ecofeminists and others advocating sweeping change were shut out. The problem was taken care of in a way that would not change anything too fundamentally—which was all to the good.

Richard Delgado, *Our Better Natures: A Revisionist View of Joseph Sax's Public Trust Theory of Environmental Protection, and Some Dark Thoughts on the Possibility of Law Reform*, 44 VAND. L. REV. 1209, 1214-15 , 1225-26 (1991). If neither the government nor "people like us" can act effectively as trustees for environmental protection, then who should oversee environmental management? How does the public trust theory freeze our thinking about environmental ethics? Do you see any signs of changed attitudes toward the environment in the past twenty-five years? The sweeping changes advocated by ecofeminists are discussed in the notes following the Lynn White excerpt in Chapter One of this anthology.

8. Some commentators have taken the public trust doctrine a step further and suggested that an affirmative duty of stewardship should be imposed on private property owners to prevent destabilizing environmental harms. This duty, although not strictly a trust, would impose limitations on the autonomy of landowners in a manner similar to the public trust doctrine. *See* ERIC T. FREYFOGLE, JUSTICE AND THE EARTH (1993); James P. Karp, *A Private Property Duty of Stewardship: Changing Our Land Ethic*, 23 ENVTL. L. 735 (1993). Can the public trust doctrine be a vehicle for stimulating a more ecological land ethic? The land ethic is discussed in detail in the Aldo Leopold excerpt in Chapter One of this anthology.

Professor Lazarus describes the development of public trust theories in Nineteenth Century American law, and the special importance of the *Illinois Central Railroad* case, which Professor Sax has called the lodestar of American public trust law. After acknowledging the trust's importance, Lazarus argues that recent developments in administrative, tort, property, and constitutional law have rendered the public trust approach unnecessary and possibly harmful to environmental interests.

CHANGING CONCEPTIONS OF PROPERTY AND SOVEREIGNTY IN NATURAL RESOURCES: QUESTIONING THE PUBLIC TRUST DOCTRINE
Richard J. Lazarus
71 Iowa L. Rev. 631 (1986) (reprinted with permission)

* * *

I. THE ORIGIN OF THE PUBLIC TRUST DOCTRINE IN AMERICAN LAW

* * *

B. Introducing the Public Trust Doctrine into the United States

The English common-law notion that the public retains certain inviolable rights to natural resources ultimately found its way into judicial opinions in the United States. Adopting the distinction first expressed in Lord Chief Justice Hale's treatise, nineteenth-century American jurists divided the interests in navigable waters into three categories:

(1) *jus publicum*—the rights of the general public; (2) *jus regium*—the royal right to manage resources for public safety and welfare (akin to our modern police power); and (3) *jus privatum*—the private right of title. The dual sovereign nature of our federal system, however, added a new twist to the *jus publicum*. From the outset, the Supreme Court described the sovereign interest of the national government in terms differing from the state government's sovereign interest, even though it described the interests of both sovereigns in property law terms. The Court termed the federal sovereign's paramount interest over commerce in interstate navigable waters the "federal navigation servitude." In contrast, the Court described the state interest generally in terms of the state's "sovereign ownership" of the bed of certain navigable waters within each state's own borders. Apart from the precise labels the Court employed, the common interest of both sovereigns in those water resources was clear in the nineteenth century. Commerce was primarily waterborne; the rivers served as highways for pioneers and supplied power for industry. Accordingly, cities and towns invariably lined major waterways, and natural ports were a prerequisite to developing a major metropolitan area.

1. Federal Navigation Servitude

Federal insistence that navigable waterways were subject to special public rights and, therefore, national sovereign authority, was first formalized when states attempted to grant exclusive franchises to navigate their waterways. Indeed, it was this type of arrangement between New York and Robert Fulton (of steamboat fame) and Ambassador Livingston that led Chief Justice Marshall to declare in *Gibbons v. Ogden*[23] that commerce in navigable waterways was of such great importance that maintenance and availability of the waterways must be within the exclusive control of the federal government. This ruling spawned a host of judicial decisions concerning the scope and significance of this special federal power, called the federal navigation servitude. These decisions occurred as the national government sought to expand the internal waterway system and in so doing often interfered with the specific plans of states and private parties.

2. State Ownership of Beds of Navigable Waters

At the state law level, the public trust doctrine took on a different character, suggesting not only that the state possessed special powers over these water resources, but also that it owed certain enforceable duties to the public as well. The Supreme Court ultimately described the nature of this state authority in 1842 in *Martin v. Lessee of Waddell*[26] as state ownership of the beds of navigable waters in their sovereign capacity.

The origins of the modern public trust doctrine thesis lie in the notion of "sovereign capacity" ownership. In particular, lurking in the background of those early judicial rulings was the suggestion that state power to alienate the resource or otherwise deny general public access is sharply restricted. This suggestion was critical to Sax's later thesis and found its roots in judicial descriptions of sovereign ownership of waterways as akin to the powers and duties of a trustee.

---

[23] 22 U.S. (9 Wheat.) 1 (1824). A previous circuit opinion written by Chief Justice Marshall in fact foreshadowed the ruling. *See* Wilson v. United States, 30 F. Cas. 239, 245 (C.C.D. Va. 1820) (No. 17,846).
[26] 41 U.S. (16 Pet.) 367 (1842).

3. *The* Illinois Central Railroad *Decision*

In *Illinois Central Railroad v. Illinois*[30] the Supreme Court squarely addressed the issue of the meaning of state sovereign ownership. The legal issue raised in that case was fairly narrow—whether Illinois could, by legislative enactment, repeal an earlier statute conveying huge portions of the bed of Lake Michigan to Illinois Central without offending the federal Constitution. The Supreme Court's reasoning in upholding the state legislature's subsequent action is not evident. The Court could have relied easily on the theory that the initial enactment was devoid of legitimate public purpose, especially given that the Court could have done so merely by deferring to the subsequent legislature's considered judgment. The four-justice majority instead expounded at length on the special nature of sovereign ownership of navigable waters to support its ruling that the state grant had been revocable. The thrust of the Court's far-reaching opinion, though certainly unnecessary for the result, is unmistakable. According to the Court, at some level a state legislature is powerless to convey into private hands a natural resource as important as Chicago's harbor. The decision, however, raises more questions than it answers.

First, the Court assumed that without title the state would be powerless to prevent use of the harbor, which the state later determined was contrary to the public interest. But the lack of power hardly seems plausible, given that state police power would regulate railroad uses of the resource and the federal navigation servitude would still provide for both maintenance of the navigability of the resource and public access. In all events, certainly no legal bar would prevent the state from exercising its eminent domain authority to repurchase the property.

The decision raises a second, even more perplexing issue. It is far from clear what source of law the Court was drawing upon to reach its result. Language in the opinion suggests that the Court was announcing a rule based on federal law universally applicable to all state legislatures. Although the tone of the opinion nearly strikes constitutional chords, the Court thirty years later described the *Illinois Central* decision as merely resting on a "matter of Illinois law."[39]

Taking the Court's subsequent characterization as correct, as we must, we then must fathom the basis for the Court's declaration of such a novel rule of state law. The Court did not cite any relevant precedent in Illinois law to support the decision. The Court merely referred vaguely to the use of sovereign trust language by state courts in their decisions discussing state ownership of the submerged beds. This in turn is followed only by the Supreme Court's naked assertion that the trust arrangement is inalienable.

The *Illinois Central* decision remains today the "lodestar"[42] guiding the modern public trust doctrine. State courts have repeatedly turned to it in the late nineteenth and early twentieth centuries to justify rejecting or at least carefully scrutinizing shortsighted or

---

[30] 146 U.S. 387 (1892). * * *

[39] *See* Appleby v. City of New York, 271 U.S. 364, 395 (1926). In *Appleby* the Court reversed the ruling of the New York Court of Appeals and held that under state law the legislature could grant land under tidal water free of the *jus publicum* and had done so in this case. *See id.* at 383-84. Accordingly, the Court held that if the state wanted to reassert its sovereign rights, it would first have to buy them back. *See id.* at 399.

[42] Sax, [*The Public Trust Doctrine in Natural Resource Law: Effective Judicial Intervention*, 68 MICH. L. REV. 471 (1970)], at 489.

even corrupt legislative attempts to convey into private hands critical coastal or inland waterway resources. And still today courts rely on the *Illinois Central* Court's reasoning to support their rulings.

4. *Expansion of the Trust Concepts*

The notion of sovereign ownership in trust originated but did not remain confined to navigable waters and their beds. Similar language cropped up in judicial opinions describing the source of special governmental authority over wildlife and public lands. In the case of public lands, the Supreme Court went so far as to suggest that trust duties included the responsibility to ensure that the resources were "not wasted."[47] Perhaps the most interesting early expansion of the trust concept, however, was its application to city streets. Many courts upheld municipal authority to allow railroads use of the streets and other public trust property. These courts often held that the trust doctrine exempted the city and its commercial licensees from liability for harm caused to adjoining property owners by transit activities. Ultimately many state courts expanded this application of the trust to promote the use of city streets by elevated railroads. Eventually the subsurface for the growing hidden infrastructure of the city was represented in the form of subways, sewer pipes, gas lines, and electric cables. California courts similarly utilized the trust concept to promote economic development, by ruling that growing cities in need of water, such as Los Angeles, had broad sovereign rights to waters within their original land. Thus, the traditional trust doctrine concept in the United States became as much a legal basis for economic expansion as for resource protection.

* * *

III. THE PAST AND FUTURE ROLES OF THE PUBLIC TRUST DOCTRINE

* * *

Assessment of the future value of the public trust doctrine must start with the candid premise that the doctrine rests on legal fictions. Notions of "sovereign ownership" of certain natural resources and the "duties of the sovereign as trustee" to natural resources are simply judicially created shorthand methods to justify treating differently governmental transactions that involve those resources. Like most legal fictions, the purpose of the public trust doctrine at various periods of American legal history and in recent years has been to avoid judicially perceived limitations or consequences of existing rules of law. The precise object of concern varied; in *Illinois Central*, it was corrupt or shortsighted state legislatures; in the nineteenth-century water rights and city street matters, it was inadequacies in absolute private property rights that denied public needs or private tort remedies that threatened municipal development; more recently, the source of worry in the environmental arena has, as Professor Sax put it, been with "insufficiencies of the democratic process."[168]

---

[47] *See* Knight v. United States Land Ass'n, 142 U.S. 161, 181 (1891); *see also* Camfield v. United States, 167 U.S. 518, 524 (1897); United States v. Beebe, 127 U.S. 338, 342 (1888).

[168] Sax, at 521.

* * *

Instead of immediately casting the fiction aside, recognizing the fictional nature of the trust doctrine is necessary to frame the debate on the doctrine's continued usefulness in natural resources law. Just as the need for legal fictions arises in the wake of changing circumstances that strain existing legal norms, so too the need dissipates when, over time, the fabric of the law is woven in a more coherent and systematic fashion in response to those initial changes. Or, alternatively, new changes may occur that similarly remove the initial justification for the fiction's creation. In this manner, a time comes when the fiction is no longer necessary. Even more fundamentally, the fiction's continued use obscures analysis and thus impedes the law's coherent development. On this basis, the future of the public trust doctrine in natural resources law must be assessed.

Assessing the public trust doctrine on this basis leads to the conclusion that the day of "final reckoning"[177] for the doctrine is here, or soon will be, and reliance upon it is no longer in order. As shown in the following sections, the law of standing, tort law, property law, administrative law, and the police power have all evolved in response to increased societal concern for and awareness of environmental and natural resources problems and are weaving a new and unified fabric for natural resources law. Whether these developments are viewed as totally independent of the doctrine or, alternatively, as somehow having subsumed the doctrine's principles does not matter. The conclusion is the same from either perspective: much of what the public trust doctrine offered in the past is now, at best, superfluous and, at worst, distracting and theoretically inconsistent with new notions of property and sovereignty developing in the current reworking of natural resources law. * * *

* * *

C. Conceptions of Sovereignty and Property and the Public Trust Doctrine

* * * At bottom, the trust doctrine is premised on a view of the nature and role of the sovereign that has little in common with the current style of government, at least in the areas of environmental protection and natural resource conservation. In particular, the doctrine assumes that absent its sovereign ownership and trustee duties, governmental powers over important natural resources would be inadequate and governmental accountability to the public for its decisions affecting those resources too limited. Recent developments in natural resources and environmental law question both of these assumptions.

To be sure, governmental power to protect the environment is not currently absolute, nor is governmental accountability for its environmentally destructive activities total. A negative assessment of the continuing utility of the public trust doctrine does not require either such extreme result. The relevant inquiry looks to the net impact of the doctrine. Here, that means asking whether in the face of recent changes in the nature and scope of governmental power, the doctrine continues to play a significant, independent role. Here again, the trust doctrine falls short.

---

[177] [L. FULLER, LEGAL FICTIONS (1967)] at 121.

1. *The Rise of the Modern Police Power State*

a. Expansion of Police Power Authority

First, there currently is little room or need for the public trust doctrine to play a meaningful role in promoting sovereign authority over environmental quality. The trust doctrine arose at a time, long since gone, when sovereign power depended on ownership and, accordingly, when courts interpreted the scope of governmental police powers quite narrowly. Then, the validity of a governmental police power restriction that adversely affected private property expectations depended on fictional categories. * * *

* * * It is now well settled that the police power is the most fundamental source of governmental authority to prevent needless environmental harm and related risks to human health and welfare. To be sure, the "police power" too could be described as a legal fiction, but unlike the trust doctrine, the police power is a live fiction that reflects current legal analysis and social values. The extent of police power authority does not depend on the application of formalistic categories of property law, but ultimately on the precise nature of both the governmental interest and the private property expectations at odds in a particular case.

* * *

The environmental protection and natural resource conservation laws of the last fifteen years broke dramatically from the traditional view of limited government and incorporated much of the New Deal vision of the rightful role of government. At the outset, the validity of the newer laws does not, as it did in the past, turn on their furthering narrow health and safety concerns; courts require only a rational relation to a goal of some "conceivable public purpose,"[234] including, for example, aesthetic values, conservation goals, or public welfare in general. * * *

* * *

2. *Modern Administrative Law*

The tremendous expansion in the nature of sovereign authority and the degree of governmental oversight does more, however, than undercut any meaningful role for the public trust doctrine in promoting governmental authority. The implications of this expansion question the central premise of the trust doctrine's origins—that the doctrine provides a needed legal basis to ensure public accountability for governmental decisions that adversely affect the environment.

Here again, hindsight suggests that the modern public trust thesis is wide of the mark. First, it did not account for developments in administrative law brewing back in 1970, in particular, the impact of environmental values on administrative law. Second, it missed the fundamental shift that occurred after infusing environmental values into the government's role in enforcing environmental protection programs.

---

[234] *See* Hawaii Hous. Auth. v. Midkiff, 104 S. Ct. 2321, 2329 (1984); *see also* Ruckelshaus v. Monsanto Co., 104 S. Ct. 2862, 2879-80 (1984).

a. Administrative Agency Decisionmaking and Accountability

Prior to and during the 1970's, administrative law underwent a significant reformation that obviated any meaningful role for the public trust doctrine. Administrative law responded to changing societal demands without resort to the doctrine's origins in Roman law public trust principles. As the subject matter of the administrative agencies' decisions steadily expanded beyond the traditional scope of purely "administrative" matters to substantive issues that affect the behavior of persons in all aspects of their social and economic lives, the basic methodology of administrative agency lawmaking fundamentally changed. * * *

* * *

Congress passed statutes that, although still containing vague mandates, took strides to dictate procedures the agency should follow in implementing the statute. Or, Congress increasingly laid out those explicit substantive matters that the agency must consider and weigh when formulating its policy. The President, similarly, in recent years has exercised his executive authority to prescribe promulgation rules for agency rulemaking procedures. The courts, however, have taken the most farreaching strides to increase agency accountability, both in response to legislative and presidential directives and at the court's own initiative.

Courts have responded in two principal ways. First, judges have strictly enforced requirements designed to promote and enhance public participation in the agency decisionmaking process, and have made it easier for a private citizen to seek judicial review of the agency's decision. At the same time, courts perceptively tightened their own standards of judicial review of the merits of agency decisions by requiring adequate consideration of all interests affected by the agency decision. The courts deferred to agency expertise, perceiving that agency decisions turned as much on questions of social policy and politics as on matters of technical expertise, and more willingly demanded, as a matter of agency rulemaking procedure, that an agency provide a more fully reasoned and articulated basis for its decision. * * *

b. Impact of Environmental Values on the Administrative Process

Judicial appreciation of society's increased concern with environmental protection and resource conservation was a primary impetus behind the administrative law developments during the 1970's. Beginning with the Supreme Court's decision in *Citizens to Preserve Overton Park, Inc. v. Volpe,*[330] courts took a "hard look" at agency decisions that implicated environmental concerns. Although the hard look doctrine may in part simply reflect the judiciary's general concern with agencies implementing vague congressional mandates involving issues of broad societal importance, such as those invariably contained in environmental laws, other more peculiar aspects of environmental concerns have been a major factor. Four aspects stand out most prominently as triggering judicial concern: (1) the lack of a ready powerful constituency able to represent the interests in environmental protection, especially the interests of future generations; (2) the inherent difficulty of measuring the value of environmental protection, let alone assessing the risk of a low

---

[330] 401 U.S. 402 (1971).

probability-high consequence environmental catastrophe, especially when compared to the more immediate and perceptible economic rewards of resource exploitation; (3) the relationship of environmental protection to human health; and, perhaps most importantly, (4) increasing awareness that modern technology has raised the stakes of incorrect short-term decisions by giving us the power to destroy irreversibly aspects of our natural environment whose importance we are only beginning to understand.

These same basic concerns are also reflected in modern environmental and natural resources statutes, which now typically rein in agency actions that potentially affect the environment. The National Environmental Policy Act of 1969 (NEPA), buttressed by the ambitious regulations of the President's Council on Environmental Quality, is the most obvious example of the modern statutes. It requires federal agencies to consider the environmental impacts of proposed actions, which include issuing federal permits, spending federal funds, and managing vast federal properties, prior to taking any such action. So too, the inclusion in many federal environmental laws of provisions that specify those actions that the agency must consider unlawful and that generally impose mandatory duties on the agencies, coupled with citizen suit provisions empowering private suits both against agencies for failing to take required action and against other private parties for violating the terms of the statute, also has dramatically increased agency accountability to the public.

These same triggers are, to be sure, comparable to those Professor Sax suggested to justify heightened judicial scrutiny in the context of the public trust doctrine. But while developments in administrative law in the environmental context confirm Sax' rationale for heightened judicial scrutiny, the developments simultaneously undercut any need to rely on trust doctrine notions. Most simply put, those special considerations related to environmental concerns have successfully spoken for themselves in the judicial arena. Thus, in *Overton Park*[349] the Supreme Court, without any need for recourse to the public trust doctrine, effectively accomplished the doctrine's objective—heightened judicial scrutiny of an administrative action that failed to consider adverse environmental impacts. Indeed, the import of the Court's reasoning practically endorsed the substantive importance of the relevant environmental considerations.

The advantages of not relying on the trust doctrine, moreover, are substantial. Most fundamentally, the excess baggage that must necessarily be carried by any litigant who wishes to make an argument based on the public trust doctrine disappears. It is unnecessary to argue at the threshold that the doctrine attaches to the resource in question. Following through attenuated chains of title to show that the trust has somehow survived is unnecessary. Similarly, it is unnecessary to work around the traditional trust purposes of prodevelopmental objectives such as promotion of commerce (which arguably was met by the roads at issue in *Overton Park*).

* * *

IV. THE FUTURE OF THE PUBLIC TRUST DOCTRINE IN MODERN NATURAL RESOURCES LAW

Mere irrelevance is not, of course, enough to justify a call to abandon public-spirited invocation of the doctrine. Little in the law, let alone legal academia, would likely survive

---

[349] Citizens to Preserve Overton Park v. Volpe, 401 U.S. 402 (1971).

such an exacting standard. Rather, the appropriate remedy depends on whether use of the public trust label has or potentially could have significant adverse effects. It is to this inquiry that the Article now turns.

Evaluating the public trust doctrine on the basis of the adverse effects criterion leads this author to conclude that continued reliance on the doctrine is ill advised. Continued use of the doctrine ultimately threatens to impede environmental protection and resource conservation goals and possibly render Pyrrhic earlier advances. Most fundamentally, the doctrine's operation exacerbates a growing clash in liberal ideology within natural resources law—between the need for individual autonomy and security, traditionally tied up in private property rights, and the demands of longer-term collectivist goals expressed in environmental protection and resource conservation laws. In addition, totally apart from destructive ideological conflicts the trust doctrine creates, relying on the doctrine is no longer sound strategy. The doctrine no longer reflects current environmental values and unduly relies on a proenvironment judicial bias. Recent Supreme Court precedent strongly suggests, moreover, that the doctrine's fiction carries little weight in the legal balance. This Article discusses these concerns—ideologic and strategic—in turn.

A. Toward a Liberal Rejection of the Public Trust Doctrine

Natural resources law is currently undergoing a major transformation. Traditionally, natural resources law was a scheme of laws riddled over time by a bizarre array of formalistic property-based doctrines designed to achieve specific social goals. It is gradually evolving into a more unified system of rules in which competing private and social goals in natural resources are openly debated and limited private rights are assigned by the government. The public trust doctrine, by inevitably depending on traditional notions of property law and trusts, conflicts with the direction that current environmental protection and natural resource conservation concerns are leading legal rules. As a consequence, the doctrine threatens to undermine the important developments in natural resources law.

1. *Erosion of a Property-Based Doctrine*

The thrust of recent developments in environmental and natural resources law has been to replace already eroding traditional notions of private property rights in natural resources with a scheme of government-administered and defined private entitlements to those resources explicitly premised on continuing sovereign regulatory authority. The history of natural resources law in this country, which influenced early environmental law, has been marked by a series of obscure legal rules rooted in a wide variety of property law doctrines. Esoteric doctrines such as the rule against perpetuities, adverse possession, abandonment, the rule of capture, the common enemy doctrine, the English rule of absolute ownership, traditional riparian law, lost grant, ancient lights (or lack thereof), the law of waste, restraints against alienation, and the Statute of Frauds, and absolute maxims such as *cuius est solum eius est usque ad coleum et usque ad inferno*, and *primus in tempore, potior est in jure* dominated the substance of legal rules defining the scope of private rights in essential natural resources such as land, water, oil, and gas. Each doctrine or maxim sought to influence either the initial allocation or the subsequent distribution of the affected natural resources in a manner designed to promote identifiable social goals.

The last one hundred years, however, have been marked by a constant struggle to free natural resources law of the older, often rigid property rules and maxims. Many of the rules once served important functions; time, however, has since passed them by. Three primary reasons for this development prevail. First, society has greatly changed and social values have changed accordingly, rendering obsolete the objectives of the old rules. These rules, like many property law rules, are weighed down by historical baggage of little continuing relevance. Second, several of the earlier doctrines were based on assumptions about the physical characteristics of resources and the limits of technology that advances in science have since discredited. Third, the pace of change in recent decades has quickened to such a level that we now require a flexibility in our legal rules that the older doctrines do not admit.

The steady erosion of these traditional property law doctrines, however, is not an isolated event. It is part of a much wider trend in the law that challenges the very notion of private property rights in natural resources. Most simply put, as a result of dramatic and accelerating social, economic, and scientific changes in this country over the last one hundred years, the public interest in protecting natural resources and ensuring the most efficient or socially optimal distribution of products has increased exponentially and has overtaken individual interests. Most persons no longer live in rural settings with ready access to private ownership rights in basic natural resources and thus most must rely on others to exercise rationally those rights. Private ownership of natural resources, moreover, does not reside as in the past with individuals often very concerned about the need to preserve sufficient resources for their children and their children's children. Increasingly, it is in the hands of corporate giants, which are guided in their decisionmaking by short-term profit maximization. Technology does not provide an outer limit on resource exploitation, but instead it has advanced to the stage that threatens exploitation of monumental proportions. At the same time, advances in other, more subtle areas of the physical, chemical, and biological sciences only recently have begun to suggest the full extent of the fragile interdependencies in our natural environment. These advances reveal the possibly irreversible consequences of manipulating the environment to meet immediate demands.

The most obvious implication of this increased public interest has been greater demand for direct governmental involvement in decisions that affect the relative availability and quality of important natural resources. The most pernicious implication is that the most central justification of private property rights in those resources is undermined. Private property rights today are justified principally on the market theory that a rational profit maximizer who owns natural resources will utilize those resources in a manner that not only optimizes his or her own interest but also society's overriding interest in the efficient use of the resource. Notions of individual personality and security, although still present, are generally mere incidental justifications for private property rights. The clear implication of these changes in social demographics and advances in science is that society cannot so easily rely on the free market premise that a private decisionmaker acting in his or her own best interest will also act in society's best interest. The private decisionmaker will be unaware of the social costs of the decision. Although this has always been true, the notion of externalities, reflected in the concept of rights created by dependencies between various property owners, has generally been a minor concern of property law, or at least it has been left largely unstated. Today those unconsidered social costs may be tremendous in the natural resources context. For example, the cost to future generations is of special concern, particularly in light of our growing exploitation abilities.

* * *

2. The Rise of "New Property" in Natural Resources Law

The clear trend in environmental law and natural resources law today is to replace traditional notions of private property rights in natural resources with an intricate scheme of government-administered entitlements and permits. This trend is most evident in developing governmental programs respecting resources that have traditionally been the object of exclusive private ownership, such as land, groundwater, and fossil fuels. Detailed land use plans restrict private decisionmaking; and even when development such as mining is allowed by law, subsequently restoring land to its approximate natural condition may be required. Groundwater, under the common law, was the absolute property of the overlying property owner and is now the object of strict state regulatory allocation under new laws. The production and exploitation of fossil fuels is not only the subject of massive regulation, but also the object of substantial taxes that effectively transfer the economic wealth of the resource to the general public.

This same trend extends to those natural resources historically considered incapable of private ownership, such as air, oceans, arctic zones, and space, but no longer so viewed in light of recent technological advances that allow, if not exclusive possession, then irreversible despoliation. Current laws direct the government to allocate rights in those resources and, in the case of pollution control laws, allow private markets in these "new property" rights in natural resources. The goal of the new property rights is to reemphasize the importance of private markets in achieving allocational efficiency once the government has had the opportunity to set the initial ground rules.

Finally, the trend toward legislative replacement of common-law rights with limited entitlements defined by the government in the first instance extends to traditional common-law tort rights as well as common-law property rights. In the environmental area, for example, statutes limit or prescribe liability for harm caused by certain environmental catastrophes. According to the courts, a "person has no property, no vested interest, in any rule of the common law."[415]

The public trust doctrine simply has no place in this emerging scheme. The doctrine finds its home in the legal analytical framework supported by traditional property dogma currently (and appropriately) being abandoned. It was essentially the public property analogue to those private property concepts, which are now eroding. The doctrine's main purpose, like notions of "qualified property" and "property affected with a public interest,"[416] long since discarded, was to provide the sovereign with a ready answer to claims of the sanctity of private property rights at a time when governmental power was itself rooted in its own property holdings. To be sure, the public trust doctrine has tremendous mystical and romantic appeal, which no doubt partly explains its revival in

---

[415] See Duke Power Co. v. Carolina Envtl. Study Group, Inc., 438 U.S. 59, 88 n.32 (1978).

[416] See E. FREUND. [THE POLICE POWER] § 373; Walker, [*Property Rights in Oil and Gas and Their Effect upon Police Regulation of Production*, 16 TEX. L. REV. 370 (1938)] at 377-79.

recent years. It must be every litigating lawyer's dream to uncover that ancient case with still-binding precedent that turns the tide by establishing in the client some invincible right. From that perspective, what is better than a right grounded in Roman law that purported to protect the quality of the natural environment and the rights of unrepresented future generations in its preservation? Still, just as notions of absolute private property rights in natural resources have been and are being eroded in the wake of modern environmental and natural resources laws, so too it is only appropriate that their public property analogues be similarly abandoned. Absolutist claims on either side of the ledger are, at best, unhelpful. At an earlier time, the doctrine no doubt served the quite useful function of focusing legal analysis on a growing public concern—preserving and conserving natural resources. That initial task of refocusing has been accomplished. The difficult problems that beset the development and implementation of modern environmental and natural resources law are no longer aided by resort to a legal doctrine, such as the public trust.

3. *The Need for Candor and Protection of Individual Rights in Natural Resources Law*

Undoubtedly, the most difficult problem facing environmental and natural resources law is to reestablish some level of certainty and security in private interests in natural resources. While traditional notions of absolute private property rights are no longer in order, defining the scope of the emerging new property rights in those resources is critical to the long-term viability of the environmental protection movement. * * *

* * *

Flexibility is becoming an essential ingredient in the makeup of laws governing private and public rights in natural resources to respond to these varied physical and sociological demands. This is especially true given the rapid pace at which new knowledge is nowadays acquired and the high costs at stake in preventing needless environmental degradation. Granted, flexibility in legal rules is often at the expense of stability that is important to individual security. So too, flexible laws are susceptible to accusations that they are vague, and thus they suffer from infirmities akin to those of the public trust doctrine. The question, though, becomes who should and how to accommodate these competing concerns. Who, in other words, is the appropriate manager of a given resource? It is here, perhaps most of all, that we find the public trust doctrine's greatest flaws—a lack of candor and a lack of an established institutional framework for lawmaking.

First, like other already abandoned property-based legal fictions, the trust doctrine finds its strength and tenacity in its resistance of candor and its refusal to compromise its principles. In this way, promoting public trust analysis runs counter to the compelling need for self-examination, candor, and flexibility in the reshaping of natural resources laws. Second, unlike the emerging scheme of new property rights in natural resources that is developing largely at the administrative level (generally instigated by the legislature and overseen by the courts), the public trust doctrine provides no ready framework for the assignment of lawmaking authority. The legal doctrine is inherently suspicious of legislative and administrative lawmaking regarding natural resources; yet, at bottom, it offers nothing much in its place. By addressing none of the critical tasks currently facing the development of natural resources law, and indeed potentially resisting those efforts, the public trust doctrine threatens to fuel the growing conflict in liberal ideology and impede the fashioning of a unified system of law.

B. Toward a Strategic Retreat from the Public Trust Doctrine

Finally, even apart from its failure to provide needed candor, and its inflexibility in the face of changing values and knowledge, reliance on the doctrine should be abandoned because it offers too tenuous a basis for protecting important environmental protection and resource conservation objectives. * * *

1. *The Failure of the Trust to Reflect Modern Environmental Concerns*

The strength of the public trust doctrine necessarily lies in its origins; navigable waters and submerged lands are the focus of the doctrine, and the basic trust interests in navigation, commerce, and fishing are the object of its guarantee of public access. Commentators and judges alike have made efforts to "liberate," "expand," and "modify" the doctrine's scope, yet its basic focus remains relatively unchanged. Courts still repeatedly return to the doctrine's historical function to determine its present role. When the doctrine is expanded, more often than not the expansions require tortured constructions of the present rather than repudiations of the doctrine's past.

Achievement of modern environmental protection and resource conservation goals, moreover, ultimately depends not so much on an "expansion" of public trust values as it may require a repudiation of the doctrine's focus and traditional values. Today, societal concerns with environmental protection and resource conservation extend beyond navigable waters to include far-ranging elements of our ecosystem, such as the ozone layer, unheard of in Roman times. Our economy no longer depends so exclusively on water navigation. Our economy "navigates" by air, by motor vehicle, and, indeed, by way of the electromagnetic spectrum. So too, the promotion of commerce, a traditional public trust doctrine objective, is hardly a focus of resource protection values. Indeed, more often than not it serves as a counterweight to those values in the formulation of public policy because of its prodevelopment bias. Finally, public access, undoubtedly the single most important public trust guarantee, is often at odds with modern environmental conservation and protection laws. Increasingly, those laws must restrict access to protect resources. One telling sign of a legal fiction's demise is that the words they represent change meaning to such an extent that, as with the trust doctrine currently, the fiction's application and substance are simply a matter of individual discretion.

In short, the way we and our laws look upon natural environment has changed fundamentally since the development of the public trust doctrine. The legal categories and social value upon which the doctrine is based have little to do with modern concern. Ultimately, the public trust doctrine does not need to be "liberated," so much as our natural resources laws, including the trust doctrine, must be freed from the past.

2. *Undue Reliance on Proenvironment Judicial Bias*

A second long-term weakness that counsels abandonment of the public trust doctrine is its implicit assumption that the judiciary is in the best position to safeguard environmental concerns and that it will in fact do so. For this reason, critics typically complain that the public trust doctrine is antidemocratic and a historical "sham" or "mask" for judicial usurpation of legislative and executive branch power. Even more fundamentally, however, good reason suggests questioning the validity of the assumption that the judiciary will lean toward environmental protection, apart from philosophical concerns about the proper workings of a democracy.

First, although it is true that judicial concern is naturally triggered by the typically unrepresented environmental interests in the political process, the courts also have demonstrated considerable concern with governmental impingements on individual security interests. Environmental concerns are not guaranteed a victory in the courts should a collision with individual security interests occur.

Second, the favorable bias toward environmental protection, exhibited by the courts in the 1970's, might not continue. In the past, courts have used the public trust doctrine to support developmental activities they favored. The vagueness of the doctrine's mandate lends to the risk that the doctrine could still further those interests. Certainly, environmental interests deserve and require a firmer and more secure position in our laws.

Finally, regardless of judicial bias or desire, courts may lack sufficient competence in the environmental arena. Questions arising in the environmental and natural resources law field can be so inordinately complex and the competing societal concerns at stake so fundamental that at some level judicial second-guessing of administrative agency action may not be particularly productive. Better solutions, suggested by critics of the judicial function in environmental matters, may reside in new modes of administrative decisionmaking that are less dependent on effective judicial oversight of agency action to ensure full representation of competing considerations. One possibility suggested is to establish surrogate representatives of varying interests within regulatory agencies. Whatever the merits of these proposals, their relevance to the wisdom of the public trust doctrine is clear. They stand for the proposition that the solutions to the sorts of difficult problems society faces in environmental areas do not lie with the judiciary, while the trust doctrine ultimately depends on the contrary thesis.

* * *

NOTES

1. Lazarus is critical of the public trust doctrine for relying too heavily on pro-environmental judicial activism. But, isn't the doctrine as much a guiding principle for the executive branch as it is for the judicial branch? How could the doctrine enable agencies to justify conservationist actions? Generally, how does legal doctrine influence, strengthen, or constrain the different branches of government and other players in the political process?

2. Is Lazarus' confidence in the permanent transformation of social values and their attendant institutional guarantees well founded? Might the need for reassertion of public rights and the government's role as public trustee reemerge? The diminution of pro-environmental sympathy in the federal judiciary has coincided with trends in administrative law that have restricted the opportunity of the public to secure the kind of searching judicial review of agency action promised in *Overton Park. See Lujan v. Defenders of*

Wildlife, 504 U.S. 555 (1992), and *Lujan v. National Wildlife Federation*, 497 U.S. 871 (1990) (denying standing to environmental groups seeking judicial review of agency behavior). Also, *Chevron U.S.A. v. Natural Resources Defense Council,* 467 U.S. 837 (1984) has helped agencies secure a deferential standard of review in cases of statutory interpretation. In the area of constitutional law, the Court has recently questioned its post-New Deal, broad interpretation of the Commerce Clause, which provides the basis for most federal environmental lawmaking. *United States v. Lopez,* 115 S. Ct. 1624 (1995) (invalidating a federal criminal law prohibiting the possession of a firearm in a school zone).

3. The Supreme Court's treatment of NEPA, one of the statutes cited by Lazarus that substitutes for the public trust doctrine in reining in agency behavior that might harm the environment, also reflects how judicial indifference or hostility to environmental goals can stymie implementation of the statutory substitutes for the public trust doctrine. In the twelve cases it has decided under NEPA, the Court has rejected the position of environmental plaintiffs every time. *See* William H. Rodgers, Jr., *NEPA at Twenty: Mimicry and Recruitment in Environmental Law*, 20 Envtl. L. 485, 497 (1990) ("In few walks of legal life has the Court demonstrated such a decided tilt in its choice of prevailing parties.") and Karin P. Sheldon, *NEPA in the Supreme Court,* 25 Land & Water L. Rev. 83 (1990).

4. Is there still a role for the public trust doctrine to play in a statutory environmental law regime as a background legal principle that guides statutory interpretation and offers a basis for making decisions in areas that fall between the cracks of patchwork legislative coverage? In particular, Lazarus states that the public trust doctrine has no place in the emerging scheme of limited entitlements to use natural resources. But, might the public trust doctrine be important in deciding the exact dimensions of the limited entitlements? *See National Audubon Society v. Superior Court of Alpine County*, 658 P.2d 709 (Cal.), *cert. denied sub nom. City of Los Angeles Dept. of Water and Power v. National Audubon Society*, 464 U.S. 977 (1983) (finding that permits to divert and use water are subject to public trust restrictions).

5. Lazarus claims that the public trust doctrine simply reinforces outmoded reliance on private property rights jurisprudence and should be abandoned in favor of the "new property" approaches that extend governmental jurisdiction to the definition and management of limited rights to environmental resources and pollution. It could be argued that Sax's attention to defining and strengthening the concept of public rights contributed to the transformation and diminution of absolutist private property rights claims. Is the public trust doctrine any more of a "legal fiction" than modern property rights regimes? Is it a closer kin to the "new property" than the old?

6. Lazarus criticizes property approaches to environmental law as too absolutist to be helpful in the modern era. Are property approaches necessarily absolutist? *See* Carol M.

Rose, *Crystals and Mud in Property Law,* 40 STAN. L. REV. 577 (1988). Is Lazarus' characterization of the public trust doctrine as absolutist an accurate reflection of Sax's articulation of the doctrine? Is Lazarus' characterization an accurate reflection of the court's articulation of the doctrine in *National Audubon Society v. Superior Court of Alpine County*, 658 P.2d 709 (Cal.), *cert. denied sub nom. City of Los Angeles Dept. of Water and Power v. National Audubon Society*, 464 U.S. 977 (1983), described in note 1 after the Sax articles?

7. Delgado's critique of Sax, in note 7 following the Sax articles, bears comparing with Lazarus. Lazarus' contention that the public trust doctrine has been effectively supplanted by other changes in statutory, administrative, and common law (property and torts), calls into question Delgado's position that the doctrine frustrated subsequent developments by erecting a premature conceptual roadblock. Could both commentators be correct? Could both be wrong?

Professor Huffman surveys some of the scholarly literature that addresses the basis for the public trust doctrine. He is critical of the expansive approaches to the doctrine and advocates a more narrow conception of public rights as easements.

A FISH OUT OF WATER: THE PUBLIC TRUST DOCTRINE IN A CONSTITUTIONAL DEMOCRACY
James L. Huffman
19 Envtl. L. 527 (1989)*

* * *

Where does the public trust doctrine fit in our bag of legal tricks? Where should we teach the subject in our law school curricula? How should lawyers and judges think about the public trust law? Is it part of trust law? Is it part of constitutional law? Is it a guideline for the judicial review of administrative action? Is it simply the police power under another name? The answer is that it is none of these, at least not in its traditional, common-law formulation. The traditional public trust doctrine is property law. It defines an easement that members of the public hold in common.

* * *

It is clear that my argument does not describe the law as interpreted by several state courts. Some state courts have expressly denied that the doctrine defines an easement. Not surprisingly, in light of the doctrine's name, some courts have assumed that it is part

---

* Reprinted with permission.

of the law of trusts. Alternatively, other state courts, and Professor Blumm in this volume,[6] have argued that the doctrine is rooted in state constitutions. Professors Epstein and Wilkinson propose that the doctrine has federal constitutional roots.[7] Professor Rodgers asserts that it is a justification for strict scrutiny in the judicial review of certain types of state actions.[8] Scholars and courts have also interpreted the doctrine as a source of authority for the state exercise of the police power. None of these explanations of the public trust doctrine withstand careful analysis.

Classification of the doctrine makes a difference to the way the doctrine is interpreted and applied, and more importantly, to the impact that the doctrine's application has upon people's reasonable expectations. The point is not that there is a correct classification of legal doctrines, but rather that ordinary people come to understand the law in ways that reflect legal classification and legal discourse. If ordinary people have sound reasons to understand the public trust doctrine as defining public easements over both public and private property, it will not serve their interests, nor the rule of law, to interpret the doctrine as something else.

The rule of law does not require that legal rules be carved in stone. In defense of modern alterations of the public trust doctrine, it is often observed that the English doctrine underwent a significant change when imported to the United States. This was, however, a change that served to protect rather than alter popular expectations. Under English law, the doctrine applied only to navigable waters, with navigability defined by the ebb and flow of the tides. In the United States, the geographical reach of the doctrine was extended to include nontidal waters that are navigable in fact. The rationale for the extension was that the purposes of the doctrine—and the preservation of the associated popular expectations—required a definition of navigability appropriate to the realities of a vast continent with numerous large rivers that are unaffected by the tides. The rule of law is served by such judicial modifications. It is not served by judicial decisions that justify unexpected outcomes by articulating an entirely new rationale for an established legal doctrine.

The point is not that there is a scientifically determinable category into which the public trust doctrine fits. The classification of legal doctrines is not like the classification of species or the arrangement of elements on the periodic chart. The public trust doctrine, like the tides that once defined its reach, has ebbed and flowed. Although some schools of legal thought seek to explain such trends in the law as precisely as scientists chart the tides in relation to the phases of the moon, the explanation for the ebb and flow of particular legal doctrines is less the domain of science or logic than the domain of politics. The law is the handmaiden of social existence. It has no life of its own. The law is what we make of it, or what others make of it, if we choose to believe that it has a life of its own. It is this reality that makes the constant pursuit of the rule of law so important.

---

[6] Blumm, [*Public Property and the Democratization of Western Water Law: A Modern View of the Public Trust Doctrine*, 19 ENVTL. L. 573 (1989)].

[7] Address by Professor Richard Epstein, The Public Trust Doctrine, Florida State University Policy Sciences Seminar (Mar. 6, 1987) [hereinafter Epstein Address]; Wilkinson, *The Headquarters of the Public Trust: Some Thoughts on the Source and Scope of the Traditional Doctrine*, 19 ENVTL. L. 425 (1989).

[8] 1 W. RODGERS, JR., ENVIRONMENTAL LAW: AIR AND WATER, § 2.20, at 162 (1986).

Recognizing the truths of legal realism does not require us to abandon the values of coherence and consistency in the law. In the case of the modern public trust doctrine, sometimes well-motivated courts and commentators would make of the law what it clearly was not in the past. By transplanting the doctrine from its traditional home within property law to the fields of trust, constitutional, administrative, and police power law, the advocates of the modern public trust doctrine seek to achieve purposes not contemplated by the traditional doctrine. In the process, they would disappoint reasonable expectations based upon the previously accepted interpretation of the doctrine. Ironically, this will all be accomplished in the name of the rule of law, through the insistence that the doctrine has always been so interpreted.

* * *

III. THE PUBLIC TRUST DOCTRINE AS CONSTITUTIONAL LAW

Although there was never any suggestion in the early public trust cases that the doctrine had anything to do with constitutional law, some modern courts and commentators have sought to link the two. Reliance on the Constitution seems to have two theoretical bases. According to one approach, the public rights of public trust law are analogous to the rights that individuals have pursuant to the due process clause and other general rights guaranteed by the Constitution. This approach is an outgrowth of the search for a constitutional basis for private actions to protect the environment. Alternatively it is argued that the public rights of public trust law are analogous to the rights of people in a democratic system of government. This view reduces the public trust doctrine to a justification for democratic action pursuant to the police power. * * *

The federal constitution says nothing of individual or public rights in the environment or in the use of particular resources, but the Supreme Court has, from time to time, evidenced a willingness to imply individual rights not expressly guaranteed. For example, in recent years the Court has articulated an assortment of implied rights within the general category of privacy. Various explanations for the constitutional right of privacy has been offered, from the ninth amendment, to the due process clause, to the penumbras of various constitutional provisions. Although Justice Black criticized the analysis as "natural law due process,"[80] it could be readily adapted to the creation of environmental rights, with reliance on authority as ancient as Bracton, who saw public trust rights rooted in natural law. The Supreme Court has never employed similar analyses to articulate constitutional, environmental rights, but some state courts have suggested that such rights exist under their constitutions, and that the public trust doctrine is the expression of those rights.

* * *

By linking the public trust doctrine to constitutional claims of right, the courts may believe that they can circumvent the constitutional protections of private property. The courts would argue that because these public rights are protected under the public trust doctrine, they predate any private claims of right. The advantage of labeling them constitutional as well as public trust rights is that constitutional rights tend to be more generally

---

[80] [Griswold v. Connecticut, 381 U.S. 479 (1965)] at 507, 524 (Black, J., dissenting).

stated and give the courts more leeway for interpretation. By linking the flexibility of constitutional interpretation with the deep historical roots of the public trust doctrine, it is possible to manufacture new rights while claiming simply to uphold existing rights.

* * *

In its earliest English origins, the public trust doctrine was the basis of private rather than public rights. The private rights were held in common by all members of the public, but they were exercised privately. Individuals navigated and fished the tidal waters of England, and individuals objected when the Crown precluded them from those waters. Clause 33 of the Magna Carta was a limit on the monarch's ability to monopolize for himself or his favorites the benefits of the tidal waters. The Massachusetts "great pond" ordinance guaranteed to all individuals the right to fish and fowl on ponds over ten acres in size. The New Jersey Supreme Court decision in *Arnold v. Mundy* rejected a claim of exclusive right to oyster beds and thus protected the rights of all individuals to work those beds.[98] The *Illinois Central* decision protected the rights of all individuals in the use of the Chicago waterfront by invalidating the state's grant of a monopoly.[99]

These individual rights derive from the law of property, not from the federal or state constitutions. They have in common with constitutional rights, and in difference from most property rights, the characteristic of being shared by all individuals. Nevertheless, they remain property, rather than constitutional, rights. Like all property rights, they benefit from the constitutional guarantees to just compensation and due process, notwithstanding that they may suffer from the tragedy of the commons. Their content, however, is defined by the law of property. The common rights of fishing and navigation must be fit into the total bundle of rights that comprise property interests in navigable waters and submerged lands.

* * *

In addition to the bold assertions by state courts that their constitutions are a source of what is clearly a common-law doctrine, two academics have proposed constitutional explanations for the public trust doctrine, and a third has suggested that the doctrine is a rule of constitutional, as well as statutory, construction.

Richard Epstein interprets the doctrine as an analogue to the eminent domain clause. Where the eminent domain clause protects private rights against takings by the state, the public trust doctrine would protect public property interests from private takings. Such private takings would be dependent upon some action by the state—a conveyance, a franchise, a recognition of adverse title—and thus, the doctrine is ultimately directed at the state although it limits private takings of public rights. This is precisely the way the doctrine functioned in the historical examples discussed above, if it is understood that the so-called public rights are rights held in common by all members of the public. Thus, Epstein's explanation of the doctrine as constitutional, though he grounds it in the equal protection clause, adds nothing to the more direct protection that these property rights,

---

[98] 6 N.J.L. 1 (1821).
[99] Illinois Cent. R.R. v. Illinois, 146 U.S. 387 (1892).

held by all individuals in common, have under the eminent domain clause of the Constitution. * * *

Charles Wilkinson has formulated the most elaborate argument for constitutionalizing the public trust doctrine. After exploring various possible constitutional and nonconstitutional sources for the public trust doctrine, Wilkinson states that "the fairest, most principled conclusion is that the public trust doctrine is rooted in the Commerce Clause or . . . the Statehood Clause. . . ."[108] He seems to prefer the statehood clause, but he links the two as "necessary to complement the implied real estate transfer that was so extraordinarily favorable to the state."[109] The real estate transfer that Wilkinson has in mind is of submerged lands under navigable waters, which new states acquired from the federal government pursuant to the equal footing doctrine. His thesis is that the public trust doctrine, like the navigation servitude, is a constitutionally mandated limit on the property rights that states acquired under the equal footing doctrine. Both servitudes afford "complementary protections to major watercourses."[111]

Wilkinson's thesis is flawed in two basic respects. First, there is no evidence that the Supreme Court viewed the public trust or the navigation servitude as quid pro quo for a generous grant of lands to new states, nor is there any reason the Court would have considered such a trade off necessary. Wilkinson's claim that the Court's recognition of state title to submerged lands was a break with the general principle that the equal footing doctrine is "a rule of political equality, not equality of actual power or real property,"[112] ignores the historical link between power over navigable waters and the political sovereignty of the state. Second, although there is an important geographical link between state title and the public trust doctrine, the public trust doctrine is not a necessary adjunct to the grant of title. The analogy that Wilkinson draws to the navigation servitude of the federal commerce power is not persuasive. The navigation servitude is essential to the federal commerce power given state title to submerged lands. The public trust servitude has no similar relation to state power. A state's title and its police power can be effectively exercised without the limits of the public trust doctrine. As demonstrated below, the Constitution is relevant to the public trust doctrine as a guarantee of the property rights inherent in the doctrine, not as a source of those rights, as Wilkinson contends.

Professor Blumm, building on the analysis proposed by Professor Rodgers, argues that the public trust doctrine can be viewed, in part, as a guide to constitutional and statutory interpretation. "While all common law rules benefit from the maxim that legislation in derogation of the common law is to be strictly construed," writes Blumm, "courts construing statutes terminating the public trust restrictions are particularly narrowly construed."[118] Blumm argues that such statutes should be narrowly construed because of the "presumption favoring public ownership and control."[119] The link to constitutional interpretation is unclear, but perhaps the argument is that constitutional provisions, even the takings clause,

---

[108] [Wilkinson, *The Public Trust Doctrine in Public Land Law*, 14 U.C. DAVIS L. REV. 269 (1980)] at 21. [*sic*]

[109] *Id.* at 27. [*sic*]

[111] [*Id.*] at 21. [*sic*] Wilkinson notes with approval that modern courts have described the public trust as both a servitude and an easement. *Id.*

[112] *Id.* at 12. [*sic*]

[118] [Blumm, *supra* note 6], at 587.

[119] *Id.*

are to be understood in light of this presumption. Blumm seeks to achieve both too much and too little with this argument.

The presumption favoring public ownership and control achieves too much. Blumm's claim that the presumption derives from the objective of efficiency may have validity in the traditional applications of the public trust doctrine, but the efficiency analysis fails when applied to many of the extensions of the doctrine. Moreover, even if efficiency is a consequence of the traditional doctrine, it is not an accurate explanation of the doctrine's historic rationale. Historically, the doctrine protected individual liberties from the abuses of monarchical power. Today the doctrine is employed to limit the acquisition and exercise of private rights in water and water-related resources, often through the abuse of sovereign power. It is a tragic irony that a doctrine intended to protect liberty is becoming a doctrine that justifies the denial of liberty.

As a tool to protect individual rights to engage in public trust uses of public trust resources, Blumm's argument for strict constitutional construction achieves too little. Those individual property rights should benefit from the guarantees of the fifth amendment eminent domain clause. There should be no question about preserving the trust "where . . . reasonably possible."[121] It should be inviolable as should any other vested property right. Blumm, like Sax, has a different constitution in mind, as his argument for the public trust "as an insulation against takings claims"[122] makes clear.

IV. THE PUBLIC TRUST DOCTRINE AS A STANDARD FOR JUDICIAL REVIEW

Blumm's quasi-constitutional argument reflects Professor Rodgers' argument that the public trust doctrine "is another version of the 'hard look' that has spread its influence so widely throughout natural resource and environmental law."[123] The concept suffers from the same shortcomings in this area as it does in judicial review of administrative actions generally. The central flaw in the hard look doctrine is revealed in Rodgers' explanation of why courts sometimes turn to procedure when substantive decisions are challenged: "Where it is difficult to prescribe a correct outcome in terms of substantive resource use, courts turn readily to process as the currency of fairness."[124] The error is in the assumption that there are "correct" outcomes in terms of substantive resource allocation.

In a democracy, the correct outcome is that which properly functioning democratic institutions prescribe. Unless there is unanimity in a decision, some members of the community will disagree with the substantive outcome, and they may well argue that it is ill-advised and even stupid, but they have no basis to claim that it is incorrect or wrong. It can be incorrect only if democracy is functioning so that a minority is in control. Rodgers, like Sax, suggests no reasons why we should suspect democratic failures in those public decisions to which the public trust doctrine has been applied. The failure is

---

[121] [*Id.*] at 588.

[122] *Id.* at 584.

[123] 1 W. RODGERS, JR., *supra* note 8, at 162.

[124] *Id.*

a political one on the part of those who now look to the courts to grant them what they have been denied in the democratic process.

As evidence of the need for strict judicial scrutiny, Rodgers quotes with approval the Illinois Supreme Court's description of a legislative approved sale of submerged lands as "self-serving."[127] What is a state legislature supposed to do, however, if not serve its own (which is to say its constituents') interests? That is the theory of representative democracy. If it does not work, we should not seek a remedy in even less democratic courts. It is self-serving to claim that public decisions about resources are particularly important and thus require the courts to impose higher standards on legislators and administrators. Every political interest group can make this claim about the public decisions about which it is concerned. There is no persuasive reason why the conservationists and environmentalists should be able to take a simple doctrine of property law and turn it into a justification for broad-ranging judicial review of legislative and administrative actions.

* * *

VI. THE PUBLIC TRUST DOCTRINE AS PROPERTY LAW

If we understand that originally all property was owned in common and title was conveyed by some means to those now holding private property rights, the public trust can be understood as an easement that the public retained at the time of transfer. If we have some other understanding of the initial assignment of property rights, we will require some other explanation of how the people came to possess this easement. Whatever our explanation of how existing rights in property came to be, the public trust can be understood as a simple easement, perhaps with limits on alienation, within the law of property. The argument is not that the public trust was originally, and has always been, the equivalent of an easement, because in its original formulation it could arguably be described as a trust. Rather, the argument is that given the current state of the doctrine, it is best understood as providing a public easement.

Although some courts have objected to describing the public trust in navigable waters as an easement, American case law, until recently, fit easily within that concept. The doctrine applied only to navigable waters and their submerged lands. It recognized a public right of use for navigation and fishing. These rights had no necessary link to the sovereign's title to waters and beds of navigable waters under English law. Indeed, under English law, as experienced by American colonists, sovereign ownership constituted a risk to, rather than a protection of, these public rights. Because the Crown possessed legal title to these resources, the King could more easily undertake to use them for his personal advantage or for the advantage of his friends and associates.

Thus, the public trust right constituted an easement that permitted public use of resources otherwise under the control of the Crown. It existed not at the grace of the King, but despite the King; and it existed even if the King chose to convey his title to private parties. The King could convey only what the King possessed, and the King possessed title to the navigable waters and submerged lands subject to the public's easement for

---

[127] [*Id.*] at 163 (quoting People ex rel. Scott v. Chicago Park Dist., 66 Ill. 2d 65, 360 N.E.2d 773 (1977)).

navigation and fishing. Bracton did not say that the King could not alienate his title in the waters and submerged lands. He said that the King could not alienate the public rights in the use of those waters and lands. There was nothing novel in that assertion. Neither the King nor any private party can alienate what they do not possess.

In the public trust doctrine's original application in the United States, the only change from English law was that the individual states took the place of the Crown as the owner of the navigable waters and submerged lands. The people retained their rights to use those waters and lands for navigation and fishing. The Revolution did not alter the property rights of individuals, whether held exclusively or in common with others. The states were successors in title to the Crown, and like the Crown, their title was subject to the public rights in navigation and fishing. In the early American case of *Arnold v. Mundy*, Chief Justice Kirkpatrick of the New Jersey Supreme Court stated not only that the state could not transfer what it did not own, but that its ability to transfer what it did own was limited by the rights of the public in fishing and navigation.[151] In other words, the alienation of navigable waters or submerged lands could not interfere with the public's exercise of its public trust rights. This is precisely the nature of an easement.

In *Illinois Central*, the Supreme Court could have been more clear concerning the alienability of lands subject to the public trust. The Court stated that an 1869 grant of submerged lands by the Illinois Legislature violated "a trust for the people of the State that they may enjoy the navigation of the waters, carry on commerce over them, and have liberty of fishing therein freed from the obstruction or interference of private parties."[152] Later the Court stated that the 1869 act "was inoperative to affect, modify, or in any respect to control the sovereignty and dominion of the State over the lands, or its ownership thereof, and . . . any such attempted operation of the act was annulled by the repealing act. . . ."[153] It might be concluded from the two statements that the alienation of the 1869 act was valid, except to the extent that it purported to be irrevocable, because if the 1869 act was itself violative of the public trust, there was nothing for the later (1873) act to repeal. If the 1869 act was invalid on its own terms, however, it was because the state purported to grant more than it possessed. The grant to Illinois Central Railroad could not be consummated as intended without limiting the common property rights of the public, and was therefore invalid.

Contemporary case law uniformly agrees with the Supreme Court's holding in *Illinois Central*. The states could alienate their interests in the waters and submerged lands of navigable waters subject to the common property rights of the public. Long before the *Illinois Central* decision, the Western States had taken it upon themselves to alienate to private parties the right to use water from navigable streams. Although navigability determined state title to submerged lands, there was never any question that the states could reduce the extent of those lands by alienation. The only restraint on alienation of either water or land was the requirement that the alienation either promote, or at least not hinder, the public's exercise of its rights of navigation and fishing. As a practical

---

[151] 6 N.J.L. 1, 73-74 (1821).
[152] Illinois Cent. R.R. v. Illinois, 146 U.S. 387, 452 (1892).
[153] *Id.* at 460.

matter, the same restraint on alienation exists for any private owner of property subject to an easement.

When viewed as a rule of property law, the public trust doctrine has a sufficiently determinable meaning to guide its application in future cases. It simply describes one of the sticks in the proverbial bundle of rights that constitutes property. Some of those rights are held privately, some are held by the state in its proprietary capacity, and some, including the rights of navigation and fishing on navigable waters, are held in common by the public. This conceptualization of the public trust doctrine has the advantage of placing control over the public rights in the hands of the public rather than making the public a mere beneficiary with control in the hands of the state as trustee. The explanation of public trust as property law does not, however, resolve the question of how the public may act to exercise its common rights. At its extreme, this is the question of whether the public may alienate its rights. In a constitutional democracy, the answer is not to be found in the law of property. The answer is to be found in the theories of constitutional and democratic government.

VII. THE PUBLIC TRUST DOCTRINE AND CONSTITUTIONAL DEMOCRACY

* * *

The dilemma of the public trust doctrine in a constitutional democracy is tied up in the so-called trustee status of the state. The rights of navigation and fishing are held by the people in common. In a democracy, the people act as an entity through the democratic legislature. The basic question is this: Can the people, acting through the democratic legislature, alienate or alter the rights that each individual holds in common with every other individual? If that right is truly an individual right, no different from the other rights protected by the Constitution, the answer is clearly no. If that right is merely the right of participation in the political process, however, the right to be equally represented in the legislature, then the answer is clearly yes.

Because the public trust doctrine in its modern formulation purports to carry the banners of trust law, constitutional rights, and governmental power, as well as property law, it is impossible to say which answer is correct as a matter of positive law. If, however, we adopt the view that the public trust doctrine makes sense only as an easement within the law of property, the conclusion must be that the state cannot act to alter or alienate the public rights of fishing and navigation, unless it acts by the unanimous consent of all who share in the common rights or compensates those whose rights are involuntarily taken. The traditional public trust rule on alienation is consistent with this conclusion. Alienation is permitted only where it promotes or does not hinder the purposes of the trust, which is to say the rights of the individual members of the public.

By confusing the property rights character of the public trust doctrine with concepts of trust law, constitutional rights, judicial review, and governmental power, the courts and commentators have opened the door to dramatic expansion of governmental power with resultant intrusions upon individual rights. The trust concept contradicts democratic theory by separating the state, as trustee, from the public, as beneficiary, as if they are two distinct entities. The constitutional rights concept invites the creation of new rights at the expense of existing rights—environmental rights at the expense of property rights.

The police power concept subsumes the very notion of public rights by equating them with the public interest. As Professor Epstein has written, "How easy it is to turn a limitation on government power into a justification for expansion. And how utterly unprincipled."[167] So too is it easy and unprincipled to sacrifice the rights of some to create rights for others. What is not easy is the principled articulation of legal doctrines so that they are both internally coherent and externally consistent with the basic values of our legal system.

NOTES

1. Professor Huffman has criticized the public trust doctrine in two other articles: *Avoiding the Takings Clause Through the Myth of Public Rights: The Public Trust and Reserved Rights Doctrines at Work,* 3 J. LAND USE & ENVTL. L. 171 (1987); and *Trusting the Public Interest to Judges: A Comment on the Public Trust Writings of Professors Sax, Wilkinson, Dunning and Johnson,* 63 DENV. U. L. REV. 565 (1986).

2. Why does it matter whether we categorize the public trust doctrine as constitutional, administrative, or property law? Can or should a legal doctrine have roots in more than one legal classification?

3. Professor Huffman argues that the public trust doctrine "is best understood as providing a public easement." How does this characterization limit the application of the doctrine? Is the limitation reasonable? What is the nature of an easement with respect to tidelands, stream beds, navigable waters, and marshlands? Could the easement concept apply to other public resources, such as public lands?

4. Does Huffman accept Sax's proposition that the public trust is needed to prevent destabilizing disappointments of diffuse public expectations about the environment?

5. In his critique of a constitutional basis for the public trust doctrine, Huffman asserts that we should not elevate public rights to constitutional status because they would interfere with preexisting individual rights. Do the existing constitutionally-protected rights coexist harmoniously?

6. Professor Rieser criticizes both Sax and Huffman:

The theories of Sax and Huffman both lack an explicit consideration of the particular social goods at issue in ecological resource allocation decisions. Sax's theory and Huffman's critique each fail to identify values fundamentally

---

[167] Epstein Address, *supra* note 7.

at issue in these cases and to discuss, in this light, the relative merits of private and public decisionmaking. Although Sax refers to a societal expectation that ecosystem functions will continue—for example, a lake will continue to be a "lake"—he does not develop this idea in more specific terms that clarify why these resources cannot be subject solely to private decisionmaking. Huffman's defense of private property, especially in its relationship to individual liberties, fails to account for the interdependence of natural systems and the vital role that human actions play in maintaining and altering these systems. Huffman might respond that if destruction of such functions results from the institution of private property, that is the necessary price we must pay for a fundamental commitment to freedom. However, such a response would be unsatisfactory because it accepts as the cost of freedom loss of an environmental network necessary for survival and the enjoyment of freedom.

Sax's theory falls just short of an explanation for the property right nature of the public expectation in ecosystem preservation. Sax's notion of "expectations held in common" appears too broad and subjective unless it is narrowed to signify a public expectation that no irretrievable changes will be made to a natural system, that enough of it will remain intact so its functions can continue. Similarly, Huffman's critique neglects the effect private property can have on ecosystem functions and the values the public gives these systems. Continuing the search for a more satisfactory account of property rights in natural systems, we turn to the sciences of ecology and economics.

Alison Rieser, *Ecological Preservation as a Public Property Right: An Emerging Doctrine In Search of a Theory,* 15 HARV. ENVTL. L. REV. 393, 417-18 (1991). Do theories of public rights or interests ultimately need to rest on the ecology of survival? Most environmental controversies involve impacts that do not threaten the survival of humans. Mark Sagoff argues that the proper basis for environmental protection is not scientific. Rather, public expectations and environmental policy are based on our culturally defined relationship with the landscape. Mark Sagoff, *Settling America or the Concept of Place in the Environmental Ethic*, 12 J. ENERGY, NAT. RESOURCES & ENVTL. L. 349 (1992). For an economic approach to the public trust doctrine, see Lloyd R. Cohen, *The Public Trust Doctrine: An Economic Perspective*, 29 CAL. W. L. REV. 239 (1992).

7. In a portion of his article not reproduced in the preceding excerpt, Huffman responds to Professor Blumm's call for a persistent evolution of the public trust doctrine to meet the felt necessities of the time. Blumm thinks that the courts should play a central role in this evolution in common law. Huffman would reserve for the legislature the power to promote evolution. Are you persuaded by Huffman's argument that legislation is a better response because it is more democratic and is constrained by the Fifth and Fourteenth Amendments? Are courts constrained by these amendments? *See* Barton H. Thompson, Jr., *Judicial Takings*, 76 VA. L. REV. 1449 (1990). The takings constraint on governmental action is the subject of the next subchapter.

D. Takings

[N]or shall private property be taken for public use without just compensation.
U.S. CONST., amend. V.

The Fifth and Fourteenth Amendments to the U.S. Constitution require that the federal and state governments provide "just compensation" for private property taken for public use. This just compensation requirement has become increasingly contentious in recent years as the Supreme Court has applied it to situations where the government regulates so restrictively that property values are substantially diminished. Environmental law has become the crucible for a constitutional debate over the extent to which property owners are entitled to compensation for dashed expectations.

Most judicial decisions in environmental law focus on interpretation of statutes and the extent to which agencies acted within the authority granted to them by Congress. In these cases, Congress can always respond to a judicial decision by enacting a new law to reverse the court's interpretation. The takings challenges to environmental regulation are not susceptible to this legislative corrective. The Supreme Court has the final word on defining the governmental actions that constitute takings. Although takings law never operates to prohibit outright the government from acting, the compensation requirement may present practical problems for a regulatory system limited by fiscal constraints.

Before the 1920's, the Takings Clause of the Fifth Amendment had not been applied where regulation restricted an owner's use of land. The modern era of regulatory takings law opened with Justice Oliver Wendell Holmes' celebrated opinion in *Pennsylvania Coal Co. v. Mahon*, 260 U.S. 393 (1922). Pennsylvania had enacted a law restricting underground coal mining where damage would occur to the surface. The law limited subsurface coal mining even where surface owners had waived their rights in their deeds to recover surface damages from mining. The court found that the regulation of private property, in this case the mineral rights, went "too far" and diminished the value of the property rights so severely that the Pennsylvania Coal Company was entitled to compensation, just as it would be if the government had physically appropriated the property in an exercise of eminent domain. Professor Carol Rose analyzes this watershed decision in Mahon *Reconstructed: Why the Takings Issue is Still a Muddle*, 57 S. CAL. L. REV. 561 (1984).

In the decades following *Mahon*, the constitutional law of takings remained a fact-specific balance with vaguely formulated rules. The important modern case best representing this approach is *Pennsylvania Central Transportation Co. v. City of New York*, 438 U.S. 104 (1978). The New York City landmark preservation law prohibited Pennsylvania Central from constructing an office tower in its airspace above the historic Grand Central Terminal. The Court, stressing that the railroad company could still make viable economic use of the existing building (Grand Central Terminal), held that the company was not entitled to compensation for its inability to develop its airspace. The Court's analysis focused on the character of the government action and the "extent of the interference with rights in the parcel as a whole." 438 U.S. at 130-31. As later cases, such as *Loretto v. Teleprompter Manhattan CATV*, 458 U.S. 419 (1982), would demonstrate, government action which has the character of a physical occupation of property, interfering with an owner's right to exclude, does constitute a taking.

Many commentators sought to provide a theoretical core around which takings law could more coherently be organized. Prominent among them was Professor Frank Michelman, who made the utilitarian argument that just compensation protects from disruption the security of expectations represented by property rights. Professor Michelman would not require compensation for a law preventing a private activity that, "when the owner first began to orient his decisions towards" the activity, was evidently in conflict with crystallized expectations of others. Frank Michelman, *Property, Utility, and Fairness: Comments on the Ethical Foundations of "Just Compensation" Law*, 80 HARV. L. REV. 1165, 1242 (1967). Professor Joseph Sax viewed the role of legislatures as facilitators of resolutions to conflicts between interests. According to Sax, courts should require Fifth Amendment compensation only when a law prohibits an activity that would have no adverse spillover effects on other people's use of other resources. Joseph Sax, *Takings, Private Property and Public Rights*, 81 YALE L.J. 149, 163-64 (1971). If there are spillover effects, then courts should respect the balance struck by legislatures.

More recently, Professor Richard A. Epstein, in TAKINGS: PRIVATE PROPERTY AND THE POWER OF EMINENT DOMAIN (1985), espoused a much more expansive scope for Fifth Amendment compensation. Professor Epstein argued that the constitutional system of limited government and protected property should require the New Deal legacy of administrative programs to compensate most targets of regulation. This more libertarian approach has enjoyed renewed attention in recent years in environmental law with the rise of the privatization and property rights movements discussed in the previous subchapters. Recent Supreme Court takings decisions have contributed to this renewal. Foremost among these is *Lucas v. South Carolina Coastal Council*, 505 U.S. 1003 (1992), which carved out a category for *prima facie* taking where a regulation deprives an owner of all economic use of the property. Where such a "total taking" has occurred as a result of government regulation, the government must compensate the landowner unless the government can show that the regulation prevents a common law nuisance. Other recent cases are discussed in the notes below.

The following article by Professor Sax analyzing *Lucas* discusses the challenge that an ecological world view presents to property doctrines, and thus to takings law. The article highlights the sources of friction between environmental law and takings.

PROPERTY RIGHTS AND THE ECONOMY OF NATURE: UNDERSTANDING LUCAS V. SOUTH CAROLINA COASTAL COUNCIL
Joseph L. Sax
45 Stan. L. Rev. 1433 (1993)*

* * *

Lucas: The Facts and the Decision

In 1986, David Lucas bought two lots on the Isle of Palms, a barrier island east of Charleston, South Carolina. Although beachfront properties had been subject to develop-

---

* Copyright 1993 by the Board of Trustees of the Leland Stanford Junior University. Reprinted with permission.

ment restrictions since 1977, Lucas' lots were landward of the restricted area and originally zoned for development as residential homesites. In 1988, however, South Carolina enacted new restrictions in the Beachfront Management Act: Construction of improvements, except for narrow wooden walkways and decks, was prohibited seaward of a setback line that was based on historic movements of high water during the previous forty years. The following legislative findings served as a basis for the Beachfront Management Act: (1) the beach/dune system along the coast protected life and property by serving as a storm barrier, dissipating wave energy and contributing to shoreline stability; (2) many miles of beach were critically eroding; (3) the beach/dune system provided both the basis for a tourism industry important to the state and an important habitat for plants and animals; (4) development would endanger adjacent property; and (5) various protective devices such as seawalls had not proven effective against the harmful impacts of development. All of Lucas' land was within the newly protected zone.

Lucas filed suit, claiming that the Act's ban on construction effected a taking of his property. Lucas, however, did not challenge the legislative findings that a ban on development was necessary to protect life and property against serious harm, nor did he question the validity of the Act as a lawful exercise of the police power. Instead, he asserted that since the Act completely extinguished his property's value, he was entitled to compensation. Lucas won in the trial court, which found that the ban had made Lucas' lots "valueless." The South Carolina Supreme Court, however, reversed. Since Lucas had not challenged the validity of the statute, the State Supreme Court accepted the legislative findings that the Act was designed to prevent serious harm and held that such a law did not constitute a compensable taking, despite the Act's impact on the property's value.

The United States Supreme Court granted Lucas' petition for certiorari on the question of whether complete elimination of value by a legislative act constituted a compensable taking, notwithstanding the purpose or validity of the legislation. In an opinion by Justice Scalia, a five member majority rejected Lucas' unqualified claim, but the Court articulated a special rule for cases of total deprivation of a property's economic value. The Court held that when legislation deprives an owner of all economic value in real property, compensation is required unless the planned development violates "restrictions that background principles of the State's law of property and nuisance already place upon land ownership."[16] Thus, the central question in these cases is whether the use restrictions were "part of [the landowner's] title to begin with."[17] The Court remanded the case so that the South Carolina court could determine whether state common law had already proscribed Lucas' intended uses. The Court observed, however, that "[i]t seems unlikely that common-law principles would have prevented the erection of any habitable or productive improvements on [Lucas'] land."[18]

The Supreme Court viewed *Lucas* as an important case. Justice Scalia's opinion extensively reviewed property theory and takings jurisprudence. Justice Kennedy concurred with the majority but felt that it adopted an overly narrow view of police power. Justices Blackmun and Stevens each wrote dissents portraying the majority opinion as backward

---

[16] [Lucas v. South Carolina Coastal Council, 112 S. Ct. 2886 (1992)] at 2900.

[17] *Id.* at 2899.

[18] *Id.* at 2901.

looking, inconsistent with precedent in the takings field, and insensitive to contemporary problems.

* * *

What *Lucas* Means

If I am correct in suggesting that the current Court intends to play a restrained role in the property area, how is Justice Scalia's aggressive opinion in *Lucas* to be understood? The case is not as far reaching as its rhetoric suggests. It does not protect all who suffer a complete loss in their property's value, for the categorical 100 percent diminution rule itself is sharply limited. Regulation that would be sustained under established common law "principles" of nuisance and property law is not affected. Presumably, states will have substantial latitude in determining the extent to which their existing legal principles limit property rights. Moreover, Justice Scalia is careful to provide assurance that *Lucas* is not a threat to conventional industrial regulation, including environmental laws such as those dealing with pollution or toxics disposal. Thus, despite its tone, *Lucas* appears consistent with the restraint the Court has generally exercised in takings cases.

What, then, is the majority's agenda in the *Lucas* case? I believe Justice Scalia felt that the case presented a new, fundamental issue in property law, and that he had a clear message which he sought to convey: States may not regulate land use solely by requiring landowners to maintain their property in its natural state as part of a functioning ecosystem, even though those natural functions may be important to the ecosystem. In this sense, while the *Lucas* majority recognizes the emerging view of land as a part of an ecosystem, rather than as purely private property, the Court seeks to limit the legal foundation for such a conception.

Lucas may thus be viewed as the Court's long-delayed answer to the decision by the Wisconsin Supreme Court in *Just v. Marinette County*,[35] one of the cases that launched the modern era of environmental law:

> An owner of land has no absolute and unlimited right to change the essential natural character of his land so as to use it for a purpose for which it was unsuited in its natural state and which injures the rights of others. The exercise of the police power in zoning must be reasonable and we think it is not an unreasonable exercise of [the police] power to prevent harm to public rights by limiting the use of private property to its natural uses.[36]

The target of *Lucas* is broader than its immediate concern of coastal dune maintenance; the opinion encompasses such matters as wetlands regulation, which recently has generated a great deal of controversial litigation. *Lucas* also anticipates cases that will be brought under section nine of the Endangered Species Act, under which private landowners may be required to leave their land undisturbed as habitat. In general, *Lucas* addresses legislation imposed to maintain ecological services performed by land in its natural state. The Court

---

[35] 56 Wis. 2d 7, 201 N.W.2d 761 (1972). Wisconsin itself may have moved away from the most extreme implications of *Just*. *See* Kmiec v. Town of Spider Lake, 60 Wis. 2d 640, 211 N.W.2d 471 (1973) (holding that a zoning classification that gave land negative value had no reasonable basis and was therefore unconstitutional).

[36] 201 N.W.2d at 768.

correctly perceives that an ecological worldview presents a fundamental challenge to established property rights, but the Court incorrectly rejects that challenge.

* * *

Lucas' Doctrinal Peculiarities Support the Majority's Purpose

The *Lucas* majority may have designed the seemingly odd ruling to isolate the ecological regulations which Justice Scalia seeks to illegitimate, without jeopardizing mainstream regulations. The majority's nuisance exception illustrates this point. Justice Scalia surely knows that nuisance law is a slippery legal concept—it has been applied to everything from brothels to bowling on Sundays. His use of nuisance law, however, is neither stupid nor careless. He invokes nuisance principles to emphasize the difference between regulations which are designed to maintain land in its natural condition and regulations which embrace conventional police power. Rather than describe how property may be used—which is the traditional function of nuisance law—this new sort of environmental regulation effectively determines whether property may be used at all. Traditional nuisance law, however broadly construed, limited use. Its protection was wide-ranging, but it did not characterize property as having inherent public attributes which always trump the landowner's rights. This traditional understanding of private property is presumably what Justice Scalia feels is embedded in our "constitutional culture."[49] In this sense, laws demanding that landowners maintain the natural conditions of their property transgress even the most broadly construed "background principles of nuisance and property law."[50]

Justice Scalia's view of traditional private property principles also explains his rejection of a harm/benefit distinction and his recognition that landowners have positive development rights. From a certain environmental perspective, making places less natural is itself "harmful." If transformation to human use is itself defined as harmful, many land uses which were previously legitimate could become unlawful. This concern leads Justice Scalia to shift from a conception of property rights that defines what owners cannot do ("harm" to others) to what they can do (develop land to produce private economic return). Ownership is thereby redefined as some irreducible right of use by the private landowner. Ownership then means at least that the owner has some right to employ the property for personal benefit, even if it thereby eliminates "benefits" that land provides in its natural state.

Read this way, Justice Scalia's opinion emphasizes four points: (1) leaving land in its natural condition is in fundamental tension with the traditional goals of private property law; (2) once natural conditions are considered the baseline, any departure from them can be viewed as "harmful," since the essence of human use of land is interrupting the land's natural state; (3) if any disruption of natural conditions can be viewed as harmful (as surely they can), then natural conditions generally could be viewed as normal and could be demanded by the state; and (4) with that predicate, states could exercise their police power to maintain natural conditions, thereby eliminating the economic value of private property to its owner.

---

[49] [*Lucas*, 112 S. Ct.] at 2900.
[50] *Id.* at 2901.

Justice Scalia's opinion raises two important questions. Are environmental regulations that require maintenance of natural conditions significantly new and different from traditional regulations? If so, how should the law respond?

III. THE DEEPER MEANING OF *LUCAS*: PROPERTY IN THE TWO ECONOMIES

There are two fundamentally different views of property rights to which I shall refer as land in the "transformative economy" and land in the "economy of nature."[52] The conventional perspective of private property, the transformative economy, builds on the image of property as a discrete entity that can be made one's own by working it and transforming it into a human artifact. A piece of iron becomes an anvil, a tree becomes lumber, and a forest becomes a farm. Traditional property law treats undeveloped land as essentially inert. The land is there, it may have things on or in it (e.g., timber or coal), but it is in a passive state, waiting to be put to use. Insofar as land is "doing" something—for example, harboring wild animals—property law considers such functions expendable. Indeed, getting rid of the natural, or at least domesticating it, was a primary task of the European settlers of North America.

An ecological view of property, the economy of nature, is fundamentally different. Land is not a passive entity waiting to be transformed by its landowner. Nor is the world comprised of distinct tracts of land, separate pieces independent of each other. Rather, an ecological perspective views land as consisting of systems defined by their function, not by man-made boundaries. Land is already at work, performing important services in its unaltered state. For example, forests regulate the global climate, marshes sustain marine fisheries, and prairie grass holds the soil in place. Transformation diminishes the functioning of this economy and, in fact, is at odds with it.

The ecological perspective is founded on an economy of nature, while the transformative economy has a technological perspective of land as the product of human effort. As Philip Fisher states in *Making and Effacing Art*:

> At the center of technology is the human act of taking power over the world, ending the existence of nature; or, rather, bracketing nature as one component of the productive total system. The world is submitted to an inventory that analyzes it into an array of stocks and resources that can be moved from place to place, broken down through fire and force, and assembled through human decisions into a new object-world, the result of work.[53]

For most of the modern era, the technological use of land has operated to end "the existence of nature." Land has been fenced, excluding wildlife so that it could instead support domesticated grazing animals, agriculture, and human settlements. * * *

Even when people acknowledged the toll of development on natural resources, giving birth to the conservation movement in the nineteenth century, there was virtually no impact on the precepts of property law. The concerns of conservation were then largely

---

[52] Several recent books employ the idea of a natural economy. *See, e.g.*, ROBERT E. RICKLEFS, THE ECONOMY OF NATURE: A TEXTBOOK IN BASIC ECOLOGY (1976); DONALD WORSTER, NATURE'S ECONOMY: A HISTORY OF ECOLOGICAL IDEAS (1985).

[53] PHILIP FISHER, MAKING AND EFFACING ART: MODERN AMERICAN ART IN A CULTURE OF MUSEUMS 223 (1991).

aesthetic, and ecological understanding was limited. Exceptions existed, especially in understanding the adverse impact of timber harvesting on watersheds, but even as to forests, conservation was largely implemented on distant lands where public ownership prevailed. The principal aim of the early conservation movement was to set aside remote enclaves as public parks, forests, and wildlife refuges, where nature could be preserved while elsewhere the transforming business of society went on as usual.

The burst of concern for controlling industrial pollution also failed to propel nature's economy onto the legal agenda. Conventional pollution laws do not challenge the traditional property system. They do not demand that adjacent land be treated as part of a river's riparian zone nor that it be left to perform natural functions supportive of the river as a marine ecosystem. On the contrary, such laws assume that a river and its adjacent tracts of land are separate entities and that the essential purpose of property law is to maintain their separateness. Thus, they assume development of the land and internalization of the development's effects; they are effectively "no dumping" laws, under which the land and the river are discrete entities.

Benefits that adjacent lands and waters confer upon each other can, with rare exceptions, be terminated at the will of the landowner, because the ecological contributions of adjacent properties are generally disregarded in defining legal rights. For example, if riparian uplands are the habitat for river creatures that come on shore to lay their eggs, landowners are perfectly free to destroy that habitat while putting the land to private use—even though doing so harms the river and its marine life. The existence of such connections between property units was not unknown (though certainly much more is currently known about their importance); rather, until recently society assumed that the termination of natural systems in favor of systems created by human effort was a change for the better. In addition, when significant ecological losses did occur, people believed that the losses could be compensated through technological means. Therefore, landowners developed upstream lands that, in their natural state, had absorbed flood waters. The adverse effects of too much waterflow on downstream lands were either tolerated or replaced technologically, as with flood control dams. Finally, when dams were built, states tried to replace instream losses with fish hatcheries.

* * *

The majority opinion correctly recognizes that a fundamental redefinition of property was possible in *Lucas*. In this light, *Lucas* represents the Court's rejection of pleas to engraft the values of the economy of nature onto traditional notions of the rights of land ownership. Justice Scalia assumes that redefinition of property rights to accommodate ecosystem demands is not possible. The Court treats claims that land be left in its natural condition as unacceptable impositions on landowners. By characterizing the demands of the economy of nature as pressing "private property into some form of public service,"[62] the Court fails to recognize that lands in a state of nature are already in public service but to a purpose that the Court is unwilling to acknowledge.

Given that the economy of nature is emerging as a prominent viewpoint, the Court should have asked whether notions of property law could be reformulated to accommodate

---

[62] *Lucas*, 112 S. Ct. at 2895.

ecological needs without impairing the necessary functions of the transformational economy.

IV. PROPERTY DEFINITIONS HAVE ALWAYS BEEN DYNAMIC

Historically, property definitions have continuously adjusted to reflect new economic and social structures, often to the disadvantage of existing owners:

> Economic development was a primary objective of Americans in the nineteenth century, but steps to promote growth frequently clashed with the interests of particular property owners. . . . Americans, in J. Willard Hurst's phrase, pre-ferred "property in motion or at risk rather than property secure and at rest." As a consequence, legislators and courts often compelled existing property arrangements to give way to new economic ventures and changed circum-stances.[63]

* * *

Examples of property law's adaptation to social changes abound. In a ruder world, nuisance law originally imposed unprecedented duties of neighborliness on owners' rights. The Kentucky Constitution once opined that "the right of the owner of a slave to such slave, and its increase, is the same, and as inviolable as the right of the owner of any property whatever."[70] In eighteenth century America, the states abolished feudal tenures, abrogated primogeniture and entails, ended imprisonment for debt, and significantly re-duced rights of alienation, as well as dower and curtesy. In the nineteenth century, to promote industrialization by hydropower mills, courts redefined the traditional rights of natural flow in water established during a preindustrial economy. The rules changed again when log-floating became a necessary way to get lumber to markets. In the arid west, landowners' riparian rights were simply abolished because they were unsuited to the physical conditions of the area. As the status of women changed, laws abolished husbands' property rights in their wives' estates.

The modern company town and the modern shopping center have generated modifica-tions to the law of trespass. In response to urbanization, legislative zoning reduced the rights of landowners. The affected landowners contested zoning statutes, claiming they were subject only to case-by-case restrictions on land use under nuisance law. The Supreme Court rejected their claim and validated zoning. Justice Sutherland wrote: "In a changing world, it is impossible that it should be otherwise."[81] Indeed, the very heart of the *Lucas* opinion—the concept that property ownership confers positive developmental rights—is

---

[63] JAMES W. ELY, JR., THE GUARDIAN OF EVERY OTHER RIGHT: A CONSTITUTIONAL HISTORY OF PROPERTY RIGHTS 6 (1992) (citation omitted).

[70] KY. CONST. OF 1850, art. XIII, § 3. Interestingly, during the abolition of slavery in America—a movement that certainly grew out of a fundamental change in societal values—great deference was shown to slaveholders' property interests, perhaps in recognition of the issue's political sensitivity. "For example, Pennsylvania's 1780 emancipation statute applied only to future generations of slaves. . . . Even then, the law postponed freedom until such slave children reached the age of twenty-eight, in order to reimburse their masters for the expenses of raising them." ELY, *supra* note 63, at 24. Lincoln originally favored emancipation with compensation, and owners were compensated in 1862 when Congress abolished slavery in the District of Columbia. Of course, the Thirteenth Amendment later eliminated slavery without compensation to owners. *Id.* at 83.

[81] Village of Euclid v. Ambler Realty Co., 272 U.S. 365, 387 (1926).

a product of a modern economy that itself destroyed common rights in property because such rights were no longer functional in a capitalist society.

V. IS COMPENSATION THE ANSWER?

Though the *Lucas* majority does not say so explicitly, its adoption of a standard based upon historically bounded nuisance and property law reflects a sentiment that a state should compensate landowners who, through no fault of their own, lose property rights because of scientific or social transformations. The *Lucas* opinion focuses on landowners—such as proprietors of barrier beaches or wetlands—who seem to be the ultimate victims of unanticipated, uncontrollable changes. Not only are their land uses restricted for historically unrecognized purposes, but also they own a type of land that, by today's standards, should never have been subject to private ownership at all.

In the past, innocent loss in the face of unexpected change did not generate a right of compensation. Most owners regulated under new laws were hapless victims of changes they could not reasonably have anticipated. Farmers could not have known that the pesticides they were using were harmful; industrialists located on rivers could not have anticipated modern water pollution laws; buyers of land now deemed unstable did not have the advantage of modern methods for detecting instability. Paradoxically the most unexpected and sweeping changes, such as the industrial revolution, left the largest number of uncompensated victims in their wake. Notions of "expectation" or the "principles" of nuisance law cannot explain the failure to compensate such owners. Why they were left to bear their losses is a profoundly interesting question.

The noncompensation norm in circumstances of social change reflects a decision to encourage adaptive behavior by rewarding individuals who most adroitly adjust in the face of change. * * * As existing uses are granted the status of compensable property rights, change becomes less desirable. A society which values change will also likely value human adaptability.

Rather than compensate all the owners disadvantaged by the industrial revolution, for example, property rules changed to promote and encourage development. The courts encouraged the process of industrialization by refraining from socializing its costs through compensation; society rewarded those owners who were best able to respond to the changing world. Noncompensation thereby promoted technological and economic innovation.

* * *

Many forms of adaptive behavior mediate the competing demands of the transformational economy and the economy of nature. Some are already familiar, such as contour plowing to prevent erosion and the clustering of subdivision developments to preserve wooded areas which provide wildlife habitat, windbreaks, and soil stability. Other, less familiar forms of adaptation exist as well. Diversification and timely divestment of lands unsuitable for development are techniques of economic adaptation. Similarly, the acquisition of tracts that are sufficiently large could make it economically feasible to preserve some land in its natural state, while other areas could be developed more intensely. Pooling several people's resources to achieve joint management and shared profits could assure that not every acre a person owns would have to be transformed from its natural state.

Such arrangements could provide alternatives to the *Lucas* majority's concerns about total economic loss. In such cases the whole might be as valuable as the pieces would have been if developed by conventional means. The loss to areas left undeveloped might be compensated by enhanced value in open space or the presence of wildlife, good fishing, and recreation.

Such opportunities will not be available in every situation. Certain individuals will inevitably be caught up in the transitional moment. These first owners to whom the new rule applies will have no opportunity to respond adaptively. At some level the problem is inescapable: Someone must always be first, and new regulation may come without much warning. But there are various nonconstitutional devices that can, and often should, be used to mitigate the burden imposed on the first rank of newly regulated owners. Exempting already developed lands from the new rules (grandfathering) is one such mechanism; allowing variances for hardships is another. Both were ultimately employed in the South Carolina law that gave rise to the *Lucas* case. A gradual phasing in of new regulations is another possible mitigation strategy. Exemption of individual homesites from subdivision regulations is another device for insulating the most vulnerable individuals, while still subjecting the majority of fragile lands to the coverage of new laws. Not every such technique will be appropriate in every situation, but these examples illustrate that there are many ways to blunt the impact of transition to new legal regimes.

VI. TOWARD A NEW DEFINITION OF PROPERTY

Public, Planned, Ecosystemic

Assuming no compensation and a willingness to look anew at the nature of rights in land, what might property rights designed to accommodate both transformational needs and the needs of nature's economy look like? They would, at the least, be characterized by the following features:

1. Less focus on individual dominion, and the abandonment of the traditional "island" and "castle-and-moat" images of ownership.
2. More public decisions, because use would be determined ecosystemically, rather than tract by tract; or more decisions made on a broad, systemwide private scale.
3. Increased ecological planning, because different kinds of lands have different roles.
4. Affirmative obligations by owners to protect natural services, with owners functioning as custodians as well as self-benefitting entrepreneurs.

To some extent, each of these changes already can be found in contemporary land use management. Extensive public regulation, active participation by the community in determining how land shall be used, and affirmative obligations imposed on private developments have increasingly become part of the land use process. The demands of the economy of nature, however subtly, have worked their way into the governance of land use. Wetlands regulation and coastal management have been in place in some states for nearly thirty years. Thus, the practice has preceded the theory, and change has occurred. After all, property is functional.

The true significance of changes being made, however, often was concealed under the all-embracing rubric of "harm." Justice Scalia was correct: "Harm" is a paint that covers any surface. Judicial failure to ask why land management had changed so much, and to produce a plausible justification for the ongoing revision of property rights, has probably been one reason landowners see themselves as victims of injustice. * * *

The Usufructuary Model

How would an owner's rights be defined in a property system that served both of the economies described here? Perhaps the closest existing model is that of usufructuary rights. The owner of a usufruct does not have exclusive dominion of her land; rather, she only has a right to uses compatible with the community's dependence on the property as a resource. Thus, for example, one may own private property rights in a navigable river to use the water, but those rights are subordinate to the community's transportation needs in the river. The private use may be entirely eliminated where the community's navigation needs so require. Usufructuary rights have already developed in water because rivers and lakes were viewed as continuous and interconnected, not as separable into discrete segments. Many people depended on the rivers and lakes while numerous individuals also held private property interests in the resources. These characteristics made water unsuitable for complete privatization.

* * *

VII. THE PROBLEM OF GOVERNMENTAL ABUSE

* * *

If the *Lucas* majority simply had suggested that heightened judicial scrutiny should be triggered when regulation deprives an owner of all economic value, I would have no quarrel with the opinion. Such a rule of thumb would single out those owners who bear the heaviest private burden of the new ecological era. One might sympathetically view such owners as having lands that never would have been privatized in an ecologically sensitive world. Moreover, when regulation leaves no opportunities for private use, it also does not leave room for adaptive behavior by owners as an alternative to demands for compensation. Such scrutiny would put regulators on notice that they too should seek adaptive solutions to avoid excessive regulation of private uses. Just how much judicial scrutiny such a standard would entail and what burden of justification on regulating governments the standard would impose are questions to which answers can evolve. Instead of responding by freezing outdated conceptions of property, as does the *Lucas* majority, by using a crabbed definition of property and its corresponding categorical rules, courts could respond with flexibility to governmental excess and to the pains unfair regulations inflict on landowners.

* * *

NOTES

1. Professor Sax's article appeared with other excellent analyses of *Lucas* by William Fisher and Richard Lazarus in a symposium published at 45 STAN. L. REV. 1369-1455

(1993). *See also,* Richard Epstein, *The Seven Deadly Sins of Takings Law: The Dissents in* Lucas v. South Carolina Coastal Council, 26 LOY. L.A. L. REV. 955 (1993); Joseph L. Sax, *The Constitutional Dimensions of Property: A Debate*, 26 LOY. L.A. L. REV. 23 (1993).

2. Sax quotes from the famous Wisconsin decision of *Just v. Marinette County* to illustrate the view of property rejected by the Court in *Lucas*. Note the connection between the public trust and takings doctrines. One view of *Just* is that the Wisconsin court found no taking when the state prohibited the landowner from filling wetlands because the public rights in the services provided by the natural wetlands predated and conditioned Just's title to the land. Under this view, state regulation to promote the public trust can never be a taking because it does not harm any right actually conferred by the state on the landowner.

3. What is the "ecological worldview" that, Sax argues, the *Lucas* Court rejected? Is it the "land ethic" described by Aldo Leopold in the excerpt in Chapter One of this anthology? Other commentators have called for a shift in worldview that would limit the expectations that owners of important natural areas have for growth and development. *See* ERIC T. FREYFOGLE, JUSTICE AND THE EARTH 45-63 (1993); J. Peter Byrne, *Green Property*, 7 CONST. COMMENTARY 239 (1990); David B. Hunter, *An Ecological Perspective on Property: A Call for Judicial Protection of the Public's Interest in Environmentally Critical Resources*, 12 HARV. ENVTL. L. REV. 311 (1988). Does the Constitution enshrine a particular view of nature, the environment, or property in the Fifth Amendment?

4. How would you respond to the two questions Sax claims that Justice Scalia's opinion raises: Are environmental regulations that require maintenance of natural conditions significantly new and different from traditional regulations? If so, how should the law respond?

5. Sax compares the two world views of the "transformative economy" and the "economy of nature." Are these the same views of the environment that Professor Rose characterizes as "given-ness" and "gift" in the Commons subchapter? In his characterization of the features of a reformed conception of property, Sax mentions that owners would function as custodians as well as self-benefiting entrepreneurs. Do affirmative custodial duties currently exist in property law? How would a privatizer argue that Scalia's view of property best promotes both entrepreneurial and custodial activities?

6. Economics is not the only social science that bears on the takings question. Professor Stake applies results from psychological experiments in his analysis of this issue. Jeffrey Stake, *Loss Aversion and Involuntary Transfers of Title, in* LAW AND ECONOMICS: NEW AND CRITICAL PERSPECTIVES 331 (Robin Paul Malloy and Christopher K. Braun eds. 1995).

7. John Locke's notions, along with much of Enlightenment thinking, epitomize what

Sax calls a "transformative economy." In his Two Treatises of Government, Locke elaborated his theories of property and labor with the notion of productivity. According to Locke, an important purpose of property is to use land most productively and leave nothing fallow or to spoil. Some revisionist readings of Locke find support for conservation and stewardship in this productivity proviso. *See* Lynton Keith Caldwell and Kristin Shrader-Frechette, Policy for Land 654-84 (1993).

8. Should the government compensate property owners whose expectations and investments are destroyed by regulation that reflects changed social attitudes toward the environment? Is Sax's answer, that noncompensation encourages adaptation, an adequate constitutional response?

9. Sax describes his model of property rights in an economy of nature as "public, planned, and ecosystemic." An economy of nature is one that accounts for the services provided by ecosystems. Why should this lead to public, as opposed to expert, technocratic planning? Why not have ecologists judge permissible uses? In his article advocating an ecological perspective on property, David Hunter argues that:

> [U]se restrictions intended to preserve the ecological integrity of sensitive lands are different from other use restrictions. In regard to the former, society's decisions are compelled by a recognition of the external ecological effects private land-use decisions can have; in the latter, they are driven by majoritarian value judgments. This insight differentiates ecologically necessary exercises of the police power and refers the inquiry to the environmental sciences. Thus, the inherent manipulability that plagues traditional takings doctrines, as exemplified by the harm/benefit distinction, is avoided.

David B. Hunter, *An Ecological Perspective on Property: A Call for Judicial Protection of the Public's Interest in Environmentally Critical Resources*, 12 Harv. Envtl. L. Rev. 311, 313 (1988). Do you agree that ecologically-based planning can or should avoid majoritarian value judgments? To what extent is the ecological or ecosystemic terminology based on actual scientific research results, or a majoritarian embrace of certain values symbolized by these concepts borrowed from the natural sciences? To what extent does Hunter's approach differ from recognizing public trust values in the ecological integrity of sensitive lands?

10. Sax describes his model of property as granting only usufructs subordinate to communitarian needs. Would a usufructuary system of property rights stifle investment? Is it reasonable to argue that lost investment in today's society is less important than impaired natural systems?

11. Sax suggests that in many ways *Lucas* is "not as far reaching as its rhetoric suggests." He contends that states will still have a fair amount of latitude in restricting property rights. But in another line of takings cases, which includes *Nollan v. California Coastal*

Commission, 483 U.S. 825 (1987), and *Dolan v. City of Tigard,* 114 S. Ct. 2309 (1994), the Court has been scrutinizing the closeness of the fit between regulations and the legitimate public purpose that justifies them. Particularly with respect to conditions attached to development permits, these decisions have placed a greater burden on government to defend its restrictions by meeting both "substantial nexus" and "rough proportionality" standards. The Court now places the burden on the government to "make some sort of individualized determination that the required dedication is related both in nature and extent to the proposed development's impact." *Dolan* at 2317-18. Suppose the *Dolan* approach were applied to a situation of a total taking. Is the *Dolan* burden an example of the heightened judicial scrutiny with which Sax has no quarrel when regulation deprives an owner of all economic value?

12. Governmental action can also enhance property values. Zoning helps make land development predictable and orderly. Zoning can thus increase the value of land by barring incompatible uses and promoting stable communities. One of the ironies of the *Lucas* case is that if it were not for the availability of federal flood insurance, building homes on barrier islands might well present too much of a financial risk. Also, Lucas' property value was enhanced by government-financed bridges and other infrastructure. See Edward Thompson Jr., *The Government Giveth,* 11 ENVTL. F., Mar./Apr. 1994, at 22; Natasha Zalkin, *Shifting Sands and Shifting Doctrine: The Supreme Court's Changing Takings Doctrine and South Carolina's Coastal Zone Statute,* 79 CAL. L. REV. 207 (1991). Should these enhancements in property value, provided by the government, be taken into consideration when courts calculate takings compensation? *See United States v. Fuller,* 409 U.S. 488 (1973) (limiting compensation for private land taken to its value without a federal grazing permit, which normally attaches to the land upon sale). Lucas settled with the South Carolina Coastal Council for $1,575,000 in 1993, when the state eventually took title. Lucas had purchased the lots for $975,000 in 1986.

13. Since 1988, when President Reagan issued Executive Order 12,630 requiring takings impact analyses for all existing and proposed federal regulation, the takings issue has moved from the courtroom to legislatures at both the federal and state level. The 104th Congress considered a number of bills that would codify the executive order. Over 40 states have considered private property rights bills since 1991. As of the beginning of 1995, twelve states had enacted property rights laws. The most prevalent version of these bills requires some form of takings impact analysis by state agencies (and in some states, local governments as well). Known as assessment or planning bills, they mandate explicit evaluation criteria and procedures for determining the extent to which a proposed governmental action could pose a risk of being ruled a regulatory taking in court. Another version of these state property rights bills, known as compensation bills, would place statutory limits on the extent to which regulatory action can reduce the economic value of private property—establishing, for example, a threshold of a 50 percent reduction in property value which would automatically require compensation. Who should decide where to draw the line between protected property rights and the extent of regulation: the courts or the legislatures? What are the implications for implementation of environmental law?

14. Although the takings doctrine is a peculiarity of the U.S. Constitution, the issue of compensation is increasingly debated in other nations. *See, e.g.,* COMPENSATION FOR EXPROPRIATION: A COMPARATIVE STUDY (G.M. Erasmus ed., 1990); Annette D. Elinger, *Expropriation and Compensation: Claims to Property in East Germany in Light of German Unification*, 6 EMORY INT'L L. REV 215 (1992); Olga Floroff and Susan W. Tiefenbrun, *Land Ownership in the Russian Federation: Laws and Obstacles*, 37 ST. LOUIS U. L.J. 235 (1993); Ann Gelpern, *The Laws and Politics of Reprivatization in East-Central Europe: A Comparison*, 14 U. PA. J. INT'L BUS. L. 315 (1993); Randal S. Jeffrey, *Social and Economic Rights in the South African Constitution: Legal Consequences and Practical Considerations*, 27 COLUM. J. L. & SOC. PROBS. 1 (1993); Ugo Mattei, *Efficiency in Legal Transplants: An Essay on Comparative Law and Economics*, 14 INT'L REV. L. & ECON. 3 (1994).

Five
Risk

In his majority opinion enjoining the Tellico Dam because of its risk to the continued existence of the endangered snail darter, Chief Justice Burger noted that:

> Congress has spoken in the plainest of words, making it abundantly clear that the balance has been struck in favor of affording endangered species the highest of priorities, thereby adopting a policy which it described as "institutionalized caution."

Tennessee Valley Authority v. Hill, 437 U.S. 153, 194 (1978). Some would make the broader claim that all environmental law (not just the Endangered Species Act) promotes a policy of "institutionalized caution." In international environmental law, this "institutionalized caution" is embodied in a concept called the "precautionary principle," an idea that environmental protection measures should be employed even in the absence of conclusive proof of environmental harm. *See generally,* Bernard A. Weintraub, *Science, International Environmental Regulation, and the Precautionary Principle: Setting Standards and Defining Terms,* 1 N.Y.U. ENVTL. L.J. 173 (1992); James Cameron and Julie Abouchar, *The Precautionary Principle: A Fundamental Principle of Law and Policy for the Protection of the Global Environment,* 14 B.C. INT'L & COMP. L. REV. 1 (1991). Because the environment is so complex, caution may be justified to reduce the likelihood of catastrophic, unforeseen, or irreversible effects. Caution aims to reduce risk. This chapter considers the extent to which environmental law can or should function to balance the risk of unwanted consequences, be they cancers or extinctions, against the rewards of particular activities.

This chapter also discusses the problems associated with deciding how much caution, or how little risk, we should accept or impose. Like cost-benefit analysis, risk management presents a special, seemingly technical language that often belies important value choices about society's aspirations for environmental law. Consider whether the debate over risk issues is really between worry-warts (the risk averse) and thrill-seekers (the risk embracing). This chapter surveys the issues in the risk debate and uncovers some of the deeper divisions in the conflicting visions of environmental safety.

In the first excerpt, Alon Rosenthal, George Gray, and John Graham introduce the technical issues, assumptions, and uncertainties associated with quantitative risk assessment. They then categorize the different risk management approaches of environmental statutes dealing with carcinogens. Most of these congressional mandates are narrative and vague, vesting considerable risk management discretion in the administrative agencies. The authors describe the difficulties that would result if Congress attempted to be more specific and uniform in setting levels of risk for society.

William Ruckelshaus goes beyond Rosenthal, *et al.* and argues that even more administrative discretion would improve decisionmaking about environmental risk. Ruckelshaus supports decentralizing risk management to provide people most vulnerable to the trade-offs with a greater voice in the outcome. That a well-respected, and the only two-time, Environmental Protection Agency [EPA] Administrator would get so involved in the debate over risk illustrates its importance in environmental law.

John Atcheson criticizes the assumption that runs through Rosenthal, *et al.* and Ruckelshaus that the EPA's mandate is risk reduction. Atcheson foresees many problems with using risk reduction as an organizing principle of environmental law, especially its "reactive policy dynamic," its false certainty, and its tendency to limit budgets for global environmental protection.

Peter Huber distinguishes between public risk (non-natural threats that are mass-produced, broadly distributed, and borne largely involuntarily) and private risk (natural or local risks subject to personal control). Huber highlights the public's irrationality in demanding lower public risk, often at the expense of higher private risk. He also criticizes institutional biases (particularly in courts) that favor older, more risky technology over newer, safer technology. Where Rosenthal, *et al.* focus on the relative institutional capacities of agencies and Congress to manage risk, Huber focuses on agencies and courts. He finds the conventional expert administrative agency to be the institution best able to handle issues of environmental risk.

Stephen Breyer shares Huber's view that risk management is an appropriate framework for environmental regulation. Breyer proposes a new kind of expert administrative entity with a small, centralized staff rationalizing risk across existing government agencies. Breyer extends his analysis to include the comparative capacities to manage risk of Congress, as well as courts and agencies.

In the final excerpt, Clayton Gillette and James Krier criticize the technocracy inherent in expert agency management of risk. They challenge Huber's assertion that courts are biased against public risk at the expense of private risk. Although written before Breyer's work, Gillette and Krier anticipate and attack many of Breyer's arguments about the institutional benefits of expert administrative entities. In particular, Gillette and Krier disagree with the assertion that existing agencies over-regulate public risk. Gillette and Krier present a different way of viewing and validating the general public's "multidimensional" judgments about risk, which include considerations of involuntary exposure, delayed effects, distribution of risk, and catastrophic potential. Gillette and Krier close with insightful observations about the relationship between democracy and technocracy.

The following article, written by researchers in the field of public health, describes how risk goals are articulated by Congress and employed by agencies implementing environmental law. The debate over "bright line" mandates versus narrative standards has assumed greater importance in the years since this article appeared.

LEGISLATING ACCEPTABLE CANCER RISK FROM EXPOSURE TO TOXIC CHEMICALS
Alon Rosenthal, George M. Gray, John D. Graham
19 Ecology L.Q 269 (1992)*

INTRODUCTION

Scientific information about the human health risks of exposure to toxic chemicals is critical to making sound regulatory decisions. The rapidly expanding information base about chemicals has complicated the task of regulators and has spawned a growing professional discipline called, alternately, risk assessment or quantitative risk assessment (QRA). A risk assessment is an analytical report that provides qualitative and quantitative indications of the human health risks attributable to exposure to an environmental agent.

The results of risk assessments now guide regulators of toxic substances in making screening, priority-setting, and standard-setting decisions. Screening decisions, which may be based on a very simple assessment, determine whether a particular chemical exposure may pose enough risk to justify a more detailed risk assessment. Priority-setting decisions identify those chemical exposures which are serious enough to justify regulation. Standard-setting decisions involve setting specific limitations on discharges to adequately protect the public from chemical exposures. The process of making priority-setting and standard-setting decisions is often called "risk management." * * *

* * *

While not unfettered, agency discretion in risk management remains extremely broad. In particular, agencies have considerable discretion in translating narrative statutes into specific risk management decisions, since narrative standards are not self-defining, and since courts generally will defer to agency efforts to translate such standards into specific actions. Legislators have responded to this situation with proposals which they hope will constrain agency risk management decisions to a narrower range of outcomes which would more closely approximate legislative aims. Since agencies make extensive use of quantitative risk assessments in risk management, a number of the newer legislative proposals would establish numerical "bright lines" to control the risk management process. The term "bright line," which is commonly used to indicate a clear distinction, has become firmly entrenched in environmental policy jargon, and refers to quantitative risk levels which are written into environmental laws.

Legislators see mandated numerical risk levels, or bright lines, as a means to reduce executive branch discretion and gain greater congressional control over risk management.

---

* Reprinted with permission.

For example, Congress might mandate that the amount of dioxin permitted in freshwater fish be reduced until the excess lifetime cancer risk to the average sport fisherman is less than one chance in a million. The idea is that by specifying the numerical level of risk for the agency, legislators could better guarantee that an appropriate degree of protection is provided to the public.

* * *

In this article, we examine the case for and the case against the use of bright lines in regulatory statutes. Our major thesis is that legislating bright lines would do little to constrain agency discretion in risk management, since agencies would retain enormous discretion in the risk assessment process. In the face of profound scientific uncertainty about cancer risk, agency risk assessors can make numerous quasi-policy judgments in deciding how chemical risks are calculated. Although Congress could constrain the discretion of risk assessors by mandating specific analytic methods and data sources, there is a real danger that such detailed legislative prescriptions would undermine scientific progress in risk assessment.

If Congress is determined to mandate bright lines, it should undertake more policy analysis to determine how to construct bright lines to achieve its public policy goals. While the most popular variant of bright line legislation would compel the reduction of lifetime cancer risks from each source of chemical exposure to less than one chance in a million lifetimes, it is by no means clear that this single approach would be appropriate in all circumstances.

Taking into account the scientific limitations of current risk assessment methods, we argue that legislators should consider bright lines as a device to guide agency priority setting, as they did in drafting the 1990 Clean Air Act Amendments rather than as a tool to control the precise level of stringency that final standards must satisfy. Legislators should also consider "fuzzy bright lines," which establish a numerical range of acceptable risk rather than a single number.

I. QUANTITATIVE RISK ASSESSMENT

* * *

Cancer risk estimates are predictions of an unknown future, rather than estimates of the future behavior of a known phenomenon. For this reason, they can be quite difficult to quantify with precision. A comparison of the prediction of car accident rates to that of cancer rates illustrates the difficulty. An estimate of the number of persons who will be killed in car accidents can be based on frequency data—actual counts of automobile fatalities over a number of years. A prediction can thus be based on the past behavior of the system. In contrast, cancer risk predictions are based on extrapolated probabilities, not on past frequencies. There are a number of reasons for this. For example, the causes of cancer are much more complex, because cancer does not develop immediately after exposure to a carcinogen, and because regulators want to know the potential risk of substances to which the public has not yet been exposed in great numbers. As a consequence, predictions of cancer risk cannot be known with similar degrees of precision.

In evaluating the seriousness of incremental cancer risks, it is useful to have a sense of perspective about the frequency of cancer. At current U.S. mortality rates, a baby born today has about a one-in-four, or 0.25, chance of contracting fatal cancer in his or her lifetime. This is the average American's baseline cancer risk from all causes. An incremental risk of one in a million, or 10^{-6}, the most frequently proposed bright line risk standard, is equivalent to a change in lifetime cancer risk from 0.25 to 0.250001.

A. Hazard Identification

The most definitive way to determine whether a compound can cause human cancer is through the science of epidemiology. Cancer epidemiology attempts to establish associations between human exposure to a suspected cancer causing agent and the frequency of cancer in the human population. The major drawback of epidemiological studies is that they cannot measure risks before those who are exposed develop cancer, but merely identify effects which have already occurred. Risk managers want to identify human carcinogens before cancer develops, before they can be discovered by epidemiology.

Furthermore, cancer epidemiology is fraught with interpretive difficulty. Cancer is a disease with a long latency period that arises from many causes, only some of which are known. Human exposures to potential carcinogens are often complex, uncertain, and poorly documented. If exposures are mismeasured, the epidemiologist will have a difficult time detecting any association between exposure and disease, even if one exists. Moreover, epidemiological studies are often plagued by confounding factors, such as smoking, by a lack of suitable control groups, and by alternative interpretations of data. Due to practical limitations on the size of studies and the large background risk of cancer, epidemiologists usually cannot detect modest cancer risks that would still be of concern to risk managers. While some epidemiological studies of animal carcinogens have been "negative," this may simply reflect the inadequate sample sizes in these studies. When epidemiologists do detect human cancer risks, they usually do so in occupational settings where historical levels of exposure have been quite high. If findings from the workplace are to be extrapolated to environmental settings, epidemiologists must resolve uncertainties about how to extrapolate tumors observed at relatively high doses to the tumors that might occur at low levels of environmental exposure.

* * *

In light of the limits of epidemiology and the need to identify hazards before they cause serious harm, scientists have resorted to animal experiments in an effort to identify agents that are potential human carcinogens. The key laboratory test used in hazard identification is the long-term rodent bioassay, which is conducted on the assumption that a rodent carcinogen may also be a human carcinogen. In addition, laboratory tests of the biological properties of chemicals provide information which can help scientists assess a chemical's potential for human carcinogenicity.

* * *

Several hundred compounds have been shown to cause cancer in animal tests. The usefulness of these studies in predicting human carcinogenicity depends on the accuracy of certain assumptions. These include the assumption that humans respond in a similar manner to rodents; the assumption that results of exposure to high doses over the relatively short lifetimes of animals are functionally equivalent to the results of exposure to low doses over human lifetimes; and the assumption that cross-species scaling methods accurately extrapolate doses given to small test animals to reflect comparable human doses. These assumptions are hotly contested within the scientific and regulatory communities, but a frequently stated rationale is that, while they may not be accurate, they are conservative—reliance upon them will minimize the chance that a carcinogen will be falsely exonerated. On the other hand, carcinogens are unlikely to be classified as carcinogens until enough high-quality, large-sample testing has been done in a variety of rodent strains and species to reveal their carcinogenic activity.

* * *

B. Dose-Response Evaluation

* * *

Perhaps the most contentious judgment in carcinogen risk assessment is how to extend the dose-response curve from the high doses to which animals are exposed in the laboratory to the lower doses to which humans are exposed in the environment. There are several well-known statistical models for fitting the animal data and extrapolating the dose-response curve to low doses. Often each model will fit the experimental animal data quite well and have at least some plausible basis in biology. The models nonetheless may yield low-dose risk estimates for the same chemical, or even from the same data set, that vary enormously, by factors of hundreds or even of thousands.

* * *

C. Exposure Assessment

Exposure assessment is the phase of a risk assessment that determines just how much exposure to a carcinogen people actually confront. Exposure can occur through a variety of routes, including inhalation, dermal absorption, and ingestion of contaminated food or water. While some sources of pollution cause human exposure through more than one such pathway, EPA risk assessments do not always consider this possibility. More recent risk assessments, however, indicate a trend to account for as many sources and routes of exposure as possible.

* * *

EPA generally uses predictive models, rather than direct measurements, to calculate the exposure of the MEI [maximally exposed individual]. In the case of a resident at a factory fenceline, a mathematical dispersion model might estimate the air concentration of the carcinogen 200 meters from the source (EPA typically assumes in such scenarios that the fenceline, and the residence of the MEI, are 200 meters from the source). In addition, the models often assume that the MEI is outdoors breathing air at this predicted concentration twenty-four hours a day for seventy years. Although no one spends his or her entire life outdoors at the fenceline of the factory, and although few factories produce the same products, or even exist, for seventy years, the MEI calculation is designed to be conservative. By overstating probable actual exposure, it provides a safety margin, giving an upper bound on the true lifetime exposure.

Use of the hypothetical MEI to set standards is extremely controversial. Critics of MEI-based standards argue that it is unsound to regulate, often at very great cost, on the basis of an inflated exposure scenario that never occurs. Supporters argue that highly exposed people, even if they are few in number, have a right to protection, and that the conservatism in MEI scenarios may be appropriate given the other uncertainties in risk assessment.

* * *

While researchers often prefer detailed monitoring of a carcinogenic pollutant to uncertain modelling, monitoring is expensive and cumbersome. Furthermore, exposure to a compound cannot be monitored unless the compound has already been released into the environment, and even then, the researcher cannot be certain that the compound will behave similarly in other environments. * * *

* * *

D. Risk Characterization

* * *

The meaning of EPA's risk estimates cannot be accurately conveyed except in light of the numerous assumptions that have been made. As two commentators have stated, risk estimates from analyses done according to EPA procedures "do not give certainty in the scientific sense, nor can they be used to establish precise numbers of persons who will be stricken with some disease."[131] However, the number that comes from the risk characterization step is often reported and used without qualification. Advocates of risk assessment constantly call for analysts to quantify and report the full range of uncertainty in a risk assessment. In fact, because of the numerous conservative assumptions built into the EPA risk assessment process (so-called "compounded conservatism"),[134] EPA has stated that a risk estimate produced in accord with its procedures should be regarded as a plausible upper bound on risk. That is, the actual risk will almost certainly lie somewhere between the EPA risk estimate and zero. The actual risk is very unlikely to be greater than the EPA risk estimate, is probably lower than the EPA estimate, and may even be zero.

Therefore, EPA states that, in addition to the risk number, a risk characterization should contain: (a) a discussion of the "weight of the evidence" for human carcinogenicity (e.g., the EPA carcinogen classification); (b) a summary of the various sources of uncertainty in the risk estimate, including those arising from hazard identification, dose-response evaluation, and exposure assessment; and (c) a report of the range of risks, using EPA's risk estimate as the upper limit and zero as the lower limit.

* * *

II. NARRATIVE STATUTES AND RISK ASSESSMENT AT EPA

Environmental statutes guide government agencies through either narrative or numerical directives. With the possible exception of the Delaney Amendment to the Federal Food,

---

[131] [Milton Russell & Michael Gruber, *Risk Assessment in Environmental Policy-Making*, 236 SCIENCE 286 (1987)] at 287.

[134] For discussion of the pitfalls of regulating on the basis of conservative risk estimates, see Richard J. Zeckhauser & W. Kip Viscusi, *Risk Within Reason*, 248 SCIENCE 559 (1990); Albert L. Nichols & Richard J. Zeckhauser, *The Perils of Prudence: How Conservative Risk Assessments Distort Regulation*, 8 REG. TOXICOLOGY & PHARMACOLOGY 61 (1988).

Drug and Cosmetic Act, which seems to compel zero risk, the existing federal environmental laws designed to reduce risks to human health due to chemical exposure use the narrative approach. These narrative statutes are generally of three types: (1) those that compel EPA to clean up the environment to the degree that is technologically achievable (often called "technology-based" statutes); (2) those that compel EPA to clean up the environment to a degree that makes sense based on a balancing of health benefits and the costs of control (so-called "balancing" statutes); and (3) those that compel EPA to clean up the environment to a degree that assures that the public health is protected, usually with some margin of safety (so-called "health-based" statutes). In some cases Congress has used more than one of these forms in a single statute.

Over the years, EPA has, through a somewhat haphazard and idiosyncratic process, translated narrative directives into decision rules for risk management based on the findings of QRA. Like the authors of several previous studies, we found some crude patterns in the numerical levels of cancer risk that affect the standard-setting process in EPA program offices. However, we argue in this section that there is no apparent relationship between how an EPA program office uses QRA and the language of the narrative statute the program implements. In other words, narrative statutes, as currently written, do not appear to inform or constrain EPA's use of QRA in risk management decisions. Indeed, we found some rather subtle yet powerful differences in how cancer risks are calculated, reported, and regulated throughout EPA which have no obvious roots in the underlying statutory mandates.

We begin with a discussion of the Delaney Clause, the only bright-line statute, and then discuss the three major categories of narrative statutes. Our intent is not to provide a comprehensive review of the relevant statutes, but rather to indicate how risk assessment and management practices vary within and across the different types of narrative statutes implemented by EPA.

A. The Delaney Clause: A Bright Line of Zero Risk

The Delaney Clause, section 409 of the Federal Food Drug and Cosmetic Act (the FFDCA),[148] is perhaps the classic example of the zero-risk statute. While EPA and the FDA have engaged in creative legal reasoning to avoid the highly stringent regulatory implications of the Delaney Clause, there is no question that the Delaney Clause is the closest Congress has ever come to including a bright line in environmental legislation. In order to understand fully the surprising role that risk assessment has played in the implementation of the Delaney Clause, it is necessary to understand how EPA and the FDA share regulatory authority over pesticides.

The FFDCA is one of two statutes which govern EPA's regulation of pesticides. Under the FFDCA, EPA sets, but does not enforce, maximum allowable levels of pesticide residues (so-called tolerances) for raw agricultural commodities, animal feeds, and processed foods. Pesticide manufacturers submit applications to EPA officials, who set tolerance levels for each chemical ingredient in a pesticide and for each food commodity on

---

[148] FFDCA § 409, 21 U.S.C.A. § 348 (West 1972 & Supp. 1992).

which a pesticide is applied. Both the FDA and the U.S. Department of Agriculture monitor the food supply and enforce the legal tolerance limits set by EPA.

Enacted in 1958, the Delaney Clause prohibits any pesticide residue "if it is found . . . to induce cancer when ingested by man or animal, or if it is found, after tests which are appropriate for the evaluation of the safety of food additives, to induce cancer in man or animal."[154] Contrary to popular perception, the FFDCA does not permit the EPA to apply the rigid approach of the Delaney Clause in setting tolerance levels for all foods. Only "processed foods with concentrated pesticides" are subject to the arguably zero-risk language; raw agricultural commodities are not. Through a fascinating combination of legal and technical maneuvers, EPA has tried to legitimize the use of QRA under the terms of the Delaney Clause.

From the beginning, implementation of the Delaney Clause was problematic. The provision appeared to prohibit pesticide residues on the basis of a mere potential carcinogenic hazard, apparently forbidding EPA from using QRA or exempting minimal risks. EPA responded to this predicament with a case of regulatory paralysis: since a finding of cancer risk under the Delaney Clause would trigger complete prohibition of the residues, EPA was reluctant to identify cancer risks under the clause. Only twice since its enactment has the agency invoked the clause to refuse a new food use of a carcinogenic pesticide.

* * *

One of the reasons behind EPA's desire to consider the magnitude of the carcinogenic risks of new pesticides is its concern about the relative carcinogenicity of older and newer pesticides. Because pesticides approved in earlier decades were not adequately tested to identify their carcinogenic potential and were grandfathered in under earlier standards, EPA is concerned that strict application of the Delaney Clause to new pesticides prevents the replacement of more dangerous older chemicals with safer new ones. Because EPA does not have the administrative flexibility to approve new pesticides that are carcinogenic, older high risk pesticides are retained on the market while less toxic alternatives are discouraged because the smaller risk they pose might still trigger a registration rejection.

* * *

B. Health-Based Statutes: The Clean Air Act

Perhaps the most famous narrative provisions in environmental statutes designed to protect public health are found in the Clean Air Act (CAA). Under section 112 of the 1970 Clean Air Act, EPA was required to set emission standards for hazardous air pollutants, such as carcinogens, that would "protect the public health" with an "ample" margin of safety.[175] EPA's efforts to implement this narrative provision using QRA between 1970 and 1990 created deep discontent in the environmental community, stimulating extensive litigation over the role of risk assessment under section 112. * * * While EPA's assessments of cancer risks may change under the 1990 amendments, EPA's historical use of QRA to manage air toxics illustrates the extent of agency discretion

---

[154] FFDCA § 409(c)(3)(A), 21 U.S.C.A. § 348(c)(3)(A) (West 1972). Identical language in other parts of the statute regulates color additives and animal drug residues. Merrill, *supra* note 10, at 3.

[175] Pub. L. No. 91-604, § 112, 84 Stat. 1676, 1685 (1970).

embedded in apparently health-based, narrative provisions. EPA responded cautiously or lethargically (depending on one's point of view) to the powerful regulatory authority contained in section 112. In 1979, EPA proposed a strategy in which it would use risk assessment in listing carcinogens for regulatory consideration, but the strategy was never finalized. In the early years of the Reagan Administration, EPA sought to delegate the air toxics issue to the states on the grounds that only local "hot spots" were likely to justify regulatory action. Later, EPA used QRA extensively to determine the extent of cancer risks attributable to various industrial sources of air toxics. While EPA's air office released numerous QRA's for public comment in the mid-1980's, the rulemaking process was very slow.

EPA delays in standard setting under section 112 have been attributed to several causes. EPA itself suggested that the "ample margin of safety test," if interpreted literally, might be construed to require zero emissions for carcinogens, which could produce massive dislocations given the pervasiveness of carcinogenic emissions by industry. If interpreted this way, section 112 would be a strict, zero-risk statute much like the Delaney Clause.

Even if section 112 did not set a zero-risk standard, some EPA officials saw the required National Emission Standard for Hazardous Air Pollutants (NESHAP) as far too expensive to justify the estimated reductions in cancer risk. This produced agency paralysis almost as severe as that produced by the strict language of the Delaney Clause. The reasons were similar: since listing could trigger extremely costly NESHAP's, EPA was reluctant to list substances without compelling evidence of widespread population risk. Some EPA officials regarded the estimated population risks from air toxics as quite small, which undercut the case for expeditious rulemaking activity.

EPA's decision to avoid section 112 listings and rulemakings sparked substantial litigation. Even when EPA did promulgate NESHAP's, it used QRA to justify emission standards that were more permissive than some desired. This also prompted environmentalists to file suit. The most important of these cases involved EPA regulation of vinyl chloride. In *Natural Resources Defense Council v. EPA*,[188] the District of Columbia Circuit Court, sitting en banc, reversed an earlier panel decision. According to the full court, section 112 requires EPA to set NESHAP's on the basis of a two-step process. First, EPA must determine "safe" levels of carcinogenic emission, without regard to cost or technological feasibility. Second, EPA may set emission standards lower than the safe emission level in order to provide an ample margin of safety to the public. Although the agency might determine that certain non-zero risk levels are safe or acceptable, it still would be compelled in the second step to determine that the final emission standard provided an "ample margin of safety" in light of scientific uncertainties about risk and possibly other factors.

* * *

C. Risk-Benefit Balancing: * * * FIFRA

Under some statutes, Congress wishes to provide EPA with broad discretion to weigh the risks and benefits of alternative regulatory choices. While these balancing statutes do

---

[188] 824 F.2d 1146 (D.C. Cir. 1987), *rev'g* 804 F.2d 710 (D.C. Cir. 1986).

not require risk assessment per se, in calling for EPA to eliminate "unreasonable risks," they imply that EPA should consider the magnitude of health risks, the anticipated reductions in risk from alternative standards, and the economic and social consequences of alternative standards. In striking contrast to statutes which set a bright line level of acceptable risk, these statutes invite EPA to make determinations of unreasonable risk which will vary from decision to decision based on a discretionary balancing of diverse factors.

* * *

New pesticides cannot be marketed in the United States unless EPA registers them under FIFRA [Federal Insecticide, Fungicide, and Rodenticide Act].[199] The statute also authorizes EPA to suspend the registrations of pesticides already on the market. EPA can withdraw a pesticide's registration only if there are labeling problems or if there are "unreasonable adverse effects on the environment," defined as "any unreasonable risk to man or the environment, taking into account the economic, social and environmental costs and benefits of the use of any pesticide."[202] In practical terms, EPA is not required to undertake a formal, mathematical cost-benefit analysis of each pesticide decision. Nevertheless, judicial review of the agency's registration decisions is influenced by the legislative intent that EPA should consider factors other than public health.

In contrast to the zero-risk orientation of the Delaney Clause, which applies to processed foods, EPA's regulation of pesticide residues on raw agricultural commodities under the FFDCA also entails risk-benefit balancing. The FFDCA directs EPA to limit pesticide residues on raw agricultural commodities to the extent necessary to protect the public health, giving appropriate consideration to other "relevant factors,"[205] including the "necessity for the production of an adequate, wholesome, and economical food supply."[206]

Under these broad statutory authorizations, EPA has used risk assessment to inform regulatory decisions about pesticides. EPA's Office of Pesticides Programs [OPP], which implements both FIFRA and the FFDCA, does not have a formal policy regarding weight-of-the-evidence classification * * *. * * *

In its exposure assessments, the OPP does not base its calculations on a hypothetical maximally exposed individual. Instead, the office achieves a high degree of conservatism in risk assessment by calculating population risk using assumptions about population exposures that, in reality, never occur. For example, when determining tolerance levels for pesticide residues, the OPP assumes a maximum number of crop applications, at the maximum rate of application, with the minimum preharvest interval. It then takes average food intake values from national consumption surveys and integrates them into its Dietary Risk Evaluation System exposure equations. The office then calculates total population risk by summing the average risk posed for each crop on which the pesticide is legally

---

[199] 7 U.S.C.A. §§ 136-136y (West 1980 & Supp. 1992).

[202] FIFRA § 2(bb), 7 U.S.C. § 136(bb) (1988). In a 1971 case, the D.C. Circuit noted that the law "places a heavy burden on any administrative officer to explain the basis for his decision to permit the continued use of a chemical known to produce cancer in experimental animals." Environmental Defense Fund v. Ruckelshaus, 439 F.2d 584, 596 n. 41 (D.C.Cir.1971).

[205] FFDCA § 408(b), 21 U.S.C. § 346a(b) (1988).

[206] Id. In an extended description of its strategy for risk management of pesticide residues, EPA interpreted this provision to require a "risk benefit standard" comparable to the standard setting approach under FIFRA.* * *

applied. For occupational exposures, the office uses surrogate exposure data based on the application method.

Since FIFRA requires EPA to balance the risks and benefits of pesticides, no strict numerical risk levels bind OPP discretion in risk management. Indeed, OPP officials do not acknowledge operating under any formal risk range. There are, however, some patterns in the risk levels which they tend to consider acceptable. The OPP tends to set acceptable risk levels for the food-consuming population within or below the range of 10^{-5} to 10^{-6}, while it tends to accept occupational risks that are less than 10^{-4} to 10^{-5}.

* * *

D. Technology-Based Statutes: The Safe Drinking Water [Act] * * *

While virtually all environmental statutes embrace protection of public health as a goal, the operative narrative standard for regulatory decisions is often a technology-based criterion. These standards seek to reduce human exposures to carcinogens to the lowest level that is technologically feasible. * * *

The Safe Drinking Water Act has numerous regulatory provisions, although its primary focus is setting drinking water standards for the nation. The statute creates two types of standards for drinking water in the United States: nonenforceable "maximum contaminant level goals" (MCLG's), which are concentrations at which no adverse human health effects are believed to occur; and enforceable standards, maximum contaminant levels (MCL's), which, according to the terms of the SDWA, must be set as close to the MCLG's as is "feasible with the use of the best technology, treatment techniques, and other means which the EPA finds after examination for efficiency under field conditions . . . are available (taking costs into consideration)."[244] While the MCLG's are derived from health-based language, the MCL's are derived from technology-based language that permits some consideration of economic impacts.

EPA's consideration of health and feasibility under the SDWA differs from the risk-benefit balancing it conducts under * * * FIFRA. The ODW [EPA's Office of Drinking Water] interprets the statute as mandating an affordability analysis of the analytical technology for detecting contaminants, and not as mandating treatment options per se. In other words, ODW tends to require the lowest levels of contaminants that can be detected with affordable analytical technology. Hence, zero or negligible risk of cancer ostensibly provides an objective function under the SDWA, with feasible detection technology acting as the key constraint on regulatory stringency.

In practice, the ODW sets MCLG's for substances that are probable animal or human carcinogens (chemicals classified as either Group A or Group B carcinogens) at zero. It sets MCLG's for Group C (possible) carcinogens on the basis of acceptable risk benchmarks (e.g., 10^{-6}) or on the basis of a noncarcinogenic endpoint with safety factors added to compensate for possible carcinogenicity. Thus, MCLG's tend to be highly protective, particularly for carcinogenic substances.

In contrast, EPA typically sets the enforceable MCL standards at the so-called "practical quantitative limit" (the PQL), the smallest quantity detectable using available analytical methods. Regardless of the technological obstacles, however, the ODW tries to ensure

---

[244] SDWA § 1412(b)(5), 42 U.S.C. § 300g-1(b)(5) (1988).

that MCL's do not impose lifetime cancer risks in excess of a range of 10^{-4} to 10^{-6}. In several cases, however, estimated residual risk from MCL's has exceeded 10^{-4}.

The QRA's conducted by the Office of Drinking Water are not based entirely on conservative assumptions. * * * The ODW bases its exposure assessments on risk to an average exposed person with no consideration of either unusually sensitive or maximally exposed populations. For example, its risk calculations assume a two-liter-per-day consumption pattern over a seventy-year lifespan, based on research which indicates that the average individual consumes 1.4 liters of water a day. The office does not consider groups with potentially higher exposures (e.g., manual laborers in Arizona) in its risk assessments.

In the final analysis, drinking water carcinogens are regulated on the basis of what agency officials believe a state drinking water program, as authorized by the SDWA, can reasonably be expected to detect. ODW officials argue that the analytical methods necessary to meet existing standards are "not inexpensive," and that small systems already cannot afford to meet the required detection limits. However, the ODW's judgment regarding what is feasible is highly subjective and state drinking water programs occasionally disagree. For example, California, Florida, and New Jersey consider EPA's MCL of five micrograms per liter * * * for benzene excessively lenient, and each of these states has set a standard of one [microgram per liter] standard instead. Critics of EPA's implementation of the SDWA argue that the more demanding MCLG's become functionally irrelevant due to the ODW's emphasis on detection technology. * * *

* * *

E. Hybrid Narrative Statutes

While some insight is gained by categorizing environmental statutes according to the type of narrative language that governs regulatory decisions, some statutes are either difficult to categorize or combine elements of each type of narrative language described above. For lack of a better term, we call these hybrid narrative statutes.

* * *

2. Superfund

Under EPA's "Superfund" program (CERCLA), which regulates the cleanup of inactive hazardous waste sites, a rather elaborate process of risk assessment and management has evolved from a somewhat ambiguous narrative statutory mandate.

The narrative directives for risk management under Superfund are found in section 121(d)(2), which sets forth a two-part standard for cleanup of hazardous waste sites. First, onsite cleanups must satisfy standards from other federal and state environmental programs that are "applicable" or "relevant and appropriate [requirements (ARAR's)] under the circumstances."[295] Second, the cleanup must protect human health and the environment.

---

[295] CERCLA § 121(d)(2)(A), 42 U.S.C. § 9621(d)(2)(A) (1988). CERCLA defines ARAR's as
  any standard, requirement, criteria or limitation under any Federal environmental law, including but not limited to the Toxic Substances Control Act, the Safe Drinking Water Act, the Clean Air Act, the Clean Water Act, the Marine Protection, Research and Sanctuaries Act, or the Solid Waste Disposal Act; or . . . any promulgated standard, requirement, criteria, or limitation under a State environmental or facility siting law that is more stringent than any Federal standard, requirement, criteria or limitation, including each such State standard, requirement, criteria, or limitation contained in a program approved, authorized or delegated by the Administrator under a statute cited in sub-paragraph (A), and that has been identified to the President by the State in a timely manner.
CERCLA § 121(d)(2)(A)(i)-(ii), 42 U.S.C. § 9621(d)(2)(A)(i)- (ii) (1988) (citations omitted).

In applying this two-part standard on a site-specific basis, the Superfund program makes widespread use of QRA.

Under CERCLA, EPA undertakes remedial actions, generally involving cleanup around hazardous waste sites that pose an environmental or public health threat. EPA utilizes QRA at two points in this process. After the agency deems a site sufficiently hazardous to rank it on the "National Priorities List," it conducts a baseline risk assessment to judge whether the health risk justifies cleanup under section 121. Once EPA decides to undertake remedial action at a site (note that here QRA serves a priority-setting function), EPA uses risk assessment to determine appropriate cleanup levels (note that here QRA serves a standard-setting function).

CERCLA does not specify which ARAR standards are applicable under any given circumstances, but in utilizing them, EPA considers the levels of risk that they represent. For example, where exposure is limited to a single substance, EPA cleanup demands are generally met by fulfilling the relevant ARAR requirement (e.g., a drinking water standard for the substance). In contrast, when a mixture is present, the agency evaluates the cumulative risk after completion of the cleanup.

Since the program's inception, EPA has conducted site-specific QRA's. These are particularly complex because sites generally house a host of chemicals to which humans may be exposed through multiple routes. EPA usually does not calculate population risks under Superfund, in part because it typically cannot determine the size of the current (or future) exposed population at a specific site. Instead, the OSW attempts to make exposure assumptions that reflect a reasonable maximum exposure (RME). This concept, which is intended to be more realistic than the "maximally exposed individual," combines upper bound and midrange exposure assumptions. For example, while the Office of Drinking Water uses a fixed two-liter-per-day estimate of water consumption for adults, a Superfund exposure assessment for sites in warm regions in theory may exceed this. On the other hand, the generic assumptions used in QRA's for Superfund sites are not always as conservative as those typically used in other EPA offices. For example, QRA's for Superfund sites assume a thirty-year rather than a seventy-year residence.

If QRA suggests action is required, Superfund allows EPA to pursue various risk management strategies. For instance, institutional controls can limit population proximity to a site through zoning restrictions. Furthermore, recent regulations establish quantitative risk ranges that guide cleanup decisions. The use of a range of acceptable risks permits the agency to use some discretion in setting standards. Although the subject of both criticism and litigation, the National Contingency Plan final rule states that, generally, remedies must reduce the threat from carcinogenic contaminants at a site until the excess lifetime cancer risk to a highly exposed individual (e.g., reasonable worst case) is within or below the range of 10^{-4} to 10^{-6}.

Historically, EPA's policy inclination under Superfund, all things being equal, has been to select remedies that produce results at the more protective end of the risk range. Therefore, when developing its preliminary remediation goals, the OSW establishes 10^{-6} as a point of departure and allows higher risk levels only if cleanup is not reasonable and practical. More recently, EPA has become more lenient. If a baseline risk assessment (BRA) shows a risk of less than 10^{-4}, the agency can make a "no action" record of decision. Nonetheless, there have been cases in which a BRA indicated risks in the higher part of the risk range, and in which EPA initiated remedial action to achieve a 10^{-6} remediation level. EPA is most likely to take such action when cleanup costs are low or when population density suggests potentially high incidence of disease.

* * *

V. NARRATIVE VERSUS BRIGHT-LINE STATUTES

* * *

A. Promoting Democratic Control

* * *

Concerned by the ambiguities and inconsistent administrative activities which narrative criteria produce, some have argued that Congress should make the critical policy judgments by mandating a numerical level of risk to which regulatory decisions must conform. According to this view, Congress has not only the prerogative, but also the responsibility, to make these crucial policy judgements. By deciding what numerical level of protection is required, Congress would replace the judgments of unelected and unaccountable administrative officials with the judgments of elected officials who are directly accountable to the public.

Regardless of one's theory of democracy, our analysis of the risk assessment process suggests that mandated risk levels per se would do little to assert democratic control over the standard setting process. The numerous semitechnical, semipolicy judgments pervasive in the calculation of carcinogenic risk could frustrate any congressional attempt to control regulatory decisions through specification of risk levels.

We saw, for example, that alternative choices of exposure assumptions and dose-response models can lead to plausible risk estimates that vary by several orders of magnitude. If agency officials believe that a statutory bright line is too stringent in a particular case, they can manipulate the risk calculation to produce a numerical estimate of risk that will allow them to justify their desired level of stringency. For example, if EPA's initial estimate of the cancer risk from exposure to formaldehyde appears to be so great as to require huge dislocations in current activities, EPA can reduce its exposure estimates by replacing the hypothetical MEI with the actual MEI, or it can reduce the cancer potency factor by censoring information about the incidence of noncancerous tumors in rats. Likewise, the agency can make more pessimistic assumptions in risk assessment if it believes that Congress has not required a sufficiently stringent level of protection from a specific risk. The large degree of scientific uncertainty permits agency risk assessors to make such changes without undermining the scientific credibility of the risk assessment process. The statutory bright line would be met, but the agencies' fundamental policy judgments would be buried in the risk assessment factors, rather than being visible in the agencies' analysis of the acceptable risk. Because courts are poorly equipped to detect such behavior, judicial review would not prove effective in countering such evasion of the congressional standard.

As long as the degree of scientific uncertainty in cancer risk assessment is large, the choice of acceptable risk levels for use in regulatory decisions will be of secondary significance. A statutorily mandated risk level could in fact mislead the public about the actual level of public health protection, which can only be ascertained by scrutinizing the risk calculation.

Advocates of bright lines are not convinced that agencies would respond by manipulating risk calculations. Administrative agencies historically have been reluctant to depart from their standard risk assessment assumptions despite pressure from both industry and environmentalists. For years, industry groups have urged, with minimal success, changes in risk assessment practice that would replace conservative assumptions with what industrial advocates believe are more realistic ones. At the same time, environmentalists have contested claims that risk assessment is too conservative and articulated reasons why cancer risk estimates might be underestimated. Interest groups and their allies on the EPA Science Advisory Board, an independent group of scientists which advises the EPA Administrator, can effectively block any policy-driven attempt to instigate wholesale departures from standard risk assessment practice.

One of the reasons that departures from standard assumptions in QRA practice historically have been rare is that existing narrative statutes provide regulators substantial discretion in making regulatory decisions—regardless of the precise numerical findings of QRA. Bright line statutes, as discussed above, shift policy decisions to an earlier stage. By giving more policy weight to quantitative risk estimates, mandated risk levels would encourage agencies to examine more closely the assumptions in their risk assessments. With bright lines occasionally compelling some uncomfortable decisions, regulators might insist that the judgment calls in risk assessments be scrutinized on a case-by-case basis, making departures from the standard assumptions more frequent. Since many departures can be justified as scientifically plausible, they might be welcomed by the EPA Science Advisory Board.

Some advocates of mandated risk levels, recognizing the influential role of assumptions and judgments in QRA, have gone further and advocated that Congress compel agencies to calculate cancer risk estimates in a particular way. According to this view, only by specifying both the maximal allowable risk level and the method of calculation can Congress ultimately determine the degree of protection provided to the public. While such an approach would shift some additional power to Congress, it poses some serious problems.

Congress lacks the attention span, expertise, and appreciation of the scientific process to prescribe methods of QRA. The potential for error in translating an evolving science into statutory QRA procedures is enormous. Moreover, as we will argue * * * below, mandating a particular QRA methodology might freeze scientific progress in risk assessment. In short, in its zeal to control executive agencies, Congress might sabotage the scientific progress that is critical to advancing the policy goals it wishes to further.

* * *

B. Promoting Public Health and Economic Efficiency

* * *

A fundamental flaw of any uniform mandated risk level is that it cannot achieve economic efficiency. The mandated level of risk will be understringent for some pollution sources and overstringent for others, depending on the marginal costs of risk reduction at each source. For example, a uniform lifetime cancer risk level of one in 10,000 will cause understringency for those sources that can achieve a one in 1,000,000 risk level at little or no incremental cost to society. In contrast, a mandated risk level of 1 in 1,000,000 will cause overstringency at those sources that can achieve a one in 1,000,000 risk level only at unacceptably high costs to society (e.g., plant shutdowns, unemployment and/or substantial reductions in standard of living).

The only case in which a uniform risk level can achieve efficiency is where the marginal cost of reducing risk at each pollution source is identical. Such circumstances are rare. Numerous studies have demonstrated huge disparities in the marginal costs of pollution control at industrial sources; these disparities result from such factors as the design of the industrial process, the age of the facility, the atmospheric and temperature conditions at the facility, and the facility's access to the capital and materials needed for pollution control. While most bright lines would prove inefficient by these criteria, a bright line could be devised that would assure some consideration of economic efficiency. For example, one could construct a bright line which required each source to reduce risk until the ratio of incremental cost to incremental risk reduction exceeds a specified value.

* * *

Finally, excessive emphasis on reducing insignificant or minute risks of chemical carcinogens necessarily diverts valuable resources needed to address more significant carcinogenic risks, as well as other, more pressing environmental problems involving protection of ecological systems and natural resources. If Congress is primarily concerned about reducing net health risks to acceptable levels, any bright line should be devised with enough flexibility to allow such risk-risk tradeoffs to be taken into account.

C. Promoting Good Regulatory Science

Some have expressed concern that bright lines might freeze scientific progress in risk assessment. From a policy perspective, it is important to consider the implications of bright lines for the scientific maturation of the risk assessment process. Those statutes that mandate use of specific technical assumptions, types of data, and mathematical models are of particular concern. In the final analysis, the scientific integrity of the regulatory process should be nurtured because it is critical to both the competence and the legitimacy of toxic chemical regulation.

We indicated earlier that there are serious gaps in scientific understanding of chemical carcinogenesis, although the information base is expanding at a rapid rate. Given these conditions, Congress should be reluctant to enact a statutory scheme that would preclude or discourage regulators from making use of additional scientific knowledge; it should certainly avoid statutory designs that would discourage development of additional information about the effects of chemical exposure on human health.

Under the prevailing narrative statutory tests, regulators have retained considerable discretion to interpret scientific information for use in risk assessment and management. Although the development of risk assessment guidelines at federal agencies has placed some constraints on the use of new scientific information (particularly on the use of mechanistic information about how chemicals cause cancer), no statute has placed explicit restrictions on an agency's ability to consider, interpret, and utilize scientific knowledge. * * *

If Congress replaces narrative statutes with numerical bright lines, administrative agencies would presumably retain the freedom to use scientific information in generating risk estimates. Hence, absent congressional direction as to QRA procedures, bright lines would not restrict directly an agency's ability to use new scientific information in QRA.

There is a danger, however, that bright lines would induce regulators to consider only that information that can be incorporated into existing mathematical models of dose-response evaluation. Narrative statutory tests provide incentives to produce mechanistic data, such as biological information on the relevance of high-dose animal tumors to low-dose human responses. Even if such data cannot readily be incorporated into standard mathematical models of risk assessment, the statutes provide the regulator ample discretion to consider such data. In contrast, bright lines might discourage consideration and generation of mechanistic data that are difficult or impossible to incorporate into standard dose-response models, unless improved models that incorporate these data can be developed quickly.

* * *

E. Promoting Administrative Consistency

* * *

The public is justifiably confused when it is told that a single risk level as estimated by different program offices in a single executive agency has multiple meanings. If the methods and assumptions used in QRA are so varied, the existence of an essential truth, which QRA purports to measure, appears dubious. Moreover, the diversity of risk levels permitted by EPA risk managers fuels opposition by citizens who resent the relative leniency or stringency of a particular decision.

The fragmentation in the federal government's current approach to risk assessment may not be all bad, however. Fragmentation allows and fosters advances in what is still a relatively immature analytic tool. As program offices and agencies experiment with different QRA approaches, new and improved methods will emerge. A monolithic approach to QRA might inhibit this process, while conveying a false sense of the accuracy and reliability of current methods of QRA.

Even if one believes that current agency inconsistency is undesirable, it is hardly clear that new legislation would improve the situation. Were Congress to amend narrative statutes to include bright lines, it probably would not choose to include a uniform level of acceptable risk in all environmental statutes. Pluralism in bright lines would be likely to emerge from Congress, reflecting the variation in political pressures from statute to statute. Congress might introduce further confusion by mandating a variety of methods for calculating risk under the various laws.

* * *

NOTES

1. Is reducing risk the same as protecting the environment?

2. If bright line risk standards are poor policy, which one of the more flexible, narrative categories is best? Under what circumstances should Congress employ health-based, risk-benefit balancing, technology-based, or hybrid standards? Are some methods more appropriate for priority-setting as contrasted with standard-setting?

3. One of the U.S. Supreme Court's most significant statements about risk assessment came in a case involving the Occupational Safety and Health Administration's (OSHA) regulation of benzene exposure in the work place. *Industrial Union Dep't, AFL-CIO v. American Petroleum Institute,* 448 U.S. 607 (1980). The Occupational Safety and Health Act required the agency to set standards "to provide safe or healthful employment or places of employment" at a level "which most adequately assures, to the extent feasible, * * * that no employee will suffer material impairment of health or functional capacity even if such employee has regular exposure to the hazard." In setting exposure levels for benzene, a known carcinogen, OSHA followed its policy of assuming no safe exposure level absent clear proof to the contrary, and accordingly set the standard at the lowest level feasible, one part-per-million. Indeed, when it sought comment on its proposed standard it did not ask for comments on whether a certain exposure level was safe, but rather on whether the proposed level was the minimum that was feasible. Justice Stevens, writing for four of the five justices who believed OSHA's standard to be invalid, expressed particular concern about the agency's failure to assess the scope of the risk posed by the stringent standard:

> By empowering the Secretary to promulgate standards that are "reasonably necessary or appropriate to provide safe or healthful employment and places of employment," the Act implies that, before promulgating any standard, the Secretary must make a finding that the workplaces in question are not safe. But "safe" is not the equivalent of "risk-free." There are many activities that we engage in every day—such as driving a car or even breathing city air—that entail some risk of accident or material health impairment; nevertheless few would consider these activities "unsafe." Similarly, a workplace cannot be considered "unsafe" unless it threatens workers with a significant risk of harm.

Id. at 642. The Court acknowledged the difficulty of determining which risks are "significant," and suggested that agencies have considerable discretion in making these threshold determinations. The Court further offered a view as to the outside boundaries of the significance determination:

> The requirement that a "significant" risk be identified is not a mathematical straightjacket. It is the Agency's responsibility to determine, in the first instance, what it considers to be a "significant" risk. Some risks are plainly acceptable and others are plainly unacceptable. If, for example, the odds are one in a billion that a person will die from cancer by taking a drink of chlorinated water, the risk clearly could not be considered significant. On the other hand, if the odds are one in a thousand that regular inhalation of gasoline vapors that are 2% benzene will be fatal, a reasonable person might well consider the risk to be significant and take appropriate steps to decrease or eliminate it.

Id. at 655. The Court also made clear that while the agency has the burden of establishing that a significant risk exists, "OSHA is not required to support its findings * * * with anything approaching scientific certainty. * * * [S]o long as they are supported by a body of reputable scientific thought, the Agency is free to use conservative assumptions in interpreting the data with respect to carcinogens, risking error on the side of overprotection rather than underprotection." *Id.* at 656.

A more recent illustration of a court overturning an agency's health-based standard for lack of sufficient risk-based justification is *Leather Industries of America v. EPA*, 40 F.3d 392 (D.C. Cir. 1994) (remanding a rule setting regulatory thresholds for toxic contaminants in sewage sludge).

4. Rosenthal, Gray, and Graham refer to the famous "vinyl chloride" decision, which established a two-step method for setting hazardous air pollutant emission standards that would protect human health with an ample margin of safety under the original § 112 of the Clean Air Act. *Natural Resources Defense Council v. EPA*, 824 F.2d 1146 (D.C. Cir. 1987) (en banc). First, the agency had to determine a level that was "safe" without directly considering costs. Second, the agency had to set the standard at a level that would assure an "ample margin of safety." *Id.* Costs could be considered only at the second step. The 1990 Clean Air Act Amendments, however, changed the method of regulating hazardous air pollutants. Now, the EPA initially sets standards on the basis of the maximum achievable control technology, without regard to safety or risk. If the residual risk to the most exposed person exceeds a one in one million risk of contracting cancer, then the standard must be revised to reduce the risk below that level. 42 U.S.C. § 7412. Is this a sensible way to address the problem inherent in regulating risk?

Frank B. Cross, Daniel M. Byrd, and Lester B. Lave propose an alternative to both the technology-based and the health-based approaches in *Discernible Risk—A Proposed Standard for Significant Risk in Carcinogen Regulation*, 43 ADMIN. L. REV. 61 (1991). To get around the "morass" of standards, goals, and procedures which delay innovation, increase the costs of doing business, and reduce the amount of potential protection, these authors propose a threshold standard of discernible risk. Under their proposal, an agency would regulate a substance only when it detects a "statistically significant" risk. Is the discernible risk standard preferable to the other narrative standards discussed by Rosenthal, Gray, and Graham? How should an agency determine a "statistically significant" risk? If you face a one in one million chance of contracting cancer as a result of exposure to hazardous air pollution, is that risk "statistically significant"?

5. The National Research Council (NRC) of the National Academy of Sciences has produced two studies that frame risk assessment practices in federal agencies. The first report, RISK ASSESSMENT IN THE FEDERAL GOVERNMENT: MANAGING THE PROCESS (1983) (commonly known as the "Red Book"), was written in response to a number of difficult rulemaking decisions involving human health risk from benzene, cotton dust, and formaldehyde. It established the four-part risk paradigm (hazard identification, dose-response assessment, exposure assessment, and risk characterization) for assessment that continues to serve as the foundation for regulation. The Red Book explicitly sought to distinguish risk assessment from risk management. More recently, the NRC published SCIENCE AND JUDGMENT IN RISK ASSESSMENT (1994), which resulted from a study mandated by Congress in the 1990 Clean Air Act Amendments. Although the study focused on risk assessment of air issues, the recommendations were more broadly applicable to EPA regulation. Overall, the NRC supported the EPA's risk assessment procedures but made many suggestions for improvement, particularly in the areas of uncertainty analysis and screening for rough estimates of risks posed by a large number of substances before engaging in more expensive analysis.

Also helpful in understanding the current scientific controversies over risk asssessment is the NRC report ISSUES IN RISK ASSESSMENT (1993). For another clearly presented review of the risk assessment process, see Chris G. Whipple, *Fundamentals of Risk Assessment*, 16 Envtl. L. Rep. (Envtl. L. Inst.) 10190 (1986).

6. Rosenthal, Gray, and Graham caution against over-emphasis on cancer risk at the expense of other, more pressing environmental problems. Yet, almost all of their examples concern carcinogens. Paul Locke persuasively argues that current risk assessment policies inadequately account for non-cancer health effects, such as birth defects, neurotoxicity, and immune system disruption. Paul A. Locke, *Reorienting Risk Assessment*, ENVTL. F., Sept./Oct. 1994, at 28. *See also* Paul A. Locke, *The Limitations of Comparative Risk Assessment,* 2 SHEPARD'S EXPERT AND SCIENTIFIC EVIDENCE 75 (1994). Recent studies link hormonal disruption and fertility decline with exposure to certain pesticides that have been regulated at levels based on cancer risk. William K. Stevens, *Pesticides May Leave Legacy of Hormonal Chaos*, N.Y. TIMES, Aug. 23, 1994, at B5.

7. The uncertainties associated with risk assessment are not limited to issues of cancer or even human health. Predicting the effects of human activities on natural systems raises many unanswerable questions. "Ecosystems are not only more complex than we think, but more complex than we can think." FRANK E. EGLER, THE NATURE OF VEGETATION: ITS MANAGEMENT AND MISMANAGEMENT (1977), *quoted in* Reed F. Noss, *Some Principles of Conservation Biology, As They Apply to Environmental Law*, 69 CHI.-KENT L. REV. 893, 898 (1994). Noss argues that the less data or more uncertainty involved, the more cautious a conservation plan must be. *Id.* Many of the stochastic issues involved in cancer risk assessment now present problems for conservation biologists seeking to manage natural resources. *See* Fred P. Bosselman & A. Dan Tarlock, *The Influence of Ecological Science on American Law: An Introduction*, 69 CHI.-KENT L. REV. 847 (1994).

In 1990, the EPA's Science Advisory Board recommended, and the Agency endorsed, a reordering of EPA priorities. The report advocated that the EPA "attach as much importance to reducing ecological risk as it does to reducing human health risk." Science Advisory Bd., U.S. EPA, Reducing Risk: Setting Priorities and Strategies for Environmental Protection 6 (1990). For a discussion of the challenges presented by an ecological risk management goal, *see* Robert F. Blomquist, *The EPA Science Advisory Board's Report on "Reducing Risk": Some Overarching Observations Regarding the Public Interest,* 22 ENVTL. L. 149 (1992); Robert L. Fischman, *Biological Diversity and Environmental Protection: Authorities to Reduce Risk,* 22 ENVTL. L. 435 (1992); NATIONAL RESEARCH COUNCIL, ISSUES IN RISK ASSESSMENT 243-64 (1993); U.S. EPA Science Advisory Board, Ecosystem Management: Imperative for a Dynamic World (EPA-SAB-EPEC- 95-003 1995).

8. Rosenthal, Gray, and Graham observe that the fragmentation of administrative authority for environmental protection results in inconsistent application of quantitative risk assessment. Are the problems of implementation and credibility that result compensated by the authors' claim that fragmentation promotes experimentation and innovation in assessment methods? What are the incentives for innovation?

9. Pressure is mounting for Congress to modify the lone bright line statute that Rosenthal, Gray, and Graham identify. Recall that the 1958 Delaney Clause calls for zero cancer risk for additives in processed foods. In 1988, the EPA attempted to exempt from the Delaney Clause certain pesticides posing a "negligible risk" of cancer. A federal appeals court ruled that the Delaney Clause requires "zero risk":

> The issue before us is whether the EPA has violated section 409 of the FFDCA, the Delaney clause, by permitting the use of carcinogenic food additives which it finds to present only a de minimis or negligible risk of causing cancer. The Agency acknowledges that its interpretation of the law is a new and changed one. From the initial enactment of the Delaney clause in 1958 to the time of the rulings here in issue, the statute has been strictly and literally enforced.

* * *

> The language is clear and mandatory. The Delaney Clause provides that no additive shall be deemed safe if it induces cancer. * * * The statute provides that once the finding of carcinogenicity is made, the EPA has no discretion.

* * *

> The EPA's refusal to revoke regulations permitting the use of benomyl, mancozeb, phosmet and trifluralin as food additives on the ground the cancer risk they pose is de minimus is contrary to the provisions of the Delaney Clause prohibiting food additives that induce cancer. The EPA's final order is set aside.

Les v. Reilly, 968 F.2d 985, 988-90 (9th Cir. 1992).

In the aftermath of *Les v. Reilly* and another Delaney Clause case, *California v. EPA,* No. 89-0752 (E.D. Cal. Oct. 12, 1994), the EPA agreed to begin proceedings to withdraw approval for the use of 36 pesticides that have been found to cause cancer in animals, but which the agency would have exempted from Delaney because they posed only negligible risk to human health. Affected chemicals include benomyl, a fungicide used on apples, citrus fruits, grapes, rices, and tomatoes. *See Proposed Settlement to Ban Carcinogens in Food Filed With U.S. District Court*, Daily Env. Rep. (BNA) No. 234, at D-6 (Dec. 9, 1994); John H. Cushman, Jr., *EPA Settles Suit and Agrees to Move Against 36 Pesticides*, N.Y. TIMES, Sept. 13, 1994, at A24.

The Clinton Administration has proposed statutory changes to reconcile the Delaney Clause with FIFRA's risk-benefit balancing. The Administration's proposal would allow use of pesticides on food crops only when there is a reasonable certainty that no harm will result. If a pesticide passes muster under this standard, which is more strict than the existing FIFRA risk-benefit balance, then it would be immune from a ban under the Delaney Clause. Environmental groups and agricultural chemical interests have each put forward their own proposals as well.

Professor Rodgers discusses the Delaney Clause in his excerpt in Subchapter A of Chapter Two.

10. Since 1981, under successive executive orders issued by Presidents Reagan (E.O. 12291) and Clinton (E.O. 12866), agencies have been required by the White House to prepare cost-benefit analyses of proposed rules. Benefits may be described in terms of reduction in environmental risk. The Office of Mangement and Budget reviews these analyses before giving agencies approval to proceed with promulgation. The implementation of these executive orders is discussed in ENVIRONMENTAL POLICY UNDER REAGAN'S EXECUTIVE ORDER (V. Kerry Smith ed. 1984), and Ellen Siegler, *Executive Order 12866: An Analysis of the New Executive Order on Regulatory Planning and Review*, 24 Envtl. L. Rep. (Envtl. L. Inst.) 10070 (1994).

The 104th Congress considered legislation that would require all major new regulations designed to protect human health, safety, or the environment to undergo a uniform analysis, involving risk assessment, characterization, and independent peer review. H.R. 9, 104th Cong., 1st Sess., Division D (1995) (Risk Assessment and Cost-Benefit Act of 1995). Under this law, agencies would be required to prepare for each major rule:

(1) An identification of reasonable alternative strategies * * *

(2) An analysis of the incremental costs and incremental risk reduction or other benefits associated with each alternative strategy * * *

(3) A statement that places in context the nature and magnitude of the risks to be addressed and the residual risks likely to remain for each alternative strategy * * *. Such statement shall, to the extent feasible, provide comparisons with estimates of greater, lesser, and substantially equivalent risks that are familiar to and routinely encountered by the general public * * * [and] comparisons of * * * similar risks regulated by the Federal agency.

(4) * * * an analysis of whether the identified benefits of the rule are likely to exceed the identified costs * * *

Id., § 421(a). In addition to these procedural requirements, an agency could not promulgate final rules unless it certified that: (1) the incremental risk reduction of any strategy chosen will be likely to justify, and be reasonably related to, the incremental costs; and, (2) alternative strategies were either less cost-effective or less flexible in allowing regulated entities to achieve the applicable objectives of the regulation. *Id.* at § 422(a). Would this law convert all environmental regulation to the risk-benefit balancing type described in the Rosenthal, Gray, and Graham excerpt and illustrated with FIFRA? John Graham supported this legislative initiative. John D. Graham, *Edging Toward Sanity on Regulatory Risk Reform,* Issues in Sci. & Tech., Summer 1995, at 61.

The EPA, while opposing the risk provisions of H.R. 9, has nonetheless "pledged to continue efforts to include more scientific information in writing regulations, for example using risk assessment to help quantify risk and balance it against the cost of regulation." Warren E. Leary, *Agencies Defend Their Records,* N.Y. Times, Jan. 7, 1995, at 8. Carol Browner, the EPA Administrator, claimed that H.R. 9 would slow and even prevent agency efforts to protect the environment: "We don't think that under the risk provisions of the 'Contract With America' that we could have banned lead in gasoline, and that would have been tragic." *Id.* (quoting Carol Browner). Other commentators have been less guarded in their criticism of the bill:

> It contains heavy handed requirements that enshrine scientific principles into law, making it nearly impossible to improve the risk assessment process when new scientific information is uncovered. The peer review provisions erect an unelected, unappointed panel to approve the work of public servants. The act creates a bureaucratic structure that has the potential to dramatically slow down all rule making. * * * It also would force agencies to devote more resources to assessment, which will take away from their ability to implement measures to actually protect the environment and improve public health.

Paul A. Locke, *Regulatory Reform and the Myth of "Realistic Risk",* Envtl. F., Jan./Feb. 1995, at 35.

11. Rosenthal, Gray, and Graham note that alternative choices of exposure and dose-response assumptions can lead to plausible risk estimates that vary by several orders of magnitude. Some of these choices have become controversial. In the area of pesticide regulation, the EPA has used risk estimates based on a 160-pound man despite studies that suggest children are at much greater risk, particularly for chemical residues on fruit. The greater risk is due to children's higher metabolic rates and greater consumption of fruit and fruit juice. Keith Schneider, *Pesticide Plan Could Uproot U.S. Farming,* N.Y. Times, Oct. 10, 1993, § 4, at 6; National Research Council, Pesticides in the Diets of Infants and Children (1993). Other subpopulations, such as some Native American groups, may have typical exposure rates well in excess of the population at large because they subsist on fish which have bioaccumulated toxic organic chemicals. As part of his executive order on environmental justice, President Clinton directed that: "Federal agencies, whenever practicable and appropriate, shall collect, maintain, and analyze information on the consumption patterns of populations who principally rely on fish and/or wildlife for subsistence. Federal agencies shall communicate to the public the risks of those consumption patterns." Exec. Order No. 12,898, 59 Fed. Reg. 7629 (1994) (§4-401). Commentators have highlighted other important value judgments embedded in the technical risk assessment process. *See, e.g.,* Donald A. Brown, *Superfund Cleanups, Ethics, and Environmental Risk Assessment,* 16 ENVTL. AFF. 181 (1988).

12. Rosenthal, Gray, and Graham are willing to vest substantial discretion in administrative agencies to manage risk. Note that in recent years, courts have been quite deferential to agency interpretations of vague environmental mandates. *See, e.g., Babbitt v. Sweet Home Chapter of Communities for a Great Oregon,* 115 S. Ct. 2407 (1995); *Chevron, U.S.A. v. Natural Resources Defense Council,* 467 U.S. 837 (1984). How much public monitoring of risk assessment is appropriate? Are the issues involved primarily ones of scientific accuracy? The next excerpt elaborates on some of these issues related to administrative discretion and public oversight.

In 1970, after creating the EPA with an executive order, President Nixon appointed William D. Ruckelshaus as its first Administrator. Ruckelshaus served three years. A decade later, during the tenure of Anne Gorsuch, the Agency's credibility was tattered by mismanagement and scandal. In 1983, President Reagan asked Ruckelshaus to return to the job of Administrator to rebuild the Agency's effectiveness and morale. Ruckelshaus' unique second term lasted until 1986. This second term featured the integration of formal risk assessment into agency decisionmaking.

RISK IN A FREE SOCIETY
William D. Ruckelshaus
14 Envtl. L. Rep. (Envtl. L. Inst.) 10190 (1984)*

It is now a commonplace of political discourse that technological advances have had a profound effect on our democratic institutions. Mass communications is the familiar example. But I would like to draw your attention to another way in which technology may impinge upon a democratic society, one that is perhaps as serious, if more subtle; one that commands a huge proportion of my own attention. I refer to the chemical products and by-products of modern technology and the potential social disruption associated with the processes we have created to control them.

When I began my current, and second, tenure as Administrator of the Environmental Protection Agency (EPA), my first goal was the restoration of public confidence in the Agency, and it was impressed upon me that straightening out the way we handled health risk was central to achieving it. Needless to say, EPA's primary mission is the reduction of risk, whether to public health or the environment. Some in America were afraid. They were afraid that toxic chemicals in the environment were affecting their health, and more

---

* Reprinted with permission.

important, they suspected that the facts about the risks from such chemicals were not being accurately reported to them, that policy considerations were being inappropriately used in such reports, so as to make the risks seem less than they were and excuse the Agency from taking action. Even worse, some people thought that the processes we had established to protect public health were being abused for crass political gain.

Whether this was true or not is almost beside the point; a substantial number of people believed it. Now in a society such as ours, where the people ultimately decide policy—what they want done about a particular situation—the fair exposition of policy choices is the job of public agencies. The public agency is the repository of the facts; you can't operate a democratic society, particularly a complex technological one, unless you have such a repository. Above all, the factual guardian must be trusted; a failure of trust courts chaos. Chaos, in turn, creates its own thirst for order, which craving in its more extreme forms threatens the very foundation of democratic freedom. So in a democracy a public agency that is not trusted, especially where the protection of public health is concerned, might as well close its doors.

I described a possible solution to this problem last June in a speech to the National Academy of Sciences. The Academy had stated in a recent report that federal agencies had often confused the assessment of risk with the management of risk. Risk assessment is the use of a base of scientific research to define the probability of some harm coming to an individual or a population as a result of exposure to a substance or situation. Risk management, in contrast, is the public process of deciding what to do where risk has been determined to exist. It includes integrating risk assessment with considerations of engineering feasibility and figuring out how to exercise our imperative to reduce risk in the light of social, economic, and political factors.

The report proposed that these two functions be formally separated within regulatory agencies. I said that this appeared to be a workable idea and that we would try to make it happen at EPA. This notion was attractive because the statutes administered by many federal regulatory agencies typically force some action when scientific inquiry establishes the presence of a risk, as, for example, when a substance present in the environment, or the workplace, or the food chain, is found to cause cancer in animals. The statutes may require the agency to act according to some protective formula: to establish "margins of safety" or "prevent significant risk" or "eliminate the risk."

When the action so forced has dire economic or social consequences, the person who must make the decision may be sorely tempted to ask for a "reinterpretation" of the data. We should remember that risk assessment data can be like a captured spy: if you torture it long enough, it will tell you anything you want to know. So it is good public policy to so structure an agency that such temptation is avoided.

But we have found that separating the assessment of risk from its management is rather more difficult to accomplish in practice. In the first place, values, which are supposed to be safely sequestered in risk management, also appear as important influences on the outcome of risk assessments. For example, let us suppose that a chemical in common use is tested on laboratory animals with the object of determining whether it can cause cancer. At the end of the test a proportion of the animals that have been exposed to the substance show evidence of tumor formation.

Now the problems begin. First, in tests like these, the doses given are extremely high, often close to the level the animal can tolerate for a lifetime without dying from toxic non-cancer effects. Environmental exposures are typically much lower, so in order to determine what the risk of cancer is at such lower exposures—that is, to determine the curve that relates a certain dose to a certain response—we must extrapolate down from the high-dose laboratory data. There are a number of statistical models for doing this, all of which fit the data, and all of which are open to debate. We simply do not know what the shape of the dose-response curve is at low doses, in the sense that we know, let us say, what the orbit of a satellite will be when we shoot it off.

Next, we must deal with the uncertainty of extrapolating cancer data from animals to man, for example, determining which of the many different kinds of lesions that may appear in animals is actually indicative of a probability that the substance in question may be a human carcinogen. Cancer is cancer to the public, but not to the pathologist.

Finally, we must deal with uncertainty about exposure. We have to determine, usually on the basis of scant data and elaborate mathematical models, how much of the stuff is being produced; how it is being dispersed, changed, or destroyed by natural processes; and how the actual dose that people get is changed by behavioral or population characteristics.

These uncertainties inherent in risk assessment combine to produce an enormously wide range of risk estimates in most cases. For example, the National Academy of Sciences report on saccharin concluded that over the next 70 years the expected number of cases of human bladder cancer resulting from daily exposure to 120 milligrams of saccharin might range from 0.22 to 1,144,000. This sort of range is of limited use to the policymaker and risk assessment scientists are at some pains to make choices among possibilities so as to produce conclusions that are both scientifically supportable and usable.

* * *

Historically at EPA it has been thought prudent to make what have been called conservative assumptions; that is, in a situation of unavoidable uncertainty, our values lead us to couch our conclusions in terms of a plausible upper bound. As a result, when we generate a number that expresses the potency of some substance in causing disease, we can state that it is unlikely that the risk projected is any greater.

This conservative approach is fine when the risks projected are vanishingly small; it is always nice to learn that some chemical is *not* a national crisis. But when the risks estimated through such assessments are substantial, so that some action may be in the offing, the stacking of conservative assumptions one on top of another becomes a problem for the policymaker. If I am going to propose controls that may have serious economic and social effects, I need to have some idea how much confidence to place in the estimates of risk that prompted those controls. I need to know how likely *real* damage is to occur in the uncontrolled and partially controlled and fully controlled cases. Only then can I apply the balancing judgments that are the essence of my job. This, of course, tends to insert the policymaker back into the guts of risk assessment, which we had concluded is less than wise.

This is a real quandary. I now believe that the main road out of it lies through a marked improvement in the way we communicate the realities of risk analysis to the public. The goal is public understanding. We will only retain the administrative flexibility we need to effectively protect the public health and welfare if the public believes we are trying to act in the public interest. There is an argument, in contradiction, that the best way to protection lies in increased legislative specificity, in closely directing the Agency as to what to control and how much to control it. If we fail to command public confidence, this argument will prevail, and in my opinion it would be a bad thing if it did. You cannot squeeze the complexity inherent in managing environmental risks between the pages of a statute book.

How then do we encourage confidence? Generally speaking there are two ways to do it. First, we could assign guardianship of the Agency's integrity—its risk assessment task—to a group of disinterested experts who are above reproach in the public eye. This is the quasi-judicial, blue-ribbon panel approach, which has a strong tradition in our society. If we have a complex issue, we don't have to think about it very much, just give it to the experts, who deliberate and provide the answer, which most will accept because of the inherent prestige of the panel.

The discomfort associated with imagining, in 1984, a conclave of Big Brothers to watch over us only strengthens my conviction that such panels cannot serve the general purpose of restoring and maintaining confidence. It turns out that the experts do not agree, so instead of an unimpeachable and disinterested consensus you get dissenting advocacy. Once again, experts have values too.

Alternatively, we could all become a lot smarter about risk. The Agency could put much more effort into explaining what it is doing and what it does, and does not, know. Here I do not mean "public involvement" in the usual and formal sense. This is embodied in administrative law and has always been part of our ordinary procedure in promulgating rules. Nor do I mean a mere public relations campaign to popularize Agency decisions. Public relations smoothes over; I think we need to dig up. We have to expose the assumptions that go into risk assessments. We have to admit our uncertainties and confront the public with the complex nature of decisions about risk.

Living in a technological society is like riding a bucking bronco. I do not believe we can afford to get off, and I doubt that someone will magically appear who can lead it about on a leash. The question is: how do we become better bronco busters? I think a great part of the answer is to bring about a major improvement in the quality of public debate on environmental risk.

This will not be easy. Risk assessment is a probabilistic calculation, but people do not respond to risks "as they should" if such calculations were the sole criterion of rationality. Most people are not comfortable with mathematical probability as a guide to living and the risk assessment lingo we throw at them does not increase their comfort. Tell someone that their risk of cancer from a 70-year exposure to a carcinogen at ambient levels ranges between 10^{-5} and 10^{-7}, and they are likely to come back at you with, "Yes, but will I get cancer if I drink the water?" Also, attitudes toward risk are subjective and highly colored by personal experience and other factors not fully captured by risk assessments.

We have research that points out that people tend to overestimate the probability of unfamiliar, catastrophic and well-publicized events and underestimate the probability of unspectacular or familiar events that claim one victim at a time. Many people are afraid to fly commercial airlines, but practically nobody is afraid of driving in cars, a victory of subjectivity over actuarial statistics.

* * *

Many people interested in environmental protection, having observed this mess, conclude that considerations of risk lead to nothing useful. After all, if the numbers are no good and the whole issue is so confusing, why not just eliminate all exposure to toxics to the extent that technology allows? The problem with such thinking is that, even setting aside what I have just said about the necessity for improving the national debate on the subject, risk estimates are the only way we have of directing the attention of risk management agencies toward significant problems.

There are thousands of substances in the environment that show toxicity in animals; we cannot work on all of them at once, even with an EPA 10 times its current size. More important, technology does not make the bad stuff "go away"; in most cases it just changes its form and location. We have to start keeping track of the flow of toxics through the environment, to what happens *after* they are "controlled." Risk management is the only way I know to do this.

In confused situations one must try to be guided by basic principles. One of my basic principles is reflected in a quotation from Thomas Jefferson: "If we think [the people are] not enlightened enough to exercise their control with a wholesome discretion, the remedy is not to take it from them, but to inform their discretion." Easy for *him* to say. As we have seen, informing discretion about risk has itself a high risk of failure.

However, we do have some recent experience that supports the belief that better information inclines people to act more sensibly. In Tacoma, Washington, we have a situation where a copper smelter employing about 600 people is emitting substantial amounts of arsenic, which is a human carcinogen. We found that the best available technology did not reduce the risk of cancer to levels the public might find acceptable. In fact, it looked as if reducing to acceptable levels of risk might only be possible if the plant closed. I felt very strongly that the people in Tacoma whose lives were to be affected by my decision ought to have a deeper understanding of the case than they could get from the usual public hearing process.

Accordingly, we organized an extraordinary campaign of public education in Tacoma. Besides the required public hearing, we provided immense quantities of information to all communications media, arranged meetings between community leaders and senior EPA officials, including myself, and held three workshops at which we laid out our view of the facts. I think most people appreciated this opportunity, and we certainly raised the level of discussion about risk. So unusual was this kind of event that some inferred that I was abdicating my responsibility for this decision, or that somehow the Tacoma people were going to vote on whether they wanted jobs or health. After some initial confusion on this score we made it clear that it was entirely my decision, and that while I wanted to hear, I was not committed to heed.

Although I suppose some would have been happier continuing in their found belief that we could provide absolute safety with absolute certainty, and were disturbed by these proceedings, in all I would call it a qualified success. Those who participated came away with a better understanding of the anatomy of environmental decisions, and local groups were able to come up with options that increased protection while allowing the plant to remain open, options that are well worth considering as we put together our final decision.

What are the lessons of Tacoma? Shortly after we began the workshops, people started sporting buttons that said, "BOTH," meaning they were for both jobs and health. I took this as a good sign, that people were attending to the balance between economic realities and environmental protection. "Both" is a good idea, and in most cases we can have it, if we are smart. Another lesson is that we must improve the way we present risk calculations to the public. There was too much tendency to translate risks of cancer into cases, with no regard to qualifying assumptions and uncertainties. Cancer threats make great headlines and the inclination to infer certainty where none exists is very powerful. We must take seriously our obligation to generate lucid and unambiguous statements about risk. Finally, Tacoma shows that we have to prepare ourselves for the other Tacomas. Environmental stress falls unevenly across the land and we have a special responsibility to people in communities that suffer more than their share. We are prepared to make the extra effort in such communities, as we did in Tacoma.

We must also improve debate on the national level. This may prove more difficult, as Washington is a most contentious place. Also, at the national level things tend to polarize perhaps more than they should, given how much we know about environmental health questions. Typically, where we obtain evidence of an environmental threat, opinion divides between those who want to eliminate the risk as quickly as possible, with little concern about cost, and those who deny the threat exists. Fights between these groups can go on for a long time, during which the object of the battle, the pollutant, remains in the environment. Acid rain threatens to become this kind of dispute.

* * *

* * * Let me now propose some principles for more reasonable discussions about risk.

First, we must insist on risk calculations being expressed as distributions of estimates and not as magic numbers that can be manipulated without regard to what they really mean. We must try to display more realistic estimates of risk to show a range of probabilities. To help do this we need new tools for quantifying and ordering sources of uncertainty and for putting them in perspective.

Second, we must expose to public scrutiny the assumptions that underlie our analysis and management of risk. If we have made a series of conservative assumptions within the risk assessment, so that it represents an upper bound estimate of risk, we should try to communicate this and explain why we did it. Although public health protection is our primary value, any particular action to control a pollutant may have effects on other values, such as community stability, employment, natural resources, or the integrity of the ecosystem. We have to get away from the idea that we do quantitative analysis to find the "right" decision, which we will then be obliged to make if we want to call ourselves rational beings. But we are not clockwork mandarins. The point of such analysis is, in fact, the orderly exposition of the values we hold, and the reasoning that travels from some set of values and measurements to a decision.

Third, we must demonstrate that reduction of risk is our main concern and that we are not driven by narrow cost-benefit considerations. Of course cost is a factor, because we are obliged to be efficient with our resources and those of society in general. Where we decline to control some risk at present, we should do so only because there are better targets; we are really balancing risk against risk, aiming to get at the greatest first.

Finally, we should understand the limits of quantification; there are some cherished values that will resist being squeezed into a benefits column, but are no less real because of it. Walter Lippman once pointed out that in a democracy "the people" as in "We the People," refers not only to the working majority that actually makes current decisions, and not only to the whole living population, but to those who came before us, who provided our traditions and our physical patrimony as a nation, and to those who will come after us, and inherit. Many of the major decisions we make on environmental affairs touch on this broader sense of public responsibility.

I suppose that the ultimate goal of this effort is to get the American people to understand the difference between a safe world and a zero-risk world with respect to environmental pollutants. We have to define what safe means in light of our increasing ability to detect minute quantities of substances in the environment and to associate carcinogenesis with an enormous variety of substances in common use. According to Bruce Ames, the biochemist and cancer expert, the human diet is loaded with toxics of all kinds, including many carcinogens, mutagens and teratogens. Among them are such foodstuffs as black pepper, mushrooms, celery, parsnips, peanut butter, figs, parsley, potatoes, rhubarb, coffee, tea, fats, browned meat, and alfalfa sprouts. The list goes on; my point is that it would be hard to find a diet that would support life and at the same time impose no risk on the consumer.

So what is safe? Are we all safe at this instant? Most of us would agree that we are, although we are subjected to calculable risks of various sorts of catastrophes that can happen to people listening to lectures in buildings. We might be able to reduce some of them by additional effort, but in general we consider that we have (to coin a phrase) an "adequate margin of safety" sitting in a structure that is, for example, protected against lightning bolts but exposed to meteorites.

I think we can get people to start making those judgments of safety about the arcane products of modern technology. I do not think we are ever going to get agreement about values; a continuing debate about values is the essence of a democratic policy. But I think we must do better in showing how different values lead rationally to different policy outcomes. And we can only do that if we are able to build up a reservoir of trust, if people believe that we have presented fairly what facts we have, that we have exposed our values to their view, and that we have respected their values, whether or not such values can be incorporated finally in our decisions. We have, I hope, begun to build that sort of trust at EPA.

NOTES

1. In a widely cited, subsequent article on the subject of risk management, Ruckelshaus recommended that:

> [R]isk management means giving the protective agencies flexibility comparable to that which managers have traditionally exercised in other spheres. This suggestion, of course, runs counter to the inclination to further restrict the discretion accorded those agencies. Administrations do vary in their priorities

and competence, so how can we ensure that this flexibility will not be misused? * * * [F]lexibility should be limited by broad public acceptance, including acceptance by individuals subject to risk, and also by more sensible and appropriate oversight.

* * *

In my view, sound public policy would give EPA the flexibility to confront and deal with risks in the local context. This flexibility would entail, first, balancing risks against the local economic impacts of controlling them; second, ensuring that our national programs that attempt to deal with local risks operate according to risk management principles; and third, involving the local public in a meaningful way in the decisionmaking process.

William D. Ruckelshaus, *Risk, Science, and Democracy*, ISSUES IN SCIENCE AND TECHNOLOGY, Spr. 1985, at 19, 31, 33.

How can agencies earn the public trust necessary to sustain more discretion?

In a response to Ruckelshaus' 1985 article, Jay Hair, then-president of the National Wildlife Federation, accused Ruckelshaus of eroding the centralized federal authority and uniformity that are fundamental to the environmental statutes. Jay Hair, *Forum*, ISSUES IN SCIENCE AND TECHNOLOGY, Wint. 1985, at 5. Would Ruckelshaus' system result in pollution havens? Would certain risks be considered significant in some parts of the country but not in others?

2. Charles T. Rubin criticizes Ruckelshaus' interpretation of the Tacoma experience. Ruckelshaus took the people's desire to have "BOTH" jobs and health as a good sign that the public was attending to risk benefit balances. Rubin notes that "BOTH"

is what they wanted all along; if they thought they could get all the jobs with no risk to health even the most extreme environmentalist or pro-plant advocate would not have rejected one merely because it came with the other. * * * It is hard to see how wanting "BOTH" does any more than restate the problem. If we dismiss the charge of simple Machiavellianism against Ruckelshaus (if people are confused enough to want "BOTH," then EPA has a freer hand), we are left with the proposition that "'BOTH' is a good idea, and in most cases we can have it, if we are smart." * * * Yet asking the question "Who says you can't have it all?" has never been the beginning of political wisdom.

Charles T. Rubin, *Environmental Policy and Environmental Thought: Ruckelshaus and Commoner*, 11 ENVTL. ETHICS 27, 48-49 (Spr. 1989). Does Ruckelshaus suggest a practical approach to problems where the tradeoffs are less tractable?

3. Another critic of Ruckelshaus was then-NRDC attorney David Doniger, now an EPA official:

When the Administrator urges the American people to accept a philosophy of deliberately trading off lives and health against the economic costs of pollution controls ("risk management"), he is both disregarding the requirements of the Clean Air Act and swimming against the strong tide of public opinion. Section 112 of the Clean Air Act embodies the public's adherence to a fundamental goal that no one should be required to sacrifice his or her life or health on account of air pollution. The testimony and written comments of so many individuals living near the ASARCO smelter in Tacoma, Washington and elsewhere around the country show that when lives and health are on the line, the general public will not accept a philosophy which abandons that goal and legitimizes such trade-offs. This philosophical and moral rejection of the Administrator's policy is not going to change, for such trade-offs are deeply repugnant to most people.

The strength of public feeling on this issue is nothing new. It dates from the 1970 enactment of the Clean Air Act and before. The Administrator's argument is also nothing new. "Risk management" appears to be nothing more than a new name for cost-benefit analysis. No matter what the name it is given, the public consistently rejects it.

* * *

My third point has to do with equity. The arsenic proposals do not address the fairness of leaving people trapped in what have been termed "islands of risk." For the people of Tacoma, who are clearly exposed to the highest concentrations of arsenic, the Administrator has deliberately framed the issue as a trade-off between allowing continued high risks of cancer or closing a plant—a grim either-or proposition. The Administrator has failed even to ask a fundamental question of fairness: Doesn't the government, representing the rest of the American people fortunate enough to live in what we think are safer places, owe some form of relief to those who are trapped in the islands of risk? When the dioxin-contaminated town of Times Beach, Missouri was judged unsafe to inhabit, EPA used Superfund monies to purchase the residents' homes, relieving them of the awful choice between their health or their homes. While the Superfund itself is not available for use regarding air emissions from ASARCO-Tacoma, doesn't the issue of fairness still need to be addressed?

* * *

Under a precautionary statute that directs EPA to play it safe rather than sorry, quantitative risk assessments are sometimes useful in indicating that a proposed control plan is clearly inadequate. They may also be used to illustrate gross inequities between the protection afforded one group of people versus another, as discussed above. But EPA's use of its current techniques to justify not applying available controls cannot be supported either as a rational application of the statutory criteria or as a sensible public health policy judgment.

David Doniger, *The Gospel of Risk Management: Should We Be Converted?*, 14 Envtl.

L. Rep. (Envtl. L. Inst.) 10222 (1984). Both Ruckelshaus and Doniger claim that public opinion supports their arguments. Can both be right?

Doniger stresses the similarities between risk management and cost-benefit analysis. Economists have noted this kinship as well. *See, e.g.*, A. Myrick Freeman III & Paul R. Portney, *Economics Clarifies Choices About Managing Risk*, RESOURCES, Spr. 1989, at 1. In particular, comparative risk analysis uses the economic concept of opportunity cost: "what society must give up in the form of other desirable things in order to pursue a desired goal such as reduced environmental risk." *Id.* What aspects of cost-benefit balancing does Doniger claim the public rejects? Doniger frames the public policy choice as whether any person "should be required to sacrifice his or her life or health on account of air pollution." Is this a fair characterization of the issue? We will return to the issue of the comparative net risk analysis in environmental policy when we examine the excerpt by Peter Huber, below.

4. In 1985, ASARCO-Tacoma had to close its smelter after it failed to reach agreement with the EPA on meeting federal air emissions standards. The story, in many ways, only begins here. Arsenic and other heavy metals contaminated the soil and groundwater of the ASARCO property. In September 1986, ASARCO and the EPA agreed on a CERCLA (Comprehensive Environmental Response, Compensation, and Liability Act) consent order requiring ASARCO to demolish the smelter structure and clean up the area. *ASARCO, EPA Reach Agreement Under Superfund on Demolition of Copper Smelter in Tacoma, Wash.*, 17 Env. Rep. (BNA) 744 (Sept. 19, 1986). A University of Washington study of the population in north Tacoma in 1986 showed that children, especially boys under the age of six, suffered from abnormally high concentrations of arsenic. *Children Found Most Exposed to Arsenic Near Old Copper Smelter in Tacoma, Wash.*, 17 Env. Rep. (BNA) 1188 (Nov. 14, 1986). The EPA suspended demolition in March 1987, alleging problems involving asbestos removal and arsenic. *EPA Halts Demolition at ASARCO Smelter Due to Problems With Asbestos Removal*, 17 Env. Rep. (BNA) 1868 (Mar. 6, 1987). A new consent decree filed in federal court at the end of 1991 established a new demolition plan and required ASARCO to reimburse the EPA for public expenses at the site. *ASARCO to Remove Contaminated Smelter Stack, Pay Past Response Costs Under Proposed Decree*, 22 Env. Rep. (BNA) 2126 (Jan. 10, 1992).

For Ruckelshaus, the guiding goal of the EPA is risk reduction. John Atcheson, who also was an EPA official, concedes that risk reduction is important but argues that it should not be an organizing principle for an agency charged with environmental protection.

THE DEPARTMENT OF RISK REDUCTION OR RISKY BUSINESS
John Atcheson
21 Envtl. L. 1375 (1991)*

I. INTRODUCTION

* * *

Increasingly, the environmental agenda is being shaped around a cost-benefit, risk reduction paradigm, with potentially profound legal, economic, budgetary, policy, and ultimately environmental implications. For example, EPA is putting in place a strategic planning process designed to resolve budget and mission conflicts, and help set a proactive policy direction. There is a debate within the Agency on whether this planning process should use risk reduction as a tool to set priorities, or whether risk reduction should be the ultimate goal in and of itself. Congress has also gotten into the act; certain parts of the new Clean Air Act are based on risk reduction—specifically, managing so-called "residual" risk where the best technologies are not sufficiently protective. The Office of Management and Budget (OMB), the President's chief fiscal agent and over the past ten years his primary policy and ideology police officer, has been increasingly using risk as the ultimate arbiter of cost-benefit decisions. In OMB's jargon, we have "environmental externalities" and "residual damages" (that is, those damages that are acceptable under a risk reduction-cost-benefit paradigm).

At the request of EPA's Administrator, William Reilly, the Agency's Science Advisory Board (SAB) recently completed a report entitled, *Reducing Risk: Setting Priorities and Strategies for Environmental Protection*. It is, in part, a critique of the 1987 EPA report, *Unfinished Business: A Comparative Assessment of Environmental Problems*. Administrator Reilly also asked the SAB to "assess and compare different environmental risks in light of the most recent scientific data . . .[,] examine strategies for reducing major risks, and to recommend improved methodologies for assessing and comparing risks and risk reduction options in the future." [3]

At a time when every attempt to set a new environmental agenda is seen as an attempt to retreat from the old, Reilly's and Deputy Administrator Hank Habicht's request showed personal courage. It also demonstrates their recognition that the environmental stakes have been raised, and that today's challenges demand new approaches. The SAB's report—a farsighted and forward looking document—helps lay the groundwork for a new environmental agenda. As good as it is, however, it perpetuates the schizophrenia in our national environmental policy regarding the role of risk. Of the SAB's ten recommendations, eight are expressed in terms that make risk reduction a goal or objective—an end, not a tool used to achieve an end.

* * *

This Essay explores what sets the environmental agenda of the next twenty years apart

---

* Reprinted with permission.
[3] [Science Advisory Bd., U.S. EPA, Reducing Risk: Setting Priorities and Strategies for Environmental Protection (1990)] at ii. * * *

from the set of problems we faced in the first twenty years, examines some of the shortcomings of a risk-dominated policy framework for dealing with the new generation of environmental problems, and briefly outlines elements of a policy framework that can help us set the right course. * * *

* * *

IV. LIMITATIONS OF THE RISK REDUCTION PARADIGM

A great deal has been written about the limits of economics as an environmental policy tool, but very little about those of risk reduction. Yet risk reduction, when framed as a goal, is just as limiting, and it may get in the way of this necessary policy transformation. Risk reduction does not allow adequate consideration of resource conservation and patterns of development, it is reactive, it is difficult to communicate to the public, and it may ultimately be resource limiting. Moreover, the level of uncertainty inherent in risk assessment makes risk reduction, as a policy, a risky business.

* * *

B. Risk and a Reactive Policy Dynamic

Risk, by its nature is reactive. It must be actively applied to a problem: therefore, one must know a problem exists. The problem must be tangible and identifiable. There is, therefore, an implicit assumption that we will apply the risk paradigm to the right set of activities. In short, we must anticipate a problem in order to decide whether we want to assess it. This presents a kind of ecological Catch-22. Clearly, the range of human activities is too broad, and the sensitivity of our biological and ecological systems too acute to allow a realistic identification of those activities that will prove to be dangerous. Even when we have correctly anticipated a problem, risk reduction is a poor policy metric if proaction is important. Quite simply, the large uncertainties inherent in risk assessments can only be managed by good data. To quote the SAB on managing uncertainty:

> As long as there are large gaps in key data sets, efforts to evaluate risk on a consistent, rigorous basis or to define optimum risk reduction strategies necessarily will be incomplete, and the results will be uncertain. For example, data on human exposure, and on the toxicity of many pollutants are seriously deficient. In particular, the lack of pertinent exposure data makes it extremely difficult to assess human health risks.[33]

May it ever be that we lack this exposure data. In the topsy turvy world of risk reduction, we must expose people to toxins, before we can protect them from toxins. If we take this tack with ecological threats, we are in for a very long twenty years—if we make it.

Risk works best when telling us where we ought not to have gone and it can tell us only a little about where we ought not go. It does nothing to inform us as to where we should be heading and what we should be doing.

And yet the next twenty years demand a proactive policy course. Our new found appreciation of just how sensitive ecological systems are tells us that "mistakes" are all too possible—even likely. And our understanding of humanity as a global force tells us

---

[33] Science Advisory Bd. * * * at 8.

that these "mistakes" may be catastrophic and irrevocable. Given these new realities, we simply cannot afford to react to problems. Yet that is precisely how our risk-dominated policies function. As each new environmental problem emerges, we first deny it, then put it in a catalogue with other problems, assess its relative risk, and go about the business of deciding whether and how to address it.

It is as if we were negotiating a river full of rapids, but with no clear idea of where the river goes, or when to expect the next set. As we successfully complete each set of rapids, we heave a sigh of relief and say, "Well, we made it so far." We can, as the SAB's Recommendation Number 3 suggests, invest in better ways of negotiating the rapids, even better ways of predicting what kind of danger is posed by a given class of rapids, but what we really need is a map. At a minimum, we should follow a policy that forces us out of the canoe, to reconnoiter as best we can where we are going, what we might encounter, and how we might avoid it.

It is not that we shouldn't rank our problems, nor that risk assessment shouldn't be one of the principal tools we use to rank them. Rather, it is that risk-based ranking should not set our agenda, it should only help us allocate resources. An agenda based on risk reduction will doom us to dealing piecemeal with environmental problems; to reacting as each new problem pops up, rather than laying the policy groundwork for anticipating and preventing environmental problems in the first instance. Our own Superfund, and the tragedy of Eastern Europe should tell us that the economic costs of reaction and remediation are too dear. Poland's Environmental Minister, for example, estimates that the cumulative drag on the Polish economy posed by fifty years of environmental neglect is equal to fifteen percent of the Polish Gross National Product (GNP).

* * *

C. Risk as Resource Limiting

Ironically, risk reduction, which was introduced into environmental policy to help make the best use of scarce resources, may actually work to limit the funds available to address environmental problems.

To understand why this is so, it is necessary to understand two different ways of viewing threats. The first looks at risks stochastically, which merely means that an attempt is made to assess the probability and frequency at which a given risky event, consequence, or action may occur. This is the approach to risk assessment that EPA has relied on to date.

EPA's use of stochastic risk assessments as a basis for defining risk reduction opportunities and allocating resources was, at least in theory, both appropriate and effective as long as we believed that the set of problems we faced were primarily associated with the human health effects of point source releases of toxics. Under this scenario, ranking problems and deciding on an appropriate magnitude of risk measured, say, by how many additional cancers were tolerable, made some sense. The presumption was that there was a level of expenditure at which the risk reducing action could not compete with other uses of that money or other opportunities to reduce risk. For example, if spending a million dollars prevented one additional cancer from pesticide exposure in foodstuffs, but prevented two additional cancers by eliminating volatile organics in drinking water, society might be justified in putting money into treating drinking water. In the context of a policy that was focused on reducing threats to human health from exposure to toxics, and based on a conceptual framework grounded in neoclassical economic theory, stochastic risk analyses made sense. When the benefits of environmental programs accrue to individuals, but the costs are borne by society, risk provides (at least in theory) a rational metric that allows us to get the most environmental benefit from a given expenditure.

But the environmental landscape looks distinctly different over the next twenty years. The scale of our concern is global, not just individual. In the context of planetary environmental problems, both the benefits and the costs accrue to society at large. The problems of balance and equity are less sharply defined. The potential costs of forgoing a particular action or program may have direct impacts on society at large, not merely a few individuals in society.

The second way to look at risks is deterministically. That is, assume the threat will occur. Where military threats are concerned, we have taken a deterministic approach to risk—we assume the worst will happen and prepare for it. This too, makes sense. Consider the alternative.

Picture if you will, some bureaucrat in Washington pondering military risks stochastically. It is 1987. Oil prices are low, there is relative peace in the Middle East. The bureaucrat decides that the chance of war in that region is five percent. Across the hall, a co-worker decides that it would take five hundred tanks equipped to handle the fine sand and other conditions peculiar to that region to fight a war there. The bureaucrats pass their reports to the boss. The boss looks at the two reports, and using stochastic risk assessment methods, multiplies five hundred tanks times five percent. Based on that careful analysis, the boss orders twenty-five tanks.

It is now 1991, and imagine that we had on hand twenty-five tanks to fight a war with Iraq. Alternatively, imagine that it is 1999, and we decided we could afford to protect only twenty-five percent of the stratospheric ozone layer, or more likely, that we could afford to halt CFCs, reduce carbon dioxide, but not address methane or nitrous oxide emissions.

The point is, given the levels of uncertainty in characterizing risks, we cannot divine acceptable levels of risk from threats that are planetary in scope; and we cannot trade off global risks. Allowing climate change but controlling stratospheric ozone depletion makes no more sense than arguing that an all out thermonuclear war against one opponent would be acceptable, but against another objectionable.

This, then, is how policies centered on risk reduction could work to limit environmental budgets. Risk reduction as a central theme sets up a policy dynamic that encourages decision makers to look at potential risks stochastically, that is through a lens of probability. It thus implicitly discounts the potential threat. It forces us to make trade offs between natural systems that are not tradable. In a sense, we end up with a net risk which is the value of the smaller risk subtracted from the larger risk. In short, it encourages a zero sum game in our budget. Environmental policies should challenge this precept, not reinforce it.

* * *

V. NEW PROBLEMS, NEW POLICIES: AN AGENDA FOR THE 1990s AND BEYOND

If the risk-reduction-cost-benefit paradigm cannot meet the environmental challenges of the next twenty years, how, then, are we to set environmental policy? What shall be the rudder that steers our course, informs our choices? A comprehensive description of the environmental polices for the next twenty years could fill a book, but a broad outline might look like the following.

A. Set a Course

First, we need to set a course, to decide on a direction. The most effective way to do this would be to choose environmental endpoints and build environmental policy around them. The choices should not be based solely on risk, nor on abstract economic theories. Rather, they should be based on science and ecology, a shared sense of what we as a society value, and a consensus on what the solutions should be. Cost and relative risk, can be a *part* of the latter.

We have already done this on an ad hoc basis. The original Clean Water Act set a goal of "fishable, swimmable" rivers by 1983. President Bush pledged "no net loss of wetlands" in his 1988 campaign. What we need to do now is to identify, on a systematic basis, the critical environmental values we need to protect. The SAB's ranking of health and ecological problems is a good starting point, but it is only a starting point. It does an excellent job of cataloguing and ranking our *current* problems. But as the SAB notes, we must begin to anticipate and prevent problems. For example, one of the most cataclysmic changes in global climate occurred about ten thousand years ago and appears to have been the direct result of changes in salinity in the North Atlantic. Lovelock notes that phytoplankton and near-shore coastal environments appear to play a critical role in the carbon cycle, and in the regulation of oxygen. Perhaps, then, we should count maintenance of sea salinities and preservation of near-shore biota in our endpoints. Doubtless there are other global ecological "keys" that we should be preserving. With a substantial increase in investment, EPA's Environmental Monitoring and Assessment Program can help inform and guide revisions to the SAB's endpoints.

Ultimately, however, the key to setting the course is to substantially improve our comprehension of ecological systems on a planetary, regional, and local level. We must invest in understanding the intricate patterns and cycles that support life and define the makeup of our atmosphere and the climate of our planet. Then we must devise means of detecting changes. We need to define environmental indicators that will tell us what is going on and put in place extensive monitoring systems that track these indicators. We also need to keep central and up to date statistics on our planet's health. As Michael Alford put it, "[i]f this is spaceship earth, we are flying it blind."[44] Above all, we must keep our goals dynamic and flexible so that we may change or revise our endpoints to reflect new scientific information, changed public values, or feedback from our monitoring efforts.

* * *

NOTES

1. In a portion of his article not excerpted above, John Atcheson discusses the uncertainties associated with risk management. In addition to the ones highlighted in Rosenthal,

---

[44] Alford & Ouelette, *The Coming Environmental Numbers Crunch*, ENVTL. BUS. J., Apr. 1990, at 3.

Gray, and Graham, Atcheson mentions the assumption that regulation will achieve one hundred percent compliance with the standards set by the EPA. Atcheson claims that noncomplying or unregulated activities create exposures that far exceed those accounted for in risk management. What level of compliance should risk assessment assume in setting standards? Is it fair to impose higher standards on complying sources in order to account for sources that escape compliance? What role should enforcement entities such as the Department of Justice, U.S. Attorneys, or state Attorneys General play in setting environmental policy?

2. Atcheson believes that risk assessment is an appropriate tool for allocating resources. Risk reduction, however, is not an appropriate goal for defining the environmental agenda. Why does Atcheson make this distinction? Particularly in the current climate of fiscal austerity, does resource allocation have the practical effect of defining the environmental agenda?

3. What is wrong with a "reactive policy dynamic"?

4. Is Atcheson persuasive in his analogy between national defense and global environmental problems, such as stratospheric ozone depletion? Are the principles of "institutionalized caution" and preparation for the worst case scenario equally applicable to both areas of public policy?

5. What does Atcheson propose, instead of risk reduction, as an alternative guiding principle for environmental protection? His examples of the proactive goals of the Clean Water Act and the Bush Administration's wetlands policy have been criticized as merely aspirational and unrealistic. Can aspirational, yet unattainable, goals serve as useful policy objectives for EPA decisionmaking?

6. Issues relating to the proper role of risk in public administration are frequently debated by both academicians and public officials. Two recent collections of essays reflect this healthy mix in the policy literature: REGULATING RISK: THE SCIENCE AND POLITICS OF RISK (Thomas A. Burke, et al. eds., 1993); and WORST THINGS FIRST? THE DEBATE OVER RISK-BASED NATIONAL ENVIRONMENTAL PRIORITIES (Adam M. Finkel and Dominic Golding, eds., 1994). Congress, as well, has been engaged in these issues. *See, e.g., Risk-Based Decisionmaking at the Environmental Protection Agency: Joint Hearing before the House Comm. on Government Operations,* 103d Cong., 2d Sess. (1994); Terry Davies, *Congress Discovers Risk Analysis,* RESOURCES, Wint. 1995, at 5.

Administrative agencies are not alone in their struggle with risk management. Courts, too, must resolve disputes related to environmental aims. Peter Huber's article compares agency risk management with judicial risk management. Huber also makes some important

observations about the disparity between quantitative risk assessment and public perceptions of risk. This disparity has been the source of much controversy in recent years.

SAFETY AND THE SECOND BEST: THE HAZARDS OF PUBLIC RISK MANAGEMENT IN THE COURTS
Peter Huber
85 Colum. L. Rev. 277 (1985)*

* * *

My arguments grow out of a single paradox of the risk economy: greater private safety
is often to be found in the greater *acceptance* of public risk. A similar paradox has been
noted once before in a related context, and it is worth reexamining the prior learning
briefly at the outset.

In *The Affluent Society*,[5] Professor Galbraith addressed the generation of public poverty
by the excess production of private wealth. Our "affluent society," wealthy enough to
secure all our essential needs, has succeeded in replacing scarcity of private goods with
abundance. But we are unable to put aside an economic system built on pervasive scarcity,
responsive to fears forged in millenia of existence in conditions of deprivation. At full
throttle, we continue to drive forward the economic machinery that created our modern
affluence, generating and then satisfying ever-increasing demands for private consumption.
Meanwhile, we continue to shun that historical enemy of private affluence—the shared
or "public" good. The result is social imbalance: too much investment in private goods,
too little in public ones. We have too many cars, too few roads to drive them on, too
much private wealth, too few policemen to protect it. A further result is that our gross
output continues to grow, but our aggregate welfare declines.

Encouraged by the regressive preferences of its legal system, our "safe society" does
with risks many of the wrong-headed things Galbraith said the affluent society has done
with goods. Wealthy and clever enough to manage risk effectively, we have freed ourselves
from the great bulk of risks that have historically plagued humankind. But our judicial
regulatory system remains responsive to fears forged in millenia of life in hostile and
hazardous surroundings. And so, through the regulatory machinery of our courts, we
continue to attack risk with determination, shunning most of all that historical enemy of
private security—the public risk. As a result, our "safe society" invests too much in private
risks, too little in public ones. We have too many wood stoves, too few central power
plants, too many cars, too little public transportation, too many natural toxins, too few
mass-produced substitutes. A further result is that our gross output of public risk steadily
declines, but our aggregate consumption of risk begins to increase.

---

* Reprinted with permission.
[5] J. GALBRAITH, THE AFFLUENT SOCIETY 190-99 (3rd ed. 1976).

I. THE ATTACK ON THE WINDMILL

* * *

Which brings us to the whooping cough vaccine, one for which especially precise risk figures are available. In recent decades the vaccine has been used to immunize almost every child in the United States. According to a report by two scientists at the Centers for Disease Control, use of the vaccine prevents an estimated 322,000 cases of whooping cough per year. An estimated 457 persons per year would die of the disease without the vaccination program; use of the vaccine reduces annual mortality to 44, for a net annual savings of 413 lives. Tragically, however, about 1 in every 310,000 recipients experiences serious, long-term brain damage. Without the vaccine there would be 29 such cases per year; vaccination raises that figure to 54 cases, an increase of 25 cases per year. The aggregate figures could scarcely be less ambiguous: receiving the vaccine increases the risk of one particular form of injury a little, but drastically reduces the risk of another.

Any rational parent of a young child knows what to do with figures like these. So does the Food and Drug Administration (FDA). The vaccine has been approved, its use encouraged by doctors, and its purchase and administration to children is funded by the federal government for indigent patients. The public subsidy is unquestionably a sound investment. Overall, according to the Center for Disease Control, every dollar invested in vaccination reaps an estimated potential savings of eleven dollars in reduced costs of treatment.

Nonetheless, Wyeth Laboratories recently decided to bail out of the whooping cough vaccine market. Wyeth cited only one reason: tort liability. There is no suggestion that Wyeth's whooping cough vaccine was more dangerous than any other United States manufacturer's. Wyeth and others have simply encountered too much regulation in the courts. They have repeatedly been held liable for complications arising from the vaccine's use, and adequate insurance has become difficult to obtain. As a result, a manufacturer that increases national wealth tenfold for every dollar of its product, one whose product contributes to saving hundreds of lives every year, has been forced by the tort system to abandon the product.

There is every reason to fear that foolishness of this order, driven by the myopia of the judicial system, will continue. If present trends are any indication, it appears that the tort system's vagaries will ultimately drive mass immunization programs out of the private sector altogether. There is only one retailer of the whooping cough vaccine left on the market, and it recently doubled its prices in response to mushrooming legal costs. A total of nineteen vaccines are now produced by only one American manufacturer. Even if the federal government replaces the private sector and manufactures and distributes existing vaccines, the health consequences could be severe. There is no reason to suppose that the old vaccines that might continue to be produced under government supervision would provide immunization at lower risk. And there is every reason to fear that innovation in the development, mass-production, and distribution of new, safer vaccines would be thoroughly stifled. The private sector heretofore has had the financial incentive to innovate in these areas. The governmental regulator, by contrast, will always know that preserving the status quo, doing as little as possible as late as possible, is the bureaucratically safe strategy. Meanwhile, of course, the unregulated, residual, all-natural hazards of contagion, comfortably immune from the embrace of the tort lawyers, will continue to thrive in the same risk market.

One must acknowledge something of a puzzle here. The vaccination industry's products, developed with the genius of modern technology and medical science, have moved steadily from one triumph over risk to the next, successfully immunizing us against dozens of humankind's most ancient and devastating perils. Why then is the industry in such bad trouble that federal liability protection is in the works? The answer is surely that the legal system has regulated not wisely but too well.

II. EXTERNALITIES, RIGHTS, AND THE SECOND BEST

* * *

A. The Inadequacy of the Present Rationales

1. *Externalities and the Second Best.* — The idea of unconsented-to risk as an abstract and absolute bad, an "externality" in all its manifestations, starts with a certain, simple appeal. Internalizing the externalities, through before-the-accident regulatory oversight or after-the-accident liability, seems like the obvious solution, as simple as it is classical. Too simple, in fact, and less classical than it may first appear.

Everything is risky, and risk is everywhere. The natural state of the world is not safety but abundant (though often natural) hazard. And in a world permeated with risk of both Nature's and man's creation, it is economically *inefficient* to treat every unit of manmade risk as an economic externality. Hazardous manmade goods impose external costs only insofar as they create more risk than they remove. If the air comes out of the factory dirtier than it went in, we may have an externality; if the drug is more hazardous than the disease it is intended to cure, its attendant risks may be viewed as external costs if borne by an uninformed consumer. But if the air comes out cleaner, or the drug removes more risk than it adds, society is receiving external benefits and should be paying the manufacturer a premium. This argument is obvious enough when we deal with a single good (clean air, good health) and a single type of risk (pollution, disease). But it is equally compelling when the factory contributes to the public safety not by cleaning the air but by manufacturing a good that makes life safer in other ways. The argument certainly applies to any hazardous consumer good whose use, though risky, removes more risk from the user's environment than it adds.

* * *

Without perfect regulatory uniformity, a rule of the "second best" is engaged in risk markets, just as in economic ones. In the economic world, competition guarantees efficiency only when *all* markets are competitive. The theory of the second best demonstrates that when many markets are not competitive, it may well be counter-efficient to attack monopolies in the remainder. And so with risk. Rigid risk internalization will promote safety only when all sources of risk within a particular risk "market" can be held to the regulatory ideal. But if most sources of risk cannot be deterred by regulation, it may well be counter-productive to attack external risks from the remaining sources. Patchy, erratic risk internalization may impose *greater* costs on the *safer* substitutes within particular markets, and so may encourage a shift in consumption toward the more hazardous.

The conclusion is hardly a radical or surprising one. In the real world, consumers choose among available substitutes—and respond when regulation alters the range of available choice. If new technologies are suppressed, old ones will continue to be used; if mass-produced goods and mass-exposure services carry special regulatory burdens, privately-produced and discrete-exposure substitutes will enjoy a competitive edge; if manmade risks are deterred, natural risks will fill the vacuum.

There is no reason to hope that the market itself will bar the way. In a regulated monopoly—electric power production, for example—it is quite certain that disproportionate regulatory burdens placed on the safer means of production will lead to use of the more hazardous. With only one producer, consumers simply have nowhere else to turn. Likewise, when risk benefits are truly "external" in the common sense of the word (as would be the case, for example, with my hypothetical factory removing more pollution from the air than it adds) the market obviously will not save the firm that is charged for the negative externalities it creates, while it receives no government subsidy for the positive ones. But even a competitive market, involving bilateral transactions, cannot correct for the regressive risk incentives that unwise regulation may create, for the simple reason that safety usually does not sell. Although there may be a small, boutique market for some safer-than-average products or services, and although safety may also sell for a few products (such as drugs) sold specifically for their risk-reducing value, relative risk, by and large, is simply ignored in the market. That, after all, is one main reason why we regulate in the first place. The market can be no better at correcting for regressive risk choices imposed by a malfunctioning regulatory system than it is at making progressive risk choices in the absence of regulation.

So we come back to the efficiency of shunning public risks. It may well be efficient to charge the manufacturer of a hazardous good, or the operator of a hazardous factory or powerplant, for all the public risk she causes—but only if we are confident that she can also charge the public for all the ambient risk that her good or service displaces. If she cannot, it may be inefficient to charge her in full measure for the external risks that attend her production. How much public risk is "too much" depends very much on how much (free) public or private safety comes into the world along with it.

2. *A Second Best for Just Entitlements.* — The view that public risks undermine the just order is equally susceptible to the same absolute-risk trap. It is a trap that transforms Jenner and Sabin (those vicious purveyors of less-than-perfectly-safe vaccines) into moral villains.

The first philosophical step in the jurisprudence of risk is uncontroversial enough. "The focus of corrective justice is on the relative distributional positions of wrongdoer and victim before and after each breach of entitlements. The picture is of a status quo, a baseline which the actor disturbs."[68] It is in defining the appropriate baseline that the stumbling begins.

One legal commentator, for example, flatly asserts what is quite typical of the genre: we all start with "individual entitlements to personal security and autonomy"; the "baseline"

---

[68] Rosenberg, [*The Causal Connection in Mass Exposure Cases: A "Public Law" Vision of the Tort System*, 97 HARV. L. REV. 851 (1984)] at 877 n. 108.

of risk, in other words, is absolute safety. This is silly. Humankind's "original condition" (to coin a phrase) is not a risk-free existence. Universal safety is most definitely not the natural order, not the starting point in human entitlements, not the condition that "should" or would prevail but for the rude intervention of antisocial men and women. The world is (or at least once was) abundantly populated with *natural* risk.

If the risk baseline is sensibly defined—in terms of what the real world (including highly risky Nature) actually offers before man's hazards come on the scene—many risk-creating activities are "just" by any conceivable moral standard. No one is deprived of any just entitlement when a manufacturer introduces into the market a vaccine that increases by X the risk of contracting one incurable disease but decreases by 2X the risk of dying from another. Of course we would prefer to get the risk-reducing benefit without the partial risk-increasing offset, and we should not allow the availability of an X risk cure to blind us to the desirability of finding an even better one. But the morality of the manufacturer's conduct cannot be gauged simply by reference to the absolute risk that she creates.

The conclusion is obvious, important, and regularly overlooked. A "just" law of risk, like an "efficient" risk economy, wastes no time with risk in the absolute. It is philosophically naive to treat every unit of manmade external risk as an infringement on just entitlements. Unjust risk-creating activities, like "inefficient" ones, comprise only those activities that *add* to the aggregate risk burden of our environment.

In developing a law of risk, therefore, it is very important to understand and confront two sets of risk facts. The first is where we are: the already-established actuality of the risk, or the risk "baseline". The second is where we may go: how public and private risk-creating activities tend to move that baseline. An essay on the law of risk simply cannot develop intelligently without carefully examining these risk facts.

B. The Risk Baseline

It is customary to set the stage in a legal article on risk by describing certain carefully selected "facts" of the risk environment that especially trouble the commentator. Every scholar, it seems, has some risk anecdote, supported by selective citation to the scientific literature, that reveals a shocking underregulation of some public risk, and that impels the commentator to prescribe new intervention by the legal community. My own description of the risk environment is somewhat longer than is usual, and somewhat more quantitative.

1. *The Relative Safety of Old and New.* — Life has been growing steadily safer in this country, and at a rapid pace. The reasons are undoubtedly complex, but the trend strongly suggests a first rule of thumb for prudent risk management: new technologies, new chemicals, new consumer products, and new industrial processes, though hazardous in themselves, are on average much safer than the old hazards they displace.

The aggregate risk trends, at least, are beyond dispute. Human life expectancy, a reciprocal measure of the background risk of dying, has steadily increased in the western world, from about twenty-eight years in A.D. 500, to fifty years in the nineteenth century, to the current figure of approximately seventy-four years. This continuous decrease in background risk has persisted without interruption even while we have developed toxic chemical wastes, nuclear power, hazardous contraceptives and drugs, the air pollution of the modern industrial state, and myriad other new technological terrors.

The risk of cancer in this country has not declined in step with the background risk, but putting aside the effects of smoking, it has held steady. The evidence here is more controversial. But, contrary to popular belief, the weight of the evidence clearly indicates that we have not undergone, nor are there any signs we are about to undergo, a cancer epidemic. Richard Doll and Richard Peto, two internationally recognized cancer epidemiologists, recently completed the most current and definitive study on the causes of the 400,000 annual cancer deaths in the United States.[76] These results have gained widespread acceptance among expert epidemiologists. There is now a solid consensus among the experts in that field that the aggregate risk of cancer death from all sources continues on a steady decline, and risks from cancer (other than from smoking) are, at worst, holding steady.

A few scientists on the fringes of the scholarly debate, and many lawyers in the mainstream of our contentious profession, are unwilling to accept the accuracy of these favorable (or at least neutral) risk and cancer trends. But the trends are real nonetheless. Explaining them is much more difficult, but the most straightforward explanation is also probably the most accurate.

First, and most important, steady improvements in our risk environment have resulted from the continuous displacement of natural hazards and toxins by artificial ones that are less potent, more carefully handled, produced in smaller quantities, or more easily controlled. One good example here is carcinogenic food. For the public risk hunter, artificial food additives may present tempting targets. But there is growing evidence that some antioxidant preservatives inhibit the formation of certain active natural carcinogens, and so may actually contribute to the decline in mortality from stomach cancer. Another example, involves the radiation burden imposed by nuclear power. The use of nuclear fuel in electric power generation in fact *removes* radiation from the environment, and therefore, once the fuel cycle is completed, reduces the aggregate risk of exposure to radionucleotides. Some drugs are carcinogenic; indeed, essentially *all* current cancer therapies are themselves carcinogenic to some degree. But the cancer you have—that the drug may cure—is usually a much greater risk than the new cancer that the drug may cause. The list of examples is as endless as the list of choices among manmade and natural substitutes that modern technology makes possible.

Second, the favorable risk trends are explained by the fact that new technology steadily displaces old technology. New products and processes, though never risk-free in themselves, usually prove to be less hazardous than the older, manmade substitutes they replace. Consider, for example, the case of electric power. Building a new power plant of any type certainly adds some quantum of risk to the environment, though the estimates of the risks attending different generating technologies vary widely. It is equally plain that when the construction of a new power plant permits an old one to be retired, the net change in the public risk books is very favorable, because the old power plants are uniformly dirtier and more dangerous. And electric power production, whatever the fuel used, contributes enormously to the reduction in background risk by displacing more hazardous oil lamps, wood stoves, and industrial steam engines.

---

[76] Doll and Peto, [*The Causes of Cancer: Quantitative Estimates of Avoidable Risks of Cancer in the United States Today*], 66 J. NAT'L CANCER INST. 1192 (1981).

There is hardly a product in use today—a car, plane, boiler, municipal water system, drug, vaccine, or hypodermic syringe—that is not many times safer than its counterpart of a generation or even a decade ago. The net change that results from any particular risk exchange may be difficult to evaluate. But actuarial tables strongly suggest that the aggregate change in our risk environment wrought by new technology has been inexorably and swiftly progressive. Innovation and technological change, one must presume, reduce risk. Nothing else satisfactorily explains the steady decrease in aggregate background risk in the past several centuries of technological transformation.

2. *The Relative Safety of Mass Production.* — The second notable fact of our risk budget is that our consumption of risk from mass production and centralized sources is completely dwarfed by our consumption of risks of private or natural origin. The reasons here are surely complex as well. But this aspect of our risk economy strongly suggests a second rule of thumb for prudent risk management: public sources of risk are often considerably less hazardous than the private or natural, discrete-exposure counterparts for which they can substitute.

Here, again, there is a wide gulf between fact and the prevailing fiction. It is popular to assume that decentralized, private risk production, the "soft" energy path, the "natural" diet, the technologically unadulterated existence, is safer. The ascendant belief is that most hazards of living are manmade, public risks, produced by large corporations and borne by unwitting or unwilling consumers. It is widely (and correctly) reported that as much as ninety percent of cancer may be due to environmental factors, and many people infer (quite incorrectly) that "environment" means pollution, occupational toxins, food additives, and other types of public risk that can be readily harnessed in the courts.

The reality is that we bear far less public risk than private or natural risk. Indeed, in proper perspective, the artificial public risks that excite so much legal commentary border on the irrelevant; their aggregate contribution to the hazards of living is somewhere between small and completely trivial. Several days or weeks of breathing our most polluted urban air add up to about two minutes of smoking a cigarette; consuming publicly-supplied drinking water in the most polluted areas of the country for a year is about as dangerous as drinking half a bottle of wine; we pay about the same risk price for privately driving one mile by car as for "publicly" flying thirty miles by jet. Although exposure to the public risks of asbestos is dangerous, the hazard is focused primarily on those who engage in a largely private pattern of risk taking—smoking cigarettes.

* * *

To those unfamiliar with the quantitative aspects of risk, at least some of these assertions will seem difficult to accept. How, for example, can innocuous wood stoves be more dangerous than a nuclear power plant? Quite easily. First, wood is a very dirty fuel, especially when burned under the poorly controlled conditions typical of the home stove. Second, the occupational hazards of gathering wood are, per unit of energy gathered, far higher than those for more concentrated forms of energy extracted under conditions of mass production and central control. Third, the bulk transportation of wood—a low-grade fuel that must be transported in large quantities—creates substantial risks. Finally, the key to the safe handling of a wood or any other energy source is containment, and wood fires are relatively difficult to contain. Fire tends to escape from a home stove far more often, and with more immediately grave consequences, than radiation from a large power plant under central control in a remote location.

If wood seems like an unfair source of comparison, energy conservation, another "private" alternative to central power production, is hazardous as well. Conservation requires home insulation, which is often not innocuous (note the unfortunate experience with both asbestos and formaldehyde foam). Insulation also traps radon gas and other natural and artificial pollutants in the home, causing significant increases in exposure to radioactive and other airborne toxins, and the occupational hazards involved in insulating homes on a mass scale are not inconsequential.

* * *

III. THE JUDICIAL ROLE IN MANAGING PUBLIC RISKS

* * *

A. The Old-New Division

Judicial review of new technological ventures sharply (and altogether unapologetically) separates the risks of new technology from the old risks in our abundantly hazardous environment. We do not convene judicial panels to pass on the social acceptability of the automobile, or of burning coal to generate electricity. And judicial review certainly wastes no time with the ancient natural hazards of pestilence, famine, drought, the cold of winter, and contagious or congenital disease. Searching judicial review of technology in practice means searching review of technological *change*. New technological risks, but not old ones, shoulder the considerable costs and delays of judicial review before they can be brought to market.

This phenomenon bears heavily against new sources of risk and thus encourages the retention of old ones. Courts rarely hand down an opinion overnight; courts drawing extensively on expert advice and adjudicating matters of vast social import tend to move with ponderous caution. Proponents of new risks thus face not only the staggering direct costs of extensive litigation but also the debilitating costs of delay. Old, already-established risks, on the other hand, bear none of these costs. The gap between the accelerated, premarket, regulatory costs imposed on new risks, and the postponed, postmarket costs borne by old ones, is often sufficient even under existing regulatory structures to freeze out ventures in new technologies. An intrusive second look by the courts accentuates the division even further.

The "go slow" judicial philosophy is not a choice between safety and risk. It is a choice in favor of old risks and against new ones. Though they may prefer to believe otherwise, the courts are incapable of saying only "no" to risk; the rejection of one risk is always the acceptance of another. To the extent that the courts are institutionally tilted against technological change, they are also, inevitably, tilted in favor of the established hazards of existing technology and the untamed natural world. Like it or not, when the courts choose to govern risks, they must choose among them.

* * *

B. The Public-Private Division

At first glance it might appear that the courts can do better when they address public risks retrospectively. Tort actions for damages invite judicial action only after the bodies have fallen. Perhaps it is easier to make sound risk choices at this stage. And perhaps not.

The favorite judicial targets for retrospective regulation are man-made risks created on a mass-production scale. Judicial risk deterrence obviously cannot be engaged when the risk creator is the Creator. Nor is it the cottage industry, the one-kitchen cannery, or the do-it-yourself home insulator who will be summoned to answer on the expansive "public law" theories of liability that some commentators would have us perfect. Mass exposure actions can be directed against the hazards of saccharin, but not against the hazards of pure sugar, against formaldehyde foam or asbestos insulation, but not against cold weather, against the polio vaccine, but not against the polio virus, against the manufacturer of the "alpha-drug" used to treat your cancer, but not against the untreated cancer itself or your basement apricot-pit distillery. Only mass-exposure defendants can practicably be called to account for the risk—as distinguished from the harm—they create, and only in the mass-exposure context do the proportional liability rules and streamlined "public law" procedures make any sense.

Mass producers are not only the preferred defendants under evolving public-risk tort law, they are also held to especially stringent standards of liability. Indeed, the very concept of strict liability was invented in the context of mass-produced consumer products; discrete actors operate under the relatively lenient standard of negligence. Looking specifically to Professor Rosenberg's proposals, only mass producers can be required to pay accelerated compensation for risk created, and it is only mass producers would be required to pay according to a proportional liability rule of causation. Retail producers of manmade risks will continue to be protected by the requirements of actual harm and preponderance-of-the-evidence proof of causation, if only to prevent everyone from suing everyone all the time. And Nature, a very large creator of risks, must, of course, remain entirely immune to liability. We have set in place, in other words, three different standards of liability to be applied against three different classes of risk producers that regularly sell in the same markets. The strictest standard applies to the wholesalers of manmade risks. The retailers benefit from a more lenient standard, and Nature enjoys the Creator's immunity.

The consequences are as one might expect. Liability rules that disfavor certain producers will either drive their risky products out of the market entirely, or inflate their prices so as to force at least marginal shifts in consumption toward less strictly regulated sources of hazard. Judicially created biases against public risks encourage, unsurprisingly enough, risk privatization. This is a risk preference that is most probably hazardous to the public's health.

* * *

NOTES

1. Huber argues that Americans irrationally choose lower public risk at the expense of higher private risk, and that the only unjust risk-creating activity is one which adds to the aggregate risk burden of our environment. How, if at all, does Huber account for distributive inequities in risk? Should risk management and environmental law address disproportionate exposure to public risk? Chapter One of this anthology discusses these issues of distributional justice.

2. Donald Hornstein faults Huber's view as begging important questions of environmental law. Hornstein believes that comparative risk analysis cannot perform the political function of goal-setting:

> Any centralized, formal system of risk analysis will lack clear superiority in decisionmaking. In part, this reflects the "cognitive" problems that will inexorably plague any system of comparative risk analysis that attempts to assess and compare all significant environmental risks. Not only will there be Herculean data gaps and processing costs, but there is considerable evidence that the experts will react to the inevitable uncertainties in the data by themselves using heuristics when they calculate probabilities.

Donald T. Hornstein, *Reclaiming Environmental Law: A Normative Critique of Comparative Risk Analysis*, 92 COLUM. L. REV. 562, 610-11 (1992). Do Hornstein's observations mean that the comparative analysis is useless in setting priorities for environmental law?

3. Hornstein also criticizes the comparative risk assessment approach for defining environmental policy in terms of trade-offs among environmental risks. He asks: "Can it really be said with confidence that the proper trade-off is between groundwater pollution and global warming, rather than between groundwater pollution and the $35 billion consumers spend annually for soft drinks?" Hornstein at 624-25. Hornstein believes the answer is "no" and explains the policy bias of comparative risk assessment:

> [R]ather than addressing the underlying causes of environmental problems, comparative risk analysis fractures what may be interconnected problems into discrete "risks" and then compares effects. Such a fractured approach misses the chance to craft holistic policies, because decisionmakers are focused on the very visible risk assessments presented to them about different risks, rather than on the more subtle boundary-drawing that made risks "separate" in the first place. Thus, even the [EPA Science Advisory Board] acknowledged that its strategies for addressing thirteen problem areas (for example criteria air pollutants, habitat alteration) could well change if the problem areas were defined differently (for example automobiles, energy-sector activities). The need to make comparisons, moreover, all but assures that any debates about boundary-drawing will miss what Amory Lovins once called the "infinite regress" of more fundamental questions that are raised when one considers, say, whether to build a big power station: "why a power station? why a big one? why more electricity? why electricity? why more?" By structuring the debate as a choice among existing ways to produce the least amount of risk (as when comparative risk analysts chart the air-pollution benefits of nuclear-

over coal-based electricity), comparative risk analysis tends to become merely a blueprint for moving society out of the fire and into the proverbial frying pan. Although the benefits of such incremental improvements may be substantial, comparative risk analysis is structured to avoid the opportunity for fashioning more fundamental alternative options (such as a world freed from voracious energy budgets) that may offer even greater benefits.

Hornstein at 625-26. Does this refute Huber's claims about the relative safety of mass production?

Hornstein views Huber's example of the whooping cough vaccine differently. Rather than compare the risks of the current vaccine to a world without a vaccine, Hornstein would look at the costs of improving the existing vaccine. Hornstein explains:

> Even small risks are economically unjustified if they can be improved in a cost-effective way. To the extent that vaccine-induced injuries occur, the costs to parents and children are real. Simply to ignore these costs, while concentrating on problems with larger aggregate risk levels, will lock in inefficiency at the margins.

Hornstein at 624.

4. Are there examples in environmental law where regulations focus on the net risk of an activity (the change in the aggregate risk burden to society) rather than the gross risk produced? Does Huber fall into the same trap that he claims has snared other commentators by employing selective anecdotes to support claims about under- (or over-) regulation? Consider this criticism by Professor Houck of another advocate of comparative risk analysis:

> Anyone with even a limited background in risk management knows many examples of under regulation, of deformed children and uncompensable suffering resulting from delayed bumper standards, unregulated pesticides, and safety levels that were compromised or, worse, not promulgated at all. While the book mentions in passing the possibility of under regulation, each case history presented, each example offered, is an example of regulation going "too far." Never not far enough.
>
> * * *
>
> How many inner-city children suffered brain impairment and death while the government re-evaluated, cost-benefitted, and otherwise delayed acting on leaded gasoline we will never know. But the number is undeniably substantial. There is another side to the risk management story, another kind of injustice beyond economic inefficiency, and it is not well represented * * *.
>
> Perhaps the most revealing discussion of this nature is that in which Judge Breyer "suggests many concrete possibilities for obtaining increased health, safety, and environmental benefits through reallocating regulatory resources." Among the suggestions are advertising the dangers of sun bathing, encouraging

changes in diet, subsidizing the production of healthier foods, and encouraging the purchase of smoke detectors. From the full list, a single, common denominator emerges: Nothing is required of anyone. One is reminded of former Secretary of Interior Donald Hodel's alternative to signing the Montreal Protocol (committing the United States to reduce the production of chlorofluorocarbons, to protect the Earth's ozone layer): floppy hats and sunscreen.

Oliver Houck, *Risk Management Gone Too Far?*, ENVTL. F., Mar./Apr. 1994, at 8, 8-9 (book review of STEPHEN BREYER, BREAKING THE VICIOUS CIRCLE (1993)). You will read more of Professor Houck's criticism of Judge (now Justice) Breyer after the next excerpt. For now, consider whether the argument about selective use of examples of under- versus over-regulation can be settled without first agreeing on a measure of success for environmental law. If not risk reduction, what? Also, consider whether Huber's preference for public risk might be used as a shield from blame by a company that harms the environment in order to earn higher profits. Would Huber agree with former Secretary Hodel?

Two years before President Clinton appointed him to the Supreme Court, Stephen Breyer delivered the Oliver Wendell Holmes Lectures at Harvard University. In those lectures, published the following year, Breyer drew on his experiences as a judge to comment on comparative risk analysis and criticize environmental regulation. Breyer focused on the relative strengths of different institutions, including courts, agencies, and Congress, in addressing the challenges of risk management in environmental law. In the "vicious circle" Breyer describes, public perception, Congressional reaction, and the uncertainties of the regulatory process reinforce each other to produce counterproductive and inconsistent results. The following excerpt from the book based on the lectures provides an institutional solution that would implement many of the reforms advocated by Huber in the previous excerpt.

BREAKING THE VICIOUS CIRCLE: TOWARDS EFFECTIVE RISK REGULATION
Stephen Breyer
(1993)*

* * *

SOLUTIONS

My suggestions * * * seek self-reinforcing institutional change, which will gradually build confidence in the regulatory system. My suggestions are based on several assump-

---

* Reprinted with permission of the publishers from BREAKING THE VICIOUS CIRCLE: TOWARD EFFECTIVE RISK REGULATION by Stephen Breyer, Cambridge, Mass.: Harvard University Press, Copyright 1993 by the President and Fellows of Harvard College.

tions: The public wants better health and more safety overall. On balance, the public would like to have more risk reduction at current expenditure or similar risk reduction at less cost, i.e., it would like more "optimizing." The current hodgepodge of results does not reflect a public that really wants dirty Boston harbors and superclean swamps; rather, such policy priorities more likely reflect the psychological and practical difficulties of making risk decisions one substance at a time. Finally, I assume a kind of "general will"—a public that "really" wants an overall result that differs from its substance-specific preferences revealed on particular occasions.

* * *

The Characteristics of a Solution

Neither the courts nor Congress seem likely to provide real solutions to the problems of risk regulation. Major nonregulatory alternatives, deregulation, taxes, labeling, or greater public participation seem insufficient. Is it possible to find administrative help within the Executive Branch? Our problems are essentially problems of good government. Is there then a better-government or bureaucratic solution to the problems posed?

There are strong reasons for believing that an answer does lie in that direction. I shall describe a possible change in administrative organization that is not a cure-all, nor a definitive answer, but, I believe, is a constructive approach. Like more radical changes, such as the creation of OMB itself (and perhaps like the creation of the Senior Executive Service), its aim is to help to realize the hope for effective government implicit in any civil service able to attract honest, talented, and qualified administrators.

The suggestion has two parts: (1) establishment of a new career path that would provide a group of civil servants with experience in health and environmental agencies, Congress, and OMB; and (2) creation of a small, centralized administrative group, charged with a rationalizing mission, whose members would embark upon this career path. Such a proposal is likely to engender objections that the proposal sounds undemocratic, elitist, ineffective, politically unfeasible, and without any practical means of implementation. Before considering those objections, however, I wish to describe the essential characteristics of such a group, how it might draw on certain positive attributes of bureaucracies, the nature of its specific mission, and several examples of related institutional experience.

The discussion in the first two chapters suggests that the design of any new administrative group would have to incorporate five features. First, the group must have a specified risk-related *mission*—not the mission of "total safety" or "zero risk," or "maintaining economic productivity," but the mission of building an improved, coherent risk-regulating system, adaptable for use in several different risk-related programs; the mission of helping to create priorities within as well as among programs; and the mission of comparing programs to determine how better to allocate resources to reduce risks.

Second, the group must have *interagency jurisdiction*. Such jurisdiction is needed to bring about needed transfers of resources, say from toxic waste to vaccination or prenatal care; otherwise, efforts to overcome resource misallocation would remain somewhat theoretical, rather like discussions about transferring money spent on aircraft carriers to health care. Without such interagency jurisdiction, the group would find it difficult to overcome the tendencies of separate agencies simply to compromise differences through a single meeting leading to a single rule determined administratively rather than scientifically, as when EPA, CPSC [Consumer Product Safety Commission], and FDA [Food and Drug Administration] recently ironed out their rat-to-man "comparative body weight" versus "comparative surface area" disagreement simply by choosing a number—body weight raised to the 3/4 power—that split the difference. Without interagency jurisdiction, the group would find itself limited in its ability to find examples of comparable risk-related problems in different areas which it could use in building its system, to suggest priorities among programs, and to look for potentially creative ways to put health resources to work more effectively.

Third, the group must have a degree of *political insulation* to withstand various political pressures, particularly in respect to individual substances, that emanate from the public directly or through Congress and other political sources. At a minimum, a group's members must enjoy civil service protection.

Fourth, the group must have *prestige*. That prestige must both attract, and arise out of an ability to attract, a highly capable staff. A capable staff is one that understands science, some economics, administration, possibly law, and has the ability to communicate in a sophisticated way with experts in all these fields.

Fifth, the group must have the *authority* that will give it a practical ability to achieve results. Such authority may arise in part out of a legal power to impose its decisions. But it may also arise through informal contacts with line agency staffs, out of its perceived knowledge and expertise, out of "rationalizing" successes that indicate effectiveness, and out of the public's increased confidence that such successes may build.

In summary, my proposal is for a specific kind of group: mission oriented, seeking to bring a degree of uniformity and rationality to decision making in highly technical areas, with broad authority, somewhat independent, and with significant prestige. Such a group would make general and government-wide the rationalizing efforts in which EPA is currently engaged. Let me now turn to why the creation of such a group might help.

Drawing upon the Virtues of Bureaucracy

The group I have in mind, composed of civil servants who are following the proposed career path, would draw strength from its ability to harness several virtues inherent in many administrative systems: rationalization, expertise, insulation, and authority.

1. *Rationalization.* Bureaucracies rationalize the problems and processes with which they work, allowing them to develop systems. For example, gradually over several decades, bureaucracies charged with setting rates for electricity, communications, and transportation have developed a complex but fairly uniform system of "cost of service ratemaking." That system does not consist simply of rules and regulations. Rather, the rules are accompanied by standards, practices, guidelines, prototypes, models, and informal procedures, all shaped to some extent by a general goal (that of replicating a competitive marketplace) but more directly guided by goals internal to the system (efficiency, fairness, fair return on investment). The system solves roughly similar problems in roughly similar ways irrespective of the particular regulatory program or regulated industry at issue.

The problems of health and safety risk regulation could well benefit from the development of a similar system. Such a system would recognize differences between, say, unusually high risks to specially placed individuals and risks to a general population. It would neither reduce all lives saved to a common dollar-value, nor claim incommensurable differences among different health programs and circumstances. Such a system would compare experience under different programs to create a uniform approach, while embodying that approach in models, examples, and paradigms that permit local variation. Ratemaking problems are somewhat simpler, yet they suggest a parallel.

2. *Expertise*. Bureaucracies develop expertise in administration, but also in the underlying subject matter. They normally understand that subject matter at least well enough to communicate with substantive experts, to identify the better experts, and to determine which insights of the underlying discipline can be transformed into workable administrative practices, and to what extent. A unified group charged with developing a system for addressing health risk regulation might bring together people familiar with science, risk analysis, economics, and administration—expertise that now is divided among different agencies, such as EPA and OMB.

3. *Insulation*. A civil service automatically offers a degree of insulation or protection both from politics and from public opinion. Of course, tenure rules tend to insulate its members, to some extent, from the force of public criticism. More important, administrators of a system can rationalize or justify particular results in particular cases in terms of the system's rules, practices, and procedures. Just as a doctor justifies a dose of bitter medicine by reference to medical theory and practice that indicate it will help the patient, so regulators explain and justify highly unpopular individual decisions, such as a decision that means a significant rate increase for the public. They do so through reference to the rules and practices of a system that, considered as a whole, helps the public by keeping rates within reason. Use of a coherent, well-worked-out system changes the focus of political questions. It becomes more difficult simply to ask, "Isn't this specific result terrible?" The relevant question becomes, "Is this a good *system*; and, if so, does the system generate this particular result?" Bureaucratic solutions, if sound and coherent, resting on well-constructed comparisons among different substances, offer administrators the promise of a modest increase in independence, through greater insulation from public criticism of individual decisions.

4. *Authority*. A bureaucratic solution offers the hope of creating authoritative decisions that may, in turn, help break the vicious circle. Respect for decisions as authoritative is not easy to create in this era of political distrust, an era that since 1970 has seen Americans' confidence in virtually every institution—government, business, the press (but, surprisingly, not the military)—plummet, and an era in which different political parties control Congress and the Executive Branch. Still, it seems to me that public respect depends not only upon the perception of public participation but also, in part, upon an organization's successful accomplishment of a mission that satisfies an important societal need. (Consider the rebound of confidence in the military during the 1980s.) If that is so, the authority or legitimacy of a particular regulatory action depends in part upon its technical sophistication and correctness, and in part upon its conformity with the law, and both parts help to determine the extent of public confidence in the regulator.

Insofar as a systematic solution produces technically better results, the decision will become somewhat more legitimate, and thereby earn the regulator a small additional amount of prestige, which may mean an added small amount of public confidence. Any such increase in trust may encourage greater legislative respect. As a central bureaucratic group attains a degree of prestige and develops contacts, Congressional committees may begin to ask it for advice in drafting legislation, thereby helping further to rationalize risk-regulation programs and expenditures. Congress might delegate it additional or broader regulatory authority. That authority may increase the agency's prestige, making it easier to attract better-trained personnel, who may in turn do a better technical job, which in turn may generate increased public confidence. These tendencies, even if only gradual, point in the right direction.

* * *

Objections

Now let me turn to five major objections that could be made to my proposal for a new, centralized bureaucratic group.

1. *It is undemocratic.* It may be objected that the proposal would grant too much power to the central Executive Branch at the expense of Congress; it is undemocratic because it disregards Jefferson's advice not to "take" power from the people but to "inform their discretion."[55]

A moment's thought, however, reveals that the proposal takes no power from Congress. The Executive Branch currently exercises the power that any such group would possess, but it does so in a disorganized, somewhat random way. Chaos is not democracy; to organize rationally the exercise of power may mean its better, but not its greater, exercise.

Success, of course, might lead Congress to delegate to the Executive Branch broader regulatory authority than it has at present. But any Congressional decision to broaden statutory mandates would have to reflect a democratically made judgment that the broader delegation would bring about results more consistent with the public's basic health and safety demands. Broad delegation is not itself undemocratic; the public often recognizes that such delegation is essential to achieve an important general public goal, say, the regulation of securities. Congress does not write statutes that direct the battle movements of individual Army tank corps, nor could the Army win battles if it did so. For reasons I have mentioned, to achieve the public's broader health and safety goals may require forgoing direct public control of, say, individual toxic waste dumps.

* * *

2. *Selection of group members is elitist.* The best defense against a charge of elitism is to point out that the word is not an argument but simply a pejorative label. One can equally well apply a different label to the principle of recruitment, such as "the search for quality and competence." Is it not worth trying to recruit highly qualified people into government? Is protecting the public health not a worthwhile use of their time? In conjunction with adequate levels of compensation and working conditions at the higher levels of the civil service, the career path that I have sketched could reasonably be expected to attract such people through its promise of increased authority, prestige, and potential accomplishment.

3. *It would be ineffective.* The most serious criticism is that proposals of this kind do not accomplish anything. They simply amount to reshuffling administrative boxes, perhaps

---

[55] Thomas Jefferson, *Letter to William Charles Jarvis*, in John Bartlett, *Familiar Quotations* 473 (14th ed. 1968).

creating a few new bureaucratic bottles out of which pours the same old, bad wine. In reply, I can only point to the nature of the administrative task, the specific agenda, the list of necessary attributes, and the inherent characteristics of the kind of organization described. The centralized administrative group in several respects offers a kind of "middle ground." It is meant to know about many different regulatory programs, yet have the mission of creating unifying models that can be adapted to suit different regulatory contexts. It is meant to have a staff that understands science and economics, yet, by rotating through a number of assignments, learns enough about Congressional politics and high-level administration so that it does not become narrowly expert. The staff is meant to work with Congressional statutes and regulatory rules, yet with a mission (and experience) that should prevent it from becoming overly "proceduralist" or "lawyer-like." It is meant to reach beyond a single agency both because risk regulation itself does so (consider OSHA [Occupational Safety and Healty Administration] and FDA, as well as EPA) and because, by doing so, it may imaginatively make connections that otherwise it might not see. It is meant as an alternative that helps to avoid both local program-oriented agency/subcommittee/interest-group fragmentation and substance-by-substance, or regulation-by-regulation, revisions based upon overly simplistic "dollars-per-life-saved" evaluations by a cost-oriented reviewing body. Examples from more centralized civil services suggest (though they do not prove) that this list of objectives is not Utopian.

* * *

The relation of the centralized administrative group to the problems of random agenda-setting and inconsistency is more obvious. The group's access to a broad range of different programs makes it more likely that less well-known programs (such as transportation for cancer checkups, or perhaps even efforts to stop the deforestation of Madagascar) will appear on agendas along with more traditional risk reduction. The group's agenda and system-building activities should help to produce uniform methods for measuring risks to humans that vary appreciably with scientific knowledge and circumstances. The group should begin to develop methods for measuring the effectiveness of similar programs in similar ways. One should expect to see the development of methods for examining the effect of one program's regulations upon another, and for inhibiting regulations that are shown to be counterproductive. More important, the group, after noticing that a little extra money spent on, say, vitamin supplements for pregnant women, or fireproofing space heaters would buy much more health safety than extra money spent on avoiding low-level radiation risks, would then ask what we should do about it. And, more generally, a politically insulated group could work with a sufficiently long time horizon to allow comprehensive regulation of risk, rather than responding in an extreme fashion to the latest health risk to catch public attention.

4. *It is politically unacceptable.* The centralization of authority that the proposal embodies will tend to weaken the ability of Congressional subcommittees (or influential agency/outside-group/subcommittee "triangles") to influence specific agency policies directly. Without some compensating degree of "group" independence from direct Presidential control, the proposal may not prove acceptable to many in the environmental community. But since many risk-related choices are, and must remain, inherently political, to insulate totally the group's major policy decisions from those of politically responsible officials is neither desirable nor possible.

Some degree of insulation can, however, be achieved, for example through the use of civil service career paths, by the professional discipline of staff members, by limiting the extent to which politically elected officials become involved in decisions about individual substances, and, if the public begins to recognize the group as a success, by a natural tendency for politicians to rely upon the group's decision as offering a partial refuge from responsibility for unpopular choices.

Nonetheless, you might still ask whether the group's work is sufficiently visible to the public—whether the group is sufficiently open to public participation to obtain the public's confidence. To some extent, of course, the group's proposals, plans, and findings would be openly available for comment and criticism. Yet one important objective is to limit the extent to which public debate about a particular substance determines the regulatory outcome, in respect to a range of substances that are not automatically or inevitably politically volatile. Is such an objective itself consistent with the building of public trust?

Remember the sharp decline in confidence in public institutions over the past twenty-five years. Recall, however, that rebuilt trust in institutions is based not simply on the public's perception of openness, but also on the ability of an institution to accomplish its mission successfully, particularly where that mission itself helps to achieve an important public purpose. Those who rebuilt confidence in the Federal Trade Commission in the 1970s did so not through public-relations campaigns but by reorganizing the Commission so that it better accomplished its important consumer-protection mission. Doing so created better morale, increased confidence, and greater prestige, all of which improved the agency's reputation and in turn helped further improve agency performance.* * *

* * *

NOTES

1. Recall that former EPA Administrator William Ruckelshaus, in his excerpt earlier in this chapter, rejected the "quasi-judicial, blue-ribbon panel approach" to rationalizing risk management and restoring public confidence in environmental regulation. He argued that it is impossible to transcend the values of the panel experts, who engage in advocacy rather than in "unimpeachable and disinterested consensus." Ruckelshaus instead suggested a number of ways to enhance and enlist public involvement in risk management. Breyer insists that an agency earns the trust of the public only if it accomplishes its mission. Breyer believes that rational risk management requires central, expert guidance. Does Breyer adequately respond to Ruckelshaus? Are Breyer's assumptions about administrative effectiveness reasonable?

2. In RISK MANAGEMENT AND POLITICAL CULTURE (1986), Sheila Jasanoff takes a cross-cultural look at the ways in which national governments reconcile democratic values with expert judgment about risk. She finds that the legal culture, which determines who participates in decisionmaking and how disputes are resolved, shapes and ultimately overshadows scientific information. Jasanoff attributes the American difficulty with reaching final risk management decisions ("closure") to the price of broader public involvement. Breyer's model for risk management is similar to the expert panel models Jasanoff studied in Germany and Great Britain. Would Breyer's proposal be feasible in the United States without a change in the political culture?

3. Because of Justice Breyer's prominence on the bench, the timeliness of his book, and the clarity with which he writes, BREAKING THE VICIOUS CIRCLE has attracted a great deal of commentary. *See, e.g.*, David A. Dana, *Setting Environmental Priorities: The Promise of a Bureaucratic Solution*, 74 B.U. L. REV. 365 (1994) (book review) (criticizing Breyer for ignoring the role that interest groups play in shaping environmental regulation and overestimating the ability of a politically insulated bureaucracy to rationalize priorities); Symposium, *Risk Assessment in the Federal Government,* 3 N.Y.U. ENVTL L.J. 251 (1995). Victor Sher, President of the Sierra Club Legal Defense Fund, employs the following parable:

> A woman is standing in front of a stream. Behind her are four risk assessors. The first is a toxicologist who says, "Go ahead and cross the stream because it's cold and swift but not toxic." The second risk assessor, a cardiologist, says, "You should cross the stream because you're young and healthy and you're not already hypothermic." The third is a hydrologist who says, "Cross the stream. I've seen streams like this and usually they're pretty smooth on the bottom." The fourth is an EPA risk assessor, who says to cross because the risks are insignificant compared to the risks of global warming and the ozone layer.
>
> The woman refuses to cross the stream, so the risk assessors pull out their charts and explain to the woman that the risks are negligible. They ask why she refuses. She answers: "Because there's a bridge right over here."
>
> The problem with risk assessment is that there is no way of getting around the problem that there are so many variables, so many unknown synergies, so many additive effects. The models are so imperfect, and our knowledge extrapolating from animal tests is so incomplete. There's no way that science can assure us safety. When you look at the existing burden of poisons in the world, the only thing we know for sure is that there is too much there already.
>
> Instead of trying to assess risks, we should be looking at alternatives that avoid risks in the first place. Like the bridge over the stream. Asking whether the cost of cleanup is worth the increment in risk is not the right question. We can never quantify what the risk really is. Instead, let's ask how can we avoid creating the risk in the first place.

Victor Sher, *Assessing Risk: A Tale of Judge Breyer and the Bridge Not Taken*, ENVTL. F., Sept./Oct. 1994, at 44. This critique of Breyer's view is similar to Hornstein's critique of Huber. Are Huber and Breyer advocating the same reforms?

4. Professor Oliver Houck is more specific in his criticism of Breyer's proposals:

The proposal of a super agency entrusted with the final say over levels of human health and safety in the United States and modeled after OMB [the Office of Management and Budget] and its Office of Information and Regulatory Affairs ignores a widely held perception that these two entities in particular—which conducted an open war against environmental regulation throughout the 1980s—departed a long way from rather fundamental notions of accountability in government. An institution acting almost entirely in secret, accessible to the president (and, historically, to those campaign contributors and others in the president's favor) and to virtually no one else, subject to no open meetings laws, no Freedom of Information Act, no notice, comment, or other rudiments of administrative due process (to say nothing of judicial review), with the power not only to second-guess the public rulemaking of existing agencies but to make their budgetary and legislative decisions as well, creates a branch of government subject to checks and balances by none of the existing branches, not even by the press.

The Risk Management process may be a mess—and it is—but taking it behind closed doors as a remedy is the kind of idea that comes up every couple of decades by people who would like to streamline government for excellent ends and either results in something like the French Revolution's Committee for the Rights of Man or dies a more quiet but equally deserving death. The genius of American government and its most important contribution to world governance since democracy itself is an open, administrative process, the vital organs of which are public participation and judicial review. As recent revelations of extraordinary, undisclosed radiation hazards by the Department of Energy provide only the latest confirmation, truth is more likely to emerge from the crucible of an open process than from the conclusions of inaccessible (to the public, anyway) "experts." And since when was any expert neutral?

Judge Breyer's choices here are stark. Either we create a new institution with the power to decide, or we have a waste of time. If the new institution has the power to decide, either it will be subject to traditional administrative process or it won't. If it will be, it will soon dissolve into the same tugs of war, litigation, politics, and public pressures (all the pressures referenced in this book, by the way, are from "the public," an uninformed public, as in "the viscitudes of public opinion"; no pressures such as those that led a federal agency deliberately to understate toxic releases from the government's Fernald, Ohio, facility for the last 15 years are alluded to) that perpetuate the existing muddle. If, on the other hand, an agency with this much clout will not be subject to administrative process, we have a new form of government indeed. New to the United States of America, that is.

What, then, is the answer to risk management? * * *

* * * [E]xamine those public health and environmental laws that work, and

those we can agree do not. For openers, in the "work" camp we can put the National Pollutant Discharge Elimination System program of the Clean Water Act, the new air toxics abatement program, and pretreatment standards under the Resource Conservation and Recovery Act. They are producing marked reductions in highly hazardous emissions. On the "not work" side we can identify, with ease and near unanimity, the Comprehensive Environmental Response, Compensation, and Liability Act (which cannot come to grips with hundreds of hazardous waste sites) and the Toxic Substances Control Act and the Federal Insecticide, Fungicide, and Rodenticide Act, which have yet to scratch the surface of new toxic substances or pesticides.

Now, why do the first approaches work and the latter fail? The ones that get the job done do not rely on or even bother with risk management. They abate toxic water and air emissions, they reduce hazardous waste concentrations, by best-available-technology engineering requirements. For the most hazardous substances (and in this more limited inquiry, risk analysis plays a more useful role)—*e.g.*, CFCs, liquids in landfills—they attempt to set no "safe level" standards. They simply ban them; at which point, invariably, and despite the dire predictions of economic inefficiency and catastrophe from the affected industries, less risk-posing substitutes appear as if by magic.

Turn now to the very few substances regulated at all by TSCA or FIFRA, and even here regulated by such facially inadequate palliatives as warning levels (for Hispanic farm workers?) (but what else can you do with a standard like "unreasonable risk"?) and to the chaos of CERCLA, blamed largely on lawyers for its extraordinary expense and unextraordinary cleanup results. Why do the lawyers litigate? For one, because the cleanup requirements are based on science so soft it would be ineffective assistance of counsel not to litigate and, for another, because no one knows what to do with the factor of costs. All of these decisions are purportedly made on the basis of risk management, with the appropriate consideration of costs, etc., by neutral experts. None of them work. Breyer has proven that if nothing else in part one. Nor will they work any better if done behind closed doors by the super experts of a super agency. The science will become no more firm, simply less visible and, with less participation, less informed. The inquiry is fatally flawed. Judge Breyer has the right question but the wrong answer. He goes too far.

In an increasing number of statutes, the Congress—the same body maligned in this book for creating and not solving the risk management problem—is solving it in a very different way. For much of the field of environmental and public health, it is banning the worst risks, adopting best available technology for the rest, and passing risk management by.

Oliver Houck, *Risk Management Gone Too Far?*, ENVTL. F., Mar./Apr. 1994, at 8, 9-10.

Are risk balancing approaches to environmental law so fatally flawed that they ought to be abandoned? Does Houck offer a viable alternative? Would Breyer subscribe to

Houck's list of EPA regulatory programs that work? How can Houck be sure that these programs do not over-regulate activities that might on balance reduce risk? How would policymakers implement a technology-based program for Superfund cleanups or pesticide registration? Professor Houck expands on the failure of risk management programs in comparison to technology-forcing regulations in *Of BATs, Birds, and B-A-T: The Convergent Evolution of Environmental Law*, 63 MISS. L.J. 403 (1994).

Houck raises the institutional dangers posed by the establishment of a "super agency" insulated from public scrutiny and accountability. Does Houck exaggerate the insulation of Breyer's risk experts? Are there institutional safeguards that fall short of the secrecy of the Department of Energy and the OMB that can protect the tenure of the risk experts and encourage rational, systematic decisions? Breyer claims that his proposal invests no new authority in the executive branch; it merely promotes organization of a systematic approach to risk in place of the current irrational, *ad hoc* approach. Would Breyer's proposal cast more rather than less light on administrative decisions concerning risk?

5. On September 30, 1993, President Clinton issued Executive Order 12,866, which established mechanisms for regulatory planning and review that apply across the executive branch to all agencies. 59 Fed. Reg. 51,735 (1993). Section 4 of the executive order establishes the Regulatory Working Group (RWG), consisting of agency heads, the Vice President, and various advisors, to serve as a forum to assist agencies in analyzing important regulatory issues, including comparative risk assessment. The RWG works closely with the OMB. Sally Katzen, the Administrator of OMB's Office of Information and Regulatory Affairs, explains that her office looks "across all executive branch agencies trying to develop and implement a coordinated approach to regulatory policy." *Strengthening Risk Assessment Within EPA: Hearing Before the Subcomm. on Technology, Environment and Aviation of the House Comm. on Science, Space, and Technology*, 103d Cong., 2d Sess. 7 (1994). Katzen explains that the RWG plans to produce a series of guidance memoranda to assist agencies in regulating risk more consistently, to the extent permitted by statutes. *Id.* at 16-17. Does this initiative begin to fill Breyer's prescription for comparative risk management?

Although explicitly responding to Huber's article, Professors Gillette and Krier concern themselves with many of the claims of institutional competence and neutrality made by Breyer. Their thoughtful article focuses on administrative behavior but also compares agencies with courts and Congress to evaluate bias and effectiveness in risk regulation. By taking a broad perspective on the risk concept and the political ramifications of expert authority, the following excerpt highlights many of the fundamental issues that will vex environmental law over the next decade.

RISK, COURTS, AND AGENCIES
Clayton P. Gillette and James E. Krier
138 U. Pa. L. Rev. 1027 (1990)*

Risk inheres in our condition. Whether brought on by nature in such forms as earthquakes and disease, or by humans with mundane machines like the automobile and high technologies like nuclear energy, hazard is ubiquitous and inevitable. Hence selective aversion to certain risks, most particularly to the manmade risks of advanced technologies, can prove to be counterproductive. Selective aversion might foreclose progressive new technologies that are, despite their dangers, on balance beneficial. A world with vaccines and nuclear power plants is not perfectly safe, for example, but might be safer than a world without. In other words, though risk by definition is costly, avoiding risk is costly as well. It entails the costs of controls and other risk-reduction measures, and at times the costs of forgone benefits (a risky new technology might guard against even more threatening natural hazards, such as disease; it might displace the greater risks of a technology already in place, or produce units of output at a lower cost than the existing technology, or both). So the objective of risk management must be not the elimination of risk, but rather the minimization of all risk-related costs.

All of this sounds platitudinous, yet it happens to be extraordinarily controversial—especially in the case of "public risks," a recently coined name for the distinctive hazards of high-tech times. Public risks have been defined as manmade "threats to human health or safety that are centrally or mass-produced, broadly distributed, and largely outside the individual risk bearer's direct understanding and control."[3] "Private risks," in contrast, are either of natural origin or, if manmade, produced in relatively discrete units, with local impacts more or less subject to personal control. In these terms, then, disease is a natural private risk; the hazards of commonplace artifacts like automobiles and wood stoves are manmade private risks. Public risks, on the other hand, originate in new or complex technologies like chemical additives, recombinant DNA, mass-produced vaccines, and nuclear power plants.

The public-private distinction is hardly perfect (consider the pollution pouring into the atmosphere from thousands of automobiles, or from thousands of wood stoves), but it is useful enough, especially for purposes of illuminating a currently important controversy that centers on the idea of cost minimization in the risk context. Public risks are precisely the risks that have recently captured the attention of the legal community and the world at large, in no small part because they give rise to such novel problems for lawyers and such grave apprehensions among lay people. Public risks have moved the legal system to relax doctrines—regarding, for example, standards of causation and culpability, burdens of proof, sharing of liability—that were designed to deal with the private risks that once dominated the landscape. And public risks have moved lay people to intensify their demands for risk control measures. These developments suggest that public risks are

---

[3] Huber, *Safety and the Second Best: The Hazards of Public Risk Management in the Courts*, 85 COLUM. L. REV. 277, 277 (1985).

subject to especially harsh treatment, yet such treatment might often be contrary to minimizing the sum of all risk-related costs. If some public risks, whatever their dangers, are in fact safer or otherwise more beneficial than the risks they would displace, then cost minimization requires open-minded efforts to encourage many of the very technological threats that current legal and popular opinion would instead deter. As a consequence, the question of what to do about public risk has become a subject of considerable (and sometimes heated) debate.

* * * [We give] particular attention to two important points of contention. The first of these has to do with attitudes. The general public, and to some degree the legal system as well, have a particular aversion to public risk. Is this justified? The second point of contention, intimately related to the first, has to do with institutions, and especially with judicial versus administrative rule. At present, the courts are playing an important part in shaping the legal response to public risk. Is this sensible?

According to one powerfully stated outlook—an outlook that runs directly against the grain of prevailing sentiments—the answer to each of the foregoing questions is a firm "no." Our actions increase, rather than minimize, risk costs. We worry too much about public risks and not enough about private ones. We control public risks with a haphazard mix of market, judicial, administrative, and legislative measures that too often proceed in the wrong direction, without coordination, and with too little reliance on agencies and too much on courts. The courts especially are said to pander to uninformed and irrational risk attitudes; their decisions show a myopic bias against new technology and in favor of its victims. New or complex technologies are subjected to a degree of scrutiny that riskier but established (often private) risk sources never underwent and could not survive. As a result, we have too much private risk and too little public risk, not more safety but less. Some of the critics advancing this line call for a reduction of the judicial role in risk assessment and management, and for more reliance on administrative agencies. Agencies, they argue, have more expertise, are more objective and rational, can be more attentive to the net effects of technological advance. Courts, they conclude, should defer to them.

This is the set of views that we call into question here.* * *

* * *

D. Judicial Competence

Even if the courts are balanced in their treatment of public risk, it does not automatically follow from this that the judiciary is a good risk management institution. The claim that the judicial system is "institutionally predisposed to favor regressive public risk choices"[85] might fail for lack of proof, but the claim of judicial incompetence would still remain.

Imagine, for example, that the risk premium exacted by the courts proves to be worthwhile. Could it nevertheless be avoided or at least made significantly smaller? Are there alternative institutions that can achieve something like the optimal amount of public risk in a more adroit (less expensive) way? For critics of the courts, the answer is yes. Administrative agencies, however imperfect themselves, would be a very considerable

---

[85] Huber, *supra* note 3, at 329.

improvement. For this reason, courts operating in the civil liability setting are implored to defer to the experts of administrative agencies that have undertaken "searching and complete . . . regulation."[88] If an agency has determined (in the course of a licensing proceeding, for instance, or through regulatory hearings) that a particular public risk is progressive, liability on the producer's part should thereafter be foreclosed so long as it meets the terms of its license or complies with applicable regulations.

* * *

IV. RISK, AGENCIES, AND EXPERTS

Since their birth a century ago, their great endorsement during the New Deal, and their extraordinary proliferation over the last fifty years, administrative agencies have come to be seen by some as the ideal institution for managing complex social problems. In principle, after all, agencies can provide what markets and courts sometimes cannot: expert regulation in the public interest. Given the complexity of public risk, the problems of market failure, and the shortcomings of the courts, administrative rule seems an obvious course to take.

Obvious, though, only if one envisions agencies in the idealized terms of the New Deal. If, instead, one is motivated—by simple curiosity, by skepticism, or by allegiance to a persistently systemic investigation—to consider how reality might depart radically from the ideal, then a rather different image comes into view. One can see that agencies, like markets and courts, are themselves easily capable of failure. The generalization is obvious, but we are interested in particulars. Most to the point here, we are interested in the possibility of agency failure of a very specific sort—a systematic tendency in favor of too much public risk. In pursuing this line of inquiry we aim to provide not an exhaustive or decisive account, but only a suggestive one. The issue is whether the courts should defer to administrative agencies in cases of public risk. Our account suggests that the answer is much more complicated than a sanitized vision of administrative decision making might suggest.

* * *

B. Access and the Problem of Capture

* * * We are concerned not simply with how agencies actually behave currently, but also with how they might be expected to behave were they granted more freedom than at present. What might the practice of risk assessment and management look like then?

* * *

Administrative power to seize the initiative is especially appealing to anyone who believes that when public agencies act, they act in the public interest. Just such a faith seems to be reflected in some of the views voiced by Mr. Huber, particularly the claim that public agencies can supply "a 'public' point of view on the problem"[101] of risk assessment and management. Less clear is the source of this public point of view, or the basis for believing that agency initiative would necessarily serve it. Assessment and

---

[88] Huber, *supra* note 3, at 334. * * *

[101] Huber, *supra* note 3, at 331. * * *

management are, as we saw, heavily dependent on a wide range of information and values. How any particular risk decision comes out is likely to turn in part on what happened to go into an agency's deliberations. Hence an abiding faith that outcomes are in the public interest requires an underlying conviction that information and values filter into and out of agencies in some evenhanded way. If, however, risk producers have a comparative advantage over risk consumers in getting the administrative ear, then agency decision making might be marred by access bias just as judicial decision making is.

The problem we have in mind is a variation on some central themes in the literature about agency "capture," a body of theory and evidence familiar enough to require only a brief account here. Capture theory proceeds from the notion that the motivations and behavior of private citizens and public officials in political markets are similar to those of producers and consumers in ordinary economic markets. Citizens (in this case, risk producers and risk consumers) and officials (here, those involved in the process of risk regulation) are assumed to be substantially self-interested and to want their private interests served by political and regulatory processes in ways that may have little in common with what would serve the larger public interest.

Self-interest is easy enough to picture in the case of risk producers and consumers, but its meaning regarding political officials, administrators in particular, is worth a few words. With respect to public actors, self-interest can mean something as obvious (and acceptable) as wanting to avoid embarrassing technical errors in the course of making decisions, as trivial as wanting to save time and effort during the day-to-day routine (in order to nurse the agency budget or enhance agency leisure), or as substantial (and possibly tainted) as wanting to advance agency or personal power and resources. Agency and personal advancement, in turn, are likely to be a function of the reactions to agency decisions by the legislative and executive branches, by the electorate, by the presumed targets and supposed beneficiaries of agency action, and by potential employers of agency personnel, whether within the government, or without.

Just as public officials have the means to satisfy the interests of private citizens, citizens have the potential to serve the interests of officials. They can provide information and points of view. They can contribute money to political campaigns and administrators' pockets. They can assemble blocks of voters. They can offer employment opportunities. These examples mix sinister elements with benign ones, but the capture argument hardly depends on the former. There is nothing sinister in the fact that various citizens might cluster into interest groups for the purpose of contributing resources. * * * Information, points of view, voter attitudes, and dollars as a measure of intensity of voter attitudes are, after all, obviously relevant to making decisions in the public interest (unless the public interest means something utterly unrelated to what the public is interested in).

That interest groups express their views by these means, then, does not necessarily imply tawdry politics; to the contrary, there might be no other practical way to discern much of the meaning of "the public interest" in a democratic system. The model is interest group pluralism and its idea that agency output (self-interest notwithstanding) will approximate the social good as long as the output results from countervailing pressures brought to bear by any number of interested groups, each of which has roughly equal access to the decision making process. Capture theory shows how the pluralist model can go wrong. Almost by definition, interest group pluralism can endorse decisions as "in the public interest" only if all the various interest groups are indeed able to voice their wants effectively. If, instead, some groups enjoy a comparative advantage in catering to administrative needs and desires (that is, if the pluralist process is too singular, not sufficiently plural), there arises the danger that agency attention will be captivated by too narrow a range of interests and be diverted from an appropriately public perspective.

Whether, and how much, bias is likely to result from asymmetric access to the administrative process depends considerably on the nature of any particular item on the regulatory agenda. In the case of public risk generally, though, the problem appears to be a substantial one, as should be obvious from our discussion of access bias in the courts. We saw in that discussion how the typical characteristics of public risk—impacts that are latent, diffuse, widely dispersed, of low probability, and nonexclusive—limit the ability of potential and actual public risk victims to gain access to the courts. Our point here is that they can also frustrate the efforts of victims to mobilize for the purpose of influencing agency decisions about risk. Whatever the objective of the mobilization effort (it might be to prepare and provide a good research product for agency consideration, or to present a convincing brief for the victim point of view, or to gather a crowd to attend public hearings, or to organize an effective lobby), considerable amounts of time, effort, and money will be required. * * * Hence the problem of mobilization remains.

Look now at the other side of the story, and consider the ability of public risk producers to muster effective interest groups. Their organizational burdens will generally be lighter for any number of well-known reasons: there are fewer potential group members; each member will usually know the identity of most others; each member is likely to have a relatively large, concentrated, and immediate stake in agency decisions, as compared to public risk victims; each has greater assets (wealth, information, personnel, facilities, and so forth) to tap than any one or several (or even many) victims; commonly all or many of the members will already be organized, say through a trade association. Taken together, these considerations facilitate effective communication, provide opportunities to monitor individual contributions and chastise noncontributors, increase the likelihood that the private benefits of group action will exceed private costs, and forestall freeriding behavior. In short, the costs of organizing collective efforts will generally be lower for the producers than for the victims of public risk, and this in turn means producers will generally enjoy a considerable comparative advantage in mobilizing interest groups and exercising influence, whether by benign or sinister means.

The foregoing analysis simply elaborates a familiar generalization. Large groups seeking agency decisions that would yield diffuse, remote, dispersed, and nonexclusive benefits are handicapped relative to small groups seeking decisions that would avoid (or fighting decisions that would impose) concentrated costs. The generalization applies to the case of risk regulation as much (if not more) as to any other, which is not to say that it is free of interesting exceptions. One can no doubt point to instances of risk regulation, and even to instances of risk-regulation agencies, that stand in contrast to our account. But we are concerned with tendencies, and especially with tendencies that would exist if there were broader deference to agency rule than at present. In this context, the problem of asymmetric access suggests that agency decisions would tend in the direction of producer interests, and thus toward too much public risk.

* * * Note that just as class actions are not an easy answer to access barriers in the

judicial setting, public interest organizations are not an easy answer in the agency setting (including within that setting judicial review of agency activity). Public interest organizations themselves require support—they are not a costless enterprise—and will, for just the reasons canvassed above, have difficulty getting it. Almost by definition, the organizations are likely to be in too short supply. * * *

C. Process and the Meaning of Risk

The last section's story was a cautionary tale, warning that a deferential attitude toward agency decisions could lead to too much public risk. The story in this section ends with the same lesson, but it begins in a very different way. We worried above that asymmetric access might distort an egoistical agency's image of the public interest. Here we abandon the assumptions on which those concerns were based, happily grant every wish of public interest theorists, and hence suppose that agencies are invulnerable to undue outside influence and selflessly dedicated to a rational vision of the social good. Still, we think, the likely result of deference to such agencies would be too much public risk, at least so far as the public is concerned.

The key to this conclusion can be found by asking an important question that all the discussion thus far has simply begged: What does "risk" *mean*? To anticipate our argument, suppose that the concept signifies different things to different people—more particularly, one thing to agency experts and another to the lay public. Suppose, in addition, that while each of these meanings is sensible, the expert definition implies levels of public risk that are, by the lay definition, almost invariably too high. It then follows that a selfless agency, determined and free (because of expansive deference) to assess and manage public risk in accord with its own conception, will end up regulating less than called for from the public's point of view. The resulting contest is, at bottom, one of competing rationalities, and its resolution is a matter of ethics and politics, not technical expertise. Nothing in the training, credentials, or legitimacy of risk assessors or bureaucrats qualifies them to settle the issue. Hence deference to agencies would grant them ground they have no right to claim. Deference would beg a central question in the control of public risk.

* * *

To begin the discussion, return to the central question: What does risk mean? We asked this, but only implicitly, many pages ago—and alluded to one answer. Risk, we suggested, can be seen as the function of expected mortality or morbidity, or what we shall here refer to as expected annual fatalities or "body counts," and in these terms many public risk technologies might indeed seem to be relatively safe. Those who favor modern technological developments do so in part precisely because they, like most experts, gauge risk in just this way. They may disagree about details, such as whether one looks at total expected deaths, deaths per person or per hour of exposure, or loss of life expectancy due to exposure, but generally speaking "experts appear to see riskiness as synonymous with expected annual mortality [and morbidity]."[118] So, for example, when technical experts are asked to rank the risks of various activities and technologies, "their responses

---

[118] Slovic, *Perception of Risk*, 236 SCIENCE 280, 283 (1983) (citation omitted). * * *

correlate highly with technical estimates of annual fatalities."[119] When experts write about relative risk, they implicitly or explicitly use body counts as the relevant measure. And, in a way seemingly consistent with the logic of their method, they insist that a death is a death is a death—1,000 lives lost in a single anticipated annual catastrophe, or through many accidents expected every year, or lost ten-fold but only once every decade on average, or lost in a single community or across the country, are all the same to them.

In the view of experts, then, risk is a one-dimensional phenomenon.* * *

For the lay person, risk is *n*-dimensional, as William Lowrance suggested in an early study. He observed that a variety of considerations in addition to expected fatalities and injuries affect people's judgments about risk: involuntary exposure, delayed effects, scientific uncertainty about the hazard in question, "dreaded" versus common hazards (for example, the threat of death from invisible radiation as opposed to an auto accident), irreversible consequences, and others.[124] Since the time of Lowrance's work, any number of studies have found "that many attributes other than death rates determine judgments of riskiness" by lay people, whose "model of what constitutes risk appears to be much richer than that held by most technical experts."[125] Thus the public is known to be concerned about risks that have catastrophic potential, that are unfamiliar, uncontrollable, or involuntary, that threaten future generations, that would concentrate fatalities in time or space, that are distinctively threatening as opposed to widespread and shared by the general population, that are manmade as opposed to natural. * * *

* * *

Disagreements between lay people and expert risk assessors cannot be attributed to simple ignorance or ineptitude on the part of either group. The divide, instead, results from fundamentally different world views. For lay people, "'riskiness' means more . . . than 'expected number of fatalities.'"[136] For experts, it doesn't. The implications of this split are hardly trivial. * * *

How might we resolve this difference in outlook, and the conflicting risk assessments that result? The easy way would be to reject one of the opposing views as senseless or irrational. The expert perspective hardly deserves this treatment, as intuition alone makes obvious: surely risk and its minimization have *something* to do with actual human loss, measured in death and illness. The sense of body counting is thus apparent. Some experts, though, are unwilling to concede that more than bodies count, and that the lay view, too, makes sense; they are generous only in their scorn. They take the easy way and dismiss "the public's understanding" as "insane" at worst, "irrational" at best. Their contempt, however, is utterly unwarranted.

Rather than discuss why this is so, we could perhaps appeal once again to intuition and leave the matter at that. Surely the characteristics that nag at the popular mind have—like body counts—*something* to do with risk, hazard, threat. It is worthwhile, however, to move beyond the intuitive and state explicitly at least a few of the arguments

---

[119] Slovic, Fischhoff & Lichtenstein, *Regulation of Risk: A Psychological Perspective*, in REGULATORY POLICY AND THE SOCIAL SCIENCES 241, 263 (R. Noll ed. 1985). * * *

[124] *See* W. Lowrence [OF ACCEPTABLE RISK: SCIENCE AND THE DETERMINATION OF SAFETY (1976)], at 86-94.

[125] Slovic, Fischhoff & Lichtenstein, *Regulation of Risk, supra* note 119, at 243. * * *

[136] Slovic, *supra*, note 119 at 270.

that support the lay understanding, partly because some of the arguments undermine the contending expert conception. Hence making out the case for the public's picture of public risk will give us grounds to reconsider body counting. Our objective is not to show that the popular perspective is best, though we happen to think it is; our purpose, rather, is simply to establish it as an obviously worthy and fully admissible point of view in the public risk debate.

Return, then, to the public's rich image of risk, and reflect for a moment on its many dimensions. People have a lower tolerance for involuntary than for voluntary exposure. Even on its surface, the concern here is easily understood, and closely related to the dimensions of uncontrollability and uncertainty. Voluntary exposure pre-supposes knowledge. Knowledge coupled with freedom of action facilitates individual choice and efforts to control events bearing on the choice. To be forced to face a risk, on the other hand, or to be ignorant of it, or to sense that no one is really in command of it, leaves one's well-being in the hands of others, or of no one. Either alternative is obviously inferior, under most circumstances, to being in charge.

Upon deeper examination, this sense of voluntariness might trivialize the true concern. Suppose my situation (say I am an unskilled worker) "forces" me to "choose" a risky occupation, in exchange for some wage premium. Is my exposure to the risk "voluntary"? Suppose, more generally, that I rightly see life as full of difficult choices. Is it sensible to say that, given my power to choose—given that any choice is "voluntary"—I should accept without complaint whatever consequences follow? The answer might be yes if the world were organized in a way consistent with ideal values and principles, but it is not. Behind the notion of voluntariness, then, there may lurk more fundamental concerns about autonomy and equality and power among individuals in the society, for it is the pre-existence of these that lets free choice be morally interesting. People perhaps are saying that some risks seem consistent with such ideals and others not, and registering the view by showing a greater acceptance of risks that they regard as "voluntary" in fundamentally important ways, as opposed to "chosen" in some narrower sense.

The foregoing account enlightens us about other popular dimensions of risk, such as the enhanced dislike of delayed (latent) effects, and of irreversible ones. Latency frustrates knowledge, and irreversibility frustrates control. They make it more difficult for us to govern our own circumstances—and also to govern our governors. How do we hold accountable officials whose mistakes or misdeeds manifest themselves only decades after a term of office? And how do we correct for what they have done, if what they have done is uncorrectable? Latency and irreversibility practically deny us the fruits of trial-and-error, perhaps the best means yet devised by which to resolve uncertainty.

What of the special dislike of manmade as opposed to natural hazards? Once again, a story grows out of what has been said thus far: Humans might treat each other with motives that Nature could never have, and this matters. Mark Sagoff develops this theme in the course of considering why the government should regulate artificial risks more strictly than natural ones, even if they are "no more dangerous" (obviously, in the sense of body counting). First, people are responsible for artificial risks, but not for natural ones, and the government's job is to regulate what people do. Second, only manmade risks can, in any meaningful sense, threaten autonomy, an additional reason to be especially wary of them. Third, the harms we suffer because of the acts of others carry special injury; we mourn the deaths from a natural flood but resent, deeply, the ones from a broken dam. We "are concerned not simply with safety but with responsibility and guilt as well."[144]

These same concerns arise in the case of those manmade risks we and others classify as "public": risks generated by highly centralized high technologies. Th[is] is especially so because public risks entail so much uncertainty (given their complexity), imply such considerable power, and are capable of such calamitous effects. The last consideration, in particular, implicates the public's aversion to the possibility of disastrous consequences and brings us to the cluster of factors that enter into what is termed "dread." Dread correlates significantly with some aspects of risk that we have already discussed, such as involuntariness and uncontrollability, but also with such others as inequitable distributions, threats to future generations, and catastrophic potential—each of which speaks almost for itself.

The idea of inequitable distributions, for example, reflects the view that just as a right thinking society should concern itself with the distribution of wealth, so too should it do so with the distribution of risk. For example, risks that might result in death or disease are often considered worth taking because they confer significant benefits not otherwise available. This risk burden may be regarded as equitably distributed only if it is borne by those who simultaneously enjoy the benefits. Burdens imposed on others, or diverted to future generations, generate worries about exploitation. Alternatively, risks concentrated in time and space might be regarded as inequitable or otherwise unacceptable because concentration can result in losses that are avoided by broader distributions. This suggests, then, a link between inequitable distributions and catastrophic potential. Concentrated risks can threaten whole communities, and the loss of a community (think of Love Canal, of Chernobyl) is the loss of a valued thing distinct and apart from the disaggregated bodies of a community's citizens.

Imagine, for instance, a decision maker who is forced to choose between two actions. The first action poses a 1 in 1000 chance of causing 100,000 deaths spread randomly across the country; the second has a 1 in 1200 chance of causing the near obliteration of a city of 100,000. A rational decision maker could obviously select the first alternative, notwithstanding its larger expected loss. Either action could cause physical injuries, the end of families, grief among survivors. Only the second, though, would provoke the "collective trauma" of disasters that wipe out neighborhoods and entire networks of relationships—losses that cannot be measured merely in terms of lives and property destroyed. The possibility of catastrophe, then, is clearly material to choices among risks. Aversion to catastrophic losses is also consistent with the commonplace observation that people are regularly willing to pay a premium in order to soften the blow of very costly (but very unlikely) events.

* * *

V. RISK, TECHNOCRACY, AND DEMOCRACY

* * *

Even supposing agencies could be much better than they are at what they do, we have

---

[144] M. Sagoff, [Technological Risk: A Budget of Distinctions (1986) (unpublished manuscript)], at 15. * * *

suggested how they might nevertheless be good at the wrong thing, resulting in more public risk than the public, for its own sound reasons, wants. This recalls the debate about attitudes and the question of what risk means. Until that question is resolved, much of the ongoing debate about how to control public risk is emphatically off the point. No one can talk sensibly about whether judicial control yields too little public risk, or administrative control too much, without knowing how risk itself is to be conceived. One conception might suggest one set of reforms, and the other another. If, for example, risk is to be measured by body counts, then agencies seem to have an advantage. But if risk means what the public would have it mean, then agencies look to be remarkably limited and courts much less so. The courts are, after all, criticized in part precisely because they accommodate the public's attitudes. A purported liability of judges and juries—that they are not experts—turns out to be an asset.

Without an understanding of what risk is to mean, we cannot begin to answer the institutional questions that lie atop that basic attitudinal puzzle. Yet even were the puzzle solved, and in favor of the expert view, and even were we to concede all the alleged advantages of expert control, still it might not follow that expertise provides the best route to safety, because expert control can give rise to special dangers.

B. The Political Risks of Technocracy

In *Ecology and the Politics of Scarcity*, the political theorist William Ophuls draws a dark picture of a future that is to be avoided, if at all, only by the exercise of extraordinary restraint. Briefly, he argues that population growth, dwindling supplies of energy and other resources, and increasing amounts of pollution promise an end to the abundance that nourished political liberalism over the last several centuries. No longer can technological advance be expected to provide the easy solutions we have learned to take for granted; if anything, technology aggravates the problem of ecological scarcity.

This image, a familiar neo-Malthusian one, differs remarkably from that found in a work like Peter Huber's *Safety and the Second Best*, making it all the more troubling that Huber and Ophuls end up at the same place when it comes to the question of control. Each would rely on management by experts. According to Huber:

> Regulatory agencies are equipped to make the risk comparisons on which all progressive transformation of the risk environment must be based. The courts are simply not qualified to second-guess such decisions; when they choose to do so they routinely make regressive risk choices. Requiring—or at least strongly encouraging—the courts to respect the comparative risk choices made by competent, expert agencies would inject a first, small measure of rationality into a judicial regulatory system that currently runs quite wild.[241]

As for Ophuls, "the mounting complexity of technology along with the staggering problems of managing the response to ecological scarcity . . . will require us to depend on a special class of experts in charge of our survival and well-being—a 'priesthood of responsible technologists.'"[242] To be sure, the critical management decisions will be

[241] Huber, *supra* note 3, at 335.
[242] W. Ophuls, [ECOLOGY AND THE POLITICS OF SCARCITY (1977)], at 159.

"'trans-scientific' in that they can only be made politically by prudent men, [but] at least the basic scientific elements of the problems must be understood reasonably well before an informed political decision is possible."[243] Such decisions, hence, will be beyond the capacity of the average citizen, who lacks the time, the knowledge, and perhaps even the intelligence "to grasp the issues, much less the important features of the problems."[244] The decisions will also be beyond the gifts of ordinary politicians. "If we grant that the people in their majority probably will not understand and are therefore not competent to decide such issues, is it very likely that the political leaders they select will themselves be competent enough to deal with these issues?"[245] Seeing the answer to be no, Ophuls turns to Plato for instruction. "Plato argued that the polity was like a ship sailing dangerous waters. It therefore needed to be commanded by the most competent pilots . . . , an elite class of guardians."[246] Ophuls concludes that "[t]he emerging large, highly-developed, complex technological civilization operating at or very near the ecological margin appears to fit Plato's premises more and more closely, foreshadowing the necessity of rule by a class of Platonic guardians, the 'priesthood of responsible technologists' . . . ."[247]

While Huber and Ophuls seem to be in remarkable agreement, there is nevertheless an important difference between the two. Only Ophuls acknowledges the "profound political issues"[248] raised by what he foresees. Society "will not only be more authoritarian and less democratic than the industrial societies of today . . . but it will also in all likelihood be much more oligarchic as well, with only those possessing the ecological and other competence necessary to make prudent decisions allowed full participation in the political process."[249] In a line, "democracy as we know it cannot conceivably survive."[250]

As it happens, Ophuls' account contains the seeds of its own destruction, for scattered throughout the pages of his book are convincing illustrations of the limits of technocracy. Robert Dahl has recently pursued exactly this point in exactly Ophuls' terms in order to remind us that reality cannot deliver on the Platonic Ideal. Guardians possessed of the necessary instrumental knowledge and moral virtue simply do not exist.[251]

Suppose, however, that they did. Might the case for technocratic control of public risk nevertheless fail even as (and because) it succeeds? By definition, technocratic management would seem to foreclose much meaningful participation by the public, yet the public's sense of alienation is at the core of the public risk problem. Recall that "dread" is a term of art for the public's sentiments about modern risks, and dread—as we saw—is itself a catchall for concerns about a lack of control. Given this, the program should be not to alienate but to include the public. Let *it* decide what *it* shall expose *itself* to, make *it* familiar with the exotic, give *it* control.

A growing body of literature advances just this view. Its authors argue that the appro-

---

[243] *Id.* at 159-60.
[244] *Id.* at 160.
[245] *Id.*
[246] *Id.*
[247] *Id.*
[248] *Id.* at 161.
[249] *Id.* at 163.
[250] *Id.* at 152.
[251] *See* R. Dahl, [CONTROLLING NUCLEAR WEAPONS, DEMOCRACY VERSUS GUARDIANSHIP (1985)], at 19-51.

priate response to public risk is to democratize the management process, specifically by increasing public participation. Because risk presents intractable problems and tradeoffs, those placed at risk should have a role in deciding which games are worth what candles. Just as participation in general is a means by which individuals can exercise control over their political circumstances and reduce their sense of civic isolation, so participation in the management of risk can reduce the sense of helplessness that arises from involuntary exposure to hazards.

The idea behind participation, then, is not necessarily to improve the technical accuracy of risk decisions, but rather to enhance the legitimacy of the decision making process. Given the stakes in questions of public risk, it is easy to see why the public should have an intimate role. And given that accuracy could actually be served by a public presence—because responsible risk assessment and management, however conceived, must depend to some degree on what the public knows, values, and prefers—public participation seems only the more appropriate.

C. The Environmental Risks of Democracy

The difficulty is that direct democratic participation poses special problems in the case of public risk. One of the most challenging items on the agenda of future debates will be to consider whether, and how, we can nourish a fragile political system while simultaneously protecting a vulnerable environmental one.

* * *

But a far deeper problem, we think, arises from the fact that truly effective participation probably requires a considerable degree of decentralized decision making and locally accessible decision forums. Public risk sources, however, typically call for highly centralized management. Their extraordinary power generates costs and benefits, and effects and side effects, that commonly reach beyond even the largest community and in some cases wrap around the globe. Given this, the idea of local control seems unacceptable. Decisions made in any one locality are likely to consider only parochial interests, resulting on some occasions in too little public risk, and on other occasions too much. Proceeding in an uncoordinated fashion, some communities will protect their own backyards and leave no place for risky but, from a larger perspective, beneficial developments. Other communities will find ways to realize the benefits of development while exporting its costs to neighbors (an example would be polluting factories using tall smoke stacks). Still others will simply accept risks that their neighbors wish to avoid, but in the nature of things cannot (a decision by one locality to accept a toxic waste dump essentially negates the decision of a neighboring community to reject the same project).

Finally, those who propose increased democratization of risk management will have to confront the fact of democracy's historic reliance on trial and error as a means of resolving uncertainty in the course of making policy. The tendency to muddle through, as Charles Lindblom called it in a well-known essay,[264] is a commonplace to close

---

[264] *See* Lindblom, *The Science of Muddling Through*, 19 Pub. Admin. Rev. 79 (1959); *see also* Lindblom, *Still Muddling, Not Yet Through*, 39 Pub. Admin. Rev. 517 (1979) (supporting incrementalism because neither revolution nor drastic policy change, nor even planned large steps, are ordinarily possible).

observers of American politics. A chief virtue of the method, which relies on trial-and-error to promote incremental learning, is its capacity to resolve uncertainty simply by the simple act of acting, even if the action is mistaken. In the case of public risks, however, muddling is also fraught with vices. The reactive technique of trial-and-error is useful only to the extent that information generated by one (successful or unsuccessful) experiment can be considered and exploited in a subsequent one. But with many public risks, the potential to learn from error is simultaneously the potential to bring about catastrophic consequences. Errors might in any event be of little educational value, thanks to latency. Latency means that what we learn, we learn late. This promotes irreversibility and limits opportunities to correct mistakes through a relatively quick series of many trials.

There are reasons, then, to avoid a participatory, incremental, trial-and-error method of muddling in favor of holistic, systematic, "synoptic" methods of expert comprehensive analysis (perfectly represented by quantitative risk assessment). These are said to be preferable when "small errors in policy can cause irreversible or even catastrophic harm."[267] Unfortunately, however, the synoptic methodology is itself troublesome, on a number of grounds. First is the widely accepted opinion that it depends on "firmness of data and consensus on goals"[268]—things hard to come by in the case of public risks. Second is the problem of latency, which might well affect even the incentives of expert analysts. Consider, for example, the mundane point that weather forecasters are regarded by careful students of such matters as being among the very best and most reliable of prognosticators. There are, no doubt, technical and technological reasons for this, such as regular advances in meteorology and the development of orbiting satellites, but there is also the intriguing fact that weather prediction is performed in such an elegant system of almost instantaneous meaningful feedback. Bad weather-folk simply don't survive. In the case of bad public risk assessors, though, latency frustrates the forces of natural selection that might otherwise help eliminate poor assessors and managers. By the time their errors are discovered, they are likely to be out of office, perhaps even deceased, making it difficult (or impossible) to hold them accountable. The absence of long-term accountability could result in shirking, laxity, and an unwarranted focus on the short term. Third is the apparent fact that synoptic decision making can itself lead to calamity, suggesting perhaps that the sheer intractability of public risk makes muddling through the lesser of two evils. Robert Dahl seems to reach this conclusion. He argues against expertise despite the dangers of bad guesses by ordinary people, comforting himself with the notion that "the opportunity to make mistakes is the opportunity to learn."[270] In the same vein, Ida Hoos, a staunch critic of systems methodology, reckons that "[m]uddling through is probably safer in the long run than the wrong cure."[271]

From the standpoint of democratic participation in risk management, a dilemma arises if views like these are rejected—if incrementalism, after close examination, is revealed as the obvious thing not to do. Active participation appears to go hand in hand with incremental decision making, suggesting that the two must stand or fall together. Muddling

---

[267] *See* Diver, [*Policy Making Paradigms in Administrative Law*, 95 HARV. L. REV. 393 (1981)] at 431.

[268] Lowi, *Deconstructing American Law* (Book Review), 63 TEX. L. REV. 1591, 1596 (1985).

[270] R. Dahl, [CONTOLLING NUCLEAR WEAPONS: DEMOCRACY VERSUS GUARDIANSHIP (1985)] at 51.

[271] I. Hoos, [SYSTEMS ANALYSIS IN PUBLIC POLICY: A CRITIQUE (rev. ed. 1983)], at 246.

through has allowed even the uninformed to play a role and learn by doing. The method is said to be "basically democratic."[272] Now, though, it might also prove catastrophic, something to be borne heavily in mind by those who argue for a greater public role in the management of modern technology.

* * *

The challenge of public risk is to devise solutions as powerful as the problems they confront, problems that courts and agencies were hardly designed to solve. We need to imagine institutional breakthroughs that match our technological ones, and we may need a new politics to replace the old. Tolerant, open-minded, penetrating argument is an excellent pathway to imagination. In these respects, though, the current debate about public risk falls short.

* * *

NOTES

1. In a portion of the article not excerpted, Gillette and Krier argue that the judicial process discourages people who are hurt by public risk from bringing their claims before courts. There is an enormous body of literature on the rules courts apply to common law claims for recovery from increased risk of cancer or other environmental harms. *See, e.g.,* GERALD W. BOSTON & M. STUART MADDEN, LAW OF ENVIRONMENTAL AND TOXIC TORTS (1994); Troyen A. Brennan, *Environmental Torts*, 46 VAND. L. REV. 1 (1993); Daniel Farber, *Toxic Causation,* 71 MINN. L. REV. 1219 (1987); Neil R. Komesar, *Injuries and Institutions: Tort Reform, Tort Theory, and Beyond*, 65 N.Y.U. L. REV. 23 (1990); Susan R. Poulter, *Science and Toxic Torts: Is There a Rational Solution to the Problem of Causation?,* 7 HIGH TECH. L.J. 189 (1993); David Rosenberg, *The Causal Connection in Mass Exposure Cases: A "Public Law" Vision of the Tort System*, 97 HARV. L. REV. 849 (1984). These works tend to confirm and expand on the hurdles for potential plaintiffs exposed to some environmental risk to secure relief in the courts. The Farber article is excerpted and discussed in detail in Chapter Two of this anthology.

2. Courts play an important role not only in common law disputes but also in reviewing agency action. The late Judge David Bazelon, who handled many cases involving review of environmental, health, and safety regulations while on the D.C. Circuit, distinguished between agency risk-taking (for which courts should grant wide discretion) and risk-disclosure (which courts should scrutinize carefully):

> With life and health at stake, there is need for a court to scrutinize agency proceedings with extreme care, despite—or because of—its limited technical

---

[272] *See* W. OPHULS, [supra note 242], 191-93. * * *

competence. To survive the court's searching scrutiny, an agency must provide adequate notice and an opportunity for objections. It should consider and address those objections, making clear what it accepts, what it rejects, and, most importantly, why. To facilitate the court's review, the agency record should disclose the full and precise basis of its decision. The agency should include its evidence, its methodology, and the assumptions that underlie its empirical inferences * * *. Finally, I would especially stress the need for an agency to disclose the uncertainty that surrounds its determinations. And by uncertainty, I mean the agency's ignorance as well as its quantitative estimates of error.

Full disclosure will undoubtedly improve the quality of information by exposing weaknesses to peer review, legislative oversight and public scrutiny. But society also requires disclosure for the same reason—or the same democratic faith—that underlies informed consent for medical procedures and warning labels for drugs and other products. Absolute safety is impossible, and benefits usually entail risks. But the electorate must have an opportunity for the final say about which risks it will bear and which benefits it will seek. * * * Experts who are beyond reach and beyond view must never be allowed to arrogate those decisions to themselves.

Bazelon, *Science and Uncertainty: A Jurist's View*, 5 HARV. ENVTL. L. REV. 209, 212 (1981). Judge Bazelon first expressed his views on the changing role of judicial review of agency action that deals with environmental risks in *Environmental Defense Fund v. Ruckelshaus*, 439 F.2d 584 (D.C. Cir. 1971) and *International Harvester v. Ruckelshaus*, 478 F.2d 615, 650-52 (D.C. Cir. 1973). The U.S. Supreme Court, however, has limited the ability of the judiciary to impose special procedural requirements aimed at improving disclosure of risk. *See Vermont Yankee Nuclear Power Corp. v. Natural Resources Defense Council*, 435 U.S. 519 (1978) (criticizing and reversing a Bazelon opinion requiring the Nuclear Regulatory Commission to employ procedures "sufficient to ventilate the issues" surrounding nuclear fuel reprocessing and disposal). Is Judge Bazelon's view consistent with the "substantial compliance" standard of judicial review of risk assessments proposed in H.R. 9, 104th Cong., 1st Sess. (1995) (§ 441)? Note that exacting judicial review does not always militate in favor of greater risk reduction. Compare *Environmental Defense Fund v. Ruckelshaus* with *Leather Industries of America v. EPA*, 40 F.3d 392 (D.C. Cir. 1994) and *Corrosion Proof Fittings v. EPA*, 947 F.2d 1201 (5th Cir. 1991). *See also* Note 3 following the Rosenthal, Gray, and Graham excerpt in this Chapter.

Does more exacting judicial scrutiny of agency disclosure mitigate some of the dangers of "technocracy"? Can or should courts review the substance (risk-taking) as well as the procedure (risk-disclosure) of agency decisionmaking?

3. Gillette and Krier express skepticism about the ability of agencies to balance fairly diffuse, remote, dispersed, nonexclusive benefits against concentrated costs. What safeguards or counterweights might correct agency bias? What management solutions are we left with if we accept the view that both courts and agencies are systematically biased against public risk reduction?

4. Why is loss of an entire community worse than more widely distributed risks? Is the loss any more than the aggregate of individuals harmed or killed? Does public perception of risk (particularly dread) indicate real concerns not accommodated by quantitative risk assessment, or does it indicate an emotional response uninformed by careful, rational reflection?

5. Concern about inequitable distribution of environmental risks has risen since the publication of the Gillette and Krier article. Public risks are borne disproportionately by low income groups and minorities, and the "environmental justice" movement has coalesced to respond to this disparity. Chapter One of this anthology excerpts and discusses the article by Richard Lazarus, *Pursuing "Environmental Justice": The Distributional Effects of Environmental Protection*, 78 Nw. U. L. Rev. 787 (1993).

6. If quantitative risk assessment measures only a single component of a multi-dimensional concern of the public, then how well could Breyer's "super agency" manage environmental policy? If Breyer's reforms are improvements over the current regulatory structure, might they be worth making even if they adopt the narrow view of risk? Does Gillette and Krier's description of risk support Ruckelshaus' proposals for greater public participation in agency decisionmaking? Is decentralization of decisionmaking possible in the modern economy? Is environmental regulation inherently elitist?

Six
International Issues

The complexity of the policy and technical issues that characterize the domestic environmental scene pale in comparison with the challenges facing international environmental lawmaking. In addition to the myriad of domestic concerns—including scientific uncertainty, tension between economic and environmental interests, and differing institutional perspectives—international lawmaking also raises sensitive issues of national sovereignty, enforceability, and diplomacy that substantially complicate the task of identifying and attempting to resolve environmental problems of international and global scope. In addition, threats to the environmental integrity of the planet—such as global warming, stratospheric ozone depletion, and loss of biodiversity—are of potentially greater magnitude than more local (i.e., national) environmental concerns. In short, the risks posed by international environmental threats are potentially more serious, yet far more difficult to manage, than are domestic environmental threats.

The articles in this chapter approach these challenges from three different angles. In the first article, Professor Edith Brown Weiss traces the development of international environmental law and highlights the changes in design and content of international agreements. Recent international efforts seek to deal more effectively with ongoing scientific developments, with global-scale environmental problems, and with the increased role of nonparties and nongovernmental organizations. In the second article, Professor Thomas Schoenbaum analyzes the international trade regime, particularly the General Agreement on Tariffs and Trade (GATT), and its impact on environmental protection measures. In the concluding article, Professor David Wirth addresses the interplay between international and domestic (United States) lawmaking, and suggests that Congress's role in domestic lawmaking has been subordinated in the development of international agreements.

For a more comprehensive analysis of international environmental issues, see ANTHONY D'AMATO AND KIRSTEN ENGEL, INTERNATIONAL ENVIRONMENTAL LAW ANTHOLOGY (1996).

The opening article provides an overview of the development of international environmental law, particularly during the past quarter-century. In addition to being a leading scholar in this field, Professor Edith Brown Weiss served as the EPA's Associate General Counsel for International Affairs during 1990-1992.

INTERNATIONAL ENVIRONMENTAL LAW: CONTEMPORARY ISSUES AND THE EMERGENCE OF A NEW WORLD ORDER
Edith Brown Weiss
81 Geo. L. J. 675 (1993)*

In 1972 international environmental law was a fledgling field with less than three dozen multilateral agreements. Today international environmental law is arguably setting the pace for cooperation in the international community in the development of international law. There are nearly nine hundred international legal instruments that are either primarily directed to international environmental issues or contain important provisions on them. This proliferation of legal instruments is likely to continue. Therefore, it is important to assess what we have done and explore where we are headed.

I. THE HISTORY OF INTERNATIONAL ENVIRONMENTAL LAW

A. Prior to 1950

Before 1900 there were few multilateral or bilateral agreements concerning international environmental issues. Relevant international agreements were based on unrestrained national sovereignty over natural resources and focused primarily on boundary waters, navigation, and fishing rights along shared waterways, particularly the Rhine River and other European waterways. They did not address pollution or other ecological issues. The dramatic exception to this pattern emerged in 1909 in the United States-United Kingdom Boundary Waters Treaty, which provided in Article IV that water "shall not be polluted on either side to the injury of health or property on the other."

In the early 1900s, countries began to conclude agreements to protect commercially valuable species. * * * Only one convention focused on wildlife more generally: the 1900 London Convention for the Protection of Wild Animals, Birds and Fish in Africa.

By the 1930s and 1940s, states recognized the importance of conserving natural resources and negotiated several agreements to protect fauna and flora generally. * * * During this period, states also concluded the well known International Convention for the Regulation of Whaling, as well as other conventions concerned with ocean fisheries and birds.

In the first half of this century there was little development and application of customary international norms to environmental issues. The classic Trail Smelter Arbitration between Canada and the United States,[14] which affirmed Canada's responsibility for the damage from copper smelter fumes that transgressed the border into the state of Washington, was the notable exception. The language of the Arbitral Tribunal has been cited widely as confirming the principle that a state is responsible for environmental damage to foreign countries caused by activities within its borders, even though in this case Canada's liability for the damage was determined in the compromise establishing the Tribunal. One of the

---

* Reprinted with the permission of the publisher, copyright 1993, Georgetown University.

[14] Trail Smelter Arbitration (U.S. v. Can.), 3 R.I.A.A. 1911, 1933 (1938) (granting damages for agricultural and timber losses); 3 R.I.A.A. 1938, 1966 (1941) (establishing environmental controls to eliminate future injurious emissions). * * *

most important aspects of the Arbitration is the Tribunal's decision that if there is a threat of serious continuing harm, the state must cease the harmful conduct (which implies that damages would not be sufficient). The Tribunal required the parties to effectuate a monitoring regime to ensure that further damaging pollution did not occur. Because the Trail Smelter Arbitration is a rare example of international environmental adjudication in this early period, it has acquired an unusually important place in the jurisprudence of international environmental law.

B. 1950-1972

During the 1950s and early 1960s, the international community was concerned with nuclear damage from civilian use (a by-product of the Atoms for Peace Proposal) and marine pollution from oil. Thus, countries negotiated agreements governing international liability for nuclear damage and required measures to prevent oil pollution at sea.

In the 1960s, environmental issues began to emerge within countries. Rachel Carson published her famous book *Silent Spring*, and comparable books were published in European countries. * * *

Internationally, during the 1960s, multilateral international environmental agreements increased significantly. Conventions were negotiated relating to interventions in case of oil pollution casualties, to civil liability for oil pollution damage, and to oil pollution control in the North Sea. The African Convention on the Conservation of Nature and Natural Resources was concluded in 1968.

C. 1972 and Beyond: The Modern Era of International Environmental Law

Modern international environmental law dates to approximately 1972 when countries gathered for the United Nations Stockholm Conference on the Human Environment, and the United Nations Environment Programme (UNEP) was established. Many important legal developments took place in the period surrounding the Conference, including negotiation of the Convention on International Trade in Endangered Species, the London Ocean Dumping Convention, the World Heritage Convention, and the first of the UNEP regional seas conventions. Since then, there has been a rapid rise in international legal instruments concerned with the environment, to the point that we are concerned today with developing new means for coordinating the negotiation and implementation of related agreements, in particular their administrative, monitoring, and financial provisions.

Since 1970, hundreds of international environmental instruments have been concluded. Including bilateral and multilateral instruments (binding and nonbinding), there are close to nine hundred international legal instruments that have one or more significant provisions addressing the environment. Within the last two years alone, there have been about a dozen highly important multilateral negotiations occurring more or less in parallel.

D. Historical Developments: The Changing Themes and Focus of International Environmental Law Agreements

The subject matter of international environmental agreements now bears little resemblance to that in agreements concluded in the first half of this century, which focused on boundary rivers, fishing rights, and protection of particularly valued animal species. Today there are agreements to control pollution in all environmental media, conserve habitats, protect global commons, such as the high-level ozone layer, and protect resources located within countries that are of concern to the international community. Moreover, the U.N. Conference on Environment and Development held last June in Rio de Janeiro, Brazil, suggests that we are entering a new phase in international environmental law in which environmental and economic issues will be joined.

The scope of international agreements has expanded significantly since 1972: from transboundary pollution agreements to global pollution agreements; from control of direct emissions into lakes to comprehensive river basin system regimes; from preservation of certain species to conservation of ecosystems; from agreements that take effect only at national borders to ones that restrain resource use and control activities within national borders, such as for world heritages, wetlands, and biologically diverse areas. The duties of the parties to these agreements have also become more comprehensive: from undertaking research and monitoring to preventing pollution and reducing certain pollutants to specified levels. Notably, there is no example in which the provisions of earlier conventions have been weakened; rather, they have been strengthened or their scope has been expanded.

The international community is increasingly aware that it is important not only to monitor and research environmental risks, but also to reduce them. Thus states have moved from international agreements that mainly address research, information exchange, and monitoring to agreements that require reductions in pollutant emissions and changes in control technology. The Protocol on Sulphur Dioxide to the United Nations Economic Commission for Europe (U.N.-ECE) Convention on Long-Range Transboundary Air Pollution calls for a thirty percent reduction in national annual sulphur emissions or their transboundary fluxes by 1993, and the Montreal Protocol on Substances That Deplete the Ozone Layer, including the 1990 Adjustments and Amendments, requires that chlorofluoro-carbons and halons, except for essential uses, be phased out by the year 2000. This emphasis on preventing pollution is likely to continue as we appreciate that the capacity of our environment to absorb the byproducts of production and consumption is limited.

The last seven years, from 1985 to 1992, illustrate the increasingly rapid development of international environmental law. During this period, countries have negotiated a surprisingly large number of global agreements. These include the Vienna Convention on the Protection of the Ozone Layer; the Montreal Protocol on Substances that Deplete the Ozone Layer with the London Adjustments and Amendments; the Protocol on Environmental Protection (with annexes) to the Antarctic Treaty; the Basel Convention on the Transboundary Movements of Hazardous Wastes and Their Disposal; the two International Atomic Energy Agency (IAEA) Conventions on Early Notification of a Nuclear Accident and on Assistance in the Case of a Nuclear Accident or Radiological Emergency; the International Convention on Oil Pollution Preparedness, Response and Co-operation; the Framework Convention on Climate Change; the Convention on Biological Diversity; the principles on forests; the non-binding legal instrument of the Arctic Environmental Protection Strategy; and the London Guidelines for the Exchange of Information on Chemicals in International Trade.

Developments at the regional level have proceeded at a similar rate. Member states of the United Nations Economic Commission for Europe have negotiated three protocols to the U.N.-ECE Convention on Long-Range Transboundary Air Pollution: a protocol providing for a thirty percent reduction in transborder fluxes of sulphur dioxides, a protocol freezing the emissions of nitrogen oxides, and a protocol controlling emissions of volatile organic chemicals. These countries have also concluded agreements on environmental impact assessment, transnational industrial accidents, and transboundary fresh waters and lakes.

* * *

At the bilateral level, many international environmental legal instruments have been concluded during this period. In North America, the United States has signed bilateral agreements with Canada and Mexico on the transport of hazardous wastes. An agreement between Mexico and the United States addresses urban air pollution problems in Mexico City. In 1991, Canada and the United States concluded an agreement to control acid precipitation. In Latin America, Brazil and Argentina concluded an agreement that provides for consultation in case of nuclear accidents in either country.

Most of these agreements were considered impossible ten years ago; some were thought impossible only months before they were concluded. The provisions in the new agreements are generally more stringent and detailed than in previous ones, the range of subject matter broader, and the provisions for implementation and adjustment more sophisticated. This history is encouraging because it suggests that the international community's learning curve as reflected in international environmental law is surprisingly steep. This should give us hope that we may be able, with some success, to address the immense challenges of global environmental change and to meet the urgent need for environmentally sustainable development.

II. THE LESSONS LEARNED

In reviewing the past forty years in international environmental law, it is apparent that countries have learned much about both the process of negotiating international environmental agreements and the desirable substantive content of the agreements.

* * *

A. Skill and Rapidity in Negotiating International Agreements

Contrary to popular myth, the international community has become very skilled at negotiating international agreements. Countries negotiated nine years (from December 1973 to December 1982) to conclude the Law of the Sea Convention, which admittedly was a herculean effort to conclude a comprehensive, detailed, and definitive agreement, which would in part codify the rules relating to the various uses of the oceans. By contrast, countries today are negotiating complicated agreements in only a few years, often developing entirely new areas of law. Countries negotiated the complex Climate Framework Convention in fifteen months (from February 1991 to May 1992). Negotiations for the Environmental Protocol to the Antarctic Treaty (which includes four detailed annexes) and for the Biological Diversity Convention required less than two years, as did the complex agreements on industrial accidents and volatile organic chemicals under the auspices of the U.N.-ECE. It is now rare for countries to need more than two years to negotiate even complicated, detailed international agreements. Agenda 21, a nonbinding instrument, offers perhaps the most striking evidence of the skill of the international community in achieving these ends. In less than two years, countries negotiated an approximately 850 page text setting forth strategies for the multiple and complex issues raised by environment and development. Thus, countries have evolved a negotiating process in the international environmental field that leads to rapid conclusion of agreements.

B. Changes in Design and Content of Agreements

International agreements have become increasingly detailed and operational. * * * The early U.N.-ECE Protocol on Sulphur Dioxide to the U.N.-ECE Long-Range Transboundary Air Pollution Convention sets forth a general obligation to reduce transboundary fluxes by thirty percent, while the new Protocol on Volatile Organic Chemicals provides far more detailed and specific reduction requirements. Similarly, very detailed obligations appear in the Montreal Protocol on Substances That Deplete the Ozone Layer and in the Basel Convention, which controls the transboundary shipment of hazardous wastes, both concluded in the last five years.

The design of agreements has also evolved. In contrast to the traditional practice of negotiating a single agreement for an issue, such as use of boundary waters, or negotiating comprehensively all of the issues in an international environmental matter, countries experimented in the first UNEP Regional Seas Convention in 1976 with adopting a framework convention complemented by at least one accompanying comprehensive proto-col. This approach has been followed in all subsequent UNEP regional seas conventions. This more open-ended framework allowed countries to begin to take coordinated actions to conserve regional seas but avoided premature negotiations on more complicated issues in the region. This piecemeal negotiation strategy was adopted by the countries of the U.N.-ECE in 1979 when they concluded the Convention on Long-Range Transboundary Air Pollution, which set forth a general framework for monitoring and exchanging informa-tion on air pollution in the region. This was followed by protocols among the U.N.-ECE countries establishing a monitoring system and controlling emissions of certain chemicals. Countries adopted a similar negotiating process to address the problem of global ozone depletion: first the Vienna Convention for the Protection of the Ozone Layer, which set forth a general framework for monitoring, exchanging information, and facilitating scientific research, followed by a more detailed Montreal Protocol setting forth a complex regime for controlling chemical depletion of the ozone layer.

* * *

C. Adjustments to Changes in Scientific Understanding

Scientific uncertainty is inherent in all international environmental law. We do not have a full understanding of the natural system or of our interactions with it. Our scientific understanding is always changing, as is our technological knowledge and know-how. Consequently, those who draft international agreements have had to design instruments and implementation mechanisms that have sufficient flexibility in order to allow parties to adapt to changes in our scientific understanding and technological abilities.

Early agreements had no special processes for adjusting to changes in the scientific understanding of the problem. Even if there were schedules attached to the agreements, they could be amended only by the traditional process of establishing a negotiating forum, agreeing upon the changes, adopting them, and then obtaining the number of ratifications required by the treaty for them to enter into force. This traditional procedure has proved to be too cumbersome to address rapid scientific advances. Later agreements have eased the process by providing for periodic meeting of the parties, for the formulation of technical changes by experts or international secretariats subject to confirmation by the parties, and entry into force by agreement of the parties without ratification. For example, the Montreal Protocol on Substances that Deplete the Ozone Layer provides for parties to meet at regular intervals to respond to new scientific findings, for regular technical assessments to be made available to parties before a meeting, and for simplified adjustment procedures by which parties can agree to reduce consumption of listed chemicals faster and further than provided in the text without having to use formal and time consuming amendment procedures.

In an effort to promote flexibility the new Climate Framework Convention provides for a standing body to provide scientific and technological advice on a timely basis. This body will provide scientific assessments of climate change and its effects, and the impact of implementing measures under the Convention. It will also identify relevant new technologies, assist in building local capacity for scientific research and assessment, and respond to scientific inquiries of the parties. * * *

* * *

D. A Systems Focus

As our understanding of the environment has grown, we have recognized that agreements need to be directed to conserving ecological systems, not only to controlling specific pollutants or conserving particular species. This insight has been increasingly reflected in international instruments.

For example, the ASEAN Convention on the Conservation of Resources addresses the conservation of ecosystems and habitats as a central means of conserving endangered species. The new Biological Diversity Convention focuses on the conservation of ecosystems and habitats in full recognition that many of the species that should be conserved are microorganisms or other species about which we know little or nothing. The 1978 Great Lakes Water Quality Agreement modified language in the 1972 Agreement to include reference to basin-wide ecosystems in the Great Lakes. The 1987 Protocol to the Agreement includes annexes that explicitly address ground water pollution and atmospheric transport of pollutants as sources of Great Lakes contamination. The change reflects the recognition that what feeds into lakes through the air and ground water is as relevant as direct discharges into the lake in determining its quality. * * *

E. Attention to Nonparties

Because the global environmental system ignores political boundaries, it is important for countries that have an impact on the global environment not to remain outside the convention system and defeat the purposes of the agreement. * * *

Traditionally, multilateral agreements usually did not include explicit incentives to join an agreement, although there may have been outside pressures to join. In the environmental agreements reached in the last two decades, in contrast, states have increasingly offered incentives in the agreement in the form of technical assistance or other positive inducements. The Montreal Protocol, the Climate Framework Convention, and the Biological

Diversity Convention provide such incentives as technical assistance, technology transfer, or building national capacity to implement the agreement.

A less common way of providing incentives is the use of negative inducements in the form of a ban on trade in the controlled substances with nonparties. As early as the 1973 Washington Convention on International Trade in Endangered Species of Wild Fauna and Flora (CITES), countries recognized that if agreements were to be effective, they needed to ensure that nonparties did not become havens for circumventing the agreement. The CITES agreement limits trade in the covered species with nonparties. This strategy has recently been revived and strengthened in the environmental agreements directed to controlling transboundary shipments of hazardous waste and to preventing ozone layer depletion, both of which include provisions prohibiting trade with nonparties. The Montreal Protocol provisions are punitive because they prohibit the parties from subtracting exports of controlled substances to nonparties from their national consumption calculations of controlled substances.

Parties to the General Agreement on Tariffs and Trade (GATT) are now considering in the GATT Environment Working Group whether the use of negative inducements by limiting trade is consistent with the GATT. Data on the effectiveness of such a provision in the CITES agreement is scattered and mainly anecdotal, but suggests that the negative inducement trade limitation has had little effect on the behavior of countries. However, because it is easier to monitor trade in ozone depleting chemicals and in hazardous wastes, trade ban provisions relating to these items may prove to be more effective.

Negative inducements in international environmental agreements also address another issue that relates to nonparties: the free-rider problem, in which a state obtains the benefits of the agreement without ever joining and incurring the costs the agreement might impose. For example, a country that declined to join an air pollution agreement or climate convention could receive the benefits of cleaner air or a stabilized climate without incurring the costs of achieving it. Trade prohibitions and positive incentives to join the agreement are also relevant to controlling this phenomenon, and the international community is increasingly recognizing this.

F. Participation of Nongovernmental Organizations

Nongovernmental organizations (NGOs) have assumed an increasingly important role in the negotiation, ratification, implementation, and enforcement of international environmental agreements. They are a primary link between the public and national governments; they let individuals try to influence the international environmental agreement process.

The presence of NGOs at official negotiations of international environmental agreements has become routine. At the Climate Convention negotiations, for example, a wide array of NGOs monitored the negotiations, distributed material, lobbied delegations, and otherwise tried to influence the negotiators. Representatives of NGOs also are appearing on official country delegations, as in the negotiations for the Environmental Protocol to the Antarctic Treaty. In the Climate Convention negotiations, an NGO, the Foundation for International Environmental Law and Development based in London, provided advice to a group of island states and served as members of their delegations.

* * *

The process of interaction among NGOs, governments, and intergovernmental organizations is complicated. NGOs try to influence national governments directly and indirectly by increasing public awareness and public pressures on national legislatures. Governments, on the other hand, use NGOs to convey positions to the public. Ministries or agencies within governments may use NGOs to strengthen their views in relation to other parts of the bureaucracy by keeping them well informed about issues and providing venues for them to express their views to various parts of the bureaucracy. NGOs provide intergovernmental organizations with important, independent communication links with national governments; and NGOs rely on intergovernmental organizations to provide information and insights that are useful in influencing national governments.

* * *

III. A CRITIQUE OF INTERNATIONAL ENVIRONMENTAL LAW TODAY

Given the rapid proliferation of international environmental legal instruments and the emergence of rules of customary international law, it is important to examine these efforts critically using an established framework. Countries are devoting considerable time and financial resources to the negotiation of legal instruments. Are the instruments effective, efficient, and equitable? Are they adequate to the tasks for which they were negotiated? These are the issues addressed below.

A. Effectiveness

Although countries have become skilled in negotiating international agreements, they are still much less skilled at making the agreements operate effectively. Some of the problems of effectiveness arise immediately after the agreement is negotiated. While countries may now be able to negotiate complicated environmental agreements in less than two years, the normal period between the time that negotiations are concluded and the agreements enter into force is likely to be three or more years. This means that it is important to accelerate the process of ratification and provide interim or provisional measures that will enable the parties to further the objectives of the convention even before it comes into effect. * * *

* * *

Sadly we have little data on the successful implementation and overall effectiveness of international environmental agreements. There have been two notable governmental efforts to address this question: the United States Government Accounting Office, which concluded that the agreements they examined were not well monitored for effectiveness,[140] and the intergovernmental report prepared for the United Nations Conference on Environment and Development, which provided a broad overview of agreements and identified several specific problems.[141] * * * Thus, there is an urgent need for further empirical

---

[140] *See generally* U.S. GENERAL ACCOUNTING OFFICE, GAO/RECD 92-43, INTERNATIONAL ENVIRONMENT: INTERNATIONAL AGREEMENTS ARE NOT WELL MONITORED (1992); *see also* U.S. GENERAL ACCOUNTING OFFICE, GAO/RECD 92-188, INTERNATIONAL ENVIRONMENTAL AGREEMENTS (1992).

[141] *Preparatory Comm. for the U.N. Conference on Environment and Development, Survey of Existing Agreements and Instruments and its Follow-up*, U.N. GAOR, 4th Sess., Agenda Item 2, U.N. Doc. A/Conf. 151/PC/WG.III/L.32 (1992) [hereinafter UNCED]. The summary and the background papers have been published in THE EFFECTIVENESS OF INTERNATIONAL ENVIRONMENTAL AGREEMENTS (Peter H. Sand ed., 1992).

research to determine whether, as Professor Louis Henkin has declared for public international law generally, "almost all nations observe almost all principles of international law and almost all of their obligations almost all of the time."[144] * * *

Making agreements effective, specifically at the national and local levels, should be a high priority of the international community; consequently it is important to identify the factors that influence compliance at the national and subnational levels. These factors include: a country's economic and social culture, as well as the structure and operation of its bureaucracy and communication among these bureaucracies; the availability of technical expertise and local technical capacity; ready access to information; the role of nongovernmental organizations; the functions and powers of the secretariat established by the agreement; whether the country participated in the negotiation of the agreement; the influence of other parties to the convention; the incentives in the agreement to encourage compliance; and the provisions for monitoring and reviewing country performance under the agreement. By increasing our understanding of the compliance process and the impact of these factors, we should be able to structure agreements, follow-up measures, and assistance so as to enhance the likelihood of more effective implementation and compliance.

B. Efficiency: The Treaty Congestion Problem

Because the international community will always have limited resources to address difficult issues, it is important that the system of negotiating, monitoring, implementing, and complying with international environmental agreements function relatively efficiently. Ironically, the success that countries have had in negotiating a large number of new international environmental agreements has led to an important and potentially negative side effect: treaty congestion. This affects the international community as a whole, particularly international institutions, as well as individual governments that may want to participate in the negotiation and implementation of agreements but have scarce professional resources.

One of the characteristics of the treaty congestion problem is operational inefficiency. It is not yet clear that we will be able to make the new system of international agreements function efficiently. Moreover, efficient operation is, in part, a function of risk assessment and presently there is no generally accepted system for assessing risks, and even more importantly, none for prioritizing them.

The transaction costs in negotiating international agreements are high. A normal negotiation may require four or five intergovernmental negotiating sessions of one to two weeks each during a period of eighteen months to two years. * * *

Many countries, especially those with limited resources, have complained about the demands these negotiations place on them for staffing and funding in order to participate in the negotiations. While the industrialized countries have provided some assistance to developing countries to participate in certain negotiations, such as the Climate Convention, such assistance has been insufficient to allow many developing countries to participate with fully staffed delegations, or sometimes to participate at all in particular sessions.

---

[144] LOUIS HENKEN, HOW NATIONS BEHAVE 47 (1979).

Moreover, the international community has not developed a systematic process for coordinating the negotiations. As Sir Geoffrey Palmer notes,

> The making and negotiation of the instruments themselves has to start anew each time. No organization commands clear power to coordinate international environmental negotiations. Each negotiation proceeds differently. . . .Such an approach carries the grave risk that on each occasion the wheel must be reinvented. Common elements are not necessarily treated the same way.[152]

The opposite problem also arises from treaty congestion—the tendency to take language from one treaty and transfer it to another because it has already received clearances from home governments, even though a different approach, or different language, might be more appropriate. There is sometimes little attention devoted to examining anew what the best approach or language might be for the special circumstances in the agreement under negotiation.

To induce coordination in the system, Palmer proposes a common institutional home for international environmental agreements.[153] But whether it would necessarily be efficient to have such a centralized arrangement is questionable; it would depend in good part on the efficiency of the structure and the operations in the institutional home. It may be possible to induce greater efficiency into the present system through more effective and widespread use of advances in information technology and other coordination measures.

With such a large number of international agreements, there is great potential for the additional inefficiency of overlapping provisions in agreements, inconsistencies in obligations, significant gaps in coverage, and duplication of goals and responsibilities. * * *

* * *

Treaty congestion has also created significant inefficiencies in implementing international agreements. Normally there are separate secretariats, monitoring processes, meetings of parties, sources of scientific advice and presentation of scientific material, financing mechanisms, technical assistance programs, and dispute resolution procedures for each treaty. At a minimum there is a need for coordination of agreements. * * *

As we look to the future, it is evident that more needs to be done to mitigate the inefficiencies in implementing international agreements. In the provisions for financing implementation of the agreements, industrialized countries favor making the Global Environmental Facility (GEF),[164] located at the World Bank, the funding mechanism for new international environmental agreements, in particular for the climate and biological diversity conventions. This proposal, which would promote efficiency, has encountered strong opposition from developing countries who argue it is inequitable unless the govern-

---

[152] Geoffrey Palmer, *New Ways to Make International Environmental Law*, 86 AM. J. INT'L L. 259, 263 (1992).

[153] *Id.* at 264. * * *

[164] The Global Environmental Facility (GEF) was established to fund projects on global warming, pollution of international waters, destruction of biological diversity, and depletion of the ozone layer. It is a three-year experiment administered by the World Bank that provides grants for investment projects, technical assistance, and to a lesser extent, research to assist developing countries in protecting the global environment and to transfer environmentally safe technologies to them. Countries with per capita income of less than $4000 a year (as of October 1969) are eligible.

* * *

ing structure of the GEF is altered to give them a substantial voice in the Facility. Others are wary of the concentration of power this would bring. This particular conflict highlights the larger equity versus efficiency dilemma, which is both ancient and widespread throughout national and international legal systems. This dilemma will likely arise repeatedly as countries attempt to bring greater efficiency into the current system of implementing international environmental agreements.

Finally, treaty congestion leads to overload at the national level in implementing the international agreements. A country needs sufficient political, administrative, and economic capacity to be able to implement agreements effectively. Today a large number of international environmental institutions, including most pointedly the numerous secretariats servicing international environmental agreements, have some claim on the administrative capacity of national states. Even industrialized states with well-developed regulatory mechanisms and bureaucracies show signs of being overwhelmed. As attention shifts to the importance of implementing and complying with the agreements that have been negotiated, this burden on the administrative capacity of states will become even more acute. Attention must be given to developing local capacity within countries to implement and comply with international environmental agreements effectively and efficiently. New technologies will be useful, but cannot substitute for other capacity-building measures, such as the training of personnel, development of economic resources, and restructuring of institutions for accountability.

C. Equity: The Source of Conflict

Increasingly, notions of equity or fairness are the focus of pointed conflict in the negotiation and implementation of international environmental instruments. For equity to have meaning, it must be defined. The traditional notion of equity that has formed the basis of numerous environmental accords is one of national sovereign rights to exploit resources within a country's jurisdiction or control, combined with rights to shared or common resources (whether for natural resources or for pollution emissions) on a first-come, first-served basis. However, this traditional equity ethic has been deteriorating, and a new ethic is in the process of emerging. The search for a consensus on a new definition of equity is likely to be one of the major factors shaping international environmental accords in the future.

The controversy over the definition of equity lay at the heart of the U.N. Conference on Environment and Development debates. The Rio Declaration on Environment and Development,[167] a nonbinding legal instrument, explicitly reflects this concern with equity. Among other things, the Principles of the Declaration address obligations intended to "decrease the disparities in standards of living and better meet the needs of the majority of the people of the world";[168] provide for priority treatment to "the special situation and needs of developing countries, particularly the least developed and those most environmentally vulnerable";[169] and recognize that "[i]n view of the different contributions to global

---

[167] Rio Declaration [on Environment and Development, June 13, 1992, 31 I.L.M. 874] [hereinafter Rio Declaration].

[168] *Id.* princ. 5, 31 I.L.M. at 877.

[169] *Id.* princ. 6, 31 I.L.M. at 877.

environmental degradation, States have common but differentiated responsibilities."[170] By contrast, twenty years earlier the U.N. Stockholm Declaration on the Human Environment[171] referred only to the need to consider "the systems of values prevailing in each country and the extent of the applicability of standards which are valid for the most advanced countries but which may be inappropriate and of unwarranted social cost for the developing countries,"[172] and, as was also expressed in the Rio Declaration, the need for financial and technical assistance.[173]

In international environmental law, the two issues that have given definition to equity are the allocation of natural resources and the responsibility and liability for pollution. Both have traditionally been based on rights acquired on a first-come, first-served basis, subject to increasing demands for equitable sharing of the burden of conserving natural resources and controlling pollution.

The right of countries to control the exploitation and use of natural resources within their own jurisdiction or control has been repeatedly reaffirmed in international legal instruments. Traditionally states have also claimed the right to exploit resources outside national borders in commonly held areas on the basis of a first-come, first-served ethic in the absence of agreement to the contrary. This method of exploiting resources is reflected in the initial allocations of the geostationary orbit, the radio frequency spectrum, international waterways, fisheries, marine mammals, birds, and ocean mineral resources. Most international agreements have at least implicitly started from this ethical presumption. Countries have then voluntarily agreed to constraints on their operational behavior affecting these shared or common resources. The two notable international agreements that did not begin with this first-come, first-served presumption, but rather started from a notion of shared responsibility for the resources at issue, are the Convention on the Law of the Sea and the Wellington Convention on Antarctic Mineral Resources, both of which resulted in complicated allocation schemes that have never gone into effect. Increasingly, however, areas once considered to be *res nullius* or belonging to no one are treated as part of the "global commons."

The second primary focus of international environmental legal instruments has been on controlling pollution. Again, states have traditionally asserted the right to pollute at self-determined levels. International instruments have limited these rights. In practice this has meant that states that were able to industrialize first, or those that have vast territories, have been able to establish pollution levels quite independently of other countries.

In instances of transborder pollution, states have the responsibility under Principle 21 of the Stockholm Declaration to ensure that "activities within their jurisdiction or control do not cause damage to the environment of other States or of areas beyond the limits of national jurisdiction."[177] But increasingly the effects of pollution are felt on a regional basis, which means that more detailed, regionally-focused control arrangements are needed.

---

[170] *Id.* princ. 7, 31 I.L.M. at 877.

[171] Declaration of the United Nations Conference on the Human Environment, June 16, 1972, 11 I.L.M. 1416 [hereinafter Stockholm Declaration].

[172] *Id.* princ. 23, 11 I.L.M. at 1420.

[173] *Id.* princ. 12, 11 I.L.M. at 1419. * * *

[177] Stockholm Declaration, *supra* note 171, princ. 21, 11 I.L.M. at 1420.

Countries have found it difficult to reach consensus on the base line year for establishing acceptable pollution levels. The problem is that countries that are beginning to industrialize and trying to reach parity with more industrialized countries do not want to be burdened with an early base line year, and those industrialized countries that have already started controlling pollution want to receive appropriate credit in the selection of the base line year. * * *

The equity issues that are most controversial in the international community concern responsibility for the prevention of harm to global resources and liability for their damage. The Rio Declaration addresses these issues in its reference to "common but differentiated responsibilities" arising from "the different contributions to global environmental degradation,"[179] and in its concern with liability issues and the polluter pays approach in internalizing environmental costs.[180]

The controversial issues in defining equity with regard to pollution control are multiple: whether to establish common or differentiated pollution control standards (as in the per capita chemicals consumption base line standard for developing countries in the Montreal Protocol), what flexibility there should be in the time frame for meeting standards (as in the ten year delay permitted for developing countries in meeting Montreal Protocol chemical phase-out requirements), the extent to which countries should be held responsible for activities that contributed to global environmental degradation in the past (for example, liability for effects of ozone depletion on inhabitants of the southern hemisphere), the extent to which a group of countries should be held responsible to particular countries who may suffer harm tomorrow from actions taken globally today (for example, the claims of island countries that industrialized countries establish a trust fund today to cover the costs of the rise of ocean levels due to global warming tomorrow), and the more general question of the responsibility of the present generation to future generations for the care and use of the planet.

In developing a new definition of equity for environmentally sustainable development, several factors and issues must be noted and addressed. First, the global environment knows no political boundaries; its components are spatially and temporally interdependent. This means that no one country or even group of countries has the capability to protect the environment over time by its own isolated efforts. Consequently, there is an incentive for all countries to reach consensus on an equitable and effective basis for allocating responsibility for maintaining the planet.

Second, developing countries have control over resources that are important to the industrialized world, just as the industrialized world has always had control over resources needed by the developing world. The debates during the Biological Diversity Convention reflect this fact; the developing countries realized that the best reserves of biological diversity lie within their boundaries. In some ways this gave them bargaining power in the negotiations.

Third, developing countries are likely to suffer most from environmental degradation. This is both because poverty is a primary source of environmental degradation and because

---

[179] Rio Declaration, *supra* note [167], princ. 7, 31 I.L.M. at 877. * * *
[180] Rio Declaration, *supra* note [167], princs. 13 & 16, 31 I.L.M. at 878-79. * * *

when rapid, human-induced global environmental change occurs, these countries have the least capacity to adapt.

Finally, future generations are, in my view, becoming a party to debates about equity. Sustainable development is inherently intergenerational, as are the agreements we negotiate. Yet future generations' interests have not been identified and adequately represented in the negotiations, the implementing measures, or in the compliance mechanisms of international environmental agreements. * * * Thus, as we consider the future, it will be important to develop an international consensus on the definition and outlines of the concept of intergenerational equity.

IV. EMERGING DIRECTIONS IN WORLD ENVIRONMENTAL LAW AND ORDER

* * *

A. The Immediate Trends

In the next two decades, the joining of environmental protection and economic development will grow. The burgeoning new field of environment and trade reflects this linkage. While trade law has operated under the relatively unified and broad framework of the General Agreement on Tariffs and Trade for more than forty years, fledgling international environmental law still consists only of many separate and disparate legal instruments. It is not surprising then that most environment and trade issues are discussed almost exclusively within the GATT context. The environment and trade issues move in two directions: environmental protection practices affect trade, and trading practices affect environmental conservation. Thus, it will be important to move to a *modus vivendi* in which environmental and trade concerns are accorded comparable legitimacy, and both are viewed as important elements of sustainable development.

More generally, in the quest for environmentally sustainable development, the focus will likely move to considering environmental concerns at the front end of the industrializing process, so as to prevent pollution, minimize environmental degradation, and use resources more efficiently. * * * If so, international environmental law will reflect this emphasis by focusing on standards and procedures for preventing pollution and minimizing environmental degradation, rather than on liability for damage, and on providing incentives to companies to use environmentally sound processes.

Second, the formulation of nonbinding legal instruments, or "soft law," is likely to increase more rapidly than the negotiation of formal international conventions. This is because when the instrument is nonbinding, agreement is normally easier to achieve, the transaction costs are less, the opportunity for detailed strategies to be set forth are greater, and the ability to respond to rapid changes in our scientific understanding of environment and development issues are more vast.

Third, the growing adoption of new approaches, duties, and procedures in international environmental accords is likely to continue. These include the precautionary principle or approach and the duties to consult with affected states, to prepare an environmental impact assessment before undertaking certain projects, to provide emergency assistance for environmental accidents or disasters, to monitor activities, and to make relevant information available.

Finally, UNCED and the 1992 Rio Declaration may be viewed as legitimizing the importance of public participation in environmental decisionmaking and of public access to relevant information. The international institutional system in which environmental legal instruments are imbedded is likely to continue to become more diverse and to include increasingly larger numbers of nongovernmental organizations of various kinds. * * *

B. The Broader Perspective

The concept of national interest, which has long been used to address foreign policy decisions, is not a very useful construct for analyzing global environmental problems in the long-term. National interest can be defined as national preferences, or the preferences of a country's decisionmakers. On the global scale these interests are often considered in terms of a zero-sum gain. The implicit assumption is that one country's national interest is necessarily opposed to another's. But when addressing global environmental issues the interest is a common one: the overall maintenance of the world's environmental systems. This becomes apparent as we look into the future because no community today can by itself conserve the planet for even its own descendants.

* * *

The international environmental agreements negotiated during the last two decades reflect a commonality of interests. In many international legal instruments, states have agreed to constrain "operational sovereignty," while continuing to retain formal national sovereignty. The conventions on ozone depletion, transboundary shipments of hazardous waste, air pollutants such as nitrogen oxides and volatile organic chemicals, and the Antarctic environment illustrate this constraint. In other agreements, states have arguably strengthened their operational sovereignty by focusing on national plans and actions and dissemination of these documents to other parties to the agreements. The recent Framework Convention on Climate Change and the Convention on Biological Diversity reflect this approach. Nonetheless in these instances, states have set up an international process for monitoring the health of the environment and for providing other benefits to parties. In the climate change convention, the international procedures are sophisticated and far-reaching, and they could lead to substantial international consideration and evaluation of national measures to mitigate climate change. Thus, the international environmental agreements examined in this article point in the same direction—a recognition of the benefits of international cooperation and an increased willingness to agree to obligations directed to protecting the environment.

While countries may share a commonality of interests in maintaining the robustness and integrity of our planet, there are deep differences among them over the equitable allocation of burdens and benefits in doing so. These were vividly displayed at the Rio Conference meeting and are reflected in more recent agreements. Moreover, states do not agree on priorities—whether to satisfy immediate needs to alleviate poverty and local environmental degradation or longer-term needs to protect the robustness and integrity of the biosphere. The clashes extend to communities and groups at the local and transna-tional levels. These clashes could intensify in the next two decades, as countries (and communities) try to reach consensus on what is equitable in the context of environmentally sustainable development. Unless resolved, they could lead to inefficient and ineffective outcomes that are inadequate to the task of conserving our global environment and ensuring sustainable development for future generations.

NOTES

1. Professor Weiss traces the international community's impressive learning curve in identifying matters of common interest and addressing them in an increasingly sophisticated manner. She closes the article in guarded, if not pessimistic, terms concerning the "deep differences" in countries' priorities on equity issues. How might such issues be addressed? How could or should they be resolved within the international community? Is this the ultimate global challenge? Compare the challenge of domestic equity issues raised in Chapter One.

2. Weiss refers to the United Nations Conference on Environment and Development (UNCED), held in Rio de Janeiro in June 1992 (also known as the "Earth Summit"). That historic meeting brought together 30,000 participants from 176 countries. Peter H. Sand, *UNCED and the Development of International Environmental Law*, C795 ALI-ABA 747, 749 (1993). UNCED generated five documents:

a. Two conventions—the UN Framework Convention on Climate Change and the Convention on Biological Diversity—which were developed before the Conference were opened for signature at the Conference;

b. A non-binding declaration of principles for forest management;

c. The Rio Declaration, a statement of 27 principles focusing on sustainable development; and

d. Agenda 21, an action agenda consisting of 40 chapters with 115 specific topics.

ALEXANDRE KISS and DINAH SHELTON, INTERNATIONAL ENVIRONMENTAL LAW 23-29 (Supp. 1994).

3. Twenty years prior to UNCED, the United Nations sponsored the Stockholm Conference on the Human Environment, and established the United Nations Environment Programme (UNEP). UNEP has played an active role in encouraging nations to address environmental problems of international and global import. But UNEP has no formal powers or executive authority. Thus, Sir Geoffrey Palmer, a leading figure in the international environmental law field, has suggested the creation of a new international organization. Geoffrey Palmer, *New Ways to Make International Environmental Law*, 86 AM. J. INT'L L. 259 (1992). Weiss makes passing reference to Palmer's recommendation, but dismisses it on efficiency grounds. *See* text at footnote 153. In light of Palmer's extensive experience in this field, not only as a scholar but also as a policymaker—he served as

New Zealand's Prime Minister, Deputy Prime Minister, Minister for the Environment, and Attorney General—his recommendation merits closer consideration.

Palmer's recommendation stems from his conclusion that the progress made in international environmental law during the past two decades is more apparent than real.

> If we consider the new instruments that have developed the international law for the environment in the last twenty years, we would be pardoned for thinking that the record is a good one. * * *

* * *

> While the number of instruments is impressive, and some of them will have slowed down degradation, it cannot be assumed that they have led to an improvement in the overall situation. A strong argument can be made that, during the time these instruments were being developed, the environmental situation in the world became worse and is deteriorating further. There is no effective legal framework to help halt the degradation. Furthermore, many international agreements do not necessarily mean many ratifications. Frequently, there appears to be a long lag in securing widespread ratification because of insufficient incentives for nations to sign up. Many other nations simply seem not to address the issues, not regarding them as of sufficient priority compared to domestic concerns. Nor is there any institutional mechanism to provide nations with incentives to comply when they have ratified. Moreover, ratification itself says nothing about whether the agreed standards are being observed. * * *

> The making and negotiation of the instruments themselves has to start anew each time. No organization commands clear power to coordinate international environmental negotiations. Each negotiation proceeds differently. * * *

> There is no institutional machinery to evaluate gaps that may be found in the international framework of agreements or to develop means of assigning priorities among competing claims for attention. Nor is there any way of ensuring that environmental issues are effectively coordinated with and integrated into other activities that may be progressing at the international level. * * *

* * *

> One of the biggest obstacles that must be overcome in international negotiations is the rule of unanimous consent. This rule impels each negotiating body to search for the lowest common denominator; it adds to the difficulty of negotiations because sometimes a single nation can resist the development of a common position and demand concessions as the price of securing unanimous consent. While it is doubtful that the rule of unanimous consent can be banished from international global negotiations, the introduction of new institutional mechanisms may provide ways around it, which would speed up the process and result in instruments of greater potency.

> What is missing from the present institutional arrangements is the equivalent

of a legislature: some structured and coherent mechanism for making the rules of international law. * * *

In sum, the methods and techniques now available to fashion new instruments of international law to cope with global environmental problems cannot meet that challenge. The emerging issues are so big and so all-embracing that current ways of doing things will not solve these problems. The institutional mechanisms within the United Nations system are not capable of handling the issues.

Id. at 262-64. In light of these problems, Palmer recommends the creation of an International Environmental Organization, modeled after the International Labor Organization. This would be in the nature of a specialized United Nations agency, empowered to impose binding international environmental regulations by a two-thirds vote, to gather information and monitor compliance with regulations, to gather "authoritative and widely representative scientific advice," and to enforce violations against noncomplying countries. *Id.* at 280-81. Regarding the crucial compliance feature, Palmer elaborates as follows:

* * * For them [measures to secure compliance] to be effective, there must be some strong incentives to join the organization and stay in it. For many countries these will probably reside in technical assistance, information, advice, technology transfer and even financial assistance for dealing with environmental problems. From a practical point of view, the sanctions should include the withholding of benefits by the organization and of direct contacts with delinquent governments, and the mobilization of the politics of shame. * * *

Id. at 281.

Can an organization of this nature address the equity issues highlighted by Weiss in the foregoing article? Can the equity, economic, and scientific issues that are intertwined in the environmental arena be addressed in a rational manner by an inherently political body? What alternatives might there be?

4. Weiss describes the increasingly significant role of nongovernmental organizations in the development of international environmental law. Professor A. Dan Tarlock suggests that "NGOs play a role which is both similar and more powerful than public interest plaintiffs in domestic law." A. Dan Tarlock, *The Role of Non-Governmental Organizations in the Development of International Environmental Law,* 68 CHI.-KENT L. REV. 61, 72 (1992). Although international environmental law gives them no formal role in enforcement,

NGOs are playing an increasing role in the enforcement of international environmental standards. * * * Paradoxically, the non-role of the International Court of Justice and the limited enforcement powers of the United Nations Environmental Program have given NGOs the flexibility to play more diverse and creative roles.

Id. at 73. In devising "debt-for-nature swaps," NGOs have made a notable contribution to the most challenging of international environmental issues, that of the equitable distribution of environmental benefits and burdens across developed and developing nations. *Id.* at 74.

* * * [L]oans [from banks to developing countries] are now a crushing debt burden for many countries and put intense pressures on countries to continue to exploit their natural resources bases. * * *

* * * [In debt-for-nature swaps], NGOs purchase from a bank a portion of the debt of developing countries faced with a write-off or write-down prospect. Developing country "paper" is plentiful and relatively cheap. The NGO must fund a debt instrument with hard currency that the developing country would like to retire as quickly as possible, often high interest, short term bonds. After the NGO purchases the instrument, it is converted into the local currency of the debtor country and the debt service is applied to purchase land threatened by development or to finance a conservation program. Debtor countries gain the benefit of servicing its debt with local rather than hard currency, subject to NGO control over the country's natural resources. Banks may deduct the original amount of the debt donated rather than the current fair market value of the debt. This strategy has been adopted by the United States government because it makes the best of a bad situation, helping developing nations with crushing debt burdens, and offers a modest way to support sustainable development projects.

* * *

Debt-for-nature swaps are unlikely to be a major vehicle for developing country debt relief but they have considerable potential to save high priority natural areas such as rain forests. From a legal point of view the most interesting aspect of debt-for-nature swaps is the creative NGO circumvention of the basic principle of international law, proclaimed by the United Nations at the height of the Cold war, that each nation has the right to exploit its natural resources. * * *

Id. at 74-75. Tarlock concludes with the suggestion that, as NGOs acquire more power in the international arena, "minimum norms of responsible environmental participation should be developed to monitor their performance." *Id.* at 75.

Agenda 21, adopted by UNCED at Rio in June 1992, encouraged the United Nations Commission on Sustainable Development to facilitate NGO participation, in part by relaxing the rules of NGO accreditation. ALEXANDRE KISS and DINAH SHELTON, INTERNATIONAL ENVIRONMENTAL LAW 14-16 (Supp. 1994).

5. Although the preceding article and notes focus primarily on the legislative aspect of international environmental law, there has also been much activity on the adjudicatory front. Some of the significant cases are mentioned in the next two articles. Before leaving the topic of NGOs, however, it bears note that NGOs have been playing an increasingly active role in international judicial proceedings. In relatively limited circumstances, NGOs may initiate litigation or intervene as a party. They may also serve as experts or witnesses in litigation brought by others. Finally, and most significantly, they may participate as amici curiae. *See* Dinah Shelton, *The Participation of Nongovernmental Organizations in International Judicial Proceedings,* 88 AM. J. INT'L L. 611 (1994).

Whereas the preceding article views international law from the perspective of environmentally-focused agreements, the next article looks at agreements focused on international trade and considers their environmental implications. The question whether international trade agreements elevate economic over environmental considerations is one of the more contentious aspects of this controversial field. Professor Thomas Schoenbaum articulates the position that international trade agreements are compatible with environmental protection, and suggests means of better harmonizing the two interests.

FREE INTERNATIONAL TRADE AND PROTECTION OF THE ENVIRONMENT: IRRECONCILABLE CONFLICT?
Thomas J. Schoenbaum
86 Am. J. Int'l L. 700 (1992)*

States should cooperate to promote a supportive and open international economic system that would lead to economic growth and sustainable development in all countries, to better address the problems of environmental degradation. Trade policy measures for environmental purposes should not constitute a means of arbitrary or unjustifiable discrimination or a disguised restriction on international trade. Unilateral actions to deal with environmental challenges outside the jurisdiction of the importing country should be avoided. Environmental measures addressing transboundary or global environmental problems should, as far as possible, be based on an international consensus.

Principle 12
*Rio Declaration on Environment and Development***

I. INTRODUCTION

The global multilateral trading system and its centerpiece, the General Agreement on Tariffs and Trade (GATT),[1] are facing a new challenge from a quite unexpected quarter. The GATT is under attack by some in the environmental community who charge that international free trade blindly fosters the exploitation of natural resources. The GATT is depicted as a sinister charter that allows "big business" a free hand to plunder the bounty of the natural world. * * * Thus, a segment of the large and influential environmen-

---

* Reprinted with permission.
** Adopted June 14, 1992, at the United Nations Conference on Environment and Development, Rio de Janeiro, UN Doc. A/CONF.151/5/Rev.1, *reprinted in* 31 ILM 874, 878 (1992).
[1] The GATT, Oct. 30, 1947, TIAS No. 1700, 55 UNTS 188, entered into force on January 12, 1948. * * *
    Under United States law, the GATT is a U.S. executive agreement, treated as a treaty obligation. *See* Proclamation No. 2761A, 12 Fed.Reg. 8863 (1947).

talist lobby has joined the growing coalition of interests seeking to scuttle what is left of international free trade.

The recent recognition of environmental quality as a global concern has highlighted the extensive interface among environmental degradation, pollution control and international trade. Passage of the Clean Air Act Amendments of 1990, for instance, led to predictions that the strengthened air standards would impose costs on United States business that would make our factories less competitive with those in other countries. The current negotiations among the United States, Canada and Mexico concerning a North American Free Trade Area (NAFTA) have prompted the objection that American companies will face unfair competition from plants in Mexico that are subject to less-stringent environmental regulations. Environmentalists also fear that polluting industries will migrate to countries with lax environmental regulations and export to nations with stricter controls.

The response to the latter concerns is to adopt restrictions on international trade in the name of environmental protection. Thus, national and international efforts to protect the planet's environment and resources clash with the goal of free international trade. This conflict is exacerbated by misunderstanding; up to now, neither environmentalists nor those concerned with international trade knew or cared much about each other's goals and values. The conflict also pits two otherwise worthy objectives against each other. We should not be forced to choose between environmental protection and free international trade; both values are essential to our future survival and well-being.

The environmentalists who argue that free trade will destroy the environment are shortsighted and wrong. * * * Analysis shows that existing GATT regulations place virtually no constraints on the ability of a nation to protect its own environment and resources against damage caused by either domestic production or domestically produced or imported products. GATT rules can also be made consistent with efforts to preserve regional and global environmental quality. Furthermore, trade liberalization, whether on a global or regional basis, will actually help the environmentalists' cause by (1) fostering common standards for environmental protection that must be observed even by certain developing countries that currently ignore environmental concerns; (2) terminating subsidies, particularly in agriculture, that are environmentally destructive, as well as inefficient; and (3) ensuring economic growth, which will create the financial means, particularly for developing countries, to control pollution and protect the environment.

The current ruckus raised by the environmentalists over GATT rules is due primarily to a GATT dispute panel's invalidation of a United States import ban on tuna from countries that do not require "dolphin-friendly" fishing methods.[13] From this ruling many

---

[13] United States—Restrictions on Imports of Tuna, Report of the GATT Panel (Aug. 16, 1991), *reprinted in* 30 ILM 1594 (1991) [hereinafter U.S. Tuna Ban]. In the eastern tropical Pacific Ocean, dolphins and porpoises travel in proximity with yellowfin tuna, usually sitting on top of the tuna. Tuna fishermen kill dolphins when they use purse-seine fishing nets that entangle and capture the dolphins, which usually panic and drown. To reduce this incidental taking of dolphins and porpoises, the United States, under the authority of the Marine Mammal Protection Act (MMPA), 16 U.S.C. §§ 1371-1377 (1988), requires that fishing fleets use marine mammal safety techniques and equipment. The MMPA also requires a ban on imports of fish caught with fishing techniques that result in the incidental killing of dolphins and porpoises. 16 U.S.C. § 1371(a)(2) (1988). The GATT panel report drew very unfavorable comment in the United States. * * *

Ironically, the GATT panel report will probably never become binding on the United States. As a technical

environmentalists have drawn the conclusion that the GATT is hostile to all natural resource conservation restrictions. This is totally false; the tuna ban violates the GATT not because of any inherent policy against conservation but because the GATT rightly protects member states from the unilateral imposition of domestic standards by importing countries through market access restrictions. Such protection is necessary even from an environmental standpoint. If every country were allowed to impose its own domestic environmental standards on other countries, the result would not be greater environmental protection but chaos and anarchy.

For the purpose of analysis, trade restrictions in the name of environmental quality may be grouped into four categories. The first category includes regulations on imports and exports adopted by all nations to safeguard their domestic resources and environment and to protect public health and safety. The imposition of such restrictions has traditionally been considered the prerogative of each sovereign state. Indeed, environmental standards actually contribute to economic efficiency since they correct environmental abuses that would otherwise distort the operation of the international trading system. * * *

Nevertheless, the imposition of environmental and safety standards in the recent past has sparked international controversy. For example, in 1989 the European Community (EC) enacted a ban on the importation of hormone-treated beef, provoking the United States to impose $100 million in retaliatory measures against European exports. A similar row recently ensued when several nations, including Zaire, Indonesia, Malaysia, the Philippines and even the United States, prohibited the export of raw logs. Moreover, differing environmental standards frequently constitute nontariff barriers to free international trade; they also may amount to disguised protectionism. What limits are appropriate for such measures? Is there a need for international norms and standards?

A second category of trade restrictions is increasingly used as a policy tool to enforce environmental standards in international agreements. Recent examples include provisions in the various international agreements to protect the earth's ozone layer, safeguard endangered species of plants and animals, and restrict the international movement of hazardous wastes, as well as in proposed agreements to protect tropical forests and stem global warming.

Even if these international trade restrictions are legitimate tools to preserve the global environment, the proliferation of such agreements raises several issues. What kinds of threats to global resources justify trade restrictions? Are the measures employed proportional to the potential environmental harms? Should nations be permitted to impose them unilaterally or should such restrictions be allowed only pursuant to multilateral agreements?

A third set of trade restrictions for environmental purposes is even more controversial. Increasingly, states with stringent environmental controls are questioning the adequacy of environmental controls in other nations. This concern is based not only on environmental considerations, but also on apprehensiveness about unfair competition from foreign companies that are not subject to strict pollution controls. As a result, a nation may employ unilateral trade restrictions to enforce national environmental objectives and to induce

---

matter, GATT panel reports are binding only when they are adopted by the GATT Council. * * * Mexico, because of political considerations, deferred bringing the panel report before the GATT Council, and on June 15, 1992, the United States, Mexico, Venezuela and Vanuatu entered into a compromise agreement to settle the dispute. * * *

other nations to adopt commensurate environmental standards. Such retaliatory measures may take the form of a surcharge or a ban on the import of certain goods.

This kind of trade restriction raises important concerns under international law. Should a country be permitted to impose its own notion of environmental quality on other nations? Are trade restrictions a legitimate way to retaliate for inadequate environmental standards?

A fourth category of environmental trade restrictions consists of controls on the export of hazardous products, technologies and waste. Events such as the accidental explosion at the Union Carbide factory in Bhopal, India, in 1984 have stimulated the search for new international standards to govern the export of hazardous chemicals, wastes and pesticides to developing countries.

Although at first glance such reforms may seem useful and uncontroversial, serious questions lurk beneath the surface. For example, how should "hazardous" be defined in drawing up restrictions on the export of technologies and products? What are the appropriate risk assessment methods? Is there a need to harmonize the rules in this regard? Should these questions be determined unilaterally or by multinational conventional regimes? What is the appropriate method of regulation: a tax, a ban or prior informed consent?

This article examines these four types of restrictions in the light of current international trade law and offers suggestions for resolving the tension between international free trade and environmental quality.

II. THE GATT

The GATT, an international organization with 106 member states, has primary responsibility for administering the complex web of legal rules, political relationships and economic policy instruments that govern world trade. Most GATT decisions are taken by consensus, rather than by vote, and the day-to-day work is done by a small, nonpolitical secretariat located in Geneva, Switzerland. In addition to overseeing the member countries' contractual commitments and obligations, the GATT sponsors periodic rounds of negotiations aimed at reducing tariffs and, more recently, reducing or eliminating nontariff barriers to trade.

Contracting parties are obliged (1) to enter into tariff commitments; (2) to extend "most favored nation" (MFN) treatment to imports from other GATT parties; (3) to give imported goods "national treatment" once they have cleared customs and border procedures; and (4) to eliminate quantitative restrictions on imports and exports. To facilitate compliance with these obligations, the GATT administers a procedure for settling disputes between member countries.

Tariff Commitments

The central obligation of GATT is the tariff "concession," which is a commitment by a contracting party to levy no more than the stated tariff on the imports of other GATT contracting parties. * * *

Most-Favored-Nation Treatment

In addition to the specific obligations that arise from tariff concessions, the GATT sets forth various general obligations that apply to trade in all products, not just those listed in the schedules. The most fundamental of these is the most-favored-nation principle contained in Article I, which requires each contracting party to grant every other contracting party treatment at least as favorable as it grants any country with respect to imports and exports of like products. * * *

* * *

National Treatment

Article III of the GATT contains the "national treatment obligation," which imposes a rule of nondiscrimination between goods that are domestically produced and those that are imported. * * *

National treatment in the environmental context was recently at issue in the *Superfund Case*,[39] which involved a provision of the U.S. Comprehensive Environmental Response, Compensation, and Liability Act (known as "Superfund") that imposed a tax on imported oil greater than the charge for domestically produced petroleum products. In defending the tax, the United States argued that the resulting discrimination was competitively insignificant and that it was for a benign purpose: to finance pollution control measures, the cleanup of hazardous waste sites. The dispute settlement panel found, however, that the GATT's national treatment policies are applicable to all taxes regardless of their policy purposes. Therefore, whether the imposition of an internal tax on imported products meets the national treatment requirement of Article III(2) depends on whether like domestic products are taxed, directly or indirectly, at the same or a higher rate. Applying this test to the taxes in dispute, the panel concluded that the petroleum tax did not satisfy Article III(2) because it levied a higher charge upon imported petroleum. As for the tax on certain imported chemicals, the panel concluded that the imported and like domestic substances bore equivalent burdens; therefore, the tax met the requirement of Article III(2).

Elimination of Quantitative Restrictions

Article XI(1) of the GATT generally prohibits the use of quotas or other quantitative limitations on exported or imported products. * * *

The permissible scope of environmentally inspired trade restrictions under these principles was recently tested in the landmark *U.S. Tuna Ban* panel decision. Pursuant to the Marine Mammal Protection Act (MMPA), the United States had banned imports of yellowfin tuna from Mexico (as well as certain other nations) on the grounds that Mexican boats were permitted to employ harvesting methods that kill dolphins, which are protected under the MMPA.

Acting on a complaint filed by Mexico, the GATT panel found that the U.S. tuna embargo violated GATT Article XI(1), which forbids prohibitions and restrictions on imports or exports. The United States sought to justify the ban as a regulation permitted under paragraphs 1 and 4 of Article III, that is, as incidental to the enforcement of the MMPA regulations on the harvest of domestic tuna. The panel conceded that internal regulations on imported products are permitted under paragraphs 1 and 4 of Article III as long as they do not discriminate between products of different countries in violation of Article I(1) and as long as imported products are accorded treatment no less favorable

---

[39] United States—Taxes on Petroleum and Certain Imported Substances, GATT, BISD, 34th Supp. 136 (1988) [hereinafter Superfund].

than are like domestic products. However, the panel construed the two paragraphs of Article III as permitting only regulations and requirements relating to *products* as such. The MMPA regulations, which concern harvesting techniques designed to reduce the incidental taking of dolphins, cannot possibly affect tuna as a *product*; therefore, the ban could not be justified. Furthermore, the panel, in obiter dicta, made the point that "a contracting party may not restrict imports of a product merely because it originates in a country with environmental policies different from its own."[52]

The panel's decision in this regard is consistent with prior cases, * * * and is based on a literal reading of GATT Article III, which permits regulations on imported products "affecting their internal sale, offering for sale, purchase, transportation, distribution or use" but excludes any regulation of the way those products are produced, created or manufactured if it leaves no residue of differentiation in the products themselves. The panel, however, upheld the U.S. Dolphin Protection Consumer Information Act, which provides that tuna products offered for sale in the United States may be labeled "Dolphin Safe" if they do not contain tuna harvested in the Eastern Tropical Pacific (ETP) by a vessel using a purse-seine net or are accompanied by documentary evidence that the net was not intentionally deployed to encircle dolphins. The panel noted that this labeling provision does not restrict the sale of tuna; tuna products may be freely sold both with or without the "Dolphin Safe" label. The labeling requirements were therefore found to be consistent with Article I(1), since all countries whose vessels fished in the ETP enjoyed equal access to the "Dolphin Safe" label.

Environmental, Health and Safety Exceptions

The GATT contains several provisions that relate directly to environmental protection, health and safety. Article XX provides in relevant part as follows:

> Subject to the requirement that such measures are not applied in a manner which would constitute a means of arbitrary or unjustifiable discrimination between countries where the same conditions prevail, or a disguised restriction on international trade, nothing in this Agreement shall be construed to prevent the adoption or enforcement by any contracting party of measures:
>
> . . .
>
> (b) necessary to protect human, animal or plant life or health; . . .
>
> (f) imposed for the protection of national treasures of artistic, historic or archaeological value;
>
> (g) relating to the conservation of exhaustible natural resources if such measures are made effective in conjunction with restrictions on domestic production or consumption . . .

There is little documentary evidence about the intentions of the negotiators of Article XX. The text apparently derived from the kinds of exceptions traditionally written into bilateral treaties of friendship, commerce and navigation. Significantly, Article XX contains no requirement that the country claiming the exception must enter into negotiations with affected countries or even provide notification. The judgment as to whether an action

---

[52] [U.S. Tuna Ban, *supra* note 13], para. 6.2, 30 ILM at 1622.

satisfies Article XX is apparently left, in the first instance at least, to the contracting party claiming it. There is no provision for safeguarding international obligations in such cases or for compensating adversely affected countries.

Nevertheless, there are important explicit limitations on the use of Article XX. A measure invoking an Article XX exception must still avoid "arbitrary or unjustifiable discrimination between countries" and must not be a "disguised restriction on international trade." In addition, subsections (b) and (d) require that the restrictions imposed must be "necessary" to accomplish their purposes. In GATT panel decisions, Article XX has been interpreted as a limited and conditional exception, and a heavy burden of proof must be carried by the party invoking its provisions. In particular, the environmental exceptions, subsections (b) and (g), have been strictly and narrowly interpreted.

The 1983 *Canada-U.S. Tuna Case*[60] grew out of the U.S. refusal to recognize the 200-nautical-mile fishing zones of coastal states with respect to highly migratory species such as tuna. To enforce this position, section 205 of the Fisheries Conservation and Management Act authorized the imposition of an import prohibition on fish products from the involved fishery if U.S. rights were violated. When Canada seized nineteen U.S. fishing vessels within its 200-mile limit, the United States responded with an embargo on tuna and tuna products. Canada complained to the GATT, arguing that the tuna ban was an import prohibition in violation of GATT Article XI(1). The United States contended that its embargo was justified under Article XX(g) because tuna was an exhaustible natural resource. The GATT panel concluded that Article XX(g) was inapplicable because there were no U.S. correlative restrictions on the domestic production or consumption of tuna. Thus, the tuna ban violated the GATT prohibition against discriminatory import restrictions because there was no evidence that it was "primarily aimed" at conservation.

The *Canada—Herring and Salmon Case*[63] involved a Canadian export ban on unprocessed sockeye and pink salmon, herring and herring roe that was challenged by the United States as an illegal export restriction. Canada attempted to justify the restriction under GATT Article XI(2)(b) as a domestic restriction "necessary to the application of standards or regulations for the classification, grading or marketing of commodities in international trade," as well as under Article XX(g). The GATT panel, however, found that the export ban was unjustifiable under the former provision because, while Canada could bar the export of fish not meeting its quality standards, it could not ban all exports of fish since some would comply with the standards. The panel also analyzed Article XX(g), finding that, while a trade measure under this subsection need not be "necessary" or "essential" to the conservation of a natural resource, it had to be "primarily aimed at" conservation to satisfy the "relating to" language of the provision. Furthermore, to be justified under Article XX(g), which requires that trade measures be made in conjunction with restrictions on domestic production or consumption, the panel interpreted "in conjunction with" to mean that a trade measure had to be primarily aimed at rendering such production or consumption restrictions effective. The panel found that the Canadian measure failed both tests.

---

[60] United States—Prohibition of Imports of Tuna and Tuna Products from Canada, *id.*, 29th Supp. 91 (1983) [hereinafter Canada-U.S. Tuna].

[63] Canada—Unprocessed Salmon and Herring, GATT, BISD, 35th Supp. 98 (1989).

* * *

The *U.S. Tuna Ban* panel, in rejecting the application of Article XX(b) and (g), restated these narrow interpretations as well. After examining the history, purposes and consequences of Article XX(b), the panel found that it focuses on the life or health of human beings, plants and animals within the jurisdiction of the importing country; it does not cover measures intended to protect the animal or plant life or health of those outside that country's jurisdiction. Furthermore, the panel noted that the U.S. measures could not be considered necessary even if Article XX(b) were construed as having extrajurisdictional effect, since other options were reasonably available, such as the negotiation of international cooperative arrangements. Turning to Article XX(g), the panel observed that because this provision requires that the measures relating to the conservation of natural resources be taken "in conjunction with" domestic production and consumption restrictions, it was intended to apply to resources within the invoking party's jurisdiction. Thus, the panel concluded that "Article XX(g) allows each contracting party to adopt its own conservation policies."[68] Moreover, the panel found that the requirement of Article XX(g) that the measure be "primarily aimed at conservation" had not been satisfied because the dolphin-taking rate imposed on Mexico was linked to the U.S. taking rate, not to any objective standard.[69]

In sum, the GATT scheme allows each contracting party only limited freedom to determine its domestic environmental policies. The measures it uses to implement those policies must not discriminate between foreign states and must not favor domestic products. Finally, GATT principles prohibit the extrajurisdictional use of trade measures to impose environmental policies and standards on other nations.

III. PROTECTING THE DOMESTIC ENVIRONMENT

The GATT recognizes that the contracting parties retain control over policies regarding health, safety and pollution, as well as natural resources, within their jurisdiction. The *U.S. Tuna Ban* panel report readily conceded that the GATT permits extensive regulation of trade for environmental purposes:

> [T]he provisions of the General Agreement impose few constraints on a contracting party's implementation of domestic environmental policies. . . . [A] contracting party is free to tax or regulate imported products and like domestic products as long as its taxes or regulations do not discriminate against imported products or afford protection to domestic producers. . . .[70]

Accordingly, several different methods may be used to apply domestic environmental policies to imports and exports.

First, Article XX(b) permits import prohibitions or restrictions to enforce domestic policies concerning human health and safety, and animal and plant conservation. However, as we have seen, such restrictions must be enforced on a nondiscriminatory basis; they must be "necessary" in the sense that other methods are not available or practicable; and their reach must be confined to the jurisdiction of the country enacting the measure.

---

[68] [U.S. Tuna Ban, *supra* note 13], para. 5.32, 30 ILM at 1621.

[69] *Id.*, para. 5.33, 30 ILM at 1621.

[70] *Id.*, para. 6.2, 30 ILM at 1622.

Within these limits, Article XX(b) may be used to justify a wide variety of environmental and health regulations on imports, including auto emission standards, product noise standards, food and drug regulations, toxic and hazardous substance regulations, and pesticide residue limits.

Second, Article XX(g) permits trade restrictions relating to the conservation of exhaustible natural resources, but such restrictions must be applied on a nondiscriminatory basis, "primarily aimed" at the conservation of the resource, enforced in conjunction with restrictions on domestic production and consumption, and aimed at conserving resources *within* the jurisdiction of the country enacting the measure. Pursuant to this exception, a nation may certainly prohibit the export of species of endangered plants and animals within its jurisdiction. It may also ban or restrict the exportation of certain natural resources, such as tropical timber, but only if the conditions listed above are fulfilled. The bans recently enacted by several countries prohibiting the export of unprocessed logs do not appear to qualify for two reasons: (1) there is no corresponding domestic restriction on consumption or timber production; and (2) the limitation of the ban to unprocessed logs indicates that it is not "primarily aimed" at conservation but has other purposes, i.e., the retention of business for domestic wood-processing and manufacturing industries.

A third source of justification for conservational trade restrictions under the GATT is Article XI(2)(a), which permits an export prohibition or restriction when there are domestic shortages. Such measures may be "temporarily applied to prevent or relieve critical shortages of foodstuffs or other products essential to the contracting party." * * *

* * *

The GATT correctly restricts environmental exceptions to regulations that fulfill environmental purposes. By excluding "disguised restrictions on international trade," the GATT properly tries to distinguish restrictions that purportedly protect the environment but really have other purposes. The difficulty lies in the lack of proper criteria for differentiating between environmentally protective trade restrictions and disguised trade barriers.

Because of the paucity of GATT determinations on this issue, it is useful to look at other nations' experience. A useful analogy is the *Danish Bottles* case,[87] a 1988 decision of the Court of Justice of the European Community that involved a Danish ban on nonreturnable containers. The measure also mandated advance approval of all beverage containers and quantitative limits on the sale of all foreign beverages in nonapproved containers. In ruling on the conformity of this regulation with the EC Treaty, the Court of Justice first determined that Article 30 of the Treaty, which prohibits quantitative restrictions on trade between member states, is limited by Article 36, the counterpart to Article XX of the GATT, which allows EC member states to enforce health and safety requirements.

The Court then scrutinized the Danish law and regulations for their conformity with Article 36 on the basis of three criteria: first, whether the aim of the measure fell within the scope of the exemption; second, whether the measure had been applied on a nondiscriminatory basis; and third, whether the measure satisfied the principle of proportionality, which requires that the protective measure be necessary to accomplish its purpose. In applying these criteria, the Court approved the nonreturnable container requirement but

---

[87] Case 302/86, Commission v. Denmark, 1988 ECR 4607.

held that the quotas on foreign beverages in nonapproved containers violated the principle of proportionality. Therefore, although foreign beverage producers were obliged to market their products in Denmark in recyclable containers, they could use their own containers without restriction.

The *Danish Bottles* case indicates how GATT Article XX might be interpreted to exclude disguised restrictions on trade from the exception. The principle of proportionality as elucidated by the Court of Justice is a useful method for determining whether a restriction invoking Article XX is legitimate.

A second way to reduce the trade friction resulting from environmental regulations is provided by the GATT Standards Code of 1979.[88] The Standards Code recognizes that differing technical standards may constitute nontariff barriers to trade and obliges members to use international standards whenever possible. Nevertheless, members are free to apply national standards where necessary to protect the environment, as well as human health and safety, as long as they do not create "unnecessary obstacles to international trade." To minimize the trade-distorting effect of differing product standards, the Standards Code (1) mandates open procedures in the adoption of product standards and testing methods; (2) requires nondiscrimination in the application of such standards; (3) approves technical assistance for developing countries; and (4) provides procedures for settling disputes. * * *

* * *

Environmentalists may object that harmonizing standards or adopting international standards is equivalent to a "lowest common denominator" approach that will result in lax requirements. Although this may once have been the case, the future should be different. In virtually all countries, there is political pressure for greater environmental controls; nations, such as the United States, Japan and the EC members, that have higher environmental standards are likely to bring increasing pressure to bear upon countries with lax controls to eliminate their competitive advantages; and there is a greater awareness of the urgency and global scope of environmental problems. Nevertheless, the GATT Standards Code suffers from the weakness of lacking an explicit mandate to deal with environmental standards. The Standards Code should accordingly be amended to require (1) that environmental protection be considered in the formulation of standards, and (2) that standards be harmonized at the highest practicable levels of protection for the environment so that no country can make its capacity to absorb pollution a feature of its comparative advantage.

In addition, GATT should hold a new negotiation on Article XX designed to conclude a side agreement that would (1) flesh out the criteria for applying the various exceptions, particularly those in subsections (b) and (g); (2) incorporate new principles of environmental protection, especially as regards the global environment; and (3) develop new principles such as those in the *Danish Bottles* case that harmonize international trade and environmental concerns.

* * *

V. INADEQUATE ENVIRONMENTAL PROTECTION CONTROLS IN OTHER NATIONS

The imposition of the costs of pollution control on companies whose manufacturing processes generate pollution may be justified on both environmental and economic grounds.

---

[88] Agreement on Technical Barriers to Trade, Apr. 12, 1979, GATT, BISD, 26th Supp. 8 (1980).

Requiring the polluter to pay ensures that those costs are borne by the polluter and the consumers of its products, not by society at large. Therefore, countries should be encouraged to implement pollution control measures either by command and control regulations or by levying a tax commensurate with the level of pollution. Not all nations will adopt such controls, however, and industries located in nations with few or none may well be able to produce competing goods at less cost.

As we have seen, in conformity with the GATT, country A may restrict the import of goods that may endanger the domestic environment, for example, hazardous wastes, toxic chemicals and products containing CFCs; but may country A single out those nations with inadequate pollution controls and adopt trade restrictions on their products—tariff surcharges, quotas or taxes—on the theory that it is removing the "pollution advantage" inherent in the products concerned?

Under existing GATT law, country A would certainly violate its GATT obligations by enacting such a "pollution equalization" measure. First, it would violate the most-favored-nation requirement of GATT Article I(1), since the surcharge, quota or tax would be levied on the basis of the geographic origin of the product. As interpreted in the *Belgian Family Allowances*[120] and *U.S. Tuna Ban* cases, differences in the laws and environmental policies of exporting countries cannot be a basis for discriminatory treatment if there are no resulting objective differences in the imported products themselves. Levying a tariff surcharge, quota or tax on imports from only certain countries would therefore violate the obligation in Article I(1) to treat "like products" imported from all GATT contracting parties uniformly.

Second, the *U.S. Tuna Ban* decision is authority for the proposition that a quota in such a case would also violate GATT Article XI(1) since it could not be justified as a regulation under Article III(4). Third, a "pollution tax" levied on imports from certain countries while exempting domestic industries producing like products would additionally contravene the GATT's national treatment clause, Article III(1), under the authority of the *Superfund* decision. Furthermore, none of these methods of burdening imports can be justified under the exceptions in GATT Article XX; subsections (b) and (g) were intended to apply only to resources and environmental conditions within the jurisdiction of country A, but the imported goods, although their production is polluting the country of origin, are not hazardous to the environment of country A. Therefore, country A cannot restrict the importation of goods merely because they were produced at what country A perceives to be excessive environmental costs.

The foregoing discussion is based on the GATT principles in Articles I, II and III that "like products" must be accorded equal treatment. Is it possible to conclude that differences in the circumstances of production of items that may have the same characteristics at the point of importation justify their treatment as "unlike products"? GATT Articles I, II and III permit differential treatment to be accorded to *unlike* products.

The concept of "like product" is not defined in the GATT, but GATT dispute settlement jurisprudence has established guidelines for determining its meaning. First, tariff classification is usually the point of departure for determining "like product." Second, the physical

---

[120] [GATT, BISD, 1st Supp. 59 (1953)]. * * *

properties of the products and their end-use characteristics may determine their "un-likeness," usually as a justification for separate tariff classifications. However, all of these distinctions are based on differences in the goods themselves, not on differences in the characteristics of the exporting countries or the mode of production in the exporting nation. No GATT decision has accepted the proposition that differences in production processes can be the basis for different tariff classifications. Indeed, the dictum of the *U.S. Tuna Ban* decision—that "a contracting party may not restrict imports of a product merely because it originates in a country with environmental policies different from its own"[130]—suggests the opposite conclusion.

Is this a flaw in the GATT system? Is the GATT hostile to environmental protection? On the contrary, the GATT rules appear to be the only workable solution. Nations face a widely differing array of economic, health, safety, social and environmental conditions. They must be allowed the right under international law to choose their own policies and priorities. To allow each country unilaterally to restrict trade on the basis of differing environmental conditions in another country would invite chaos and retaliation. Further-more, if unilateral trade restrictions were permitted for environmental reasons, they could also be used to combat all manner of national socioeconomic policies. Permitting such actions would reduce international trade to a power-based regime that would have no stability or rationality.

Nevertheless, the GATT should accommodate environmental protection and should not permit contracting parties to use lax environmental regulations as an instrument of comparative advantage. There are several ways to do so without permitting unbridled unilateralism, which would destroy international free trade. The best solution would be for the GATT to open a new negotiation to conclude an environmental code that would set out minimum levels of pollution control and environmental quality with respect to certain key economic sectors, such as import-sensitive industries. As an incentive for nations to subscribe and adhere to such international standards, (1) violations could be defined as countervailable subsidies under the GATT, and (2) adequate pollution control could be made a criterion for granting a nation benefits under the Generalized System of Preferences and, in the case of the United States, the Caribbean Basin Initiative.

VI. THE EXPORT OF HAZARDOUS PRODUCTS, WASTES AND TECHNOLOGIES

The growing worldwide concern over hazardous products, wastes and technologies has manifested itself in restrictions on international trade. Not only have import restrictions on hazardous goods increased, but recently exporting countries, motivated by domestic and international political pressures, have undertaken on their own to restrict the "export of hazard."

In general, exporting countries employ three approaches to dealing with the export of products, wastes and technologies. First, they may ban the export of products that are barred from use in their own territory. Second, they may permit the export of those products under regulations that require prior informed consent. Third, exporting and

---

[130] U.S. Tuna Ban, *supra* note 13, para. 6.2, 30 ILM at 1620. * * *

importing nations may negotiate multilateral approaches to the problem that adopt harmonized or international standards for dealing with the risks involved.

The impetus to adopt export restrictions was accelerated by the Bhopal disaster of 1984, in which poison gas escaping from a Union Carbide plant killed twenty-two thousand people. The catastrophe stimulated a congressional response and a vigorous debate over whether to apply stricter standards to U.S. companies operating in foreign countries.

Another focus of concern is the export of pesticides, which is regulated by the Federal Insecticide, Fungicide, and Rodenticide Act (FIFRA). The Act requires the registration of all pesticides sold in interstate or foreign commerce. Before an unregistered pesticide may be lawfully exported from the United States, the foreign purchaser must acknowledge in writing that the chemical is unregistered for use in the United States. This written statement, which the exporter is required to obtain, must be submitted to the Environmental Protection Agency, which, in turn, forwards copies to U.S. embassies in the importing countries for submission to appropriate officials. FIFRA also requires the EPA to notify foreign governments and international agencies when the registered status of a pesticide is canceled or suspended. Exported pesticides must also be adequately labeled as registered or unregistered under U.S. law. Export of unregistered pesticides, therefore, is permitted only under a system of notice that requires prior informed consent.

The export of hazardous wastes has also received great attention from the international community. The Basel Convention on the Control of Transboundary Movements of Hazardous Wastes and Their Disposal (Basel Convention) requires detailed notification and consent of the receiving country as a precondition for authorizing international waste shipments. Upon receipt of an exporter's notice of intent to ship hazardous waste, the competent authority of the exporting country must provide the intended importing country, as well as any transit countries, with written notification of the proposed shipment. * * * The importing country and any transit country must submit a written response consenting to the shipment, denying permission for it, imposing conditions or requesting further information. Furthermore, the Convention provides that parties must prohibit the export of the waste whenever there is reason to believe that it will not be managed in an environmentally sound manner. The Basel Convention has been adopted by over a hundred countries. * * *

The GATT is actively engaged in addressing the issue of export of hazardous substances. The GATT proposal, which is embodied in a separate code to which members would accede, would allow individual GATT members to decide whether their domestic restrictions on hazardous products should be extended to exports. If a member state so decides, it is required to notify GATT and to publish in full all laws, regulations and decisions relating to the products concerned.

This approach is an excellent solution to the "export of hazard." The GATT proposal wisely avoids the substantive aspects of hazardous product regulation and concentrates on transparency, providing a clearinghouse for the notification and publication of restrictions. Whether to restrict a particular hazardous product and the nature of any such restrictions are sensibly left to more specialized forums and to the individual GATT members themselves.

CONCLUSION

Contrary to the alarmist claims of some environmentalists, there is no inherent conflict between international free trade as it has evolved under the aegis of the GATT and protection of environmental quality. The GATT recognizes and contains policy instruments that can be used to protect domestic and global natural resources; the GATT and environmental protection are largely compatible.

Nevertheless, the current tension between environmentalists and free international trade points up certain problems that must be addressed. The environmentalists should realize that international free trade is essential to world economic progress, which is in turn necessary for the protection of environmental values, particularly on a global scale. Environmentalists must also educate themselves in the GATT principles so that they can accomplish their objectives through GATT-permissible methods rather than through discriminatory import bans, export prohibitions, discriminatory taxes and unilateral trade sanctions that violate the GATT.

For their part, those who are concerned with the GATT system should acknowledge the necessity and immediacy of environmental goals that did not exist at the time GATT principles were formulated. In addition, they must recognize that the relationship between GATT law and environmental protection needs to be clarified and extended. The GATT should authorize the working group on the environment to prepare for a full-fledged negotiation among the contracting parties. Among the actions that might be considered by the working group are the following:

(1) conclusion of a side agreement on GATT Article XX to define currently ambiguous criteria and resolve conflicts of interpretation;

(2) utilization of the GATT Standards Code to provide a forum for harmonization of environmental standards and regulations;

(3) amendment of the GATT Subsidies Code to define the scope of countervailing duties for natural resources and pollution subsidies;

(4) conclusion of a new GATT environmental code to address the issues of multinational environmental agreements and minimum levels of pollution control for import-sensitive industries;

(5) promotion of the new GATT code on the export of domestically prohibited goods and other hazardous substances;

(6) agreement on the criteria for considering differing environmental standards as a basis for tariff differentiation; and

(7) agreement on standards and criteria for "eco-labeling," commercial advertising and packaging relating to the ecologic characteristics of products.

These clarifications and modifications can easily be handled within the existing GATT framework; no fundamental revision of the Agreement is required to accommodate environmental values. Environmentalists, in turn, should end their alliances with protectionists and instead embrace the GATT as an important instrument to enhance global environmental quality.

NOTES

1. Does Professor Schoenbaum convince you that, under the existing regime of international law, the promotion of trade and the protection of the environment are mutually compatible objectives? To what extent is his thesis of compatibility dependent on his suggested changes in GATT provisions, as written and as construed?

2. Other commentators are less sanguine about the potential for harmony between these two international values. As articulated by an attorney with Public Citizen Litigation Group:

> The environmental community's objections to subjecting environmental regulations to the trade regime stem not solely from the processes by which trade rules are adopted and implemented, but also from the incompatibility of existing and proposed trade rules with effective solutions to pressing environmental problems. This incompatibility derives both from the divergent goals and philosophies of the two regimes and from the particular precepts that are embodied in existing and proposed trade rules.

Patti A. Goldman, *Resolving the Trade and Environment Debate: In Search of a Neutral Forum and Neutral Principles*, 49 WASH. & LEE L. REV. 1279, 1288 (1992).

3. Does the *U.S. Tuna Ban* case support Goldman's view? Does the panel's narrow reading of both Article III(1) and (4), which permit nondiscriminatory domestic regulations on imported products, and Article XX(b) and (g), which authorize nondiscriminatory domestic regulations to protect human, animal or plant life and to conserve exhaustible resources, imply a working presumption against environmental restrictions that impinge on free trade? To what extent will "clarifications and modifications" of GATT, as suggested by Schoenbaum, address such underlying presumptions? Does the *Danish Bottles Case*, decided not under GATT but under somewhat-analogous provisions of the European Community Treaty, provide persuasive precedent for interpreting GATT Article XX in a more environmentally-friendly manner in the future?

4. In light of the *U.S. Tuna Ban* precedent, how difficult would it be to justify under GATT Article XX(b): A domestic moratorium on the harvesting of marine mammals? A toxics disclosure provision such as California's Proposition 65? Would the possibility of negotiating international agreements to address those issues eliminate the "necessity" needed to justify domestic environmental restrictions under GATT?

5. Anyone critical of the apparent supremacy of international trade over environmental protection considerations must also note that several international agreements designed specifically for environmental protection invoke trade restrictions as effective enforcement mechanisms. Section IV of the Schoenbaum article, omitted from the above excerpt, addresses that aspect of the relationship between trade and environmental protection.

One of the international agreements that employs trade restrictions is the Convention on International Trade in Endangered Species of Wild Fauna and Flora (CITES). Parties to CITES may prohibit the import and export of endangered and threatened wildlife species. Insofar as such prohibitions might conflict with GATT, which controls? Schoenbaum states that as between countries that are parties to both GATT and CITES, the CITES provisions will survive as they postdate the inconsistent GATT provisions. As between a party to both treaties and a party to only one, the treaty to which they are both parties will govern. Thus, as between two GATT members where only one is a party to CITES, an endangered species import or export ban will be vulnerable to challenge under GATT.

6. Concomitant with the ever-growing package of environmental regulations on both the domestic and international levels, there has also emerged a heightened interest in using economic incentives to achieve environmental objectives. Focusing on the international front, Robert Housman and Durwood Zaelke suggest the creation of an international system of incentives and disincentives in order mutually to reinforce trade and environmental policies. Robert F. Housman and Durwood J. Zaelke, *Making Trade and Environmental Policies Mutually Reinforcing: Forging Competitive Sustainability*, 23 ENVTL. L. 545 (1993). The authors, both affiliated with the Center for International Environmental Law, propose the use of "environmental countervailing duties" that importing countries could impose on products manufactured without adequate environmental controls. The duty would be equal to the subsidy that the product was effectively enjoying as a result of imposing the environmental costs of production on society, rather than internalizing such costs. While conceding that the system poses administrative challenges, that it requires careful monitoring to prevent blatant protectionism, that it could burden developing countries, and that it raises the prospect of one nation seeking to impose its own values on others, Housman and Zaelke maintain that a countervailing duty system could be sufficiently well structured to minimize such negative effects. They also recommend the paired use of incentives—along with duties, or disincentives—to encourage the internalization of environmental costs during production.

7. Since the Schoenbaum article was published in 1992, additional international agreements designed primarily to facilitate trade have been negotiated. While environmental issues were prominent considerations, there remains substantial controversy as to the adequacy of the mechanisms for preserving strong domestic environmental standards.

One such agreement is the North American Free Trade Agreement (NAFTA), signed in December 1992 and ratified by Congress in 1993. The negotiation of an acceptable environmental side agreement played a key role in the congressional debate. North American Agreement on Environmental Cooperation, 32 I.L.M. 1480, *reprinted in* THE NAFTA SUPPLEMENTAL AGREEMENTS (U.S.Government Printing Office ed. 1993). The side agreement calls upon each country to "ensure that its laws and regulations provide for high levels of environmental protection," to "strive to continue to improve those laws and regulations," and to "effectively enforce its environmental laws and regulations through appropriate governmental actions." *Id.,* Articles 3 and 5. It also establishes a Commission for Environmental Cooperation to assist in the implementation of the agreement.

Another is the Uruguay Round of Multilateral Trade Negotiations, concluded in December 1993 and approved by Congress in December 1994. In the Uruguay Round, the GATT nations established a World Trade Organization and, under its auspices, a Committee on Trade and the Environment.

For an explanation and critique of these developments, see Jennifer Schultz, *The GATT/WTO Committee on Trade and the Environment—Toward Environmental Reform*, 89 AM. J. INTL L. 423 (1995). *See also* Judith H. Bello and Mary E. Footer, *Symposium: Uruguay Round—GATT/WTO*, 29 INTL LAW. 335 (1995); Steve Charnovitz, *The NAFTA Environmental Side Agreement: Implications for Environmental Cooperation, Trade Policy, and American Treatymaking*, 8 TEMP. INT'L & COMP. L. J. 257 (1994).

8. A number of voluntary international efforts have been launched to encourage companies to achieve consensus environmental standards that may go beyond legally-mandated requirements. For example, the International Organization for Standardization is developing a wide range of environmental guidelines—known as ISO 14000. A comprehensive examination of such voluntary efforts and related requirements can be found in Ridgway M. Hall Jr. and Kristine A. Tockman, *International Corporate Environmental Compliance and Auditing Programs*, 25 ENVTL. L. REP. 10395 (1995).

Whereas the Schoenbaum article addressed the relationship between international trade and environmental protection, the next article focuses on the relationship between international environmental agreements and domestic environmental law. Professor David Wirth brings to his scholarship nearly a decade of law practice, with the State Department and with the Natural Resources Defense Council. In this article, he highlights the potential for conflict, both substantive and procedural, between international and domestic law.

A MATCHMAKER'S CHALLENGE: MARRYING INTERNATIONAL LAW AND AMERICAN ENVIRONMENTAL LAW
David A. Wirth
32 Va. J. Int'l L. 377 (1992)*

I. INTRODUCTION

It is now axiomatic that environmental law is among the most rapidly growing, innovative areas of the international legal system. Recent compendia identify hundreds of international agreements dealing, directly or indirectly, with environmental concerns. Multilateral negotiations addressing depletion of the stratospheric ozone layer, international trade in toxic wastes, and the integrity of the global climate have attracted enormous attention from governments and the public in the United States and abroad. Resulting legal instruments, such as the 1987 Montreal Protocol on Substances That Deplete the Ozone Layer

---

* Reprinted with permission.

and the 1989 Basel Convention on the Control of Transboundary Movements of Hazardous Wastes and Their Disposal, have generated considerable optimism about the potential for international law effectively to mitigate global environmental risks.

Multilateral discussions now often supplant national statutory and regulatory schemes crafted in the late 1970s and early 1980s as the preferred fora for federal policy-making on such environmental hazards as stratospheric ozone depletion and exports of hazardous wastes. Tackling international environmental problems like ozone destruction and overseas shipment of wastes in a global context has obvious benefits. A multilateral setting provides a unique opportunity to design effective and efficient international legal structures that advance critical environmental goals while simultaneously reflecting the needs and expectations of all countries.

This trend toward multilateral resolution of international environmental questions has generally been lauded. Less well appreciated is the potential for tension and even clashes between the procedure and substance of international and domestic legal frameworks. Considerable differences exist between the international and national legal orders. Many bedrock principles of domestic environmental and administrative law—including notice to the public, an opportunity to be heard, and judicial review to assure reasoned decision-making—are reflected poorly, if at all, in the international legal system. Indeed, the notion that any of these components might be essential to the integrity of international legal processes, including international environmental decision-making, borders on heresy. In extreme cases, decisions that could directly affect the health and well-being of people within the United States could be lifted out of domestic decision-making processes and placed in a legal context that barely acknowledges the existence of individuals. In other circumstances, the power of an individual state to take measures to preserve natural resources within its own jurisdiction or shared resources of the global commons may be constrained.

* * *

In exploring this relatively uncharted area of the law, this Article evaluates the relationship between international agreements and domestic public law in the context of environmental decision-making. First, relevant procedural and substantive doctrines of international and domestic law are examined to clarify the nature of the interactions between the two legal systems. Then, several case studies of serious discontinuities between international developments and domestic public law are analyzed. Finally, after the examination of these generic doctrines and concrete examples, recommendations are made for narrowing these divergences and encouraging smoother relationships between the international and national legal regimes.

II. TWO LARGELY INDEPENDENT LEGAL SYSTEMS

* * *

A. Trends in International Environmental Law

Legal obligations in the international environmental field arise principally through international agreements, among which the "legislative" instruments of binding multilateral agreements have assumed principal importance. * * *

Multilateral agreements in the environmental area increasingly articulate specific and often complex regulatory schemes with measurable, crisp procedural and substantive requirements for implementation by individual states. These multilateral instruments are analogous in many ways to domestic regulatory structures in their precision. For example, the 1985 Helsinki Protocol on Reduction of Sulfur Emissions or Their Transboundary Fluxes by at Least Thirty Per Cent requires each state party to accomplish a uniform percentage cutback in pollution, measured from an agreed base year, by a firm deadline. The 1988 Sofia Protocol Concerning the Control of Emissions of Nitrogen Oxides or Their Transboundary Fluxes sets out highly specific technology-based standards for pollution control. The 1989 Basel Convention on the Control of Transboundary Movements of Hazardous Wastes and Their Disposal mandates detailed procedures governing the export of municipal trash and toxic detritus. * * *

Although the products of these multilateral undertakings may bear considerable resemblance to domestic environmental statutes or regulations, the processes by which these multilateral instruments are formulated do not. * * * Public scrutiny of and access to international processes may be difficult or even non-existent. Although some scientists, businesspeople, and non-governmental organizations have managed to carve out niches for themselves as observers or advisers to multilateral institutions, policy and practice among international organizations regarding public participation remains very uneven and has not been standardized. Although some documents may circulate informally, distribution of proposals for and drafts of multilateral agreements and other important instruments may also be confined to governments.

Measures taken to arrest the depletion of the stratospheric ozone layer illustrate the major differences between the international legal order and the domestic law of the environment. The Clean Air Act formerly directed the Environmental Protection Agency (EPA) to respond by regulation if there was reason to believe that human activities damaging the ozone layer might endanger health and environment. Acting pursuant to this mandate and in response to considerable public concern, in 1978 EPA, through a notice-and-comment rulemaking proceeding, prohibited nonessential uses of ozone-destroying chlorofluorocarbons (CFCs) such as spray aerosol propellants.

In the mid-1980s it became apparent that this limited ban on a small number of CFC uses was insufficient to address grave threats to the integrity of the stratospheric ozone layer, which by then was seriously disrupted by a continent-sized "hole" over Antarctica. After being prodded with a lawsuit, the Executive Branch took up the issue again, but this time in a multilateral arena, the United Nations Environment Program (UNEP). The resulting Montreal Protocol on Substances That Deplete the Ozone Layer, which sets out a precise numerical reduction schedule for chemicals that may deplete the ozone layer with firm deadlines, is now widely regarded as an effective, potentially global solution to the problem of ozone depletion.

Substantial differences in process accompanied this transition to an international forum for crafting legal requirements for reductions in emissions of ozone-depleting chemicals. EPA implemented the Protocol through a domestic rulemaking, much as it had the 1978 spray propellant ban. The new regulatory proceeding, however, was significantly different from, and much more constrained than, the earlier one. This time many important issues in the rulemaking had already been decided in the multilateral negotiations sponsored by

UNEP. As the principal mechanism for domestic policy-making, that international process did not afford the same procedural guarantees as a domestic rulemaking. As a substantive matter, moreover, EPA interpreted the Montreal Protocol as both a floor and a ceiling. The international commitments in the Protocol precluded weaker regulation of the eight enumerated ozone-depleting chemicals, and strategic and prudential considerations inherent in international bargaining counseled against more stringent controls.

B. The Domestic Law of Foreign Relations

An international agreement, including an environmental pact, is both binding under international law and, like a statute, "the supreme Law of the Land." * * * Although the responsibilities of the United States remain intact on the international plane, a number of doctrines may nonetheless vitiate the force of international legal requirements within the United States. Congress may enact legislation that supersedes commitments in an international agreement or that violates customary international law. The courts may invalidate international agreements on domestic legal grounds. As a matter of domestic law, the Executive Branch may take actions inconsistent with customary international legal standards.

At least one supplementary principle operates to ameliorate discontinuities that might otherwise be created by these doctrines. When it is possible to reconcile a statute and international law, whether originating in agreement or custom, domestic law is construed so as not to conflict with the international duty. Congress is thus presumed to act consistently with international law and the international legal responsibilities of the United States.

Although an international agreement and Congressional legislation are of equal legal authority, the formulation of international commitments differs considerably from domestic statutory enactments. The President, as the "sole organ of the nation in its external relations," has the exclusive power to "make Treaties"[43]—in effect, simultaneously to define both the national law and the international legal obligations of the United States. The Constitution requires the advice and consent of the Senate, by a two-thirds majority, to ratification of concluded international agreements. The President negotiates the treaty for the United States and then presents it as a concluded agreement to the Senate for its *post hoc* advice and consent to subsequent ratification. * * *

The Executive Branch also enters into a distinct and very large category of "executive agreements" on behalf of the United States that, unlike treaties concluded under article II, section 2 of the Constitution, do not require subsequent Congressional endorsement. A subset of executive agreements, so-called "sole" agreements undertaken by the President in reliance on his own constitutional authority, does not require legislative participation either as a precondition to negotiation or subsequent to conclusion. * * *

* * *

III. DISCONTINUITIES BETWEEN THE INTERNATIONAL AND DOMESTIC LEGAL SYSTEMS

The international legal system, like national law, is constantly changing. International responsibilities of the United States may be affected by orders and judgments of the

---

[43] U.S. Const. art. II, § 2. * * *

International Court of Justice, decisions of international arbitral tribunals, binding international agreements, the evolution of customary standards and norms, and other multilateral instruments. Difficulties can nevertheless arise at the interface between international and national law. These interstices in the legal framework fall into at least two generic categories. First, developments on the international level may diverge from existing domestic legislative and regulatory schemes. Second, the implementation of international duties at the national level may encounter legal complications. This section examines case studies of each type of discontinuity.

A. Executive Agreements Affecting Domestic Environmental Regimes

The principle that an international agreement and a statute should be reconciled whenever possible finds its most frequent application where there is an apparent conflict between an earlier international agreement and a later statute. However, two recent cases—both of which interpret environmental statutory schemes—suggest that courts may construe the requirements of existing domestic law in light of a subsequent international agreement. This approach can on occasion disrupt existing legislative and regulatory structures in unpredictable and arguably unintended ways when, as in each of these cases, international obligations are contained in an executive agreement entered into based on the Executive Branch's unilateral interpretation of a statute and without Congressional approval or participation.

In *Japan Whaling Association v. American Cetacean Society*,[60] the Supreme Court construed the Packwood Amendment to the Magnuson Fishery Conservation and Management Act and the Pelly Amendment to the Fishermen's Protective Act of 1967 in light of a subsequent executive agreement[63] with Japan. The existence of that agreement was decisive in the Court's rejection of arguments that a federal official had violated a statutory directive.

Shortly after World War II, more than forty nations entered into a multilateral agreement known as the International Convention for the Regulation of Whaling that created the International Whaling Commission (IWC). The IWC has the power to set limits on the harvesting of various whale species. An "opt-out" procedure allows each nation party to the Whaling Convention unilaterally to reject these quotas, rendering them legally ineffective with respect to that country. Although the quotas are binding on member nations that do not opt out, the IWC nevertheless has no power to impose sanctions for violations.

The Pelly and Packwood Amendments attempt to reinforce the Whaling Convention on the domestic level by requiring the Secretary of Commerce to monitor the whaling activities of foreign nationals and to investigate potential violations of the Whaling Convention. Upon completion of this investigation, the Secretary must promptly decide whether to certify conduct by foreign nationals that "diminishes the effectiveness" of the Whaling Convention. After certification by the Secretary, the Packwood Amendment directs the Secretary of State to reduce the offending nation's fishing allocation within the United States' fishery conservation zone by at least fifty per cent.

---

[60] 478 U.S. 221 (1986).

[63] Agreement Concerning Commercial Sperm Whaling in the Western Division Stock of the North Pacific, Nov. 13, 1984, United States-Japan T.I.A.S. No. 11,070.

In 1981, the IWC established a zero quota for harvests of sperm whales. During the next year, the Commission ordered a five-year moratorium on commercial whaling to begin in the 1985-86 season and to continue until 1990. Japan filed timely objections that effectively relieved it, as an international legal matter, from compliance with the sperm whale quotas for 1982 through 1984. Nonetheless, the potential sanction under the Pelly and Packwood Amendments by the United States threatened Japanese whaling for the 1984-85 season. After extensive negotiations, the United States and Japan concluded an executive agreement in which Japan agreed to catch no more than 400 sperm whales in each of the 1984 and 1985 seasons. Japan also agreed to cease commercial whaling by 1988, three years after the date specified by the IWC. In return, the United States agreed not to certify Japan under the Pelly and Packwood Amendments.

Suit was brought by several environmental organizations to compel the Secretary of Commerce to certify Japan. The Supreme Court, reversing both the District Court and the Court of Appeals, decided that the Secretary had no mandatory duty to certify in response to IWC quota violations. Although the bulk of the opinion deals with the construction of the Pelly and Packwood Amendments, it is clear that the chosen interpretation was strongly influenced by the existence of the agreement with Japan as an acceptable, if alternative, means of achieving the statutory goal.

The international agreement at issue in this case was an executive agreement, entered into on behalf of the United States by the President without consent or input from the Congress. Neither of the applicable legislative enactments authorized the negotiation of the agreement, nor was the particular agreement with Japan endorsed by the Congress either before or after its conclusion. Although the question remains the subject of considerable debate, some authority suggests that such an agreement must be consistent with existing legislation. The Court avoided this problem by interpreting the conflict out of existence, but simultaneously contorted the statutory framework.

Greenpeace USA v. Stone[70] is among the most recent cases addressing environmental effects outside the United States under the National Environmental Policy Act of 1969 (NEPA). The court in that case made clear that its conclusion that NEPA did not apply was strongly influenced by an agreement that the court found had been made between President Bush and Chancellor Kohl of Germany.

* * *

Like the agreement in *Japan Whaling*, the Bush-Kohl arrangement in the *Greenpeace* case was concluded without Congressional participation. Indeed, by comparison with the instrument in *Japan Whaling*, this "agreement" was never reduced to a single written instrument and was closer to a unilateral statement of purpose. * * *

* * *

The United Nations Economic Commission for Europe (ECE), has been working for more than a decade on questions of air pollution, especially acid rain as a regional problem in Europe. After negotiations sponsored under the ECE's auspices, a Convention on Long-Range Transboundary Air Pollution (LRTAP), was concluded in 1979. An ancillary

---

[70] 748 F. Supp. 749 (D. Hawaii 1990), *appeal dismissed as moot*, 924 F.2d 175 (9th Cir. 1991).

Protocol Concerning the Control of Emissions of Nitrogen Oxides (NO_x) or Their Transboundary Fluxes, designed to address one of the principal precursors of acid rain, was signed in Sofia in 1988. Another Protocol Concerning the Control of Emissions of Volatile Organic Compounds (VOCs) or Their Transboundary Fluxes, intended to control one of the main causes of photochemical smog pollution, was signed in Geneva late last year. After articulating a nebulous commitment to "limit and, as far as possible, gradually reduce and prevent air pollution," the LRTAP Convention sets out a general framework for cooperation, consultation, and exchange of information on air pollution. By contrast, the NO_x Protocol states an overall obligation to level off emissions at 1987 levels by 1994, and enumerates precise engineering requirements for mobile and stationary sources of nitrogen oxide pollutants. Likewise, the VOC Protocol contains overall emissions targets and timetables, supplemented by detailed technological requirements.

In structure and level of detail, the LRTAP Convention and the NO_x and VOC Protocols are very much analogs, in the field of acid rain and tropospheric air pollution, to the Vienna Convention and Montreal Protocol on stratospheric ozone depletion. The United States, as a domestic legal matter, entered into both the Vienna Convention and the Montreal Protocol as treaties within the meaning of the Constitution after Senate advice and consent to ratification. The LRTAP Convention and the NO_x and VOC Protocols, however, were undertaken as executive agreements without Congressional participation. Likewise, after the enactment of the acid rain provisions of the Clean Air Act Amendments of 1990, the United States concluded a new pact with Canada on acid rain as an executive agreement. However, unlike its practice in the preparations leading to the Montreal Protocol, the Executive Branch gave no public notice in the Federal Register of, and did not solicit comment on, any of these agreements. Despite the lack of formal notice, the Executive Branch has informally consulted with interested members of Congress and the public with respect to these air pollution pacts concluded as executive agreements.

* * *

"Locking in" the status quo at the international level through unilateral action by the Executive Branch may constrain future legislative or administrative action in a manner arguably inconsistent with Congressional intent. Both statutory and constitutional avenues for petitioning the Executive for regulatory modifications may be compromised. The lack of formal notice may deprive the public of an opportunity to comment on a policy-making juncture at least as important as many administrative regulations.

B. Recent Developments on Trade

A number of recent examples of significant discontinuities have arisen between international trade regimes and national environmental legal requirements. Indeed, an unexpected and vociferous public debate has erupted over the application of existing international trade agreements to environmental matters and the contents of proposed trade pacts. While it is too early to identify all of the nuances that may arise, the examples discussed in this section suggest that the interface between international trade law and the domestic law of the environment will continue to generate significant legal questions.

The General Agreement on Tariffs and Trade (GATT),[98] the principal multilateral

---

[98] General Agreement on Tariffs and Trade, Oct. 30, 1947, arts. XI.1 & XX(b), 61 Stat. (5), (6), T.I.A.S. No. 1700, 55 U.N.T.S. 194 [hereinafter GATT], reprinted in 4 BISD [Basic Instruments and Selected Documents]. * * *

instrument governing international trade relations among states, explicitly exempts from its coverage measures "necessary to protect human, animal or plant life or health."[99] Partially as a result of a bitter dispute between the United States and the European Community (EC) over the use of hormones to promote growth in cattle, the ongoing revisions to the GATT known as the Uruguay Round of Trade Negotiations explicitly treat certain measures to protect public health, such as limitations on pesticide residues in food, as potential trade barriers. Under the rubric of "harmonization" of "sanitary and phytosanitary measures," the Uruguay Round would explicitly subordinate this category of regulatory activity to the GATT international trade regime. Moreover, domestic regulatory activity on issues like pesticide residues would be subject to international scrutiny through compulsory adjudicatory or "dispute settlement" mechanisms under the GATT. As the current United States statutory scheme for controlling contaminants in food does not anticipate an international review procedure, it is far from clear what effect this new development will have on domestic law and regulation in this area.

* * *

In the mid-1980s EPA, acting on evidence that the fumigant ethylene dibromide (EDB) causes cancer, genetic mutations, and adverse reproductive effects in human beings, banned that pesticide for use on domestic produce. By contrast, in response to assertions from the Department of State that the ban would damage the economies of friendly exporting countries, EPA promulgated a tolerance * * * that continued to allow residues of thirty parts per billion (ppb) of EDB in imported mangoes. The District of Columbia Circuit, concluding that EPA's reliance solely on concerns of foreign affairs in the establishment of a pesticide residue limitation was arbitrary and capricious, granted a petition for review and set aside the mango tolerance.[120] On remand, EPA claimed that the continued tolerance for imported mangoes was justified by ongoing cooperative efforts with food-exporting nations to assure that fruit and vegetables enter the United States free of pests such as the Mediterranean fruitfly, diseases, and unsafe levels of pesticides. Moreover, mango-producing nations were channelling export revenues into the search for alternatives for EDB. Accordingly, EPA concluded that revoking the EDB tolerance would pose greater risks to the food supply than continuing that requirement. After EPA provided assurances with respect to the limited term of the standard for imported mangoes, the court approved the tolerance.[121]

* * *

IV. STRENGTHENING THE NEXUS BETWEEN INTERNATIONAL AND DOMESTIC LAW

This uneasy interface between international and national law has potentially far-reaching, but as yet largely unappreciated, implications. Consider an example that illustrates

---

[99] GATT, supra note 98, art. XX(b) (exception "[s]ubject to the requirement that such measures are not applied in a manner which would constitute a means of arbitrary or unjustifiable discrimination between countries where the same conditions prevail, or a disguised restriction on international trade.") * * *

[120] Nat'l Coalition Against the Misuse of Pesticides v. Thomas, 809 F.2d 875, 883 (D.C. Cir. 1987).

[121] Nat'l Coalition Against the Misuse of Pesticides v. Thomas, 815 F.2d 1579 (D.C. Cir. 1987).

some possible ramifications. Assume that the contracting parties to the GATT have accepted the current text on sanitary and phytosanitary standards from the Uruguay Round of Trade Negotiations. Assume further that, in response to new scientific evidence of the high risk of cancer associated with this product, the pesticide Zap-Em is removed from the market pursuant to the Federal Insecticide, Fungicide, and Rodenticide Act (FIFRA). EPA cancels Zap-Em's registration and bans its residues on domestic and imported foodstuffs by revoking the existing tolerance for the product. Ruritania, also a party to the GATT, initiates a dispute settlement proceeding in that body, alleging that the prohibition on residues of Zap-Em in Ruritanian food exported to the United States is stricter than relevant international standards and, to the extent the ban is more stringent than those requirements, is scientifically unjustified and, therefore, a violation of the GATT. A panel established in accordance with the GATT's dispute settlement provisions finds that EPA's ban on Zap-Em constitutes a non-tariff barrier to trade in violation of that agreement.

The Executive Branch is now presented with the unfortunate choice between lifting the ban or continuing to violate international law. If the former is chosen, the resulting tolerance-setting proceeding could raise unique questions because of its unusual impact on foreign policy. * * *

Solely due to the foreign affairs context of the later rulemaking, the procedural guarantees accompanying this second tolerance-setting proceeding are entirely different from the process that established the tolerance for Zap-Em in effect before the ban. Although perhaps a particularly virulent example, this hypothetical scenario illustrates the profound discontinuities that can arise when issues ordinarily governed by domestic statutory structures emerge in an international context. At least two initiatives would tend to minimize these divergences between the international and national legal systems while preserving the integrity of the international obligations of the United States: (1) encouraging greater Congressional participation in international agreements not expressly authorized by statute; and (2) regularizing public participation in international regulatory processes at the national and international levels.

A. Congressional Participation in International Agreements Not Expressly Contemplated by Statute

The *Japan Whaling* and *Greenpeace* cases demonstrate the disruptive effect international agreements can have on domestic legislative regimes. Existing statutory and regulatory schemes can mesh smoothly with treaties and executive agreements authorized by the Congress through legislative participation in defining the terms of those international instruments. Moreover, Congressionally-sanctioned international agreements have the imprimatur of the legislative branch as the law of the land. By contrast, executive agreements not expressly contemplated by statute, even if not strictly inconsistent with existing law, can nonetheless modify or even frustrate the operation of existing legislation and regulation without the participation of the legislative branch.

That an "agreement can be given effect without the enactment of subsequent legislation by the Congress," as set out in State Department policy,[145] is not by itself necessarily

---

[145] [11 F.A.M. § 721.3, reprinted in 1 Michael J. Glennon & Thomas M. Franck, United States Foreign Relations Law: Documents and Sources 205 (1980)].

sufficient evidence of consistency with Congressional intent as expressed in an existing legislative scheme. Nor does that test provide adequate legal justification as a matter of course in the absence of express prior statutory authorization for the choice of an executive agreement instead of either an article II, section 2 treaty or a Congressional-Executive mechanism requiring the participation of the legislature. The mere existence of statutory authority in a particular area does not consequently imply that an executive agreement that has domestic legal effect and that purports to rely on that authority is consistent with the underlying Congressional purpose. Further, reliance on an executive agreement not expressly contemplated by statute could be questionable when implementation is intended to be accomplished by new regulations or rulemakings pursuant to existing statutes. In such a case, the international agreement could compromise the regulatory process, thereby undermining important principles of administrative law like those in the APA. Finally, even when both statutory and regulatory authorities are in place, the choice of an executive agreement would be inappropriate because of its tendency through international processes to constrain future legislative and administrative choices.

However, as State Department policy also recognizes, resolution of the historically delicate question of "choice of instrument" is quite sensitive to context. In such situations, silence, indifference, or acquiescence by the Congress can carry legal significance. To overcome potentially difficult questions concerning the necessary threshold level of Congressional interest and thorny interbranch disputes that can arise on a case-by-case basis, Congress ought to consider enacting legislation that would articulate the requisite legislative concern for each executive agreement not previously authorized by statute that falls within the enumerated powers of the Congress and that is intended to have domestic legal effect. Legislative participation in formulating and giving domestic legal effect to international agreements within realms of statutory concern will almost by definition tend to assure greater consistency with overall statutory purposes. * * *

* * *

B. Regularized Public Participation on the National and International Levels

Perhaps the most obvious divergences between international and national law involve considerations of process. For example, if the Uruguay Round proposals on harmonization of sanitary and phytosanitary standards are adopted, GATT dispute settlement mechanisms will become a forum in which United States regulations on pesticide residues could be challenged as a matter of international law. However, unlike domestic legislative, administrative, and judicial processes, those mechanisms are secret and inaccessible to the public. * * *

As more environmental threats that are governed by or overlap with domestic regulatory structures are addressed in the international arena, there is a commensurately increasing need for improved processes for public participation on the international level. To ameliorate the effects of resulting discontinuities, multilateral fora like GATT might adopt rules of procedure that regularize and greatly expand public access to, and public accountability of, their law-making, law-enforcing, and adjudicatory processes. Without question, improved access and public participation at the international level is the most desirable way to reconcile these disparities, while simultaneously furthering the larger public policy goals of improving the legitimacy and accountability of the international legal system.

However, much can also be done at the purely national level in the absence of progress on the international level or until multilaterally agreed-upon measures are implemented.

First, the APA's foreign affairs exception should be reevaluated. The underlying justification for that provision is no longer warranted, if it ever was. The foreign affairs exception is a crude and unsophisticated mechanism governing a sphere of the law that has become increasingly nuanced and complex. Environment, like foreign trade, clearly falls within the enumerated powers of the Congress. The national legislature has reacted to both issues with complex webs of statutory and regulatory directives. For that reason, both areas are fundamentally different from traditional security and foreign affairs concerns like the conduct of war and the recognition of foreign governments entrusted by the Constitution to the President. Likewise, international undertakings on both environmental and foreign trade matters governed by statute are well within the reach of Congressional law-making authority. Accordingly, the unusual deference to the Executive Branch contained in the APA exception merely because of the international context for decision-making is not warranted.

Second, Congress should replace the sweeping APA exemption with comprehensive new legislation that articulates how basic principles of American public law will be applied in a foreign affairs context. At a minimum, this legislation should establish standards for distinguishing between those domains—such as war and recognition of foreign governments—that are appropriate for an exemption like that currently in the APA and those—like environment—that are not. For the latter category, outcome-neutral procedures analogous to notice-and-comment rulemaking and judicial review under the APA should be established, with processes tailored to meet the needs of governmental decision-making in national, bilateral, and multilateral contexts. * * *

V. CONCLUSION

Employing international processes to address international environmental risks is obviously sensible, desirable, and in some cases necessary. Improving the efficacy and accountability of multilateral mechanisms to make them responsive to serious global threats, like stratospheric ozone depletion and greenhouse warming, should be a top priority from both legal and policy perspectives. At least for now, however, there is also a risk that critical principles of separation of powers, public participation, and democratic decision-making will be compromised merely because an environmental issue has been removed to an international forum. These fundamentals, which are essential to the integrity of our governmental structure, are by no means confined to environmental law. Although the international environment is probably the best example of the discontinuities between international and domestic law, virtually any area of Congressional power and action can engage these crucial questions.

International initiatives can be effective, efficient, and in some cases indispensable vehicles for furthering environmental and other national and international goals. But that is not a sufficient justification for subverting our democratic principles and fundamental governmental structure by shielding unilateral, often secret action by the Executive Branch (where only one official, the President, is directly accountable to the public) from Congressional, public, and judicial review. Legal processes for otherwise desirable international environmental undertakings should be altered to ensure that Executive Branch activities on the international level are accountable to the Congress and to the public at large, as measured against the same basic principles that apply to legislative or administrative actions.

Through its own inattention, by Executive Branch design, or both, the Congress has been marginalized in the negotiation and implementation of many international environmental agreements. Areas within the enumerated powers of Congress, of which environment is clearly one, should not be usurped by the Executive Branch merely because they arise in an international context. Those matters, like environment, governed by domestic statutes are clearly distinguishable from those within the Executive's plenary powers. Our constitutional system of separation of powers anticipates and can accommodate a larger role for the legislature in the category of international concerns that simultaneously fall within the plenary powers of the Congress. Moreover, greater involvement of the legislature will tend to produce significant incidental benefits. As a legal and practical matter, greater opportunities for Congressional input will ameliorate or eliminate discontinuities between the international and domestic legal systems. Over time, a higher level of legislative participation might even encourage greater public accountability of international processes generally.

NOTES

1. Refer to the articles cited in note 7 following the Schoenbaum article to assess the impact of the final version of the Uruguay Round provisions on the issues raised here by Professor Wirth.

2. Does the Zap-Em hypothetical posed by Wirth in part IV indicate that GATT, as amended by the Uruguay Round, effectively clipped the EPA's powers under FIFRA? The final Uruguay Round provision concerning sanitary and phytosanitary measures recognizes the parties' rights to adopt domestic measures to protect human, animal, and plant health—but only where such measures are "necessary," are "based on scientific principles" and are "not maintained without sufficient scientific evidence," and "are not more trade restrictive than required to achieve their appropriate level of protection, taking into account technical and economic feasibility." 1994 World Trade Organization Agreement on Sanitary and Phytosanitary Measures, Articles 2:2, 2:3, and 5:6. *See* Ernst-Ulrich Petersmann, INTERNATIONAL AND EUROPEAN TRADE AND ENVIRONMENTAL LAW AFTER THE URUGUAY ROUND 36-37 (1995). Under this regime, what options are available to the EPA when it receives scientific information suggesting—but, inevitably, not conclusively—that Zap-Em may be carcinogenic to humans? Does the marriage between international and domestic law in this case result in a least-common-denominator approach to environmental regulation?

3. What consequences might result from greater congressional involvement in international lawmaking? Would the international community have concluded the broad range of international agreements, and even so would the United States have had the same degree of input and participation, if domestic procedures had been grafted onto the international scene? Can Wirth's concerns be addressed without significantly hampering the government's practical ability to negotiate and enter into international agreements?

4. As the Wirth article indicates, the President has at least two different procedural options for bringing international agreements back home. One option is the treaty which, pursuant to Article II, Section 2 of the Constitution, must be approved by two-thirds of the Senate. Another option is the executive agreement (or congressional-executive agreement), which requires simple majority support from both houses of Congress. In a comprehensive article tracing the historical practice, first relying exclusively on treaties and then shifting dramatically to the use of executive agreements, Professors Bruce Ackerman and David Golove critically examine the fragile constitutional status of executive agreements. *See* Bruce Ackerman and David Golove, *Is NAFTA Constitutional?* 108 HARV. L. REV. 799 (1995).

Case Index

Index